Lucy Toulmin Smith, Richard Kyngeston

Expeditions to Prussia and the Holy Land made by Henry earl of Derby (afterwards King Henry IV.)

In the Years 1390-1 and 1392-3. Being the Accounts Kept by his Treasurer during Two Years

Lucy Toulmin Smith, Richard Kyngeston

Expeditions to Prussia and the Holy Land made by Henry earl of Derby (afterwards King Henry IV.)
In the Years 1390-1 and 1392-3. Being the Accounts Kept by his Treasurer during Two Years

ISBN/EAN: 9783337169183

Printed in Europe, USA, Canada, Australia, Japan

Cover: Foto ©ninafisch / pixelio.de

More available books at **www.hansebooks.com**

EXPEDITIONS
TO
PRUSSIA AND THE HOLY LAND
MADE BY
HENRY EARL OF DERBY
(AFTERWARDS KING HENRY IV.)

In the Years 1390-1 and 1392-3.

BEING

The Accounts kept by his Treasurer during two years.

EDITED FROM THE ORIGINALS BY

LUCY TOULMIN SMITH.

WITH INTRODUCTION, NOTES, AND INDICES.

PRINTED FOR THE CAMDEN SOCIETY.

M.DCCC.XCIV.

COUNCIL OF THE CAMDEN SOCIETY

FOR THE YEAR 1894-5.

President.

THE RIGHT HON. THE EARL OF CRAWFORD, K.T., LL.D., F.R.S., &c., &c.

JAMES J. CARTWRIGHT, ESQ., M.A., F.S.A., *Treasurer.*
REV. J. SILVESTER DAVIES, M.A., F.S.A.
REV. J. WOODFALL EBSWORTH, M.A., F.S.A.
JAMES GAIRDNER, ESQ., *Secretary.*
SAMUEL RAWSON GARDINER, ESQ. M.A., LL.D., *Director.*
REV. F. A. GASQUET, D.D.
DAVID HANNAY, ESQ.
REV. WILLIAM HUNT, M.A.
ARTHUR W. HUTTON, ESQ., M.A.
J. BASS MULLINGER, ESQ., M.A.
REV. CHARLES NEIL, M.A.
J. E. L. PICKERING, ESQ.
H. C. SOTHERAN, ESQ.
HENRY R. TEDDER, ESQ.
PERCY M. THORNTON, ESQ., M.P.

The COUNCIL of the CAMDEN SOCIETY desire it to be understood that they are not answerable for any opinions or observations that may appear in the Society's publications; the Editors of the several Works being alone responsible for the same.

[NEW SERIES NO. LII.]

CONTENTS.

	PAGE
PREFATORY NOTE	v.
INTRODUCTION: The Manuscripts . . .	ix.
The Teutonic Order and its relations to England	xi.
Crusades into Prussia	xvi.
References in Chronicles . . .	xix.
Language of these Accounts . .	xxiii.
Narrative and Itinerary for 1390-1 .	xxv.
The Barbary Crusade; Derby at Calais .	xxxvii.
Men on the Reysa; actual strength . .	xlii.
The Winter Household . .	xlv.
Narrative and Itinerary for 1392-3 .	xlvii.
Men on the Second Journey . . .	l.
More Funds	liv.
Narrative resumed	lvi.
Itinerary 1392-3	lxxii.
Henry's position in England and Abroad .	lxxx.
Derby's Household	lxxxvii.
Money and Coinage	xcviii.
APPENDICES A, B. Extracts from Chronicles .	cvi., cx.
LIST OF ERRATA	cxiii.
TEXT. PART I.	
Writ appointing Treasurer of War . .	1
Writ ordering audit of Treasurer's Accounts .	2
Monies received, 1390	3
Provision for the Journey to Prussia .	5
Wardrobe in England, Loveney's Account .	34

CONTENTS.

	PAGE
Boatage and Shippage	36
Expenses of Household and of Reysa, Aug. 8-Oct. 20	38
Household Expenses at Königsberg	57
,, ,, ,, Brandenburg, &c.	69
,, ,, ,, Elbing, &c.	70
,, ,, ,, Dantzic	72
Wardrobe in Prussia	88
Provision in Prussia for Ships and Return to England	95
Silver Articles	100
Kitchen Requisites in Metal	101
Household Expenses (Prussia) entered on Brevement rolls	102
Gifts, Chamberlain's Accounts	104, 113
Money for play at dice	115
Alms and Oblations	116
Wages of Knights, Esquires, and Valets	118, 133, 137
,, ,, Gromes	136, 141
,, ,, Knights and Esquires for the Reysa	131
,, ,, Minstrels	132, 137, 141
Allowance for loss on Florins	142
Summing up of Expenditure	142

TEXT. PART II.

Receipt of Treasurer for 3,000 marks	147
Writ ordering audit of Treasurer's Accounts	148
Monies received	149
Provision for Second Journey	151
Expenses in Prussia	163
Expenses in the Mark	184
,, from Frankfort-on-Oder to Bohemia	187
,, in Bohemia	188
,, from Vienna to Friuli	195
,, at Portogruaro, &c.	204
,, at Venice	211

CONTENTS.

	PAGE
Provision at Venice for Voyage to Palestine	220
Expenses on Voyage by Rhodes, &c., to Palestine and back to Venice	224, 231
Expenses at Venice, Treviso, and neighbourhood	233, 239
,, in Piedmont and Savoy	241, 247
,, ,, Burgundy	249
,, ,, France	251
,, on return to England	254
A Parcel of Daily Accounts omitted	258
Belechere	259
Purchase of Horses	262
Money for play at dice	263
Wages	264
Alms and Oblations	273
Skippage, *i.e.* Transport by Water	278
Wardrobe Expenses	279
Gifts throughout the Year	289
Allowances to Treasurer	291
NOTES	293
INDEX I., PERSONS	315
INDEX II., PLACES	327
INDEX III., GLOSSARIAL	334

In the notes, &c., reference is made to the two following editions:—*Froissart*, edited by M. Kervyn de Lettenhove, Brussels, 1867-77, 25 vols.; *Rymer's Fœdera*, published by Churchill, 1704-1732.

PREFATORY NOTE.

THE two Wardrobe Accounts now printed in their entirety for the first time have been hitherto known to but a few writers, who have, however, used them as important sources of information. Beltz in 1841 made use of both, among other Duchy accounts, for his notice of Henry IV. in youth;[a] Mrs. Everett Green ransacked them for her " Lives of the Princesses " (1851);[b] but although the journeys to which they relate are known from chronicles, it was not till the late Professor Pauli, then of Rostock, recognised their interest and value for students of the history of Prussia and of the Teutonic knights that any considerable attempt was made to publish their contents. In December, 1868, the large mass of non-public documents and records belonging to the Duchy of Lancaster, and hitherto kept at the office of the Duchy, were presented by the Queen, as Duchess of Lancaster, to the nation, and were transferred to the Public Record Office. Previously to this, however, in 1856, Dr. Pauli, in the course of his researches on English history at the Duchy office, found and re-discovered the first book of accounts in question, viz., those of 1390-91. He communicated a paper containing an excellent sketch of the contents of this to Dr. Pertz, who read it at a meeting of the Berlin Academy of Science on 6 August, 1857;[c] and furnished another, consisting of such extracts from the MS. as he had had time to make, relating especially to the Prussian details, which was

[a] " Memorials of the Order of the Garter," p. 239.
[b] Vol. iii , pp. 304-308.
[c] Printed in the " Monatsberichte der Königlichen Akademie der Wissenschaften zu Berlin," (1857) 1858, p. 406.

published in the collection "Scriptores Rerum Prussicarum,"[a] set on foot in 1861 by Dr. Theo. Hirsch, Max Töppen, and E. Strelke. In the first of these papers Professor Pauli expressed his regret that he had not succeeded in finding the similar account for Derby's voyage of 1392-3, which was known from some of the chroniclers. On a visit to England some years later Professor Pauli had the pleasure of seeing this account also, and published an analysis and reports upon it in the "Nachrichten" of the Royal Society of Science of the University of Göttingen in 1880 and 1881.[b] Through his friend the late Mr. Alfred Kingston, of the Public Record Office, and Secretary to the Camden Society, he procured a copy of the two manuscripts entire, and set about preparing them for publication by that society. At this time Dr. Pauli was Professor of Modern History at Göttingen. He made considerable progress with the work, principally as regards the first account, even having written an Introduction in English, which bears the date 23 July, 1881. Unhappily, however, the scholar's hand was stayed; before his enthusiastic pen could finish his task he died, in the beginning of June, 1882, at the age of fifty-nine.[c]

The unfinished work was thus thrown back for a time, the Society being unsuccessful in their first attempts to find an editor to take it up. Finally, however, on overtures made by Professor H. Prutz of Königsberg, it was arranged that the work should be brought out simultaneously by the Historical Society of East and West Prussia and the Camden Society,[d] I undertaking the English,

---

[a] Vol. ii., 1863, pp. 788-792. The collection contains 5 volumes, issued at Leipzig between 1861 and 1874.

[b] "Nachrichten v. der Kgl. Gesellschaft der Wissenschaften," Göttingen, 1880, No. 8; ib. 1881. No. 11.

[c] The Council of the Camden Society, at their meeting on 7 June, referred to the intended publication in a resolution of condolence and regret. See *Athenæum* for June 10 and 17, 1882.

[d] The title of the German edition is "Rechnungen über Heinrich von Derby's Preussenfahrten, 1390-91 und 1392," hsgn. von Dr. Hans Prutz, Professor an der Universität zu Königsberg. Publication des Vereins für die Geschichte der Provinzen Ost und Westpreussen. Leipzig, 1893.

Professor Prutz the German edition. The two editions are independent as regards everything but the text; as regards the text, the English edition gives the two Accounts entire, the German (depending upon my collation) gives the whole of the first Account, but only so much of the second (about half) as concerns Germany and the journey thence to Venice.

Professor Prutz has been ready for some months, and I owe him and our Society an apology for the delay on my part. When, however, the considerable difficulties of the work are looked at, involving much textual labour, and very much research for elucidation; a work perhaps rather rashly and ignorantly undertaken in my zeal for the honour of English editors on English ground, and having to be carried on amongst other occupations; considering also that the later portion of the second journey offered problems, some of which have proved the hardest of the whole—I trust that the delay will be found excusable. My aim has been to present a good text, according to the manuscript, together with such necessary aids as may make it serviceable to students, and thus to render the work, I hope, not unworthy of the eminent scholar and lover of English history to whom it owes its inception.

When the transcript and papers were handed over to me it was found that much remained to be done; to begin with, no collation on the MS. had been made, though surely Dr. Pauli must have intended this. How essential it was the result showed. The whole thus requiring revision, it seemed best to prepare the edition on my own basis, using the few annotations, explanatory of a few personages, places, and obscure words, as far as possible.[a] Dr. Pauli's introduction not in my judgment now meeting the requirements of the case, and yet possessing a claim on the reader of this work, is not printed in its original form, but a large part of it is embodied in my own, with [ ] to distinguish the writer;[b] the

[a] These are denoted by the letter P, except two or three at the foot of the text that have escaped me.

[b] Some amplifications and a few corrections in expression, due to the English of a foreigner, were unavoidable.

same has been done with some extracts from chronicles, intended by way of appendix. Past labour thus, it was hoped, would not be lost, and would be treated in a reverential spirit.

My best thanks are due to many kind friends for assistance; to Professor Prutz for advance sheets of his edition,[a] to Frau Pauli of Göttingen for placing her husband's notes and papers at my disposal, and to Mr. F. B. Bickley of the British Museum and Mr. C. Trice Martin of the Record Office for reading through the proof-sheets of the text with much care. Nor can I refrain from acknowledging the kindness of Dr. S. R. Gardiner, Mr. James Gairdner, and Mons. Paul Meyer, with ever ready aid and friendly counsel on various knotty points.

[a] I have availed myself in several instances of the notes of Professor Prutz (though I sometimes disagree with his conclusions), and have chiefly followed his identifications of place-names on German soil, which correspond with those of Dr. Pauli.

INTRODUCTION.

The Manuscripts.—The Accounts printed in the present volume are preserved among the rich stores of the records of the Duchy of Lancaster, now in the Public Record Office, where they form part of the " Ministers' Accounts" of the Duchy, and are known as of Class XXVIII, 1st bundle, Nos. 6 and 7. No. 6 is a folio (12 in. long by $8\frac{3}{4}$ wide) of eight quires of parchment, containing sixty leaves (a few only are blank), written in a regular neat official hand, ruled and bracketed, with titles and some marginal notes written large, according to the manner of early accounts. The old soft leather cover, into which the quires were stitched, remains; the two writs (pp. 1, 2) authorising the special Treasurer and the audit of his accounts being attached by their ends to the edge of one side, while the outside is inscribed with the title of the book, the inscription being on a piece of parchment stitched on to the leather. The book has seen much use, and the cover is coming to pieces, but the interior is in good condition. This contains the receipts and expenditure of Henry, Earl of Derby, eldest son of John of Gaunt (Duke of Aquitaine and Lancaster), over his journeys and his household abroad from the 6th May, 1390, to April 30, 1391, about nine years before he became king. No. 7, containing forty-four leaves of rather larger size ($15\frac{3}{4}$ in. long by $11\frac{1}{2}$ in. wide), is also in its original parchment cover, having likewise two documents (see pp. 147, 148) attached to one side; the form of the account for the most part resembles that of No. 6, and the cursive handwriting is generally clear, but it contains some evident errors, showing that the clerk employed by the treasurer on the second occasion was more careless, or perhaps had greater difficulties to contend with among his vouchers and originals than the clerk of the first account (they do not appear to have been written by the same, the hands differ). No. 7 contains Henry's receipts and expenditure over his journeys and household abroad for the year 16 July, 1392, to 16 July, 1393. In both cases a few weeks of life in England are included, but on the whole they are records of nearly two years of foreign travel and sojourn. Both manuscripts are well preserved and in good condition as far as the interior is concerned; they are, there is no doubt, the official accounts presented by Derby's Treasurer, Richard Kyngston, before the auditors of the Council of the Duchy, and passed by them, to be laid up in the private archives of the Duchy along with other accounts of the like nature.[a]

[The books were evidently made up after the return of the earl from a number of memoranda and jottings on slips or small rolls of parchment and paper set down by those concerned in the receipt and issue of the money as their bills of account.[b] These were arranged by the treasurer and copied out under the heads] which are given in the table of contents, [the monies accounted for on each page being invariably summed up at the bottom of the page]. If the scribe were not extremely careful inaccuracies would be sure to arise in small matters, and this is indeed found to be the case, especially with regard to dates and the names of unfamiliar places; occasionally also with prices and sums of money. The figures, as usual at the period, are written according to Roman numeration, and in trying to rectify them this must be taken into consideration. Both books with their numerous items of constant recurrence are written in close contractions, a fact which has occasioned doubt in some words of obscurity or unknown gender. For the present

[a] For the purpose of illustrating this work, and of resolving doubtful or explaining obscure words, I have had frequent recourse to other accounts of Henry, or of his father, still in the same collection. These are referred to by the abbreviations D. of L., cl., bdle., for Duchy of Lancaster, class, bundle.

[b] See after, p. xc.

volume it was determined to print the text extended, as more
generally readable, and for greater certainty the extensions are
indicated in *italic* type till near the end of Part I., except in a few
doubtful cases where the contraction is retained.[a] The old spelling
has been carefully adhered to, but the promiscuous use of capital
initials is reduced to modern usage, and punctuation introduced.
The total sum of each original page has been usually set in the
margin to allow the full page more clearly to appear, every small
original annotation being carefully inserted as helping to understand the document. Two only of this class are not constantly
printed, the sign p^r. = probatur, occurring at the bottom of each
page, after the total (see pp. 9, 113); the other, being the
invariable repetition of the sum total written very small at the
edge of the lower margin, was of course unnecessary; but both
deserve mention as connected with the system of checking the
accounts.

Both books have been collated throughout on the MS. twice,
besides frequent reference again to correct doubtful points.

The Teutonic Order and its relations to England.—
The Order of Teutonic knights had its origin in a hospital founded
by citizens of Bremen and Lubeck at Jerusalem in 1128. On the
capture of Jerusalem by the Saracens in 1187 the hospital
disappeared, to be revived at Acre in 1190 under a new military
monastic brotherhood, following the Augustinian rule, with vows
to tend sick pilgrims and fight the pagans. Henry Walpot was
the first grand master, 1190. Attaining power and influence
in 1230 they undertook a crusade against the heathen Prussians,
and in 1237 absorbed the " Brothers of the sword," who possessed
Courland, Semgallen, and Livonia. On the fall of Acre in 1291
they removed their chief seat to Venice, and finally, in 1309,
established it at Marienburg on the Vistula, being then also

---

[a] The italic indications were abandoned at this point on account of the needless
further expense, the contractions being of the same character throughout.

masters of Prussia and Pomerelia. Pomerania was to follow later. The grand master of the Order with the treasurer and the grand commander lived at Marienburg, the marshal at Königsberg, the grand hospitaller at Elbing, and the trappier at Christburg, the four latter being respectively "commanders" or preceptors of the towns. Other towns had also their commanders, as Ragnit, Insterburg, and many others.[a]

Unlike the Templars and the knights of St. John the Teutonic knights had no property in England, but almost from the beginning of their entry into Prussia the English kings granted them an annual subsidy (40 marks or 80 gold nobles) in lieu of land, which was continued nearly two hundred years, not without some breaks. Henry III., after having granted, presently annulled the grant; but it was restored by Edward I., who twice confirmed it. Under Edward III. the payment, which then seems to have been due at the house of the Order at Coblentz, having lapsed during three years, Grand Master Kniperode wrote to that king reminding him of the subsidy and its arrears, whereupon Edward issued a charter reciting previous grants and assuring the money in future. In it he acknowledges the hospitality which the masters and brethren of the order had shown "nostratibus per dictum hospitale transeuntibus sepius gratanter et benevole," but does not particularize Coblentz.[b]

During the fourteenth century, but especially in the second half,

[a] For descriptions of the officers of the Order and their functions, with chronological lists of names, see Voigt's "Namen-Codex der Deutschen Ordens beamten," Königsberg, 1843.

[b] Six documents making and confirming this annual grant are printed from the Charter, Liberate, and Patent Rolls (English Record Office) in "Archives de l'Orient Latin," vol. i., pp. 416-422. They are of the dates Henry III., 1235; Edward I., 1279 and 1285; Edward III., 1359; Richard II., 1389; and Henry IV., 1404. The letter from Kniperode is printed from the archives of Königsberg, by J. Voigt, "Codex Diplomaticus Prussicus," Königsberg, 1848, vol. iii., p. 117, who also gives Edward III.'s charter (under date 1360). M. Perlbach (Alt-preussische Monatsschrift, xviii., 1880, p. 226) gives notes from the Liberate Rolls of the payment orders made in thirteen years of Henry III., viz., from 1235 to 1261.

INTRODUCTION.

trade between the Hanse towns of the German and Prussian coasts and those of England, such as Boston, Lynn, Hull, and York, was frequent and considerable. These towns were near their highest prosperity, full of craft-gilds and activity. Dantzic, which came under the Teutonic Order early in the century, depended for much of her commerce upon English demand, exporting thither corn and wood, while sheltering the English cloth business and merchants within her walls;[a] on the other hand it is known that many houses in Boston were held by foreign merchants.[b] From our Accounts we learn that Derby, in 1390 and 1392, had dealings both in Dantzic and Königsberg with English merchants (acting for the most part as "factors") who seem to have been settled there. John Whytyk, John Trepland of York, and John Bever at Dantzic, John Squirell at Königsberg.[c] The interests of York in the Prussian trade were of such importance that when, on a case of grave dispute in 1388, King Richard sent three envoys to Prussia to treat of a basis of agreement, one of these was a citizen of York, another of London, and the third a clerk. The treaty drawn up by these three is dated Marienburg, 21 Aug., 1388, as between the King of England and Conrad Zolner de Rotenstein, Grand Master of the Teutonic Order, and received due confirmation on both sides.[d] Besides enrolment among the state archives the treaty was carefully

---

[a] Th. Hirsch, "Danzigs Handels-und Gewerbsgeschichte," Leipzig, 1878, pp. 99, 100.

[b] T. Allen's "Hist. of County of Lincoln," 1836, vol. i., pp. 219, 222, 224.

[c] See pp. 72 **29**, 97 **29**, 61 **16**. That Trepeland (pp. 40, 175, &c.) was an English merchant of York is proved by a bond dated at Dantzic, 13 March, 1391, under which he and a German merchant lent money to John Beaufort and other English knights, then on a short reysa with the Teutonic order. Hirsch, "Danzigs Handels-u. Gewerbsgeschichte," p. 234, note 983. (I owe this interesting reference to Professor Prutz).

[d] See all the documents in Rymer, vol. vii., pp. 588, 599-601, 647, 739. Professor Prutz gives a valuable sketch of the action of the Grand Masters Kniperode and Rotenstein in regard to the complaints of the merchants, and of the negotiations which led to the treaty of 1388 above mentioned. "Rechnungen," introduction, pp. xxix.-xxxiii.

CAMD. SOC. c

entered at full length in the municipal records of the city of York."

The political relations between the Order and her neighbour Lithuania had from the middle of this century been warlike; Winric de Kniperode, Grand Master (1351 to 1382), took prisoner a Lithuanian prince in battle; King Olgierd and his brother were the most implacable enemies of the Order. But when by the marriage of Olgierd's son Jagello, Grand Duke of Lithuania (recently baptised as Uladislas), to Hedwig, the young Queen of Poland, on 17 Feb., 1386, those two countries became united, and Grand Master Conrad von Rotenstein made a treaty offensive and defensive with him, peace seemed in view. The Order feared to be overshadowed by these two powerful states. Jagello held a national assembly at Wilna, his own capital, in 1387, his people were baptised, and he made his brother Skirgal or Skirgello lieutenant-general of the Duchy. This appointment, however, aroused the jealousy of his cousin Vitold, the ambitious Prince of Samogitia, and other near provinces; he tried to surprise Wilna, and in 1388 brought his wife and children to Prussia as hostages, applying to the Grand Master for aid. Here was the opportunity for the Order to find their gain in the dissensions of their enemies. The Order took the side of Vitold, an alliance was concluded between them on 19 January, 1390,[b] and under the command of the Marshal Rabe they took the field against Jagello. After a short campaign, in which they had some success, they returned to Prussia. But the enemy then fell upon the possessions of Vitold, one town after another falling into their hands, the strong fortress Grodno costing them a six weeks' siege. Vitold, however, succeeded in bringing about an alliance between his people of Samogitia and

---

[a] In the oldest book, marked $\frac{A}{V}$, fos. 131-3, where I saw it in the year 1882. The same volume contains a curious indenture for the sale of the "quarter of a ship call James," and the fish in it, by Jasper Groudham, skipper, of Dantzic, to two merchants of York and Beverley, in 1459 (fo. 184).

[b] Wigand v. Marburg, Scripl. rer. Pruss. vol. ii., p. 640.

the Order, which was settled at Königsberg on May 26, 1390;[a] and thus strengthened, another campaign was determined on. Foreign help was welcome, perhaps invited, from knights of France, Britain, and Belgium. It was in acceptance of this call that Henry Earl of Derby took his way to Prussia in July, 1390, a journey of which the first of the present accounts gives the details. It is hardly to be called a crusade, it was a military expedition in aid of a friendly power brought about by political necessities.

At the beginning of Derby's expedition, on 10 August, when Lancaster Herald took his father's letters to Marienburg (p. 40/7) Conrad Zölner von Rotenstein (1382-1390) was still Grand Master, but he was ill, and died at Christburg on the 20th of the same month. Conrad von Wallenrod had been Marshal from 1382 to 1387; he was made Grand Commander in 1387, and after the death of Rotenstein he acted as vicegerent, till on 21 March, 1391, he was elected Grand Master, which position he occupied at the time of Derby's second but short visit to Prussia in August, 1392. He died in the following year. Engelhardt Rabe was Marshal of the Order from 1387 to Nov. 16, 1392; he it was who now led the allied armies against the Lithuanians Jagello and Skirgal.

Besides the several journeys of notable Englishmen to Prussia, Henry the elder Earl of Derby and John Beaufort,[b] another of Derby's kinsmen, his uncle Thomas of Woodstock, Duke of Gloucester, was commissioned by the King in 1391, and received licence on 5 Sept. to impress ships and sailors at Orwell Port (near Harwich) to take him and his company to Prussia, with powers to treat "de quibusdam materiis et negotiis" between the King and the Grand Master. His knights and squires had their letters of protection on 23 Sept., but this expedition, quite separate from Derby's, never reached its destination. Gloucester set out, says Walsingham, against the desire of the English people,

[a] Voigt's "Geschichte Preussens," vol. v., pp. 538, 539.
[b] See pp. xiii. note c, xvii.

who feared the King's tyranny in his absence; but his vessels encountering violent storms touched on the Danish, Norwegian, and Scottish coasts, and he finally reached Tynemouth, happy to escape with life, and got home to his house at Pleshy.[a] His herald Croyslett, however, was in Prussia in November (p. 107), he appears in Derby's accounts more than once. We also hear of a Scottish knight, Douglas, and the English Clifford meeting in Königsberg in 1391, when they had a tragic quarrel, in which Boucicaut took up the cause of the slain Douglas, mentioned by several writers.[b] The intercourse between the two countries was therefore by no means rare at this period.

Crusades into Prussia.—[The[c] Teutonic knights, who conquered and annihilated the heathen Prussians, and with the brilliant spirit of political organizers planted a great German colony in the vast territories between the Vistula and the Memel, had been in permanent intercourse with the English Government ever since the days of Henry III. Their Grand Masters, by courtesy princes of the Empire, but representing in reality at the head of the Order the sovereignty of an independent state, appear to have enjoyed regular subsidies of forty marks a year from the kings of England for promoting the Christian faith.[d] During the reign of Edward III., when, after the fall of Acre in 1291, the crusades to Palestine had long been at an end, it became the fashion among the higher nobility and gentry, especially when an unwelcome truce interrupted the wars in France, to fulfil their vows by joining either the kings of Spain in a raid against the Moors or the Prussian

---

[a] French Rolls, 15 Ric. II., m. 16, 15, 14, printed in Rymer, vii., 705, 706. Walsingham, "Hist. Angl.," ii., 202.

[b] *E.g.* "Le livre des faicts du Mareschal de Boucicaut," ed. Michaud et Poujoulat, p. 232, Wigand v. Marburg, p. 644. Boucicaut made three journeys to Prussia, "Le livre," pp. 225, 232.

[c] Dr. Pauli's "Introduction" begins here, and ends p. xxxiv.

[d] See note before p. xii. also Dr. Pauli's "Geschichte von England," iv., p. 616, and his "Pictures of Old England," p. 134. –L.T.S.

knights against their pagan neighbours.[a] We learn from Knighton that Henry earl of Derby and duke of Lancaster, great-grandson of Henry III., in 1351, when the fighting in France ceased for awhile, resolved to go to Prussia instead. He started with a large retinue by land, but being stopped by a set of freebooters or moss-troopers of noble descent, had to pay a high ransom.[b] A contemporary German chronicler, Henricus de Hervordia, gives a very curious account how the vanguard of the little army conducting the treasury of the earl eastward, had a sharp rencounter in the territory of the bishop of Paderborn with a gang of Westphalian knights, who defeated and robbed the Englishmen in a most disreputable manner.[c] This attack appears to have arisen out of a quarrel between the earl and Otto duke of Brunswick, as to which details are given by Knighton and Walsingham (see also Rymer, v., 742, and Leibnitz, in "Script. rer. Pruss." ii., 47-30).

[Knighton continues, that the English duke, in spite of his check in Westphalia, pursued his pilgrimage to Prussia, but was much disappointed by the tidings that just before his arrival a truce for several years had been concluded between the Christians and their heathen enemies. A charter, issued by him from Stettin, January 15, 1352, is extant in a Berlin manuscript,[d] but he evidently soon returned.

How popular these crusading expeditions to the Baltic regions must have been during that chivalrous period is well known from Chaucer's Prologue to his " Canterbury Tales." The gentle knight had fought with the infidels in Egypt and Armenia, in Granada and Tlemecen,—

---

[a] " Et exinde multi Angligenae et Francigenae transierunt ad Sprueiam ad bellum campestre assignatum die parasceves proximo sequenti inter regem Hispaniae et paganos;" a rather mutilated passage. Knighton's Chronicle, in Twysden's " Decem Scriptores." col. 2583.

[b] *Ibid.*, col. 2603, years 1351 and 1352.

[c] H. de Hervordia, a Dominican born in Westphalia, died October 9, 1370; see his " Chronicon," ed. Aug. Potthast, Göttingen, 1859, p. 286.

[d] Printed in " Script. rer. Pruss.," ii., 516, note.

xviii   INTRODUCTION.

> ' Ful often tyme he hadde the bord bygonne,
> Aboven alle nacyouns in Pruce.
> In Lettowe hadde he reysed and in Ruce,
> No cristen man so ofte of his degre."

It is most significant that a word of High-German descent, *reise*, *journey*, which was the technical term in Prussia for a warlike expedition,[a] and which, in fact, had conveyed the particular meaning of a pilgrimage to the holy sepulchre since the days of Walter von der Vogelweide,[b] had crept into the English language by Chaucer's time with special reference to a Prussian crusade.

The "Canterbury Tales" were not yet published, though the poet, as is well known, was already intimately connected with the noble house of Lancaster, when early in the year 1390 the grandson of the elder Henry by the mother's side, Henry earl of Derby, the first-born of John of Gaunt, duke of Lancaster, proposed likewise to have a *reise* with the Teutonic knights. He was at that time about twenty-five years old, had already three sons by Mary de Bohun, and with the earldom of his maternal grandfather an establishment of his own at Bolingbroke Castle.[c] Whether in memory of the prowess of old Derby, or from the desire to be out of the way of the incessant political struggles, which, owing greatly to the intrigues of his father and his uncles, distracted the reign of his cousin Richard II., we know for certain that the young earl at this period of his life went abroad repeatedly. Capgrave ascribes his pilgrimages to the molestations to which he had been exposed at home.[d] Certainly he had no thought of occupying the

---
[a] The various extracts in Ducange under "reisa" show that it was a general word for a military expedition, not confined to Prussia.—L.T.S.
[b] " Möht ich die lieben reise gevaren über se." About 1228.
[c] I believe this statement to be a mistake; Bolingbroke seems to have been his home in 1390-1 it is true, but important documents are dated from Peterborough, and in 1392-3 it is Peterborough whence he started and to which he returned with his baggage. See pp. 2, 143, 148, 254, 270, &c., and p. lxxxiv.—L.T.S.
[d] " De Illustribus Henricis," ed. Hingeston, pp. 98, 99. "Orta autem seditione inter Ricardum regem et quinque dominos, qui vulgariter dicti sunt domini de campo, hic vir magnificus post multas molestias sibi intentas, mare transiit, loca sancta devoto

throne himself, when, like his ancestor, he first joined the Teutonic knights in the year 1390, and two years afterwards] set out on a pilgrimage to the Holy Land.

It is extraordinary that Dr. Pauli, with Henry's accounts before his eyes, omits any mention or notice of the crusade to Barbary. Yet there can be no doubt, from the comparison of dates and the sequence of events that Henry set out to go to Barbary in the first place, and that, knowing of the war going on in Prussia, he intended also to join that later. On this subject see further, p. xxxvii.

References in Chronicles.—Several English writers mention these voyages, but the first of 1390 attracted more attention than that of 1392. Walsingham, in "Ypodigma Neustriæ,"[a] has merely a short paragraph on the siege of Wilna, but in his History gives some detail, crediting the English prince with the lion's share of glory. Henry, he says, in 1390 went to Le Pruys, where with the help of the Marshal and "Wytot" he conquered the army of the King of Lettow, taking four dukes and killing three, with more than three hundred of the more valiant of the enemy. He took the city "Wille" [Wilna], on the walls of which his men were the first to mount. The castle of Wille was besieged five weeks, but on account of the illness which troubled the army the Masters of Pruys and Livland would not longer continue the siege. Eight people of Lettow were made Christians; and the Master of Livland took away three thousand prisoners into his country.[b]

Walsingham's account is wanting in minor dates, but it is worthy to be placed beside those of the Teutonic chroniclers, and gives the main outlines of the campaign. Knighton has but a

affectu visitans . . . . Videns igitur dicta- Henricus sibi periculum imminere, litem temporalem in peregrinationem sanctam vertit." John Capgrave, an Augustinian priest of Lynn, was born 1393, and wrote temp. Henry VI.—L.T.S.

[a] Rolls edition, p. 361.
[b] "Hist. Anglicana." *See* Appendix A,

short mention, the most noticeable part of which is his mistaken statement that Derby took a thousand men to Prussia.[a] Capgrave refers to the journey of 1390 in both his books; in the Chronicle by a few lines which really relate to the battle of Aug. 28 at Kawen;[b] in his "Illustrious Henries" he speaks of the same conflict in general terms under the old idea of combating the enemies of the cross.[c]

The above passages relate to the expedition of 1390 (Part I. hereafter). Capgrave is the only English writer who speaks of the journey of 1392; in his life of Henry IV. he gives a detailed narrative of the journey through Europe to Jerusalem and back which is confirmed in nearly every particular by this Account (Part II.), while helping to understand it.[d] John of Posilge also has a few lines on the subject.[e] Other valuable references are found among the Venetian State Papers, French Rolls, and several other Duchy of Lancaster accounts.

[Besides the scanty English chronicles some contemporary writers in the dominions of the Teutonic Order notice the visits of the young English prince and other distinguished foreigners, principally Scotch and French. These works have been edited in the excellent collection of *Scriptores rerum Prussicarum*, Leipzig, vols. ii. and iii., 1863 and 1866. First are the Latin Annals of the Franciscan convent at Thorn, which after 1360 were continued by an unknown inmate of the house, whose exactness in dates is beyond praise.[f] Relying on these and some other narratives, but chiefly on his own excellent resources, John of Posilge—a parson at Eilau about 1372, who died 14 June, 1405, after having been for twenty years official of Riesenburg, in the diocese of Pomerania

---

[a] Knighton's Chronicle. *See* Appendix A.
[b] *See* Appendix A. Kawen, now Alt Kowno.
[c] "De Illustribus Henricis," Rolls ed., p. 99.
[d] *Ibid.*, pp. 99-101. *See* Appendix B.
[e] "Scriptores rerum Prussicarum," ii., 182. *See* Appendix B.
[f] *See* Appendix A.

—wrote a chronicle in Latin, afterwards translated into German, beginning with the year 1360. This author shows lively interest in minute details as well as large views concerning affairs at home and abroad; indeed he appears to be the most important witness to the grandeur of the Teutonic government in Prussia, and to its high military success just before its fatal decline. Another contemporary, Wigand of Marburg, a herald in the service of the Order till about 1411, after 1394 composed a rhymed chronicle in German. But the original being unfortunately lost, his work is represented merely by an inferior translation into Latin and by a late German extract.[a]

The most valuable records by far, however, of the two journeys of young Henry of Lancaster are his own two Wardrobe Account Books. It is well known to scholars in the medieval history of England that documents of this class, viz. audited accounts of the keepers or treasurers of the king's wardrobe, and occasionally, too, of a prince's or nobleman's, occur now and then as early as the reign of Henry III., and increase in number and importance during the reigns of the Edwards. Though a few of them have been published in *Archæologia* and elsewhere, they are hitherto far from being accessible. A complete collection of all still extant in public or private archives would open indeed an invaluable store for exploring the ways and means, the demand and supply, the manners and customs, the history of prices, the public and private economy in the course of the fourteenth century.[b]

The payments being issued regularly by the hands (per manus) of some official of the earl for the benefit (pro) of the various people belonging to the retinue, or of the sellers of provision, of merchants, mariners, the representatives of the various trades,

---

[a] *See* Appendix A.

[b] A good many accounts of royal and private wardrobes, priories, gilds, and other bodies, have been printed by various societies, as the Antiquaries, Surtees, and Camden, and the Roxburghe Club, besides the work of foreign editors, as Douet d'Arcq. T. Hirsch, &c.—L.T.S.

workmen, clericals, musicians, mendicants, etc., the reader not
only obtains a survey of the manifold officers of the household, but
an insight into its requirements while travelling by sea and land.
Sir Hugh Waterton, chamberlain, presided over the establishment.
Richard Kyngeston, archdeacon of Hereford, was the treasurer.
As clerk of the household [?] acted William Haver, who died,
however, at Königsberg. A great number of men with christian
names and English surnames serve in the stewardship, in different
branches of the household with all its more honourable pursuits for
men and horses, in the stables, the kitchen, the buttery, pantry,
poultry, falconry, etc. From the lists of wages about a dozen
knights may be discerned. There are esquires and valets, a troop
of bowmen and other attendants of the military profession, enlisted
evidently for the *reise*. Six minstrels, a trumpeter, and five other
musicians receive regularly their pay. Derby and Lancaster
heralds accompany the earl. Even some vestiges of a private
chapel, both on board the ship and in Prussian quarters, are
recognisable.[a]

The exact number of the little army of 1390, generally indicated
as the earl's household and family, cannot be calculated, since many
attendants are not accounted for by name, but are comprised with
their superiors. Knighton's *armata manus M electorum militum*,
is certainly overrated. The local chronicler, John of Posilge,
mentions 300 soldiers, and distinguishes "many good bowmen."
Two large vessels were sufficient to convey the party from Boston
to Dantzic.[b] They had German owners,[c] as the names of the
skippers testify. The Easterlings and other members of the Hansa

---

[a] For more detail as to Derby's household and the composition of his little army,
see further, pp. xlii., xlv., xci., xcii.—L.T.S.

[b] Cf. p. 37 **21, 24**, and p. 87 **22, 24**. Some of the party, however, had to go
as passengers in a third vessel, see p. 37 **27**.—L.T.S.

[c] This does not appear to be proved; the vessels probably were English, with
German captains. In any case the vessels were only hulls, and had to be fitted up
with cabins and other accommodation at Derby's expense (see pp. 26, 27, 157 **17** to
158 **6**), as we know was the case at Venice in 1392.—L.T.S.

were enjoying at that time the full development of the celebrated league of German cities, which may be said to have ruled the markets of the Scandinavian kingdoms and of the Flemish and Dutch municipalities. They carried on a very lucrative trade with England by means of their old establishments or factories, at London, Boston, Lynn, Hull, and Newcastle.

Language of these Accounts.—It is very instructive to gather from the names of the hundreds of persons who had to be paid in wages for their labour and in prices for their goods the overwhelming predominance of the Low-German or Saxon element over the people of Slavic or Prussian and Lithuanian extraction. The christian names, taken mostly from some calendar saint, adopt generally the form which is still in use along the coasts of northern Germany. The surnames, unless arbitrarily supplied by the clerk to the original Hankin, Henrik, Claus, are taken either from the various trades and handicrafts, or from some distinguishing quality, or from the town and province of the owner. However, beyond Pruceman, Pruce, Sameland, there is a certain class of names like Kinge Jekell, Pege Peegolt, Hok, Prak, Burrek, which doubtless suggest the original inhabitants of the country. Others, like Jacob Outremar and Kyrsten van Hostrych, allude at least to an immigration from considerable distances. Now and then among the numerous names from Dantzic the reader lights on an Englishman resident at that place].[*]

The surnames of the Englishmen here met with may be divided into three classes, and the same remarks apply to all ranks of society; *first*, those named after a place, as Henry of Bolingbroke, William Willoughby, Peter de Melbourne ; *second*, those drawn from their office or occupation, like Adam Baker, Henry de coquina, William Kage-maker ; and *third*, those whose names of whatever origin had already become crystallized into true surnames, such as John Cudworth, Robert Krakyll, Henry Maunsell. Many of all three kinds

---

[*] *See* before, p. xiii.

occur in the accounts, and it is interesting to note how easily names of the first two slip into the third class by omission of the *le* or *de* denoting qualification. It may be remarked also that though a man was known chiefly by his occupation he sometimes had a proper surname as well, *e.g.*, Lawrence of the kitchen and of the scullery in 1390-1 was, there can hardly be doubt, the same as Lawrence Travers in 1392-3, while in John Fyssher the baker we have a true surname. An important fact demonstrated by the study of the place appellations is, that the men with whom Derby surrounded himself, his household officers, esquires, and valets—whether household or military—were drawn from the towns, manors, and villages of his own or of the Duchy possessions. This cannot perhaps be traced in all cases, but it is patent in so many that the general statement may be taken as true; it is what we should expect in the feudal society of the fourteenth century.

It may here be said that the identification of the foreign names, both of persons and places, has in many cases been a matter of no slight difficulty; the safest guide is perhaps the phonetic, putting oneself into the place of an Englishman in a foreign land who tries to write down what he hears. The mistakes of the scribe misreading some letters are accountable for a good deal.[a]

[The language, or rather the jargon, in which the accounts are written throughout at first sight seems to be Latin. It is the Latin grown up from the Pipe, the Fine, and the Liberate rolls, common in the Exchequer, but much degraded by attorneys and brokers, who were accustomed by long usage to adopt the vernacular term for any object that could not be specified by a word of Latin descent. Hence, owing to the use of abbreviations

---

[a] The word erroneously **printed** Siron, p. 288 **8**, is an example; the first letter resembling nothing **definitely**, I at first **took** it for G, then for S; there is no hint to help in locating the place. In making the Itinerary, I **found** that the party must have passed, in all **probability**, through Verona, **and** turning once more to **the MS.** saw that the letter is an imperfect V, the *a* **having** a turned end (unfortunately not printed) **should** be expanded *na*.

(according to ancient custom), the impossibility of writing out at full length some of the inflexions; hence, too, the favourite use of the French article *le* before a French or English word without the least distinction of gender.* For all these languages, English of course most freely, are mixed up with the Latin substance. Many difficulties arise, moreover, from the indifferent system of orthography, so that certain archaic words and their meaning are not at all easily ascertained. Add a difficult reading now and then, and under such circumstances there always remain a few words which in the end baffle palæographical and historical ingenuity.]

The Latin of these accounts seems to cause much surprise to our foreign friends. Yet it is not so very different in kind, though more in degree, from that of numerous other records, especially accounts, kept in England, some of which must have come under Dr. Pauli's eye. From the standpoint of a classic scholar no doubt the law Latin, and much ecclesiastical Latin of the Middle Ages (such for example as that in the registers of the Knights of St. John at Malta) is barbaric; but for England, viewed as the common official written medium in a country where two languages, French and English, were spoken for two hundred years, it could not help sharing the elements of those living tongues which it had to represent. Life naturally conquered learning. As this official Latin had again in turn considerable influence on the vocabulary of modern English, the study of it is not without much interest for the unclassic student.

Narrative and Itinerary for 1390-1 (*Part I*).—We must now endeavour to find the sequence of events amidst the, at first sight, very confused mass of items comprised under the principal heads into which the accounts are classed. To supplement and define Dr. Pauli's short sketch the itinerary of the journey will be useful, about the dates in which, after the 19th July, there

---

* It is curious that the habit of using the French article *le* before certain nouns survived even through the 17th century. In the Administration Books of Wills at Somerset House, ships are often thus indicated, as le New Milford, 1671, le Defyance, 1696, le Africa galley, 1700, and others.—L.T.S.

is little difficulty. Where no dates are given the names of the towns trace Henry's progress. The further sections as to *Barbary* and *Men on the reysa* attempt to throw a little more light on points not here alluded to.

The appointment of Kyngston the treasurer was signed on 6th May, for the voyages to be made "in the parts of Barbary and of Pruz." How the expenses were met will be shown further on, though the receipts of course stand at the head of Kyngston's account.

[The first entries (p. 5) are for purchases dated London the 5th and 6th May (1390). It appears that earl Henry first went] by the old road to Dover, the same that the Canterbury pilgrims took, viz., [by way of Dartford, Rochester, Ospringe, and Canterbury to Dover, whence he crossed to Whitsand and Calais (pp. 6, 7). Here he remained about three weeks, after sending a message to Paris in order to obtain a safe conduct from the King of France. Items for the kitchen at Calais,[a] for large quantities of wine and beer, victuals

---

[a] Calais, taken by Edward III. in 1347, was by this time well settled by Englishmen and under an English municipality (Chronicle of Calais, Camden Soc., pp. xxiii., xxiv.). The house which Eustache de St. Pierre had occupied in rue Pedrowe had been granted to the elder Henry of Lancaster in 1361 (Kervyn's Froissart, vol. 23, p. 74). John de Lancaster, esquire, had the custody of Merke Castle, close by, in 1391-2 (French Roll, 15 R. II. m. 12), so that the family, no doubt, had a home there to receive them on their frequent visits, whether the younger Henry had a house of his own or not (p. 7,**6**). He was there at least twice in 1390, at St. Inglebert justs in March-April, and for Barbary in May. The Lantern-Gate was the principal entrance to the town; the prison near it, to whose inmates Derby was generous (p. 8 **28**), I have not found named elsewhere. One of the churches of Calais, central in situation, was dedicated to St. Nicholas; was it a warning light hung on the tower of this church for which Derby gave alms in the ship on his return to England (p. 37 **10**)? There was a good deal of *pontage* or toll to be paid here by ships on arrival and departure (p. 37 **11, 19**); a source of funds resembling that insisted on a few years later, 1397 and 1432, for the repair of the haven (Rot. Par. iii. 374, iv. 105a). As to "Paradis" and the haven, see further note, p. 297. Places near Calais named in our text are Gravonyng or Gravelines, on the Flemish frontier, where butcher's meat was bought (pp. 9, 11), and Whitsand or Wissant, a few miles south-west of Calais, where Derby's "harness" or luggage appears to have been landed and carted to Calais (pp. 7, 8). This was an ancient town and landing-place; in 1184 Prince Richard sailed from Dover to Witsand (Eyton, Court of Henry II., p. 260).

INTRODUCTION.   xxvii

and provender of different kind, are entered at Calais between the
13th and 31st May. In the meantime two other messengers had been
despatched, one from Calais to Hertford[a] and back, between the 23rd
and 28th May, and another to London and back (pp. 12, 13), as
was Derby Herald to the court of France.] Levnthorpe, Derby's
receiver-general, was also sent over to Hertford, probably just preceding his master's return (p. 123). [From these references we
conclude that Henry, who no doubt had crossed the channel with
a complete establishment of men and horses, must originally have
intended to proceed] to Barbary.[b] But his plans were altered, as
shown further on. [Derby therefore had to return about the first
of June the way he came, travelling by Dover, Canterbury, and
Dartford to London. While he himself, it seems, went on to see
his father and his own family at Hertford and Berkhampstead, at
the castles of Kenilworth and Bolingbroke, his servants were ordered
to make the necessary preparations for the sea voyage, and to purchase at London and at Hull large stores of provisions and a
quantity of chattels and utensils, all of which were directed to
Boston. On the 8th July the master of the earl's ship and his men
in port there receive remuneration.[c] Much carpentry had to be
done to make the ships ready (p. 27). In the meanwhile Henry
lodged and baited at various places, no distinct date being added or
the purpose hinted at. However, all the time his retinue, his
horses, live cattle, and whatever else was required for the voyage
had found their way to the place of embarkation, to be shipped
there just before the feast of St. Margaret (20th July, p. 27). This
is indeed the last date mentioned on English ground.

It must have been the 8th August when the ships, after passing the
German Ocean, the Sound,[d] Copenhagen (p. 97/**25, 28**), and a

---

[a] Hertford was one of the principal seats of John of Gaunt.—L.T.S.

[b] Dr. Pauli's words were "to proceed by land through Flanders and Germany."
But he had ignored the Barbary episode.—L.T.S.

[c] P. 20 **4**. "Magister navis et servientes sui." These may not be the same as the
skipper and his "nautes."—L.T.S.

[d] Though, of course, the ships passed through the Sound, it is not named here.
"Le Sond," on p. 97, is the Hanse town Stralsund.—L.T.S.

large tract of the Baltic, sighted the Pomeranian coast at Leba], where Derby sent three of his trusty men on land. He himself, with part of his company, landed a little further on at Rixhöft, where they immediately had a meal (p. 38) ; the rest went on by sea to Dantzic (p. 39/**7**). Derby rode in a cart as far as Putzig, there bought a horse and saddle, [and spending the night of the 9th in a mill near the road, he and his party reached Dantzic on the 10th, where they stayed till the 13th of August] (pp. 39, 40) apparently putting up at the house of Lord de Burser. Here Derby must have learnt that Rabe had already started, and he lost no time in pushing on. Lancaster herald immediately took horse with letters from Derby's father to the Grand Master at Marienburg (40/**6**), while the rest [had to wait till the horses, the harness, the arms, and the entire outfit had arrived from the ships, and to purchase fresh stores and horses for the Reysa and the journey towards Königsberg." Crossing the Vistula (p. 44/**4**) without staying at Marienburg, they spent the night of the 13th at the village of Schönberg ; [on the 14th they stopped for the night at Elbing, rode the next day through Braunsberg and Brandenburg, and arrived on the 16th at Königsberg (pp. 44, 45), while the heavy luggage and part of the household were transported to the same destination on the shallow waters of the Frische Haff by prames, the flat boats of the country.[b]

[a] At Dantzic prames were hired, repaired, and fitted up to convey the heavy stores and fresh victuals, beer, etc., by water to Königsberg (pp. 40-42)—where they did not arrive in time (46,**34**)—and thence, partly dragged by men and ropes overland (p. 48 **14**), to the Curische Haff and down the Memel towards the seat of war. They also brought away the sick on 27th August (pp. 50,**32**, 51,**12**, 54,**2**, 55,**5**).

Thirteen hired carts and carters conveyed Derby's land stores and armour from Dantzic to Königsberg (pp. 43 **22-27**, 45 **5**) ; but he also bought seven new waggons (carucæ) to carry victuals for the Reysa, with horse-harness thereto, which were shipped on the prames (p. 44 **8-17**).—L.T.S.

[b] From Königsberg everything was not sent on by the prames ; a large number of baggage-carts, driven by Prussian carters, were hired ; no less than eighteen of these took baggage to Insterburg Castle (p. 51 **17**), where the stores were left under the care of a Prussian during the campaign (p. 53 **25**), while another train of twenty-

INTRODUCTION. xxix

The prince, for whose service during the campaign the Grand Master had appointed two knights (heers, herren), to whom Derby paid a good round sum (pp. 54/**20, 31,** 106/**8**), started again on the 18th, slept at Cremitten, passed through Tapiau, dined (? the 19th) at Norkitten and entered the *Wyldrenesse*, now called the Grauden forest, lying between Insterburg and Ragnit, the wild frontier marches which separate Prussia from Lithuania proper, on the 21st August.][a]

On 22 August he came up with the allied forces under Marshal Rabe (p. 50/**31**), probably near Ragnit, and by the 24th they arrived at the Memel river, crossing it here or somewhat further up. Derby seems to have been welcomed with minstrelsy by the Master of Livland's musicians—that Master having joined the army (p. 105)—and to have received, either then or while before Wilna, several presents from the marshal and other knights, as two or three coursers, an ox, four sheep, and two peacocks (the last three no doubt for his table). At Königsberg two tents, and a horse to carry them, had been hired for his use on the Reysa (p. 50/**3, 27**), for service and guard about which he had two Prussian valets from Ragnit (p. 105/**17**).

On the 25th August the combined army lay before Georgenburg. On the way thither, while near Trappöhnen on the Memel, news had come to them of the death of Rotenstein, the Grand Master. They also learned that Skirgal lay with a strong force further on, near where the Nerya (Wilia) falls into the Memel. A surprise was resolved on; leaving the lesser folk and the extra horses to continue with the vessels[b] up the Memel and the Wilia towards

---

two, each with four horses and a man, were employed in carrying victuals and baggage on to the reysa itself (p. 54 **22**). Their payments were regulated by the two Teutonic Herrs mentioned in the next paragraph.—L.T.S.

[a] Here it was found that some at least of the victuals must be transferred to horses' backs, as the carts could not get through the forest (p. 50 **27**).—L.T.S.

[b] Our text says that the sick were sent away in the prames on 27 Aug. (p. 51 **11**): they must have been among Posilge's "geringe volk." See extracts from Posilge

CAMD. SOC.   e

Wilna, the choicest from the armies were selected; they marched on through the forest towards Old Kowno, and fording the Wilia fell upon Skirgal, forcing him to retreat with great loss. Many were killed in crossing the ford, and Henry lost one of his young knights, Sir John Loudcham, whose body was taken to Königsberg (p. 53/**30**, see after p. 303). Much booty, including 200 saddled horses, fell into the victors' hands, while three dukes and eleven boyars were taken prisoner. This battle took place on Sunday the 28th August.

Wilna, upon the Wilia (now in Russia), the capital of Lithuania and an important seat of trade, was strongly fortified. It consisted of the city on a hill, called by Posilge the outer or "upper house," built of wood (*castrum ligneum*, Wigand), and not walled (*castrum non muratum*, Annals of Thorn), which sheltered numerous inhabitants and merchants; and after this the *castra murata* (Ann. Thorn), walled or built with stone. The first, which must have been extensive and strong, was stormed by the three armies, who had previously made a bridge over the Wilia, and in a few days, *i.e.* on 4 Sept., it was won. This, as the chroniclers Posilge and Walsingham say, was greatly due to Henry of Lancaster, who had many good bowmen, and one of whose Englishmen it was who first planted his flag upon the walls of the city (p. 105/**10, 24,** Walsingham). Fire and terrible slaughter finished the destruction, Karigal, another brother of Jagello, was killed, and numerous prisoners made.

The army then sat down before the two stronger forts, but in spite of mines and engineers[a] and all efforts, the defence was so powerful that at the end of nearly five weeks[b] they were not taken.

and Wigand (Appendix A) for the account of this battle, which has been mixed up with the siege of Wilna by some other writers.

[a] See p. 106 **1**. The miners worked under the shelter of a machine called *sus* (105 **21**), so named because, says William of Malmesbury, "after the manner of a sow they proceed to undermine the foundation of the walls." *See* Ellis, Original Letters, 2d. Ser. i., p. 33.

[b] Posilge says the siege lasted five weeks all but two days.

INTRODUCTION.   xxxi

The besiegers then, compelled by sickness, want of powder, and the late season combined, abandoned the attempt, and returned to their various countries, Derby setting his face towards Königsberg. Walsingham says that eight Lithuanians were made Christians, so that probably Derby took them to England with him from Wilna. The accounts give several items. He bought two boys (p. 52/**26**), who were under the care of a woman named Ferwey or Farys, at Königsberg and Dantzic (pp. 68, 92/**21**); another woman named Wendell or Wendchull had the charge of three boys at Königsberg till Feb. 10 (pp. 65/**6**, 67/**24**, also 90/**20**); while the bailiff of the bishop's house at Dantzic had others in his ward, who may have been the six Lettows for whom pilches or fur coats were bought (pp. 113/**13**, 91/**30**). One was specially named Henry Lettowe, for whom, as well as for Lettish women and children, many items of clothing were provided (pp. 89/**1**, 90/**34**, 91/**29**, 92/**20**). This effort toward substantial conversion is worth notice. What gain to the Order the siege brought about it is hard to say; a charter still exists wherein the Polish king Jagello recognises the services of the general who defended his forts and city, gratitude and courage being by no means confined to the Christians.[a]

[The Earl of Derby returned much the same way he came. Castle Coluwa near the entrance of the Wilia into the Memel, Insterburg and the Wilderness, Tapiau (whence he sent his man John Gylder with letters to England and back, p. 108/12), where the last night was spent, are again mentioned, before Henry and his people re-entered Königsberg on the 20th October.[b] Besides the loss of Sir John de Loudcham, two of his knights were taken prisoners by the enemy, for whose liberation Derby herald was about November despatched with letters to Jagello, King of Poland (p. 108/**3**)]. Professor Prutz prints at the end of his Introduction an interesting letter (preserved in the Königsberg archives)

[a] See Appendix A, p. cx., *note*.
[b] About this time he visited Arnan, where the chapel of St. Katherine was, as Professor Prutz points out, a place of pilgrimage (p. 53,**18**).—L.T.S.

which passed between Conrad von Wallenrod and Henry as to these prisoners, on February 22, 1391, in which Henry tried to get the good word of an eminent Pole, who happened to be at the time in Marienburg, on their behalf with the King, but unsuccessfully. Derby herald was sent to Poland again from Dantzic apparently just before Derby left, in March (p. 111/**21**); but whether the prisoners ever obtained their freedom, or who they were, we do not know.

An entry on the French Rolls is of some interest here as tending to show that Henry may not when he started from England have intended remaining abroad through the winter, viz. a grant dated 4 Dec., 1390, whereby he gave letters of attorney to eight of his people at home, Loveney and Lewnthorpe being of the number, to run in any English court for a year.[a] This legal document must have been rendered necessary in consequence of his prolonged absence.

[The prince spent nearly four months, including Christmas and the New Year, at Königsberg, a sojourn about which many interesting details may be gathered from the treasurer's entries. There were tournaments and hunting parties (pp. 108/**22**). The prince was presented repeatedly with horses and hawks, with deer, three young bears, a wild bull, perhaps an elk (pp. 108/**30**, 109, 111/**3, 10, 15**). Many members of the court had to be provided with fur dresses. The amount of music he had to listen to seems amazing, for minstrels, fiddlers, and musicians of all sorts were almost continually in attendance upon him. In February, 1391, we find him moving again. At least part of his household was transferred to Brandenburg on the 9th, and to Braunsberg on the 10th of that month. On the 14th at Dirschau, on the 15th they revisited Dantzic, the most flourishing city of the country and a principal member of the Hansa, where they stayed about six weeks.

It appears that in Dantzic Henry had to take quarters for his

---

[a] French Roll, 14 Rich. II., m. 8.

INTRODUCTION.   xxxiii

large company in two places, one a house in town that belonged to a burgess named Klaus Gottesknecht (pp. 73/**9**, 111/**1**; the *hospitissa* on p. 96/**2**, **12** may have been his wife), where he and his court had lodgings; the other for the larger portion of his retinue was a little out of the city towards the west, being the mansion of the bishop of Leslau or Cujavia, on a hill or rather a ridge of downs formerly called Old Gorka and later the Bishopsberg, at present one of the strong citadels of the fortified city. The old episcopal castle was destroyed by the citizens later, in the year 1415, but it seems to have been a rather dilapidated place, without doors, or the doors without hinges and locks, as early as 1391, since the rooms had to be restored for human habitation and fitted up in many respects.^a It is fascinating to glance by means of these accounts at the occupations and the manner of living taken up by numerous Englishmen for some length of time in a populous and thriving town, carrying on a very brisk trade with their own country. The most trifling and the most costly expenses for the enjoyment of life and for the approaching voyage homeward, or for the church services,^b which last naturally increased towards

---

^a *See* pp. 72,**13**, 75,**5**, 79,**15**, **30**, 86 **23**. Derby himself stayed at both houses, his residence at the old bishop's house being proved by the item (p. 85 **23**) respecting the *camera et aula*, *i.e.* the lord's own room there, also by the care taken in fitting up the kitchen (p. 79,**21**). I believe that he stayed at Godesknecht's first, until the bishop's house could be put in order; and the torches borne before him from the town to the house may have been on the occasion of his removal. There was a woman hostess or housekeeper in the house, at least in March (p. 83,**13**, **22**, 77,**10**, 111,**16**), and probably all the time.—L.T.S.

^b Among other things, during seven days (probably in Easter week) Derby made a "pilgrimage" in Dantzic itself, visiting and offering at four churches daily, by which he would, like others who performed the same pious duty, obtain the absolution "a pena et a culpa" granted by the Pope, Boniface IX. The indulgences were to be obtained by visiting these churches, and Derby took the advantage of this. (It was in 1390 that Boniface issued his bull against the abuse of the indulgence system by pardoners and quæstors. Jusserand's "English Wayfaring Life," pp. 313-321, 433). No crusading vow, or absolution from it, as imagined by Dr. Pauli ("Pictures of Old England," p. 137), is referred to.

Passion Week, are entered with ever equal and minute accuracy.* Two ships again under the command of Prussian masters (pp. 98/**1, 4**), but with English pilots from Boston (p. 143), were chartered in good time. A number of carpenters (pp. 76, 79, etc.) had to be engaged to erect cabins for men, stables for the animals, and cages for the hawks, of which Henry took home quite a collection, either gifts of his knightly hosts or of his own purchase. After stores of every kind and in very large quantities, purchased from John Bever and other principal merchants of the place, had been taken on board, and Easterday (March 26) had been spent with festivities and liberal offerings, some of which continued till the end of the month, the prince embarked once more, about the 31st March, from which day till the 30th April no expenditure is dated.

With the exception of an occasional charge spent in playing at dice (p. 115/**20**) there is not a word about pastime during a long and tedious voyage, which, however, seems to have proceeded prosperously, though we do not know the exact date of arrival. Henry and his men disembarked again at Kingston-upon-Hull, some of the baggage and victuals being sent on by coasting vessels to Boston (pp. 98/**5**, 99/**20**). All wages for this account terminated with the 30th April, except those of the treasurer Kyngston who was paid up to 18 Jan., 1392. In the month of January, 1392, the accounts were made up at Peterborough, and audited (? at Bolingbroke) between the 1st and 19th of the same month (pp. 2, 143).

Göttingen, 23 July, 1381. R. PAULI.]

---

* The last days of his stay in Dantzic, we learn from Professor Prutz, who prints four letters existing in the Königsberg archives addressed by Wallenrod to the " Duke of Lancaster" (apparently meaning Henry), were somewhat occupied by a dispute that had arisen between one Claus Makenhagen, a subject of the Duke of Stolpe, and some Englishmen at Schonen, the great factory for salting herrings and the herring trade in the south of Sweden. Coming to Dantzic, the man was trapped and imprisoned, and Henry, having it is supposed taken the part of the Englishmen, was appealed to that Claus might be set free and indemnified. He was liberated, but the end of the story does not appear. Prutz, "Rechnungen," pp. lxxiv., ci.-ciii.

Through the haze of numerous undated items we can trace Henry's movements a little further. Some of his baggage was brought by a boat across the Humber from Hull to Barton (where was the principal ferry), and thence was carted right across Lincolnshire southwards to Bolingbroke; Derby himself with some of his party rode the same way, all supping "with haste" at Caistor (pp. 98/**15**). The rest of the baggage was brought to Boston, and thence carted the much shorter distance to Bolingbroke *viâ* Thornton. Richard Catour, who had been to Prussia, had to be buried at Hull, and masses said for him (pp. 99/**29**, 117/**25**); perhaps he had died on board or just after landing. There were expenses at Barton also for a meal for John Beaufort, Thomas Swinford, and others, soon after crossing from Hull, having probably come separately (pp. 100/**3**). Arrived at Bolingbroke, Henry was not long before he made a pilgrimage to Bridlington, where, as Walsingham[*] tells, great miracles had been worked at the tomb of John the late prior there, giving alms and oblations at this tomb (p. 117); his way from Bolingbroke lay through Horncastle, Louth, Caistor, Barton-upon-Humber, Hull, Beverley, and Watton, all which places are here named (pp. 98-100, 117/**1**). In the January following he was at Peterborough (pp. 2, 143).

ITINERARY I., 1390-91.

Date.	
1390.	
May 5, 6	Purchases at London, 3 ; Treasurer for War appointed, 1.
,, 9—31	Archers and men collected at Calais for Barbary expedition, Derby being there also (see after, pp. xxxix., xl.).
,, ? 18	Elmham and Stokes sent to Paris for safe conduct, 8,**17**, 20,**9** (see after, p. xlii.).
June 5	Derby with his suite returned to England (see after. p. xlii., *note b*). Preparations for voyage to Prussia, chiefly at London, Hull, and Boston.

[*] "Hist. Anglicana," under year 1389, p. 189

xxxvi   INTRODUCTION.

Date. 1390.		Modern Name.	Name in MS., page of text, etc.
July 8—19		At Boston, vessel engaged, 20,**4** ; carpenters making it ready 26, 27.	
„ 10—19		At Boston. Treasurer Kyrgston here, 27.	
„ 19		From Boston, Derby sailed, 27, cf. Pomfret's wages, 127.	
Aug. 9		Leba, Rixhöft	Leba, Ross henid or Rooshed, landing there, 38 ; cf. wages, 128.
„ „		Thro' Brück and Putzig	Weste, Pusk, to Dantzic, 38, 39.
„	9, 10	At Dantzic	Dansk, 39, 104 ; Lancaster herald sent to Marienburgh, 40,**7**.
„	13	„ Schönberg	Schonebergh, evening, 44, 45.
ᵃ „	14	„ Elbing	Melwyn, 44, 105.
„	„	„ Braunsberg and	Bronesbergh, 44.
„	„	„ Brandenburg	Brambergh, 44.
„	16	„ Königsberg	Conyngburgh, 45.
„	18	„ Cremitten	Cremeton, 50 ; crossed the Pregel. Beginning of the " Reysa," 131.
„	„	„ Tapiau	Tapion, 50.
„	„	„ Norkitten	Neuerketon, 50.
„	21	„ Insterburg	the beginning of " le Wyldrenesse " or forest, 49, 50 ; baggage left, 53 **25**.
„	22		Derby met Marshal Rabe, probably near Ragnit on the Memel, 50;**31**, 53 **10**.
„	24		On banks of the r. Memel, 51,**2**.
„	25	At Georgenburg	Jorgyngburgh, Castle, 51.
„	27		The sick sent back in the prames, 51,**12**.
Sunday, Aug. 28		Near Alt Kowno "ultra ripam de le Memel," fight with the Lithuanians, 51,**33**.	
ᵇ Sept 4		At Wilna	le Wylle,ᶜ 51. Five weeks' siege.
Cir. Oct. 7		Retreat began, by way of Coluwa (Coln.) on the Wilia, 52 **33** ; Village on the Haff, near Ragnit, 53 ; and Instreburg 53.	

ᵃ The date p. 44 is misprinted 15, it should be Aug. 14, that on p. 105 should also be 14 instead of Aug. 13.

ᵇ John of Posilge gives 4 Sept. as the day when "they came before Wilna." The 5th Sept. is the nearest in our text.

ᶜ Le Wylle (51, 53), as well as Welle elsewhere (105, 106), denotes Wilna. The old name for the river Wilia was Nerga or Nerya.

INTRODUCTION.   xxxvii

DATE. 1390.	Modern Name.		Name in MS., page of text, etc.
Oct. 20	Tapiau		Tapiewe, 53.
	(Arnau)		Capella St. Katerine, 53, **18**.
,,	At Königsberg		Conyngburgh, servants making ready, 57.
,, 22	,, ,,	Derby	here; end of the Reysa, cf. 131, 62 **23**.
Cir. Nov. 1	,,	,,	Birth announced of Humphry, Derby's fourth son, 107.
Dec. 25, etc.	Königsberg		Christmas spent here, 67, 68.
Feb. 9	,,	quitted	for Dantzic; cf. 67, 69.
,, ,,	At Brandenburg		Bramberg, 69.
,, 10	,, Braunsberg		Brounesbergh, 69.
,, 11	,, Elbing		Melwyn, 70.
,, 13	,, Marienburg		Maryngburgh, 71; at St. Anne's chapel of the Order there, 116, **22**.
,, 14	,, Dirschau		Darsowe, 71.
,, 15	,, Dantzic		Dansk; ? getting ready the Bishop's house for Derby, 72 **13**, 74, **22**, etc.
,, 16	,, ,,		Derby in Gottesknecht's house, 73.
Mar. 26, Easter Day.	,, ,,		Lent and Easter here, 72-83, 110, 111.
Mar. 31	,, ,,		Daily oblations till this day, 117, **5**.

The Barbary Crusade: Derby at Calais.—We must now reconsider the events of the first half of 1390. In 1389 the Genoese, finding their commercial navigation still threatened by the Moorish corsairs of Barbary, in spite of the recent successs of the Sicilians against the pirates, applied to France for aid to punish them. An embassy was sent to Charles VI. at Toulouse towards the end of that year, proposing to send an expedition to take the city El Mahadia (near Cape Africa, Tunis), and thus to strike a central blow. The warlike spirits of France were fired, Charles consented, and Louis II. de Clermont, duke of Bourbon, the king's uncle, took the lead of this new crusade. In March, 1390, he was in Paris raising money for the voyage to Barbary. Recruits poured in from France, Spain, and England in such numbers that the Genoese, whose part it was to find ships and to provision the expedition, could not supply enough bread and corn, and the date and port of rendezvous were therefore changed; instead of Genoa about June 24, all were to meet at Marseilles on 1 July, 1390. It must be noted that Froissart states that those who lived furthest from Genoa began to set forth about the middle of May. He adds, " Si misrent bien ung mois ou environ à là venir avant que ils fuissent assemblées." Louis' preparations were successful, and the expedition was ready at the time intended.

Among the English volunteers who actually went were John Beaufort (son of Lancaster and Catherine Swinford), with twenty-four knights and gentlemen and a hundred archers.[a] Henry Lancaster's eldest son had also intended to join the crusade, as proved by the accounts in this volume, which also prove that he did not actually go.[b] In this same year, 1390, from 20 March to 24 April, three French knights, Jean le Meingre, brother of Marshal Boucicaut, Regnault de Roye, and the Sire de Sempy,[c] had held the justs of St. Inglebert near Calais, which were attended by many English; among these were the brothers Henry and John, who, according to the Baron Pichon, took their turn on 20 April.[d] Froissart[e] narrates that the English returned all together, and presumably the brothers were among them. They had then opportunity while in Calais for these justs to learn the proposals and

---

[a] As to the Barbary crusade, *see* " France en Orient," par J. Delaville le Roulx, i., 166-176 ; Froissart, ed. Kervyn de Lettenhove, vol. 14, pp. 154-159.

[b] Sir John Hayward, whose " Life of King Henry IV.," was published in 1599, was quite aware of the Barbary expedition, but he mixed it with the events of the Reysa of 1390 in most curious confusion. His relation up to the landing in Barbary — save that he makes Derby go — is pretty correct ; then in describing the action he imports the battle at Alt Kowno (without the name), with the slain dukes and soldiers and prisoners as in Walsingham, as well as the five weeks' siege and other circumstances at Wilna, only he calls the city Tunis ! *See* pp. 30, 31.

[c] Derby afterwards sent the Sire de Sempy a gift of a palfrey, doubtless in acknowledgment of his courtesy (p. 34, l. 25).

[d] " Joutes de St. Inglebert," at end of " Partie inédite des Chroniques de St Denis," Paris, 1864, p. 73.

[e] Ed. Kervyn, vol. 14, pp. 150, 151.

arrangements for joining the Barbary expedition; and they returned to England to make or to complete their own preparations.

The very first document in connection with the present accounts is the appointment by Derby of a special Treasurer for War, dated at London, on 6th May; in this he expressly states that he is undertaking voyages into Barbary *and* Prussia, showing that from the beginning not only was the idea of joining the Barbary crusade seriously entertained, but that he intended to make both expeditions. He must therefore have begun preliminaries before this date, and it is of course possible that several undated payments which fall within the year here accounted for may have actually been incurred before the 6th May. Among these may be the letters to some great French official, represented by the erroneous term "senescallus Francie."[a] It is also likely that Derby should have sent his herald to the French king (p. 15, l. 4) for a safe conduct to Barbary quite at the beginning of May, if not earlier. Whether the August reysa in Prussia had been actually determined on before the alliance with the Samaites, signed on the 26th May,[b] may be doubtful, in view of the hostilities and losses which immediately preceded that treaty; but it is clear that Henry or his father must have kept themselves informed of the troublous state of the country and the perplexities of the Teutonic Order from early in the year. And news of the serious need of the knights may have reached Henry in May and have moved him to give up altogether the Barbary crusade.

A careful examination of the pay lists for 1390-91 (pp. 118-127) further supports the assumption that Derby went to Calais early in May for the purpose of joining the crusade to Barbary. His connection Thomas Swinford, with about twenty esquires and three or four principal officers of his household, were with him at Calais, as it appears, from May 9 till May 31 (some remained a few days later), each providing one or more archers. Two archers are

---

[a] *See* note on p. 297.   [b] *See* before, p. xv.

named on their own account, Bodendale and Prendergast; besides these Lord Willoughby sent two, and Lord Bagot ten. All these were paid by Derby; in the case of Bagot's men he even paid their return back to England, five on 25 May, five on 2 June (pp. 118, 122). The fare also of others was paid back to Dover (p. 36/**9**). Moreover, the pay of all these archers, whose number amounted to forty-one, was made at the rate given for *extra curiam*, 1s. a day, except in the case of six who received *infra curiam* pay, viz. 6d. a day. Why should he have incurred this expense? The inference is strong that they had been engaged for military service which was not fulfilled indeed, but that nevertheless they had to be paid before discharge. Boatage was paid for the return of the knights, esquires, and archers to Dover (p. 36/**11**). Compare too the last item but one of Kyngston's receipts for 1390-1 (p. 4), where he accounts for the value of 16 bows sold in Calais remaining from those provided "for the journey to Barbary," and the large sum, £29 6s. 10d., paid in London by Loveney, the clerk of the Wardrobe, for cloth for Derby's esquires and valets—in which last term may be included the archers[a]—"for the journey to Barbary" (p. 35/**20**). Again, the first item of wardrobe matters bought in England this year was for 80 bows and 6 broad bows (p. 34), which without very close calculation appears to allow sufficient supply for the archers of both expeditions, especially when it is considered that little indication is given of archers having been taken on the Prussian reysa (it is remarkable that only six are mentioned, besides

---

[a] The archers on service *infra curiam* were sometimes designated archer-valets, *valetti sagittarii*, cf. the items of those who went on the reysa (p. 128), where *valettus* and *sagittarius* are with one exception (which proves the rule) used indifferently, and all are paid at 6d. a day. Of those who were at Calais on service *extra curiam*, only one bears both designations, viz. Thomas Toty's man, called *sagittarius* till 31 May and *valettus* 1-10 June (pp. 118, 123), again proving that an archer was a shooting valet. Other valets were distinguished as " valets of the chamber," etc. (p. 129). In 1392 the king ordered that all the valets, and even servants below that grade, of his household should practise with the bow. Rymer, vii., p. 721.

the "gunner sagittarius" who first gained the walls of Wilna pp. 105, 128). It is clear therefore that Derby made considerable preparations with the full intent of going to Barbary, and the most reasonable explanation of the presence of so many of his archers and esquires in Calais for three or four weeks in May seems to be that he had them there ready for that expedition. Had he meant them for Prussia, with the first intention of taking the road thither through France, as supposed by Professor Prutz, why did he not take them for that reysa when he actually started in July? It is hard to believe the archers could have been on the reysa without his paying them; on the other hand, of the esquires who were in Calais eleven did accompany Derby to Prussia and were with him throughout the year.[a]

Besides the above, there were many others at Calais in Derby's pay, chiefly from 9 to 31 May, and a few beyond into the first days of June; these were valets and various officers and subordinates, many of whom afterwards went to Prussia.[b] The whole number thus paid (including archers and esquires) was about 120 persons, of whom but a very small proportion, such as Jenico, Elmham, and Stokes, performed merely occasional service.

It is evident again, from the terms of the writ of audit, that something had been done towards the Barbary journey, it is not ignored as though it had been entirely dropped. Kyngston also (p. 3) speaks of his account as for the "voyage ordained to the parts of Barbary," as well as for the voyage going into Prussia. Lastly, we know that Derby sent his herald to the King of France for a safe-conduct to go to Barbary (see p. 15,4). Conclusive

---

[a] These were John Assheley, John Cope, J. Dalyngrugge,* Rich. Dancaster,* Thomas Gloucester, Roger Langford, Ralph Rochford,* Wm. Sewardby, Ralph Staveley,* Thomas Toty, and John Waterton. The four marked by an asterisk had been at the justs of St. Inglebert in April.

[b] About twenty valets and servants of various grades, from John Countershaw at 6d. a day to John Walker and his ten fellows at 2d. a day each, are only mentioned as at Calais, or there and returning to England; a few, as Langdon, Syde, and Wolfley were abroad with Derby again in 1392-3.

evidence of this is furnished by Whitteby's accounts, where it is found that the Duke of Lancaster made a gift of 20 florins of Arragon (= £6 13s. 8d.) to " Derby heraldo domini comitis Derbye eunti Regi Francie pro uno salvo conducto adquirendo pro dicto comite eunti versus partes Barbarie " (D. of L., cl. 28, bdle. 3, No. 2). Though this payment was not made till a year and half after the event, the fact was incontestable.

Derby commissioned his treasurer, Kyngston, on 6 May, 1390, for his voyages to Barbary and to Prussia (p. 1). From 9 to 31 May his men were ready in Calais; some time in May he sent Elmham, a man of trust accustomed to treaty, together with John Stokes, probably with an escort of three archers,[a] from Calais to Paris, again to seek a safe-conduct from the King of France. Elmham is the only man the pay of whose archers began so late as May 18, which affords ground for believing that they were on the special service of escorting their master on his Paris mission, during at least part of the three weeks they were retained. Derby himself was at Calais till 5 June, when he returned to England.[b]

There were thus, apparently, two attempts by Derby to procure a safe-conduct through France in 1390; perhaps Elmham's journey had reference to the Prussian undertaking; perhaps its object was to carry out the final negotiations as to Derby's part in the Barbary expedition.[c] Whether the influx of volunteers rendered his adhesion unnecessary is only matter of conjecture; it is reasonable to

[a] See notes *Elmham* and *Stokes*, after, p. 295.

[b] The date is not directly given, but may be gathered by comparing the dates of the cook's wages and those of other servants, on p. 125. with those of Payne, Staveley, and others, *infra curiam* at Calais and *infra curiam* in England, p. 126.

[c] It is, of course, possible that Derby's herald accompanied Elmham, and that the entries (pp. 8-17, 20-9, 15-4) refer to one and the same mission, which in that case certainly related to Barbary: the terms leave it doubtful. Elmham and Stokes were paid at once separately, the herald (a regular retainer) received the chief part of his fee long after, as shown above. Bourbon himself was not in Paris at this time; moving about while preparing, he was at Turin from 17 to 19 May (" France en Orient," i., 172).

suppose, as before suggested, that the Teutonic expedition offered at this juncture much stronger inducements. That the attempts were in some way rendered unnecessary may be inferred from the result; Derby changed his intentions, and did not pass through France at all this year, nor till his return from Palestine in 1393. The *personnel* of his following at Calais, and of that which actually went to Prussia, differed so much as to warrant the belief that if he at first sought a safe conduct for the purpose of leading his Prussian expedition through France, it must have been for the smaller and less important contingent; and that, going back to England to gather a stronger force, shipping direct from an English port was found to be a more convenient and safer means of transit.

Men on the Reysa; actual strength.—Taking the pay-lists given on pp. 128-133, we find that the knights who were of Derby's retinue for the reysa (18 August to 22 October, sixty-six days), and who (except Loudeham) received 2s. a day for that service, were—

<ul><li>Peter Bucton.</li><li>Hugh Waterton.</li><li>Thomas Swynford.</li><li>John Norbury.</li><li>John Loudeham.</li><li>Thomas Erpingham.</li><li>Thomas Rempston.</li><li>John Clifton.</li><li>Richard Goldsburgh.</li><li>John Loveyn.</li></ul>

To these we must add William Willoughby, who received his pay in a lump sum on Oct. 28, just after the end of the expedition (p. 106/**12**). This pay (£10) may have included an archer (he was paid separately for two archers sent to Calais, p. 119).

Erpingham took an esquire, Bucton and Swinford an archer (or archer-valet) each, H. Waterton and Norbury two archers each.[a] Clifton, Goldsburgh, and Loveyn were only paid for these sixty-six days, and we do not hear of them again, except that Clifton was repaid the purchase of a chess-board and men for Derby (p. 113/**17**).

[a] These are the only archers mentioned as connected with the Prussian reysa.

Loudeham was killed in the battle on 28 August. Besides the other officers of the household[a] there were on the reysa sixteen esquires, who for that service were paid 1s. a day, with Lancaster herald and master William Cook, both paid at the same rate (Derby herald is not entered as on the reysa itself). Of valets of the chamber, and of other grades, twenty-five were *infra curiam* throughout the reysa (eight of these same men are called "gromes" on a later page), and to complete all, the six indispensable "minstrels." The numbers thus stand, *for the reysa* itself—

Knights 11, their men 7	18
Officers of household (not knights) . .	4
Esquires, and two at their pay . .	18
Valets of the chamber, gromes, &c.. .	25
Minstrels	6
	71

Many of these, chiefly Derby's personal followers, were on service during the whole stay abroad in 1390-1, some also in England and Calais previously performed various services, and received their pay accordingly. Besides these, we find casual mention of a few others who received gifts "pur le Reys," the Zealand, Dampier, and Croyslett heralds (p. 107), two Prussian knights (106/**8**), two Prussian valets from Ragnit (p. 105/**17**), an esquire of Dantzic (p. 106/**30**), and Derby's host, whoever he was, at Königsberg, who was " cum domino in le Reys " (p. 111/27); of these, however, only the three heralds came from England. There were also miners and engineers, how many is not stated (pp. 105/**20**, 106/**1**). Several minor valets and servants who are mentioned as receiving gifts in Prussia, though they do not seem to have got regular pay, such as John del Ewery, Robert Jonson (of the buttery) (p. 108/**25**), W. Fyssher (baker), Graceless, Syde, Byngeley, Thomas Waterton, Geoffry (baker), John Colle, must have swelled the retinue from

---

[a] See after, p. xcii.

England; and we get a few indications that some at least of the knights and officers had their own servants too, such as Norbury, Kyngston the treasurer, and Morley, one of the chief valets (pp. 110/**11, 32**), John Davy, and Sir John Loudeham (pp. 99, 143/**3**). In scanning the long list of *Dona* (pp. 104-115) the names of many of those who received regular pay, either upon the Reysa or at other times, appear; besides those of many others who had but temporary employment in one place or another, such as boatmen, minstrels, and messengers, all or the greater part not from England; care must be taken therefore not to count these in reckoning the number that Henry took with him. If we add these 16 Englishmen, and allow 10 miners and engineers as Derby's contribution to the siege, we get close upon a hundred. In allowing for the servants of knights and officers we must take into account the probability of their being hired in Prussia on arrival in a majority of cases, which would save the expense of sea and land transport; Lord Erpingham is expressly said to have a " Richard ducheman " *i.e.* a German servant (pp. 49, 60), and several "duche" men are mentioned (see Index I.).

Thus to make up even the 300 men supposed by Posilge to have been taken by Derby to Prussia, the most moderate estimate of the chroniclers, we must allow (1) for a large number of menials and servants, say one " famulus " taken by each of the esquires and chief valets ; (2) the ten knights had probably each his own retainers at his own expense, Derby paying their lord only. Many of these, even of the servants, may have been bowmen, like those of Richard's household two years later. We may thus perhaps allow for a certain number of bowmen here unaccounted for; but there seems no escape from the conclusion that the actual number was really smaller than 300. 150 to 200 seems to be nearer the truth.

The Winter Household.—After the Reysa was over Derby retired to Königsberg, where he took up his abode from about 22 Oct. (pp. 131, 62/**23**, 63/**15**) to 9 February (p. 69/**13**) ; he

then moved on to Dantzic, where he stayed from 15 February till
31 March, perhaps a few days longer (pp. 72, 117/**5**). During all
this time, *i.e.*, 1 Nov. to 30 April, the pay-lists show that he had a
large retinue with him, no less than from sixty to sixty-three persons had regular pay, so that he must have kept up a large establishment. Besides the ten officers of the household marked (see after,
p. xcii.), there were Erpingham, Swinford, Dalingridge, Norbery, and
Sir John Malet,[a] knights; fourteen or fifteen esquires,[b] besides the
Master Cook, and Derby the herald—the latter taking esquire's pay
of 7d. a day when merely *infra curiam*. There were also twenty-
five valets receiving regular pay, twenty of whom had been on the
reysa, doubtless some few had remained at Königsberg (we find an
item for laundry "before the lord returned from the reysa,"
p. 54/**13**). Some of these, and nine others besides, to the number
of twenty-two, received livery, *i.e.* a pilch or warm gown, at the
New year p. 112), a few also received horses at that time. Add
the six regular minstrels, and allow for some casual supernumeraries, and we get the total of between 70 and 80 persons paid
forming Derby's winter's establishment abroad.

Habbegood and Catour, two of the valets of the chamber, paid
at the highest rate, 6d. a day, died during the year; Habbegood
soon after the return to Dantzic in the beginning of November
(cf. 107/**17**, 130/**3**), and Catour perhaps at sea or just on the return
to England, for his wages were paid up till April 30 (pp. 99/**29**,
140/**7**). Oblations and a mass of requiem performed at Hull about
this time may have been on his account (p. 117/**25**). These, with
Hauer and the knight Loudeham, mentioned on pp. xliv., xcii.,
make up the tale of the dead in 1390-1.

---

[a] *See* note *Malet*, p. 308.
[b] The esquires were Houghton, Langeford, Cope, Toty, Gloncestre (John or
Thomas), Rocheford, Chelmeswick, Staveley, Dancastre, John Waterton, Hasildene,
Rygmayden (William or Richard, perhaps both), Bugge, Assheley. Reginald
Curteys, who also performed some duties connected with the household at Königs-
berg and Dantzic (pp. 102,20, 104,1), had esquire's pay from 1 January.

Narrative and Itinerary for 1392-3.—(*Part II.*)
The motive for Derby's second year of travel may have resembled that assigned by Capgrave in 1390, viz., a desire to avoid political troubles at home. He must have heard of the still frequent campaigns of the Teutonic knights, and with a desire for action have determined to go again to Prussia in order to join them in what expedition might be on foot. On 27 June, 1392, the king's letters of protection for a year were granted to Derby and his companions Hugh and Robert Waterton as then about to go abroad; and on 6 Feb. following Derby's letter was renewed also to last a year, he being then described as "tarrying abroad."[a]

Preparations were made then at Lynn[b] for aid in another reysa, and Kyngston was re-constituted treasurer for war on 15 July (p. 148/**30**), viz., the day before our second account opens, though he charged for a week's wages previously, being the time he took in coming from Hereford to Lynn (p. 291). John, Duke of Lancaster, who had, on 1 July, at Leicester, granted to his son Henry 2000 marks a-year, to be paid quarterly out of the receipts arising from his possessions at Tutbury and Bolingbroke, the first payment to be made at Michaelmas 1392, on 19 July advanced (*prestita*) the whole 2000 marks, adding to them a gift (*donum*) of 1000 more, both expressly "for his voyage to Prussia." This we learn from the accounts of Whitteby, the Duke's receiver-general,[c] and the receipt given by Kyngston for this money (p. 147) is one of the documents attached to his second account. Leunthorpe, Derby's own receiver-general, for the same purpose, paid over to Kyngston

---

[a] French Roll, 16 Rich. II., mems. 14, 6.

[b] While at Lynn, Henry had some communication with Henry Spencer—the crusading Bishop of Norwich (1370-1406), the firm and able man who had led a campaign against the Flemings nine years before, and who in his own episcopate bore hard upon the Lollards—but what message the valet Freeman brought back we cannot tell (p. 270 **15**).

[c] D. of L., cl. 28, bdle. 3, no. 2 (two leaves from the end).

£100 on 20 July,[a] and with these funds Derby set sail from Heacham, 14 miles north-east of Lynn, on 24th July.[b]

A great part of his stores were bought at Lynn, where also the three ships (p. 278) which carried him and his company were fitted out (p. 157) Several of his men were at Lynn some time making ready (p. 270). Spices were bought in London (p. 160), some baggage was brought from Peterborough[c] in four boats, which seem to have taken three days about it (p. 151/**21**, **26**), while ten boats were hired to tow the ships from Lynn to Heacham (p. 159/**11**).

The voyage appears to have been quicker than that of 1390, the vessels arriving on 10 August at Putzig and Dantzic, at which last Derby stayed a fortnight. Probably one of the three houses at which he and his party stayed (p. 259) was the house of Gottesknecht, his host the former time (p. 180/**14**). On 25 August he started from Dantzic, passed through Dirschau to Elbing, where he was the guest of the Augustinians for perhaps two days, making offerings at the abbey on the 29th, reached Braunsberg on 31 Aug. and arrived at Königsberg once more on 2 September. We get little help from the chronicles as to what he did while here, or why he made so short a stay. For he left Königsberg on either 3 or 4 Sept., and returning through the same towns was back in Dantzic probably by the evening of 7th. But Capgrave,[d] relating that "as the lords of the province were not friendly to his desire, he left them," seems to indicate the truth that the Grand Master and his allies did not want Henry's services this time; and this view is confirmed by Wigand, date about June 1392, who says that many nobles, Percy of England, and others, then were there wishing to help Vitold, but that he turned them back when they got as far as

[a] D. of L., cl. 28, bdle. 3, no. 5, fo. 5 v°.; and after, p. 149.

[b] This date is due to Capgrave (see Appendix B). Our account shows Derby at Heacham on 20 and 21 July, playing at dice and evidently waiting (p. 263). See note, p. lxxx.

[c] Sometimes shortened to Burgh, as on p. 151, cf. p. 162,**10**.

[d] See Appendix B.

Tzuppa (between Insterburg and Kowno), as he did not need them.[a] Derby's visit to Königsberg therefore, only a few months later, may have been in order to see and hear for himself at headquarters whether anything further could be done, and the immediate hopelessness of action must have driven him back to Dantzic at once to take measures of another kind. A significant item in Kyngston's account shows that the Order paid him a considerable sum, £400, towards his great charges undertaken on their behalf (p. 149/**20**). The Marshal Engelhardt Rabe appears to have met him at Dantzic (though Kyngston had to go to Königsberg for the money), and thus they parted at least on fair terms.

Posilge's improbable assertion that in consequence of a quarrel at Dantzic, in which Derby's men killed Hans, a countryman, he left Prussia to avoid the revenge of the friends, is not borne out by these accounts. Derby paid the rector of the church of Dantzic,[b] by agreement, for the burial of Hans and his servant, while he and his household gave oblations and alms to the poor on the occasion (pp. 166-7, 273), all which are peaceable and regular actions, and evidently settled the matter. The date of the payment is apparently 25 August, so that the incident happened before Derby went to Königsberg, during his first fortnight in Dantzic. Moreover, the second stay in Dantzic of Derby or some of his people extended over twenty days, making a sojourn in Prussia of about six weeks in all.

Prof. Prutz, relying on an entry in the "Annals" of Thorn (evidently misdated 1391),[c] inclines to the opinion that strife as to the right of bearing the banner of St. George was the cause of

---

[a] "Multi etiam negotiatores erant ibi, et peregrini nobiles, sc. dominus Perse de Anglia, etc., qui proponebant ire in Ritterswerder in succursum Wytandi, quos remisit ad sua, cum venissent ad Tzuppam, dicens: se non egere auxilio eorum, quia convertisset se et revertuntur in Königsberg." Script. rer. Pr., ii., p. 618.

[b] The Marienkirche, says Professor Prutz.

[c] "Dux de Lankasten Anglicus fuit in Prussia et habuit multas contentiones pro vexillo sancti Georgii, sed non obtinuit." (Script. rer. Pruss. iii., p. 168.)

INTRODUCTION.

Henry's change of plan. St. George was the chief patron saint of the Teutonic Order; his was the banner under which Englishmen also went to battle, and they had for the last fifty years especially considered him as their patron, since Edward III. had founded the Order of the Garter dedicated to his honour. Other nations also had their orders of St. George. But on their own territory, and in the reysas on their behalf, the Teutonic knights insisted that they should have precedence, and alone among contingents from other nations should bear St. George's banner. Naturally this led to contention; the English had been prohibited in 1364, and in the summer of 1392 difficulties had again arisen when, in addition to the banner borne by the Order's officer, Lord Percy had unfurled his flag at the head of his Englishmen, peace being only partially restored by Witold and his wife.[a] Setting aside the probability that the entry in the "Annals" of Thorn really refers to the troubles with Percy, Henry might have felt his English dignity offended if he, more powerful than Percy, could not gain the right contended for. On his first and effective visit he seems to have given way peaceably, as we find him making a gift of a dozen yards of blanket to "le Here" who carried the banner, who can be no other than the Teutonic knight (p. 89/**28**). But the accounts give us no clue as to what happened on this matter on his second visit, except that at Lynn he had made two "getens" or pennons of worsted and buckram, with the arms of St. George, presumably to take with him (p. 152/**28**). From the materials, however, these were most likely provided as ensigns to hang out of the two chief ships.[b]

Men on the Second Journey.—Capgrave says that Henry took with him about 300 men (the same number was set down by

---

[a] Wigand, Script. rer. Pruss. ii, pp 541, 646, 648.

[b] Fifty years later the Earl of Warwick had "a gyton for the ship of eight yards long." See a valuable article on flags in Retrospective Review, 2d Ser., vol. i., pp. 111, 114, 115. *Guydhome, guydon, gyton,* are three forms of the word there found, which the accounts have as *geten.*

INTRODUCTION.   li

Walsingham for the first voyage). An analysis of the accounts for 1392-3, and especially of the pay-lists (pp. 264-272), must, as before, be our guide, which will give general results, without, indeed, assurance on many desirable details. Altogether we find mentioned eighty-seven men, all but a few of whom he must have taken with him,[a] viz.:

> *Knights and officers*, 10.
> Otto Granson.[b]   Ralph Rochford.
> William Willoughby.   Richard Kyngston.
> Hugh Waterton.   Hugh Herle.
> Peter Bueton.

Erpingham apparently joined him on 23 Sept. at Schonee, just as he had left Dantzig, and an Austrian knight, Ralph de Vienna, joined him on 6 April at Venice or Treviso, and travelled to England with him. Another knight, Peter Scinlatour, he met with on his travels. His chaplain, Hugh Herle, receives wages only till Sept. 30, but as we find him at Prague towards the end of October, he was probably with Derby all through, the wages standing over. Kingston, too, was continually with Derby, but for the eight weeks from 1 Oct.—24 Nov., 1392, he took no wages, an omission I cannot explain.

Esquires 15, the two heralds Lancaster and Derby, Master William Cook and William Pomfreit, clerk of the kitchen, made up 19. (Of the esquires eleven had also been on the journey of 1390.)[c]

Valets 49, including as before pages and valets of the chamber

---

[a] The most part received wages from the 21 July, 1392.

[b] See note on p. 309.

[c] The esquires were R. Chelmswyke, Peter Melbourne, R. Staveley, T. Toty, John Payne, T. Gloucester, Robert and John Waterton, the bastard Granson, Francis de Lombardy, R. Dancaster, W. Gyse, T. Goter, W. Rygmayden, Edm. Bugge. Toty and Payne were constant attendants, evidently trusted men; Bugge and Gyse only appear now and then at the end of the accounts. Lancaster herald joined him in April, 1393.

INTRODUCTION.

of various grades, also John Fisher the baker, to which add 7 minstrels and 2 henksmen, 58. (Of this division 24 had been on the journey of 1390.)

Thus finding a total of 80 men who sailed from Lynn, which is somewhat higher than the computation (before, p. xliv.) for 1390, we must again count upon servants of the squires and dependents, &c., of the knights to make up near the number attributed to the expedition. In this case, as in that, it is difficult to find the 300, even if we consider that many who were of the company received no wages but simply lived at their master's expense,[a] a large undeterminate body for whom the great quantities of meat, bread, beer, and wine were purchased. That this was the case sometimes may be inferred from an expression on p. 272/**6, 14**, where we find that several valets and pages had no wages paid them from the 1 Jan. till 17 Feb.—a period which came in the midst of 119 days for which they were paid - because they were " super expensis domini." In other words they were boarding at his expense while he was away on his voyage from Venice to and from the Holy Land.

Being returned to Dantzic, and the determination taken to go thence to Palestine, some of the party and stores had to be sent home to England as no longer needed, and those chosen to go on had to be arranged and horsed. A ship was despatched homewards towards the end of September, the master of which, Ludkyn Drankmaistre, received 100 marks or £66 13s. 4d. for her hire (p. 279), the English pilot, John Benet, one of Derby's men, only receiving four marks for the whole voyage (p. 162/**3**). This vessel brought to England (?) Robert Waterton, Derby's master of the horse, and his brother John, the four esquires, Rygmayden, Bugge, Gyse, and Goter, about six minstrels, twenty-six[b] valets of the

[a] The figures of the Duke of Clarence, cited on p. **xc.**, confirm this view.
[b] This list is based on the dates for which wages were paid (pp. 267-9), and a note in the margin of p. 267 shows that this is a true general guide, although some of the details are not clear. R. Waterton, for instance, was only paid till 13 Aug., he may

horse (as Morley), of the kitchen including John Fisher the baker, and of various degrees; the two chief valets of the wardrobe, John Dyndon and John Dounton having charge of their lord's wardrobe, *i.e.*, his armour and military trappings (pp. 179/**32**, 257/**19, 23**). Last, not least, lord William Pomfreit, the clerk of the kitchen, a responsible man, accompanied them, for it was into his hands at York on 12 November, after their arrival, that Leunthorpe paid the 100 marks for the freightage of the ship direct out of Derby's funds at home (p. 162/**22**), so that this money did not pass through Kyngston's account (pp. 279, 290).ᵃ When the vessel arrived at Hull the baggage was sent overland to Lynn and thence by boat to Peterborough (p. 162); and Pomfreit sold the victualing stores returned, the money for which he later handed over to Kyngston (p. 151/**5**).

John Dyndon's wages *infra curiam* ceased on 22 Sept., and his wages *extra curiam* were for eleven days after his master left Dantzic, during which time he had to hire a room in which to keep the "garderoba" till they should sail (pp. 268/**20**, 179-80). Derby therefore left Dantzic on 22 Sept., while his followers sailed for England on 3 Oct.; and the twenty days on p. 259/**10** must be reckoned from the 3 Sept., the day he left Königsberg, as his second stay in Dantzic could not have been more than fifteen or sixteen days.

The remaining retinue with which Derby travelled forward was thus pretty numerous, seven chief officers and knights, about ten

therefore have been sent away earlier than the rest; he seems to have joined Derby again on 1 June, 1393, when he had reached Chambery. About half the men, including the four esquires and the minstrels, were paid from 21 July till 15 Sept.; the rest, among whom were Dyndon and Fisher, from 21 July till 22 Sept. Travers of the scullery and Kikkeley the cook did not return with these, see p. 210, 212.

ᵃ In Leunthorpe's Account for 16, 17, and 18, Rich. II. (D. of L., cl. 28, bdle. 3, no. 5, fo. 5 vº), he enters, "per manus Willielmi Pountfreit clerici coquine ejusdem hospicii [domini]. lxvj li. xiij s. iiij d.; pro frecto vnius nauis a Portu de Dansk in Prucia vsque portum de Kyngston super Hull cum garderoba domini et parte familie sue, per indenturam ipsius Willelmi datum apud Ebor. xij die Novembris anno xvjº."

esquires, of whom Toty seems to have acted as master of the horse for a time (p. 257/**12**), the two heralds, and about twenty-five to thirty valets and servants, Shelford, Gilder, and Harpeden being valets of the chamber (p. 208); Crakyll, the trumpeter, too, was not forgotten. Jacob, the guide, was hired to take them through the unaccustomed lands. Between forty and fifty in all, besides supernumeraries, of whom we have no account, and casuals here and there along the route.

More Funds.—Starting anew on a distant journey additional funds had to be provided, and for aid in their transmission the Lancasters, father and son, had recourse to the Lombards. The name Lombard was used in the thirteenth and fourteenth centuries as a general term for Italian merchants of Tuscany and Lombardy; among the cities which sent forth into other countries members of their flourishing *societates* were Lucca, Florence, Genoa, and Venice.[a] Several entries on the Rolls of Parliament show how their success in England, like that of the Jews, excited the jealousy of the natives.[b] The exchange and storage of money was in their hands in Italy from early times, and became extended and regulated as commerce grew and the passing to and fro of crusaders and pilgrims increased. Derby had sent a messenger from Calais to Lombardy early in 1390, doubtless on some financial affair (p. 17/**2**) Several un-named Lombards are mentioned in Kyngeston's account for 1392-3, from whom articles had been purchased or loans made, one of these men was at Jaffa (see Index I.). The Albertini (p. 150) seem to be the same as the *Alberti*, one of the chief and most ancient of the families of Florentine merchants, flourishing from the thirteenth to sixteenth centuries.[c] They must

---

[a] *See* list in "Les Lombards en France," a useful treatise by C. Piton, Paris, 1892, p. 39, also "Archives de l'Orient Latin," vol. ii., *Documents*, p. 209.

[b] Rot. Par., ii. 137, iii. 626, v. 144, in Edw. III., Henry IV., and Henry VI.

[c] S. L. Peruzzi, "Firenze e i banchieri Fiorentini." Firenze, 1868, p. 145. We find a "Paulus Albertini socius mercatorum" in 1258, 42 Hen. III., referred to in Rymer, i. 656.

have had a branch in Venice; here Derby's attorney (for he was not yet returned from Palestine) on 2 Feb. 1392-3 procured 8,888 ducats in exchange for £1,333 6s. 8d., for which the duke's officers had given bond at Leicester on the previous 28 November to Matthew, one of the partners of the Alberti, and to Dyne of Florence (p. 150).* No doubt this was paid through their London house, where Matthew may there have represented the firm; a few years later express mention is made of Philip Alberti (with other Florentine merchants) dwelling in London, obtaining licence to make a certain transaction with their partners abroad (7 Hen. IV., Rymer, vol. viii. 441), and twice at least before this, Henry IV. procured money for war through the means of Genoese and Florentine merchants, of whom Philip Alberti was one. (Rymer, viii. 359, 383). The phrases "Lombards ou Albertynes," and "marchands d'Albectyn," used on the Rolls of Parliament show the ideas attached to their name, though the distinction might not be clear (iii. 627, v. 276).

Derby obtained money in the same way again from Nicholas de Lucca at Venice on 12 April, 1393 (2095 ducats in exchange for 500 marks sterl.), and from Francis Neerle in France, after June 3 (2,000 francs for 500 marks). These two names do not occur in any of the lists given by Piton or Peruzzi, nor elsewhere that I can find, and the account of Whitteby for 17th Rich. II., which might throw light on both, is unfortunately missing. Besides

* In the account of Whitteby, Lancaster's receiver-general, for 15 and 16 Rich. II., ending 2 Feb. (D. of L., cl. 28. bdle. 3, no. 2), is the following item : " Et Matheo domino lumbardo, vni ex consorciis domini Antonii d'Albertis, et Jaketto Dyne de Florencia pro escambio monete Anglie in 8888 dokettis novis de Venys et 2s. 8d. in sterlingis vel valore, precio doketti 3s., solvende domino comiti Derbye vel Janico Dartache scutifero seu alio attornato suo sufficiente potestate habente, apud Venys in festo purificationis B. M. [2 Feb.] anno 16°, per securitatem cuinsdam obligacionis per Johannem Walcote, Johannem Leycestre cives Londonienses et predictos Matheum et Jakettum facte," to Whitteby and three others, the bond bearing date at Leicester, 28 Nov., 1392. A note in the margin indicates that Kyngeston, Treasurer for War, answers for this money.

these sums Derby received various gifts and contributions on his way which will be mentioned later.

Narrative Resumed.—A safe conduct was obtained from the Duke of Stolpe for the passage through his territory (p. 179), part of Pomerania, he being probably unfriendly; it is the only one that seems to have been required. Leaving Dantzic on 22 Sept. Derby arrived the same day at Schonee, where he halted two or three days. At various points along his journey some of the chief valets were sent on a day or two a-head to provide supplies or otherwise make ready for the arrival of their lord; this had been done on 5 Sept. from Braunsberg returning towards Dantzic (p. 170/**23**), and now again at Schonee (p. 183/**30**). This, which may have been a constant practice but is only occasionally noted amongst the items, renders the exact dating of a few stages of the journey doubtful, and in some cases the servants seem to have gone to places (foraging) where the lord never went. Mistakes have been made by the clerk in dates here and there while copying the groups of *parcellæ*, as well as in rendering names of places; the itinerary has been drawn up after careful study and comparison of all these circumstances, and is, I believe, substantially correct; but parts must be taken with caution.

Leaving Schonee on 25 Sept. Derby passed through Hammerstein and on the 27th came to Poleschken, three miles beyond Polzin. Here in the Mark, now Neumark, he passed successively through Schievelbein, Dramberg, Arneswald, Landsberg, and Drossen, where he quitted its borders and reached Frankfort-on-Oder on 4 October. Passing Goban and Triebul he entered Bohemia at Gorlitz on 7 October and thence made his way to Prague on 13th. Here at the Court of King Wenceslas [a] (brother to Anne, Queen of England) he stayed eleven days; went with him for three days to Zebrak or Bedeler, a favourite country residence (p. 191/**7**); paid devotional visits on 20 and 21 Oct. to the ancient Castle Hrad-

---

[a] See note, p. 310.

INTRODUCTION.   lvii

schin of the city (p. 274/**29, 30**), and again gave offerings at the relics in the castle at Karlstein, " the proud monument of the dead Cæsar '*ᵃ* (p. 275/**4**). Bernau was probably visited also from Prague about 19 Oct. (pp. 260, 274). Several important purchases were made at Prague of cloth and clothing for Derby himself and the two henchmen; goldsmiths' ware, silver-gilt collars, and a belt; two super-altars for Derby's chapel; and considerable sums paid for tables and scutcheons of Derby's heraldic arms, both on wood and paper, and for painting them. Lancaster Herald painted these arms in Derby's room at Prague, and again at Vienna (pp. 190/**26**, 279, 280), and much care seems to have been taken by the heralds to have these insignia always painted or hung in the lord's hall or room wherever he made a stay of any length.

By 26 Oct. Henry was again moving to Brod (whence he took two coursers to England, p. 292), and on to Czaslau the same day. In daily stages he passed through two other cities, arriving at Brünn, the capital of Moravia, on the 29th. Here, instead of going direct to Vienna, he turned eastwards; and from Göding, where he and part of his men appear to have crossed the river March, he took horse with Wilbram northwards to Weisskirch (a few miles east of Olmütz) and back, apparently in two days and a half (p. 193/**15-18**). The reason for this detour is not indicated; it may have been made in order to visit some personage connected with the reigning house of Moravia and Friuli. Jodocus, first cousin to Wenceslas of Bohemia, was at this time Margrave of Moravia, and his brother John Sobieslaw, who had been Bishop of Olmütz, was Patriarch of Friuli.[b]

Vienna was reached and the Danube crossed on 4 November[c]

[a] Pauli, " Nachrichten," as before, p. 349, no. 14, of 1881.
[b] Anderson's " Royal Genealogies," *Bohemia ;* Gams' " Episcopi Eccles. Cathol.," *Aquileja. See* after, p. 308.
[c] At this point several dates give much difficulty. I have set the originals down in the Itinerary, fearing to change too much, but I believe from the 29 Oct. the

(p. 194/**14, 25**). Here he must have hastened to meet the Duke of Austria (Albert of Hapsburgh), who sent letters with his own to the Senate of Venice asking to let him have the hull of a galley with tackle, in order to go to Palestine. At once he despatched his steward Sir Peter Bucton, Sir Peter Solatour (or St. Latour)[a], esquire Payne, Mowbray herald and others, with 14 horses to Venice to arrange for and provision the galley for the voyage (p. 201/**28**); they were paid for this ten days' service on 13 Nov. p. 202/**3**; the same party incurred some expenses at St. Daniel apparently a few days later, p. 220/**15**). John Redington the Prior of St. John of Jerusalem in England was possibly one of the "others," or met them later; and these ambassadors, taking the letters, obtained the vessel, which the College of Signory granted (on 18 Nov.), to be fitted up and in good order, free of expense. Derby was to arm and provision it at his own charge, which included putting in the cabins (p. 219/**31**), and was not allowed to take any merchandise nor any passenger beyond his own men.[b] Bucton and Redington made an agreement with them for the navigation from Venice to Jaffa and back again, for the sum of 2,785 ducats,[c] so that their generosity, which they made the most of, does not appear very great.

The stay in Vienna was but short, four days, long enough however to permit of communication with the king of Hungary, about 6 Nov., who had a house across the river (p. 195/**13**). He was

following would be a more correct reading. as two days then are unaccounted for; and on the other hand Derby must surely have arrived in Vienna before 4 Nov., which obliges him to get the Duke of Austria's letter the same day. 29 October at Brünn, 30 Göding, 31 Weisskirch, 1 November Driesen, 2nd Schönkirchen, 3rd Vienna, where he stayed four nights at the cost of Albert III (p. 150/**17**), so that he would leave Vienna on 7 Nov. The visit to the King of Hungary, and the receipt of money from Albert's officers, are both set down for 6 Nov.

[a] I have not succeeded in identifying this knight.

[b] Venetian State Papers. ed. Rawdon Brown, vol i., no. 107, and see Pref. lxxxii.: the grant is printed at length in "Archives de l'Orient Latin," ii. p. 238.

[c] P. 279, l. 3. The word *eis* must refer to the Signory, who were owners of the galley.

INTRODUCTION. lix

Sigismund, younger brother of Wenceslas of Bohemia, both connected with Derby through their sister queen Anne. Leggings (caligæ) embroidered like his livery were made for Derby soon after (p. 285/**32**). The Duke of Austria hospitably paid for his entertainment (p. 150/**15**), and sent one of his esquires with Derby to Venice (p. 285/**13**); it is possible that this esquire came in company with the knight lord Ralph of Vienna (p. 265), whose wages, like those of some others, may not be exactly set down.

Derby now took his way leisurely to Venice; as for his previous embarkations at Boston and Lynn, the vessel would require time to be prepared. Taking a south-westerly course through Austria, Styria, and Carinthia he passed many towns by daily stages; between Leoban and Knittelfeld, Kyngston and two of the valets were left at St. Michael with 13 carriage horses for a night (p. 198/**21**). Through Friesach, St. Veit, and Feldkirch, he supped at Klagenfurt, breakfasted next day at Villach, and supped the same evening at Arnoldstein. At Malburgeth on the morning of 18th Nov.,[a] he reached Pontafel and the confines of Friuli in time for supper. In this mountainous and rugged country the difficulty with the vehicles was great, much grease was used, yet the wheels and other parts were broken, and at length Henry had to exchange his carriage for two small ones on account of the narrow way (p. 202). An old carriage was sold for three florins (p. 150/**29**). Where the Patriarch John of Friuli entertained him, as noted by Capgrave, does not appear; no trace is found of a visit to Udine, the capital, but Kyngston enters money for a night's expenses received from the Patriarch's marshal (p. 150/**20**).

Passing through Venzone (or Peusseldorf),[b] San Daniele and Spillimbergo, he appears to have made the long ride on 21 Nov. from Spillimbergo through Sacile to Conigliano, whence on the even-

[a] See note, p. lxxiv.
[b] See same note. From Venzone it seems that Wilbram, one of the chief valets, and purveyor for the horses, went to Cividale, on the Austrian boundary of Friuli and fell sick there (pp. 210,**30**, 260,**31**). See p. 310.

ing of the 22nd, Treviso, recently come under Venetian dominion,
was reached. Here was a couple of days halt;[a] servants were then
sent forward with baggage, crossing the Piave at night through
Ponte di Piave (Pontegla) and Motta on the Livenza to Portogruaro,
where they arrived on the 24 Nov. (p. 204), Derby, himself, perhaps not till next day (p. 205). Here at Portogruaro, and not at
Venice, Derby established his people and horses under the chief
care of Wilbram and Toty, in winter quarters for the four months
ending March 31, 1393 (pp. 210, 211). Here, on 26 Nov., they
sold by auction twelve oxen no longer needed (p. 150/**31**). Hence
they went to various places foraging and buying—a man riding
with Harpeden "in patriam" or fatherland, as the Venetians
designated Friuli then and centuries later[b] (p. 210/**19**)—to
Cavallino on the 28th, Lio (probably Lio Major) on 29th Nov. and
1 Dec. (p. 211/**17**), to Portlown, which seems to be Pordenone
(p. 210/**12**), and probably again to Treviso. Barges and boats from
Portogruaro to Venice were frequently hired to carry men or baggage
(pp. 206/**20**, 207/**19**, &c.); and one curious item shows that it
was a hard winter, nine men had to be employed to break the ice
between the cities (p. 207/**21**).

But there were many purchases and much business to be done
in Venice, and Derby went there on 1st Dec. (p. 211/**16**), staying
twenty-one days (p. 218/**28**) at a house on the Isle of St. George
(pp. 211/**15**, 219, 220, &c.). On Nov. 30 the Signory voted
300 ducats to give Derby a public reception,[c] which would involve
some state honours. Capgrave says he was entertained by the
Doge himself. Derby gave oblations on the 2 Dec. at St. Mark's,[d]
also on his first visit to the Doge[e] there, and another time they

---

[a] See note as to Chishon, p. lxxv.
[b] Peter Heylin's "Cosmographie," 1670. p. 120.
[c] "Venetian State Papers," i. no. 108, "Archives de l'Or. Lat.," ii., *Documents*, p. 236. See also Capgrave, Appx. B.
[d] P. 275, l. 18, where *November* is obviously an error for *December*.
[e] Antonio Vernieri, Doge from Oct., 1382—Nov., 1400.

performed the same pious duty together (pp. 275/**30**, 276/**2**); indeed, at various times during his two sojourns, he visited and offered at many of the Venetian churches, where several holy relics were commonly shown to pilgrims.ᵃ About this time Kyngston appears to have received some money from the Prior of St. John, who also supplied more while on board ship, probably at Rhodes (p. 150/**1**); this money must have been in exchange for a sum paid to the priory or chief preceptory of St. John at Clerkenwell, London, by the Duke of Lancaster. The preceptors of that order being in the habit of transmitting the yearly revenues arising from their distant provinces to the chief house in Rhodes would give the English preceptor facilities for this financial assistance.ᵇ

A house was hired as a larder for a week, apparently at Portogruaro (p. 207/**32**), beds hired for the valets, meat was salted, butts of wine bought, spices, bread which was put in barrels, poultry, and other provender. But most of this provided at Portogruaro (pp. 204-211) seems to have been for consumption during December, when there was much passing backwards and forwards, and part, doubtless, was for expenses during Derby's absence. Some officers preceded him to Venice to make ready (p. 206/**20**). The expenses noted in Venice, both for his stay on going and that on returning from Palestine, are heavy. Litter for beds was brought from Sta. Lucia to St. Giorgio (p. 211/**14**), and on arrival various things were bought at Lio, a village on the neighbouring coast, or the Lido.ᶜ Coals were brought to warm the house (pp. 218/**16**, 219/**20**), fish, poultry, roes, fruit, spices, and other dainty food, besides the meat, bread, and wine of daily need, were largely bought, apart from the provision for the voyage. Derby probably gave as well as received entertainment. St. Nicholas was another point of importance in Venice, where Derby and his

---

ᵃ See "Itineraries of W. Wey," printed by the Roxburghe Club, pp. 52, 53.

ᵇ Cf. the Computus of the English prior in 1328, and his remittances to the Bardi and Peruchi, "Hospitallers in England," Camd. Soc., 1857, p. 219.

ᶜ See note a, p. lxxvi.

chief men had to do. In Wey's time, seventy years later, the port of departure was near St. Nicholas Church,[a] and it may be that Derby's galley lay there, and that he and his party were rowed to it from St. Giorgio (pp. 219/**33**, 220).

The provision for the voyages seems large. Mowbray and Harpeden, with two guides, went to markets and fairs in the country round buying oxen for salting; 2,250 eggs, with live poultry, and a house with cages and food for them, were collected; casks for water, cheese, oil, potted ducks, fish, vegetables, condiments, spices, 2,000 dates, 1,000 pounds of almonds, sweet confections and sugar of many sorts, choice wines in amphoræ and in butts, biscuit and fresh bread, for which 40 sacks were bought on the Rialto and brought to the bakery (p. 222/**19**), four barrels full of various fruits bought from Francis the "fruterer" (p. 223), butter, and fuel, with other things, were put on board the vessel. A lamp was hung in the cabin, a mattrass, feather bed, and bolster provided, together with warm clothing (pp. 280/**30**, 281/**18**). Lastly, a store of wooden-ware for the kitchen and pantry, besides bowls, cups, and pots of earthenware, and four pairs of tin flasks to put wine in (pp. 220-224).

It is rather difficult to ascertain which of his party Derby took with him on this pilgrimage; the probability seems to be that about 8 or 10 men stayed with the horses at Portogruaro (p. 210), and that the rest of his company, perhaps 40 or 50, with supernumeraries,[b] went. The two Gransons, Solatour (p. 263), Prior Redington, Erpingham, Willoughby, Mowbray the herald, with some esquires and valets, are named on one point or other of the voyage, and the pay-lists, imperfect though they may be, tell a little more. A good number must have accompanied him, and the stores bought at headquarters for a voyage of some weeks need not therefore surprise us.

---

[a] This appears to be a place on the Lido, near the Hebrew burial ground, east of the city, on a map of Venice of 1540, which shows also two other churches of the name.   [b] *See* before, p. liv.

INTRODUCTION. lxiii

Venice was one of the principal ports of departure for pilgrims to the Holy Land in the 14th and 15th centuries, and the route now followed by Derby differed but little from that laid down in the "Informacyon for Pylgrimes" of about 1430, printed by Caxton,[a] or from Wey's "Itineraries" in 1458 and 1463, from and to Venice. Unfortunately, Kyngston's accounts give nearly all the items for this interesting part of the journey undated; it appears that on shipboard wages were not paid, and things bought at the ports touched at are grouped together indiscriminately.

Sailing from Venice about the 22nd or 23rd December, we find him giving oblations on Christmas Day at Zara, on the Dalmatian coast (p. 277); his course thence lay past Lissa, Corfu, and Modon, at the south of the Morea; thence straight to Rhodes, apparently without touching at Candia, as was often done (no mention is made of Candia either going or returning). Occasion was taken at these points to have the linen for the table, pantry, and buttery washed, an item that often occurs throughout the accounts. At Modon oblations were offered and skins of wine bought. At Rhodes must have been a little stay; in this fertile island, inhabited by the Knights of St. John since 1300, and carefully cultivated, fresh supplies were procured, and some repair made to the rudder, as well as to parts of the lord's armour (p. 283/**7**), while doubtless Henry, who gave oblations (p. 278/**4**), visited the Grand Master Heredia in his palace, having Redington with him. But he more likely stayed here on his return voyage, and now pressed on to Jaffa, where fish were bought, and an ass was hired to carry food to Ramah, where more was bought, enough to satisfy several men. Henry the henchman, a guide Antonio, Mowbray the herald, a scalk or servant, the valet Gilder, Bucton the steward, and Kyngston the treasurer (225, 226), and perhaps Chelmeswyke an esquire (p. 277/**10**), are all who can be traced to have accompanied Henry to Jerusalem). They must, it seems, have gone on foot, no word is found

---

[a] Reprinted by the Roxburghe Club, 1824.

of mule or horse hire or baiting, except one horse hired by the
henchman from Ramah to Jerusalem (about twenty-four miles), and
an ass for the same youth on the return. It is disappointing to find
so little said of what was done at Jerusalem, the goal of pilgrimage
now reached; only the items of wax candles bought there for
Derby and others by "the guardian," *i. e.*, the guardian of the Holy
Sepulchre (p. 226/**2**, **4**), indicate that he made the regular visits
prescribed to pilgrims. Of the offerings usually made at each of
the traditional spots we only get one glimpse, viz., six ducats paid
by Henry at the Holy Sepulchre (p. 278/**4**), unless the oblation made
"super montem" for which Chelmeswyke handed him a ducat,
refer to the Mount of Olives (p. 277/**10**). This is the more surprising
because Derby shows himself throughout both journeys habitually
giving alms and oblations at churches, shrines, and monasteries
that he came by, and it seems impossible that he should have
omitted these, the most important of all to the faithful. Capgrave
says, as he would of course believe, that Derby visited the Sepulchre and other holy places. We must therefore conclude that, as
in the case of Thomas Swinburne noted below, no other religious
dues were required.

The visit was evidently a short one, but perhaps as long as was
then usual, and he hoped to come again; the Earl of Warwick,
who also had a galley by special permission in 1393, was only ten
days between landing at Jaffa and re-embarking.[a] From want of
dates we cannot tell the duration of Derby's visit; fresh food was
bought at Jaffa, and he sailed straight to Famagusta in Cyprus.

---

[a] "Venetian State Papers," i. no. 163. Two other English knights who visited
Palestine in 1392 were William de Lisle, a king's gentleman who set out early that
year (French Roll, 16 Rich. II., m. 8), and Thomas de Swinburne, an ancestor of the
poet of to-day, Mayor of Bordeaux, who sailed from Venice on 2 Sept., going by
way of Alexandria, which he reached on 20 Oct. He was at Jerusalem from 11 to
17 Dec., 1392. See the narrative and expenses of this journey by his man, Thomas
Brygg, printed in Archives de l'Orient Latin," ii., *Doc.*, p. 378. The only religious
dues paid by this party were, on entering the Holy Sepulchre and coming out of it,
six and a half ducats and a few grossi.

INTRODUCTION.   lxv

Thus ended his visit to the Holy Land; his wish to go there again was known and caught up by Shakespeare, whose play has erroneously made the world think he never went at all. In a letter written to the Emperor of Abyssinia after he became king (without date) Henry speaks of his continual hope once again (*iterato*) to visit the Holy Sepulchre in person;[a] a letter which receives additional interest in connection with these accounts.

At Famagusta Derby seems to have been lodged in the castle (pp. 229/**9**, 230/**3**); in another place "hospicium domini" is mentioned (p. 228/**3**), but this may have been at the capital, Nicosia, whither Prior Redington, Lord Granson, and other knights and esquires went as embassy to the King of Cyprus, James I. of Lusignan (p. 226/**27**). Capgrave informs us that the king received Derby with honour, but how long he stayed we cannot say. Fear of the plague, which had devastated Cyprus in 1392,[b] does not appear to have affected him. It is difficult to separate the items relating to Cyprus from those as to Rhodes, but judging from their number the time spent in both islands was short; this could not indeed be otherwise out of a voyage which occupied but three months altogether, one part of which (from Venice to Jaffa) was usually allowed to take between six and seven weeks. Some repair had again to be made to the galley (p. 226/**25**), and a cabin made for a leopard (p. 229/**3**), a royal beast which it is reasonable to suppose was presented to Derby by the king of Cyprus. Many items occur henceforward on account of the leopard and his keeper, who travelled home to England (p. 256/**15**), perhaps to be added to the collection of wild beasts already kept in the Tower since the days of Henry I.[c] Henry had also with him falcons, either brought from England as part of a nobleman's outfit or bestowed by some of

---

[a] "Royal and Historical Letters of Henry IV.," ed. F. C. Hingeston (Rolls Series), vol. i. pp. 421-2.

[b] "Archives de l'Orient Latin," ii. 275.

[c] "History of London," W. J. Loftie, 1883, ii. 146. As to the leopard in the text, *see* pages in Index iii.

his noble hosts, and a parrot, probably given him by one of his eastern hosts, appears in Italy on his homeward route with a cage hung by a cord (p. 285/**19, 24,** p. 286/**28**).[a] But the best token that he had fulfilled his pilgrimage was a converted Turk or "Sarasin," whom he brought back from Rhodes, baptised by the name of Henry, and for whom a bed, a pilgrim's gown or sclaveyn, a toga, and several pairs of shoes were provided at divers times and places.[b] Together with Herle the chaplain and others, and Derby's baggage, he eventually found his way to Peterborough by the end of June (p. 254/**17**).

It must have been while in Cyprus that the Doge of Genoa, Antonio Montaldo, presented Harry with a butt of wine (p. 230/**3**). Leaving Famagusta, they sailed round to Bafas on the south-west side of Cyprus, and thence to Rhodes. Here oblations were again given (pp. 275/**27,** 276/**6,** 278/**5**), especially at the church and holy relics of the knights (p. 277/**11**), and eight wooden scutcheons of arms painted by Mowbray herald were hung up in the castle (pp. 227/**2-6,** 283/**11**). After more purchases of food, and the gifts of bread and a butt of wine by the Grand Master at Lango or Cos, a flourishing island near Rhodes also belonging to the knights (p. 230/**10**), the ship made for Modon, where three great butts of its famous Romoney wine were bought (p. 230/**24**), and alms were given to the poor (p. 278/**20**); touched at Corona, also in the Morea, passed Corfu, Ragusa, where more alms were distributed (p. 278/**19**) and provender bought (p. 231/**6**), the island Lesina, the ports Zara and Pola, and arrived once more at Venice about 20 March. The

---

[a] The entry as to the parrot on p. 292 is puzzling. Almandia seems to mean Alemannia, but unless we consider that the Swiss may have been included under this name in the common language among the Savoyards—which is not impossible—there is no point along Derby's route homewards from Italy near enough to permit of the parrot being lost among them. On the other hand, if we take Thos. Dent's search to have been, not for a lost bird, but to fetch it, whether gift or purchase—the journey from any part of the route before Venice would have incurred more expense than the item gives.

[b] See Index i., *Henry.*

ship's patron or captain had evidently made a good market for himself, as his kind did in Wey's day, with the various articles sold in the galley, chiefly wines of Romoney and of Mark, by his servants to Derby's people (p. 232). He had a wife, for whom Kyngston bought a purse (p. 284/**21**).

Henry again took up his abode at St. Giorgio (p. 234/**5**), where he stayed till 10 April, put up his arms in the hall there, besides eight more escutcheons hung at St. Mark's, as memorials of his visit. On the 31 March the Signory voted that 100 ducats should be spent in honour of his return " so that he may go back to his own country well pleased with us."[a] How this was spent we do not see here, but there was much cleansing and washing of house and linen, and purchase of provender against the festival of Easter on April 6 (pp. 235, 236), Italian pastry-cook and butcher being employed. Many oblations too were made (p. 277), and gifts to the poor distributed (p. 284/**25**). But already on 3 April preparations were begun for removing to Treviso (p. 236/**30**), and the steward, the marshal, Toty and others were sent there to make ready, and a boat was hired to fetch the horses and other servants from Portogruaro to Treviso, four days work in all (p. 236). Boats were hired to take Derby and all his family from Venice to Meistre, where Derby supped on 12 April, but his baggage set forth on the 11th, taking two days on the way (p. 237/**26**, **30**). From Meistre to Treviso carts and horses were hired, and it seems that Derby put up at Treviso at the friars' convent, for his baggage was carted thither (p. 237/**23**, see also p. 240/**26**). But a good deal of carpentering had to be done at doors, cupboards, and the dresser (p. 239).

At Treviso they stayed till 28 April (p. 238/**25**), Kyngston remaining meanwhile in Venice (p. 240/**20**), during which time there was mending of horse gear and making ready for the journey. Many fine stuffs, furs, silks, and linen, had been bought in

[a] "Archives de l'Orient Latin," ii., Doc., 239; "Venetian State Papers," i. no. 110.

lxviii   INTRODUCTION.

Venice, collars of silver and of silver-gilt, and a collar and coin
of gold (pp. 284, 285, 286/**17**), which needed chests and packing,
and the goldsmith brought his things to Treviso (p. 240/10).
On 20 April a cage was bought for the parrot (p. 286/**28**), a hat
for the leopard (p. 240); and finally on 28 April they left Treviso,
the falcons borne on horseback for Vicenza, the luggage in cars
for Padua. Passing **through** Noale on 29th the next stages are
Padua, Vicenza, and Verona, but n**o**ne of these are dated, and
little halt can have been made, for we find Mowbray the herald
at **Milan on 1** May, probably, however, preceding his master
(p. 287/**5, 6.** compare p. 242 **25**). This date is, however, almost
certainly wrong, and we should rather read 11 May, for Mowbray
and Harpeden were preceding their lord by a day and night (see
also p. 243/**19**); and he seems to have reached Milan about 12
or 13 May (p. 211). This date allows time for the three last
stages. After Verona, Lodi and Pavia were reached, where an
injured chest and saddle were mended, and a case made to hold
four **cups** fashioned of ostrich eggs (p. 241/**26**); oblations were
made at both (p. 277). At Milan, where Gian Galeazzo Visconti
now held sway, Derby made some few days' stay; Capgrave says
he was entertained by the count,* who showed him the tombs of
St. Augustine, Boethius, and of his own uncle Lionel, Duke of
Clarence, who had married Gian's sister and had died in Milan.
While here too, he acted as mediator between the count and a
house of friars, probably Augustinians (like Capgrave himself),
with whom some cause of quarrel had arisen, and succeeded in
pacifying the matter; it is possible that this may have been the
Augustinian house at Pavia, where he had given offerings (p. 287/
29). Silks and goldsmiths' wares were purchased in Milan, and
a great glove for the falcon (p. 287), also that for which Milan
has so long been renowned, velvet, some of **it** cloth of velvet and
gold (p. 288).

On o**r** about 17 May Derby quitted Milan, and passing through

* He was made duke in 1396.

Vercelli and Chivasso (where he had more silver collars) arrived
at Turin on 21 May, where he gave alms at St. Anthony's (p.
77/**27**), Rivoli on 22, and Avigliano the same day. Hence
three mules loaded with baggage were sent on over the mountains
to Troyes, in Champagne, whence it was probably carted to Paris
p. 254/**22, 25**). Lord Otto Granson, who would have his own
reasons for avoiding Savoy at this time (see after p. 309) must
have left him some weeks before, perhaps reaching Burgundy by
another route from Venice (the last we heard of him was at
Cyprus); here from Avigliano Derby sent a messenger on business
to him (p. 246/**19**). Approaching the mountains he appears to
have remained at Susa three days, 23 to 25 May; he crossed Mont
Cenis and reached Lanslebourg on 26 May, St. Michel and Fontrouverte (to the west) on the next day, arriving at La Chambre
on 28 or 29 May. On 30 at Aiguebelle he must have passed
through Chambery[a] on his way to Yenne on the Rhone, where he
was on 1 June. From Susa onwards he had given frequent alms
to the poor and others on his way, to the lepers on the mount at or
near that place, and now to a hermit on the Mont du Chat, near
Yenne (p. 276). Crossing the Rhone, Derby rested at Rossillon
2 June, St. Rambert 3rd, and reached Bagé on 5th, near which it
appears that he crossed "the water between Savoy and Burgundy"
(p. 247), i.e., the Saône,[b] entering the ducal dominions on his way
to Macon. So on he went by daily stages, thro' Burgundy and
Champagne,—now the departments of Saône-et-Loire, Côte d'Or,
Aube, and Seine-et-Marne,—to Paris, which he gained on 22 June,

---

[a] See note, p. lxxviii.
[b] On the "Atlas Historique de la France," by Aug. Longnon, "France in 1380"
(livr. iii., 1889), Savoy is shown to extend at that period far into the present department of Ain, and though the northern boundary is not very clearly defined, Bagé
appears to be in Savoyard territory. The Rhone would therefore be far too easterly
to have been the "water" of limitation referred to, which would seem here to have
been the Saône. With the boundaries of Piedmont, Savoy, and Burgundy on that
map, the rough groupings of items in the text (pp. 246-249) mainly agree.

a three weeks' journey from Yenne. It is noticeable that he did not pass through Dijon, the capital city of Burgundy, where twenty-nine years before Philip the Bold, son of King John of France and uncle of Charles VI., had inaugurated a new line of dukes and his own long rule. Perhaps Philip was in Flanders or elsewhere at this time. When at Chalon-sur-Saône (where he gave oblations, p. 276), 8 June, Derby sent forward Walter Juteburgh (who had been his messenger to Granson in Burgundy on 22 May) with some of his household officers to Paris, no doubt to make ready for him. Others still preceded him as heretofore (see *e.g.*, pp. 251/**29**, 253/**16**, 255/**24**). Drawing near Paris, at Troyes, he visited the church of St. Antony (p. 276/**19**), and he was at Grand-puits, near Nangis, by 19 June. Here a division was made; Hugh Herle, Derby's chaplain, with two other clerics and the Turk, &c. were despatched with a falcon and a quantity of baggage from Melun on the Seine to Calais by water, *i.e.*, they were boated down the Seine and round by the coast, paying toll on the river; and from Calais to Peterborough (p. 254/**16**).

When Derby arrived in Paris it is probable that the uncles of Charles VI., the dukes of Berri and Burgundy, were there, perhaps too his own father, on business connected with the treaty of peace; and, says the chronicle, he went to see the city under the guidance of the former.[a] The three years' truce between the English and the French powers, made in 1389, had in April of this year been prolonged to Michaelmas 1394, public proclamation of which was ordered on 26 June.[b] There had besides long been attempts at forming a lasting treaty of peace, for which Richard II. had given his safe conduct, several times renewed, permitting the French dukes to go into Picardy; in that of 5 August,

---

[a] Under date 1393, "Ce temps pendant, vint a Paris le filz au duc de Leucastre veoir la noble cité au conduit des diz ducs, oncles du roy de France." "Chronique des Quatre premiers Valois," ed. S. Luce, p. 335. This collocation is pointed out by Professor Tout.

[b] Rymer, vii. p. 748.

1393, he specifies also the English dukes, Lancaster and Gloucester, as having lately been concerned in the affair,[a] although they appear not to have been fully authorised till 12 Sept. But Derby made a so short a halt in Paris—two nights at most—that he cannot have seen or done much there; his horse's gear needed repair, and some purchases were made for his wardrobe, which included a ring with a balais ruby (pp. 257/**27**, 287/**21-25**). On the 24th June we find him at Amiens giving oblations, also alms to a poor madman (pp. 276, 277), and he placed his scutcheon in the house where he stayed (p. 287/**31**); on 28th he was at Calais (p. 258), and on 30th crossed over to Dover (pp. 254, 256). A balinger was hired at Calais, pontage, portage, and boatage to the ship paid as usual (p. 279/**5-9**), and at Dover four boats had to carry the men and baggage, including the leopard, ashore (257/**15**).

From Dover Derby went by the old road through Canterbury, breakfasted at Sittingbourne on 1 July, was at Rochester with his leopard on 2nd, gave alms at Ospringe the same day (p. 276), was at Dartford on 3rd, and in London by the 5 July. This was slow travelling for a man who was accustomed to move rapidly, but it was perhaps a stately progress and welcome home to the popular young earl after the long and difficult pilgrimage. In London a few purchases were made at a goldsmith's (p. 288); after this the accounts say no more of his movements; so in London we leave him. Wages were paid up to the 13 July (pp. 270-272); Kyngston came up to town in October to certify the loans made by the Lombards while abroad, and was occupied there from January to March following in making up his accounts, which he afterwards gave in at Leicester (p. 292).

[a] Rymer, vii., pp. 741, 752, 753, 766.

lxxii   INTRODUCTION.

ITINERARY II., 1392-93.

Date. 1392.	Modern Name.	Name in MS., pages of text, &c.
July 16—24	Preparations at Lynn for the voyage, 152, 156, &c., 270.	
„ 19	Derby at Lynn, 278 ; Treasurer Kyngston receives money for the journey there, 147.	
„ 20, 24	Derby at Heacham, Norfolk, 159, 263.	
„ 24	Derby took ship at Heacham (Capgrave, *De. Ill. Hen.*, p. 99).	
? Aug. 10	Landed at Putzig	Putsk, 171/**12**.
Aug. 10	At Dantzic	Dausk, 163, cf. 258, stay of 15 days, 259 **6**.
„ 25	Leave Dantzic, 166	
„ 25, 26	At Dirschau	Darsowe, 167, 273
„ 28, 29	„ Elbing	Melwyn, 167, 273 ; guests of Augustinians there, 259 **20**.
„ 31	„ Braunsberg	Bronnesburgh, 167.
Sept. 1	„ Heiligenbeil	Helebell, Helipill, 167, 273.
„ „	„ Brandenburg	Brandeburg, 167.
„ 2	„ Königsberg	Conynsburg, 168.
„ 3	„ „	171, 274 ? returned this day.
„ 4	„ Brandenburg	Brondeburgh, 170.
„ 5	„ Braunsberg	Bronnesburgh, 170 ; Harpeden, &c., sent forward, 170 **23**.
„ 6	„ Elbing	Melwyn, 170 ; chapel of St. George there, 274.*
„ 7	„ Dirschau	Darsowe, 171.
? Sept. 7 or 8	„ Dantzic	Dansk, cf. 180 **14**.
Sept. 14	„ „	Dausk, 172-180, 274 **11**, **13** : stay of 20 days, p. 259 **8**, but this appears a few days too much.
„ 22	Left Dantzic, p. liii.	
„ 22, 24, and 25	At Schöneck	Seonee, 263, 183, 259 ; Cudworth sent forward, 183 **30**.
„ 26	„ Hammerstein	Hamestede, 184, 259.

* Several of the dates on p. 274 are evidently wrong, especially l. 8, Elbing, on Sept. 1 ; l. 22, Schonee, on 15 Sept. ; l. 23, Landsberg, on 18 Sept. ; l. 24, Zittau, on 20 Sept.

INTRODUCTION. lxxiii

Date. 1392.	Modern Name.	Name in MS., pages of text, &c.	
Sept. 27	At Poleschken (3 m. beyond Polzin)	Polessine, Polyschene, 184, 259.	
,, ,,	,, Schievelbein	Scheuelbene, 185, 279.	
,, 28	,, Dramberg	Drawyngburgh, 185, 260.	Le Mark.
,, 29, 30	,, Arneswald	Arneswold, 185, 260.	
Oct. 1	,, Landsberg	Londesburgh, Londesper, 186, 260.	
,, 2	,, Drossen	Dresse, 186.	
,, 4	,, Frankfort-on-Oder	187, 260.	
,, 5, 6	,, Goban	Gobin, 187, 260.	
,, 6	,, Triebul	Treboll, 188, 260.	
,, 7	,, Görlitz	Gorlech, 188, 260. Enter Bohemia.	
,, 9	,, Zittau [a]	Zitaw, 189, 260.	
,, 10	,, Niemes	Nemance, 189, 260.	
,, 11	,, Weisswasser	Whytwater, 189, 260.	
,, 12	,, Jung-bunzlan	Bronnslowe, 190, 260.[b]	
,, 13—24	,, Prague	Prake, 190.	
,, 22	,, Karlstein	Charleston, Prague, 275.	
,, 19 or 22	,, Berne [c]	Bernau, 260, 274, visited from Prague.	
	,, Bettlern or Zebrak	Bedeler, 191, visited from Prague, 3 days.	
,, 26	,, Brod	Preda, 192, 260.	
,, ,,	,, Czaslau [d]	Chastelet, 192, 260,	
,, 27	,, Dentschbrod	Deuchebrede, 192, 260.	
,, 28	,, Meseritsch	Mederess, Misserich, 192, 260.	
,, 29	,, Brünn	Bronne, 193, 260.	
,, ? 30	,, Göding	Gedding, 193.	

[a] The date, 7 Oct., at Zittau, p. 188, if correct, may refer to purchases made by servants sent forward a day or two, belehere was paid on the 9th, the more probable date for Derby's presence there.

[b] The date on p. 260, "Bronnslowe," 23 Oct., is evidently wrong, as shown by the direct statement of days at Prague, p. 190. 29. The preceding item, Berne, is misplaced. There are so many mistakes in dates and names on this and the following page, that their testimony must be taken with caution. For instance, 10 Nov. is stated to be Sunday, and on p. 202 14th is said to be Saturday, and 15 November Sunday; none are, however, correct, the Sundays in November, 1392, falling on 9, 16, 23, and 30 days of the month.

[c] Probably Bernau, a village near Saaz. Dr. Pauli identified it with Alt-Bernatitz; there are two villages of this name, one near Pilsen, the other near Czaslau.

[d] Identified by Dr. Pauli.

lxxiv   INTRODUCTION.

Date. 1392.	Modern Name.	Name in MS., pages of text, &c.
Nov. 1	At Weisskirch	Wiskyrke, 193.
„ 2	„ Driesen	Drysing, cf. 193, 260.
„ 3	„ Schönkirchen	Sconekirke, 193, 260.
„ 4—7	„ Vienna ª	Wene, 150 **17**, 194, 195, 260. Four nights' stay. On 4 Nov. steward Burton and party went forward to Venice, ten days' business, 201, 202.
„ 8	„ Traiskirchen	Arskirke, 196, 260.
Sunday, Nov. 9	„ Nenukirchen	Newekirke, 196, 260.
Nov. 10	„ Mürzzuschlag	Mersolach, 197, 260 **22**.
„ 11	„ Kindberg	Kimber, 197, 260.
„ 12	„ Leoban	Lowbon, 197, 260.
	St. Michael,	the Treasurer and a party here, *extra curiam*, 198 **21**.
„ 13	At Knittelfeld	Knettesfeld, 198, 260.
„ 14	„ Judenburg	Jondenburgh, 199, 260.
„ „	„ Newmarkt	Newmark, 202.
„ 15	„ Friesack	Friesak, 202.
„ „	„ St. Veit (Styria)	Seintfete, 202
Sunday, Nov. 16ᵇ	„ Feldkirch	Felkirke, 200, 260.
Nov. 16	„ Klagenfurt	Stamford, 202, supper.
„ 17	„ Villach	Fillak, Fellowe, 200, 202, 260, breakfast.ᶜ
„ „	„ Arnoldstein	Horleston, 202, supper.
„ ? 18	„ Malburgeth	Malberget, 200, 260.

ª *See* note on these dates in Introduction, p. lvii.

ᵇ I give the true Sundays here, not the erroneous days of the text. It would appear that the date, 18 Nov., at Feldkirch, p. 200, must certainly be wrong, the 16 Nov. is more likely to be right. If Friesack and St. Veit were reached on 15 Nov., Feldkirch, the next stage, would be gained on 16th, and at Klagenfurt (Stamford) Derby supped the same day (p. 202 **24**). For Villach, the next stage, two dates are mentioned, 17 Nov. is the nearest, on which day also Arnoldstein was reached. As the travellers must have arrived at Malburgeth next, before getting to Pontafel, where they supped on the 18th, we are forced to the conclusion that they were there on the morning of the 18th, instead of the 19th or 20th as variously given in the text. They might then reach Venzone (stated by a note of Dr. Panli's to be the Italian name for Peusseldorf, and thus to be the place intended by Posidolfe) on the 19th, and San Daniele on the 20th—not on 22 Nov., as on p. 260.

ᶜ *Prandium*; sometimes the word used is *jantaculum*, both I take to answer to the lunch or first meal of the day.

INTRODUCTION. lxxv

Date. 1392.	Modern Name.	Name in MS., pages of text, &c.	
Nov. 18	At Pontafel	Pontafle, 203, supper.	
„ 19	„ Venzone (Peusseldorf)	Posidolfe, Posilthorpe, 203, 260.	
	„ Cividale [a]	Civitas hostr' [*i.e.* Austriæ] Guydel, 260, 210, **30**.	In Friuli.
„ 20	„ San Daniele	260.	
„ „	„ Spillimbergo [b]	Spillingberk, 203, supper.	
„ 21	„ „	„ „ breakfast.	
„ „	? Ghiarre	Gecur, 203, boatage.	
„ ? 21	Sacile	Cysele, Gisill, 201, 260.	
„ 21	At Conigliano	203, supper.	
„ 22	„ „	„ breakfast.	
„ „	„ Treviso	Trevise, 203, supper.	
Sunday, Nov. 23	„ Treviso ;	203, 260.	
„ „	"Chichon" [c]	260.	
Nov. 24	„ Treviso	203.	
„ „	„ Ponte de Piave	Pontegla, 203, servants at night.	
	„ Motta, on Livenza	Mote, 203.	
„ „	„ Portogrnaro	Portgruer, 204.	

[a] On p. 260, l. 30, next after Posilthorpe—which Pauli states to be Venzone (*see* last note)—we have "civitatem hostr," which seems to be Civitas Austriæ or Cividale in Friuli (*see* Stubbs' ed. of Hoveden's Chronicle, iii., p. 195, note [Pauli], also Ferrarius, Lexic. Geog. s. v. *Forum Julium*). But it does not appear possible that Derby himself should have gone there if his next stages were San Daniele and Spillimbergo. We must explain the entry by supposing that one of his men went there, and another as to John Wilbram, sick at Guydel (p. 210), which I already take to be Cividale, confirms this view. This latter is not dated absolutely. Or was it here that the Patriarch entertained Derby one night, as shown in Kyngston's receipts ? The dates do not seem to allow of it.

[b] Between Spillimbergo and Conigliano lies Sacile, which no doubt is intended by the Cysele and Gisill of our text, but the date there given is 24 Nov., impossible if those given for Conigliano and Treviso are right. Leaving Spillimbergo in the morning, the travellers seem to have crossed the Meduna, near Basaldella, then the Zellini, the stony beds of which, called *Ghiarre* on Vallardi's modern map, may perhaps be intended by the word Gecur (p. 203,**16**), thence to Sacile and Conigliano in one day is a long stretch, but the dates of the extremes are precise.

[c] Chichon I cannot identify ; it may be some place at or near Treviso ; the payment of "belchere" apparently indicates some place where Derby stayed. No belchere is set down for Treviso, where he seems to have stayed for a couple of days.

lxxvi   INTRODUCTION.

Date. 1392.	Modern Name.	Name in MS., pages of text, &c.
Nov. ? 25	At Portogruaro	Derby himself arrived, 205.
,, 28	,, ? Cavallino	Gaverley, 209, purchases here.
,, 29	,, Lio,ᵃ or the Lido	Leo, 209, purchases.
Nov. 29ᵇ till Mar. 31	,, Portogruaro	Establishment here for the winter, 210, 211.
Sunday, Nov. 30	,, Venice	purchases, 220, 211.
Dec. 1	,, ,,	Derby himself stays twenty-one days, 211, **16**, 218, **29**, 275, **18**.ᶜ
,, ,,	,, Lio, or the Lido	Leo, 211, purchases; Derby here first day.
,, 23	? Sailed from	Venice, 218.ᵈ
,, 25	At Zara ᵉ	Jarr, 277.
	,, Lissa (island)	Lisea, 224.
	,, Corfu	Corfu.
	,, Modon, Morea	224.
	,, Rhodes	Rodes, 225.
(? cir. 27 Jan.)	,, Jaffa	Jaffe, 225.
	,, Ramah	Rames, 225.
	,, Jerusalem	225, 226.

ᵃ A map of La Frioul of 1778 (by Majeroni et Capellaris) gives the *Lio del Cavallino*, the point of land between the Lido and the mouth of the Piave river, also a small place called Lio Major at the north-east end of the Laguna of Venice. P. Heylyn's Cosmographie, 1670, p. 123, speaks of the forts or castles of Lio as on one of the openings in the Lido, near which ships lay at anchor. The word is a form of Lido from the latin *litus*, the *d* between vowels dropping out in the Venetian dialect.

ᵇ The date, *October* 29, p. 210, must be a slip of the pen for *November*, as the "ibidem" in the sentence refers to Portogruaro. The same may be said of *October*, p. 211, l. 7.

ᶜ On p. 275, November 2 must be an error in the MS. for December 2.

ᵈ From Venice to Zara, perhaps, occupied more than one day: as the date at Zara is fixed, allowing two days from Venice, we get the 23rd as the probable date of departure.

ᵉ It is singular that no dates were kept from the time Derby left Venice at the end of December till he returned thither in March, with two exceptions, an item for oblations given at Zara on 25 Dec., and in February two items for money lost at play in the galley, but in what part of the voyage can only be approximately conjectured. (A few dates of wages in February were kept, pp. 267, 272.) In the few conjectural dates I have been guided by Wey's dates when he went the same voyage in 1458; from Venice to Jaffa took him four weeks and four days. See "Itineraries of William Wey," Roxburghe Club, 1857, p. 57.

INTRODUCTION. lxxvii

RETURN JOURNEY.

Date. 1392-3.	Modern Name.	Name in MS., pages of text, &c.
	At Ramah	Rames, 226.
(? cir. 6 Feb.)	„ Jaffa	Jaffe, 226, 232.
(? cir. 9 Feb.)	„ Famagusta	Famagost, 226 **17**; castle there, 229, 230 **3**. }
	„ Nicosia	Embassy to king of Cyprus, 226 **29**. } Cyprus.
	„ Bafas	Baffa, 230.
(? cir. 19 Feb.)	„ Rhodes	"redeundo," 227, 228.
	„ Cos (Lange)	Langow, island, 230.
Feb. 23, 25	In the galley, but no place is named, 263, 264.	
	At Modon, Morea	Modhom, 230, 278.
	„ Corona, Morea	Cornona, 231.
	„ Corfu	231.
	., Ragusa	231 **6**, 278 **19**.
	., Lesina, island	Lissinner, 231.
	„ Zara	Jar, 231.
	„ Pola	232.
Mar. 20	„ Venice	284, furs bought there.
Mar. 21 till April 10	„ „	nine days, 233.
April 6	„ „	and twelve days, 234.
April 11 till April 28	„ Treviso	Easter Day, 236.
	„ „	Servants, &c., 238, **25**, 241.
April 12	„ Meistre	Meistre, Derby sups there on way to Treviso, 237 **12**.
? April 12	„ Treviso	Derby there, 238.
April 28, 29	„ Noale	Norwall, Nowall, 241, 264.
	„ Padua	Pado, Padowe, 240, 278.
	„ Vicenza	Wycens, 240, 276, 287.
	„ Verona	Viron', *printed* Siron,ª 288.
May 1 (? 11)	„ Milan	Mowbray forward here, 287, **5**, **6**; cf. 242 **25**.
„ 10	„ Lodi	Ladde, Lauda, 241, 276.
„ „	„ Pavia	Pauy, 241.
„ 13—? 16	„ Milan	Melane, 241, 287, **12**.ᵇ

ª The initial letter is badly formed, hence the error. This is the only mention of Verona, through which Derby must have passed.

ᵇ The MS. has xxj Maii, but apparently the copyist should have written xvj; it is clear that Derby was at Turin on 21 May, and would therefore probably have left Milan on 17 or 18 May

CAMD. SOC.

INTRODUCTION.

DATE. 1393.	Modern Name.	Name in MS., pages of text, &c.
May 18	At Vercelli	242.
,, ,,	,, Chivasso	Chevaux, 242.
,, 21	,, Turin	Toryn, 242, 261, 276.
,, 22	,, Rivoli	Rynols, Ryweles, 247, 261.
,, ,,	,, Avigliano	Avylan, Avelan, Velayn, 243, 246, 261.
,, 23—25	,, Susa	Sehusa, 243, 261, 276 (Last town in Piedmont).
,, 26	,, Lauslebourg	Launcebrugge, 244, 261 (Enters Savoy).
,, 27	,, St. Michel	St. Michael, 245, 261, 276.
,, ,,	,, Fontronverte [a]	Farneworth, west of St. Michel, 244, 261.
,, 28 or 29	,, La Chambre [b]	Chambourell, Chambour, 245, 261, 278.
,, 30	,, Aiguebelle	Egbell, 245, 261, 276.
,, 31	,, Chambery	Chambonry, Chambry. 245, 247.
June 1	,, Yenne	Jan, 245, 246, 261 ; Mont du Chat, 276.[c]
,, 2	,, Rossillon (Ain)	246, 261.
,, 3	,, St. Rambert ,,	Sarombert, 247, 261.
,, 4	,, ? Pont d'Ain ,,	Pompinet, 247, 261 ; Fownteney, Breme.[d]
,, 5	,, Bagé-le-Chatel	Bagea, 248, 261 (Leaves Savoy).
	" Aqua inter Saboldiam et Burgundiam," ? the Saône,[e] 247.	
,, 6	At Macon	248, 261.
,, 7	,, Tournus [f]	Turnays, 249, 261 (In Burgundy).

[a] This place is spelt Fonauerte on Tavernier's map of 1630. The same map gives Rinolle for Rivoli ; both forms are nearer to those of the accounts.

[b] The clerk who wrote out the accounts must have confused two places here ; La Chambre, passed on the way north from Aiguebelle, and Chambery, which lies half-way between Aiguebelle and Yenne. The confusion of dates on the four days' May 28-31, in the two accounts given on pp. 245-7 and 261, confirms this view : he took Chambour, Chambonry, and Chambourell to mean one place, viz., La Chambre, and having May 31 vacant he put in Floren (p. 261) from an item ten days further on. (I can find no place answering to the name Floren on this part of the route.) Chambery, from its situation and importance, must have been one of Derby's stations on either 30 or 31 May.

[c] The Mont du Chat rises between Yenne and the Lac du Bourget. Derby seems to have crossed the Rhone at Yenne.

[d] The stations between St. Rambert and Bagé are very uncertain ; I can only conjecture Pompinet to represent Pont d'Ain, a likely situation ; but Fownteney and Breme remain unidentified.

[e] See before, p. lxix.

[f] Tournus (in Latin Trenochium) lies on the direct route between Bagé and

INTRODUCTION. lxxix

Date. 1393.	Modern Name.	Name in MS., pages of text, &c.
June 8 or 9	At Chalon-sur-Saône	Chalons, 249, 261; Juteburgh and others sent forward to Paris, 247.
,, 9	,, Beaune	Beaune, 250.
,, 10	,, Floreyn	250 and ? 261, **15**.
,, 11	,, Chanceaux (Côte d'Or)	Chauce (*printed* Chaucc), 250, 261.
,, 12	,, ? Montbart (Côte d'Or)	Mencyllambard, 251, 261.
,, 13	,, Chatillon-sur-Seine (Côte d'Or)	Chastelon, 251, 261 (Last town in Burgundy).
,, 14	,, Bar-sur-Seine (Aube)	Berce, 251, 261.
,, 15	,, Troyes	252, 261.
,, ,,	,, Pavillon (Aube)	Graunt Pavelon, 252.
,, 16	,, Mariguy-le-Châtel (Aube)	Marin, Marine, 252, 261.
,, 17	,, Nogent-sur-Seine	Nougent, 253, 261.
,, 18	,, Provins (Seine et Marne)	Province, 262.
,, 19	,, Graud-puits (Seine et Marne)	Grauntpuisse (near Nangis), 258, 262.
	Part of the company sent from Melun to Calais, 254.	
,, 20	At Brie-comte-Robert	Bricounte, Vicount-Robert, 262, 253.
,, 21	,, Charenton	Pountecharcton, 262, 254.
,, 22	,, Paris	262.
,, 24	,, Amiens	Amyas, 254, 276, 278.
,, 28	,, Calais	Caleys, 258.
,, 30	,, Dover	254, 256.
July 1	,, Canterbury	255.
,, ,,	,, Sittingbourne	255.
,, 2	,, Rochester and Ospringe	256. 276.
,, 3	,, Dartford (Kent)	256.
,, 5	,, London	257.

Chalon-sur-Saône. The word in the MS. is contracted; in the first instance the sign resembles that used for *ra*, while in the second it is plainly that signifying *ur*, and here Turnays ought to have been printed. The dates of the two entries, as in some other cases, do not exactly agree, but are sufficiently near; both must refer to the same place.

List of dates according to the MS., which need to be corrected; see also notes to Itinerary II.

P. 193 **21**, 29 November here should evidently be 29 *October*.

P. 200 **3**, apparently this should be 16 *November*.

P. 210 **23**, Octobris should be *November*; on 29 Oct. they were at Brünn.

P. 245 **27, 30**, these should be 30 *May*, when, as shown by pp. 261, 276, the party were at Aiguebelle. Line **29**, *Chambery* 31 *May* is most likely intended (see *note*, p. lxxviii.).

P. 253 **4**, the succession of places in the journey shows that this should be 17 June, as on p. 261.

P. 263 **4**, November should be *December* (on 1 Nov. Derby was in Moravia).

P. 273 **2**, this date, 28 July, evidently leaves too little time for the voyage to Dantzic, and as we see that Derby was at Heacham on 24 July, whence he probably sailed that day (Capgrave says in the feast of St James the Apostle, of which 24 July was the eve), he could not have gone back to Lynn four days later. The scribe might easily mistake xxiiij for xxviij, and I propose to read it 24 July. Derby's ships were towed from Lynn to Heacham, 159 **11**.

P. 275 **18**, the same error as on p. 263, November written for *December*.

P. 287 **12**, this should probably be the 16 *May* (xvj instead of xxj); on May 21 Derby was in Turin.

Henry's Position in England and Abroad.—The picture that may be formed from these accounts of Henry of Bolingbroke as a young noble and his surroundings is, perhaps, more comprehensive than may elsewhere be found. As the eldest (and only legitimate) son of the able and powerful John of Gaunt he was one of the most important princes in England, moving among the flower of knighthood of his time at home and abroad; grandson of Edward III., and through his mother, Blanche, also descended from Henry III., he was heir to the great wealth of his maternal grandfather, Henry,[a] the first Duke of Lancaster, as well as to numerous grants made to his father, John, and added to the duchy.

---

[a] Henry left two daughters, co-heiresses; Blanche, the younger, married John of Gaunt (died in 1369, her only son, our Derby, being but three years old); Matilda, the elder, married William of Bavaria, and died in 1362, when her estates fell to her sister Blanche and husband, John being created Duke of Lancaster.

Born 30 May, 1366, Earl of Derby, he bore the principal sword, *Curtana*, at the coronation of his cousin, Richard II., in 1377. He was married as a boy of fourteen or fifteen (between 1380 and 1382)[a] to Mary de Bohun (also a child under her mother's care), through whom he inherited the earldoms of Hereford and Northampton, and the seigneury of Brecknock, with great estates, that lady being one of the two co-heiresses of the wealthy Humphrey de Bohun.[b] He thus occupied in every way a princely and a remarkable position, and was able to command from the fiefs and lands which owned him as lord a large following of knights and gentlemen, even during the lifetime of John of Gaunt. The interests of father and son must have run closely together in matters concerning the duchy, of which he was Warden in 1388.[c] From an early age his father had appointed certain officers to his household, and one of the most striking facts brought out by the inquiries as to who were the persons and names met with in these accounts is the continuity of their employ. The same men who surrounded Derby as a youth looked after his interests and shared in some measure his pursuits—as the Watertons, Bucton, Herle, Leventhorpe, and others—were his faithful friends and companions in later years, some remained with him till the end. Besides his immediate " family," as the accounts call his own men, there were those who, like Erpingham, nine years his senior, Staveley, Rempston, Willoughby, Thomas Swinford his brother's half-brother, and Otto Granson,[d] were his companions in arms and on his travels, some of whom also shared his fortunes when king. And among them we find men moving whose names have been immortalized by the poets, whose friends they were; the Sire de Sempy, by

[a] Ramsay's " Lancaster and York," i., p. 158.
[b] Mary died in 1394, the year after her husband returned from Palestine. The share of the Bohun possessions which she brought him was added to the Duchy of Lancaster by her son, Henry V., in 1414, Rot. Par. iv., p. 48b.
[c] Doyle's " Official Baronage," ii., p. 316.
[d] See notes at end of the text, pp. 293-313, for details as to these and the other names above.

Eustache Deschamps; Sir Peter Bucton and Otto Sire de Granson, by Geoffry Chaucer.[a]

Of his relatives we get but few glimpses in the accounts, Duke John chiefly appears as supplying money, or requiring to be certified of loans abroad (pp. 3, 147, 149, 292), and as writing to the Grand Master (p. 40); he was at Leicester with his son in the early part of 1390 (p. 31/**31**). Derby gave his father a bow from Newark (p. 31/**2**), and the Duchess Constance presented her stepson with a palfrey (p. 8/**3**). One peep at Derby's wife giving oblations with him at Lincoln—probably in the cathedral (p. 27/**28**), and the sailor announcing to him the birth of his fourth son[b] when at Königsberg in November, 1390 (p. 107), are all that we learn of his own hearthstone. John Beaufort, his half-brother, then about fifteen, is once referred to, and his uncle, Thomas Duke of Gloucester[c] (who had married Eleanor Bohun, Derby's sister in-law) comes on the stage through his herald, Croyslett. Heralds, in fact, remind us of more than one important family connection. Zealand, the herald with Derby on the Reysa (p. 107) must in some way have represented there the adherence or friendship of Albert, Count of Holland and Zealand, Duke of Bavaria (1377-1404), brother and successor to the William who had been husband to Derby's aunt, Matilda. Dampier, Horne, and Swethe, are other heralds named; the first was on the Reysa to represent, probably, one of the Lords of Dampierre,[d] the others made shields of arms at Königsberg; none of them are mentioned in the lists of Francis Thynne.[e]

It is evident that abroad, at the various courts which he visited,

[a] See pp. 300, 309.
[b] This item gives the nearest date yet known for the birth of the "Good Duke Humphry." See Ramsay's "Lancaster and York," i. p. 159.
[c] See before, p. xv., and p. xiii., note.
[d] There was a Dampierre in Normandy and another in Champagne.
[e] "Of the Duty and Office of an Herald," 1605, printed at the end of "Guillim's Heraldry."

Derby was treated not merely as a noble but as a prince of high rank and much consideration. This would naturally be the case in 1390, arising from the occasion of his journey and his success in it. On his second journey, when he found that further stay in Prussia was useless, the circumstance that he would pass the courts of several sovereigns, friendly through ties of marriage, probably weighed in his decision of the route to be followed to Venice. The family party which dominated this side of central Europe were connected with him through Anne queen of England. Anne, Wenceslas of Bohemia and Sigismund king of Hungary were all children of the emperor Charles IV.; Albert duke of Austria had married, as his first wife, another daughter (d. 1373), while the margrave of Moravia and the patriarch of Friuli were nephews to the emperor, and first cousins to all of these. In an age when family alliances were part of the strength of politicians, this conjunction would not escape the keen eye of a man like Henry, brought up among statesmen and accustomed to the interests, wider than those of his own island, which the affairs of France, Flanders, and Spain, and of the Teutonic knights had brought into the lives of his own relations, and to Englishmen generally. He already had some reputation, and was well received by the Venetian republic, with an eye to their own interests. When he reached Milan he could claim relationship with the Visconti, count of Vertus, through his uncle Lionel, the count's brother-in-law, who lay buried there. Whom he met in France is hidden from us; probably no eminent personage till he came to Paris.

As has been seen, he moved along with considerable retinue and state, sending heralds or other officers before him, both to announce his arrival and to provide food and lodging. The herald, sign of dignity and family, accompanied him throughout; and it would be interesting to know whether any of the numerous scutcheons painted by this officer with Derby's arms or those of his knights, and left behind at many of the resting places, still exist.

It is difficult, without more research into records than can now be made, to say what part of the duchy possessions exactly were assigned to Derby at the time of these accounts, or indeed to state what were his usual places of abode. Bolingbroke, his birth-place, seems to have been the headquarters of the family. The castle, built in the time of Stephen, and attached to the earldom of Lincoln (which John of Gaunt enjoyed in right of his wife Blanche), was a spacious building with prisons and four towers, the " prime seat " of the duchy, where all the records were kept, and in one of the towers of which the yearly audit of the duchy accounts was held.[a] It is in accordance with this that Henry's stores and baggage on return from his journey were sent to Bolingbroke (p. 98), and he seems to have returned there himself for a time. But we find him oftenest at Peterborough; he was there in 1390 before starting for Prussia (p. 30); again for making up the accounts with Kyngston in January, 1391-2 (pp. 2, 143); he started thence in July, 1392, and thither returned a year afterwards, while his first daughter Blanche had been born there in the spring of 1392.[b] At Berkhampstead, an ancient royal castle, he had his children in 1402,[c] but whether it were here or at Peterborough that his son Humphrey was born during his absence there is nothing to show, communication between this place and his father's castle of Hert-ford[d] is all we see of it (p. 28). He stayed at Leicester, probably coming there to meet the council (p. 32, 31/**30**). Lincoln and Leicester were two of his father's principal seats. From Kenilworth (which had belonged to his mother Blanche) Kyngston

[a] Harl. 6829, fo. 161. a MS. of the 17th century, written before 1661. See T. Allen's " History of Lincoln," ii., p. 104.

[b] Ramsay's " Lancaster and York," i., p. 159. In Leynthorpe's accounts too is an item for the expenses of two valets and a horse carrying £322 of the lord's money (evidently revenue) from Brecknock to Peterborough, in October, 1392, i.e., while Derby was travelling. D. of L., cl. 28, bdle. 3, no. 5, fo. 10 b.

[c] See after, p. 293.

[d] John kept Christmas at Hertford in 1389; Ar. Collins' " Hist. of John of Gaunt,' London, 1740, p. 60. He had been living at Kenilworth Castle in 1377. Walsingham, " Hist. Angl.," Rolls ed., i., p. 339.

fetched the treasure in florins of Arragon given by John of Gaunt towards the reysa, taking it by way of Southam (Warwickshire), Towcester, Stratford, Dunstable, St. Albans, and Barnet to London for exchange (p. 33, 18/**23**). Derby himself must have been there too after his return from Calais in June, 1390 (cf. p. 125/**10**, 31/**27**, 127/**1**).

The Lancasters had a house or houses in Calais and one or more in London; but John's palace of the Savoy, descended from Queen Eleanor, had been burnt by the mob in 1381, and we do not distinctly see where they now came when business brought them to town.[a] Probably they made no long stay there;[b] like the king they seem to have moved frequently from place to place within their own domains.[c] In Boston, whence Derby sailed on his first voyage, his father possessed a house called Gishours Hall, which afterwards passed to Thomas Beaufort.[d]

As with the earldom of Northumberland in 1512,[e] the business of the duchy of Lancaster was governed by a Council, of which we find mention as waiting at Leicester for Derby five days in the

---

[a] See after note, p. 301.

[b] They were both in London from 22 Nov. to 9 Feb. in 1396, as is shown by the waferer's wages. D. of L., cl. 28, bdle. 3, no. 6.

[c] The reason for this is well shown in Grostête's "Rules for the Countess of Lincoln," written 1241, which teaches how to arrange the sojourns, for so many weeks and according to the advantages of each manor, and so as not to overburden any. Rule 26, "Walter of Henley," ed. Lamond, p. 145.

[d] P. Thompson, " History and Antiquities of Boston," 1856, pp. 55, 59.

[e] Northumberland Household book, pp. vi., 50. When Henry IV., in the first year of his reign, separated the Duchy from the Crown possessions, he continued it under the administration of a chancellor and council, which it still retains. See 30th Report of the Deputy Keeper of Public Records, p. 1, et seq.; "Charters of the Duchy of Lancaster," ed. Wm. Hardy, 1845, pp. 103, 138, 142. The council, however, does not appear in the charters under this shape or name. It would be highly interesting to inquire into the composition of this council, probably formed of the chief officers of the duchy, and to compare it with the king's council of 1305. See F. W. Maitland's " Memoranda de Parliamento 1305 " (Rolls Series), 1893, introd. pp. xxxvi., xlvii.; and compare " Rolls of Parl.," vol. iv., p. 176 b; vol. v., pp. 383, 384 a.

CAMD. SOC.

spring of 1390 (p. 32); and again, it is by the precept of the Council that Otto Granson received his high pay in 1392 (p. 264). In Leventhorpe's account for 1391 the chamberlain and council are stated to have been at Peterborough [a] when his salary was given; it thus does not appear to have been stationary; probably it met at one place or the other to suit the convenience of father or son. For both Derby's voyages ways and means had to be considered. As has been seen, large sums were supplied by his father.[b] It may be convenient here to recapitulate the sources of supply for these expensive journeys.

1. Journey of 1390-1. The total receipts of this year were £4,383 8s. 3¼d. (*See* pp. 3, 4.)

John of Gaunt at first gave his son two sums in gold florins of Arragon, together 25,000 florins. This treasure must have been some of that which he brought back from Spain in the autumn of 1389, "47 mules laden with chests of gold,"[c] as part of the indemnity paid him by the King of Castille for renouncing his claims in that country. Part of the florins were not of full value, so that on exchange there was a loss of £132 16s. 3¼d. on the estimated value of the whole, viz. £2,777 15s. 6½d. (*see* pp. 142, 3. Four thousand marks = £2,666 13s. 4d.). £2,777 15 6½

On May 8 and 13, from Derby's own officers, *i.e.* chamberlain, treasurer, and receiver-general, sums amounting to 833 6 8
On June 13, duke John again gave his son (expressly for the voyage to Prussia) . . . 755 11 6
The sale of remainders produced . . . 16 14 7
(Of this a balance of £8 3s. 5½d. remained.)

£4,383 8 3½

---

[a] D. of L., cl. 28, bdle. 3, no. 4 (a roll).
[b] *See* pp. xlvii. lv.
[c] Knighton (Twysden's ed.), p. 2677; Walsingham, "Hist. Angl.," ii, p. 194.

II. Journey of 1392-3. Receipts, £4,915 5 0¾.

Balance from the account of 1390-1 [a] . . .	£8	3	0¾
John of Gaunt gave his son 3,000 marks . .	2,000	0	0
Derby's receiver-general	100	0	0
Marshal of Prussia	400	0	0
John of Gaunt at Venice three times, about December, March, and April 12 . . .	2,008	2	10
Ditto again in France	333	6	8
Given towards expenses by the Duke of Austria and Patriarch of Friuli	19	10	0
Profits on exchange	27	6	8
Sales of old things and remainders . . .	18	15	10
	£4,915	5	0¾

It is thus abundantly plain that Derby could have done nothing without his father's aid; Spanish gold sent him to Prussia the first time, and for the second journey the duke's wealth supplied no less than £4,341.

Derby's Household.—A study of the method of the accounts discloses that Derby's establishment—whether at home or abroad, for the continuity was kept up—was modelled on the same plan as the king's, viz. that found in *Fleta*, book 2, chapters 14-24. This compendium of English law, drawn up in the latter part of the thirteenth century from Bracton's great work, *De Legibus*, of the previous reign, embodies certain regulations for the king's court and household not in Bracton, nor as far as yet known to be found elsewhere. Mr. F. M. Nichols, on the evidence of these chapters, considers that *Fleta* must be the work of some official employed in the household of Edward I., conversant with the royal officers and their duties.[b] The rules themselves may be much older, as they are

---

[a] The 5d. was omitted in entering this balance in 1392-3. *See* pp. 149-151.
[b] "Britton," edited by F. M. Nichols, 1865, Clar. Press, introd. xxvi. The chapters above referred to (lib. ii., c. 14-24) are not part of the *Fleta* chapters found in

exemplified in perfect working already in the royal Wardrobe (*i.e.* household) Accounts of the 28th year of Edward I., which were printed by the Society of Antiquaries in 1787.[a] In those accounts the items are grouped or classified under heads according to the officers and their functions; and these general heads, some identical, some modified and subdivided—the duties of the officers becoming more defined as they increased and divided—are found in royal and princely household accounts down to at least Queen Mary.[b] How far great lords usually adopted this arrangement of household would of course depend on their estate in rank and wealth;[c] a comparison between several Lancaster and royal accounts show that the difference was but one of degree.[d]

Both theory and practice in the great households placed one man at the head as responsible for all payments, collecting and recording all accounts daily or weekly. *Fleta* calls him the treasurer or clerk of the wardrobe, and so he appears in 28 Edw. I;[e] and in the Household Ordinances of Edw. II., 1323;[f] treasurer of the household is the title in 21 Edw. III., and under Edw. IV.[g]

The bursar of a priory appears to have discharged very much the

Walter of Henley (*see* ed. E. Lamond, 1890, Dr. W. Cunningham's Introd., xxxi., xxxii.). But the duties of the Steward in one of these last (cap. 72) should be considered in connection with other household officers.

[a] With valuable notes by John Topham, who refers to *Fleta*.

[b] *See* a curious Table of Expenses for seven specified years between 1539 and 1560, Add. MS. 27,449, fo. 1. An account of the officers and the fees due to each, earlier than Edward I., is given in " Liber Niger Scaccarii " (? Hen. II.), Hearne, 2nd ed., vol. i., pp. 341-359.

[c] It is to be traced, much amplified, in the valuable "Regulations for the Northumberland Household" of 1512, edited by Bp. Percy in 1827, who also refers to *Fleta*, and the resemblance between the households of the king and the nobility, and notes "the establishing a system of domestic æconomy" by our ancestors. Pref., pp. vi., ix.

[d] *e.g.* Loveney's accounts of Derby's Great Wardrobe. D. of L., cl. 28, bdle. 1, Nos. 2 and 5 ; account of S. Bache, treasurer, *ib.* bdle. 3, no. 6.

[e] Wardrobe Accounts, p. 16.

[f] Chaucer Soc., ed. F. J. Furnivall, 1876, p. 6.

[g] "Collection of Household Ordinances." Soc. of Antiquaries, 1790, pp. 3, 56.

same kind of office.[a] Bishop Swinfield employed a chaplain in 1289.[b] The accounts of Thomas Earl of Lancaster, in 1313, seem to have been kept by his "cofferer,"[c] an officer assistant to the treasurer. The most interesting and instructive comparison to be made with the present accounts is perhaps to be found in the Ordinances for the household of George Duke of Clarence, the ill-fated brother of Edward IV., made 9 Dec., 1469, a few months before his marriage.[d] Here the duties of a numerous staff are set out under the chief officers, steward, treasurer, controller, and chamberlain, as in the royal households. At the end of the ordinances are lists of the persons and horses of the prince's retinue after his marriage, when he went a journey—" in his riding "—apart from these of his "standing household," the last, left with his wife, being set forth in another list.[e] These are worth attention as showing the establishment of a prince, whose rank differed little from Derby's, scarcely eighty years later. The difference of state attendant on a duke and an earl—Derby was not Duke of Hereford till 1397—would count for something, and eight decades may have introduced a little change in details, though not so much as had grown up between the time of *Fleta* and Derby; but with all allowance made the resemblance in the establishments of the two young nobles is so apparent that the light thrown upon the Derby accounts by the Clarence Ordinances is valuable.

Clarence had the same "accountable officers," also clerk of the kitchen, marshal of the hall, butler, &c. The men accompanying him in residence were said to be " in the court," sometimes one or other would be "departing out of the court;[f]" in Derby's case

---

[a] *See* "Durham Household Book," Surtees Soc., 1844, Pref. pp. viii., ix.
[b] "Swinfield's Household Expenses," Camden Soc,. p. 3.
[c] Harl. MS., p. 293, fo. 76 *b*; this is evidently an abstract noted from the original account; it is printed in M. Gregson's "Portfolio of Fragments," 3rd ed., 1869, p. 44.
[d] "Household Ord." as before, pp, 87-103.
[e] *Ibid.* p. 98-101. There is also an estimate of a year's expenses.
[f] "Household Ord.," p. 93.

the phrases *infra curiam* or *extra curiam* are frequently and carefully used to indicate the right to lower or higher wages, and show clearly that the "court" moved with and accompanied the lord's presence abroad or at home; this is another analogy with the royal household. Clarence's retinue on "his riding" was for a peaceable journey (he was married at Calais, and leaving his wife there went to England), while that of Derby was for war; but we get a similar enumeration of knights, esquires, valets, grooms, henchmen, pages, and many serving besides, to the number of 183 persons, "wherof at wages and clothing," it is expressly said were only 105 persons. Fifty horses of various kinds were taken; as as "standing household" with his duchess he left 144 persons with 43 horses.[a] The figures of the journey retinue are important, and support the results arrived at in previous pages as to the strength of Derby's companies;[b] two-fifths of Clarence's party received neither payment nor livery, giving their service in return merely for food and lodging, and we may deem the unpaid members of Derby's expeditions to have been in somewhat of the same proportion.

According to *Fleta*, the Treasurer of the Wardrobe, with a controller, keeps record of the household expenses, calling in every night the steward, chamberlain, purveyors, and clerks of the different offices to answer for their expenditure for the day over food and every other particular. He himself is responsible for the following heads of expenditure: purchase of horses, carriages, &c.; gifts, alms, and oblations; wages of knights and archers; messengers, foreign fees, presents or accommodations; and the wardrobe expenses proper, which comprise purchase of cloth, furs, wax, spices, linen, &c., also jewels, foreign expenses, ambassadors, falconers. In succeeding chapters the officers and their duties are specified,[c] and the arrangement of these supply a key to the understanding of much in Derby's accounts.

[a] "Household Ord.," pp. 98, 99.
[b] See before, pp. xlv, lii.
[c] Selden's *Fleta*, lib. ii., caps. 11-24.

INTRODUCTION.

It is clear that by the end of the fourteenth century some of the titles set down were treated as abstractions for classification, not necessarily represented by persons, although the old method of calling in the daily items was adhered to. This is shown by the use of the phrase "super officio," as "super officio scutellarie," "super officio salsarie;" two instances of the first occur on p. 23, ll. 3, 24, in which different men are paid, and in a second on p. 22, l. 7, the person paid is a woman.

The ordinary treasurer of Derby's household when at home was Simon Bache, whose "Jornale," or daily account for 1396-7, the twelfth year of his holding the office (Derby being Duke of Hereford), still exists.[a] In appointing a special treasurer "for war" on his military expeditions Derby again may have followed royal precedent, instances of which under one of the first Edwards, and in the first and second years of Richard II., are mentioned on the Rolls of Parliament [b] (the appointment of the last, however, was compelled by the people). During part of the stay abroad, Kyngston deputed the keeping the daily accounts (dietæ) to several others, whose written rolls he used as vouchers afterwards (pp. 102-104).

The following are the chief officers of Henry's household [c] named in these accounts:—

Thomas Herdwyk, clerk, auditor of accounts of Derby's officers and servants (D. of L., cl. 28, bdle. 3, No. 5). [He was also auditor to John of Gaunt's officers.]

Thomas de Wombewell, auditor (p. 148/**5**) and "supervisor terrarum domini in Anglia" (*ib.* No. 5, fo. 7).

---

[a] D. of L., cl. 28, bdle. 3, no. 6. This account is kept in the same fashion as Kyngston's, being literally a journal of items, run-on exactly like his, with two days' items in a page and the sam at the bottom of each page. Many of the same names of domestics occur in both.

[b] Vols. i., 463a ; iii., 7b, 38a.

[c] Those who accompanied him on the journeys are indicated by the asterisk ; Leventhorpe went to Calais in 1390 (p. 123). *See* notes at end of the text (pp. 293-313) for details as to many of the above.

Simon Bache, clerk, treasurer of the household (sometimes called Symkyn Bache).
Robert Hatfield, esquire, controller of the household.
John Lernthorpe (Lewn- or Leunthorpe), receiver-general.
*Peter Bucton, knight, steward.
William Loveney, clerk of the great wardrobe.
*John Dyndon, valet of the wardrobe.
*Hugh de Waterton, knight, chamberlain.
**Richard de Kyngeston* (or Kyngston), archdeacon of Hereford, treasurer for war.
Robert de Waterton*, esquire, master of the horse or marshal [a] (marescallus, *e.g.* p. 86/12**).
*Hugh Herle, chaplain and confessor.
*(John) *Derby le herald*.
* *William Pomfreit*, clerk, chief clerk of the kitchen.
*John Payne, esquire, botiller.
*John Dounton, armourer.
* *William Hauer*, clerk of the lord.[b]
Sir *John*, almoner.[c]

[a] I have not found any traces of the marshal of the hall, a distinct officer. Perhaps one of these acted as his sub-titute abroad. All early household books mention this necessary officer. It was John Russell, " marshal in hall" to Derby's son, Humphry duke of Gloucester, who, about 1440-50, wrote the famous rhyming " Boke of Nurture," which tells so much about life in the hall and the chamber, and the duties of the officers in his days. See this in " The Babees Book," ed. F. J. Furnivall, 1868, Early Eng. Text Soc., p. 115.

[b] Although called "clericus domini" (p. 5), Haver occupied but a subordinate position, as is proved by the rate of his wages, those of a valet of the chamber (p. 126); his duties seem to have been to write out the daily bills or *parcellæ*, and he was sent after Lord Thomas Percy, apparently for a debt, for his fare from Dover to Calais (*skippagium*), in the early summer of 1390. He was with Derby at Calais in June, 1390, then again in England, and in August must have been in Prussia, but not on the reysa (p. 130). In the winter of 1390, we hear of his death and burial at König-berg (p. 111), which must have occurred before 9 Feb., when Derby left that city.

[c] Henry gave alms frequently on his journeys, as was the general custom, through various hands, yet the name of his almoner or of the office occurs but once

The following are the heads of expenditure, though we cannot always be sure of the persons who held the office. It is likely that two, or possibly three accounting clerks served for all the offices:—

Office of the hall and chamber.—Repairs and cleaning in making ready the lodging; hooks to hang lights, rushes, tables, and trestles, washing and care of the nappery [a] or table linen, bed, and care of the chamber. Henry Morley and William Harpeden were evidently two of the chief valets of the chamber, John Schelford and others. Nuport was valet of the Body in 1390 (p. 124). In 1392 Maye and Hamond were pages to the valets of the chamber (p. 272).

Richard del Ewery, valet, must have borne the office of his name, with probably a yeoman under him. John del Ewery is also named.[b]

Clerk of the kitchen.—Meat bought in carcase, as oxen, sheep, calves, pigs, and an occasional kid or wild boar; fish—salt, stock and fresh of all kinds (including a porpoise); flitches of bacon; salt, are the chief objects; but he was also responsible for the beating of stock-fish (p. 22), for empty barrels and casks to hold water and victuals. Robert Burton was clerk of the kitchen under William Pomfret,[c] he helped the treasurer to make out his accounts

---

(p. 273, 4), and then only as "dominus Johannis," which I take to be equivalent to his title as a priest. I have not found this officer in other accounts, and do not know his second name; his duty would be to gather up the remnants from dishes and tables to be given away to the poor, for which baskets or buckets were provided; also to distribute old horses, cloths, and money. *Fleta*, lib. ii., cap. 23; see also Grostête's "Rules for the Countess of Lincoln's Household," in "Walter of Henley," ed. Lamond, pp. 135, 139, and cf. the Clarence Ordinances, pp. 89, 90.

[a] Sometimes this is found under the Spicery.

[b] The Ewery was a side-board in the hall at which the company washed hands before sitting down to meat. *See* "Old English Cookery," in the Quarterly Review, Jan., 1894, p. 86.

[c] Besides Master William Cook, at the pay of an esquire, 7d. or 8d. per day, two other cooks occur, William Pulter and William Kikkeley, at 4d. and 3d. a day, as well as casual cooks and a page or serving man, Henry. Gifts were given to waferers, or makers of wafers, a dainty sweet, at Königsberg, in January, 1390-1 (p. 109).

(pp. 103, 115). Possibly too the clerks of the kitchen answered for the expenditure under the three following heads, viz.:—

Office of the saucery.—Mustard, vinegar, and verjuice, of which many gallons were used, barrels to put them in, mustard seed, sometimes also vegetables and oatmeal (p. 239).

Office of the poultry.—Poultry dead and alive, and the food of the latter on board ship, capons, occasional partridges, geese, eggs and dairy products; herbs and flour are not infrequent items.

Office of the scullery.—Wooden and pewter dishes, platters and cups, earthen and brass pots, mortars and pestles, buckets, troughs, the fitting up of a dresser and a hearth and other like arrangements about the kitchen or larder, and fuel, *i.e.*, wood and coal. Robert Spaigne and Laurence Travers, seem to have been the chief valets of the scullery.

Clerk of the spicery.—Spices of all kinds, sugar, confections, honey, almonds, dried fruits, wax worked and not worked, tallow candles, strainers, canvas, ink and quires of parchment, linen for the pantry, buttery, and kitchen, with some other miscellaneous articles. This clerk must also have answered for the

Office of the chaundry, in which wick, soap, tallow, candles, and torches were provided and made. John Whytelock, probably the same as John del Chaundry, seems to have been the valet in charge (p. 78/**16**).

Clerk of the buttery.—Wine of various kinds, with casks and carriage, and its care generally. Also beer and barrels, and occasionally mead. Besides John Payne, esquire, Robert Jonson was in the buttery, and there must have been others.

Clerk of the pantry.—Bread, flour, corn, multure (*i.e.* the cost of grinding), canvas and bolting or sifting, sacks or barrels for the bread or flour, and the costs of making and baking bread. John Fysher was the chief baker (pp. 75, 80); but there were several others employed, besides a pie baker, and at Königsberg and in Venice pastry cooks, Hans Edeyne and Francisco.

Clerk of the marshalcy.—Hay, oats, the shoeing of the horses, saddles, and horse gear generally, transport of fodder and victuals on the reysa, purchase and care of horses. Besides Robert de Waterton, Thomas Toty acted as master of the horse on the journey in 1393 (p. 257), and Thomas Swylington and John Wilbram were two of the principal valets.

Clerk of the great wardrobe.—As Loveney, who filled this office, did not go abroad, it is likely that Kyngston himself answered for the expenditure under the titles purchase of Horses (p. 262); Alms and Oblations (pp. 116, 273); Wages (pp. 118, 264), and Belchere (p. 259), aided of course by those who actually spent the items, such as the chamberlain and the steward, who often sent in their voucher, " nunciante camerario," &c.

Silver vessels (p. 100) and metal kitchen vessels (p. 101, including a pair of stocks) were also on the first journey treated separately, and on the second journey Shipping Expenses (p. 278).

While Derby was still in England Loveney answered for his wardrobe expenses (pp. 34-36), but the chaundry and the spicery were at this date taken out of his office. There remain however many things in his sphere of responsibility which go beyond the modern idea of the word "wardrobe"—which, it may be said, is here out of place—but which accord with *Fleta*. Besides cloths and stuffs, silk, woollen, and linen, &c., and furs given out or purchased for the lord and his "family," and the making of the garments, the clerk of the wardrobe took cognisance of shoes and footgear; saddlery and the housing of horses; flags and banners, and heraldry; armour, including bows and arrows; all sorts of package for these various things; jewelry and goldsmith's ware; money spent at play (p. 263); and perhaps falconry; besides frequent travelling expenses. During the journeys John Dyndon (who in Loveney's accounts of 1391-2 is called " cissor robarum domini ") [a] acted as clerk (pp. 88, 179, 257) while John Dounton was " custos armature " (p. 257, see index).

---

[a] D. of L., cl. 28, bdle. 1, no. 2, fo. 2.

The Chamberlain answered for Gifts in 1390-1 (pp. 104, 113), and probably, though not so expressed, also in 1392-3 (p. 289).

The men who carried out these various offices, valets, grooms, or pages,[a] formed the bulk of the household, together with a few more to be pointed out, but from the accounts alone it is impossible to specify with certainty, except in a few cases, which names belong to the relative offices.

The *two Henksmen* or henchmen, Bernard and Henry Tylman[b] (in 1392-3 only). One of these went with Derby to Jerusalem.

The *Minstrels*.—Of these Derby had six in his regular pay all through 1390-91, two trumpeters, three pipers, one nakerer (player on the naquaire or nacaire, a kind of cymbal). In 1392 he also took six musicians, three trumpeters, and three pipers, different men, except perhaps John the trumpeter; but he sent them back to England at the end of September, only retaining one trumpeter, Thomas, who accompanied him on his journeys across Europe (p. 271). They appear as a kind of military band.

Their names were—

---

[a] After Edward III.'s time the officers were allowed by degrees "to chose and suffer suche yonge apt persones to lerne to serve and to help the yomen and groomes," and these pages had acquired a recognised status by 1461. "Household Ordinances." p. 65. We see a few in Derby's household, in the kitchen, &c.

[b] Henks-men, Henx-men, or Hench-men were, it seems, minors, sometimes wards, boys or orphans of gentle family who were placed under the care of a king, noble, or gentleman to be brought up in his household, usually with their own special attendant; their wardrobe and other expenses being provided by their guardian. See "Household Ordinances," Soc. Ant., pp. 44, 45. "Edward II.'s Ordinances," Chaucer Soc., pp. x., 17, § 25, "Babee's Book," p. ii., and "Notes and Queries," Ser. 7, iii., p. 312, where Canon Jackson prints an account of 1452, and ib. Ser. 8, iii., p. 194. The earliest instances of the word hitherto remarked are those recently pointed out from Wardrobe Accounts of 1378-9, 1400, 1420, &c. in "Notes and Queries," Ser. 8, vol. iii., pp. 389, 478. To which may be added, besides those in our text, another in Loveney's Wardrobe Account for 14 and 15 Ric. II. (1391-2), where we have Bernard, Walter, and Yonge, Derby's henksmen. D. of L., cl. 28, bdle. 1, no. 2, fo. 10 v°.

INTRODUCTION.   xcvii

1390-1.

John Brothir, trump.
Robert Crakyll, do.
William Byngeley, piper.
William de York,   do.
William Algood,   do.
Master John, nakerer.

1392-3.

John, trumpeter.
Thomas Aleyn, do.
Thomas, do.
John Algood, piper.
John Smyth,   do.
John Aleyn,   do.

Their pay was 4d. a day, the same as that of valets of the chamber, and when on military service they had 6d. a day.[a]

Robert barbour in 1390-1 was probably his master's barber valet; and Nicholas and John leche, each named once in 1392-3, are the only mentions of any doctors.

Regarding the valets, on the first journey ten seem to have been properly valets of the chamber, paid 6d. a day during the reysa, 4d. ordinary pay; five were of less degree, receiving 4d. on the reysa, 3d. ordinary pay; ten were of less degree again, and generally classed as "gromes," receiving 3d. a day on the reysa, 2d. ordinary pay. It is not easy to distinguish so certainly the men on the second journey, but there appear to have been 20 valets at 4d. a day for a considerable part of the time.[b]

---

[a] They had gowns of russet, rayed with blood and tan cloth, in 1391. (Loveney's Wardrobe Accounts, D. of L., cl. 28, bdle. 1, no. 2, fo. 4v°.) It may be re-called that the Lancasters owned Tutbury, where a large society of musicians or "minstrels" held a yearly court on 15 Aug., with sports, having a king and four assistants, whose object seems to have been to promote and encourage skill in good music in the five counties of Stafford, Warwick, Derby, Leicester, and Nottingham. John of Gaunt, in 1380, gave them a charter, with certain privileges over members of their profession. See Plot's Staffordshire, 1686, pp. 435-440. Perhaps Derby drew his band from these men.

[b] The upper valets appear to have been gentlemen of good family, though probably not, as in the days of Bracton, "the young heirs that were to be knighted, were comprehended under the title of *Valetti*," as Selden recalls; perhaps they were coming down a little in the social scale, though we see Chaucer both valet and esquire between 1367 and 1373 (Furnivall's Preface to "Edw. II.'s Ordinances," p. xii., Chaucer Soc.), for as Selden points out, under Statute 23 Henry VI., c. 14,

All the paid men from the highest to the lowest received extra wages on the reysa, and any officer employed on his lord's affairs out of court received higher pay for those days than when in court.

Money and Coinage.—Strictly accounting for the sums entrusted to him, showing loss and profit by exchange, as well as expenditure in the various countries through which Derby passed, Kyngston had frequent memoranda made on his accounts of the rate of exchange against English money. The summings up of the pages and heads of expenses are regularly reduced into money sterling on the first account, only occasionally so on the second. The English noble of 6s. 8d. was the standard coin of computation; the mark of 13s. 4d., money of account, was also sometimes used. Pounds, shillings, pence, halfpence, and farthings are the other English money used. In Italian states the ducat was the standard of computation. The following tables collect together the notes of names and values with the pages where they are to be found.[a]

Spain.—The gold florins brought from Arragon did not, in 1390-1, all realise the full value at first estimated, which caused the considerable loss of 8½d. on every mark English.

Page.	Foreign.	English.
3,142	Gold florin of Arragon	2s. 2¼d.
	3 florins	6s. 8d.
142	1 florin	2s. 1¼d.
277n. 289.	In 1392 it fell still lower, 2s.	

(1411). the valet was excepted from those who were capable of being made knights, and therefore could not be chosen knight of the shire, "Titles of Honour," 1631, p 831.

[a] Numismatists and manuals naturally concern themselves more with the actual coins than with the written signs of their currency; I have had considerable difficulty in identifying some signs in these accounts, and must beg indulgence if I have fallen into error. I beg to express my thanks for kind hints and assistance on these points to Dr. H. Dannenberg of Berlin, M. J. Delaville le Roulx, M. Prou of the Cabinet des Médailles, Paris, and Mr. C. W. C. Oman of Oxford.

INTRODUCTION.   xcix

Prussia.—The moneys of the Teutonic Order in these accounts are the mark, scot, shilling, pfennig (denarius), vierchen.

    p. 184.   mark = 24 scot or 60 shillings   6s. 8d.
              scot = 30 pfennige, or $2\frac{1}{2}$ shillings.
              shilling = 12 pfennige.
      61.   ferk. or vierchen = 4 pfennige.
    57, 66, 70,
    101, 113,   26 scot until 7 Jan. 1390-1   6s. 8d.
    67, 88,
    93, 95   25 scot 7 Jan. until Mar., 1390-1[a]   6s. 8d.
    95, 98, 184   24 scot in Mar. 1390-1, and Sept.
              1392 .   .   .   .   6s. 8d.
              With the noble at 24 scot, 9 pfennige   1d.

The vierchen only occurs twice, it was the quarter of a half-scot.[b] The scot is generally considered by German authorities to have been only a money of account.[c] Grunau, a chronicler of early in 16th century, records that it was struck by Winric von Kniperode (1351-1382), but gives conflicting statements as to its value, which, coupled with the fact that it has quite disappeared, led F. A. Vossberg to think that it was the half-scot of fifteen pfennige that was actually coined by Winric. Into the merits of the question we cannot enter here; but it may be remarked that many isolated small payments were made in the scot alone, which tends to show that it was a real coin, such as for belchere, p. 259/**26, 29**; alms, p. 117/**2**; oblations, p. 274/**11**; gifts to a servant, a tumbler and others, p. 109/**5, 10, 14**, to say nothing of numerous items in the general expenses in Prussia, *e.g.* pp. 174-177.

The Mark (Neumark).—Here were the mark, shilling, and penny (no scot); but the money was " moneta vocata f" (p. 187) exclusively used within the limits of the Mark. There is much

    [a] This was still the value of the English noble in 1399, "Treszlerbuch," quoted in Vossberg, p. 76.
    [b] Theo. Hirsch, "Handels und Gewerbsgeschichte," p. 240.
    [c] F. A. Vossberg, "Geschichte der Preussische Münzen," Berlin, 1843, p. 83; Hirsch, as above, p. 241.

INTRODUCTION.

difficulty in the explanation of this *f.*, evidently a local designation. Dr. H. Dannenberg, the well-known numismatist of Prussia, suggests (in which also Dr. Menadier, of the Cabinet of Medals at Berlin, concurs) that the *marca denariorum* of North Germany, or money really coined, in opposition to the uncoined lump-metal and money of account, was here designated. The mark being coined into smaller pieces, the pfennige or pence, the currency became known by the name of these coins, it was the " pfennige geld." And to the Englishman's ear the initial sound of this would be f. The question arises, however, whether this sort of money was confined to this part of Brandenburg; did not the rest of North Germany share in its diffusion ? Blanchet[a] states that "in the 14th century the Margraves struck a great quantity of pfennigs," and Leitzmann[b] says that several towns in Brandenburg, as Drossen and Frankfort-on-Oder, purchased the right of striking the pfennig for ever, ("sogenannten ewigen pfennig,") which show that the coinage of this piece was actively going on in the latter half of the century in the margravate. But in this currency were there also shillings ?

There seems to me another alternative ; that the f. may betoken the money called *Finkenaugen*, which was coined at Salzwedel in the Mark. Schmieder says that this had been struck since 1314 ; a thin coin stamped on one side only, the edge was raised like a ring, with the stamp in the centre looking out as it were from an eye, hence the name Finkenaugen,[c] augenpfennig (eye-penny) or okelpfennig.[d] In the time of Charles IV., 18 finkenaugen were worth a Bohemian grossus ; and in 1360 2 mark finkenaugen were worth 2½ Rhenish gulden. Besides Brandenburg this money had currency in Pomerania, Mecklenburg, and Dantzic. " Die mrc.

---

[a] "Numismatique du Moyen Age." 1890. tom. ii., p. 128.

[b] "Wegweise der Münzkunde des Königreichs Preussen," 1865. p. 15.

[c] Apparently a contraction of pfennigen-augen.

[d] "Handwörterbuch der gesammten Münzkunde ;" Nachtrag, Berlin. 1815. pp. 137, 138.

finekenoug'," or as Hirsch says, "the mark F.," occurs in an account of 1409 from the Königsberg archives, quoted by Vossberg,[a] where it is stated to have been worth 6 scot Prussian. Here we can trace that the name spread from the pfennig upwards to the mark, and presumably to whatever other money, as the shilling, was connected with them. The Englishman knew what a Prussian penny was, and put it down as d., *denarius*; he knew that here in the Mark too were pence and shillings, &c. (though of less value), and put them down as d. and s., but this queer word which he very likely did not understand he never attempted to write in full, but carefully distinguished every item paid in such money by ff. (which simply means F.) or f.[b]

This identification is not wholly satisfactory because the mark f. in these accounts is worth 8 scot prus., not 6 scot (cf. with Prussian money); and because we have no reason why that particular money should only have been found current in the Mark by Derby's people, and not also in Pomerania and other parts of Brandenburg. But greater knowledge of local conditions of the time might explain this, and I venture to think that this may be the " *moneta vocata* F."

p. 184-7.   mark = 16 shillings f.   .   2s. English.
   „   shilling (? = 12 pence f.) .   2d.   „
   275.   12 pence .   .   .   1½¼d. „
   187 n.   3 mark 4 shillings.   .   6s. 8d. „

(See this money also in some items on pp. 259, 260, 261.)

Bohemia.—Florins, grossi, pence.
p. 188,} 261 . florin = 20 grossi   .   3s. 0d. English.
   273.}
   191.   grossus = 6 pence   .   .   1¾¼d. „
   275,} 277. 2 florins 4 gr., or 44 grossi .   6s. 8d. „
   289.}

---
[a] "Preussen Münzen," p. 76. See also Hirsch, as before, p. 213; he, however, takes Finkenaugen to be a place.
[b] Mr. Oman, however, inclines to think, with Dannenberg and Menadier, that the mark f. is the mark of pfennige, not of the finkenaugen.

INTRODUCTION.

Hungarian money.—Florins, guldens.
p. 194.   florin   .   .   .   .   3s. 3½d.
   204, 151. gulden = 1 Austrian florin   .   3s.

Austria.—Florins, grossi, pence.[a]
   p. 151.   florin   .   .   .   3s.
      196, 199. 2 florins 4 grossi   .   6s. 8d.
      204. 21 gros. 4d. = 1 florin.

Friuli.—Ducats, lire, soldi, denarii, which were the currency of Venice (pp. 204/**21**, 206, 208 *notes*, 211). 4 li. 5 sol. = 1 ducat.

Venice.—Ducats, libre or lire, solidi or soldi, denarii; bagatini, pichioni.[b]
   p. 213, 217. 4 lire 12 den. = 1 ducat.
      283, 290. 1 ducat   .   .   3s. 2d.
      215, 225. 2 ducats 9 soldi   .   6s. 8d.
      286. 8 lire 11 soldi   .   .   6s. 8d.
      277, 278. 1 lira   .   .   9¼ 1/10 d. or 9¼d.
      289. 24 soldi[c]   .   .   11d.
      358. 28 soldi 2 den.   .   .   1s. 1¼d.

The bagatino only occurs twice (pp. 221/**9**, 281/**15**); no clue is given as to its value, although 500 bag. are named. The date given by Hazlitt for the appearance of this small bronze or copper coin is about 1400 to 1410;[d] while Canon Dionisius quotes a statute which he believes to show the Venetian bagatino was current in

---

[a] These appea to resemble the Bohemian money in value; in one note the scribe calls the sum paid in Austria " moneta boemici," p. 203.

[b] The piccolo of the Italian states, answering broadly to the grossus of the German countries, is only represented in these accounts by the pichon or picchione of Milan.

[c] In nearly every north Italian state 12 den. = 1 soldo, 20 soldi = 1 lira. Schmieder, " Handwörterbuch der gesammten Münzkunde," p. 427.

[d] In the reign of Michele Steno. "Coins of Venice," *Antiquary.* vol. 9, p. 253. See the same writer's " Coinage of the European Continent," 1893, p. 184.

INTRODUCTION.　　　　ciii

Verona about 1371.[a] Papadopoli indicates that the name bagatino was later applied, and found in documents after 1460, referring to the ancient silver denaro or piccolo.[b]

Rhodes and the East.—The Venetian money had currency in the Levant; besides, there were in circulation grossi siccez, aspers, and besants.

    p. 225.　4 li. 12d. = 1 ducat, ven.
       225, 227.[c]　18 grossi siccez = 1 ducat.
       258, 289/**26**.　1 grossus sic. . . . $2\frac{1}{12}$d. or $2\frac{1}{9}$d.
       258.　27 aspers . . . 3s. $0\frac{3}{4}$d.
       225, 229, 283.　28 aspers = 1 ducat.
       278, 289.　1 asper . . . $1\frac{11}{48}$d. or $1\frac{1}{216}$d.
       226, 227.　10 besants[d] = 1 ducat.
       258.　1 besant . . . $3\frac{3}{4}$d.

Milan—Pichon; sizan = sixain or sexino; imperiale. The coins of Venice and Milan sometimes intermingled. The pichon

---

[a] In Zanetti, tom. iv., pp. 353, 361-2.

[b] N. Papadopoli, "Del Piccolo e del Bianco, antichissime monete Veneziane," Venezia, 1887, p. 9.

[c] Other pages, 229, 277, 278 note (where the grossi are gr. sic.), 283. The gros siccet appears to be the gigliato struck by the Turkish emirs of Asia Minor, a Latin coin copying the gigliato of Naples and intended for circulation among both Christian and Turkish ports of the Levant. Analogous to the grossus, it was distinguished by the addition of *sikket*, the Arab word for *coin* or *mintage*. Another suggestion is that siccez = *siculi*, and that this was a name for the gigliati of the kings of Naples and Sicily, *regis Siciliæ*, or for the gigliati struck in Rhodes in imitation of them by Villeneuve (1319-1346). About this date two aspres = one gigliato (Schlumberger, "Num. de l'Or. Lat." p. 240); in our account 28 aspers = 18 grossi siccez (p. 289), showing the gros. sic. to be worth $1\frac{5}{9}$ aspers. The asper is a well-known Turkish coin. There is one instance of the half gros. sic. (p. 225, l. 20 and *note*), which may refer to the demi-gigliato.

[d] According to Schlumberger $1\frac{1}{2}$ gigliati or 3 aspres were worth 1 besant. "Numismatique," p. 240. P. Lambros states that excepting in Cyprus no besants were struck, and that in Rhodes and elsewhere the besant was only a money of account, "Monnaies inédites de G. M. de Rhodes," Paris, 1877, p. 9.

is here found in use at Venice, Verona, Pavia, and Milan (pp. 283/**28**, 288); it appears to be the Milanese *picchione*, worth 18 imperiali (or denarii), struck at Milan, and is referred to in proclamations of G. Galeazzo Visconti of 1391, and an ordinance for the mint at Pavia, 1400;[a] a name not well known, it is taken by Canon Dionisius to have been the same as the picciolo.[b] The sexino of Milan was worth 6 imperiali (see the same proclamations); there was, later, a sixain in Cyprus, first struck under King Janus (1398-1432).[c] The denaro imperiale was a Milanese coin dating from the twelfth century, commonly known by the second word only; the lira d'imperiali contained 20 soldi, each soldo 12 denari or imperiali.[d] The values in the accounts are—

p. 288. 22 pichons 1 sizan = 1 ducat.
    289. 6 pichons . . . 10½d. English.
    286. 1 pichon . . . 1¾d. ,,
    288. 1 sizan . . . 1¾d. ,,

Of the "moneta imperiali" we have here, soldi (p. 287/**11**), grossi (pp. 241, 242), and denarii (p. 252, *note*).

p. 243, 247. 14 grossi = 1 ducat.
    288. 32 soldi = 1 ducat.
    289. 12 soldi . . . 1s. 3d.
    Thus 1 soldo was worth 1¼d.

Savoy, Burgundy, and France.—Franc, blanc, and the scutum (écu) or corona (p. 277/**2**). Some ducats and grossi were also used.

p. 249, 251, 262. 24 blanc = 1 franc.
    262. 27 blanc = 1 scutum . . 3s. 4½d.

---

[a] Printed in Argelatus, "De monetis Italæ," 1750, tom. iii., p. 59.
[b] "Delle Monete di Verona," in G. A. Zanetti's "Nuova Racolta" (in continuation of Argelatus), 1786, tom. iv., p. 327 *note*, col. 2.
[c] G. Schlumberger, "Numismatique de l'Orient Latin," 1878, pp. 181, 182.
[d] C. Doneda, "Delle Monete di Brescia," Zanetti, tom. iv., pp. 417, 418.

278, 288.	1 scutum or corona	.	3s. 4d.
289.	2 scuta . .	.	6s. 8d.
277.	1 blanc . .	.	1½d.
151.	1 franc. . .	.	3s. 4d.
249} 253}	12 grossi = 1 ducat.		

There yet remain several matters of high interest in these accounts, to which attention should at least be directed; details concerning food, conveyance by land and water, dress, and many more. But this introduction has already outrun its limits, and the reader will consult his convenience by turning to the *Glossarial Index*, where the principal subjects of domestic economy, &c., are grouped, together with a few explanatory words, under such heads as Fish, Fruits, Meats, Spicery, Armour, Textiles, Games, Horses, Horse-gear, Shipping, Carpentry, Weights and Measures, &c., which will give some idea of the store of valuable material for the historian. Lists of prices of various articles, and of wages, might be drawn up, but these and other like omissions are now left to the care of the reader, who has the text before him.

The indices to *Persons* and *Places* give the means of further checking the itineraries and the conclusions arrived at in the foregoing pages. About a dozen place-names remain unidentified, in spite of all research. Three knights, Ecton, Elys, and Scinlatour, and Lord Robert Elkington, among the persons of upper rank, are little known, nothing could be found about them; the Tylman and Yonge families (henchmen) are worth further search; but future investigations about these and other names may prove more fruitful, especially if made among the contemporary records of the Lancasters.

A list of *errata* discovered as the work went on is prefixed, the reader is requested to correct them with the pen on the respective pages.

L. TOULMIN SMITH.

Highgate, *March*, 1894.

APPENDIX A.

Extracts from Chronicles, English and German, relating to the
Expedition of 1390-91.

Walsingham's Historia Anglicana. Rolls ed. vol. ii.
pp. 197-98.—Dominus Henricus, comes de Derby, per idem tempus
profectus est in Le Pruys; ubi, cum adjutorio marescalli dictæ
patriæ, et cujusdam Regis vocati Wytot devicit exercitum Regis de
Lettowe, captis quatuor Ducibus, et tribus peremptis, et amplius
quam trecentis de valentioribus exercitus supradicti pariter inter-
emptis. Civitas quoque, vocata Wille, in cujus castellum Rex de
Letowe, nomine Skirgalle, confugerat, potenti virtute dicti comitis
maxime, atque suorum, capta est. Namque qui fuerunt de familia sua
primi murum ascenderunt, et vexillum ejus super muros, cæteris vel
torpentibus vel ignorantibus, posuerunt: captaque sunt ibi, vel
occisa, quatuor millia plebanorum, fratre Regis de Poleyn, inter
cæteros, ibi perempto, qui adversarius noster fuit. Obsessumque
fuit castrum dictæ civitatis per quinque hebdomadas; sed propter
infirmitates quibus vexabatur exercitus, Magistri de le Pruys et de
Lifland noluerunt diutius expectare. Facti sunt Christiani de
gente de Lettow octo, et Magister de Lifland duxit secum in suam
patriam tria millia prisonum.

Knighton's Chronicle. Twysden's "Decem Scriptores,"
col. 2,737.—1390; ad festum sancti Jacobi [25 July] Henricus
comes Derbeye primogenitus Johannis Ducis Lancastrie cum armata
manu M. electorum militum, armigerorum, et valettorum arripuit
iter versus Pruciam et mense Aprilis rediit cum magni honoris
tripudio et omnibus Christianis excellenti gaudiflua expeditione.

Capgrave's Chronicle. Rolls' ed. p. 254.—In this yere Ser
Herry, erl of Derby, sailed into Prus, where, with help of the
Marchale of Prus, and of a kyng that hite Witot, he ovyrcam the

kyng of Lettow and mad him for to fle. Thre of his dukes he took, and foure dukes he killid, with many lordes and knytis, and swieris mo than thre hundred.

Annales Thorunensis, Scriptores rerum Prussicarum, III. pp. 164, 165, 168.

Anno 1390 . . . Eodem tempore marscalcus⁎ fuit cum magno exercitu ante Vilnam et cum eo dominus de Lankasten Anglicus, qui cum suis venerat per mare circa festum Laurentii. Et similiter   Aug. 10. iverunt ibidem illi de Livonia et Wytaut cum Zamaytis. Et ceperunt primum castrum Vilne non muratum et interfecerunt multos; sed murata castra non obtinuerunt. Et fuit longa reysa, ita quod illi de Thorun exiverunt in vigilia Laurentii et redierunt   Aug. 9. in vigilia Symonis et Jude.   Oct. 27.

Anno 1391 dux de Lankasten Anglicus fuit in Prussia et habuit multas contentiones pro vexillo sancti Georgii; sed non obtinuit.ᵇ

Chronicle of John von Posilge.—Scriptores rerum Prussicarum, III., pp. 164-167.

Anno domini 1390 . . . Item in desim jare vor assumpcionis Marie qwam der herezoge von Langkastel ken Pruszin czu   Aug. 15. schiffe ken Danczk wol mit III. hundert mannen, und koufte pferd unde schickte sich dorczu, und czog reyse mit dem marschalke vor dy Wille. Und als das heer qwam uf den Trappen,ᶜ bynnen des starb meister Conrad Czolner von Rotin-   Aug. 20. steyn au senthe Bernharden tag in syme achtin jare der meisterschaft. Do dem marschalke die botschaft qwam, do volczogin sie glich wol. Nu wart yn czu wissen, das Skirgal stark lage uff der Nerye; do funden sie desen uffsacz, das sie die schiff die Mymmel uf lysen geen, und lysen die ledigen hengeste und das

---

⁎ Engelhard Rabe.

ᵇ The German knights always claimed the exclusive right of carrying St. George's banner; in 1361 they would not permit a party of English crusaders to bear it. Wigand von Marburg, Scrip. rer. Pruss. ii., p. 511 and note [Pauli].

ᶜ Trappöhnen on the river Memel.

geringe volk vaste hin czin; und schossin sich us die bestin in
deme heere, unde ezogin durch die wiltnisse bobin Kawen, do
Skirgal lag und irre beyte, und wuste nicht das sie ym alzo no
worin. Des qwam der marschalk obir eynen vort, und troffen
Skirgal ungewarnet, das her kume dovan qwam gerant uf das hus
czu Wissewalde. Und ym worden vil lute abegeslagen an dem
vorte; und vingen dry herezogen und cylff bayoren; die santhen
sy heym ken Pruszen. Ouch wordin yn genomen II^c gesatelter
pferd. Und dis geschach uff sente Augustini tag. Und von
dannen czog der marschalk, als in die schiff qwomen unde sich
usrichten, vor die Wille. Und machten czwu brucken obir die
Nerye, und belogen das hus mit dryn heren: dy von Lyfflant mit
eyme here, Wytowt mit den Samaythen und Littowen, der vil
qwomen czu im gevlogen, mit dem andern, und der marschalk
mit den von Pruszen mit dem dritten here. An dem virden tage
Septembris qwomen sie vor die Wille und richtin czu ere
buchszen, bliden und tumeler, und sthormeten das obirste hus
mit craft und gewonnen is obirhoupt. Us deme huse woren bobin
II^m mensche gefangen und geslagen, und das fur wart so gros,
das mit enander do vortarb, wend grose kouffenschatz dorynne
was, und die lute alumb doryn woren geflogen, das unczelich was,
dy dorynne vortorbin und vorbranten. Dy andern huser worin
gar w l bemannet mit geschosse und buchszin, und wertin sich
vintlichin also, das man dovor lag vumff wochen ane czwene tage,
und kunden der ander huser nicht gewynnen. In deme here was
genug futers und spyse von fleysche und mels, das dy Littowen
und Samaythin czufurten; man mochte sicher von dem here
rytin bynnen sechs mylen und holen was man bedorfte, ungehin-
dert. Ouch woren vele Dutscher und Polan uf deme huse, dy
sich deste menlicher wertin; sie weren ane houpt hinweg geloutfen,
were das rechte hus gewonnen von den herren von Pruszen. Nu
was das pulver also gar vorschossen und ander ding vorthan, das
man dovon muste czin. Ouch was der herre von Lantkastel von
Engelland mit aldo, der vil guter bogenschutezin hatte, dy gar

wol totin, und her ouch gar menlich mit den sinen, und qwam czu groszim geschefte die reyse, nemlich als das obirste hus wart gewonnen. Und also alle ding wol volant woren mit der hulfe und willen des herren, do czogin sy weder heym czu lande, und vorloren nicht me wen xxx man dy reyse, die do worden geslagen und irschossen.[a]

Chronicle of Wigand von Marburg.—Scriptores rerum Prussicarum, II., pp. 642, 643.

Deinde per marschalkum predictum fit reysa et cum multis peregrinis, signanter cum filio Anglici ducis Lankasten Comes de Terpi, etc. Wytaudus dux interfuit, et Samayte ascendunt citra Mimilam. Dux vero Schirgal stetit parte ex altera prope antiquum Kawen, ut prohiberet transitum christianis, nec potuit, quum vadum invenerunt et pertransierunt et quam cito terram tetigerunt, pagani in fugam se dederunt, quos christiani persequuntur et multos occiderunt. Tres quoque duces ducunt captivas cum multa preda, quam ab eis abstulerunt.

Dehinc veniunt prope Willam,[b] primumque Ragnitarum vexillum pertransivit aquam, ubi quidam miles Johannes de Lutam[c] fuit occisus. Impugnantes castrum ligneum[d] cito vicerunt, ubi inter multos occisos quidam rex nomine Karigal[e] interfuit. Et accipiunt christiani multa bona in castro. Pons fit trans Nergam,[f] et multi cum negociis veniunt ad exercitum de paganis et ut christiani mutuo negociantur. Dux Conradus[g] cum telo occiditur; stete-

[a] This account agrees in many respects with the official report, sent by Conrad of Crallenrod, Grand Commander, to the king of the Romans, printed by Voigt. "Codex Diplomaticus Prussicus," iv., n. 80 [Pauli].

[b] *i.e.* Wilna.

[c] John de Londeham, see pp. 23, 143, 303.

[d] "Castrum Vilne non muratum," Ann. Torun; "das obirste hus," John von Posilge.

[e] A brother of Jagello, baptized as Ka-imir.

[f] The river Wilia.

[g] A relative of Witowd, duke of Samogitia.

runtque v septimanis in continuo agone[a] nocte dieque et pugna, et ex utraque parte multi sunt occisi; dumque se converterent ad partes, captivati et occisi sunt ultra 7000 pro majori parte paganorum. Et Livoniensis,[b] qui huiusmodi facta fecerat, ad sua, Wytaud et Samayte et Pruteni quilibet in terram suam rediere.

APPENDIX B.

Extracts relating to the expedition of 1392-1393.

John Capgrave, De Illustribus Henricis, p. 99.

Iterum autem, A.D. 1392, idem venerabilis dominus, adhuc vivente patre, mare transiit versus Prusiam, concomitantibus sibi, ut dicitur, ferme trecentis viris. Et in festo Beati Jacobi Apostoli, navem apud Hecham, prope Lennam, ascendit; et felici navigio terram desideratam intravit. Ubi cum favorem dominorum provinciæ suo desiderio non sensisset amicabilem, relictis illis, Venetias applicuit, et deinde Jerosolimam. Ibi quoque Loca Sancta cum magna devotione veneratus est, pauperes Christi magna clementia recreabat, et quosdam captivos, multo dato pretio, ad terras fidelium secum reduxit.

Dignum autem duxi hic enucleare, per quas terras et per quos principes, ad optata littora pervenit. Totum enim hunc annum solemni peregrinatione expendebat: in quo quidem labore ita provide se suosque gubernabat, ut placabilis Deo, honorabilis regno, amicabilis quoque iis in quibus conversabatur, prædicaretur.

Nam de Prusia versus Hungariam, per Poloniam, aliasque provincias diversas, pertransivit, ubi, a rege Hungarorum honorabiliter receptus, magnis muneribus decoratus est. Deinde Dux Austri benigne sibi occurrit, viam simul et victualia condigno favore minis-

[a] See Charter of Jagello (Wladislav II.) dated Dec. 4, 1390, to Clemens of Mostorzow, Vice-chancellor of Poland, who had defended Wilna, SS. rer. Pruss., ii., p. 613 note.
[b] Wennemar of Bruggenoie, master of Livonia.

trans; et hoc per omnes magnates in dicta pereginatione fiebat. Nam et dux Venetiarum cum galeis sibi per aquam occurrens, cum in proprium palatium suscepit, in Candiam, et in Rodis, ac in Jerusalem conducens, totiusque peregrinationis suæ comes individuus extitit. Visitatis quoque Sepulchro Sancto et aliis locis sacrosanctis, ad Ciprum reversus est, honorifice ibidem a rege illius insulæ receptus et deductus. Apud Papiam quoque et Mediolanum cum duce hospitabatur, peregrinationem suam dulcissimo contubernio confortans. Comes enim Virtutum (nam et tali titulo tunc gloriabatur) ipsum ad castrum ubi corpus beatissimi patris Augustini quiescit, introduxit; quod, non sine magna contemplatione, dux noster amplexatus est. Ibi et corpus summi philosophi, necnon et theologi, Boëtii conspexit; ibi et corpus Leonelli, quondam ducis Clarenciæ, et avunculi sui, vidit tumulatum. Nam et sic moriens dictus Leonellus servis suis mandaverat, ut cor suum et ossa ad Conventum Clarensem, ordinis fratrum heremitarum Sancti Augustini in Anglia, transferrentur, carnibus suis cum visceribus coram sepulchro Doctoris eximii devote relictis. Et quoniam dominus Virtutum, dux scilicet Mediolanensis, offensus erat fratribus, propter quasdam canonicorum et Abbatis querelas, ita ut ad mille marcas multare eos meditaretur idem dux, aut occasione accepta, a loco illo ejicere, pius et venerabilis dominus iste Henricus pacis vias invenit, offensam pacavit, indignationem removit, et, dato fratribus suæ munificentiæ donario satis gratifico, ab eis recessit. Transactisque Transalpinis partibus, per regem Boëmiæ et duces Almaniæ, in Franciam devectus est; ubi non diu tardans, tandem ad terram suam nativam devenit.

John v. Posilge, Script. rer. Prussicarum, III., p. 182.—
[1392] Item dornoch uf den herbst qwam der here von Lantkastel in das lant, und wolde gereyset habin mit den herrin. Nu slugen dy synen eynen erbarn knecht tot czu Dansk, der hys Hannus von Tergawisch, hie us demelande. Do besorgete sich der herre vor synen frunden das sie das wordin rechen, als sy an hatten gehabin, und czog weder us deme lande ungereyset.

LIST OF ERRATA.

PAGE.	LINE.	
xliii.	31	*for* chess *read* backgammon.
1	5	of title, *for* 1 May *read* 6 May.
4		*delete* note *b*. The addition in the text is correct.
19	10	*for* pasti *read* paste.
25	3	*delete the semicolon*.
28	3	⎫
31	1	⎪
37	20	⎪
39	7	⎪
106	14	⎪
115	13	⎪
120	26	⎬ *for* Stanele *or* Stancley *read* Staveley.
126	23	⎪
128	20	⎪
134	28	⎪
138	31	⎪
266	23	⎪
276	31	⎪
277	2	⎪
278	8, 16, 19	⎭
33	16	*insert* semicolon *after* Arogonie.
35	15	*for* Westnall *read* Westvall.
37	2	*for* Cato *read* Catour.
44		*in margin, read* August 14 *for* 15.
51	14	*insert* comma *after* sequente.
53	30	⎫
88	25	⎬ *for* Londeham *read* Loudeham.
142	21	⎪
143	3	⎭

ERRATA.

PAGE.	LINE.	
86	16	*for* Mende *read* Mende.
102	25	*delete the first semicolon.*
105		*in margin, read* August 14 *for* 13.
106	11	*for* Kempston *read* Rempston.
131	17	,, ,, ,, ,,
156	10	,, gemens ,, gemens.
158	7	,, Bannche ,, Blaunche.
179	24	*delete* * sic.
213		note b, *for* libri *read* libra.
268	4	*in margin, for* July 1 *read* July 21.
249	8	*for* Tranes *read* Tranes (? Turnes).
261	21	,, Tranays ,, Turnays.
246	32	⎫
250	26	⎬ *for* Chance *read* Chance.
251	7	,, Chanse ,, Chanse.
261	23	⎭
253		*in margin, for* pl *read* bl.
254	21	*insert comma after* tollage.
254	21	*for* la Ryne *read* la ryne (=rive).
260	7	,, Gobin ,, Gobin.
270	33	,, Brakill ,, Crakill.
272	17	,, Hound ,, Hamond.
276	7	,, Landa ,, Landa.
277	28	,, ,, ,, ,,
283	24	,, Accaby ,, Attaby.
288	8	,, Siron ,, Virona.

COMPOTUS RICARDI KYNGESTON clerici, Thesaurarii domini Comitis Derbeye pro viagio suo ordinato vsque partes Barbarie et pro viagio suo eunte versus partes Prucie, eundo, morando ibidem, et redeundo a vj die Maij anno terciodecimo vsque vltimum diem Aprilis anno xiiij°, per ccclx dies.

[6 May, 1390—30 April, 1391.]

TREASURER'S ACCOUNTS OF THE EARL OF DERBY'S EXPEDITIONS.

PART I.

EXPEDITION TO PRUSSIA,

1 MAY, 1390—30 APRIL, 1391.

Writ appointing Richard of Kingston, Archdeacon of Hereford, treasurer for the war and journeys. London, 6 May, 1390.

/ Henry de Lancastre, Conte de Derby, de Herford[a] et de North-   fo. 2.
ampton, Seigneur de Brekenok, a touz ceaux qi cestes noz lettres
5 verront ou orront, saluz. Sachez nous pur la ferme affiance que
[nous auons[b]] enuers la persone de nostre tres cher clerc sire
Richard de Kyngeston, Arcediaken de Herford, confiantz de sa seen
et loialtee ly' avoir ordeigne et assigne nostre Tresorer pur la
guerre pur cestes viages [que][b] nous feumes ordeignez de faire en
10 les parties de Barbarye et de Pruz, donantz a ly plein pouer par ces

---

[a] Herford, *i. e.* Hereford. Henry was Earl of Hereford and of Northampton, and Lord of Brecknock in Wales in right of his wife Mary, daughter and co-heiress of Humphrey de Bohun, whom he married between 1380 and 1386. See *Rot. Par.* iv. 46a, 176b. In *Doyle's* Official Baronage the earliest date given at which Derby styled himself Earl of Northampton is 1397, but this writ shows that he did so before the death of his wife, which happened in June 1394 (*Tout* in Dict. Nat. Biography).

These two writs are stitched to the edge of the front cover of the book containing the accounts, and lie folded in. Their order is reversed above to suit the dates.

[b] End of line torn in MS.

CAMD. SOC.   B

presentes de toutes les deniers assignez p*ur* nos dispences en et p*ur*
les dites viages receyv[oir et] paier p*ur* noz ditz costages et dispences, p*ar* lordeignance de n*ost*re trescher et tresame Bachiler
Monsieur Hugh de Waterton n*ost*re Chambrelein et autres de
n*ost*re Conseil, et de toutes autre choses f*ai*re que au dit office 5
appartient, p*ar*ensi toutes voies q'il respoigne a nous par voie
d'accompte deuantz nos auditours de toutes les sommes quelles il
issent receyuera, come l'ordre d'accompte demande [et] requiert.
Ces presentes a durer a n*ost*re voluntee. Done a Londres le vj iour
de May, l'ann du regne n*ost*re *Seigneur* le Roi Richard second puis 10
le Conquest d'engleterre treszisme.

Writ ordering the audit of Richard of Kingston's Accounts.
Peterborough, 1 January, 1391-2.

/ Henry de Lancastre, Conte de Derby, de Herford et de Northampton, *Seigneur* de Brekenok, a n*ost*re tresame Clerc sire Thomas 15
Herdwyk auditour des accomptes de noz ministres et officers,
saluz. Come nous p*ar* noz le*tt*res patentz avons ordeigne et
assigne n*ost*re trescher clerc sire Richard de Kyngeston, arcediaken de Herford, n*ost*re Tresorer p*ur* la guerre p*ur* cestes noz
darreins viages vers les p*ar*ties de Barbarye et en Pruz, sicome en 20
mesmes les le*tt*res est contenuz pleinement ; Nous vous mandons
que vous preignez dehuc* et raisonable accompte de n*ost*re dit
Clerc de toutes les sommes quelles il ad receu et paie p*ur* noz costages et dispences p*ur* noz ditz viages, et que vous ly facez dehuc
allouuance en son accompte de toutes les deniers quelles il p*ar* son 25
serement ou p*ar* recorde de n*ost*re trescher Bachiler Monsieur
Hugh de Waterton n*ost*re Chambrelein, et autres de n*ost*re Conseil,
a celle foitz ad paie p*ur* noz costages et dispenses suisdites. Et
cestes noz le*tt*res vous ent serront garrantz. Done souz n*ost*re seal
a Petreburgh le primer iour de Januer, l'ann du regne n*ost*re 30
Seigneur le roi Richard seconde puis le Conquest d'engleterre
quinzisme.

/ Compotus Ricardi Kyngeston, clerici, thesaurarii Domini Henrici Comitis Derbeye, pro viagio suo ordinato usque partes Barbarie, et pro viagio suo cunte versus partes Prucie, eundo, morando ibidem, et redeundo, a vj die Maii, anno regni regis Ricardi secundi tertio-decimo vsque vltimum diem Aprilis proxime sequentem, anno eiusdem Regis quarto decimo, per ccclx dies, utroque die computato, per commissionem domini, datam London. vj die Maii anno xiij° &c., et per unam litteram domini de huiusmodi compoto capiendo, remanentem cum dicta commissione huic compoto annexatam.

Recepta Denariorum.

De Illustrissimo principe Johanne Duce Aquitanie et Lancastrie patre suo, ut de dono suo sibi facto super expensis et custibus suis pro viagio suo predicto, ut in precio xxiiij M¹ Floreyns auri d'Aragonie, videlicet iij precio j noble, et sic vj ad j marcam, recepto per manus Thome Tutbery clerici et thesaurarii dicti domini Ducis, per indenturam suam datam . M¹M¹M¹M¹ marc.

De predicto Johanne, Duce Aquitanie et Lancastrie, ut de dono suo sibi facto pro viagio predicto, ut in precio M¹ floreyns, precio ut supra, recepto per manus eiusdem Thome, per indenturam suam supradictam . . . . cxj li. ij s. ij d. ob.

De predicto Johanne, Duce Aquitanie et Lancastrie, ut de dono suo sibi facto post viagium suum factum de partibus Prucie supradictis, ut pro debitis suis persolvendis diuersis personis, ut in vadiis, prestitis, et aliis custibus persolvendis, receptis denariis per manus Roberti Whytby, generalis receptoris eiusdem Ducis, per indenturam ipsius Roberti, datam

4   THE EARL OF DERBY'S EXPEDITIONS.

*Pagine Londoñ. xiij die Junii anno regni regis Ricardi
n' Dxxxiij li. secundi quarto decimo   .   .   .   .   D cclv li. xj s. vj d. st.ᵃ
fo. 4   / De Hugone Waterton milite, camerario domini, ut
de denariis receptis de exitibus vltimi compoti sui pro
expensis suis in viagiis suis predictis, per vnam in-   5
1390.   denturam ipsius Hugonis datam viij° die Maii anno
tertio decimo .   .   .   .   M¹ marc. st.
De Simone Bache clerico et Thesaurario hospitii
domini ut de denariis de ipso receptis pro viagiis predictis, per indenturam suam datam apud Douere viij°   10
1390.   die Maii, anno tertio decimo   .   .   .   .   .   c marc. st.
De Johanne Lewnthorpe generali receptore domini
ut de denariis de ipso receptis in officio suo super expensis pro viagiis predictis, per indenturam datam apud
, 1390.   Caleys xiij° die Maii anno tertio decimo .   .   .   c li. st. 15
De diuersis victualibus remanentibus post viagium
de Prucia in Angliam venditis diuersis personis
prout patet per parcellam super hunc compotum ex-
aminatam, vltra diversa victualia liberata Simoni
Bache Thesaurario hospicii, unde idem recepit xiij li. vij s. xj d. st. 20
De clerico regis prouisore victualium apud Caleys
pro xvj arcubus remanentibus de prouidenciis domini
versus viagium de Barbaria, precio pecie iij s. iiij d. .   liij s. iiij d.
De furfure proueniente de flore facto apud sanctum
Botulphum pro prouidenciis de dicto viagio de Prusia,   25
sic vendito in gross   .   .   .   .   .   .   xiij. s. iiij d.
Summa Pagine Dcccl li. xv d.

Summa totalis Receptorum M¹ M¹ M¹ M¹ ccc ⁱⁱⁱⁱj. iij li. viij s. iij d. ob.ᵇ

ᵃ St. i.e. *sterlinges*. English money is called sterling throughout the accounts.
The spelling sterlinges occurs in full at the end of Part II. of the accounts, I therefore use it throughout where necessary.

ᵇ This total is short by £50 of the addition of the two pages, instead of £4383 8s.
3½d., it should be £4433 8s. 3½d.; no doubt the *l.* following the Dccc in the second
summa was omitted by oversight. The sum owed by the treasurer at end of the
year's account, viz. £23 11s. 1⅞d., shows that the above total was really accounted
for. *See* p. 142.

[Fo. 1 v°. is blan

*Expense pro providenciis contra viagium Prucie fo. 5.
cum expensis hospicii familie domini; cum equis,
vesselamentis, et aliis neccessariis emptis pro
dicto viagio; prout patet consequenter per parcellam factam per manus Willelmi Hauer Clerici
Domini.*

Thome Grofton pro vj barhides ab ipso emptis apud Londoñ,
vj° die Maii, xv s. Et per manus Gamelyn Cofferer pro v paribus   May 6.
cofres, vnde ij paria nigra, ab ipso emptis ibidem eodem die, lxiiij s.
Super officio scutellarie per manus Roberti Russe pro j ladel et j   Respondet.
dressyng knyf ab ipso emptis eodem die, iij s. iiij d. Et per manus
Willelmi Hauir pro regardo sibi facto ibidem, nunciantibus camerario et
senescallo, xx s. Clerico speciarie per manus Willelmi Hauir pro
iij^{bus} quaternis pergameni cum coreo ligatis, xj s. vij d.; pro j botel
cum encausto, xiij d.; pro v solidis et ix contours, xvj d.; pro j busta
pro eisdem imponendis, ob.: pro iij poyntell, j d.; pro iij^{bus} quaternis papiri, xviij d., et pennis, iiij d., per ipsum emptis ibidem
eodem die, in toto, xv s. xj d. ob. Edmundo Bugge pro j equo
grey ab ipso empto apud Londoñ, v^{to} die Maii, lx s. Et Ricardo   May 5.
Kyngeston pro j equo albo ab ipso empto, c s. *Et per manus
Willelmi Wollaton pro j equo sorello ab ipso empto ibidem pro le   * — * Respondet
somario, lxvj s. viij d. Et per manus Symonis Swan pro j equo   istis equis.
ballido ab ipso empto ibidem, xlvj s. viij d. Et per manus Willelmi
Loueney pro j equo bay ab ipso empto eodem* die, lxvj s. viij d.
Clerico marescalcie per manus Johannis Drayton pro ferris unius

* In the MS. this title stands in the margin. A short form, "adhuc expense pro
providenciis contra viagium Prucie," is written in each margin, both sides of the
first twelve leaves, by way of running title.

palfre et somarii panetrie, xiiij d. JOHANNI Payn pro burnyshyng vj pecia um argenti, j pecie auri cum cooperculo, et emendacione unius eweri deaurati fracti, iiij s. Et per manus Gamelyn pro j case pro^a j cipho auri imponende, x d. CLERICO speciarie per manus Willelmi Norton pro diversis speciebus ab ipso emptis, prout continetur in j billa de papiro, l s. CLERICO marescalcie per manus Johannis Smyth pro ferris unius equi somarii pro thesaurario, viij d. THOME Grafton pro j male ab ipso empto ibidem pro le cuphous, viij s. CLERICO panetrie per manus diuersorum pro pane, vino, servisia, piscibus salsis et recentibus, ab ipsis emptis apud Dartford pro familia domini ibidem comedente, per compotum cum eisdem factum ibidem, in toto, vj s. v d. CLERICO panetrie per manus diuersorum pro pane albo ab ipsis empto ibidem, iiij d. CLERICO Buterie super vino per manus Johannis Taverner pro ij potellis ^b et j quarta vini Vasconie, xxij d. ob. Clerico Buterie super servisia, per manus diuersorum pro v galonibus servisie, x d. CLERICO speciarie pro candelis cepi, iij d. ob. CLERICO coquine per manus Blacdon pro piscibus per ipsum emptis ibidem, xvj d. SUPER officio scutellarie pro busca, j d. CLERICO marescalcie per Johannem Gelow pro feno, x d.; pro iij^{bus} bussellis et j pecco auenarum, xix d. ob.; pro pane equino, iij d. CLERICO panetrie per manus Willelmi Hostiler, pro pane, vino, seruisia, carne boum multonum et vitulorum, una cum pulteria ab ipsis emptis apud Ospryng; et cum pane equino empto ibidem et apud Dartford pro cena domini, in toto, x s. ij d. CLERICO coquine per manus Bussyn pro piscibus recentibus per ipsum emptis apud London, ij s. vj d. CLERICO speciariarum pro iij vlnis de cannevas, xv d. SUPER officio aule et camere, pro servisia et pane emptis pro familia domini per viam inter Rouchestre et Canterbery, xj d.; et pro saculo empto pro argento in eodem ponendo, iij d. ob. CLERICO marescalcie per manus Gilberti Hostyler pro feno ab ipso empto 30

---

^a *Et* in the MS., but *pro* seems to be the word intended, and necessary for the sense.

^b This *p* evidently means pottle, not pint. Two quarts make a pottle, and the price of this item was thus 4¼d. a quart.

apud Canterbery, vj d., et pro iij bz. auenarum, xviij d. Et
pro pane equino, iiij d., et pro litura, vj d. CLERICO Buterie
super vino, per manus eiusdem pro iij quarte* vini Vasconie, * Sic.
vij ob. CLERICO speciarie pro candelis cepi, j d. ob. Johanni
5 Boteman pro batillagio et cariagio harnesie domini de navi   Summa pagine xx
vsque hospicium domini apud Caleys, xviij d. CLERICO mares-   li. xvij s. ob. p
calcie per manus Saunder Cadeller pro emendacione celle   batur.
/ somarii apud Douere, ix d. Et pro conductione equorum inter fo. 5 v^{m}
London et Douere pro cariagio harnesii domini, iiij s. st. Et per   Respondet.
10 manus Ricardi Sadeler pro vij somariis sadellis ad xij s., iiij li. iiij s.;
et pro j cariage sadelle, x s.; et pro j cella pro somario de euphous,
xvj s.; vna cum emptione poles, girthes, sursengles et aliis necessariis,† ab ipso emptis apud London, xxv s. iij d., in toto cum supradictis, vij li. CLERICO panetrie per manus Johannis Payn pro   † ['The MS. has
15 pane, vino, servisia, carne, piscibus, per ipsum emptis apud Whit-   necc'ia.]
sand, xiiij s. ij d. JOHANNI Waterman et sociis suis pro pountage
apud Douere, vj s. viij d. Et diversis portatoribus portantibus harnesia domini extra Douere usque ad nauem, xij d. Et per manus
Willelmi Louency pro j equo nigro ab ipso empto pro j somario
20 pro la tressourye, iiij li. Et Johanni London' pro vadiis suis   Respondet.
extra curiam, misso de Douere vsque Caleys pro providencia
ibidem facienda erga aduentum domini, per iiij dies, capiente per
diem viij d., ij s. viij d. Et Rakebrond pro cariagio harnesii domini
de Whitsand usque Caleys, vj s. viij d. CLERICO marescalcie per
25 manus Johannis Gylder pro ij quarteriis auenarum per ipsum emptis
apud Caleys, vj s. viij d. CLERICO panetrie per manus London pro
pane albo per ipsum empto apud Caleys, iiij s. CLERICO buterie
super servisia per manus eiusdem pro iiij^{or} barellis servisie per
ipsum emptis ibidem, xij s. iiij d.; et pro cariagio dicte servisie,
30 iiij d. CLERICO coquine per manus eiusdem pro piscibus salsis et
recentibus per ipsum emptis ibidem, xij s. iij d. SUPER officio
scutellarie, per manus eiusdem pro vC de billette per ipsum emptis
ibidem, una cum cariagio dictorum, iij s. vij d. SUPER officio
pulletrie per manus eiusdem pro iijC ouis, xv d. CLERICO marescalcie

per manus eiusdem pro iiij^or quarteriis auenarum, le quarteria ad iij s., in toto xij s. Et pro cariagio dictarum auenarum, iiij d. CUIDAM valetto domine Ducisse Lancastre presentando domino unum palfrey, de dono domini apud Dartford, xl s. Et cuidam garcioni dicte domine custodienti dictum palfredum, de dono domini ibidem, 5 xiij s. iiij d. Diuersis nautis pro batillagio harnesii domini apud Whitsand, de naui in le hauen, una cum custuma dicti harnesii, nunciante camerario, xij s. ET pro pane, vino, seruisia, et carne mptis ibidem pro hominibus gallicis in aduentu domini illuc, vj s. Et diuersis portatoribus pro pountage apud Caleys, vj s. viij d. 10 CLERICO coquine per manus Willelmi Harpeden pro carne boum et multonum, piscibus salsis et recentibus per ipsum emptis ibidem, xx s. viij d. Et per manus eiusdem pro caponibus, gallinis, pulcinis, cum lacte et butiro per ipsum emptis ibidem, xvj s.ⁿ CLERICO speciarie per manus Willelmi Hauir pro xj pellibus pergameni iij s., et 15 pro j quaterno papiri ryal xij d., per ipsum emptis ibidem, in toto iiij s. DOMINO Willelmo Elmham militi et Johanni Stokes scutifero domini cuntibus cum litteris domini de Caleys vsque Paryse ad Regem Francie, pro uno salvo conducto habendo pro domino; pro expensis suis, C s. CUIDAM Draper de Caleys pro xxiiij virgis de 20 rubano motteley, precium le vlna xv d., ab ipso emptis pro garcionibus stabuli domini et aliis somptermen, xxx s. Eidem pro xvij virgis j quarterio de blanket ab eodem emptis pro eisdem garcionibus domini, pretium virge, xvj d., minus in toto viij d.,* xxij s. iiij d. Eidem pro j virga et j quarterio de blu fryse ab eodem emptis pro 25 penons, ij s. j d. CLERICO speciarie per manus Willelmi Hauir pro vj lib. amigdalorum per ipsum emptis apud Caleys, xx d.; et pro iiij lb. dattilorum, xiiij d. DIVERSIS hominibus incarceratis in quadam prisona iuxta Lanternegate apud Caleys de dono domini ibidem, vj s. viij d. CLERICO coquine per manus diuersorum pro 30 dimidio carcoisii bouis, xv s., et pro x carcoisiis multonum, xxvj s. iiij d., ab ipso emptis ibidem, in toto xlj s. iiij d. SUPER officio pulletrie per manus Henrici Bocher pro iij anguillis,† iiij s. vj d. CLERICO

---

* This item was omitted but added in the margin.

coquine per manus Bartholomei Grauenyng pro v carcoisiis multonum ad ij s. vij d. ab ipso emptis ibidem, xij s. xj d. Clerico coquine per manus Henrici Bocher pro viij carcoisiis multonum xx d., et pro vij carcoisiis multonum xviij s. viij d., ab ipso emptis
5 ibidem, in toto xxxviij s. viij d. SUPER officio pulletrie per manus eiusdem pro iij agnis ab ipso emptis ibidem, iiij s. vj d. CLERICO marescalcie per manus Johannis Walker pro expensis unius palfredi albi inter London et Douere per compotum secum factum apud Caleys, xiiij d. Et per manus Johannis Dounton pro expensis
10 ij somariorum inter London et Douere per compotum factum ut supra, una cum conductione unius garcionis ad ducendum dictos somarios, et ferrura eorundem, ij s. x d. Et per manus j garcionis stabuli pro tares, feno, et pane equino emptis pro somariis domini in naui pro prebendis dictorum somariorum
15 inter Douere et Caleys, viij d. CLERICO coquine per manus Ricardi Messenger pro carne boum multonum vitulorum et porcellorum, piscibus salsis et recent-bus, per ipsum emptis apud Caleys, a xiij die Maii usque xvj^m diem eiusdem mensis, utroque computato, in toto lxj s. ij d. SUPER officio pulletrie per manus
20 eiusdem pro aucis, caponibus, gallinis, pullis, pulcinis, ouis, lacte et butiro per ipsum emptis ibidem una cum vadiis Willelmi Harpeden, in toto lxxvj s. iij d. ob. CLERICO speciarie per manus eiusdem pro j stopa et di. mellis per ipsum emptis ibidem, xix d. SUPER officio scutellarie, per manus eiusdem pro ij duodenis viij
25 discorum ligneorum per ipsum emptis ibidem, ij s. iiij d. ROBERTO Chalons de dono domini apud Caleys, nunciante camerario, xiij s. iiij d. JOHANNI Londoñ de dono domini apud Caleys, nunciante camerario, vj s. viij d. CLERICO coquine per manus Willelmi Porteher pro j carcoisio bouis ab ipso empto ibidem, xvj s. ij d.
30 SUPER officio scutellarie, per manus R. Spayn pro ix saccis cartonum, le sacca ad vj d., per ipsum emptis ibidem, iiij s. vj d. Et per manus eiusdem pro M^l bilettes, per ipsum emptis ibidem eodem

* The sum of each page is usually followed by this sign p', meaning probatur. I do not repeat it in print.

die, vj s. viij d. CLERICO speciarie per manus diuersorum pro iij vlnis tele Flandrie, ij s. j d.; pro ij virgis tele flandrie, xviij d.; pro vj s. vlnis cannevas, iij s., emptis pro naperons pro magistro coquine et aliis de coquina; et pro ij virgis frisii viridis emptis pro le countyngburd, iiij s., in toto x s. vij d. CLERICO buterie super 5 vino, per manus Sandhill pro j potelo dimidio vini Vasconie per ipsum emptis apud Douere, xv d. Et per manus eiusdem super seruicia, pro pane, ouis et seruisia, emptis ibidem pro Camerario Thesaurario et Senescallo, v d. CLERICO panetrie per manus Roberti Jonson pro iiijC blaundreles per ipsum emptis apud 10 Caleys, ij s. iij d. CLERICO buterie super seruisia per manus eiusdem, scilicet j olla terrea pro vino imponendo, ij d. CLERICO Marescalcie per manus eiusdem pro ferrura j equi ibidem somarii buterie, vj d. Et per manus Johannis Gylder pro j carectata feni, ij s. viij d.; pro cariagio carectate feni, xx d.; pro j bussello de 15 breen una cum emptione de leueyn pro equis domini, v d. per ipsum emptis, in toto iiij s. ix d. IOHANNI Flokton de dono domini apud Caleys, receptis denariis de Johanne Waterton, nunciante camerario, xiij s. iiij d. Et cuidam barbitonsori flegbotomanti dominum, de dono domini, nunciante ut supra, vj d. CLERICO buterie super vino 20 per manus diuersorum pro lxxvj stopis vini Rochelle ab ipsis emptis ibidem, le stopa v d., xxxj s. viij d. Clerico buterie super seruisia, per manus Roberti Smyth de Gofforth pro vj barellis seruisie continente la barella xxiiij galones, ad iij s. iiij d., summa xx s. CLERICO marescalcie per manus Johannis Eluer pro xj quar- 25 teriis iij bussellis auenarum ab ipso emptis ibidem, quarterius ad iij s. iiij d., xxxvij s. xj d. CLERICO hospicii per manus Willelmi Mannyngs pro iiij barellis seruisie ab ipso emptis ibidem, le barellus continente xxiiij galones ad iij s. iiij d., xiij s. iiij d. Et pro cariagio dicte seruisie de la hauen vsque hospicium domini, viij d. 30 CLERICO coquine per manus diuersorum pro carne boum multonum et vitulorum, ab ipsis emptis apud Caleys ab xv die Maii vsque xxiij diem eiusdem mensis, lxj s. iiij d. Clerico coquine per manus Ricardi Mensenger pro carne boum multonum vitulerum por-

EXPENSES IN ENGLAND AND CALAIS.   11

cellorum, et sagino per ipsum emptis apud Caleys vsque xxv^m diem
Maii, in toto vj li. iiij s. ix d. SUPER officio pulletrie per manus May 25.
eiusdem pro aucis, caponibus, gallinis, pullis, puleinis, ouis, lacte,
butiro, et aliis victualibus per ipsum emptis ibidem usque dictum diem,
5 in toto iiij li. xv s. vij d. ob. CLERICO speciarie per manus ciusdem
pro j pane suiguri caffretin, pondere ij lb. 1 qrt., lb ad xviij d., per ipsum
empto ibidem, iij s. iiij d. ob.; et pro ij virgis tele flandre ix d., in toto
iiij s. j d. ob. CLERICO buterie super vino, per manus Martyn Tauerner pro lxix stopis vini Rochelle ad v d. ab ipso emptis ibidem, xxviij s.
10 ix d. Et per manus eiusdem pro cxj stopis vini Rochelle ad iiij d.,
xxxvij s. CUIDAM scutifero Comitis de Seintpoul de dono domini apud
Caleys xxv^to die Maii, nunciante Camerario, lxvj s. viij d. CLERICO May 25.
marescalcie per manus Willelmi Grenok, pro feno ab ipso empto
ibidem, xvj s. viij d. CLERICO panetrie per manus Johannis Payn   Summa pagine
                                                                   xxxviij li. iij s.
15 pro blaundellis et cariagio seruisie ab ipso emptis ibidem, ij s. v d.   ob.
/ CLERICO coquine per manus Hankey, Bocher de Grauonyng pro iij   fo. 6 v°.
carcoisiis multonum ab ipso emptis ibidem, ix s. vj d. CLERICO
speciarie, per manus Hankyn Spycer, pro iiij lb. di. di. qr.* sucri   * [That is, four
caffretin lb. ad xviij d., vj s. xj d.; pro di. lb. sucri siprei, iiij d.; pro   pounds and five-
                                                                                eighths.]
20 ij lb. gyngere, ij s. x d.; ij lb. piperis, ij s. x d; ij lb. canelle, ij s. vj d.;
di. lb. clowes, ij s. iiij d.; pro ij lb. dattilorum, vj d.; et pro j lb.
racemorum de corene, vj d., ab ipso emptis ibidem, in toto xviij s.
ix d. CLERICO marescalcie per manus Johannis Gylder pro x qr.
ij l z. auenarum per ipsum emptis apud Caleys, le quarter ad iij s.,
25 xxx s. ix d. Et Marescallo per manus Roberti Waterton pro
diuersis medicinis per ipsum emptis apud Caleys una cum bayte
equi domini apud Lullyngham, in toto iiij s. v d. ob. Et per manus
Ricardi Daueson pro pane equino per ipsum emptis apud Douere,
una cum diuersis medicinis per ipsum emptis pro j somario officii
30 infirmo, vj d. CLERICO Marescalcie per manus Augusti en Kenburghe pro feno, auenis litura, et pane equino ab ipso emptis apud
Caleys, pro x somariis domini per unam noctem, v s. ij d. Et pro
cariagio fimii extra stabulum somariorum officii, xj d. CLERICO
speciarie per manus Johannis Chaundeler pro xxiiij lb. candela-

rum cepi, lb. ad ij d., iiij s. SUPER officio scutellarie, per manus Johannis Gromet pro M¹ bylettis ab ipso emptis ibidem, ix s. CLERICO coquine per manus eiusdem pro vij bz. salis ab ipso emptis ibidem, vij s. viij d. Et per manus Maryon Fyssher pro iijC allecibus, pretium iij s., et pro iij morrudis v s. ab ipso emptis ibidem, in toto viij s. Clerico Marescalcie per manus magistri Hans Ferrour pro ferrura equorum, domini apud Caleys, xiiij s. iij d. SUPER officio scutellarie, per manus Roberti Spayn pro herbis ab ipso emptis ibidem, iiij s. vj d. Et pro cariagio busce de la hauen vsque hospicium domini, viij d. SUPER officio salserie per manus eiusdem pro xj galonibus de sinape vergous et vinegre, le galo ad viij d., vij s. iiij d. Et per manus eiusdem pro iiij bz. floure per ipsum emptis ibidem, iiij s. iiij d. CLERICO panetrie per manus Walteri Baker pro pane albo ab ipso empto ibidem, xiij s. Clerico panetrie per manus Alani Tanfeld pro pane albo ab ipso empto ibidem, lxiij s. vj d. Thome Pybaker pro recompensatione sibi facta laboranti in pasteria per iij vices, vna cum expensis bosce sue, propter recompensationem, iij s. iiij d. CLERICO marescalcie per manus Outeredy de Caleys pro vj qrt. vj bz. auenarum ab ipso emptis apud Caleys, le qrt. ad iij s., xx s. iij d. CLERICO Buterie super vino per manus Johannis Payn pro vj stopis vini per ipsum emptis apud Whitsand, ij s. vj d. CLERICO coquine per manus Hankyn Bocher pro vj carcoisiis multonum ab ipso emptis ibidem ad ij s. ij d., xiij s. CLERICO Marescalcie per manus Johannis Martyn pro vij qr. v bz. auenarum, qr. ad iij s.. ab ipso emptis ibidem, xxij s. x d. ob. Fratri Johanni de Sutton de dono domini apud Caleys, iiij s. vj d. JOHANNI Payn pro factura unius pixidis de argento pro treacle imponendo pro domino, iij s. iiij d. Magistro Willelmo Cook pro factura unius alterius pixidis de argento pro treacle imponendo ut supra, iij s. iiij d. SUPER officio scutellarie, per manus Thome Norkyn pro M¹ vC bilettorum ab ipso emptis ibidem, ix s. viij d. CLERICO Buterie super seruisia, per manus Johannis Stanerle pro iij barellis seruisie ab ipso emptis, le barellus ad iij s. iiij d., in toto ix s. ij d. ROBERTO Hethcote pro vadiis et expensis suis a xxiij° die Maii vsque xxviij diem eiusdem mensis, utroque computato, eunti

de Caleys usque Hertford et redeunti ; vz. pro batillagio suo
inter Caleys et Douere, et pro conductione equi inter Douere
et Hertford, et de ibidem vsque Douere, per compotum secum
factum apud Caleys, in toto xiiij s. ij d. Et Ricardo Mensenger
5 pro battillagio suo inter Caleys et Douere, eundo et redeundo
suo versus Caleys, xxvij s. x d.; et pro conductione equi inter
Douere et Londoñ et redeundo, vj s. viij d., per compotum secum
factum apud Caleys, in toto xxxiiij s. vj d. RICARDO Dancastre de dono domini pro factura unius pixidis argenti pro
10 treacle imponendo pro Domino, iij s. iiij d. CLERICO speciarie
per manus Willelmi Hanir pro xxi foliis papiri realis per ipsum
/emptis ibidem, x d., Et per manus Willelmi Puffyn pro cera
per ipsum empta ibidem, ij d. JOHANNI LEVNTHORP* pro battillagio suo versus Douere et redeundo versus Caleys, unacum
15 conductione equorum inter Hertford et Dovere et eundo et redeundo,
et una cum expensis suis in nauibus per compotum secum factum
ibidem, nunciante camerario, xvij s. ij d. CLERICO coquine per
manus Willelmi Harpedeñ pro carne boum multonum et vitulorum
ab ipso empta apud Caleys, a xxv^{to} die Maii vsque vltimam diem
20 eiusdem mensis, utroque computato per compotum secum factum
ibidem, in toto cxv s. xj d. ob. SUPER officio pulletrie per manus
eiusdem pro aucis, caponibus, gallinis, pullis, pulcinis, et aliis
victualibus per ipsum emptis ibidem ut supra, iiij li. xv s. vij d. ob.
SUPER officio aule et camere per manus Margerie Brounham pro
25 lauacione naprie et pannorum lineorum domini apud Caleys,
iiij s. CLERICO marescalcie per manus Petri Sadeler pro stuffura
vj somersadeles, ij s. vj d., et pro viij burrowez, j sursengle, et j
pare raynes, ij nouis tailliatis pro sursengles iij s. iiij d., ab ipso emptis
apud Caleys, in toto v s. x d. SUPER officio scutellarie, per manus
30 Ricardi Spayne pro i qr. de j m^l bilettorum ab ipso empta ibidem,
xx d. Et pro ij cordis per ipsum emptis pro aqua trahenda iiij d.
et pro di. bz. floure vj d. Et pro cariagio busce de naui vsque
hospicium domini, xviij d. Et pro herbis, xviij d. SUPER officio
scutellarie, per manus Thome de Warwick pro vij galonibus di.

Summa pagine x
x s. iiij d.
fo. 7.
lewnthorp.

May 25-31.

cenap*is*, ver*gous*, et vinegre ab ipso empt*is* ib*id*em, le ga'o ad vij d. *ob.*, iiij s. viij d. Super offic*io* scut*ellarie*, per m*anus* Will*el*mi Harpeden p*ro* iiij saccis carbon*um* per ipsum empt*is* ib*id*em, ij s. CLERICO speciar*ie* per m*anus* Iohannis Chaundeler p*ro* xxij libr*is* cere op*er*ate ab i*p*so empt*is* ib*id*em, le lb. ad 5 viij d.–xiiij s. viij d. Johanni Chaundeler de Caleys pro esiamento habito in hospic*io* suo per vij dies ib*id*em, nunc*iante* senescallo, vj s. viij d. CLERICO coq*ui*ne per m*anus* Mot de Curterykes pro vj morr*udis* x s. pro ij C. allec*is*, pret*ium* xx d. ab ipsa empt*is* ib*id*em, xj s. viij d. CLERICO speciar*ie* per m*anus* Johannis Chaun- 10 deler p*ro* vij lb. candelar*um* cepi, xiiij d. CLERICO coq*ui*ne per m*anus* Gyles Sotyng*es* p*ro* j carcoisio bou*is*, xxix s, et p*ro* exit*ibus*[a] iiij m*u*lton*um*, iiij d. ab ipso empt*is* ib*id*em, in toto xxix s iiij d. CLERICO panetr*ie* p*er* m*anus* diuer*sorum* pro pane albo ab ip*s*is empt*is*, xlij s. vij d. Clerico panetr*ie* sup*er* seru*isia*, per m*anus* 15 Johannis Fader p*ro* v barell*is* seru*isie* ab ipso empt*is* ib*id*em, le barellus ad. iij s. iiij d., xvj s. viij d. Et per m*anus* Geliane Moubray pro l barello et xviij gal*onibus* serv*isie* ab ipsa empt*is* ib*id*em, le barell*us* ad iij s. vij d.,—vi s. iij d. Et pro cariag*io* dicte seru*isie*, ix d. CLERICO buter*ie* super vino per Yngram Northouer pro vij[xx] 20 viij stop*is* vini Rochell ab ipso empt*is* ib*id*em, le stopa ad v d., lxj s. viij d. JOHANNI Kent de Caleys pro j stab*u*lo ab ipso conducto ap*ud* Caleys p*ro* equis do*m*ini xiij s. iiij d. CLERICO buter*ie* per m*anus* Thome Turnor pro v duoden*is* ciphor*um* ab ipso emptis, iiij s. JOHANNI Lynne pro portag*io* pont*is* ap*ud* Caleys, 25 vj s. JOHANNI Mowbray pro esiamento habito in hospicio suo ap*ud* Caleys, xvj s. viij d. HANKYN Stedeman portanti litt*eras* do*m*ini vsque senescall*um* Francie, de dono do*m*ini ap*ud* Caleys, nunc*iante* Camerar*io*, xx s. DIUERSIS naut*is* ap*ud* Caleys pro batill*agio* harnes*ii* do*m*ini de la Hauen vsq*ue* ad pippem 30 stant*em* in le Ras ib*id*em, vj s. viij d. CLERICO coq*ui*ne per m*anus* Johannis Bussyn p*ro* p*is*cibus recent*ibus* per ipsum

---

[a] In the MS. this reads "pro iiij exit. m. iiijd." The sense appears to require the transposition as above.

EXPENSES IN ENGLAND AND CALAIS. 15

emptis ibidem, iij s. viij d. ob., et pro qrt. multonis vj d., et pro
j pecia bouis iij d., in toto iiij s. v d. ob. SUPER officio pulletrie per manus eiusdem pro lacte, butiro et ouis per ipsum emptis   Summa pagine
ibidem, vij d. ob. DERBYE le Heraud de dono domini apud Caleys   xiiij s. xj d.
5 / eo quod iuit versus regnum Francie, nunciante Camerario, xxvj s.   fo. 7 vº.
viij d. CLERICO panetrie per manus Ricardi Sandhill pro pane
albo per ipsum empto apud Douere, ij s. ij d. CLERICO buterie
super vino, per manus eiusdem pro j sextario iij potellis di. vini
Vasconie, altero per ipsum empto ibidem, sextarium ad ij s. viij d.,
10 v s viij d.* CLERICO marescalcie per manus Roberti Waterton pro
feno per ipsum empto ibidem per ij noctes, vj s., et pro litura xiij d.,
et pro iij quarteriis auenarum ad diuersa precia, ix s. iiij d. SUPER
officio scutellarie, per manus Ricardi Spayn pro busca per ipsum
empta ibidem, xx d, et pro herbis, ij d. ob. THOME Gumme pro
15 portagio pontis vsque naues ad tractandum equos extra naues
apud Douere, vij s. Et per manus eiusdem pro cariagio harnesie
domini extra le hauen vsque hospicium domini in villa, xij d.
CLERICO buterie super seruisia, per manus Ricardi Sandhill pro
xix galonibus seruisie, le galo ad ij d., summa autem iij s. ij d.
20 CLERICO speciarie pro j lb candelorum cepi, ij d.; diuersis nautis
pre batillagio domini et familis sue extra le Rood apud Douere vsque
le Hauen, ij s. vj d. CLERICO panetrie per manus Phillipi Hosteler
pro pane albo ab ipso empto apud Canterbury, ij s. vij d. CLERICO
buterie super vino per manus Willelmi Tauerner pro ij sextariis
25 iij potellis di. vini Vasconie ab ipso emptis ibidem, sextarium ad
iij s. iiij d., ix s. Clerico buterie super seruisia per manus eiusdem
pro xviij galonibus seruisie, le galo ad ij d., summa autem iij s.
CLERICO speciarie pro j lb. candelarum cepi, ij d. SUPER officio
scutellarie, per manus Phillipi Hosteler pro busca ab ipso empta
30 ibidem, ij s. vj d., et pro ij bz. carbonum, iiij d., et pro herbis j d.
SUPER officio salserie pro vergeous iij d. et pro sale ibidem emptis

---

* There appears to be some error in the figures of this item. The sum does not agree with the price. The sextar contained five pottles, as shown by an item for Gascon wine a little further on. But the prices of this wine varied.

iij d. CLERICO marescalcie per manus Phillipi Hostyler pro feno ab ipso empto ibidem ij s. ij d., et pro litura xij d., et pro j qr. iiij bz. di. auenarum, le quarterium ad iiij s., vj s. iij d., et pro pane equino v d. CLERICO panetrie per manus Payn pro pane et vino per ipsum emptis apud Ospryng pro baytyng domini, xij d. CLERICO buterie 5 super vino, per manus eiusdem pro j sextario j qr. vini Rochel per ipsum emptis apud Newyngton, sextarium ad ij s. viij d., in toto ij s. x d. SUPER officio pulleterie, per manus eiusdem pro ij pulcinis iij d., et pro ouis j d., per ipsum emptis ibidem, in toto iiij d. CLERICO coquine per manus Ricardi Messenger pro carne bouum multonum et 10 vitulorum, piscibus salsis et recentibus, et sale per ipsum emptis a primo die Junii vsque vj^{um} diem eiusdem mensis, vtroque computato, per compotum secum factum apud Dartford, in toto cv s. viij d. Gloucestre Marscallo, nunciante Camerario, xx s. CLERICO panetrie per manus Nicholai Tauerner pro pane albo ab ipso empto apud 15 Dartford, xxiij d. CLERICO buterie super vino, per manus Thorne, Tauerner pro iij sextariis vini Vasconie ab ipso emptis ibidem, le sextarium ad ij s. iiij d., x s. Clerico buterie super seruisia, per manus Johannis Crull pro vij galonibus di. seruisie ab ipso emptis ibidem, xiiij d. CLERICO speciarie per manus Nicholai Tauerner 20 pro j lb. candelarum, ij d. SUPER officio scutellarie, per manus eiusdem pro busca ab ipso empta* ibidem, xij d. et pro herbis, j d. SUPER officio salserie per manus eiusdem pro cenape empto ibidem xx d. et pro litura, vj d. Et pro j qrt. iiij bz. auenarum, le qrt. ad iiij s., vj s. Et pro pane equino, ij s. iij d. CLERICO coquine per manus 25 Johannis Crull pro sale, ij d. Clerico coquine per manus Willelmi Hykelyng pro iij congris per ipsum emptis apud Boloigne, iij s. iiij d. DIUERSIS officiariis thesaurarii de Caleys de dono domini ibidem nunciante Camerario, liij s. iiij d. SUPER officio aule et camere per manus diuersorum pro sirpis ab ipsis emptis xix d. 30 CLERICO marescalcie per manus diuersorum pro conductione equorum ad diuersa loca inter Douere et London iiij s. ij d., et pro baytyng domini et diuersorum suitorum equitandorum cum eo inter Douere et London ad diuersa loca iij s ix d. ET

pro cariagio feni apud Caleys, viij d. JOHANNI / Fodryngay fo. 8.
de dono domini apud Caleys eo quod recessit versus Lumbary,
nunciante camerario, vj li. vj s. viij d. SUPER officio pullterie
per manus Willelmi Harpeden pro ancis, caponibus, gallinis,
5 pullis, pulcinis, ouis, lacte, et butiro per ipsum emptis a primo   June 1—8.
die Junii vsque viij diem ciusdem mensis, per compotum secum
factum apud London, una cum vadiis suis, in toto. lviij s xj d.
ob. CLERICO coquine per manus eiusdem [pro] piscibus et aliis
victualibus per ipsum emptis apud London per ij dies, iij s. ij d.
10 Et per manus Ade Catour pro j pecia bouis, xx d., pro ij carcosiis
multonum, iiij s. iiij d., et pro sale ij d., in toto vj s. ij d. CLERICO
panetrie per manus Ricardi Sandhill pro pane albo per ipsum empto
ibidem, ij s. v d. CLERICO buterie super vino, per manus eiusdem pro j sextario iij potellis di. vini Vasconie per ipsum emptis
15 ibidem, sextarium ad iij s. viij d., v s. CLERICO buterie super
seruisia, per manus eiusdem pro xxv galonibus seruisie, le galo ad
j d. ob, summa autem iij s. j d. ob. SUPER officio scutellarie, per
manus Talleworth pro j qr. busce ab ipso empto ibidem, xj d., et pro
herbis, j d ob. SUPER officio salsarie, per manus eiusdem pro
20 vergeous [et] vinegre emptis ibidem, iij d. CLERICO speciarie pro
j lb. candelarum cepi, j d. ob CLERICO Marescalcie per manus
Martyn Hosteler pro feno ab ipso empto ibidem, ij s. j d. et pro litura
xviij d. et pro qr. ij bz et di. auenarum, le qr. ad iiij s., v s. iij d ; et
pro pane equino, xiiij d. ob. CLERICO buterie super seruisia, per
25 manus Willelmi Turnour pro ej qr. ciphis ligneis ab ipso emptis
apud Kenillworth, vij s. vj d. HUGONE Herle pro oblacionibus   Oblaciones.
domini cotidie a ix die Maii vsque vij diem Junii, vtroque   May 9—June 7.
computato, ij s. vj d., et per manus eiusdem pro magna oblacione
domini per idem tempus in diebus festiualibus, iiij s.; et in eleemo-
30 synis domini datis diuersis pauperibus per idem tempus, x s j d.
CLERICO speciarie per manus Willelmi Harpeden pro croco per
ipsum empto inter London et Kenillworth, iij d. CLERICO coquine
per manus Henrici Busshen pro carne boum, multonum, et vitulorum, caponibus, gallinis, et pulcinis per ipsum emptis apud

Scintalbon, v s. iij d. CLERICO panetrie per manus Johannis
Hosteler pro pane albo ab ipso empto apud Scyntalbon, ix d. CLE-
RICO buterie super vino, per manus Thome Tauerner pro ij potellis
j quart vini Vasconie ad diuersa pretia, xxj d. Clerico buterie
super seruisia, per manus Johannis Hosteler pro vj galonibus ser- 5
uisie, xij d. CLERICO speciarie pro j lb. candelarum cepi, ij d.
CLERICO coquine pro congro et morrudis, vij d. SUPER officio pulletrie pro ouis emptis ibidem, iij d. SUPER officio scutellarie, pro
busca empta ibidem, iiij d. CLERICO panetrie per manus Sandhill pro bayting camerarii thesaurarii et familie domini apud 10
Donstaple, viij d. ob. ET per manus eiusdem pro pane albo empto
apud Fenystratford, vj d. CLERICO buterie super seruisia per
manus eiusdem pro vij galonibus seruisie emptis ibidem, x d. ob.
CLERICO coquine pro sale, j d. SUPER officio pulletrie, per manus
Cudworth pro ij aucis, vij d. SUPER officio scutellarie, per manus 15
eiusdem pro busca empta ibidem, iiij d.ᵃ CLERICO panetrie per
manus Johannis Broun pro pane albo ab ipso empto apud Touceter.
CLERICO buterie super seruisia, pro vij galonibus seruisie emptis
ibidem, x d. ob. CLERICO speciarie pro j lb. candelarum cepi, ij d.
CLERICO coquine per manus Johannis Bocher pro j carcosio multonis, 20
xix d., et pro sale j d. SUPER officio scutellarie pro busca, iiij d.
CLERICO panetrie per manus Sandhill pro bayting camerarii et
thesaurarii apud Southam, iij d. ob. LANCASTRE le heraud de
dono domini apud Caleys, xl s. CLERICO buterie super seruisia,
per manus Johannis Attehalle pro ij ollis coreis galoners, et 25
pro vj ollis coreis potellers, ab ipso emptis apud London, x s. viij d.
RADULPHO Steynour de Westmonasterio pro j nova aula ab ipso
empta ibidem, iiij li. vj s. viij d. ROBERTO Busse pro x caudrons,
vnde iij grossi, cum ferro ligateo ab ipso emptis apud London,
iiij li. xij s. iiij d. Et Ricardo Smyth pro vj broches, unde ij 30
parvi, pro ij paribus rakkes pro caudrons pendendis / ponderantibus in toto xxij lb., ab ipso emptis ibidem, lb. ad j d. ob. qʳ,
minus in toto iij d., xxx s. viij d. Et Johanni Gylder pro emenda-

Respondet.

*ugine
x s. iij d. ob.
fo. 8 vᵒ*

ᵃ This item is written twice over in the original.

NECESSARIES PROVIDED IN ENGLAND. 19

cione un*ius* cerur*e* dun par trossyngcofres* pro auro imponendo dat*i*
Du*ci* Lanc*astrie*, iij d.   THOME Stranston p*ro* ij lb. et d*i*. de corde
viride ab ip*s*o empto pro sua nova aula, xx d.   CLERICO speciar*ie*
p*er* man*us* Will*elmi* de Norton pro vj lb. d*i*. qr. ginge*r*, le lb. ad
5 xxij d , xj s. ij d. ob.; xj lb. *di*. d*i*.-qr. chare de coyns ad xij d., xj s.
vij d. ob.; pro iiij lb. pynenade ad xiiij d., iiij s. viij d.; pro ij lb.
carawey ad xiiij d., ij s. iiij d.; pro ij lb. ginge*r* en confyt ad xij d.
ij s.; pro ij lb. clowes en confyt ad iij s., vj s.; pro iij lb. cytronade
ad iij s., ix s.; pro ij lb. gobete real, ij s.; pro iiij lb. sucr*i* plat, roug*e*
10 et blank, iiij s.; pro vj lb. sucr*i* candy, xxiiij s.; pro iij lb. past*i* real
ad xviij d., iij s vj d.; pro ij lb. anneys en confyt, ij s.; et pro ij lb.
gariselet, ij s.; pro ij lb. ginge*r* madrean, ij s. iiij d.; pro ij lb. penydes,
ij s.; p*ro* ij lb. drage real, ij s. viij d.; p*ro* jlb. notemug, xviij d.; pro
ij quart*ernis* papir*i*, ij s. iiij d.; pro ij lb. cere rub*re*, xvj d.; ab ipso
15 empt*is* apud London iiij*to* die Jul*ii*, pl*us* in to*to* ij d., iiij li. xvj s.   • 4 July.
viij d.   Et p*er manus* eiusd*em* pro xviij pell*ibus* pergameni*ab ipso
emptis ibid*em*, iiij s , et p*ro* pounc*i*, j d., in toto iiij s. j d.   THOME
Grafton pro j clothsake magno ab ipso empto ibid*em*, xvj s.   THOME
Leueret pro ij carect*is* ab ipso conduct*is* de Londoñ vsque Boston
20 car*iantibus* diuer*sa* nec*essa*r*ia* ibid*em* empta pro viagio domini, p*er*
conuenc*ionem* sec*um* factam ibid*em*, lxxiij s. iiij d.   CLERICO buter*ie*
super vino, per man*us* Joh*ann*is Payn pro xxj dol*iis* vini Vasco*nie*
per ips*um* empt*is* apud Hulle; una cum rollagio, kranagio, et conductio*ne* un*ius* boot ad ducend*um* dicta dol*ia* vsq*ue* nauem et pro
25 runag*io* dicto*rum* dol*iorum* p*er* compot*um* sec*um* fact*um* apud
Boston, in toto cxxiij li. vij s. viij d.*   Et pro batillag*io* dicti vini   • Vin*um* cxxi
de Hulle usque Boston, lxxvj s. vj d.   JOHANNI Norbery de dono   vij s. viij d. qu
domini apud London, vj li. xiij s. iiij d.   CLERICO buter*ie* per man*us*
Joh*ann*is Payn p*ro* j barella par*ua* de crospays ibid*em* empta, v s.
30 JOHANNI Clokmaker pro j panier per ips*um* empto ad car*iandum*

* The money-box of old times was probably double, *i.e.*, with two divisions like
the modern cash-box, hence it is spoken of as "a pair of packing coffers" with one
lock. The French "d'un" slips from the writer's pen naturally after the word
"cerure." "Five pair of coffers" are one of the first purchases named. See before,
p. 5 (fo. 1).

j clokke de London vsque Bolyngbroke, viij d. JOHANNI Boteman pro batillagio equorum et harnesiorum domini de la Whithall vsque le Clot per xij millaria, ij s. vj d. Et pro portagio harnesii domini vsque hospicium domini apud Boston, ij d. MAGISTRO nauis domini et seruientibus suis, de dono domini apud Boston viij die Jullii, xl s. Et diuersis carpentariis operantibus in eodem naui pro diuersis cabans faciendis, de dono domini. xiij s. iiij d. CLERICO coquine per manus Johannis Fyssher pro lvij morrudis ab ipso emptis ibidem, l. s. DOMINO Willelmo Ehnam et Thome Stokes pro expensis suis in itinere, missis de Caleys usque regem Francie pro j sauc conduyt pro domino querendo, per compotum factum, nunciante Camerario, xiij li. iij s., deductis inde Cs. per ipsum prius receptis et antea allocatis, viij li. iij s. Et per manus Thome Fyssher pro xlviij styks anguillarum ab ipso emptis apud Boston, le styk ad iiij d., minus in toto viij d., xv s. iiij d. CLERICO coquine per manus Willelmi Wyrcestre pro xl multonibus ab ipso emptis ibidem, lxxij s., deductis inde pro exitibus dictorum multonum, xiij s. vj d. per compotum secum factum apud Boston, lviij s. vj d. SUPER officio scutellarie, per manus Johannis Cudworth pro iiijM¹ bilettorum per ipsum emptis ibidem, xxxiiij s. Et per manus Johannis de Colton pro ix qrt. di. carbonum, le quarterium ad xiiij d., minus in toto iiij d. ob., x s vj d. CLERICO panetrie per manus Thome Geffrayson de Sutton pro lxxj qrt. frumenti, le qrt. ad vj s. viij d., xxiij li xiij s. iiij d.* Et per manus Thome Jonson pro xvij quarteriis j busello frumenti ab ipso emptis, le qr. ad vj s. iiij d., minus in toto v d., Cviij s. ob. SUPER officio scutellarie, per manus Thome Fosdyke pro j hausak, et j schaue ab ipso emptis ibidem, / ij s. viij d. Et per manus Johannis Bladesmyth pro j dressyng knyf ab ipso empto ibidem, iiij s. CLERICO speciarie per manus Johannis Clerke pro l. vlnis de cannevas, le vlna ad vj d., xxv s. CLERICO buterie super vino, per manus Thome Swan pro iiij doliis vini Vasconie veteris, dolium ad xl s., plus in toto vj s. viij d., viij li. vj s. viij d. Clerico buterie super seruisia per manus Payn pro xij barellis de ber per ipsum emptis apud Boston, lxvj s. Et per manus

NECESSARIES PROVIDED IN ENGLAND. 21

Johanne Kemp pro iijC galonibus seruisie ab ipsa emptis ibidem, le galo ad j d. ob., autem deductis [iijs.]ª xxxiiijs. vj d. Et pro ix barrellis vacuis emptis pro seruisia imponenda, iij s. ix d. Et pro portagio vini et floure vsque nauem, iij s. viij d. Clerico buterie super vino,
5 per manus Payn pro ij sextariis di. picheria vini albi per ipsum emptis pro ollis unius dolii, sextarium ad ij s. viij d., v s. viij d. CLERICO Panetrie per manus Bartholomei Walsoken pro viij vlnis cannevas pro cibano faciendo, pro bultyng iij s. xj d., et pro xxxix virgis de sakcloth ad faciendum xxv sakks pro farina imponenda,
10 virga ad iij d. ob., xj s. iiij d. ob. Et pro multura iiij^xx vj qrt. frumenti, le qrt. ad iiij d., xxviij s. viij d. CLERICO coquine per manus Herman Coke pro C stoks ᵇ wynterflysh, xxvj s. viij d , pro C stoks halfwaxen, xviij s., ab ipso ibidem [emptis] in toto xliiij s. viij d. Et per manus Johannis de Freston pro xviij qrt. ij bz. salis
15 ab ipso emptis, le qrt. ad iiij s. lxxiij s.; et pro cariagio dicti salis, ij s. ij d. Et pe- manus Alani Bakster pro j porco magno de saguine ab ipso empto ibidem, vj s. viij d. CLERICO buterie super vino per manus Johannis Payn pro xv sextariis vini Vasconie per ipsum emptis, sextarium ad ij s. viij d., xl s. CLERICO coquine per manus
20 Thome Semond pro x flyckes de bacoñ ab ipso emptis apud Bolyngbroke, xij s. vj d. CLERICO speciarie per manus Adam Wikerell pro iiijC di. lb. ᶜ amygdalorum, cᵐ ad xviij s., iiij li. xij d.; pro C lb. rys x s.; pro xiiij lb. gingeris ad xviij d., xvj s. iiij d.; pro xiiij lb. piperis ad xxij d., xxv s. viij d.; pro xiiij lb. canelle, xiiij s., pro x lb.
25 sucri sipre ad viij d., vj s. viij d.; pro vij lb. iij qrt. sucri caffretin, xj s. vij d. ob.; pro vj galonibus mellis ad viij d., iiij s.; pro j lb. croci,

---

ª That is, discount was allowed of one shilling on the hundred gallons.

ᵇ This word may be scoks = shocks, a shock being a parcel of 60, generally employed in purchases in Prussia in these accounts (it will be noted that the vendor in this item bears a Teutonic name). The letters c and t in the MS. are indistinguishable. But further on, we undoubtedly have stokes, meaning fish, where scok is inapplicable. See p. 29, l. 18; p. 31, l. 32.

ᶜ That is, four hundredweight and a-half. This seems an immense provision of almonds, but they were used as a digestive, as well as in cookery. See Babee's booke, ed. Furnivall E. E. T. Soc. p. 124, 168, 267.

xvij s.; pro di. lb. macz, ij s.; pro di. lb. clowes, ij s.; pro di. lb. quibibbes, ij s. vj d.; pro j lb. caundres, ij s. x d.; pro xl virges de streynours ad iij d., x s. ; pro j lb. comyn, iiij d., et pro vj lb. floure de rys, viij d.; per compotum secum factum apud Boston, in toto x li. vj s. vij d. ob. Et per manus Ricardi Chaundeler pro cx lb. 5 cere operate, centena ad lvj s., ab ipso emptis lxj s. Et pro factura dicte cere, ij s. iiij d. Super officio salserie, per manus Matilde Massyngham pro xxxvj galonibus vinegre ab ipsa emptis ibidem, xxiiij s.; pro j bz. de mustardseed iij s., et pro ij barellis parvis pro dicto vinegre imponendo, xvj d., in toto xxviij s. iiij d. Clerico 10 coquine per manus Thome Wrangill pro iij bobus [a] ab ipso emptis apud Boston, lxj s. viij d. Et per manus Johannis Wynch pro v bobus ab ipso emptis ibidem, l s. ij d. ob. Et per manus Johannis Coke pro x bobus per ipsum emptis ibidem, vj li. xv s. Clerico coquine per manus Johannis Grey pro lvj barellis vacuis ab ipso 15 emptis pro carne aqua et aliis victualibus imponendis, le barellus ad v d., xxiij s. iiij d. Et per manus eiusdem pro v doliis vacuis pro aqua imponenda, xj s. Super officio scutellerie, per manus Ricardi Couper pro ij plankes ab ipso emptis pro j dressour faciendo, iiij s. vj d. Et pro ij pesteles, viij d. Et pro j barello pro saguine imponendo, v d. 20 Et per manus ejusdem pro ligatione dicti barelli et v doliorum et pro mundacione eorundem, xiij s. iiij d. Et per manus Ricardi Smyth pro xj cheynis ab ipso emptis ad pendendum caudrons super dictos j cheynos, iij s. viij d. Clerico coquine per manus Willelmi Wrake et socii sui pro labore suo operante in lardero apud Boston cum 25 Johanne Cudworth per vij dies di., capiente quolibet per diem iiij d., v s. Eisdem pro verberacione ij C stokes,[b] viij d. Et pro fugacione boum de Holbech vsque Boston, xij d. Clerico panetrie per manus Ricardi Couper pro hedynge iiij doliorum pro floure imponendo, et pro hopes et schauyng dictorum doliorum, viij s. 30 iiij d. Et per manus eiusdem pro strycage et stouwage xij dolio-

[a] The word in these three items is written bou', as though bonibus were intended.
[b] This appears to mean the beating of 200 stock-fish, an article of food so salt and dry that it required to be well beaten before cooking.

rum vini et floure, x s. vj d. Et pro runagio xxiiij doliorum et j pipe,
ij s. vj d. Clerico coquine per manus Wircestre pro xiij flickes
de bacon per ipsum ibidem emptis, xxvj s. iij d. Super officio
scutellerie, per manus Johannis Cudworth pro ij mortars per ipsum
5 emptis ibidem, vij s. Johanni Peyntour pro pictura lxviij paueys
domini de Willeby, per conuentionem factam cum eodem, xiij s.
iiij d. Super officio salsarie per manus Malkyn Mustarder pro
vij galonibus cenapis ab ipsa emptis ibidem, le galo ad v d., plus
in toto j d., ij s. xj d. Et pro xj galonibus et di. vergeous ab ipsa
10 emptis ibidem, v s. ix d. Super officio scutellarie, per manus Cudworth pro cxv discis ligneis per ipsum emptis ibidem, iiij s. viij d.
Super officio salserie per manus Ricardi Couper pro ij barellis ab
ipso emptis pro cenape et verges imponendo, ix d. Clerico coquine
per manus Rogeri Loft pro j boue ab ipso empto ibidem, xvij s.
15 Et pro j carcosia bouina ab eodem empta, xj s. Clerico panetrie
per manus Fyssher pro ij barellis et j hoogeshed vacuis per ipsum
pro floure imponendo xviij d. Clerico buterie super seruisia per
manus Cawod pro j barello vacuo per ipsum empto pro aqua imponenda pro potacione domini, viij d. Et pro ligacione vj barellorum
20 pro seruisia imponenda, viij d. Johanni Cudworth pro portagio
diuersorum victualium domini per diuersas vices vsque naues, per
compotum factum apud Boston, in toto xv s. iiij d. Et pro
cariagio harnesie domini de Boston vsque Chopechyre, iiij s. Super
officio scutellarie per manus Johannis Tyler pro j herthe per ipsum
25 facto in naui, vij s. viij d. et pro portagio tegularum pro dicto herthe,
iiij d. Johanni Coke de dono domini apud Boston, nunciante Camerario, xl s. Diuersis nautis de Boston pro touyng nauem domini de
la hauen apud Boston, xlvj s. viij d. Clerico buterie super vino,
per manus Johannis Gasteyn pro vino ab ipso empto ibidem, iij s.
30 iiij d. Johanni Couper pro factura unius kist pro speciebus imponendis, xvj d. Clerico panetrie per Johannem Baker de Boston
pro furnagio frumenti apud Boston, vij s. Clerico speciarie per
manus Johannis Coke pro xj virgis tele Flaundre ab ipso emptis
apud Boston, virga ad ix d., viij s. iij d.; et pro ix virgis tele

Flaundre, v s. iij d. Et pro vj virgis tele Flaundre, iij s. Super officio scutellarie per manus eiusdem pro viij trowes ab ipso emptis pro officio coquine, ij s. vj d. et pro j gratour, xvj d. Johanni Botman pro batillagio harnesii domini de Boston vsque Chopcherye, vij s. ij d. Super officio scutellarie pro ij ladels et ij scomers, iij s. x d. 5 et pro ij ceruris et x rynges et xij staples et j fryengpan et j rostern, iij s. iiij d. Et pro cariagio aque recentis de Boston vsque nauem vsque Chopchyre, vj s. viij d. Clerico coquine per manus Thome Bache pro xx multonibus ab ipso emptis, xxxvj s. viij d.; et pro j carcosio bouis x s., et pro fugacione dictorum multonum de 10 Boston vsque Chopchyre, xij d. Clerico panetrie pro bultyngclothes, iiij s., et pro pane emptis apud Boston, iij s. iiij d. Johanni Godfrey per manus Cudworth pro M^l bilettorum, xiij s. Bartholomeo Walsaken pro xliiij virgis de cannevas, le virga iij d. ob., in toto xij s. x d. Johanni Clerk pro ij tonnellis, pris de tonnello iij s., in toto vj s. 15 Gilberto Page pro ij tonellis j pipa, et in toto, viij s. Willelmo Halden pro iiij tonnellis, pris de tonnello iij s. iiij d., in toto xiij s. iiij d. Margeret de Flet j pipa, ij s. Willelmo Franch pro j tonella j pipa de Rynen, vj s. Galiard de Gaston pro j tonella, iij s. iiij d. Roberto Gobon pro j tonella et j pipa de Rynen, in toto vj s. Johanni 20 Temman pro xij virgis de cannevas, in toto vj s. et pro pakthred, ij d. / Johanni Coke pro iiij tonellis, precium le tonella, iij s., in toto vj s. Clerico coquine per manus Rogeri Atteloft pro j bone ab ipso empto ibidem, xj s. x d. Clerico marescalcie per manus Willelmi Smyth pro j qr. ij lb. de ferro operato, xx d. Johanne Webbe pro 25 viij vlnis de cannevas, le vlna vj d., in toto iiij s. Clerico marescalcie per manus Johannis Roper pro diuersis cordis ab ipso emptis ibidem, vj d. Duobus valettis pro mundacione le larderhous, vj d. Item pro conductione unius equi Cudworth ad videndum boues quando fuerunt empti apud Freston, ij s. Item pro pastura xx boum 30 per tres septimanas, xv s. et pro clausura dicte pasture, xij d. Clerico panetrie per manus Johannis Cok pro pane, seruisia, carne et piscibus, per iiij vices ab ipso emptis apud Bolyngbroke, et in aliis locis diuersis pro frumento cariando, iiij s. viij d. Item pro cariagio

NECESSARIES PROVIDED IN ENGLAND.

eiusdem frumenti, ix s. Johanni Portour pro portagio xv tonellarum de villa vsque le boltynghous, xv d. Clerico panetrie per manus Johannis Ryle pro pane, carne, seruisia emptis; pro bulters per ij dies, xiiij d.; et pro mundacione xx doliorum pro farina imponenda, 5 xxij d.; et pro clauibus a le bultynghous, v d. ITEM j valetto qui deliberauit frumentum, xij d. CLERICO marescaleie per manus Johanne Kent pro sewyng de diuersis saccis, vj d. ITEM pro cariagio frumenti de le bultynghous vsque nauem, ij s. ITEM vj valettis pro mundacione hospicii domini apud Boston, xij d. ITEM 10 pro crochetes ad aulam, emptis ad pendendum le docere et les tapetos in dicta aula domini apud Boston, iij d. ob. ITEM pur straynours emptis ibidem per manus Johannis Coke pro bultellis, iij s. ix d. JOHANNI Coke laboranti circa emptionem frumenti et aliorum victualium diuersorum per xij dies capienti pro se et valettis, per diem xij d., in toto 15 xij s. SUPER officio pulletrie, per manus Willelmi Harpeden pro iij qr. farine auenarum per ipsum emptis ibidem, xxiiij s.; et per manus eiusdem pro iij M¹ iiij C ouorum per ipsum emptis ibidem, xxij s.; et per manus eiusdem pro xxx ston casei per ipsum emptis ibidem, xx s.; et per manus eiusdem pro xxxvj ston butiri per ipsum emptis ibidem, 20 xxxvj s. Et vj bz. salis pro dictis ouis custodiendis emptis ibidem, iij s.; et per manus eiusdem pro iij qr. fabarum per ipsum emptis ibidem, xx s.; et per manus eiusdem pro vj bz. pisarum pro potagio faciendo, ij s.; et per manus eiusdem pro ij doliis vacuis per ipsum emptis ibidem pro dictis pisis imponendis, vij s. CLERICO mares-
25 calcie pro diuersis saccis per ipsum emptis ibidem, iij s. SUPER officio pulletrie per manus Willelmi Kagemaker, pro iij cages ab ipso emptis ibidem pro pullis imponendis, x s. SUPER officio pulletrie, per manus Willelmi Harpeden pro iij duodenis caponum per ipsum emptis ibidem, ix s: et per manus eiusdem pro xvj duodenis 30 gallinarum, xxxij s.; et per manus eiusdem pro ix duodenis pulcinorum per ipsum emptis ibidem, ix s. et pro putura, x s. et pro cariagio dicte pulletrie, iij s. iiij d.; et per manus eiusdem pro iij trowes per ipsum emptis, xij d. JOHANNI Smyth pro iiij lokes per ipsum emptis ibidem, xij d.; et eidem pro haspes et gemewes ab

26 THE EARL OF DERBY'S EXPEDITIONS.

ipso emptis pro diuersis doliis, viij d.; et pro expensis domini per
dictum Willelmum Harpeden emptis[a] per ij dies, ij s. viij d.; et pro
pendicione de dictis gages,[b] vj d. SUPER officio pulletrie per manus
W. Harpeden pro ij duodenis gallinarum per ipsum emptis ibidem,
iiij s. JOHANNI Clerke pro cxv waynscot pro factura cabans et 5
diuersorum necessariorum in naui, xxvij s. Et pro vj waynscot, xv d.
Et pro De ferris operatis, ij s. j d. THOME Harwod pro xlvi deles

Summa pagine xix li.   ab ipso emptis ibidem ad faciendum diuersa necessaria in naui,
iij s. viij d. ob.   xlix s. x d.; et pro j ligno magno ad emendandum le bot, ij s.

fo. 10 v°.   / VALERIANO Carpenterio pro M¹ De clauorum per ipsum emptorum 10
ibidem, iiij s. ij d.; et pro M¹cc spyks, vj s., in toto x s. ij d. Et pro
diuersis arboribus per ipsum emptis pro certis necessariis faciendis,

* Sic.   xxvij s. iij d.; et pro portagio corundem,* xvj d. Et pro lxxij deles
per ipsum emptis, le dele xij d., lxxij s.; et pro portagio corundem,
xij d. Et pro cxj waynscot per ipsum emptis, le piece ad ij d. ob., 15
in toto xx s. x. d. Et pro portagio corundem ad nauem, vj d. Et
in diuersis instrumentis ferreis, videlicet gemewes, haspes, hokes et
staples pro lecto domini pendendo pro altare in naui, iiij s. x d.
WALTERO Jonson pro emendacione vnius bot pro naui domini
per ij dies, capienti per diem viij d, ij s.; et tribus hominibus oper- 20
antibus per j diem secum, capientibus inter se per diem xx d.; et
v hominibus operantibus circa le dit Bot per ij dies, capientibus
inter se per diem ij s. vj d., v s., per compotum cum eisdem factum;
in toto una cum iiij d. datis eisdem ad potandum, ix s.; et pro
j galone tar, vj d. JOHANNI Carpenter pro meremio ab ipso 25
empto pro le Bot emendendo, iij s. iiij d.; et pro ferro operato et
clauis emptis pro dicto Boot, xxij d. JOHANNI Clerk pro De bord
ab ipso emptis ibidem, xij s. vj d. RICARDO Broun pro De bord ab
ipso emptis ibidem, xij s. vj d. BERTELMEW Walsokeñ pro xij
deles, prec. xiij d., et sic in toto, xiij s. THOME Harwod pro viij 30
deles prec. xiij d., in toto viij s. viij d. SUPER officio scutellarie

[a] Empt. in MS., but solutis must be intended.
[b] Gages, i.e., the cages named in a previous item. These were for the poultry on ship-board kept for consumption during the voyage.

NECESSARIES PROVIDED IN ENGLAND.

per manus Walteri Turnour pro CC. ciphis ab ipso emptis ibidem,
viij s. vj d. (CLERICO marescalcie per manus Johannis Jacson
pro xx qr. auenarum ab ipso emptis ibidem, le qr. ad ij s. vj d., l s.)[a]
VALERIANO Carpenterio cum vij sociis suis operantibus in naui circa
5 cabans domini facturam. die veneris proximo post festum sancti   July 8.
Thome martiris[b] capienti pro se per diem viij d., et pro quolibet socio suo vj d., per conuentionem secum factam ibidem, in toto   July 9.
iiij s. ij d. Eidem Valeriano cum ix sociis die sabbati operantibus per totum diem, capiente pro se ut supra, et pro quolibet socio
10 suorum ut supra, in toto v s. ij d. Eidem Valeriano pro vj diebus
cum ix sociis, capiente pro se ut supra et pro sociis suis ut supra,
xxxj s. Et in stipendiis trium carpenteriorum Johannis Bell
operantium ibidem per ij dies circa diuersa necessaria in naui, quilibet capientis ut supra, iij s. Et in stipendiis xiij carpenteriorum   July 18.
15 operantium in dictis nauibus die lune ante festum sanctæ Margarete[c]
circa diuersa necessaria ibidem facta, quolibet capiente ut supra, in toto
vj s. vj d. VALERIANO magistro carpenterio pro ij diebus, viz. die
lune et die martis, capiente pro se ut supra, et pro vij sociis   July 18, 19.
operantibus die martis circa diuersa necessaria in nauibus, quolibet
20 socio capiente ut supra, in toto iiij s. x d. EXPENSE factæ per
Thesaurarium guerre apud Boston pro se et diuersis officiis et parte
familie domini per x dies, viz. a x die mensis Julii vsque xix[m]   July 10-19.
diem eiusdem mensis utroque computato, pro providenciis faciendis
ibidem pro domino versus Pruciam, iiij li. iij s. ij d. ob. SUPER
25 officio pulletrie, per manus Johannis Coke pro 1 qrt. sepi per ipsum
empto ibidem, viij s. SUPER officio buterie, per manus Johannis
Payn pro j pipa de vino rubeo per ipsum empta apud Boston,
liij s. iiij d. SENESCALLO pro oblacionibus domini et domine apud
Lincolne, x s. Item in elemosynis datis ibidem per manus eiusdem
30 ex parte domini, vj s. viij d. (ITEM Senescallo pro conductione

---

[a] A pen has been struck through this entry, and this noted in the margin,—"quia
venduntur ad hospicium."
[b] The translation of St. Thomas the Martyr was on July 7.
[c] July 20 was the day of St. Margaret the Virgin.

28   THE EARL OF DERBY'S EXPEDITIONS.

equorum et pro *passagio* vltra Humber et le Wasshe per *diuersas* vice[s] super *negocium* domini, xvj s. vj d.)[a] Et apud Writel pro lu*sibus* domini ibi*dem*, per manus Rad*ulphi* Stanele*y*, xx s. Item dat*i* domino pro j anulo a g*er*manland,[b] vj s. viij d.   Et pro obla-
cione domini apud Canterbure per manus eiusdem, x s.   Item Barbi- 5 tonsori regis apud Kenyngton per *manus* eiusdem, iij s. iiij d.   Et datum bargeman domini ducis Lancastrie in exi*tu* suo versus Barbari*am*, vj s. viij d.   Item dat*um* in conductione equ*orum* inter Hertford et Barkamstyd, vj s. viij d.   Item en baytyng et con-
ductione eq*uorum* in veniendo de Caleys apud London, xiij s. iiij d. 10 / Clerico mareseu*cie* per *manus* Johannis Hosteler pro feno ab ipso empto apud London pro iiij equis domini existentibus ibidem cum thesaurario pro providenciis factis, v s. iij d., et pro pane equino, viij d.   Et pro iij qr. iij bz. auenar*um*, le qrt. ad iij s. iij d., per ipsum emptis ibidem, xj s. v d. ob.   Et pro ferrura equorum ibidem, 15 xvj d.   Johanni Gylder pro pane, vino, seruisia, et carne per ipsum emptis apud Warwicum, xix d.   Et in pane equino per manus eiusdem ibidem empto et feno, viij d. ob., et pro baytyng apud Buntyngford, iij d.   Super officio baterie et pulletrie, pro iij galoni-
us seruisie, le galo ij d., vj d.; et pro ij pullis, iij d., pro carne vitu- 20 lorum et multonum ibidem empta, x d.; et pro croco, ob., pro busca, j d., pro farina auenarum, ob., pro candelis cepi, j d., pro lecte,[c] j d., pro feno, iiij d., pro ij bz. j *pecc*o auenar*um*, xiij d. ob., pro pane equino empto ibidem, iiij d., et pro iij qrt. vini, vij d. ob.; in toto iiij s. iiij d.   Et per manus Gylder pro pane albo per ipsum empto apud 25 Caxton, ij d. ob.; pro v galonibus seruisie di., le galo ij d., xj d.; pro iij pulcinis emptis ibidem, vj d., pro j capone, v d., pro carre bo*u*m,

Summa pagine
xxiiij li. xj s. iiij d. ob.
fo. 11.

---

[a] A pen has been run through this entry. " quia scrib*itur* inferius."

[b] Germany is hardly intended here, the mark of contraction is that usually sig- 30 nifying *ra*, and the word thus reads *granmanland*; besides, further on (fo. 39) we have a gift to the "heraldo de Almann*ia*." Prof. Prutz suggests that we should read Kermanland, *i.e.* Kerman, a province of Persia, whence turquoise and other precious stones were brought in the middle ages.   See Heyd, *Hist. du Commerce du Levant*, vol. ii. p. 653.

[c] *Lecte* seems to be meant, a bed was not the concern of the buttery.

iiij d., pro croco, ob., pro busca, j d. ob., pro crem, iiij d., pro pescods, j d., pro feno, auenis et litura, viij d., in toto iij s. vij d. ob. Et per manus ciusdem pro pane albo empto apud Huntyngdon, iij d., pro di. potelli vini Vasconie, vj d., pro v galonibus seruisie, x d., pro feno,
5 v d. ob., pro ij bz. et j pecco auenarum, xiij d. ob., pro pane equino, vj d. ob., pro j capone, v d., pro iij pulcinis, vj d., pro carne boum et multonum, ix d., pro ginger, j d., pro pescods, ij d., in toto v s. vij d. ob. Et per manus ciusdem pro pane albo empto apud Peturburgh, iij d., pro iiij gal. seruisie, viij d, pro sale, j d., pro pipere et
10 croco, j d., pro herbis, j d., pro busca, j d. ob., pro piscibus salsis, v d., pro stoks, iij d., pro anguillis, viij d., pro welks, iij d., pro allecibus, iiij d., pro feno et pane equino, ix d., in toto iij s. xj d. ob. Et per manus ciusdem pro pane albo empto apud Spaldyng, ob., pro seruisia, j d. ob., pro busca et candelis, iij d, in feno, ij d. ob., pro ij bz.
15 auenarum, xj d., in toto xviij d. ob. Et per manus ciusdem pro seruisia empta apud Crowland, v d. Et pro pane albo empto apud Boston, iiij d. ob., pro cericis, iiij d., pro iiij gal. seruisie di, ix d.; pro morrudis et stoks, allecibus, anguillis, et welks, croco et pipere, ij s. x d.; pro j anguilla grossa, viij d.; pro feno et pane equino, vj d., in
20 toto v s. v d. ob. CLERICO panetrie per manus Johannis Payn pro pane albo per ipsum empto apud London, ij s. CLERICO buterie per manus ciusdem pro x gal. vini, vj s. viij d.; pro vj gal. seruisie, ix d., in toto vij s. v d. CLERICO panetrie per manus Payn p o pane albo per ipsum empto apud Boston, xij d. ob. CLERICO buterie per
25 manus ciusdem pro vj gal. iij qrt. vini, v s. vij d. ob.; et pro iiij gal. et di. seruisie, ix d. CLERICO coquine per manus magistri Willelmi Coke pro j pyke per ipsum empto ibidem, xviij d.; et pro De allecibus poudris, xx d. et per manus ciusdem pro j styke di. anguillarum, xiiij d.; et per manus ciusdem pro carne, ouis, et vj
30 pullis, xij d.; et per manus ciusdem pro lacte, ouis, et piscibus salsis, xvj d. SUPER officio scutellarie, per manus Roberti Spayne pro ix fagottis, iiij d. ob. Et per manus ciusdem pro herbis et sale per ipsum emptis, ij d. ob. CLERICO marescalcie per manus Roberti Chalons pro diuersis baytynges equorum domini apud London, Hertford, et

Pulerich, ij s. ij d.; et per manus ejusdem pro expensis equorum domini apud Boston, vz. in feno, littera, pane equino, et auenis, xiiij d. ob. Et per manus Johannis Syde pro baytynge unius maler domini de Dertford vsque Rooston, ix d. Et pro emendacione vnius selle vnius maler domini, vj d. CLERICO 5 panetrie per manus Johannis Payn pro pane albo per ipsum / empto apud Huntyndoñ, xij d. ob. CLERICO buterie per manus eiusdem pro iiij galonibus vini, iiij s. Et pro v galonibus seruisie, vij d. ob. CLERICO coquine per manus Johannis Cooke pro carne boum multonum et vitulorum ab ipso empto ibidem, xix d.; pro j 10 capone iij d. ob., iij aucis xv d., et ix pullis xiij d., in toto ij s. vij d. ob. Et eidem pro di. pecci salis, j d. ob. Clerico coquine per manus Roberti Spayne pro xij fagottis per ipsum emptis, vj d. Et per manus eiusdem pro herbis et farina per ipsum emptis, j d. CLERICO panetrie per manus Johannis Payn pro pane albo per 15 ipsum empto apud Sleford, xij d. CLERICO buterie per manus eiusdem pro v galonibus vini, v s., pro ij galonibus seruisie, iiij d., in toto v s. iiij d. CLERICO coquine per manus Roberti Saintpyr pro ij pykes, stok, anguillis, piscibus salsis et recentibus, ab ipso emptis ibidem, vj s. x d. CLERICO marescalcie per manus Johannis 20 Norbyre pro baytynge equorum domini apud Pulerich, xiij d. Et per manus Johannis Rede pro feno, pane equino, et auenis ab ipso emptis apud Sleford, vj d. SUPER officio scutellerie, per manus Roberti Spaigne pro focali, sale, ouis et herbis, xij d. CLERICO marescalcie per manus Johannis Syde pro baytynge j maler domini 25 de Rooston vsque Lincoln ad diuersa loca, x d. Et per manus Roberti Chalons pro expensis iij equorum domini existentium apud Lincoln per ij dies et ij noctes, pro feno, littera, pane equino, et auenis, per compotum cum eodem factum, xvij d. Et pro baytyng equi domini de Peturburgh vsque Lincoln, vj d. CLERICO buterie 30 super vino, pro j galone vini cariando cum domino de Rooston vsque Huntyngdon, x d. CLERICO marescalcie per manus eiusdem pro expensis equi domini apud Melton per j noctem, viz. in feno, littera, pane equino, et auenis, vij d. ob. Et per manus Thome Osteler pro

Summa pagine lxxiiij s. xj d.

fo. 11 v°.

expensis j hakenay conducti pro Stanoley per idem, iij d. JOHANNI
Norbury pro j arcu per ipsum empto pro domino apud Newark et
dato domino Duce patre domini, vj s. viij d. Eidem pro tot denariis
per ipsum liberatis domino pro lusu suo ad talos apud Leycesteriam,
5 nunciante Camerario, xiij s. iiij d. Domino Willelmo Wyluby pro
conductione ij equorum de Bronn vsque Lincoln pro domino, vna cum
expensis domini et baytynge equorum per viam de Brun et apud Lincoln
per j noctem, x s. NICHOLAO de Camera pro elemosinis domini
distributis per diuersas vices ad diuersa loca, xij d. CLERICO mares-
10 calcie per manus Roberti Chalons pro baytynge ij equorum domini
de Ketilthorpe vsque Kenillworth et deinde vsque Bolyngbroke, vna
cum ferrura equorum domini per idem tempus, xj d. Et per manus
Johannis Syde pro baytynge vnius maler et pro ferrura ciusdem,
vna cum locione pannorum lineorum domini per idem tempus, xvj d.
15 Clerico marescalcie per manus Nicholai Osteler pro expensis xj
equorum domini existentium apud Newark, et expectanti dominum ibidem per ij dies et ij noctes, viz. in feno, littura, auenis et
pane equino, vna cum ferrura dictorum equorum per idem tempus,
per compotum cum eisdem factum ibidem, viij s. x d. Et per manus
20 Johannis Peke pro expensis dictorum equorum existentium apud
Melton per j noctem, pro feno, littura, auenis, pane equino per compotum cum eodem factum, iij s. viij d. Et per manus Willelmi
Hosteler de Lincoln̄ pro expensis viij equorum domini existentium
apud Lincoln̄ per j noctem, videlicet in feno, litura, auenis, pane
25 equino, per compotum cum eodem factum ibidem, iij s. vj d. Et per
[manus] magistri Willelmi Cook pro conductione vnius equi de
Kenillworth vsque Bolyngbrok vna cum expensis hominis sui, nunciante camerario, v s. DOMINO pro conductione equorum pro se et
parte familie sue, de Donere vsque Londoñ, xiij s. iiij d. CLERICO
30 panetrie pro expensis domini et partis familie existentium apud
Leycesteriam post recessum domini Ducis Lancastrie patris domini;
viz., pro pane albo, viij d. Et in diuersis piscibus, salmon, stoks,
welkes et aliis, iiij s. viij d. Et in butiro, ouis, fabis et poudre
de gynger, xij d. Et in vadiis Willelmi Harpedeñ per iij

Summa paginæ
cliij s. iij d. ob.

fo. 12.

dies, per diem ij d., vj d. Et pro conductione j equi de Ley-
cestria vsque Boston pro cariagio necessarie pulletrie, viij d.
/ CLERICO panetrie per manus Th. Mylner pro pane albo ab ipso
empto apud Leycestriam per idem tempus, xj d. CLERICO buterie super seruisia, per manus Margerie Clasenwryght pro ix
galonibus seruisie ab ipsa emptis ibidem, xiij d. ob. Et eidem [pro]
ciphis ab ipsa emptis, iiij d. CLERICO speciarie per manus Thome
Wakfeld pro pipere, croco, gynger ab ipso emptis ibidem, xij d.
Et per manus Nicholai Channdeler pro j lb. j qrt. cere ab ipso
emptis ibidem, una cum emptione j lb. candelarum cepi, x d. ob.
CLERICO coquine per manus Willelmi Alstrey pro j carcoisio di.
multonum ab ipso emptis ibidem, ij s. vj d. Et eidem pro carne
boum ab eodem empta, viij d. SUPER oficio pulleterie, per manus
eiusdem pro vij pulcinis ab eodem emptis, x d. Et eidem pro herbis
et farina ab ipso emptis ibidem, j d. Et eidem pro ij caponibus ab
ipso emptis, viij d. CLERICO marescalcie per manus Gyseley pro
auenis ab ipso emptis ibidem, xx d. Super officio scutellarie, per
manus Johannis Grene pro fabis ab ipso emptis, ij d. CLERICO
Garderobe per manus Henrici Dauentre pro j par' ocrearum ab
ipso empto pro domino, iij s. iiij d. CLERICO marescalcie per
manus Giseley pro feno per ipsum empto pro v equis domini ibidem
per j noctem, vij d.

EXPENSE[a] partis consilij domini expectantis dominum apud Leycestriam per v dies vnacum expensis xj equorum domini; videlicet:— CLERICO panetrie per manus Thome Baker pro pane albo ab
ipso [empto] ibidem, ij s. iiij d. CLERICO buterie super seruisia, per
manus Johannis Gyseley pro xxiiij galonibus seruisie ab ipso emptis
ibidem, iij s. iiij d. Clerico buterie super vino, per manus Willelmi
Ympyngham pro ix galonibus et di. vini ab ipso emptis ibidem, ix s. vj d.
CLERICO coquine per manus diuersorum pro carne boum ouium
et vitulorum ab eisdem empta, vnacum diuersis piscibus ab eisdem
emptis per compotum cum eisdem factum ibidem, vij s viij d. ob.

10

15

20

25

30

* These paragraphs are not in the original, where the items all run on. I intro-
duce them for the sake of separation.

SUPER officio pulleterie, per manus Gyseley pro ij caponibus, ij aucis, vj pulcinis, ij s. j d., et pro farina ab ipso empta, ij d. ob. CLERICO speciarie per manus eiusdem pro croco, pipere, et gynger, per ipsum emptis, xij d. CLERICO marescalcie per manus Gyseley pro
5 feno, litura, et pane equino, iiij s. ij d. SUPER officio scutellarie, per manus eiusdem pro sinapi ab ipso empto, ij d. Et per manus Gyseley pro focali per ipsum empto ibidem, xij d. CLERICO marescalcie per manus eiusdem pro v qrt. ij bz. auenarum, precium qrt. iij s., xv s. ix d. Et per manus Johannis Ferrour pro ferrura
10 equorum domini ibidem, xix d. Et per manus Johannis Sadeler pro emendacione diuersarum sellarum domini ibidem, xij d. CLERICO garderobe per manus Gyseley pro j lb. candelarum cepi ab ipso empta, j d. ob.

EXPENSE^a thesaurarii venientis cum thesauro domini de Kenill-
15 worth vsque Londoñ pro excambio ibidem faciendo de florenis Arogonie apud Southam, pro se et familia domini in pane, seruisia, pane equino pro ij somers domini cariantibus dictum thesaurum, vj d. ob. CLERICO panetrie per manus Gylder pro pane albo, vino, seruisia, carne et ij pullettis, xxij d. per ipsum emptis apud Tou-
20 cestre. ET pro pane equino et feno pro ij somers, v d. ob. et pro pane empto apud Stratford, ij d. et pro iiij galonibus sernisie, vj d., in toto xiij d. ob. ET super officio pulletrie pro ij pullettis, iij d., pro carne multonum et vitulorum, x d.; pro croco, ob.; pro busca, j d.; pro farina auenarum, ob.; pro candelis cepi, j d.; pro feno,
25 iiij d.; pro ij bz. j pecco auenarum, xiij d. ob.; in toto iij s. ij d. ob. Clerico panetrie per manus Johannis Gylder pro pane, seruisia, carne, busca, et croco per ipsum emptis apud Dunstaple, xix d. ob. Et in pane equino et feno emptis ibidem, iiij d. ob. Clerico panetrie per manus eiusdem pro pane, ij d., pro vino, iiij d., et seruisia, vj d.;
30 pro carne boum, et multonum, viij d.; pro j capone, iiij d.; pro poudre, j d., pro farina auenarum, ob.; pro busca, j d., pro candelis cepi, j d., pro feno, iij d. ob., pro ij bz. auenarum, xij d., pro pane equino, iij d., per ipsum emptis apud Seynt Alboñ, in toto iij s. x d. Clerico panetrie per manus Johannis Gylder pro pane, seruisia, et

pane equino per ipsum emptis apud Barnett, v d. ob. CLERICO
marescalcie per manus Johannis Smyth apud Dunstaple pro ferris
equorum domini ab ipso emptis ibidem, vij d ob.

    Summa pagine lxxviij s. iiij d.

Summa omnium parcellarum in vij foliis precedentibus vsque 5
huc   Dxiij li. vj s. ij d. ob.
Inde pro vino empto pro providenciis viagii per manus Payn
butellarii   Cxxvij li. iiij s. viij d.
Et in frumento empto pro predictis providenciis, xxix li. xvj d.
Et in donis datis per diuersas vices in diuersis parcellis. 10
Et in equis, aula, vessellamentis emptis per diuersas vices.
Et in expensis hospicii familie domini cum aliis minutis neccessariis.

GARDEROBA IN ANGLIA, PER MANUS LOUENAY.

/ Super officio garderobe, per manus Willelmi Louenay pro iiij^{xx} 15
arcubus per ipsum emptis ad xij d., iiij li.; pro vj arcubus latis, xij s.;
pro canabo empto pro trussura corundem, iij s., et pro j casula mezal
empta pro trussura iiij garbarum sagittarum latarum, xvj d.; et pro
j pare sengles corei de Hungaria cum plustula pro trussura predictorum arcuum, xviij d.; pro canabo empto pro j housia j palfredi 20
xiij d. per ipsum empto apud London (in toto iiij li xviiij s. xj d.*)
ET per manus Henrici Pontfreit pro j sella cum j freno ab ipso
emptis ibidem ad dandum Regi Francie, vj li. xiij s. iiij d. ET per
manus Ricardi Sadeler pro j cella noua empta pro j palfrey ad
dandum domino de Seynpe de Fraunce, lvj s. xiij d. Cuidam 25
aurifabro de Caleys pro j signeto auri ab ipso empto, vna cum factura
eiusdem signeti et engraue cum j plume et j coler, xxviij s. ET
per manus Willelmi Louenay pro iij virgis taffate per ipsum emptis
apud Caleys pro pensels lancearum domini, virga ad x d., ij s vj d.;
et pro iij virgis taffate de blodeo, emptis in grosso pro portatoribus 30

corumdem pensellorum, ij s iiij d.; et pro j vncia di. frengie stricte
albe et blodee empta pro eisdem, iij s iiij d , in toto viij s. ij d. Et
per manus Johannis Dounton pro emendatione gladii domini apud
Caleys, iiij d. Et per manus Willelmi Louenay pro factura unius
5 goune longe auri de Cypre ibidem, iij s. iiij d., et pro furratura dicte
goune, ij s., in toto, v s. iiij d. Et per manus Willelmi Louenay pro
factura j goune pro Hans Stedeman, nunciante camerario, xiiij d.
Cuidam sissori de Caleys pro factura unius goune pro domino
ibidem, xviij d. Johanni Dounton pro j gros poyntes, iij s.; pro
10 j pelle caprino, xvj d.; pro j pelle ovis, vj d.; pro iiij^e clauis
paruis, xiiij d.; pro j pare de thourkeys, xij d.; pro j pelle nigro pro
scabards, x d.; et pro ij chesett pro trencher harnes, vj d., per ipsum
emptis apud London, in toto viij s. iiij d. Johanni Cle de Londoñ
pro vj pannis ab ipso emptis apud Londoñ, lj li. vj s. viij d ; et pro
15 ix vlnis Westnall ad vij d. emptis pro trussura dictorum pannorum,
v s. iij d.; et pro vj vlnis cannevas, le vlna ad v d., ij s. vj d.; et
pro pakkyng dictorum pannorum, vj d. Et pro j corde empta pro
eisdem, ij s. iiij d.; ab ipso emptis ibidem per compotum secum
factum ibidem, in toto, lj li. xvij s. iij d. Et pro certis pannis
20 emptis per manus Willelmi Louenay apud Londoñ pro scutiferis
et valettis domini pro viagio versus Barbariam, per compotum secum
factum ibidem, xxix li. vj s. x d. Et Johanni Walker pro expensis
ipsius et equi sui de London apud Boston, iij s. iiij d. Et liberate
domino apud Caleys pro lusibus suis ibidem, v flor. et di., vz. xiiij s.
25 viij d. Eidem apud London in domo Orwell extra Bysshopsgate,
xiij s. iiij d. Item liberati domino pro lusibus suis ad tales in naui
versus Pruciam, xxxiij s. iiij d. Eidem quando exiuit de naui versus
terram in Prucia, xl s. Et liberati domino Petro Buctoñ pro conduccione iij equorum de Fosshediche vsque Boston super negocio
30 domini ex precepto patris sui, ij s.; et pro conduccione iij equorum
de Bostoñ vsque Lincolñ et redeunte, ex precepto eiusdem, iiij s.; et
pro passagio apud le Wusshe, xij d : et pro conduccione unius equi
de Bostoñ vsque Hulle, xij d. Et pro conduccione iij equorum de
Bostoñ vsque Lincolñ et redeunte, iiij s. vj d.; et pro passagio et

repassa*gio* de Humbre, ij s. Et liberati a le Trumpet per *manus* eiusdem, ij s., in tot*o*, xvj s. vj d.

Sum*m*a to*talis* Garderobe ciiij li. vij s.

BATILLAG*IUM* CU*M* CONDUCT*IONE* NA*V*IU*M* PE*R* DI*V*E*R*S*AS* VICES INTER CALEYS ET DOU*ERE* ET PRO VIAG*IO* 5 VERSUS PRUC*IAM*.

[fo. 13.
[fo. 13 v°.
blank]ᵃ.

/ Bosse pr*o* batill*agio* domini et p*artis* famili*e* sue int*er* Dou*e*re et Caleys, p*er* ij vices, vj li. vj s. viij d. Eidem pro batill*agio* militu*m*, scuti*ferorum*, et sagitt*ariorum* in redeu*ndo* vsque Douere, 1 s. Saundre Kyleys pr*o* batill*agio* equoru*m* domini de Douere vsque 10 Caleys, lxxiij s. iiij d. Eidem pro batill*agio* xj equoru*m* scut*iferorum* d*o*mini, xxij s. ij d. Richard Barge pr*o* batill*agio* equoru*m* militu*m* et scut*iferorum* int*er* Douere et Caleys, lxxj s. iiij d. Eid*e*m pro batill*agio* x equoru*m* Johan*nis* ap Herry et sociorum suoru*m*, nunci*ante* camerario, xlij s. vj d. Petro Dounce pr*o* batill*agio* 15 equoru*m* int*er* Douere et Caleys, lxv s. iiij d. Willelmo Sparr pr*o* batill*agio* equoru*m* senescalli et alioru*m* int*er* Douere et Caleys, lxiij s. iiij d. Eidem pr*o* batill*agio* d*o*mini et p*artis* familie sue int*er* Caleys et Douere, vna cu*m* iiij s. vj d. dat*is* eidem pro j caban fact*a* pr*o* domino, lxxviij s. x d. Eidem pr*o* batill*agio* equoru*m* 20 domini et officiarior*um* suoru*m* int*er* Caleys et Douere, lxx s. Johan*ni* Bode pr*o* batill*agio* equoru*m* int*er* Douere et Caleys, xlvj s. viij d. Eidem pr*o* batill*agio* equoru*m* int*er* Caleys et Douere, xliiij s. v d. Johan*ni* Bate pr*o* batill*agio* equoru*m* int*er* Douere et Caleys, lxj s. iiij d. Thome Retfuwe pr*o* batill*agio* equo- 25 ru*m* int*er* Douere et Caleys, xlvj s. viij d. Wyslake pr*o* batill*agio*

ᵃ On the blank however was written an item, afterwards crossed through, "q*ui*a in al*ia* p*ar*te folii," and is in fact the last on the leaf. But it is more detailed here.
ᵇ Will*i*elmo Hauer eunte de London vsq*ue* Wodestok ad prosequendu*m* d*o*m*i*no Thome Percy pr*o* skipp*agio* domino de Douere vsq*ue* Cales*iam* pro expensis suis et pro conduct*ione* j equi p*er* iiij dies, iij s. iiij d."

BOAT HIRE AND EXPENSES. 37

equorum inter Douere et Caleys per ij vices, iiij li. ix s. j d. Petro
Jonson pro batillagio Ric. Cato de Douere vsque Caleys, xx s.
Willelmo Hoges pro batillagio xxxij equorum de Caleys vsque
Douere, xlj s. ij d. Johanni Page pro batillagio harnesii domini
5 et equorum scutiferorum, lxviij s. x d. Johanni Marschall pro
pontagio apud Douere in primo aduentu domini versus Calesiam,
xiij s. iiij d. Thome Kent pro portagio ibidem, vj s. viij d. Johanni de Sandewych pro batillagio harnesii domini, v s. Et pro
portagio harnesii et famulorum domini de villa ad nauem, iij s. iiij d.
10 In elemosynis datis pro lumine Sancti Nicholai in naui per
manus Ricardi Dancastre, xx d.; pro pountagio apud Caleys in
primo aduentu domini ibidem et in recessu suo versus Douere, xx s.
Et pro batillagio et portagio harnesii domini ibidem in primo
aduentu ipsius, vj s. viij d. Et pro batillagio in recessu suo versus
15 Douere et portagio harnesiorum diuersorum, vna cum familia sua,
v s. viij d. In elemosynis datis pro lumine Sancti Nicholai in
redeundo de Calesia vsque Douere, per manus domini Hugonis Herle,
xx d. Item apud Douere, in batillagio domini harnesii et familie
sue, vj s. viij d ; et pro pountagio, x s.; et pro portagio, vj s. viij d.
20 Et in cariagio hernesii Senescalli Staneley et sociorum suorum
apud Caleys, vj s. viij d. Item Herman, skypper de Dansk, pro
skippagio domini et partis familie sue de Boston vsque Dansk,
xxvj li. Et Hankyn, skypper, pro skyppagio senescalli, partis
familie domini, et diuersorum harnesiorum, xiij li. Et ij[bus] lodesmen
25 conductis pro eadem naui de Boston vsque Dansk, iiij li. Et iij[bus]
lodesmen conductis pro naui domini de Boston vsque Dansk, vij li.
Et Hankyn Brome pro skyppagio domini Johannis Ecton, militis,
les Thrumpers[a] Henrici Mansell. et Morley, vj li xiij s. iiij d. Et
pro diuersis batellis conductis ad towandum nauem domini de portu
30 apud Boston vsque Chopchire, xlvj s. viij d. Et pro batillagio
diuersorum hernesiorum in festo Sancte Margarie de portu vsque   July 20.

---

* Thrumps in original. Trumpours or trumpers is the word used in these accounts,
for our modern trumpeters.

Chopchyr.. v s. Et pro ij^{bus} carect*is* conduct*is* de Boston vsque Chopchyr cu*m* pane et al*iis* victual*ibus* eodem die, vna cu*m* diu*ersis* harnes*iis*, viij s. Willelmo Hauer pro conduct*ione* eq*uorum*, eunte pro batillag*io* de Caleys ut extra, iij s. iiij d.

Su*m*ma *totalis* Batillag*ii*, Cxviij li. xij s.   5

EXPENSE HOSPICII CUM PROVIDENCIIS FACT*IS* P*R*O LE REYS CU*M* BATILLAG*IO* ET CARIAG*IO* ET CUST*UBUS* DE PRAMES.*

PRUCIA.

fo. 14. /In expens*is* Roberti Waterton, Thome Toty, et Johannis Payn, missor*um* de dom*i*no de naui versus Lebe, cum conduccione ij 10 carect*arum* de ibidem vsque Dansk, xxvj s. viij d. st. Et in expens*is* domini cum parte famili*e* sue apud vnum paruum villagi*um* iuxta le Ross heuid, ad primum aduent*um* suum ad terram in Pruci*a*, per manus Ricardi Dancastr., iij s. iiij d. st. Et in iij carect*is* conduct*is* pro domino et parte famili*e* sue de ibidem 15 usque Pusk, x s. st. Item in expens*is* domini et part*is* famili*e* sue apud Pusk per manus ejusdem, vj s. viij d. st. Et pro v carect*is* conduct*is* de ibidem vsque Dansk pro domino et parte famili*e* sue, xvj s. viij d. st. Et in expens*is* domini apud quoddam molendinum
augst 2. vbi dominus pernoctauit in vigili*a* Sancti Laurencii, viij s. iiij d. st. 20 Et pro j equo empto pro domino, cum j sella, de j Pruci*ano* apud Pusk, xx s. Et in expens*is* camerarii, thesaurarii, Swynford et aliorum diuersorum officiariorum et part*is* famili*e* domini, qu*an*do venerunt primo ad terram, iuxta le Roos hed in j paruo villag*io*, in pan*e*, beer, mede, pisc*ibus* et busca, v s. viij d. st. Item pro con- 25 duct*ione* j equi de ibidem vsque Pusk pro harnesio domini carian*do*, xvj scot.^b Et pro conduct*ione* ij carect*arum* de Weste vsque Pusk,

---

* This title stands in the margin in the MS., and is so continued, prefaced by the word "adhuc," on the margin of many leaves like a running title.

^b This is the first item for which foreign money is mentioned.

EXPENSES IN PRUSSIA. 39

xxij scotz. Et pro conductione iij carectarum de Pusk vsque
Dansk pro eisdem, lxiij scot. Et in pane, beer, caseo et ouis apud
Pusk, xij s. pr.* Et in expensis thesaurarii, camerarii, et partis   *[Pr. stans
familie domini in j paruo villagio vbi pernoctarunt, xvj scotz. Et   *Pruciani.*]*
5 pro batillagio domini de naui vsque terram, xiij s. iiij d. st. Et pro
batillagio camerarii, thesaurarii et partis familie domini, xiij s.
iiij d. st. Et pro expensis Radulphi Stancley et sociorum suorum
de mari usque Dansk, et pro conductione equorum vna cum les
pipers, xj s. st. CLERICO panetrie pro pane albo empto apud Dansk
10 per manus diuersorum pistorum, iij marc xvij scot. CLERICO
buterie super vinum pro ollis luteis emptis ibidem, v scot. Et
cuidam tauerner de Dansk pro xxiiij stopis vini expenditis per
dominum apud hospicium domini de Burser, j marc. st. Et eidem
pro cccij stopis vini emptis per manus Johannis Payn, et expensis
15 in hospicio domini ibidem per tempus predictum, le stopa j scot, in
toto xij marc. xiiij scot. CLERICO panetrie pro pane albo empto
apud Dansk per manus Johannis Payn pro tempore quo stetit
dominus ibidem, xxxj s. en.ᵃ CLERICO buterie per manus eiusdem
pro vj barellis de bere per ipsum emptis, le barellus iij s. vj d. en; in
20 toto xxj s. en. Et eidem per manus eiusdem pro ij barellis de
methe, ij marc v scot. CLERICO coquine per manus magistri
Willelmi Cook pro diuersis victualibus per ipsum emptis in festo   August 10.
Sancti Laurencii, xiij s. iiij d. en. SUPER officio pulleterie per
manus Willelmi Harpeden pro iijC ouorum, xviij s. pr.; et eidem pro
25 j pecca farine auenarum, iij d. en.; et eidem pro butiro et lacte, vj d.
en.; et eidem pro sepis, j d. en. CLERICO speciarie pro xj lb. candelarum cepi emptis ibidem tempore predicto, xiiij s. pr. CLERICO
coquine per manus diuersorum, pro ij carcoisiis boum ab ipsis emptis
apud Dansk, lxxiiij scot. Et per manus eorundem pro xij
30 carcoisiis ᵇ multonum ab ipsis emptis ibidem, cix scot. Et pro

  ᵃ This contraction, used but a few times, can only mean *English;* the scribe
perhaps misgave the familiar *sterling* at first while writing both foreign and English money. It was however soon resumed, *en* hardly occurs again.
  ᵇ This is "casis" in the MS., but carcoisiis seems intended.

Summa paginæ x li.
viiij d. st., et in
monete Pruciane
xxxvij marc. vj scot.
xx d. pr., que faciunt
monete Anglice
xj li. ix s. iiij d. ob.

fo. 14 v°.

August 11.

August 12.

August 13.

portagio diuersorum victualium ibidem, vij s. iiij d. pr. ET
CLERICO marescalcie per manus Hankyn Ferrour pro ferrura
equorum domini ibidem, viij s. pr. ET CLERICO coquine
per manus Hankyn Fyssher pro piscibus recentibus ab ipso
emptis ibidem, iiij marc. iij s. xxij d. pr. Et pro conductione 5
j vnius equi de Dansk vsque Maryngburgh pro Lancastria le heraud
portante litteras domini Ducis Lancastrie vsque Magistrum Prucie,[a]
vj s. viij d. st. CLERICO coquine per manus Willelmi Harpeden,
xj die Augusti ibidem, pro iij duodenis gallinarum, vj s. st. Et eidem
pro v duodenis pulcinorum, v s. iij d. en. Et per manus eiusdem pro 10
iij capriolis, xxx s. pr. Et per manus eiusdem, xij die eiusdem mensis, pro iijC ouorum, xviij s. pr.; et pro sepi et lacte, ij d. en.; et
eodem di. pro pisis, iiij d. en.; Et pro ijC ouorum xij s. pr. Et xiij°
die pro butiro, lacte, et creem, xvij d. en. CLERICO marescalcie pro
auenis ibidem emptis pro equis domini per manus Thome Swylyng- 15
ton, ix s. st. Et pro prandio Thesaurarii et aliorum officiariorum
ibidem dimissorum aretro dominum xiij° die Aug., ij s. en.
INCERSIS carpentariis pro emendacione del prames cariantum victu
alia domini de Dansk vsque Conyngburgh, per vij dies., x marc.
pr. xiij scot. Et pro lx deles emptis per Johannem Trepeland pro 20
prames cooperandis, le piece ad ij scot., in toto v marc. pr. JOHANNI
de Pusk pro xlvj deles emptis per manus Johannis Bener pro dictis
prames, le piece ij scot., iij marc. pr. xx scot. Et eidem pro clauis
emptis pro eisdem, j marc. di. pr. Et per manus eiusdem pro lignis
per ipsum emptis pro eisdem prames, xxj scot. Et pro iiij ankeres 25
conductis per xv dies per Jacobum Poppyn, ij marc. pr. Et pro
ij ankeres per manus eiusdem conductis per xj septimanas, v marc.
pr. di. Et pro vj seyles pro dictis prames per xv dies, i marc. di
pr. Et pro conductione de ij seyles per ix septimanas en le
Reys, per manus eiusdem, iiij marc. di. pr. Et pro v ropes 30
magnis et v lynes parvis pro les ankeres et seyles emptis per
manus eiusdem, iiij marc. xix scot. Et pro ij ropes magnis emptis

[a] The Grand Master Conrad Zölner von Rotenstein, who died August 20, 1390. [P.]

EXPENSES IN PRUSSIA.

de Bast per manus ciusdem, xxj s. pr. Et pro meremio empto
per manus ciusdem pro dictis prames faciendis, ij marc. vij scot.
pr. Et per manus ciusdem pro clauis per ipsum emptis pro dictis
prames, j marc. xv scot. viij d. pr. Et per manus ciusdem pro
5 pakthred per ipsum empto, iij s. pr. Et Nicholao Sprank, carpentario, pro pixe, tar et lini per ipsum emptis, et pro stipendio suo
operante in les prames per iij dies, per compotum secum factum, in
toto j marc. vij scot. JOHANNI Beuer pro vij carucis nouis per
ipsum emptis apud Dansk pur le Reys, le piece j marc. x scot, in
10 toto ix marc. xxij scot. Et pro portagio corundem ad les prames,
xij scot. Et pro portagio meremii et les deles ad les prames, xxj
scot. MARTINO DE LAKE pro iij^{bus} capistris et aliis hernesiis de
ipso emptis pro equis tractandis in dictis carucis, iij marc. di. v scot.
HANKYN SCONFELD pro tar et pixide ad imponendum dictum tar,
15 ab ipso emptis ibidem, pro dictis carucis, xvij scot. JACOBO
SAMLAND pro diuersis ferris operatis ab ipso emptis ibidem, pro
dictis carucis, iij marc. xiiij scot. CUIDAM mulieri comoranti juxta
hospicium domini, pro coquina ab ipsa conducta ibidem, pro tempore quo dominus stetit ibidem, iiij marc. pr. Et hospitisse domini
20 ibidem pro belechere pro tempore quo dominus stetit ibidem, x marc.
pr. Et seruientibus ipsius ex precepto senescalli, j marc. pr.
CUIDAM homini vocato Glouekyn pro mattis ab ipso emptis pro
cooperatione prames pro saluacione victualium domini, per manus
Johannis Payn, xiiij scot. iij d. pr. Et per manus ciusdem pro
25 fructibus per ipsum emptis ibidem, xiij s. pr. Et pro ij carucis
conductis pro cariagio diuersorum cofres thesauri domini et
armature sue, iij s. iiij d. st. Et pro ij batellis* conductis pro
cariagio hernesii de Wyslee vsque rypam ibidem, vj s. viij d.
/ HERMAN Baker et diuersis pistoribus pro† pane vocato bysquyte
30 ab ipsis emptis ibidem, per manus Johannis Beuer, v marc.
vij scot. Et pro diuersis barellis emptis per manus diuersorum
pro dicto pane imponendo, viij scot. HANS Couper pro barelhedes
et pro imposicione corundem in dictos barellos, v scot. Et portagio dicti panis, vj scot. CLERICO speciarie per manus Johannis

Summa pagine
x d. et monete
ciane iiij^{xx} j. n
xix scot. viij. d
faciunt Anglie
xxv li. iij s. iiij
q·.

fo. 15.

* MS. has *pat*
† The MS. ha

Whytyk pro diuersis speciebus ab ipso emptis apud Dansk, x marc.
di. ij scot. xx d. pr. Et per manus eiusdem pro zinzibero empto
ibidem, v marc. xv scot. ET CLERICO coquine per manus eiusdem
pro salmone, wyche et anguillis salsis ab ipso emptis ibidem, xl
marc. xiij scot. Et pro ixC stokfissh ab ipso emptis ibidem, xj 5
marc. xiij scot. CLERICO speciarie pro cannevas per ipsum empto
ibidem, xxij scot. SUPER officii scutellarie, pro j besage per
manus eiusdem empto ibidem, iij s. st. Et pro portagio dictarum
piscium ad les prames, v scot. GYS FARREWYK pro ij barellis
anguillarum salsarum ab ipso emptis ibidem per manus Johannis 10
Wytyk, iiij marc. pr. ET pro portagio diuersi hernesii domini
de rypa vsque hospicium domini, iij s. iiij d. st. JACOBO CREMER
pro ij barellis de sturion ab ipso emptis ibidem, per manus
Johannis Trepeland, viij marc. viij scot. Et eidem Jacobo pro
xij bacons et j barello de sale ab ipso emptis ibidem, viij marc. 15
xv scot. JOHANNI Beuer pro xij bacons per ipsum emptis ibidem,
et pro ij barellis carnis salse, ix marc. viij scot. JACOBO HERMAN
pro x bacons et iiij barellis carnis salse ab ipso emptis ibidem, per
manus Jacobi Poppyn, xiij marc. xj scot. iij s. pr. Et Hans
Baker pro iiij flykkes ab ipso emptis ibidem, per manus Johannis 20
Payn, iij marc. pr. HANKYN Harghdych pro ix bacons ab
ipso emptis ibidem, per manus Johannis Trepeland, v marc vj
scot. Et Herman Baker pro pane albo ab ipso empto ibidem,
pro diuersis seruientibus domini existentibus in les prames ad
custodiendum victualia et hernesia domini de Dansk vsque 25
Conyngsburgh, xiiij scot. Et pro carne recenti pro ipsis empta
ibidem et aliis victualibus, iiij s. vj d. st. CLERICO buterie
super vino, per manus Johannis Payn pro j dolio vini Renyss
continente vij aunz di. per ipsum empto apud Dansk, x li. st. Et
eidem pro j dolio albi vini Renyss, continente iiij aunz. di, vj li. 30
xiij s. iiij d. Et eidem pro j dolio vini de Osey similiter per ipsum
empto ibidem, x li. st. Et pro carecta conducta ad cariandum
dictum vinum de celario domini apud Dansk vsque aquam, et de
aqua vsque Conyngsburgh, di. marc. pr. Diuersis laborantibus et

EXPENSES IN PRUSSIA. 43

adiuuantibus ad carectandum dictum vinum, di. marc. pr. Et cuidam
couper conducto ad flandum dicta ij dolia, pro quolibet dolio x s.
pr., in toto xx s. pr. Et cuidam naute pro cariagio xviij doliorum
vini de Dansk vsque Conyngburgh, ex conuencione facta cum eodem
5 in parte solucionis xj marc. pr., ij marc. pr. Diuersis hominibus
de Dansk pro vj^{xx} barellis de bere ab ipsis emptis ibidem, precium
le barellus di. marc. pr., plus in toto viij scot., lx marc. viij
scot. Cuidam homini de Dansk pro xxiiij barellis de meed ab
ipso emptis ibidem in grosso, xxvj marc. di. pr. Diuersis
10 carectariis pro cariagio dicte bere et meed de loco vbi emebatur
vsque portum apud Dansk, ij marc. di. pr. Et Johanni Payn
pro j dolio vini Renys, continente ij aunz. di. per ipsum empto
ibidem, viij marc. di. pr. Cuidam portanti vinum de villa ibidem
vsque hospicium domini, v s. pr. Cuidam couper pro emendacione
15 dictorum doliorum de bere et mede ex conuencione facta cum
eodem, di. marc. pr. CUIDAM naute pro factura des plaunches
/ in naui vbi supra dictas bere et mede iaceret, iij marc pr. CUIDAM
lotrici de Dansk pro locione mapparum domini pro tempore quo
dominus stetit ibidem, ix s. pr. Et cuidam vocato Gardebrand pro
20 bacons et sale emptis ab ipso ibidem, vj marc. Diuersis hostelers
eo quod homines non soluebant pro expensis suis ibidem, xiij s.
iiij d. st. viij scot. HUGONI Cremeton carectario et xij sociis suis,
cum xiij carectis cariantibus diuersa harnesia, victualia, necessaria
domini, et partem familie domini de Dansk vsque Conyngburgh,
25 quolibet de xij capienti pro se et carecta, xx s. st. vj scot ; et dicto
Hugoni capienti pro se et carecta iiij marc pr., eo quod cariavit
armatura domini per compotum cum eis factum, in toto in moneta
Anglica, xiiij li st. xij scot. CUIDAM pictori pro j scuto empto pro
domino ibidem per manus Roberti Waterton, x scot. Et per
30 manus eiusdem pro j sacco correo per ipsum empto ibidem pro
ferris equinis cariandis pro le Reys, vna cum saccis correis emptis
per manus eiusdem [a] ibidem pro vexillis domini portandis et custodiendis, xxv scot. Et per manus eiusdem cuidam celario pro j

---

[a] The MS. has empt, here again, but it seems to be an error for eiusdem.

44 THE EARL OF DERBY'S EXPEDITIONS.

malesadell ab eodem empta ibidem pro harnesio domini cariando, j marc. di. pr. Et pro j freno per ipsum empto ibidem pro dicto male sadell, viij scot.

Et pro batillagio domini, equorum suorum, et tocius exercitus sui apud aquam juxta Dansk, vj s viij d. st. JOHANNI Payn apud 5 Schonebergh in pane albo per ipsum empto ibidem, xj scot. Et eidem pro j barello de bere per ipsum empto ibidem, di. marc. pr. ET clerico coquine per manus Hankyn Fyssher pro piscibus recentibus per ipsum emptis ibidem, j marc. pr. CLERICO marescalcie per manus Johannis Morley pro feno et auenis per ipsum emptis 10 ibidem, xj scot. Hospiti domini ibidem pro belechere, di. marc. pr. JOHANNI Payn pro pane albo per ipsum empto apud Meluyn, xvij scot. Et eidem pro lxxij stopis vini ibidem emptis et expenditis [die] dominica ad prandium, viz. in vigilia Assumptionis Beate Marie, iij marc. pr. Et eidem pro j barello de bere per ipsum 15 empto ibidem, di. marc. pr. Eidem pro fructu empto ibidem pro domino, vj s. pr. CLERICO marescalcie pro feno et auenis ibidem emptis per manus Johannis Morley, xvj scot. Hospiti domini ibidem pro belechere, xxvj s. viij d. st. Et seruientibus suis ex precepto senescalli, di. marc. pr. JOHANNI Payn pro pane albo 20 per ipsum empto eodem die apud Bronesbergh, xvj scot. Eidem pro ij barellis de bere emptis eodem die et in crastino pro prandio domini, j marc. pr. Eidem pro xxv stopis vini per ipsum emptis ibidem, le stopa j scot, in toto xxv scot. Eidem pro cxxvj stopis vini per ipsum emptis ibidem ad cariandum cum domino vsque 25 Brambergh, cxxvj scot. Eidem pro fructu empto ibidem pro domino, iiij s pr. CLERICO marescalcie pro auenis ibidem emptis per manus Johannis Morley, ix scot. Hospiti domini ibidem pro belechere, xiij s. iiij s. st. Et seruientibus ibidem, xx s. pr. Item apud Brambergh pro pane albo per ipsum empto ibidem, xiij scot. 30 Eidem pro ij barellis de bere per ipsum emptis ibidem, j marc. pr. Et pro fructu ibidem empto per manus eiusdem, iiij s. pr. Et pro auenis emptis per manus Johannis Morley, viij scot. Hospiti domini ibidem pro belechere ex precepto senescalli, j marc. di. pr.

August 15.

Et pro batillagio thesaurarii et partis familie domini venientis cum illo de Dansk, vna cum ij carectis cum diuersis harnesiis domini, ij s. st. Et in expensis ipsius apud Schonebergh die sabbati ubi pernoctavit, iiij s. st. Item viij carectariis laborantibus cum domino de Dansk vsque Conyngburgh et reuertentibus vsque Dansk, pro stipendiis suis, cuilibet corum vij, viij scot, et magistro illorum xij scot, in toto ij marc. xx scot. Cuidam armourerio pro emendacione diuersarum armaturarum domini, et pro diuersis necessariis habitis ibidem [apud] Dansk per Johannem Dounton, x s. st. Eidem pro poyntes emptis ibidem, iij s. pr. / CLERICO coquine per manus Willelmi Harpeden pro carne boum, multonum, porcorum, et vitulorum per ipsum empta inter Dansk et Conyngburgh per iij dies, viz. a die dominico in vigilia assumptionis Beate Marie vsque diem Martis ad cenam ibidem, per compotum secum factum ibidem, lxvij s. iiij d. Super officio pulleterie per manus eiusdem pro gallis, pullis, pulcinis, columbellis, capriolis, agnellis, ovis, lacte, pisis, et aliis victualibus tangentibus officium suum per tempus predictum, per ipsum emptis ibidem, per compotum secum factum, v. marc. viij scot. Et pro ferrura equorum domini inter Dansk et Conyngburgh, per manus Johannis Morley, vij scot.

Diuersis pistoribus pro pane albo ab ipsis empto apud Conyngburgh et ibidem expendito per iij dies, per manus Johannis Payn, xlvj s. viij d. st. Et pro pane albo empto ad cariandum cum domino versus Cremeton, xxviij scot. CLERICO buterie per manus Johannis Payn super vino pro CCiiij^{xx} stopis, le stopa xxxij d., ibidem expenditis pro tempore quo dominus stetit ibidem versus le Reys, xij marc. x scot. xx d. pr. CLERICO coquine per manus Willelmi Harpedene pro carne boum, multonum, porcorum, et vitulorum per ipsum empta et expendita ibidem pro tempore quo dominus stetit ibidem, per compotum secum factum ibidem, vna cum emptione piscium recentium et salsorum expenditorum per tempus predictum, xj marc. xviij scot. SUPER officio pulleterie per manus Willelmi Harpeden pro gallis, pullis, pulcinis, columbellis, capriolis, agnellis,

Summa pagine xvij li. xvj s. st monete Prucia xxxvj marc. v j s. pr.; que fac xj li. v. s. viij d qr. st.

fo. 16.

August 14–16.

ouis, lacte, pisis, herbis, et sale et aliis victualibus tangentibus officium suum, per ipsum emptis et expenditis ibidem per tempus predictum, vij marc. **xxiij scot. xviij** d. CLERICO speciarie per manus Ricardi Catour pro diuersis speciebus vna cum cera operata per ipsum emptis et expenditis ibidem, per compotum secum factum ibidem, ij marc. xj scot. CLERICO marescalcie per manus Johannis Morley pro feno et auenis, vna cum ferrura equorum domini ibidem, et pro iiij horscombes, xv scot. ij s. iij d. JOHANNI Payn pro fructu per ipsum empto ibidem pro domino per tempus predictum, xj s. pr. Et lotrici lauanti mappas comensales et alia necessaria domini per idem tempus ibidem, ix s. pr. Hospiti domini ibidem pro belechere pro tempore quo dominus stetit ibidem versus le Reys, lxvj s. viij d. st. Et seruientibus ipsius ibidem, di. marc. pr. SUPER officio garderobe per manus Johannis Dountoñ, pro slypyng gladiorum domini, vna cum vaginis corundem ibidem, x scot., et eidem pro mailez pro plates domini per ipsum emptis ibidem, vj s. viij d. st. Et eidem pro j hous pro le baner et j autre pro le penoñ, xix scot. Et eidem pro j par bowges pro leggharneys domini, iiij scot. Et eidem pro emendacione sirotecarum domini, iiij scot. SUPER officio garderobe, per manus Henrici de camera pro xxiij vlnis panni linei per ipsum emptis ibidem pro domino, le vlna, ij scot., in toto xlvj scot. CLERICO marescalcie per manus Johannis Morley pro j pare styrop., et styrop lethres, viij s. pr.; et per manus eiusdem pro iij panellis nouis pro cursore domino, xx s. pr.; et pro stuffura xj sellarum domini, xj scot. et pro j pare styropp., viij s. pr.: et pro ij capistris et iiij gyrths, xvj s. pr.; et pro iij reynes et iij brase, xij s.; et pro iiij sursengles, x s. pr.; et pro grees pro equis domini, iij s. pr.; in toto j marc. xvij scot. ij s. pr. CLERICO marescalcie per manus Ricardi Catour pro feno et auenis pro les somers domini et iiij equis quos ipse emebat ibidem pro cariagio domini per terram, per compotum secum factum ibidem, iij marc. vj scot. ij d. pr. CLERICO buterie per manus Johannis Payn pro viij doliis vini per ipsum emptis apud Conyngburgh pro le Reys de nouo, eo quod les prames non venerunt ibidem tempestiue, le dolium ij marc.

Summa pagine, ix li.
viij s. iiij d. st., et
monete Prucinne lj
marc. ix. scot. j d.;
que faciunt Anglice,
xv li. xvj s. j d. ob.
st. pr.

fo. 16 v°.

xviij scot, in to*to* xxij marc. Et pro j pipa de Ryneschwyn con-
ti*nente* iij aunez et di. per manus eiusdem empta ibidem, l'aune pro
vj marc., in to*to* xxj marc. Et pro iij barellis vini de Ryn*esch* contin*entibus* ccclxxvj stopas, le stopa xxxiiij d., in to*to* xvij marc.
5 xviij scot. iiij d. pr. Et per manus ejusdem pro ij barellis ferrers,
j de Rynyshwyn continente xxix stopas, precium stope xxxiiij d., in
to*to* j marc. ix scot., iiij d. minus; et l'autre barell contin*ente* xxix
stopas de landewyn, precium stope xxxij d., in to*to*, j marc. vij scot,
ij d. minus. Clerico but*er*ie per manus Ricardi Catour pro iiij
10 lastes cum di. de bere, xij barellis pro le last, et le barellus pro di.
marc. pr., liiij barellis, in to*to* xxvij marc. pr. Clerico buterie per
manus eiusdem pro vj barellis de mede per ipsum emptis ibidem, j
marc., ij scot, in to*to* vj marc. di. CLERICO panetrie per manus
eiusdem pro pane albo et bysquyte et viij barellis de farine frumenti
15 per ipsum emptis ibidem pro dicta Reys, per compotum secum
factum ibidem, xviij marc. ix scot. iij s. CLERICO coquine per
manus eiusdem pro lij bacons per ipsum emptis ibidem pro dicto
viagio, le piece di. marc., in to*to* xxvj marc. Et per manus eiusdem
pro xiiij bou*ibus* per ipsum emptis ibidem pro dicta prouidencia, le
20 piece, iij marc. viij scot., in to*to* xlvj marc. xvj scot. Et per manus
eiusdem pro xxvij multonibus per ipsum emptis ibidem pro dicto
facto, le piece ix scot., in to*to* x marc. xv scot. Et per manus
eiusdem pro flatfyssh, samone et allecibus de Scon, vna cum v
caudis castorum per ipsum emptis ibidem, per compotum secum
25 factum, xxx marc. pr., ij s. iiij d. Et per manus eiusdem pro
j barello de sturion per ipsum empto ibidem, iiij marc. ij scot. Et
per manus eiusdem pro ij barellis de codlyng salso per ipsum
emptis ibidem, iij marc. pr. Et per manus eiusdem pro portagio
dictorum victualium ad les praines, xviij scot. SUPER officio
30 pulleterie, per manus Willelmi Harpeden pro xxx duodenis pullorum
per ipsum emptis ibidem pro le Reys, duodena pro xx d. st., in
to*to* l s. st. Et per manus eiusdem pro xxxijC ouorum per ipsum
emptis ibidem, centena ad xj d. ob. qr., in to*to* xxxj s. iiij d. st.

Et per manus ciusdem pro sep[a] ibidem per ipsum empt. pro dict͞
facto, v s. st. Et per manus ciusdem pro v barellis pisarum albarum
et viridium per ipsum emptis ibidem, le barell. pro xxxiiij d., in
toto, xiiij s. ij d. st. Et per manus ciusdem pro ordeo empto pro
dictis pullis, x s. st. Et pro j somerario empto per manus ciusdem 5
pro officio suo ibidem, xl s. st.[b] Et per manus ciusdem pro ij
girthes ij wayntes et ij hokes pro les paniers pro pullis, ij s. j d. st.
CLERICO marescalcie per manus Ricardi Catour pro Cl shephul
auenarum per ipsum ibidem emptis ad cariandum versus le Reys in
les prames, le shephul ad ij s. pr., in toto v marc. pr. Et pro xxxij 10
sackes per ipsum emptis ibidem pro dictis auenis imponendis, j marc.
viij scot. Et pro ferris equinis per ipsum emptis et clauis pro
equis domini versus le Reys, iiij. marc. x scot. Et pro iij cabul per
ipsum emptis ad tractandum les prames versus le Memele cum
hominibus, v marc. xj scot. Et pro presepibus ouinis in les prames, 15
j marc. di. Et pro ij cages pro pulletria pur le Reys per ipsum
emptis ibidem. j marc. xvj scot. Et pro xij falsibus per ipsum emptis
ibidem pur le Reys, xliiij scot. Et pro xxxvj sygles, le piece pur iij s.,
in toto j marc. xix scot, vj d. pr. Et eidem pro funibus cum quibus
boues ligabantur in pastura per viam, j marc. di. pr. CLERICO scut- 20
ellarie per manus ciusdem pro j dolio butiri empto per manus ciusdem
ibidem, ij marc. di. pr. Et pro ij barellis aceti per ipsum emptis ibidem,
xxij scot. Et per manus ciusdem pro ij barellis salis per ipsum
emptis ibidem, iij marc. Et pro j barello pleno porro[rum] per
ipsum empto ibidem, xxiiij scot. Et pro C casiis per ipsum emptis 25
/ ibidem pro le Reys, iiij marc. pr. Et pro viginti barellis vaccnis
per ipsum emptis ibidem pro diuersis victualibus imponendis, xxvj
scot. Et pro x l. securibus per ipsum emptis ibidem, le piece pro

[a] The word sep' may mean either sepis (for cepis), onions, or sepo (for cepo) tallow, fat. We have a similar item below, " barello pleno porrorum " for 24 scot. Fat may have been used for preserving the eggs, to which there seems reference in the last clause of this somewhat obscure item.

[b] An item is here written and struck out because it occurs in another place.

EXPENSES IN PRUSSIA.   49

viij s. pr., in toto v marc. viij scot. Et pro ij barellis cum pomis et
piris per ipsum emptis ibidem pro le Reys, xv scot. Et pro xxxvj
stopis sinapis per ipsum emptis ibidem pro le Reys, le stopa ad xij d.
pr., in toto xiiij scot. xij d. pr. Et pro portagio dictorum victua-
5   lium ad les prames per diuersos portours, xviij scot. Et cuidam
couper pro emendacione et cooperacione dictorum barellorum pro
victualibus, xiiij scot. Et Hans Prcciano pro fugacione boum et
multonum versus le Reys, cum famulo, et stipendiis suis ibidem,
iiij marc. viij scot. ij s. pr. Et pro expensis viij carectariorum
10 conductorum de Dansk vsque Conyngburgh pro carecta domini, et
redeuntium vsque Dansk, xj scot. Et per manus ciusdem Ricardi
pro iiij equis per ipsum emptis ibidem ad portandum victualia
domini in le Wyldrenesse, viij mare. xx scot. Et pro j barello de
tar per manus ciusdem empto ibidem, viij scot   Hankyn Bocher
15 pro xvj multonibus ab ipso emptis ibidem pro le Reys, le piece viij
scot. di., in toto v marc. xvj scot. Super officio scutellarie, per
manus Roberti Spayn pro farina empta per ipsum tangente officio
suo, x scot. Et Johanni Squyrell pro j tabula comensali cum j
pare tresteles et j tabula pro altari et j longo scabello vna cum scac-
20 cario per ipsum emptis ibidem pro le Reys, xxvj scot. Et Johanni
Dyndon pro panno albo et blodeo ab ipso empto ibidem pro coopertura basenetti domini, vna cum factura ciusdem, vj s. viij d. st.
Johanni Duffeld, pro emptione diuersarum herbarum ibidem
pro tempore quo dominus stetit ibidem, x s. pr. Roberto del Botel-
25 larie pro x l. bykeres per ipsum emptis ibidem, x s. pr.; et pro
emendacione mantice panetrie, iij s. pr.; et pro j pare botels de
tyn per ipsum emptis ibidem, x s. pr.; in toto viij s. scot. iij s. pr.
Ricardo Ducheman famulo domini Thome Erpyngham, eo quod iuit
cum officiario domini de Dansk vsque Conyngburgh pro conductione
30 j equi, et expensis suis ibidem, vj s. viij d. st.; et eidem pro j cappa
de beuere empta pro domino apud Conyngburgh, iij s. iij d., in
toto x s. st. Ricardo Catour pro lx vlnis panni linei per ipsum
emptis ibidem, ad cariandum versus le Reys pro diuersis necessariis, le vlna ad xxvj d. pr., in toto ij marc. iiij scot. Et pro

CAMD. SOC.   H

xx vlnis panni linei, per Henricum de camera emptis ibidem pro
necessariis domini le vlna ad iij s., in toto j marc. pr. Henrico
Samland pro ij tentoriis conductis pro domino versus le Reys,
xiij s. iiij d. st. Et pro diuersis cordis emptis pro les tentes per
manus eiusdem, iij scot. ij s. JOHANNI PAYN pro ij barellis de 5
bere per ipsum emptis apud Cremeton, vbi dominus pernoctauit die
Jouis xviij° die Aug. incipiendo viagio suo versus le Reys, xxiiij
scot. Et pro feno ibidem empto per manus domini Willelmi
Pountfreyt pro lvj equis, xx scot. Et pro xxxiiij shephull auenarum
ab Hugone Cremeton emptis, le shep. j scot., in toto xxxiiij scot. 10
Et eidem pro belechere, xij scot. Et per manus domini Willelmi
P. ex precepto camerarii pro beer per viam, v scot. Et per manus
eiusdem pro expensis exercitus domini, in presencia Burton scutiferi
senescalli, v s. j d. pr. Et in expensis thesaurarii et partis familie
domini, vna cum iij^{bus} somers domini apud Tapiou eadem nocte, 15
vij s. viij d. st. Et pro j magno luce[o] empto ibidem per manus
Ricardi Catour pro prandio domini apud Neuerketon, xij scot.
Et pro j luceo empto ibidem per manus eiusdem, vj scot. Et pro
aliis diuersis piscibus per ipsum ibidem emptis, ij marc. ij
scot. Et per manus eiusdem pro butiro, caseo, et lacte, per 20
ipsum emptis ibidem, ix. scot. j s. pr. ET JOHANNI Payn pro
pane et bere per ipsum emptis ibidem, xlij scot. viij d. Et
pro feno et auenis ibidem emptis pro equis domini ibidem,
j marc. iiij scot. Et hospiti ibidem pro belechere, xij scot. ij s.
/ Andree Strousburgh pro ij equis per ipsum emptis pro cariagio 25
domini in le Wyldrenesse ad portandum victualia, eo quod caruce
non poterunt vlterius transire, vij marc. di pr. Et pro j equo
empto per manus thesaurarii et [Johannis] Norbyre ad portandum
tentoria domini, vna cum j sella cum eo empta ibidem, vj marc. di.
Et per manus Ricardi Catour pro pane, bere, bacon, et auenis per 30
ipsum emptis die lune proximo sequente, in primo aduentu domini
ad Marescallum,[a] pro eo quod les praines non venerunt, iij marc. xv
scot. Et pro ij luces et aliis piscibus emptis per senescallum et

---

[a] Engelhard Rabe, marshal of the Teutonic order.

EXPENSES IN PRUSSIA. 51

Magistrum Willelmum Cook, die mercurii proximo sequente super   August 24.
ripam de le Memele, j marc. v scot. vj d. pr.   Et pro iiij bovibus et
ij multonibus emptis per Nichel Pruceman die Jouis proximo
sequente, vbi dominus iacebat coram Castello de Jorgyngburgh,   August 25.
5 iij marc. xiij scot. ij s. Et pro ij barellis de bere ibidem emptis per
manus eiusdem, j marc. x scot.   Et pro pane, ouis, et pulcinis per
ipsum emptis ibidem, j marc. iij scot.   Et pro iiij luces et aliis piscibus
emptis per manus senescalli et domini Willelmi de Wylughby, die
veneris proximo sequente, ix scot.   Et pro j rete empto ibidem eodem   August 26.
10 die per manus camerarii, di. marc. pr.   Et pro piscibus recentibus
emptis die Sabbati proximo sequente pro thesaurario, Rochford et   August 27.
aliis infirmis dimissis in les prames, vij s. pr.   Et pro iij multonibus vj
gallinis emptis per manus Andree Strousburgh vltra ripam de le   August 28.
Memele die dominico proximo sequente post conflictum Paganorum,
15 xiiij scot. xij d. pr.   Et pro pane et bere per ipsum emptis ibidem,
j marc. ij scot.   Et pro gallinis emptis per manus diuersorum die
Martis, die Mercurii, et die Jouis proximo sequentibus, xxiij s. pr.   Aug. 30, 31, Se[p]
Et Andree Strowsburgh pro pane, farina, et melle, sale, et ouis per
ipsum emptis a v die Sept. vsque xj diem eiusdem apud le Wylle,   September 5-11.
20 iiij marc. v scot.   Et per manus eiusdem pro vj bullokes et iiij
multonibus per ipsum emptis ibidem per tempus predictum, iiij
marc. xvij scot.   Et per manus eiusdem pro gallinis, pulcinis, et aucis
per ipsum emptis ibidem per idem tempus, xvij s. pr.   Et per
manus Nichel Pruceman pro pane, farina, melle, et sale per ipsum
25 emptis ibidem, a xj° die Sept. vsque xxiiij diem eiusdem mensis,   September 11-24
iiij marc. xix scot. ij s. v d. pr.   Et per manus eiusdem pro vij
bullokes et xij multonibus, vna cum ouis, sale, et sepis per ipsum
emptis ibidem per tempus predictum, viij marc. di.   Et per manus
eiusdem pro gallinis et iiij porcellis per ipsum emptis ibidem tempore
30 predicto, xxxij s. pr.   Et pro j vacca empta per thesaurarium pro
lacte habenda* pro domino ibidem, di. marc. pr.   Et pro vij capriolis   [Sic].
per ipsum emptis ibidem, tempore predicto, xxv s. vj d.   Et per
manus Andree Strowsburgh et Nichel Pruceman pro pane, farina,

52   THE EARL OF DERBY'S EXPEDITIONS.

Sept. 25-Oct. 7.

et melle per illos emptis a xxv die Sept. vsque vij^m diem Octobris, vtroque computato, xij marc. di. viij scot   Et eisdem pro xij bullokes et xv multonibus ab ipsis emptis ibidem per tempus predictum, ix marc. xx scot.   Et eisdem pro ouis, caseis, et gallinis; et aucis, porcellis, et capriolis per ipsos emptis ibidem per tempus 5 predictum, iiij marc. xvij scot.   Et Johanni Payn pro nucibus per ipsum emptis ibidem, pro tempore quo dominus stetit ibidem, xiij scot.   Et pro pane empto ibidem per manus eiusdem, j marc. iiij scot., et pro v galonibus mellis per ipsum emptis de j Lettowe ibidem, xviij scot.; pro cera per ipsum empta ibidem per diuersas 10 vices, xix scot.; et pro iij capriolis per ipsum emptis ibidem, vij scot. viij d., in toto iij marc. viij d.   Et per manus senescalli pro pane per ipsum empto ibidem per diuersas vices, ij marc. viij scot. Et pro iiij aucis et xij gallinis per ipsum emptis per diuersas vices ibidem, xiij scot.   Et per manus Camerarii pro pane per ipsum 15 empto ibidem, xxix s. pr.   Et Claus Schoneman, carectario baterie domini, pro pane per ipsum empto ibidem per diuersas vices, vij marc. xxj scot. ij s. pr.   Et per manus eiusdem pro v bullokes et viij multonibus per ipsum emptis ibidem, iij marc. ix scot. ij s. pr.

Summa pagine ciij marc. vj scot. j d. pr.; que faciunt xxxj li. xv s. v d. st.

Et per manus thesaurarii pro pane empto ibidem vna cum j barello 20 de bysquyte, iiij marc. di. xxiiij s. pr.   Et per manus eiusdem pro vj galonibus mellis per ipsum emptis ibidem, xxj scot.

fo. 18.

/ Et per manus eiusdem pro iij bullokes et iij bacons per ipsum emptis ibidem per diuersas vices, iij marc. viij scot.   Johanni Assheby et Thome Knape pro cera ab eis empta per manus domini 25 Willelmi P., xx s. pr.   Et cuidam homini de Lettowe pro ij pueris ab ipso emptis per dominum, j marc. pr.   Et per manus domini, Willelmi Chewworth pro nucibus per ipsum emptis ibidem pro domino. v s. pr.   Et per manus Henrici Maunsell pro j multone per ipsum empto ibidem, vij s. vj d.   Et per manus Johannis 30 Codeworth pro j couerter pro le dressour et j magno securo per ipsum emptis ibidem, vj s. pr.   Johanni Brank, Pruciano, pro j multone ab ipso apud castrum de Colu. in reuentu domini de le

Wylle empto, vj scot.; et pro boue ab ipso empto ibidem, xv scot.;
et pro gallinis ab ipso ibidem emptis, xxiiij s., in toto j marc.
vj scot. xviij d. Et per manus magistri Willelmi Cook pro diuersis
victualibus per ipsum emptis in le Wyldrenesse per diuersas vices,
5 xxvij s. pr. Cuidam homini de Lettowe pro roches ab ipso emptis
apud le Haff, v s. iiij d. pr. Cuidam piscatori ibidem pro diuersis
piscibus recentibus ab ipso emptis ibidem, xv s. viij d. Et per
manus Thesaurarii et Johannis Norbery pro pane, gallinis, mawlard,
columbellis, ouis, et caseis per ipsos emptis in quodam villagio
10 juxta le Hoff magistri de Reynet*, j marc. ij s vj d. Et in expensis
camerarii, thesaurarii, et partis familie domini apud
Tapeowe vbi pernoctarunt xx° die Octobris versus Conyngburgh,   October 20.
xiij s. iiij d. st. Et per manus Thome Knapp pro expensis ipsius et
iij sociorum suorum expectantium dominum ibidem cum iiij cur-
15 seres per iiij dies, xiij s. iiij d. st. Et pro j carecta ibidem conducta
pro domino Willelmo P. et parte familie domini vsque Conyngburgh,
iij s. iiij d. st. Et in expensis camerarii, thesaurarii et
equorum domini apud Capellam sancte Katerine, xj s. pr. Et in
expensis senescalli et maioris partis familie domini et equorum
20 domini euntium per terram de la Memele vsque Conyngburgh, per
manus Roberti Burton scutiferi senescalli per v dies, in pane,
bere, carne recenti et salsa, pullis, pulcinis, candelis, busca, feno,
auenis et litura, vna cum belechere per viam, in toto xj marc. vj scot.
xviij d. pr. Et per manus Ricardi Catour cuidam Pruciano custo-
25 dienti bona domini in Castro de Instreburgh tempore quo dominus
stetit in le Reys, j marc. pr. Et per manus eiusdem pro j carecta
conducta pro dictis bonis cariandis vsque Conyngburgh, vna cum
expensis carectarii, ij marc. iiij scot. Et per manus eiusdem
cuidam ministro Marescalli carianti corpus domini Johannis de
30 Londeham de la Memele versus Conyngburgh, di. marc. pr. Et
per manus Johannis Duffeld pro victualibus per ipsum [emptis]
apud Tapiewe, x s. pr. Et cuidam homini pro lx ouis ab ipso
emptis apud le Memele in recentu domini, iij scot. di. Et Nicholao

* Raguit, on the borders of Prussia and Lithuania.

de Prake, notario ville de Conyngburgh pro labore suo scribendo
les prames et carectas versus le Reys, vj s. viij d. st. Et per manus
Johannis Leuyngton pro feno, auenis, stramine, et aliis necessariis
per ipsum emptis in le Reys in diuersis locis per compotum secum
factum, vij marc. xv scot. viij d. pr. Item in diuersis expensis 5
factis per manus Johannis Payn de Welle vsque Conyngburgh, viz.
in pane, vino, beer, carne, et piscibus ad diuersa loca, per compotum secum factum apud Conyngburgh, iiij marc. pr. Et per
manus eiusdem pro j dolio vacuo pro vino imponendo, per ipsum
empto ibidem, x scot. Et per manus eiusdem pro j barello de beer 10
per ipsum empto et dato nautis domini Marescalli[a] venientibus cum
domino de la Haff vsque Tapiou cum j batella, xx scot. Cuidam
lotrici lauanti mappas apud Conyngburgh ante adventum domini
de la Reys, viij scot. Clerico marescalcie pro xxij sackes
per ipsum emptis ibidem pro pane, victualibus et aliis 15
necessariis in eisdem cariandis versus le Reys, xxj scot.
/ Clauk Schone carectario vna cum xvij sociis cariantibus diuersa
harnesia, necessaria, et victualia de Conyngburgh vsque Instreburgh versus le Reys, quolibet capiente pro se et carecta sua j marc.
xvj scot, per compotum cum eis factum per duos heers assignatos 20
per Marescallum Prucianum, pro domino pur le Reys, in toto, xxx
marc. pr. Hankyn Markesworth carectario vna cum xxj sociis
conductis ad seruiendum domino in le Reys cum carectis suis, et
qualibet carecta cum iiij equis et j famulo, pro diuersis victualibus et
necessariis domini cariandis quilibet per ix septimanas, quolibet 25
capiente pro se, famulo, et carecta in septimana per ordinationem
Marescalli, xlij scot, per compotum cum eis factum per dictos
duos heers assignatos pro domino ut supra, in toto cvj li. xiij s.
iiij d. st., iiij scot minus. Petro Schulkes cum ij[bus] carectis et vj
equis, capienti pro se et pro ij equis per ix septimanas per par- 30
cellas examinatas, per compotum secum factum per dictos heers, in
toto xix nobl. x scot. Hansk Adam cum ij[bus] carectis et vj equis,
capienti vt supradictus Petrus per idem tempus, xix nobl. x scot.

Summa [pagine]
xxxvj s. viij d. st., et
de moneta Pruciana
xxxvij marc. xiiij scot.
ij s. v d.; que faciunt
monete Anglice,
xj li. xj s. vj d. ob.

fo. 18 vº.

* i.e. Mareschal Rabe, see before, p. 50, note.

EXPENSES IN PRUSSIA.

Hans Schulshe carectario cum vj sociis, et quolibet corum cum vna carecta et ij^{bus} equis, per ix septimanas, capiente per septimanam xxj scot., per compotum secum factum per dictos ij heers, in toto xvij li. st., iij scot. minus. Heyn Kogeler de Dansk cum xvij sociis
5 laborantibus in vna prama de Dansk versus regnum de Lettowe per xj septimanas, quolibet capiente per septimanam, x scot. per ordinacionem Marescalli, per compotum cum eis factum per dictos ij heers, in toto iiij^{xx}.ij. marc. di. pr. Worsten Warderer cum xvj sociis in alia prame per idem tempus ad eundem locum, capientibus
10 ut supra, iiij^{xx}.ij marc. d. pr. Et pro conductione istarum duarum nauium per idem tempus, xx marc. pr. Hanke Holste cum xij sociis laborantibus in alia prame de Dansk versus regnum per viij septimanas capientibus per septimanam vt supra, in toto xliij marc. viij scot. pr. Et pro naui sua per idem tempus, v marc. pr. Hanke
15 Scheffer cum xv sociis venientibus de Dansk vsque Conyngburgh, per iij septimanas, quolibet capiente per septimanam ut supra, in toto xx marc. pr. Heyne Colendorf cum xv sociis venientibus vt supra et redeuntibus per iij septimanas, quolibet capiente vt supra, xx marc. pr. Et pro conductione istarum duarum prames per idem tempus,
20 vj marc. pr. Nikoll Zymmermann cum xiij sociis laborantibus de Conyngburgh versus regnum cum j prame et ibi morantibus per ix septimanas, capientibus per septimanam vt supra, lij marc. di. pr. Et pro conductione nauis per idem tempus, iiij marc. di. pr. Hanke Semeland cum xiij sociis laborantibus vt supra cum j naui
25 per vij septimanas, capientibus per septimanam vt supra, per compotum cum eis factum per dictos ij heers, in toto xl marc. xx scot. Et pro conductione nauis per idem tempus, iiij marc. di. pr. Jacob Schele cum vij sociis laborantibus in parua naui per ix septimanas, capientibus vt supra, in toto xxx marc. pr. Et pro con-
30 ductione nauis per idem tempus, iiij marc. di. p. Hanke Hoult cum vj sociis laborantibus in vna naui per iiij septimanas, quolibet capiente per septimanam vt supra, in toto xj marc. xvj scot. Et pro conductione nauis per idem tempus, ij marc. pr. Martyn de Lake cum ix sociis laborantibus in j naui per

viij septimanas, capiente quolibet per septimanam vt supra per compotum cum eis factum vt supra, xxxiij marc. viij scot. Et pro conductione nauis per idem tempus, iiij marc pr. Hermann Kuer cum xj sociis laborantibus in j naui per ix septimanas, quolibet capiente per septimanam vt supra, per compotum cum eis factum vt supra, in toto xlj marc. di. pr. Et pro conductione nauis per idem tempus, iiij marc. di. pr. Hanke Heynrych cum vij sociis laborantibus in j naui per iiij septimanas, quolibet capiente per septimanam vt supra, per compotum cum eis factum ut supra, in toto xiij marc. viij scot. Et pro conductione j nauis per idem tempus, ij marc. pr. Claus Pruciano cum vij sociis laborantibus in j naui per iiij septimanas, / quolibet capiente per septimanam x scot., per compotum cum [eis] factum &c., xiij marc. viij scot. Et pro conductione nauis per idem tempus, ij marc. pr. Henrych Lange pro paracione mensarum, viij scot. Et pro ligacione ferrea pro dicta mensa empta, v scot. Longbeyn cum viij sociis laborantibus in j naui per xxiiij dies, quolibet capiente per diem j scot., per compotum cum eisdem factum vt supra, in toto xij marc. xviij scot. Et pro conductione nauis per idem tempus, j marc. pr. Claus Krozier cum ix sociis laborantibus in j parua naui per v septimanas, quolibet capiente per septimanam ut supra, in toto xx marc. xx scot. pr. Et pro conductione nauis per idem tempus, ij marc. di. pr. Jacob Poppyn magistro omnium nauium laboranti cum nauibus per xj septimanas, capienti per septimanam j marc. pr., per compotum secum factum per les heers, in toto xj marc. pr. Henke Loge socio suo le lodesman de aliis nauibus per idem tempus, capienti per septimanam xx scot., in toto ix marc. iiij scot. Item Kunge Jekell magistro nauis, redeunti de Konyngburgh versus Dansk cum vna naui per iij septimanas, capienti per septimanam vt supra, per compotum secum factum vt supra, in toto ij marc. di. pr. Pege Peegolt socio suo, le lodesman de alia naui per idem tempus, capienti per septimanam xv scot., per compotum secum factum vt supra, in toto j marc. di. ix scot. Petro Hausmere magistro alterius nauis per idem

---

Summa pagine cxxxvj li. vj s. viij d. st., et de moneta Pruciana Dlviij marc. j scot.; que faciunt Anglice clxxj li. xiiij s. j d. q° st.

fo. 19.

5

10

15

20

25

30

EXPENSES AT KÖNIGSBERG.

tempus, cap*ienti* p*er* diem xx scot., p*er* compo*tum* secum fact*um* vt sup*ra*, in to*to* ij marc. di. pr. Cuid*am se*rianti ville *ac* Dansk cunti ex p*re*cepto maior*is* et consilii ville de Dansk ad expediend*um* les prames, et existent*i* cum eisd*em* p*er* xj sep*timanas*, capienti p*er*
5 septi*manam* di. marc. pr., in to*to* v marc. di. pr. Claus Carpent*ario* laborant*i* in nau*i* et exis*tenti* cum d*o*mino in le Reys per xj septi*manas*, cap*ienti* per septi*manam* xv scot., in to*to* vj marc. xxj. scot.

S*um*ma pagine—xxviij. li. viij s. v d. ob. st., de iiij^{xx}xij marcis
10 ix scot. Pruc*ianis*.

S*um*ma exp*ensarum* v foliorum precedenti*um* vsque huc in Prucia p*ur* l*e* Reys, le noble ad xxvj scot., toto computato in moneta Anglica, DCiiij^{xx} li. xiij s. xj d. ob. st., vnde pro cariagio et batillagio et custubus de prames—CCC xxxvj li. ix. s. ij d. ob. q^n.

15   EXPENSE HOSPICII APUD CONYNGB*URGH*.

/CLERICO BUTERIE super beer, per man*us* Joha*nnis* Cawode pro iij pottes de methe p*er* ipsum emptis apud Conyngb*urgh* xx die Octobris, vj s. pr. Et p*er* manus eiusdem pro lxvj bykeres per ipsum emptis ibidem, xviij s. pr. CLERICO SPECIARIE per
20 manus cuiusdam lotricis pro locione mappar*um* aule ib*i*dem, vj s. pr. Joha*nni* Cawode pro vna cerura cum quatuor kliketes per ipsum emptis pro hostio buterie ib*i*dem, xij s. pr.; et per manus eiusdem pro iiij trowes per ipsum emptis ibidem pro officio buterie, viij s. pr; in to*to*, viij scot. Et per manus
25 eiusdem pro C bykeres per ipsum emptis ibidem, xxiiij s. pr. RICARDO KYNGESTON clerico thesaurie pro vij doleis et iij pipis vacuis per ipsum emptis ibidem, pro diuersis officiis, j noble. Et per manus diuersorum pro portagio vini, beer, et aliorum victuali*um* ib*id*em per diuersas vices, iij marc. x scot. iiij d. Clerico coquine
30 per manus Ricardi Catour pro j dolio Wych[a] per ipsum empto

fo. 19 v.
Conyngb*urgh*.
20 October.

---
[a] Probably Wyshmar or Wismar beer. See Wyshmer beer on p. 81, l. 14.

ibidem, iiij marc. pr. SUPER officio scutellarie, per manus Roberti Spayne pro tegulis et lyme, vna cum posicione vnius furneys in coquina, j marc. x scot pr. CLERICO coquine per manus Willelmi Harpeden, pro ij parpoys per ipsum emptis ibidem, ij marc. viij scot. Et per manus Ricardi Catour pro j boue per ipsum empto 5 ibidem, j marc. xvj scot. Et per manus eiusdem pro xviij mul tonibus ad vj scot, iiij marc. di. pr. CLERICO buterie super beer et methe per manus Johanni Payn, pro j dolio de beer empto ibidem, xj scot. SUPER officio aule et camere, per manus Eudith lotricis pro locione tam mapparum quam pannorum lineorum 10 domini, a primo die Nouembris vsque xix^m diem Decembris, per conuencionem cum eadem factam, j marc. vj scot. Johanni Edenham, portario pro j magna cerura pro media porta per ipsum empta ibidem, xiiij s. pr. CLERICO buterie super beer per manus Payn, pro iiij laste de bere per ipsum emptis ibidem, xx marc. pr. 15 Johanni Edenham pro vna cerura per ipsum empta ibidem pro porta versus rypam, iij scot. Clerico buterie super vino, per manus Alfons Broke pro xxxviij fattes vini, le fatte ad iiij marc. pr., clij marc. pr. Clerico buterie super beer, pro CCC bykeres per ipsum emptis ibidem, centena ad viij s. pr., xxiiij scot. Et pro portagio 20 iij barellorum de methe, iij lastes de beer et viij fattes vini ibidem, xxxiiij s. pr. Et pro xl verrez de glas per ipsum emptis ibidem, viij scot. vj s. viijd. Et pro ij corphes per ipsum emptis ibidem pro officio panetrie, viij scot. Et pro iij barellis de methe per ipsum emptis ibidem, le barellus ad j marc. iiij scot., iij marc. di. 25 Et pro j laste de beer empto ibidem per manus Johannis Cawode, v marc. vj scot. Et pro j laste de vino de Ryne* per manus Johannis Payn empto ibidem, vij marc. viij scot. Et pro iij securibus emptis per manus Ricardi Catour pro coquina, vj scot. Johanni Fyssher pro j parua parura et j grater per ipsum emptis ibidem, 30 ix s. pr. CLERICO buterie super beer, per manus Johanni Cawode pro v stopis de beer per ipsum emptis ibidem, xx d. Et pro j stopa de methe per ipsum empta ibidem, viij d. Et per manus eiusdem pro portagio iiij barellorum de beer, iiij s. pr. Et pro bykeres per

[margin: 1 November. 19 December.]
[margin: * [i.e., Rhenish wine.]]

EXPENSES AT KÖNIGSBERG. 59

ipsum emp*tis* ib*idem*, iiij s. pr. **Et pro ij** stop*is* de meth*e per* ip*sum*
emp*tis* ib*idem*, ij s. pr. SUPER officio **scute***ll***erie,** p*er manus*
Rob*erti* Sp*a*yne pro j carecta carbonu*m* **per** ip*su*m empt*a* ib*idem*,
xiij scot. Et Bartho*lomeo* Colyer pro carboni*bus* ab ip*s*o empt*is*
5 ib*idem per manus* ciusd*em*, xij scot. Et **per** m*anus* ei*usdem* **pro**
carboni*bus per* ip*s*um empt*us* de Hans Satemer*e*, **xij scot.** Et
Hankyn Stere*ff* **pro** carbon*ibus* ab **ip**so empt*is* ib*idem* **per manus**
eiusd*em* Rob*er*ti, **iij s.** iiij d. Et a **Hans** Stenefeld /pro vna carecta
carbonu*m* **per** ip*s*um empta ib*i*dem, **xij scot.**   Et **pro** car*i*ag*io*
10 ciusd*em*, **viij d.** Et a **Gyse Fethir pro j fothir carbonum** ab ip*s*o
empto ib*idem*, **per manus Laurencii** de scut*ellaria*, **xj scot.** xij d.
Et hospiti ib*idem* **pro carbon*ibus*, ligno, et aliis** necessariis propter
ysum domini in hospicio suo ib*i*dem, ab ip*s*o empt*is p*er manus
Rob*er*ti Spaigne, xvj marc. vj scot. Et pro discis et platiers per
15 manus eiusdem ib*idem* empt*is*, **xij scot.**   Et Bartho*lomeo* Hoppemere pro ij fothir carbonu*m* ab **ip**so empt*is* ib*idem*, **j** marc. **viij scot.**
Et cuida*m* matrone **pro vasis ligneis ab ipsa per clericum coquine**
ib*id***em** empt*is*, **xvj scot.** Et **pro ij carectis carbonum** emptis
ib*idem, per manus* **Roberti** de **scutellaria,** de Bartelet Van-
20 daleyt, j marc. pr. Et Bartho*lomeo* Prueia*n*o **pro iiij fothir**
carbonu*m* ab **ip**so empt*is* ib*idem*, **per manus Roberti de scutel-**
*lar*i*a*, **ij** marc. **j** s. pr. Et p*er* m*anus* eiusd*em* **pro** carbon*ibus*
per ip*s*um empt*is* ib*idem*, pr*o* Habbegod et **Knyghton, xij** scot.
Et p*er* m*anus* eiusd*em* **pro j fothir carbonum per** ip*s*um empto
25 ib*id*em de **Hans Colyer, xij** scot. j s. Et hospiti domus domini
ib*ide*m **pro** lignis ab **ip**so empt*is* ib*idem*, in coquina et vndique in
domo combust*is*, que non sunt inter predicta ligna et focali*a* com-
putat*a*, vj marc. pr. Et p*er manus* Rob*er*ti **Spayne** pro **ix stopis**
de vinegre per ipsum ibidem empt*is*, **xix s.** pr. Et **pro vj** stop*is*
30 de vinegre per m*anus* eiusd*em* empt*is* **ibidem, xij s.** pr.   Et
Ph*ilipp*o Peter pro vinegre ab **ip**so **empto** p*er manus* **ciusdem**
ibidem, p*er* diuers*as* **vices** per compotu*m* secum **factum ibidem, iiij**
marc. pr. Et **pro xij** stop*is* sinapis **per** ip*s*um empt*is* **ibid**e**m** de
eodem, **xviij s. vj d.** pr. Clerico speciarie **pro xxiiij lb.** candel-

Summa pagine
ccxiiij marc. vij
xiiij d. Pruciau*i*
que faciunt An*n*
lxv li. xix s. j d.
sterling*es*.

fo. 20.

arum ibidem emptis per manus Wytelok, xxiiij s. pr. SUPER
officio scutellarie, pro[a] xij stopis aceti per manus Roberti Spayne
ibidem emptis, xxiiij s. CLERICO speciarie pro vj^{xx} lb. candelarum
de cepo ibidem emptis per manus eiusdem, ij marc. pr. CLERICO
marescalcie per manus Johannis Leuyngton pro xvj carucis feni
per ipsum emptis ibidem de Baydot Spruce,[b] iiij marc. xvj scot. pr.
Et per manus eiusdem pro xix carucis feni per ipsum emptis de
Hans Geykyn ibidem, caruca ad iiij scot., iiij marc. iiij scot. Et
per manus eiusdem pro lvj schephel auenarum per ipsum ibidem
emptis, le shephell ad ij s., j marc. xx scot. ij s. pr. Item a Claus
Eueret pro xxx shephel auenarum, le shephel vt supra, j marc. pr.,
ab ipso emptis ibidem. Et Christoforo Vndreland pro xxvj shephel auenarum ab ipso emptis per manus eiusdem, xx scot. ij s. pr.
Et per manus eiusdem pro j fothir litture per ipsum empto ibidem,
vj scot. SUPER officio scutellarie, per manus Roberti Spayne pro
iiij trowes per ipsum emptis ibidem, in toto iiij s. pr. CLERICO
panetrie per manus Johannis Cawode et Johannis Braillefford pro
pane albo per ipsos empto de diuersis pistoribus ibidem, a v^{to} die
Nouembris vsque vij^m diem Januarii, per compotum cum eis factum
ibidem, xxxix marc. xv scot. pr. RICARDO, famulo domini Thome
Erpyngham, eunti cum Roberto Waterton et Ricardo Catour pro
prouidenciis faciendis in primo aduentu domini ibidem, nunciante
camerario, pro j equo et expensis suis de Dansk vsque Conyngburg
per v dies, j marc. pr. vij s. SUPER officio pulletrie, per manus
Jacoby Fauconer, pro xx gallinis per ipsum emptis ibidem pro les
haukes domini, le gallina ad xxj d., xx s. pr. HANS LORELL pro
mundacione latrine camere domini, vj s. pr. /MAGISTRO Willelmo
Cook pro aqua ardente per ipsum empta apud Conyngburg, v scot.
ROBERTO Spayne pro ligno et clauis per ipsum emptis ibidem pro
la lardre, viij s. pr. SUPER officio scutellarie, per manus Laurencie
de scutellarie, pro xx pottes de terra per ipsum emptis ibidem, ij s.

---

[a] MS. has per.
[b] Baydot the Prussian may be intended, but the words are clearly as above printed.

EXPENSES AT KÖNIGSBERG.

et ferk[a] pr. Et pro iij bolles et iij trowes, iiij s. qr. (vz. iiij d.), emptis ibidem per manus eiusdem. SUPER officio pulletrie, per manus Willelmi Harpeden pro C ouis per ipsum empta ibidem, viij s. pr. CLERICO marescaleie per manus Walteri Ferrour pro
5 xij mannis nouis ab ipso emptis ibidem pro equis domini, x scot. Et pro xxxv mannis ab ipso emptis ibidem pur le store, xiiij scot. ij s. pr. Et eidem pro stipendio suo per mensem, capienti in septimana vj scot., in toto j marc. pr. CLERICO coquine per manus seneschalli, pro iiij bobus per ipsum emptis ibidem de Hans Crokeler,
10 le piece ad ij marc. xv scot., x marc. di. pr. Et per manus eiusdem pro viij porcis per ipsum emptis ibidem, le piece pro xij scot., iiij marc. viij scot. CLERICO speciarie per manus thesaurarii, pro lxxvj vlnis panni linei per ipsum emptis ibidem, pro mappis et towales faciendis pro aula et camera, le vlna pro j scot., in toto iij marc. iiij
15 scot. Et per manus eiusdem pro lxiiij vlnis panni linei emptis de Johanne Squyrell mercatore Anglico pro eodem officio, le vlna ad ij s., ij marc. viij s. Et per manus eiusdem pro cxlv vlnis panni linei per ipsum emptis de vxore hospitis domini ibidem, pro officiis panetrie, buterie et coquine, le vlna ad ij s., iiij marc. xx scot. pr.
20 Et per manus Ricardi de la Ewerye pro CC lb. di. de cera operata de Claus Spicer emptis, le lb. ad iij s. ij d., x marc. di. iij s. iiij d. pr. CLERICO buterie super vino, per manus Johannis Payn pro v fattes vini per ipsum emptis ibidem, le fatte ad iiij marc. pr., xx marc. pr. SUPER officio pulletrie, per manus Hans Fauconer
25 pro xij gallinis per ipsum emptis pro les faucones ibidem, xvj s. pr. CLERICO marescaleie per manus Hans Ferrour pro ferrura equorum domini in le huntyng, xij s. CLERICO buterie super beer per manus Johannis Cawode, pro iij laste et iiij barellis de beer, le laste ad v marc. vj scot., xvij marc. di. pr. Clerico buterie super
30 vino per manus Johannis Payn, pro ij fattes vini per ipsum emptis ibidem de Henrici van Manere, le fatte ad viij marc., in toto xvj marc. pr. CLERICO speciarie per manus Edithe Laundour pro locione map-   Jan. 1—Feb.

[a] Above this word is written "vz. iiij d.," indicating, it seems, that the Prussian fathing is worth 4d. The following item has the same.

parum domini a festo circumcisionis domini vsque in festum Purificationis Beate Marie Virginis, j mare. ix scot. iiij s. pr. Hans Wyndrawer pro portagio xxvj fattes vini, per convencionem cum eo factam, j mare. iiij s. pr. CLERICO coquine per manus Willelmi Harpeden pro ij porpays per ipsum emptis ibidem de Hans Mynter, ij mare. viij scot. pr. Et per manus eiusdem pro allecibus albis per ipsum emptis de eodem ibidem, ij mare. vj scot. SUPER officio scutellarie per manus Laurencii de scutellaria pro j fothir carbonum per ipsum empto ibidem, v. die Dec., xij scot. Et per manus eiusdem pro vij fothir carbonum emptis de Hans Rothir, le fo·hir ad xij scot., iiij mare. di. pr. Et per manus Roberti Spayne pro vasis ligneis emptis ibidem de Matañ Sholk, x scot. Et per manus eiusdem pro iiij fothir carbonum ibidem emptis, le fothir ad xij scot., ij mare. pr. Et per manus Laurencii de scutellaria pro iiij fothir carbonum per ipsum emptis de Petro Edwynnes, xxvj scot. Et pro j fothir carbonum per ipsum empto ibidem, xij scot. Et per manus Roberti Spayne pro vasis ligneis per ipsum emptis ibidem, iiij mare. vj scot. pr. Et per manus Laurencii de scutellaria pro j fothir carbonum per ipsum empto ibidem, xij scot. Et Petro Pruciano pro iiij fothir carbonum ab ipso emptis ibidem per manus eiusdem, xxxvj scot. ij s. pr. CLERICO speciarie /per manus thesaurarii pro diuersis speciebus, confeccionibus, et amigdolis per ipsum emptis ibidem de Claus Spycer, a xxiij° die Octobris vsque xv^m diem Nouembris, per compotum secum factum, xiij mare. pr. xvj scot. iij s. ij d. CLERICO coquine per manus Roberti Burton pro iiij bobus per ipsum emptis de Hans Cremeton, le piece ad ij mare. di., x mare. pr. Et per manus eiusdem pro viij porcis per ipsum emptis de eodem, le piece ad xiiij scot., iiij mare. xvj scot. pr. Et pro vno apre per manus eiusdem ab ipso empto ibidem, j mare. pr. CLERICO marescalcie, per manus Hans Elchyn pro xx fothir feni ab ipso emptis ibidem, le fothir ad v scot., iiij mare. iiij scot. pr. Et per manus Heyne Hogull pro vj fothir feni ab ipso emptis ibidem, le fothir ad iiij scot. ij s., j mare. xij s. pr. Et per manus Nichel Frost pro lxx shephull auenarum ab ipso emptis

ibidem per Johannem Leuyngton, le shephul j scot., ij marc.
xxij scot. Et per manus Claus Howman pro xxj shephull auenarum ab ipso emptis ibidem per dictum Johannem, le shephul
ij s. ij d., xviij scot. vj d. pr. Et pro xiiij busellis auenarum ab
5 ipso emptis per eundem Johannem, le shephel ad ij s. iiij d.; xiij
scot. ij d. Et per manus Cleykyn Pruciani pro lx shephull auenarum ab ipso emptis per manus ciusdem Johannis, le shephel ad
ij s. iiij d., ij marc. viij scot. Et Claus Howman pro iiij fothir
straminis pro littura ab ipso emptis ibidem, per manus ciusdem
10 Johannis, j marc. pr. viij scot. CLERICO speciarie per manus
Ricardi de la Ewerye pro CCxllb. candelarum de cepo per ipsum
emptis ibidem, le lb. xij d., iiij marc. Et per manus Wytelok pro
sope per ipsum ibidem, tempore quo dominus stetit ibidem, viij
scot. ij s. SUPER officio aule et camere, pro sirpis emptis per
15 manus Henrici Morley in primo aduentu domini de le Reys, liij s.
pr. Et per manus Brailleford pro sirpis per ipsum emptis erga
festum Omnium Sanctorum pro aula et cameris domini, j marc. pr. Nov. 1.
SUPER officio scutellarie, per manus Laurencii de scutellaria pro
sinapio, verious, oleribus, herbis, et farina auenarum per ipsum
20 emptis de quadam matrona vocata Edwynes, a festo omnium
sanctorum vsque vigilium Natalis Domini, per compotum secum 1 Nov.—24 Dec
factum, iiij marc. pr., iiij s. minus. Claus Semeland pro viij tabulis
comensalibus pro aula et camera domini ibidem, le piece ad vj scot.,
ij marc. pr Et eidem pro vj paribus trestellorum per ipsum
25 factis, xiiij scot. Et eidem pro lxxvij deles ab ipso emptis per
manus Ricardi Catour ad faciendum coquinam magis largam, et ad
faciendum scutellariam in eadem coquina, et ad faciendum appenticium supra hostium celarii, et alia necessaria in aula, le piece ad
viij s., x marc. pr. xvj s. pr. Et eidem pro ligno ab ipso empto
30 pro eisdem faciendo, j marc. xvj scot. pr. Et pro clauis emptis per
manus eiusdem Ricardi pro dictis necessariis faciendis, ij marc.
iiij scot. Et iiij carpentariis existentibus circa facturam eorundem
ibidem, pro stipendiis suis, quolibete capiente in septimana xiiij
scot., iiij marc. xvj scot. pr. Et Petro Loreyn carpentario facienti

les maungours in stabulis domini, et j cuppeburde in aula, et emendandi diuersa necessaria in panetria et in camera domini per diuersas uices, pro stipendiis suis, per compotum secum factum, j marc. pr. xviij scot. CLERICO marescalcie per manus Hankyn Ferrour pro melle, lynesede, co.nyne, lino, grees, et alumglas, roseyne, coperos, per ipsum emptis ibidem, pro albo cursero domini sanando, per diuersas vices, per compotum secum factum, vna cum stipendiis suis, viij scot. iiij s. viij d. / HANS Crochemere pro portagio ij laste de beer et iiij barellorum de methe, ix scot. iiij d. pr. Johanni Cawode pro j cera pro cista buterie per ipsum empta ibidem, ij scot. Et per manus eiusdem pro j candelabro pro buterie, ij s .pr. Et per manus eiusdem pro CC bykeres per ipsum emptis ibidem erga festum Natalis Domini, xx s. pr. CLERICO buterie super vino per manus Johannis Cawode, pro xxij stopis vini garnade per ipsum emptis ibidem, le stopa ad iiij s., j marc. x scot. iij s. pr. Et per manus eiusdem pro calce per ipsum empta ibidem, ij scot. WILLELMO Harpeden pro expensis suis per iij dies circa prouidencias faciendas erga festum Natalis Domini, vna cum conductione vnius equi, j marc. vj scot. viij d. pr. Et eidem pro putura pulletrie per ipsum empta ibidem, xxj s. pr. CLERICO buterie super beer per manus Johannis Payn, pro iiij laste de beere per ipsum emptis ibidem erga festum Natalis domini, le laste v marc., vj scot. xxj marc. pr. Et per manus eiusdem pro iiij fattes vini per ipsum emptis ibidem de Henrico van Torne, le fatte ad v marc., iiij scot. xx marc. xvj scot. Petro Breker pro portagio de iiij laste de beer, xxij scot. SUPER officio sentellarie per manus Roberti Spayne, pro xliij shephell farine frumenti per ipsum emptis ibidem, de Hankyn Edeyne, pasteler, pro diuersis pastelleriis in domo suo factis, de xxij^o die Octobris vsque xxij^m diem Januarii, le shephel pro vj scot., x marc. xviij scot. Et per manus eiusdem pro busca, vna cum furnagio, eciam cum stipendio predicti Hankyn per idem tempus, per compotum secum factum, xiiij marc. vj scot. Et per manus eiusdem pro j conke et j bokete per ipsum emptis ibidem tangentibus officium suum, iiij s. pr.

CLERICO coquine per manus Willelmi Harpeden, pro skaldyng
porcorum et porcellorum, a festo omnium sanctorum vsque festum   1 Nov.—25 Dec.
Natalis Domini per Petrum Moore factum, per compotum secum
factum, j marc. viij scot. Et per manus eiusdem pro allecibus per
5 ipsum emptis ibidem x° die Decembris, ij marc. vj scot.   CUIDAM 10 Dec.
matrone vocata Wendell custodienti iiij pueros domini de Lettowe
per vj septimanas, capienti pro quolibet in septimana iiij scot.,
iij marc. pr. CLERICO speciarie per manus Ricardi Walpole pro
locione mapparum aule et camere ibidem, xxij scot. pr.   CLERICO
10 marescalcie per manus Hankyn Ferrour pro ferrura equi domini
ibidem, vj scot.   CLERICO speciarie per manus Ricardi Catour pro
cera et melle, et oleo, per ipsum emptis ibidem de hospitio
thesaurarii, tempore quo dominus stetit ibidem, xj marc. xvij scot
CLERICO speciarie per manus Wytelok pro CCCCxl. lb. candelarum
15 de cepo, per ipsum emptis ibidem de Wendehull, chaundeler, erga
festum Natalis Domini, le lb ad j s. vij marc. viij scot. Et per   25 December.
manus Ricardi de la Ewerye pro D^c di. vij [557] lb. cere operate,
le lb. ad xl d., erga festum Natalis Domini, xxx marc. xvj scot. pr.
xx d.   Et CLAUS Kesseleyn pro lxxvj vlnis panni linei ab ipso
20 emptis ibidem, pro mappis aule et aliis necessariis in panetrie et
coquina, le vlna ad ij s., ij marc. di. ij s. pr. Et per manus Ricardi
Catour pro lxx vlnis per ipsum emptis ibidem de Jacobo Pewtrer,
le vlna ad ij scot., ij marc. xxij scot. Et per manus thesaurarii pro
lxxij vlnis panni linei per ipsum emptis de hospitio suo pro vsu
25 domini, le vlna ad xxvj d, ij marc xiiij scot. xij d. Et per manus
Johannis Cawode pro clarebagges per ipsum emptis ibidem, iiij s
pr.   CLERICO speciarie per manus Ricardi Catour pro j pare
de balance ad ponderandum diuersas species, vna cum diuersis
ponderibus pro eisdem, xviij scot. CLERICO coquine per manus   Summa pagine
30 Roberti Burton pro iiij porcis ab ipso emptis ibidem de Hans   cxlj marc. j scot.
Rocheforthe, le piece ad xij scot. ij marc.   Et per manus eiusdem   ij d. pr., que faci
pro v vitulis per ipsum emptis ibidem de eodem, xxv scot. Et per   Anglice xliij li.
manus eiusdem / pro j boue per ipsum empto ibidem de Hankyn   ij d. st.
Cartere, j marc. xvj scot. Et per manus thesaurarii pro xij   fo. 22.

bacons per ipsum emptis ibidem de Claus Crochemere, le piece ad xij scot, in toto vj marc. pr. Et per manus eiusdem pro vno apre per ipsum empto ibidem de eodem, j marc. ij scot. SUPER officio pulletrie, per manus Jacoby Fauconere pro xxx gallinis per ipsum emptis ibidem pro les haukes domini, xxx s. pr. CLERICO coquine 5 per manus Ricardi Catour pro pinguedine per ipsum empta ibidem, tempore quo dominus stetit ibidem, per compotum secum factum, xiij scot. iiij s. pr. SUPER officio scutellarie per manus Roberti Spayne pro j stak focalis per ipsum empto ibidem de Jacobo van Hale, ix marc. pr. Et per manus eiusdem pro xiiij 10 fothir carbonum per ipsum ibidem emptis de eodem, vij marc. x scot. xx d. Et pro cariagio de focali, di. marc. pr. Et per manus eiusdem pro vasis ligneis emptis erga festum Natalis Domini ibidem, iij marc. xv scot. Et per manus Roberti Spayne pro aceto per ipsum empto ibidem vsque vigiliam Natalis Domini, 15 de Henrico Torne, iiij marc. viij scot. CLERICO speciarie per manus Wytelok pro candelis, carbonibus et expensis suis per v dies circa facturam certorum luminum ibidem, ix scot. CLERICO buterie super beer et methe, per manus Johannis Cawode, pro vj barellis de methe per ipsum emptis ibidem, le barellus ad j noble, 20 vj marc. di. pr. Clerico buterie super vino, pro xxxvj stopis vini de* garnade per ipsum emptis ibidem, vsque ad vij^m diem Januarii, de Henrico van Torne per compotum secum factum ibidem, le stope ad iiij s., ij marc. x scot. j s. minus.

24 December.

7 January.

Summa pagine xliiij marc. ij s. ij d. Pruciane, que faciunt An- 25 glice xiij li. xj s. st.

Summa expensarum in foliis precedentibus apud Conyngburgh, le noble ad xxvj scot., vsque huc, CCviij li. x s. viij d. st.

* MS. has le.

EXPENSE HOSPICII APUD CONYNGBURGH.

Hic incipit le noble ad xxv scot.

    / CLERICO panetrie *per manus* Johannis Payn *pro* pane albo *per*
ipsum empto apud Conyngburgh de diuersis pistoribus, a vij° die
5 Januarii vsque x^m diem Febr., per compotum cum eis factum, xxxij
marc. x scot. Et CLERICO buterie super bere, *per manus* Johannis
Cawode *pro* iij lastes de beer *per ipsum emptis* ibidem, de Jacobo
Van Brandyk, le laste ad v marc. iiij scot., xv marc di. Et *per*
manus eiusdem *pro* ij barelles de methe *per ipsum emptis* ibidem,
10 le barellus ad j marc. ij scot., ij marc. iiij scot. SUPER officio scutellarie *per manus* Roberti Spayne *pro* j stak focalis *per ipsum*
empto ibidem de Jacobo van Reyneth, v marc. viij scot. Et Hans
Cartere *pro* cariagio eiusdem, v scot. Et *per manus* eiusdem *pro*
scutellis ligneis *per ipsum emptis* ibidem de Hans Bramburgh, xiij
15 scot. Et *per manus* eiusdem *pro* aceto *per ipsum empto* ibidem de
Henrico Van Torne, ij marc. v scot. Et *per manus* eiusdem *pro*
farina frumenti *per ipsum empta* ibidem de Hans Pasteler, *pro*
pastellis faciendis a xxij° die Januarii vsque x diem Febr. per
compotum secum factum ibidem, j marc. xviij scot. Et *per manus*
20 eiusdem *pro* busca, furnagio, et stipendio dicti pasteler *per idem*
tempus, per compotum secum factum, j marc. di. pr. Et *per manus*
Laurencii de scutellaria *pro* sinape, verious, oleribus, et herbis, et
caboches *per ipsum emptis* ibidem de quadam matrona vocata
Wendehull, a die Natalis Domini vsque x^m diem Febr., per com-
25 potum secum factum ibidem, iiij marc. viij scot. SUPER officio
aule [et] camere *per manus* Johannis Brailefford *pro* sirpis *per ipsum*
emptis erga festum Natalis Domini, xiiij scot. CLERICO speciarie
per manus Wytelok *pro* wyke *per ipsum empto* ibidem *pro* torches
faciendis ibidem, xxxj s. pr. Et *per manus* Reginald Curteyn
30 *pro* x vlnis de streynour, x s. pr. Et *per manus* eiusdem *pro*
diuersis bagges *pro* diuersis speciebus imponendis *per ipsum emptis*

Vsque huc nobil
xxvj scot.
fo. 22v°
1391, Jan. 7—Fe
.

Jan. 22—Feb. 1

Dec. 25—Feb. 1

68   THE EARL OF DERBY'S EXPEDITIONS.

Dec. 25—Feb. 11.

January 1.
xx
Summa pagine iiij,
xvij marc. vij scot.
ij s. pr., que faciunt
Anglice xxxj li. ij s.
xj d. ob. qr. st.
fo. 23.

ibidem, x s. pr. Et pro CCxxxiij lb. candelarum de cepo per ipsum emptis ibidem de Heyne, chaundeler, a die Natalis Domini vsque xi^m diem Febr, per compotum secum factum ibidem, le lb. ad j scot., iiij marc. xxj scot. vj d. pr. Et per manus Wytelok, pro crochetes per ipsum emptis ibidem ad pendendum les torches, iiij s. 5 pr. Et per manus thesaurarii pro diuersis confectionibus et sugre per ipsum emptis de Jacobi Cremeton van Torne, xij marc. pr. Et per manus eiusdem pro j box de anys confecto per ipsum empto ibidem de Jacobi Cremer, iiij scot. Johanni Fisher pro quodam conke per ipsum empto ibidem pro officio suo ibidem, v s. 10 pr. CLERICO coquine per manus Ricardi Catour pro skaldyng porcorum et porcellorum a die Natalis Domini vsque x^m diem Februarii, per compotum secum factum ibidem, iij marc. iiij s. pr. CUIDAM matrone vocate Ferwey pro custodia ij puerorum de Lettowe per x septimanas, capienti pro quolibet in septimana ij scot., 15 xl. scot. SUPER officio pulletrie pro xxv gallinis emptis per manus Jacobi Fauconere pro les faucons domini ibidem, xxxj s. pr. CLERICO matescaleir pro ferrura equi domini ibidem a festo Circumcicionis Domini, iiij scot. Claus Semeland capienti pro domo compacta pro camera Jacobi Fauconere et pro j magna domo pro les faucons 20 domini per xvj septimanas, capienti in septimana xld. st., iiij marc. st. / HOSPITI de Conyngburgh pro hospicio suo tempore quo dominus stetit ibidem, per conuencionem secum factam per senescallum, xx li st. Hankyn Hoke, Pruciano carretario cum xv sociis suis cariantibus harnesia domini, necessaria, victualia, et les Lettowe, et 25 seruientes buterie et camere domini ibidem, quolibet capiente pro se et carecta, de Conyngburgh vsque Dansk iij marc., per conuencionem cum eis factam, xlviij marc. CLERICO buterie super vino per manus Johannis Payn, pro ij fattes vini per ipsum emptis ibidem de Johanne Squyrell mercatore Anglico, viij marc. pr. 30 CLERICO speciarie per manus Johannis Scorell pro xj stone cere per ipsum emptis ibidem de Claus Sandyk, le stone ad j marc. xvj scot., xiij marc. iij s. ix d. pr. CLERICO buterie super beer, per manus Johannis Cawode pro iij last de beer per ipsum emptis

ibidem, le last ad v marc. ij scot., xv marc. vj scot. CLERICO
buterie super vino, per manus eiusdem pro iij sattes vini albi per
ipsum emptis ibidem, le satte ad iij marc. v scot., xij marc. xv scot.
Claus de Prake pro clauis et serramentis per ipsum emptis ibidem
5 ad pendendum hostia coquine ibidem, j marc. pr. Et per manus
Johannis Brailleford pro j tabula per ipsum empta ibidem, pro le
dressour in coquina, xviij scot. Et per manus Johannis Cawode
pro piris, pomis, et nucibus per ipsum emptis ibidem per diuersas
vices pro tempore quo dominus stetit ibidem, per compotum secum
10 factum ibidem, ij marc. di. pr.

EXPENSE APUD BRAMBURGH ET ALIBI.

CLERICO panetrie per manus Johannis Payn pro pane albo per
ipsum empto apud Bramburgh ix° die Feb., xvj scot. Et per   February 9.
manus eiusdem pro beer per ipsum empto ibidem, xxviij scot.
15 Et per manus eiusdem pro methe per ipsum empto ibidem, x scot. j s.
CLERICO marescalcie per manus Thome Swyllyngton pro seno,
auenis, et littura per ipsum ibidem emptis pro xvj equis, xv scot.
ij s. pr. Et pro belechere ibidem, xiij s. iiij d. st. CLERICO panetrie
per manus Johannis Payn pro pane albo per ipsum empto apud
20 Brounesbergh, x die Febr., xiij scot. CLERICO buterie super beer,   February 10.
per manus eiusdem pro ij barellis de beer per ipsum emptis ibidem,
j marc. pr. Clerico buterie super vino, per manus eiusdem pro
xxxvj stopis vini, le stopa ad j s., xxxvj s. pr. Et per manus
eiusdem pro ix stopis de methe, le stopa ad viij d., vj s. pr.
25 CLERICO coquine per manus senescalli pro piscibus per ipsum
ibidem emptis, ij scot. CLERICO marescalcie per manus Thome
Swyllyngton pro seno, auenis, et littura per ipsum emptis ibidem pro
equis domini vt supra, xvj scot. vj d. pr. Et per [manus] eiusdem pro
serrura equorum domini ibidem, iiij s. pr. SUPER officio pulletrie,
30 per manus Willelmi Harpeden pro sepis et alleis per ipsum emptis
ibidem, xviij d. CLERICO panetrie per manus Johannis Payn pro

70   THE EARL OF DERBY'S EXPEDITIONS.

February 11.

Summa pagine xx li.
xiij s. iiij d. st., et
moneta Pruciana
cxxv marc. xv scot
iij d. pr., que faciunt
xl li. iiij s. st.

pomis et piris per ipsum emptis ibidem, iiij s. pr. HOSPITI ibidem pro belechere, ij marc. pr. CLERICO panetrie per manus Johannis Payn pro pane albo per ipsum empto apud Meluyng, die Sabbati, xj^o die Febr., xxj scot. CLERICO buterie super vino, per manus Johannis Payn pro ij fattes vini per ipsum emptis ibidem, xij marc. di. Clerico buterii super beer et methe pro v barellis de beer per ipsum emptis ibidem, ij marc. xxij scot., le barellus ad xiiij scot. Et per manus eiusdem pro vj stopis de methe per ipsum emptis ibidem, le stopa vt supra, iiij s.

EXPENSE APUD MELUYNG ET ALIBI.   10

fo. 23 v°

12 February.

/ HANKYN Portour pro portagio vini & beer ibidem, iij scot. CLERICO panetrie per manus Johannis Payn pro pane albo per ipsum empto ibidem die dominica xij die Februarii, xliiij scot. CLERICO buterie super vino nichil, quia emitur in grosso die precedente, et beer similiter. Clerico buterie super methe per manus eiusdem pro xij stopis de methe per ipsum emptis ibidem, le stopa ad viij d., viij s. CLERICO speciarie per manus Ricardi Catour pro amigdolis, fyges, dates, et sugre per ipsum emptis ibidem, xj scot. Clerico buterie per manus Johannis Cawode pro j schok de bykere per ipsum empto ibidem, xjs. CLERICO coquine per manus famuli Johannis Payn pro j porpeys per ipsum empto ibidem, xij scot. CLERICO buterie per manus Johannis Payn pro piris, pomis, et nucibus per ipsum emptis ibidem per duos dies, xj s. pr. SUPER officio salserie, per manus Roberti Spaigne pro farina frumenti per ipsum empta pro pastello ibidem faciendo, vna cum busca, furnagio et stipendio pastellarii, xv scot. ET PER manus Laurencii de scutellaria pro oleribus, herbis, pisis et aliis salsis per ipsum emptis ibidem per idem tempus, vj scot. ij s. pr. CLERICO speciarii per manus cuiusdem lotricis lauantis mappas aule et camere per idem tempus ibidem, vj s. pr. CLERICO marescalcie per manus Thome Swyllyngton pro feno, auenis, et littura per ipsum emptis ibidem, per tempus quo dominus stetit ibidem, in toto j marc. di. ijs.

Et per manus ciusdem pro grees et talowe per ipsum emptis ibidem
pro equis domini, iiij s. pr. Et per manus ciusdem pro ferrura equorum domini ibidem, iij s pr. Hospiti pro belecher ibidem, xl s. st.;
et seruientibus suis, j marc. pr. CLERICO panetrie per manus Jo- *Expense apud*
5 hannis Payn pro pane albo per ipsum empto, die lune xiij die Febr. *Meluyng et alibi*
apud Maryngburgh, xiiij scot. CLERICO buterie super vino, per *13 February.*
manus ciusdem pro xviij stopis vini, le stopa ad xv d., ix scot.
CLERICO buterie super beer et methe per manus ciusdem, pro
j barello de beer per ipsum empto ibidem, xiiij scot. Et pro por-
10 tagio ciusdem, xij d. pr. Et per manus ciusdem pro xj stopis de
methe per ipsum emptis ibidem, le stopa vt supra, vij s. iiij d. Et
pro pomis et piris per ipsum emptis ibidem, iij s. pr. CLERICO
coquine per manus thesaurarii pro j porpeys per ipsum empto
ibidem, xij scot. CLERICO maresculcie pro feno, auenis, et littura
15 per Thomam Swyllynton emptis ibidem pro xvj equis domini, xv
scot. Hospiti ibidem pro belecher, j marc. di. pr.; et seruientibus
suis, viij scot. CLERICO panetrie per manus Johannis Payn pro
pane albo per ipsum empto apud Darsowe die Martis xiiij° die Febr., *14 February.*
xiij scot. ij s. pr. CLERICO buterie super bere et methe, per manus
20 ciusdem pro j barello de beer per ipsum empto ibidem, xiiij scot.
Et pro xvj stopis de methe, le stopa vt supra, x s. viij d. pr. Et
pro pomis et piris per ipsum emptis ibidem, iiij s. pr. CLERICO
maresculcie per manus Thome Swyllyngton pro feno, littura, et
auenis, per ipsum emptis ibidem pro equis domini, vt supra, xv
25 scot. xj d. Et per manus ciusdem pro ferrura equorum domini
ibidem, ij s. pr. HOSPITI ibidem pro belechere j noble; et seruientibus suis ibidem, vj scot. Et pro grees et talowe ibidem emptis
pro equis domini, iiij s. pr. CLERICO speciarie per manus Whytelok pro iiij lb. candelarum de cepo per ipsum emptis apud Bram-
30 burgh, le lb. xvj d., v s. iiij d. pr. Et per manus ciusdem pro v lb.
candelarum de cepo per ipsum emptis apud Brounesbergh, le lb.
vt supra, vj s. viij d. pr. Et per manus ciusdem pro xvij lb. candelarum de cepo per ipsum apud Meluyng emptis, le lb. vt supra,
xxij s. viij d. pr. Et per manus ciusdem pro vj lb. candelarum de

72   THE EARL OF DERBY'S EXPEDITIONS.

Summa pagine xxij marc. v scot. ij s. v d. pr., que faciunt Anglice vij li. ij s. iiij d. ob. st.

cepo per ipsum emptis apud *Maryngburgh*, le lb. vt *supra*, viij s. Et per manus eiusdem pro v lb. candelarum de cepo per ipsum emptis apud Darsowe, le lb. vt *supra*, v s. iiij d. pr.

[EXPENSE HOSPICII DOMINI APUD] DANSK.

fo. 24.

15 February.

/ CLERICO panetrie per manus Johannis Gylder pro pane albo per ipsum empto apud Dansk, die Mercurii xv° die Febr., j marc. pr. CLERICO baterie super beer, per manus eiusdem pro iiij laste de beer per ipsum emptis ibidem, le laste ad v marc., xx marc. pr. Et per manus eiusdem pro vj fattes vini albi per ipsum emptis ibidem, le fatte ad iiij marc., xxiiij marc. pr. Et per manus eiusdem pro ij schok byketes per ipsum emptis ibidem, xx scot. Et per manus eiusdem pro j tabula pro panetria cum ij restes, et pro mundacione panetrie in manerio *Episcopi* ibidem, xiij scot. Et per manus eiusdem pro sale per ipsum empto ibidem, ij scot. Et per manus eiusdem pro j pare botelles de *Anglia* per ipsum empto ibidem, iij s. iiij d. st. Et per manus eiusdem pro j cera pro hostio panetrie, j corf et ij sprygelles per ipsum emptis ibidem, in toto xix scot. iiij d. pr. Et per manus eiusdem pro j stopell pro j boteil per ipsum empt' ibidem, ij s. HENRICO Laghmere pro portagio de les vj fattes et iiij lastes de beer, xl scot. Cuidam lotrici lauanti mappas aule et camere in vltimo aduentu domini ibidem, xij s. pr. Johanni Gylder pro j cera pro le seler per ipsum empta ibidem, vj scot. Super officio scutellarie, per manus Roberti Spayne pro xij lastes carbonum per ipsum ibidem emptis, le laste ad vij scot. vj d., iij marc. xiiij scot. Et per manus eiusdem pro j stak de focale per ipsum empto ibidem de ballico manerii *Episcopi*, viij marc. di. pr. Et per manus eiusdem pro scutellis ligneis per ipsum emptis ibidem, xv scot. CLERICO marescalcie per manus Johannis Whytyk mercatoris Anglici pro j magno stak feni per ipsum empto ibidem de Petro Tweyfrend de Dansk, v marc. pr. Et per manus eiusdem pro iiij fothir straminis per ipsum emptis

EXPENSES AT DANTZIC. 73

ibidem pro lectis et pro littura equorum, le fothir ad vij scot.,
j marc. iiij scot. Et per manus ciusdem pro lx shephell auenarum
per ipsum ibidem emptis, le shephell ad xxv d., ij marc. ij scot.
Super officio scutellarie, per manus Roberti Spayne pro iiij trowes   Expense apud I
5 et ij bolles per ipsum emptis ibidem, xij s. pr. CLERICO speciarie
per manus Whytelok pro lx lb. candelarum de cepo, le lb. ad j s.,
j marc. pr. Et per manus thesaurarii pro diuersis confectionibus
per ipsum emptis ibidem, iiij marc. viij scot. Item in diuersis
expensis factis ibidem in hospicio Godesknawt per manus Willelmi
10 Harpeden, die Jouis xvj° Febr., pro cena domini ibidem facta: in   16 February.
primis CLERICO panetrie pro pane albo per ipsum empto ibidem,
x scot. CLERICO buterie super beer et methe, per manus ciusdem
pro j barello de beer per ipsum empta ibidem, xiiij scot. Et per
manus ciusdem pro iij stopis de methe per ipsum emptis ibidem, le
15 stopa vt supra, iij s. pr. CLERICO coquine per manus ciusdem pro
CC. allecibus per ipsum emptis ibidem, v scot. x d. Et pro codelynges emptis ibidem, vj scot. Et per manus ciusdem pro xij
pykerelies per ipsum emptis ibidem, j marc. di. Et per manus
ciusdem pro xxx bremes per ipsum emptis ibidem, xxiij scot. Et
20 per manus ciusdem pro tenches et roches per ipsum emptis ibidem,
iiij scot. xij d. Et per manus ciusdem pro j porpeys per ipsum
empto ibidem, viij scot. Et per manus ciusdem pro C di. anguillarum per ipsum emptis ibidem, x sec t. Et per manus ciusdem   Summa pagine
pro lx roches per ipsum emptis ibidem, vj s. pr. Et per manus   iiij^{xx}j marc. xij
25 ciusdem pro pisis et onyons per ipsum emptis ibidem, v s. pr.   xj d. pr., que fo
Clerico coquine / per manus Willelmi Harpeden pro xvj anguillis   xxvj li. xx d. st
poudrez per ipsum emptis apud Dansk, viij scot. xvj d. pr.   fo. 24 v°
CLERICO speciarie per manus ciusdem pro iiij lb. de dates per ipsum
emptis ibidem, iiij scot. Et per manus ciusdem pro iiij lb. de fyges
30 per ipsum emptis ibidem, ij scot. SUPER officio salsarie per manus
ciusdem pro j pecco farine frumenti per ipsum empto ibidem, iiij
scot. pr. Hankyn Porter pro portagio dictorum victualium vsque
hospicium domini, iiij s. pr. Eidem Willelmo pro iiij bykeres per
ipsum emptis ibidem, iiij s. Cuidam cupario pro ij boketes et ij

CAMD. SOC. L

skeppes emptis ibidem pro elemosina domini custodienda, vij s. viij d. JOHANNI Dyndon pro alblaster strynges per ipsum emptis ibidem pro domino, viij scot. Et per manus eiusdem pro frenges vnius lancie per ipsum emptis ibidem, vj scot. Et per manus eiusdem pro singulo lourice per ipsum empto ibidem, ij scot. HANS Haydon pro cariagio harnesii domini de villa vsque manerium Episcopi, iiij scot. SUPER officio scutellarie, per manus Roberti Spayne pro diuersis barellis vacuis per ipsum emptis ibidem pro diuersis necessariis in coquina, iiij scot. xij d. Et per manus eiusdem pro ij fattes vacuis per ipsum emptis ibidem, pro stepyng yn, xvj scot. Et per manus eiusdem pro iiij wynfattes per ipsum emptis ibidem pro diuersis necessariis ibi lem, viij scot. CLERICO buterie per manus Johannis Cawode pro mattes et stramine per ipsum emptis ibidem pro buteria, xiij s. pr. HEYNE Logere pro portagio de watertonnes vsque manerium Episcopi, iij s. pr. Et eidem pro portagio ij fattes aque ibidem, ij scot. In expensis Whytelok faciendi torches et torteys in villa de Dansk, per iiij dies, iiij scot. JOHANNI Gylder pro verres per ipsum emptis ibidem, ij marc. xviij scot. Cuidam valetto custodienti le Stewe manerii Episcopi, v s pr. CLAUS Cremere pro portagio j last de bere de villa vsque manerium Episcopi, vj scot. Hayne Caryer pro cariagio aque de villa vsque manerium Episcopi, a xvº die Febr vsque vᵐ diem Martii, ij marc. pr. SUPER officio scutellarie, per manus Roberti Spayne pro farina frumenti per ipsum empta ibidem de Hans Tollenere pro diuersis pastellis faciendis, a xvº die Febr. vsque xxvjᵐ diem Martii, v marc pr. Et pro busca et furnagio vna cum stipendio suo, ij marc. Et per manus eiusdem pro aceto per ipsum empto de Henrico Van Torne ibidem, iij marc. di. pr. Et per manus eiusdem pro iiij pestelles per ipsum emptis ibidem, viij s. pr. Et per manus eiusdem pro emendacione vj cuuarum tangentium officium suum, vj s. pr. Et eidem pro emendacione cultellorum coquine, ij scot. Et eidem pro iiij boketes et iij botellis pro croco, vj s. pr. Et per manus eiusdem cuidam lotrici lauanti pannos de scutellaria, v s. pr. Et per manus Johannis Dauid pro iiij

Feb. 15—March 5.

Feb. 15—March 26.

EXPENSES AT DANTZIC.

vrinales et cotom per ipsum emptis ibidem, xj s. pr. HANS Carpentario pro viij deles. meremio, et clauis per ipsum emptis ibidem, vna cum factura eiusdem, xxij scot. Et pro cariagio eorundem, ij s. Willelmo Kykeley pro j cera per ipsum empta ibidem pro porta
5 manerii Episcopi versus villam de Dansk, viij s. pr. Johanni Whityk pro iij ceris et emendacione iij cerarum per ipsum ibidem emptis, viij s. pr. Adam Baker pro furno suo conducto, per manus Johannis Fysshcr a xv° die Febr. vsque vltimam diem eiusdem per conuentionem secum factam ibidem, j marc. di. pr. Et per manus
10 Johannis Fysshcr pistoris domini pro j bultyngtonne per ipsum empto ibidem, iiij s. pr. CLERICO coquine per manus Johannis Whytyk pro xviij lampreys per ipsum emptis ibidem, le piece ad ij scot., j marc. di. pr. SUPER officio aule et camere, per manus Johannis Braillefford pro viij tabulis magnis per ipsum emptis ibidem, pro
15 tabulis comensalibus in aula et in camera, le piece ad vj scot., ij marc. pr. Et per manus eiusdem pro meremio et stipendio carpenterii facientis trestelles pro dictis tabulis per v dies, xij scot. Et per manus eiusdem pro viij deles per ipsum emptis ibidem ad faciendum scabella in aula et in camera, le piece ad iij s., xxiiij s. pr. Cuidam
20 carpenterio pro factura eorundem, v scot. Et per manus eiusdem pro crochetes per ipsum emptis ibidem pro aula pendenda, iij scot. Petro Breker carectario pro cariagio vini et beer per diuersus vices de Dansk vsque manerium Episcopi, per conuencionem secum factam per Johannem Gylder, xlij s. pr. CLERICO speciarie per manus
25 Whytelok pro factura xj stone cere operate pro torches et torticiis ibidem, xxv scot. Et per manus eiusdem pro C lb. candelarum de cepo per ipsum emptis ibidem, le lb. ad j s., j marc. xvj scot. CLERICO buterie super methe, per manus Payn pro iiij barellis de methe per ipsum emptis ibidem, le barellus ad j marc. ij scot., iiij marc. viij scot.
30 Et per manus eiusdem pro xij fattes vini albi per ipsum emptis ibidem, le fatte ad iiij marc. di., liiij marc. pr. Et pro cariagio eorundem, vj scot. Et pro cena domini in villa de Dansk, dominica tertia quadragesime, per manus Simeonis, vj marc. vj scot. HENRICO Hertyk pro xj scok deles ab ipso emptis ibidem per Robertum

Feb. 15—Feb. 2

Summa pagine xxiij. marc. x s. ij s. pr., que faci Angliee vij li. x j d. st.
fo. 25.

Feb. 26.

Hayden pro diuersis necessariis faciendis in nauibus, le scok ad
iij marc. pr., xxxiij marc. pr. Et pro mercimio empto ab eodem
pro diuersis necessariis faciendis in nauibus, v marc. xviij scot.
JOHANNI Beurre pro iij scok deles ab ipso emptis ibidem pro
dicto facto, le scok vt supra, ix marc. pr. Et eidem Johanni pro
xl trees magnis ab ipso emptis ibidem pro eodem facto, iiij marc.
xvij scot. Et pro cariagio dictorum deles et les trees per terram eo
quod non potuerunt cariari per aquam, j marc. xv scot. JACOBO
Outremare pro CCC waynscot ab ipso emptis ibidem pro cabans
faciendis in naui domini et in aula, le C ad ij marc. vj scot., vj marc.
xviij scot. pr. MERKEWORTH Cleykyn pro clauis ab ipso emptis
ibidem per manus Roberti Huidone pro les cabans et aliis necessariis
in naui faciendis, vj marc. ix scot. Et eidem pro hokes et barres
ab ipso emptis ibidem per dictum Robertum, j marc. pr. Et eidem
Roberto pro ij barelles de pyche per ipsum emptis ibidem pro diuersis
necessariis in naui, xj scot. Et per manus eiusdem pro x stone lini
per ipsum emptis ibidem pro eodem facto, xxiij scot. j s. Et in
batillagio eiusdem Roberti de Dansk vsque nauem existentem super
carpenterium ibidem, ex precepto senescalli per diuersas vices, xv
scot. ij s. pr. Et eidem Roberto pro expensis suis per xvij dies in
naui, capienti per diem j scot. ex precepto senescalli, xvij scot.
Edwardo Thome pro hokes, hynges et haspes pro hostiis buterie in
naui domini et in aula, et pro catenis et hokes ad pendendum lectum
domini in le caban domini, et aliis necessariis per ipsum emptis ibidem,
xiij scot. ij s. pr. Et pro batillagio eiusdem ad nauem per diuersas
vices, vj scot. / SUPER officio scutellarie, per manus Laurencii de
scutellario pro vj laste carbonum per ipsum emptis apud Dansk, ij marc.
vj scot. SUPER officio salserie, per manus Roberti Spayne pro vinegre
per ipsum empto ibidem pro tempore quo dominus stetit ibidem, per
compotum secum factum ibidem, viij marc. di. pr. Et per manus
eiusdem pro iiij carucis focalis per ipsum emptis ibidem, caruca ad
vj scot., j marc. pr. Et per manus eiusdem pro cheynes schanes
per ipsum emptis ibidem, j noble xiij scot. CLERICO speciarie
per manus cuiusdam lotricis pro locione pannorum capelle domini

Summa pagine
Cxliiij marc. xxj scot.
prueinne, que faciunt
Anglice xlvi li. vij s.
ij d. ob. q^a.

fo. 25 v°.

EXPENSES AT DANTZIC. 77

ibidem, x s. pr. Et per manus Johannis Peek pro factura sepulcri
in die Parasceues, palmis, emendacione pixidis, vj scot. iij s. pr. March 24.
Cuidam mason facienti furnum in coquina nauis domini vna cum
lapide, lym, et stipendio suo per idem tempus, j noble iiij scot.
5 Ricardo Catour pro victualiis senescalli et thesaurari prandentium
in naui, xviij die Martii, per ipsum emptis ibidem, xviij s. pr. March 13.
Et per manus ciusdem pro batillagio corundem pro ij vices, xxj s.
pr. CLERICO speciarie per manus cuiusdam lotricis lauantis linth-
eamina et alia necessaria domini vsque diem Dominicam [in] Ramis March 19.
10 Palmarum, per compotum secum factum ibidem, xij scot. HOSPI-
TIJSE domini ibidem pro implemento dolii vini per manus Johannis
Payn, xij scot. JACOBO Fauconere pro xlvj gallinis per ipsum
emptis ibidem pro les haukes domini, xliiij s. pr. CLERICO
buterie super vino, per manus Johannis Cawode pro lxvj stopis
15 vini de Lebe per ipsum emptis ibidem, le stopa ad iiij s., iiij marc.
viij scot. iiij s. pr. Et per manus ciusdem pro xxxviij stopis vini
dulcis per ipsum emptis ibidem, le stopa ad xl d., ij marc. vj si
viij d. pr. CLERICO speciarie per manus Ricardi Catour pro ij
panibus de sugre per ipsum emptis ibidem, ij marc. xvij scot.
20 CLERICO marescalcie per manus Roberti Waterton pro ferrura
equorum domini, tempore quo dominus stetit ibidem, xxxv s. pr.
CLERICO coquine per manus Ricardi Catour pro ij kempes de
rubiis allecibus per ipsum emptis ibidem de quodam mercatore
Anglico, ij marc. pr. Et per manus ciusdem pro albis allecibus
25 per ipsum emptis ibidem, viz. viij barellis, le barellus ad j marc.
iij scot., ix marc. pr. CLERICO marescalcie per manus Johannis
Leuynton pro j stak feni per ipsum empto ibidem, viij marc. xv
scot. Et per manus ciusdem pro lxviij shephull auenarum per
ipsum emptis ibidem de Hans Meykyn, le shephull ad j scot. ij marc.
30 di., viij scot. Et per manus Thome Swyllyngton pro xlvj shephull
auenarum per ipsum emptis ibidem, ix° die Martii, le shephull ad
xxviij d., j marc. xviij scot. ij s. iiij d. pr. SUPER officio scutellarie,
per manus Roberti Spayne pro xv fothir carbonum per ipsum
ibidem emptis, le fothir, vj scot. di., iiij marc. ij s. ix d. Et per

78   THE EARL OF DERBY'S EXPEDITIONS.

manus Laurencii de scutellaria pro ij tonellis carbonum per ipsum
emptis ibidem, iiij scot. Et per manus eiusdem pro iij carucis
carbonum per ipsum emptis ibidem, carueа ad vj scot. vj d., xviij
scot. xviij d. Hans Portour pro portagio vnius barelli de vinegre
de villa vsque manerium Episcopi, ij s. x d. Et per manus   5
Roberti Spayne pro viij carectis lignei focalis per ipsum emptis,
xvj s. st. Et per manus eiusdem pro viij laste carbonum per ipsum
ibidem emptis, iiij marc. viij scot. Et pro cariagio eorundem de
villa vsque manerium Episcopi, xviij scot. Et per manus eiusdem
pro CC scutellis per ipsum emptis ibidem erga festum Pasche et pro 10
naui, j marc. pr. CLERICO panetrie per manus Johannis
Gylder pro pane albo per ipsum empto ibidem, a xvij° die
Febr. vsque xx^m diem Martii, xxiij marc. pr. Et per manus
/ Johannis Payn pro j pipa vini rubii de Gasconia per ipsum empta
ibidem de quodam mercatore Anglico, vij nobles di. Johannis 15
Whytlok pro emendacione vnius clothesak tangentis officium
suum, ij s. iij d. CLERICO buterie super bere et methe, per manus
Johannis Gylder pro j laste de beer per ipsum empto ibidem, v
marc. pr. Clerico buterie super vino, per manus eiusdem pro ij
fattes vini per ipsum emptis ibidem, x marc. pr. Et pro cariagio 20
dictorum vini et beer de villa vsque manerium Episcopi, vj scot.
Et per manus eiusdem pro xiiij stopis vini de Garnade per ipsum
emptis ibidem, precium le stopa ad iiij s., xxij scot xij d. pr.
SUPER officio scutellarie per manus Roberti Spayne pro sale per
ipsum empto ibidem de Henryk Burrek, iiij marc. pr. Et per 25
manus Laurencii de scutellaria pro sinape, oleribus, caboches, et
aliis herbis et lekes, vna cum aliis salseriis per ipsum emptis ibidem
a xvij° die Febr. vsque dominicam Ramis Palmarum, per compotum
secum factum ibidem, iiij marc. viij scot. CLAUS BENHOW magistro
carpenterio operanti in naui per iij septimanas circa diuersa neces- 30
saria ibidem facienda, capienti per septimanam xviij scot., ij ma. c. di.
vj scot. Et iiij sociis suis laborantibus ibidem per idem tempus,
quolibet capiente per septimanam x scot., v marc. pr. Et Mattes
van Ostremark, carpenterio, per ij septimanas pro se et iiij sociis,

capienti pro se in septimana, xiiij scot., et quolibet sociorum capiente in septimana viij scot. per idem tempus, in toto iij marc. xx scot. Hankyn Merenb, carpenterio laboranti in naui per ij septimanas cum iij sociis, capienti pro se in septimana viij scot., et quolibet 5 sociorum capiente in septimana vij scot., per tempus predictum, ij marc. x scot. Jacob Casseleyn carpenterio laboranti in naui per j septimanam cum v sociis, capienti pro se xviij scot. per septimanam et pro quolibet sociorum suorum x scot., in toto ij marc. xx scot. Cuidam pictori pictanti arma domini in hospicio domini ibidem, di. 10 marc. pr. Et pro batillagio Roberti Pepour versus nauem, iiijs. pr. Clerico speciarie pro canella empta per manus Johannis Whytyk ibidem, iij marc. pr. Johanni Gylder pro tractura j laste de bere, xv s. pr. Clerico coquine per manus Ricardi Dancastre pro ij porpeys per ipsum emptis apud nauem, j marc. ij 15 scot. Johanni Whytyk pro emendacione diuersarum cerarum in manerio episcopi et pro clauibus pro eisdem, xvj scot. Et per manus ciusdem pro carbonibus per ipsum emptis ibidem, iij marc. xiiij scot. Et per manus ciusdem pro cariagio diuersorum victualium et aliorum necessariorum contra aduentum domini per ipsum 20 facto, ij marc. v scot. Et per manus ciusdem pro vj lignis magnis et x deles ad faciendum diuersa necessaria in coquina, larderia et scutellaria, xiiij scot. ij s. iiij d. pr. Et pro plastre et lapide ibidem emptis per eundem, iij scot. x d. Et per manus ciusdem pro henges, hokes, et clauis et cera per ipsum emptis pro eisdem 25 officiis, xv scot. iij s. ij d. Et per manus ciusdem pro xx barrellis vacuis per ipsum emptis ibidem pro diuersis necessariis, xvj scot. Et pro cariagio corundem, ij scot. Et per manus ciusdem pro xxiiij tonellis vacuis per ipsum emptis ibidem pro farina imponenda, le tonella ad ij scot., ij marc. pr. Et per manus ciusdem cuidam 30 carpenterio vocato Claus Rodebrond operanti in dicto manerio per x dies, capienti per diem j scot. di., xv scot. Et per manus eiusdem pro vj quarternis papiri per ipsum emptis ibidem, di. marc. pr. Et per manus eiusdem pro ij corfes de figes et de reysyngs per ipsum emptis ibidem, iij marc. viij scot.

Summa pagine lxviij marc. v. scot. que faciunt Angl xxj li. xvj s. vj d.

fo. 26 v°. / Clerico speciarie per manus Ricardi Catour pro oleo et diuersis speciebus per ipsum emptis ibidem per diuersas vices, xiiij marc. xvij scot. Et pro portagio eorundem, iij scot. Johanni Fysher pro x bultyng clothes per ipsum emptis ibidem, iiij scot. Et per manus eiusdem pro carbonibus per ipsum emptis et expenditis in le bultynghous, vna cum candelis et beer et aliis victualibus ibidem expenditis per xv^{am} circa bultyng frumenti pro provideneiis domini faciendis versus Angliam, xj scot. ij s. iiij d. pr. Et per manus eiusdem pro cariagio frumenti et siliginis de molendino vsque le bultynghous per diuersas vices, xxvj scot. Et per manus eiusdem diuersis molendinariis ad expediendum, xij scot. Clerico speciarie per manus Whytlok pro carbonibus, candelis de cepo, circa facturam torches et torticiorum in domo moniale ibidem, et pro stipendio cuiusdam sibi auxiliantis, ix scot. ij s. pr. Et pro lewyn pro dictis terches et torticiis per ipsum emptis ibidem, xxij s. pr. Et per manus eiusdem pro j ladele de ferro et ij ferris ad faciendum dictos torches et torticios, iiij scot. ij s. pr. Domino Hugoni Waterton pro cena domini apud Dansk die

March 21. Martis proxima post dominicam [in] Ramis Palmarum, in toto xx s. st Clerico marescalcie per manus Huet Rubuc pro v shok et di. straminis ab ipso emptis ibidem per Johannem Leuyngton, xj die Martii, le schok ix s., xij scot. j s. Super officio scutellarie, per manus Laurencii de scutellaria pro ij hameres pro stokefyssh per ipsum emptis ibidem, vj scot. Johanni Gylder pro cariagio iiij tonellarum de bykeres, iiij s. pr. Et per manus eiusdem pro cariagio di. laste de beer de villa ibidem vsque manerium Episcopi, xij scot. Clerico buterie super vino per manus Johannis Gylder pro xij stopis de Rynyswyn per ipsum emptis ibidem, xxv s. pr. In batillagio eiusdem Johannis de ibidem vsque naues per diuersas vices in negocio domini faciendo, vj. scot. Et in batillagio seneccalli et thesaurarii de villa versus naues, viij s. pr. Johanni Cawode pro ij schok de bykeres per ipsum emptis ibidem de Hogle, bykermaker, xiiij scot. Et per manus eiusdem pro iij tonnes per ipsum emptis ibidem pro dictis bykeres

et al*iis* imponend*is*, iiij scot. Et *per manus* eiu*s*dem *pro* tractu*ra*
de iiij l*aste* de beer v*sque* naue*m*, viij s. pr. CLERICO *speciarie per*
manus Edeyne Laundour lauanti*s mapparum* et towell*s* bu*terie* per
tem*pus* quo domi*nus* stetit ib*idem*, viij scot. Hans Yong*s*rowe
5 *pro* p*ortagio* iij tonell*arum* vini Gasc*onie* de Dansk vsq*ue* nau*em*,
xviij scot. Et eid*em pro* cariag*io* xxix *s*atte*s* de landewyn, xvj
scot. Et eidem *pro* cariag*io* iij *s*atte*s* de landwyn ad bark, ix s.
pr. Roberto Hethcote *pro* corda per ip*s*um empta ib*idem pro*
lecto d*omi*ni, ix s. pr. CLERICO p*a*netrie *per manus* Joh*a*nnis
10 Fy*ss*h*er pro* xl *s*hephull farine frumenti per ip*s*um empti*s* ib*i*dem
de Petro Tweyfrere, le *s*hephull ad vj scot, ix mare. CLERICO
buterie per *manus* Johannis Payn *pro* j *s*atte vini per ip*s*um
empto ib*idem*, v marc. ix scot. Et per *manus* ciusdem *pro* di. last
de Wy*s*hmer beer *per* ip*s*um empto ib*idem*, le barell*us* ad xv scot,
15 iij marc. xviij scot. Et *pro* portag*io* co*r*undem de villa vsque man-
erium Epi*s*copi, iiij scot. CLERICO speciarie *per manus* Wytlok *pro* iiij*xx* lb. candel*arum* de cepo per ip*s*um empti*s* ib*idem*, le lb. ad
j s., j marc. viij s*c*ot. Et *pro* *s*ope empto per ip*s*um ib*idem*. x s. pr.
/Balliuo manerii Epi*s*copi *pro* stramine ab ip*s*o empto ib*i*dem, et *pro*
20 tractura aq*ue* de villa vsque ad manerium Epi*s*copi, a xvij die
Febr. vsque xvij*m* diem Mart*ii*, per *manus* the*s*au*ra*r*ii*, iiij nobles
viij scot. Quatuor valetti*s* portanti*bus* vj ba*r*ello*s* de beer de
villa vsq*ue* manerium Epi*s*copi, v scot. SUPER officio scutellarie
per *manus* Roberti Spayne *pro* vj *s*hephu*l*l et di. farine frum*enti* p*er*
25 ip*s*um empti*s* ib*i*de*m* de Hans Rother*s*ord, le *s*hephul *pro* vj *s*cot.,
xxxix scot. Et *per manus* eiusdem *pro* j pipa et j barello per
ip*s*um ib*idem* empti*s* pro aqua imponend*a* in naui*bus*, ij marc.
xiiij scot. Joh*a*nni Fy*ss*h*er pro* cariag*io* farine de le bultynghous
vsq*ue* ripa*m*, xj scot. Cuid*am* lotrici lauant*i* mappa*s* aquar*ii* ib*idem*,
30 xxviij s. pr. CLERICO bu*terie* super vino per *manus* Gylder *pro* xij
stopi*s* vini de g*a*rnad*e* per ip*s*um empti*s* ib*idem*. le stopa ad iiij s.,
xlviij s. pr. HANS Skypher *pro* batill*agio* d*o*mini de villa vsq*ue*
naue*s*, xiiij die Mart*ii*, xiij scot. JACOBO SALSALE *pro* portag*io*
vj laste de beer de manerio Epi*sc*opi v*s*q*ue* ripam, capi*enti pro* le

Summa pagine
xlvj marc. ij s. iij
pr., *que* faci*unt*
Angli*ce* xiiij li.
xiiij s. vij d. ob. -
fo. 27.

February 17—M 17.

March 14.

laste, ix scot, xviij d., ij marc. di, iiij s. pr. CLERICO panetrie per manus Johannis Fyssher pro pane albo per ipsum empto ibidem de Hans Yongfrowe, iiij marc. ij scot. Et per manus eiusdem pro furnagio, busca, et stipendio suo tempore quo dominus stetit ibidem, v marc. di. CLERICO buterie super vino per manus Johannis Gylder pro ij fattes vini per ipsum emptis ibidem, xj marc. xij s. pr. CLAUS carpentere cum sociis suis laborantibus per viij dies circa diuersa necessaria in hospicio domini, capientibus per diem, iij s., xlviij s. pr. CLERICO coquine per manus Willelmi Harpeden pro xx anguillis per ipsum emptis ibidem, ij marc. pr. SUPER officio pulletrie, per manus Willelmi Harpeden pro x C di. ouorum per ipsum emptis ibidem, in toto j marc. x scot. Et per manus eiusdem pro tribus duodenis et ix gallinarum per ipsum emptis ibidem, j marc. vj scot. Et per manus eiusdem pro vj perdicibus per ipsum emptis ibidem, le piece ad ij s., iiij scot. ij s. pr. Et per manus eiusdem pro v stopis de crem per ipsum emptis ibidem, le stopa ad xvj d., iij scot. Et per manus eiusdem pro xviij stopis lacte per ipsum emptis ibidem, le stopa ad iiij d., vj s. pr. Et per manus eiusdem pro portagio dictarum, ij s. pr. Et per manus eiusdem pro vj maulards per ipsum emptis ibidem, le piece ad ij s. xij s. pr. Et per manus eiusdem pro ix gallinis per ipsum emptis ibidem, le piece ad ij s., xviij s. pr. Et per manus eiusdem pro xiiij caponibus per ipsum emptis ibidem, le piece iiij s., plus in toto iiij s., lvj s. pr. Et per manus eiusdem pro iij agnellis per ipsum emptis ibidem, ix scot. Et per manus eiusdem pro j maulard per ipsum empto ibidem, ij s. pr. Et per manus eiusdem pro iiij duodenis paruorum* anium, iiij s. pr. Et per manus eiusdem pro j vitulo per ipsum empto ibidem, iiij scot. Et per manus eiusdem pro x C ouorum per ipsum emptis ibidem, centum ad viij s., j marc. xviij scot. Et per manus eiusdem pro iij gallinis per ipsum emptis ibidem, le pece ad ij s., vj s. pr. Et per manus eiusdem pro j salmone per ipsum empto ibidem, iiij scot. WILLELMO HARPEDEN pro expensis suis circa prouidencias faciendas per quinque dies, per compotum secum factum apud

* [Sic].

Summa pagine xliiij marc. xij scot. iij s. pr., que faciunt xiiij li. v s. j d. sterlingos.

fo. 27 vº.

Dansk, capienti per diem j scot., in toto v. scot. Hans Carpentere pro se et duobus sociis per iiij dies laborantibus in naui, quolibet capiente per diem ij scot., j marc. pr. Duobus Prucianis portantibus fattes et barelles pro aqua de manerio Episcopi vsque
5 nauem, iiij scot. Clerico coquine per manus Ricardi Catour pro carne recente per ipsum empta ibidem, xxv° die Martii, j marc. March 25. xiij scot. Decem carectariis cariantibus harnesia domini de manerio Episcopi vsque rypam, xviij scot. Clerico coquine per manus Ricardi Catour pro xviij multonibus per ipsum emptis ibidem, le
10 piece ad vj scot , iiij marc. di. pr. Et per manus eiusdem pro ij bobus per ipsum emptis ibidem de Kyrsten van Hostrych, iiij marc. pr. Et per manus eiusdem pro j boue per ipsum empto ibidem, xxiiij die mensis Martii, de hospitissa domini ibidem, March 24. j noble viij scot. Hans Cruse pistori pro pane, carne bouina,
15 salsa, et bacons ab ipso emptis per manus Johannis Payn ibidem, pro prouidenciis domini versus Angliam, xxj marc. xiiij scot Et per manus eiusdem pro j dolio buteri per ipsum empto ibidem ab eodem, j marc. xj scot. Et per manus Willelmi Harpedene pro x bacons per ipsum emptis ibidem et pro pinguedine recente empta
20 ibidem pro eadem prouidencia, v marc. viij scot. ij s. pr. Clerico coquine per manus Ricardi Catour pro vj vitulis, j multone et iij agnellis per ipsum emptis ibidem de hospitissa domini, ij marc. pr. vij scot. Super officio pulletrie per manus Willelmi Harpeden pro iij perdicibus et ij maulard per ipsum emptis ibidem, viij scot. Et
25 per manus eiusdem pro iij gallinis per ipsum emptis ibidem, vj s. pr. Heyn Gromette pro batillagio thesaurarii de Dansk vsque naues et redeunte, iiij scot. Clerico coquine per manus Ricardi Catour pro ij bobus per ipsum emptis ibidem, ij marc. iij scot. Et pro batillagio dicti Ricardi versus naues, iiij s. pr. Super officio
30 pulletrie, per manus Willelmi Harpeden et Johannis Knyghton pro ordio per ipsos empto ibidem pro pullis, gallinis, et pulcinis, iij marc. pr. Claus Heyngere pro cariagio vini et beer de manerio Episcopi vsque rypam, xx s. pr. Hans Bocher per manus camerarii pro v barellis carnis salse per ipsum ab ipso emptis ibidem,

iij nobles. SUPER officio pulletrie, per manus Willelmi Harpeden pro xiiij duodenis gallinarum per ipsum ibidem emptis, duodena ad ix scot xviij d., iiij marc. di. vj scot. iij s. pr. Et per manus eiusdem pro ij^{bus} duodenis per ipsum emptis ibidem, xvij scot. xviij d. pr. Et per manus eiusdem pro xxxC ouorum per ipsum 5 emptis ibidem, centena ad viij s, iiij marc. pr. HANS HEYNGLE per manus Roberti Spaigne pro xv barellis vacuis ab ipso emptis ibidem, le barellus ad vj s. pr., j marc. di. pr. Et pro portagio dictorum barellorum et de ij cages pro pulletrie, ij scot. ij s. pr. SUPER officio pulletrie, per manus Willelmi Harpeden pro butiro 10 per ipsum empto ibidem, iij scot. Et per manus eiusdem pro j schok ouorum ibidem empto, iiij s. Et pro iij perdicibus per ipsum emptis ibidem, vj s. pr. Et per manus eiusdem pro j maulard per ipsum empto, ij s. pr. Et per manus eiusdem pro ij gallinis per ipsum emptis ibidem, le piece ad xxij d., iij s. viij d. Et per 15 manus eiusdem pro iiij agnellis per ipsum emptis ibidem, ix scot. Et per manus eiusdem pro v duodenis et ij gallinarum, le piece ad xxiij d. per ipsum emptis ibidem, v li. xviij s. x d. Et per manus eiusdem pro x C ouorum per ipsum emptis ibidem, C^a ad viij s., j marc. xviij scot. Et per manus eiusdem pro vj agnellis per 20 ipsum emptis ibidem, xij scot. Et per manus eiusdem pro iiij shephull ordii pro putura per ipsum emptis ibidem, viij scot. Et per manus eiusdem pro ij shephul ordii emptis ibidem, / iiij scot. ij s. pr. Et per manus Willelmi Harpeden pro v perdicibus per ipsum emptis apud Dansk, le piece ad xxvj d., iiij scot. 25 x s. pr. Et per manus eiusdem pro vj duodenis gallinarum per ipsum emptis ibidem, le piece ad xx d., vj li. xv s. pr. CLERICO buterie super vino, per manus Johannis Cawode pro xxj stopis vini de garnade per ipsum emptis ibidem, le stope ad xl d., j. marc. iiij scot. SUPER officio scutellarie, per manus Laurencii de scut- 30 ellaria pro ij fothir carbonum emptis per ipsum ibidem, le fothir ad xij scot., j marc. pr. Et per manus eiusdem pro xij last carbonum per ipsum emptis ibidem, le last ad vij scot., vj d.; iij marc. xiiij scot. vj d. pr. Et per manus eiusdem pro busca empta

EXPENSES AT DANTZIC.

ibidem, ij marc. pr. Et per manus eiusdem pro ligno pro hostilia
per ipsum empto ibidem, vj scot. Et per manus ciusdem pro
focali per ipsum empto ibidem, ij marc. vj scot. Et per manus
ciusdem pro focali per ipsum empto ibidem de Nykell Dyscher
5 apud le Bergh Episcopi, viij marc. iij scot. Et per manus Laurencii de scutellaria pro iij quarteriis focalis per ipsum emptis
ibidem, j marc. xx scot. Et per manus Roberti Spaigne pro
focali per ipsum empto ibidem de Claus Neverfronde, ij marc. di.
iiij s. pr. Et per manus Laurencii de scutellaria pro xj fothir car-
10 bonum per ipsum emptis ibidem, le fothir ad xj scot., v marc. pr.
j scot. Et per manus Ricardi Catour pro busca per ipsum empta
ibidem, iiij marc. pr. Et per manus ciusdem pro sale per ipsum
empto ibidem de Henrico Loge, iiij marc. di. pr. Et per manus
Laurencii de scutellaria pro aceto per ipsum empto ibidem pro
15 prouidenciis de Henrico Van Torne, iiij marc. viij scot. Et per
manus eiusdem pro sinape et aceto, oleribus et herbis, per ipsum
emptis ibidem, iiij marc. di. iiij s. pr. Et per manus ciusdem pro
scutellis ligneis, trowes, bolles, boketes et trestelles, iiij marc. pr. Et
per manus Whytloke pro sope per ipsum empto ibidem pro naui,
20 ij scot CLERICO speciarie per manus ciusdem pro Cxviij lb. candelarum de sepo per ipsum emptis ibidem, le lb. ad j s. j marc. di.
xj scot. vj d. SUPER officio aule et camere, per manus Johannis
Braillefford pro sirpis per ipsum [emptis] ibidem pro aula et camera
domini in manerio Episcopi, tempore quo dominus stetit ibidem,
25 ij marc. ix scot. ij s. iiij d. pr. Et per manus ciusdem pro clauis
per ipsum emptis ibidem pro diuersis necessariis emendandis in
officio suo, xij s. pr. HANS KESSELEYN carectario carianti diuersa
necessaria coquine et pulletrie et aliorum officiorum de manerio
Episcopi vsque ripam per diuersas vices, ij marc. vj scot. CLERICO
30 speciarie per manus cuiusdam lotricis lauantis mappas aule
et camere ac etiam diuersorum necessariorum domini, viij scot.
ij s. pr. CLERICO buterie super beer, per manus Johannis Gylder
pro ij laste de beer per ipsum emptis ibidem, le last ad v marc. pr.
v scot., x marc. x scot. Et pro iiij barellis seruisie Anglice per

ipsum emptis ibidem, le barellus ad iiij s. ij d. st., in toto ij marc.
di. pr. Et per manus Johannis Payn pro ij barellis de methe per
ipsum emptis ibidem, le barell ad j marc. pr., ij marc. pr. Et per
manus eiusdem pro xx lb. de dates per ipsum emptis ibidem, le
lb. ad ij scot., xl scot. Et per manus eiusdem pro j pane de
sugre, ij marc. vj scot. Clerico marescalcie pro ferrura equorum
domini per manus Thome Swyllyngton ibidem, iiij scot. ij s. pr.
/ CLERICO coquine per manus Ricardi Catour pro piscibus per ipsum
emptis apud naues per diuersas vices, ij marc. xix scot. Et per
manus Willelmi Harpeden pro pane, vino, piscibus, fructibus et
focali, per ipsum emptis ibidem pro Senescallo, Thesauro, Toty,
Marescallo et aliis diuersis officiariis ibidem per ij dies, vna cum
Magistris nauium, xxxviij s. pr. Et in batillagio eorundem, viij
scot. Et per manus senescalli pro piscibus per ipsum emptis apud
Dansk, xiij s. iiij d. st. HANS Boteman pro batillagio domini de
Dansk vsque Mende per manus Norbery, iij s. iiij d. st. ROBERTO
SPAYNE pro iij paribus trestellorum per ipsum emptis ibidem, xij
scot. Et per manus eiusdem pro ij fattes pro carne salsa et piscibus
per ipsum emptis ibidem, viij s. pr. Et per manus eiusdem pro iiij
haspes et ij bendes pro cloos boketes pro naui per ipsum emptis
ibidem, iiij s. pr. Johanni Peek pro j basket et j bokete per ipsum
emptis ibidem, iiij s. iiij d. HANS Carpenterio pro emendacione
coquine et aliarum domorum in manerio Episcopi vj scot. ij s.
iiij d. pr. SUPER officio scutellarie, per manus Roberti Spaigne
pro xiiij barellis per ipsum emptis ibidem pro aqua recente imponenda in nauibus, xxviij scot. Edwyne Moreyn sewster pro filo ab
ipsa empto ibidem et pro factura de xxj sakes et emendacione de
xiij veteribus sakks, per manus Thome Swyllyngton, vj scot. Et
per manus eiusdem pro iiij bolles, ij boketes, iij lepes, et corda pro
eisdem, j scope et ij gymbottes, xiij s. j ferdkyn (pr. iiij d.) pro nauibus.
Et per manus eiusdem pro x tonellis aque pro equis, xl. s. pr. Et
pro portagio eiusdem, iiij s. pr. Et pro meltyng de sepo et iiij lb.
pinguedinum, vj s. pr. CLERICO marescalcie per manus eiusdem
pro ij nonis fenis pro equis domini ibidem, emptis per ipsum, ij s.

et ij ferdkyn. HANS SHONE per manus Roberti Hethecote pro
expensis vnius battelle de Dansk vsque naues cum bonis domini,
vij s. pr. CLAUS KORME Van Ederyke pro j lb. de cotem ab ipso
empta ibidem, vj s. pr. Et per manus Ricardi de Ewerye pro
5 j chawfour per ipsum empto ibidem, vj scot. CLERICO coquine per
manus Willelmi Harpeden pro piscibus per ipsum emptis ibidem,
in toto j marc. iij scot. Et per manus eiusdem pro j vitulo per
ipsum empto ibidem, vj scot. Et per manus eiusdem pro j agnello,
per ipsum empto ibidem, vj scot. Et pro lx pykes per ipsum emptis
10 ibidem, xxij scot. Et per manus eiusdem pro iij vitulis per ipsum
emptis ibidem, xix scot. di. Et pro iij agnellis per ipsum emptis
ibidem, xij s. pr. Et pro j barello vacuo empto ibidem, j scot.
Et pro portagio dictorum victualium ad nauem, j marc. xvij s. pr.
Et pro ij mattes ibidem emptis, iiij s. pr. Et soluta per manus
15 Ricardi Catour pro j dolio carnis salse, xx scot. HEYNE WEGLE
pro ponderacione carnis ibidem et piscium salsorum ad naues, viij
scot. Cuidam dryuer pro fugacione boum ibidem, vij s. pr.
CLERICO marescalcie per manus Thome Swyllyngton pro x
fothir feni per ipsum emptis ibidem, le fothir ad vj scot.,
20 ij marc. di. pr. Et per manus eiusdem pro xlvj shephull auenarum per ipsum emptis ibidem, le shephull ad ij s. pr., j marc. di. ij s.
/ EDWARDO THORNE le lodesman nauis domini pro viagio domini
de Prucia vsque Angliam, per conuentionem secum factam ex
consensu camerarii et senescalli, C s. st. Roberto Haydon le lodes-
25 man nauis aule domini pro stipendio suo, capienti ut supra, C s. st.
Et per manus Johannis Beuere pro xiiij lanternis per ipsum emptis
apud Dansk per naui domini versus Angliam, le piece ad v scot.,
ij marc. di. x scot. JOHANNI CAWODE pro piris, pomis et nucibus
per ipsum emptis ibidem per diuersas vices pro tempore quo
30 dominus stetit ibidem, per compotum secum factum ibidem, ij marc.
xxj scot. CLERICO buterie per manus eiusdem pro ij laste de beer
per ipsum emptis ibidem, le laste ad v marc. vj scot., x marc. di.
CLERICO buterie super vino, pro ij fattes vini albi emptis ibidem
per manus Johannis Gylder, le fatte ad iiij marc. v scot., viij marc.

Summa pagine
xx marc. xvj scot
ij d. Pruciane, qu
faciunt Anglice
vj li. xij s. iij d. o
fo. 29.

x scot. Et *pro portagio dicti* vini et beer vsque manerium Episcopi, viij scot. ij s. iiij d. pr. CLERICO coquine per *manus* Ricardi Catour *pro* iiij porpeys et codelyng per ipsum emptis ibidem, xxxiiij scot. CLERICO speciarie per manus Johannis Beuere pro vj stone et di. cere non operate per ipsum emptis ibidem, le stone 5 ad j mare, xviij scot., xj mare, xxj scot. Et pro factura eiusdem cere, vij scot. ij s. pr. Et per manus eiusdem pro wyke per ipsum ibidem pro eadem cera facienda, xj s. vj d. pr. Et pro expensis thesaurarii, Ricardi Catour, et Willelmi Harpolene et aliorum in hospicio apud Dansk per vj dies post recessum domini, 10 vj s. viij d. st. JACOBO Fau onere pro iiij duodenis gallinarum per ipsum emptis pro les haukes domini in naui, xl s. pr. Et per manus eiusdem pro tiebles per ipsum emptis ibidem ad cariandum les haukes, xiiij scot. CLERICO coquine per manus senescalli pro diuersis piscibus per ipsum emptis in le Wysle, xiiij s. viij d. st. 15

Summa pagine xj li. xvj d. st., et monete Pruciane xl marc. iij scot. x d. pr.; que faciunt xij li. xvj s. x d. ob. sterlingorum.

Summa expensarum vij foliorum precedentium vsque huc in Prucia, le noble ad xxv scot., CCCxxxv li. xiiij s. viij d. qr. sterlinges.[a]   20

GARDEROBA DOMINI IN PRUCIA.

fo. 31v°.

November 4.

• [The MS. has *vno*].

/SUPER officio Garderobe, per manus Johannis Dyndon pro iij virgis panni rubii per ipsum emptis apud Conyngburgh, virga ad x s., pro domino iiij° die Nouembris, de executore Johannis de Londeham militis, xxx s. st.; et pro v virgis panni nigri per ipsum 25 emptis ibidem ad vsum domini, virga ad vj s., xxx s.; in toto lx. s. st. Et per manus Petri Tweytord pro vna* duodena panni nigri ab ipso empta ibidem pro domino per manus Henrici de Garderoba, vij nobles, xxij s. pr. Et per manus eiusdem pro panno

[a] The next two leaves, (fos. 29 v° to 31 (four pages), are blank in the MS.

WARDROBE EXPENSES IN PRUSSIA. 89

linco per ipsum empto ibidem pro mulieribus et infantulis de
Lettowe, iiij nobles di j scot. Et per manus eiusdem pro iij^{bus}
vlnis et di. de kersey per ipsum emptis ibidem, xj s. viij d. pr. Et
per manus thesaurarii pro iiij pannis de serico per ipsum emptis
5 apud Dansk in festo Sancte Elizabete, xx marc. pr. Et per manus
Johannis Dyndon pro xxiij^{bus} virgis panni nigri de Lyra per
ipsum emptis ibidem pro domino, x nobles. Et per manus eiusdem
pro vno rolle de satyn nigri empto pro domino ibidem, v marc. Et
pro j duodena de stragulis pro ministrallis per manus Johannis
10 Scorell empta apud Conyngburgh, iiij marc. pr. Et per manus
Johannis Dyndon pro v virgis de scarlet per ipsum emptis ibidem,
x nobles. Hans Wyghtman pro cariagio albi panni de Dansk vsque
Conyngburgh per conventionem secum factam ibidem, iiij marc.
di. pr. Et per manus Henrici de garderoba pro xxv vlnis panni
15 linei de Prucia per ipsum emptis ibidem, le vlna ad iiij s. pr., pro
domino, j marc. xvj scot. pr. Et pro tonsura vnius duodene de
stragulis pro ministrallis, per thesaurarium, iiij scot. Et pro panno
laneo empto ibidem per Duffeld et Laurencium de coquina, nunciante camerario, j marc. iij s. pr. Et pro camisiis, sotularibus, et
20 caligis ibidem emptis pro eisdem, j noble. Et per manus Johannis
Dyndon pro xij vlnis panni linei per ipsum emptis ibidem, le
vlna ad v s, j marc. pr. Et per manus thesaurarii pro vij vlnis
panni lanei per ipsum emptis ibidem, le vlna ad iij s. pro Willelmo
Fyssher, baker, nunciante senescallo, xxj s. pr. Et per manus
25 Henrici de garderoba pro xxxvj vlnis de blanket, per ipsum emptis
ibidem pro duplicatione juparum domini, le vlna ad iij s., j noble
xlviij s. pr. Et per manus eiusdem pro j duodena de blanket per
ipsum empta ibidem pro le heret qui portauit vexillum Sancti
Georgii in Lettow, virga ad x s., ix marc. st. Et pro blanket empto
30 ibidem pro duplicatione juparum Willelmi Fyssher, xxiiij s. pr.
Et per manus Johannis Dyndon pro ij pannis de serico per ipsum
emptis ibidem pro domino, xv marc. pr. Et per manus Henrici de
camera pro panno blodeo per ipsum empto de Henrico Malkoñ,
ij nobles, j s. minus. Et pro factura panni Henrici de coquina et

CAMD. SOC. N

Duffeld, xvj s. pr. Et per manus Johannis Dyndon pro x vlnis de tapheta rubia per ipsum emptis, le vlna ad viij scot ibidem, iij marc. viij scot. Et per manus eiusdem pro v vlnis de tapheta blodea per ipsum emptis ibidem pro vexillis domini, le vlna ad viij s., xl s. pr. Et per manus eiusdem pro xxiij vlnis panni 5 linei per ipsum emptis ibidem ad vsum domini, le vlna ad x scot, ix marc. xiiij scot. Et pro tonsura dicti panni, xij s. pr. Et pro viij lb. de cotom ibidem emptis ad vsum domini, le lb. ad viij s. viij d., j marc. ix s. iiij d. pr. Et pro filo empto ibidem, iiij s. pr. Et per manus Johannis Dyndon pro j vlna et iij quartiers de fustyan 10 / per ipsum emptis apud Conyngburgh, vij s. pr. Et per manus ciusdem pro drawyng-yerne per ipsum empt' ibidem, iiij s. pr. Et per manus eiusdem a brawederere pro j manche, pro frenges et laces pro vsu domini, viij marc. pr. Et per manus Henrici de Camera pro coreo per ipsum empto ibidem pro le doublet domini, 15 ij s. pr. Et per manus eiusdem data pellipario pro furrura ad vsum domini, xvj scot. Et per manus eiusdem pro j virga de fustyan per ipsum empta ibidem ad vsum domini, viij s. pr. Et per manus eiusdem pro iij paribus sotularium per ipsum ibidem emptis pro les Leptows,* iiij scot. Thome Goter pro conductione vnius equi 20 portantis furruram domini de Dansk vsque Conyngburgh, xvj scot. Et per manus Roberti Waterton pro ij paueys per ipsum emptis ibidem, xx scot. Et per manus Henrici de Garderoba pro karde et panno lineo pro les standardes per ipsum emptis ibidem, vna cum factura ciusdem, j marc. viij scot. xij d. Et per manus 25 ciusdem pro ix vlnis et j quartier de karde per ipsum emptis ibidem, le vlna ad iiij s. pr., xxxvij s. Et per manus eiusdem pro serico albo et blodeo, vz. xvj node per ipsum emptis ibidem pro domino, xiiij scot. j s. pr. Et per manus Johannis Scorell pro j vlna di. de blanket, precium xiij s. di., et pro j vlna et di. de b'odeo de 30 Lyra, precium xiij scot. di., pro caligis pro Johanne Rauene nepote marrescalli, j marc. ij scot. ij s. vj d. pr. Et pro sotularibus pro eodem ibidem emptis, iiij s. pr. Et soluta pro sotularibus per Henricum de camera pro Henrico Lettowe, nunciante senescallo,

iij s. pr. Et per manus Johannis Dounton pro j cofre per ipsum
empt' ibidem ad imponendum scuta domini, xvij scot. Et per
manus Johannis Dyndon pro iij vlnis panni blodei per ipsum
emptis ibidem, nunciante senescallo, pro les Lettows, xxv s. pr. Et
5 per manus Jacobi Fauconer pro viij vlnis panni lanei pro les cages
de fawcons per ipsum emptis ibidem, xxxij s. pr. Et pro j topynet
de j basinet empto ibidem per Robertum Waterton, vna cum emendacione zone domini, v nobles. Et per manus Johannis Dyndon
pro j furrura per ipsum empta ibidem de beuere pro domino, ix
10 nobles, ij scot. minus. Et per manus ciusdem pro iij virgis iij
quartiers panni nigri de Lyra per ipsum emptis ibidem pro domino,
xiiij s. viij d. st. Et per manus ciusdem pro j furrura de martynet
pro jupa domini nigra per ipsum empta ibidem, viij marc. xxij scot.
Et pro factura dicte furrure et pro furracione j pair pynsons, et pro
15 xxiij bestes pro complemento corundem emptis ibidem, le beste ad
iiij s., j noble iiij scot. Et per manus ciusdem pro iij virgis panni
nigri de Lyra pro capicio domini per ipsum emptis ibidem,
xiiij scot. Et pro filo empto ibidem, x s. pr. Et per manus
ciusdem pro j pare corkes per ipsum empto ibidem pro domino,
20 iij s. pr. Et per manus Johannis Dyndon cuidam pellipario
pro j pilche de beuere per ipsum empto ab ipso ibidem, xx
nobles. Johanni Norberye pro j jupa quam dominus accepit
/ ab ipso, ex precepto domini, C s. st. Et per manus Johannis
Dyndon pro xv vlnis panni linei per ipsum emptis apud Conyng-
25 burgh ad vsum domini, die Jouis in Cena Domini, xv scot. Et
data Bernard Hansemann pro factura jupe sue nunciante camerario, x s. pr. Et pro sotularibus suis, iij s. pr. Et per manus
Ricardi Catour pro camisiis, sotularibus et aliis necessariis emptis
per ipsum pro Henrico Lettowe ibidem, nunciante senescallo,
30 xx s. pr. Et per manus ciusdem pro pylches pro vj Lettows per
ipsum emptis ibidem, nunciante camerario, ij marc. xxj scot. Et
per manus ciusdem pro sotularibus et capiciis pro eisdem per ipsum
emptis ibidem, di. marc. pr. Et per manus Johannis Dauyd pro
ix vrinales pro domino per ipsum emptis ibidem, xxij s. vj d. pr.

Summa pagine
lxvj marc. vij -cc
x d. pr., que facit
Anglice xx li. vii
st., le noble ad
xxvj scot.

fo. 32 v°.

March 23.

pr. Et per manus Johannis Dyndon pro ij furruris de grys per ipsum emptis ibidem, quolibet de xij tymbre, **xvij marc.** pr. Et per manus ciusdem pro chalkyng dictis furruris, vij s. pr. Et per manus ciusdem pro ij furres de
5 meniuer, quolibet eorundem de xij **tymbre,** per ipsum emptis ∫apud Conyngburgh, vij marc. pr. Et per manus Johannis **Doun**ton pro ij ceturis garderobe domini per ipsum emptis ibidem, **viij scot.** Et pro emendacione diuersorum harnesiorum domini ibidem, iiij scot. Et per manus Ricardi Catour pro j pare sotularum per
10 ipsum empto ibidem, iiij s. pr. **p[ro]** Bernard Hansemann, nunciante seneschallo. Et per manus Johannis **Dounton** pro fabricacione de frenge de baners, viij **scot.** Et per **manus** Jacobi Fawconer pro j cage pro les faweons, xvj **scot.** Et per manus Willelmi Harpeden pro iij pylches per ipsum emptis ibidem, pro
15 iiij valettis in coquina, xviij **scot.**, nunciante seneschallo. Et per manus Johannis Dounton pro j house pro scuto domini per ipsum empta ibidem. ix scot. xij d. Cuidam pictori de Conyngburgh pro pictacione de vij vexillis magnis et ij paruis **vna cum** tabulis clipeis et aliis necessariis domini, per compotum secum factum ibidem,
20 xxxiiij **marc.** viij scot. Et eidem **pictori pro** factura tabellarum pendentium in hospicio domini ibidem, j noble **x scot.** Et per manus Johannis Dounton pro j scuto **domini** per ipsum empto apud Brounesbergh, viij scot. Et per manus thesaurarii pro ij merrours de Parys per ipsum emptis apud Conyngbergh pro domino,
25 xxiij s. **viij d. st.** Et per manus Henrici de garderoba pro j pylche albo per ipsum empto ibidem pro domino, **x s. st.** Cuidam homini de Conyngburgh, facienti domino j **jupam** de beuere, nunciante camerario, **vj marc.** pr. Et per manus Johannis Dounton pro fabricacione j alblaste pro domino, j s. **pr.** Ricardo Sump-
30 termann pro expensis suis eunti versus Marreburgh cum **panno albo** magistro Prucie, **vna cum** expensis equi sui, x s. pr. **Roberto Hoghet** pro expensis suis et equi sui de Conyngburgh vsque **Maryngburgh** per vij dies, eundo et redeundo cum panno albo

Summa pagine lxxij marc. vij s. xij d. Prucianc, faciunt Anglice xxiij li, ij s. viij st. ; le noble ad xxv scot.

fo. 33.

Et per manus eiusdem pro j basum per ipsum empto ibidem, vj s.
pr. Et per manus eiusdem pro j lb. de cotom per ipsum empta
ibidem, ij s. pr. Et pro ij vrinales per ipsum emptis ibidem, ix s.
pr. Et per manus eiusdem pro cotom per ipsum empt' ibidem,
ij s. pr. Et per manus Johannis Dyndon pro vj vlnis panni nigri 5
per ipsum emptis ibidem pro domino, le vlna ad viij scot., ij mare.
prue. Et per manus eiusdem pro j furrura de meniuer per ipsum
empta ibidem pro domino, de Hans Moket pellipario, vij mare. di.
pr. Et pro filo per ipsum empto ibidem, vij s. pr. Et pro furrura
dicte jupe, vj scot. Et per manus Ricardi Catour pro jakker, 10
doubletes, et aliis necessariis per ipsum emptis ibidem pro Henrico
Wallowe, Bernard Hansemann, et Guylmyne, nunciante senescallo,
vj nobles, xxxij s. pr. Et per manus domini Hugonis Herle pro
diuersis expensis per ipsum factis pro cariagio harnesii domini de
hospicio Magistri hospitalis de Conyngburgh vsque hospicium 15
domini ibidem, per compotum secum factum ibidem, j noble xxv s.
pr. Et per manus Johannis Dounton pro vno barella per ipsum
empto ibidem pro harnesio domini mundando, viij scot. Et pro
mayles ad faciendum braas pro domino, xiij scot. Et per manus
Ricardi Catour pro factura camisiarum mulierum et puerorum de 20
Lettowe, iiij scot. Cuidam matrone vocate Furys custodienti
duos pueros de Lettowe, nunciante camerario, per j mensem,
capienti per septimanam xvj s., j mare. iiij s. Et per manus
Henrici de Camera pro crochetes per ipsum emptis ibidem pro
lecto domini, xij s. pr. Et per manus Johannis Dounton pro j 25
brake de mayle per ipsum empto ibidem, x scot. Et pro j rest pro
domino, vij scot. Et per manus Johannis Dyndon pro j furrura
de grys per ipsum empta ibidem de vj tymbre, et de ij tymbre de
meniuer, xij nobles. Et tradita domino Hugoni Herle pro calice
imponendo et pro crismate, j virga panni, precium vij s. pr. 30
Et per manus Johannis Dounton pro clauis et coreo per ipsum
emptis ibidem pro harnesio domini faciendo, x scot. Et per manus
Jacobi Fauconer pro j pelle de coreo ab ipso empta ibidem
per Johannem Dounton, pro sirotecis faciendis pro domino, x s.

pr. Et per manus Johannis Dyndon pro ij furruris de grys per ipsum emptis ibidem, quolibet de xij tymbre, xvij marc. pr. Et per manus eiusdem pro chalkyng dictis furruris, vij s. pr. Et per manus eiusdem pro ij furres de
5 meniuer, quolibet eorundem de xij tymbre, per ipsum emptis *apud Conyngburgh, vij marc. pr. Et per manus Johannis Dounton pro ij ceturis garderobe domini per ipsum emptis ibidem, viij scot. Et pro emendacione diuersorum harnesiorum domini ibidem, iiij scot. Et per manus Ricardi Catour pro j pare sotularum per
10 ipsum empto ibidem, iiij s. pr. p[ro] Bernard Hansemann, nunciante senescallo. Et per manus Johannis Dounton pro fabricacione de frenge de baners, viij scot. Et per manus Jacobi Fawconer pro j cage pro les faweons, xvj scot. Et per manus Willelmi Harpeden pro iij **pylches** per ipsum emptis ibidem, pro
15 iij valettis in coquina, xviij scot., nunciante senescallo. Et per manus Johannis Dounton pro j house pro scuto domini per ipsum empta ibidem, ix scot. xij d. Cuidam pictori de Conyngburgh pro pictacione de vij vexillis magnis et ij paruis vna cum tabulis clipeis et aliis necessariis domini, per compotum secum factum ibidem,
20 xxxiiij marc. viij scot. Et eidem pictori pro **factura tabellarum pendentium** in hospicio domini ibidem, j noble x scot. Et per manus Johannis Dounton pro j scuto domini per ipsum empto apud Brounesbergh, viij scot. Et per manus thesaurarii pro ij **merrours de Parys** per ipsum emptis apud Conyngbergh pro domino,
25 xxiij s. viij d. st. Et per manus Henrici de garderoba pro j **pylche albo** per ipsum empto ibidem pro domino, x s. st. Cuidam homini de Conyngburgh, facienti domino j jupam de beuere, nunciante camerario, vj marc. pr. Et per manus Johannis Dounton pro fabricacione j alblaste pro domino, j s. pr. Ricardo Sump-
30 termann pro expensis suis cunti versus Marreburgh cum panno albo magistro **Prucie**, vna cum expensis equi sui, x s. pr. Roberto Hoghet pro expensis suis et equi sui de Conyngburgh vsque Maryngburgh per vij dies, eundo et redeundo cum panno albo

Summa pagine lxxij marc. vij s. xij d. Prucianr, faciunt Anglice xxiij li, ij s. viij st.; le noble ad xxv scot.

fo. 33.

94 THE EARL OF DERBY'S EXPEDITIONS.

versus le comaundo*ur*, xxxvj s. pr. Et in expensis Joh*ann*is Asshel*ey* p*er* id*em* tempus capi*entis* vt supr*a*, euntis cum panno albo versus le comaundo*ur* de Reynet, xxxvj s. pr. Et per *manus* Bernard*i* Hansemann pr*o* j par*e* calcari*um* per ip*s*um empto ib*idem*, ij scot. pro ij par*ibus* styropes, et j pair styrope leth*er* per ip*s*um emptis ibid*em*, xviij s. Et pro iiij panellis nouis pro curserio domini p*er* ip*s*um emptis ibid*em*, xxxij s. pr. Et eid*em* pro stuffura xvj cellar*um* domini ibid*em*, xviij scot. Et per *manus* eiusd*em* pro v capistris et vj gerthes, iiij braas et iiij reynes pro frenis, et iiij horscombes, xvij scot. ij s. pr. Et per *manus* Johannis Dounton pro emendacio*ne* gladiorum domini, vna cum ij vaginis nouis pro eisd*em*, xiiij scot. Cuid*am* ferrour vocato Hans existent*i* cum domino pro xj septi*manis*, capi*enti* per septimanam vj scot., per conuencion*em* secum factam per Rob*er*tum Waterton, ij marc. xviij scot. Et per *manus* Johannis Dounton pro ix vlnis et j qu*a*rtier de canevas per ip*s*um emptis ibid*em*, xiiij s pr. Et per *manus* eiusd*em* pro vj vnc*iis* de serico per ip*s*um emptis ibid*em*, di. marc. pr. Et per *manus* eiusd*em* pro ix vlnis de sendell*o* blod*e*o per ip*s*um emptis ibid*em*, j marc. di. Et per *manus* eiusd*em* pro j vncio de serico, ij scot. Et per *manus* eiusd*em* pro vj vlnis de sendello blodeo, di. *marc*. / Et per *manus* Johannis Dounton pro xvj vlnis de canevas per ipsum emptis ibid*em*, xvj s. pr. Et per *manus* Rob*er*ti Waterton cuid*am* cellario de Conyngburgh pro emendacio*ne* cellarum domini et aliorum neces*sa*riorum domini, xxvj s. pr. Et per *manus* Johannis Dyndon pro iij vnciis de serico blod*eo* et albo per ip*s*um emptis ibid*em*, vij scot. Et per *manus* ejusdem pro vj vnciis de rubio serico, xiij scot. Et per *manus* Rob*er*ti Waterton pro j cella per ip*s*um empta apud Dansk pro domino, j noble. Et pro v capistris per ip*s*um emptis ibid*em*, xxij scot. Et per *manus* ejusdem pro j webbe de kerches, surcengles et reynes per ip*s*um emptis ibid*em*, xij scot. ij s. pr. Cuidam homini de Dansk pro quadam balista ab ipso empta ibid*em* pro domino, xvj scot.

Summa pagine lxvij marc. j scot. vj d. peucanc*que* faci*unt* Anglice xxj li. ix s. st., le noble ad xxv scot.

fo. 33 v°.

Summa pagine iiij marc. xvij scot. xviij d. pr., que faciunt xxx s. iijd. st., le noble ad xxv. scot.

Summa totalis Garderobe in partibus Prucie, cviij li. xvj s. j d. qr. st.

5 Prouidencia domini in Prucia pro nauibus et aliis Victualibus.

Clerico panetrie per manus Johannis Payn pro pane albo per ipsum empto apud Dansk et expendito in nauibus, tempore quo dominus stetit ibidem in portu, et empto pro stauro in nauibus, xxj
10 marc. pr. v. scot. Clerico buterie super vino, per manus eiusdem et Johannis Gylder pro xxxij fattes vini albi per ipsos emptis ibidem, le fatte ad iiij marc. vj scot., Cxxxvj marc. Et per manus eiusdem pro j fat vini de Osey per ipsum empt' ibidem, xviij marc. xxij scot. Et per manus eiusdem pro j fat vini de Gernade per
15 ipsum empt' ibidem, vj marc. di. pr. Et per manus eiusdem pro ij fattes vini albi per ipsum emptis ibidem, xj marc. Et per manus eiusdem pro ij barrellis ferreres vini de Lepe, vz. lj stope per ipsum emptis ibidem, iiij marc. x scot. Et per manus eiusdem pro xxvj stope vini de Lepe per ipsum emptis ibidem, ij nobles. Et per
20 manus eiusdem pro x stope vini per ipsum emptis ibidem, xvj scot. Et per manus eiusdem Johannis Payn pro x last de Wyschemere beer per ipsum emptis ibidem, le laste ad vij marc., lxx marc. Et per manus eiusdem pro j barello de methe per ipsum empto ibidem pro nauibus, j marc. iiij scot. Et per manus eiusdem pro
25 ij laste de Dansk beer per ipsum emptis ibidem pro nauibus, le fatte ad v marc, x marc. Et per manus eiusdem pro iiij barellis seruisie per ipsum emptis ibidem, le barellus ad iij s. viij d., xiiij s. viij d. st. / Clerico coquine per manus Ricardi Catour pro carne bouina salsa, per ipsum empta apud Dansk, pro nauibus, vj marc. vj scot.,
30 Et per manus eiusdem pro xxix bacons per ipsum emptis ibidem

Clerico buterie beer et serucie.

Summa pagine CCiiij^{xx} iij marc. iij scot. vj d. pr., faciunt Anglice iiij^{xx} xiij li. vij s. ob. st., le noble a xxiiij scot.

fo. 34.

de Johanne Beuere, ix marc. vj scot. pr. Et per manus eiusdem pro xj bacons per ipsum emptis ibidem de hospitissa ibidem, v marc vj scot. Et per manus eiusdem pro x bacons per ipsum emptis ibidem de Poul Toren, iiij marc. xiiij. scot. Et per manus eiusdem pro x bacons per ipsum emptis ibidem de Hans Bucher, iiij marc. xviij scot. Et per manus eiusdem pro xvj bacones per ipsum emptis ibidem de eodem Poul de Toren, vij marc. xiiij scot. Et per manus eiusdem pro ij bacones per ipsum emptis ibidem in foro, xxj scot. Et per manus eiusdem pro j bacon per ipsum empto de pistori domini ibidem, di. marc. pr. Et per manus eiusdem pro xiiij peciis carnis bouine salse per ipsum emptis ibidem de hospitissa de Dansk, xxxviij scot. Et per manus eiusdem pro iiij multonibus salsis per ipsum emptis ibidem, vna cum di. multone, xxxj scot. di. Et per manus magistri Willelmi Cook et Ricardi Catour pro vij barellis carnis bouine salse per ipsos emptis ibidem, v marc. vj scot. Et per manus Cutteys et eiusdem Ricardi pro vj barellis carnis salse per ipsos emptis ibidem, iiij marc. vj scot. Et per manus senescalli et Haydoñ pro vj barellis carnis salse per ipsos emptis, iiij marc. vij scot. Et per manus Ricardi Catour pro j barello multonis salse per ipsum empto ibidem, xxj scot. Et per manus eiusdem pro vj bobus per ipsum emptis ibidem, le piece, iij nobles vj scot., xix nobles di. Et per manus eiusdem pro occisione eorundem, viij scot. iiij s. Et per manus eiusdem pro xxx multonibus per ipsum emptis ibidem, le piece ad xiiij scot., xvij marc. di. Et pro putura eorundem j marc. vj scot. Et per manus magistri Willelmi Cook et dicti Ricardi pro xij barelles allecium alborum per ipsos emptis ibidem, le barellus ad j marc. iij scot., xiij marc. di. Et per manus eiusdem Ricardi pro ij barellis de salmone salso per ipsum emptis ibidem, viij marc. xv scot. Et per manus eiusdem Ricardi et Willelmi Harpeden pro iiij kynerkynes de salmone salso per ipsos emptis ibidem, xxxvij scot. Et per manus magistri Willelmi et dicti Ricardi pro ij barellis de sturion per ipsos emptis ibidem, vij marc. di. pr. Et per manus eorundem pro ij shok de platfysshe magna per ipsos emptis ibidem, ij marc.

EXPENSES ON RETURN TO ENGLAND. 97

xvij scot. Et per manus corundem pro iiij shok de platfysshe parua per ipsos emptis ibidem, j marc. di. Et per manus Johannis Whytik, mercatoris, pro CCC stokfisshe per ipsum emptis ibidem, ix marc. ix scot. Et per manus Ricardi Catour pro j sturioun fresshe
5 et j purpeys per ipsum emptis ibidem, v nobles, xj scot. Et per manus thesaurarii pro ij porpeis per ipsum emptis in mari,[a] xij scot. Et per manus Ricardi Catour pro j shok de codelyng fresshe per ipsum empt' apud naues, viij s. iiij d. st. Et per manus eiusdem pro j shok de platfisshe per ipsum [empt'] ibidem,
10 xiij scot. Et per manus eiusdem pro j kynerkyn anguillarum per ipsum empt' ibidem, xj scot. Et per manus eiusdem pro j cade allecium rubrorum per ipsum empt' ibidem, j marc. pr. Et per manus thesaurarii et Payn pro iij cades allecium rubrorum per ipsos emptis ibidem, ij marc. xxij scot.
15 /SUPER officio pulletrie, per manus Willelmi Harpeden pro v shephell farine auenarum per ipsum emptis apud Dansk, j marc. vj scot. Et per manus eiusdem pro xxiiij shephell pisarum per ipsum ibidem emptis, iiij marc. pr. Et per manus eiusdem pro xij shephell de onyons per ipsum emptis ibidem, j marc. di. pr. Et
20 per manus eiusdem pro ij cages pro pulletria per ipsum emptis ibidem, j marc. xiiij scot. Et per manus eiusdem pro j dolio butiri per ipsum empto ibidem, j marc. viij scot. Et per manus eiusdem pro oleo per ipsum empto ibidem, vij nobles, viij scot. CLERICO coquine per manus Hans Gosseleyn naute aule domini pro piscibus
25 per ipsum emptis in le Wysle et in le Sonde per diuersas vices, xiij s. iiij d. st. Et eidem pro j farcost per ipsum conducto ibidem ad adiuuandum ipsum vltra le Wysle, v nobles. Et per manus ejusdem pro j lodesman in la Hauen ex precepto domini, iij s. iiij d. st. JOHANNI BEUERE mercatori de Dansk pro DC lx shephell farine
30 frumenti per ipsum emptis ibidem pro prouidenciis domini versus Angliam, centena ad xij marc. di., iiij^{xx} ij marc. di.; et eidem pro xl shephell siliginis per ipsum emptis ibidem, le shephell, v s. iiij d.

Summa pagine
Clij marc. iiij se
iij d. Pruciane.
faciunt Anglice
l li. xiiij s. v d.
le noble ad xxii
fo. 34 v°.

Providencia de :

[a] The word is mar'. It is hardly likely to stand for marcatum here, as forum is used previously for market.

CAMD. SOC.   O

pr., iij marc. di. iij s. iiij d.; in toto iiij^{xx} vj marc. iij s. iiij d. pr. **HANS
GOSSELYN** naute aule domini pro nauiagio seneschalli et partis
familie domini et equorum domini de Prucia vsque Angliam,
lv li. st. HENRICO HERTYK pro nauiagio domini de Prucia vsque
Angliam, iiij^{xx} li. Item soluti pro j farecost de Hull ad cariandum
victualia domini vsque Boston, lxvj s. viij d. Et cuidam altero farecost ad cariandum victualia domini ibidem, xl s. **Cuidam** portour
pro portagio harnesium domini de naui vsque terram apud Boston,
vj s. Item data iiij carectariis cariantibus harnesium domini de Hull
vsque Bollyngbrok, xj s. **viij d.** Johanni Dauid pro expensis suis 10
de Bullyngbrok vsque Hull, **xx d.** Et eidem pro conductione vnius
batelle de Hull vsque Barton, viij d. Et eidem pro conductione
ij equorum de Barton vsque Bullyngbrok, iij s. iiij d. Et pro
expensis dictorum ij equorum per viam, viij d. Et pro expensis
dictorum equorum apud **Bullyngbrok, vj d.** Johanni Gylder pro 15
cena domini, certorum militum, et armigerorum suorum equitantium
versus **Bullyngbrok** cum festinacione per ipsum empta apud **Castre,**
vna cum expensis equorum domini, necnon pro cena certorum
carectariorum et suorum equorum cariantium harnesium domini
vsque **Bullyngbrok, viij s. x d.** Item **soluti** pro j carecta abbatis 20
de Thorneton et pro victualibus hominum et equorum ibidem, viij d.
Et **soluti** carectario, de dono domini ibidem, iij s. **iiij d.** ITEM
soluti per manus Johannis Gylder apud Whatton, pro pane, vino,
et seruisia per ipsum emptis ibidem, pro baytyng domini et partis
familie sue, xviij d. Et pro expensis Laurencii de scutellaria, 25
Bruillefford, Henrici Page coquine, Roberti del Botery, ij garcionum
archiepiscopi et ij carectariorum, iij s. iiij d. In expensis [equi] domini
apud Beuerley, Brydlyngton vna cum fertura eiusdem, vj d. ROBERTO
HOWE pro caponibus, gallinis, pullis, pulcinis et columbellis per
ipsum emptis apud Barton, xxiij d. JOHANNI WYNDESORE pro 30
portagio carnis de naui vsque terram, iiij d. Et per manus eiusdem
pro grees per ipsum empto apud Hull, v d. Et per manus Henrici
Maunsell pro baytyng apud **Sytyngburne, j d.**; et apud Rouchestre,
j d.; apud London, iij d.; apud **Leycestre, iiij d.** Item apud **Melton**

EXPENSES ON RETURN TO ENGLAND.

/ Mowbray pro pane equino per ipsum empto ibidem, v d. ob. ; **apud** fo. 35.
Donstaple j d. ; in toto xvj d. ob. Et per manus Thome Knappe
pro expensis iij equorum domini apud Bartoñ pro baytyng, ij d. ;
apud Castre pro expensis vj equorum per noctem in feno et littura,
5 viij d.; et pro iiij bz. auenarum per ipsum emptis ibidem, **ij s. viij d.** ;
apud Horncastell pro baytyng iiij equorum iiij d. ; **et pro ferrura**
eorundem ij d.; in toto, iiij s. WILLELMO Kykeley pro expensis
suis de Hulle vsque Bollyngbrok, vna cum batillagio super Humbre,
et pro conductione equorum suorum per idem tempus, per compotum
10 **secum factum, iij s. iiij d.** In expensis camerarii, thesaurarii **et**
partis familie domini existentium ibidem per j diem et ij noctes, in
pane albo empto ibidem per **manus** Johannis Gylder, iiij s.; pro
j barello di. seruisie, le barellus ad v s., vij s. vj d.; **pro carne boum**
et multonum emptis ibidem per manus eiusdem, v s., et **pro ij capo-**
15 **nibus**, vj gallinis per ipsum emptis ibidem, xxij d.;' pro vj pulcinis
per ipsum emptis ibidem, xij d., **et pro** farina auenarum, j d., **pro**
busca empta ibidem, xij d.; et pro candelis emptis ibidem, iiij d.,
et pro x **galonibus** vini, le galo ad viij d., vj s. viij d.; in toto
xxvij s. v. d. Et per manus Johannis Gylder liberati **valetto**
20 domini in pane et victualibus suis, existenti in les craieres ad custodiendum **harnesia** domini de Hull versus Boston, **vj s. viij d.** Et
pro batillagio famulorum et harnesii domini de naui versus terram,
et reportagio harnesii domini ad les craiers, vj s. viij d. Et pro
batillagio **camerarii**, thesaurarii et aliorum famulorum domini de
25 Hulle versus Bartoñ, vj s. viij d. Et pro batillagio equorum domini,
eodem modo, ij s. Et pro batillagio domini ibidem, iij s. iiij d.
Et pro conductione equorum ibidem pro domino, vj s. viij d. Et
pro expensis factis circa Ricardum Catour, Johannem Dauy, et
famulum ipsius,* iiij s. Et pro sepultura ipsius Ricardi, xxviij s. j d. • [Sic].
30 Et pro pane empto apud Barton per manus Johannis Gylder, ij s.
viij d. Et pro j barello seruisie empto ibidem per manus eiusdem,
v s. Et pro vj galonibus seruisie emptis ibidem, xij d. Et per
manus eiusdem pro vj galons vini ibidem emptis, le galo ad viij d.,
iiij s. Et per manus eiusdem pro carne boum et multonum empta

ibidem, iiij s. vj d. Et pro iiij caponibus, iiij gallinis, vj pulcinis, iij duodenis columbellarum, iij s. iiij d. Et pro sale et busca emptis ibidem, x d. JOHANNI GYLDER pro expensis Bewford, Swynford, et aliorum scutiferorum et sumptermen domini pro pane albo empto ibidem, xv d.; pro ij pipis et di. vini emptis ibidem, xx d.; pro 5 vij galonibus di. seruisie emptis, xv d.; et pro piscibus recentibus emptis ibidem, xij d.; pro stokfyssh emptis ibidem, x d. ob.; pro ray empt' ibidem, ix d.; et pro piscibus salsis emptis ibidem, ij d.; pro ouis et lacte emptis ibidem, vj d.; et pro j lb. amydoni, iij d.; pro saffron empt' ibidem, j d.; pro butiro empto ibidem, iij d.; pro 10 sale empto ibidem, ob.; pro busca empta ibidem, iij d.; pro feno et pane equino emptis ibidem, xviij d.; et pro ferrura equi domini ibidem, ij. d. ob.; in toto, x s. ob. Et per manus eiusdem pro candelis cepi per ipsum emptis ibidem, vj d.; et in cepo ij d., in toto viij d. In expensis Thesaurarii et partis famulorum domini apud 15 Louthe, iiij s.

Summa pagine vj li. xvj s. iij d. st.

Summa prouidenciarum et conductionum nauium in redeundo versus Angliam in ij fol. vsque huc, CCCxxx li. vj s. x d. st.; vnde de conductione nauium, Cxxxv li.

VASA ARGENTEA. 20

fo. 35 v°. / In primis soluti pro vj skales argenteis, ponderis viij li., xviij s. iiij d. st. et viij scot. pr. Et pro factura eorundem, iiij marc. pr. xxj scot. Et pro xiij cocliaribus argenteis ponderis iiij marc. iiij scot. pr., et pro factura eorundem, xxxvj scot., in toto v marc. pr.
January 7. xvj scot. Et vij° die Januarii pro ij^{bus} spyceplates argenteis, pon- 25 deris xx marcarum iij fferthynges, le marc. pro ij marc. vj scot., in toto xlvj marc. xvj scot. xv d. pr. Et pro j chargeour, iij discis, et j saweere, ponderis xx marc. de troye, xlv marc. Et pro factura de les spyceplates, chargeours, disches, et saweere, vna cum xij scutis armorum domini circa les spyceplates existentibus, xlij 30

GOLD AND SILVER WORK.   101

marc. pr. xij scot. Et pro j saler argenteo pro sale imponendo, ponderis iij marc. di. st, et pro factura eiusdem ij marc. pr., in toto lix s. viij d. st. Et pro auracione eiusdem et de les spyce-plates, per manus Johannis Payne, ix nobles, iij s. iiij d. Et pro
5 cathena domini, ponderis vj^{xx}xj marc.,[a] et in factura eiusdem, xxvij nobles, in toto Cxliiij marc. vj s. viij d. st. Et pro j couercle de argento, ponderis ij marc. english, iiij marc. xij scot. pr.; et in factura eiusdem, j marc. di. pr. Et pro vj floribus domini deauratis, ponderis xj marc. vj scot.; et pro factura
10 eorundem, xv marc., in toto xxvj marc. vj scot. pr. Et pro vij floribus domini ponderis xviij marc. iiij scot.; et aurifabro pro eisdem vij floribus faciendis, xvij nobles. Et pro burnyshyng del pieces, ix scot. Item aurifabro faciendo flores domini, pro auro ad eosdem, vj nobles. Item aurifabro pro deauracione cathene Johannis
15 Dalyngrugg, militis, v nobles. Item eidem pro emendacione cathene domini, j noble xx scot.

Summa pagine, Cxxj li. xvj d. st., et monete Pruciane Ciiij^{xx} xvj marc. xvj scot. xv d. pr.; que faciunt Anglice lx li. x s. iiij d. ob. st., le noble ad xxvj scot.

20   NECESSARIA ET VESSELAMENTA PRO COQUINA.

/ In primis date a Hans Peutrer de Conyngburgh pro xij pottes   fo. 36. de peutre, ponderis ij petrarum, xl lb. pro petra, la lb. ad iij s., in toto xij li. pr.[b] Item eidem pro lx discis, ponderis iij petr. xv lb., le lb. ad iiij s., in toto xxvij li. pr. Et pro aliis lx discis, ponderis
25 iij petr. xxvj lb., xij s. pr.[c] Et pro xxx sauseriis ponderis x lb.,

---

[a] The MS. has the word nobles here by mistake.

[b] In this and the following items, taking the marc at 24 scot, we find the li. or pound Prussian money to be worth twenty scot.

[c] In this and the next items there appear to be some errors or omissions, and it is difficult to see what the total 65 li. refers to.

papiro content*as*, vt in Ciiij marc. iij scot. ij s. iiij d. pr.; que *faciunt* Anglice, xxxij li. xij d.

Et in diuersis cust*ibus* et expensis dicti hospicii in officio speciarie factis per manus Curteys, prout patet per parcellas et per dictas in quodam rubio papiro contentas et super hunc comp*utum* examinatas, vt in CCxxij marc. xxij d. pr., que faciunt Anglice lxviij li. vj s. iiij d. st.; le noble ad xxvj scot., videlicet per totum tempus quo dominus stetit in partibus Prucie predictis. 5

Summa pagine de parcellis et abbreuiamentis, CCCiiij^{xx} ix li. vj s. v d. ob. qr. st. 10

DONA DATA CONTENTA IN ROTULO OSTENSO DOMINO PER CAMERARIUM.

fo. 39. / Hankyn Steresman de naui domini versus Pruciam de dono domini apud Dansk, xiij s. iiij d. Et diuersis ministrallis ibidem
August 11. die Jouis in crastino sancti Laurencii, nunciante camerario, vj s. 15
viij d. Et ij wafreres ibidem eodem die exist*entibus*, nunciante camerario, xij d. Et cuidam homini portanti litteras de castello de Halyngburgh vsque regnum Anglie, xiij s. iiij d. Et diuersis sergeantes de Dansk, laborantibus super providenciam domini faciendam ibidem, xiij s. iiij d. Et diuersis botemen nauis domini de 20
dono domini quando venerunt cum corpore Christi de naui vsque Dansk, vj s. viij d. Et domino Hugoni Waterton ibidem de dono domini, x li. Et Johanni Norbery ibidem de dono domini, x li. Et domino Ricardo Kyngeston thesaurario ibidem de dono domini ibidem, lxvj s. viij d. Johanni Payn de dono domini ibidem, xl s. 25
Magistro Willelmo Cook de dono domini ibidem, xl s. Diuersis
August 10. ministrallis in festo Sancti Laurencii per manus Johannis Payn ex preceptis domini, j marc. pr. Cuidam ballino de Dansk eunti cum Johanne Payn ad monstrandum ei vina, bere, et mede et alia necessaria tangentia officium suum ibidem, j marc. pr. Diuersis 30

ministrallis apud Meluyng die dominica in vigilia *Assumptionis* August 13. Beate Marie, nunciante camerario, j marc. pr. Item Beuere de Dansk eo quod laborabat circa prouidenciam domino apud Dansk, xx s. st. Johanni Whytwyk pro eadem causa, vj s.
5 viij d. Johanni Gray eo quod laborabat cum domino de Dansk vsque Conyngburgh, xxvj s. viij d. Cuidam Gallico presentanti dominum cum j cursero ex parte cuiusdam militis Francie, nunciante camerario apud Conyngburgh, xiij s. iiij d. Roberto Barbour de dono domini apud Dansk, xiij s. iiij d. Cuidam valetto
10 domini de Bourser, eo quod recepit vexillum primo super muro ciuitatis de Welle, xl s. Cuidam homini de Prucie eo quod inuenit vnum noche domini ibidem, iij s. iiij d. Cuidam garcioni domini Marescalli eo quod presentauit dominum cum vno cursero ibidem, xiij s. iiij d. Diuersis ministrallis magistri de Nyueland[a]
15 facientibus ministraleiam ibidem, de dono domini, x s. Cuidam valetto domini Camaundour de Kerseburgh[b] presentanti dominum cum j cursero, vj s. viij d. Item ij valettis Prucianis de Reynete existentibus cum domino per totam reisam[c] circa tentoria sua, ij noble, ij flor. v s. iiij d. Cuidam cryour domini Marescalli ibidem
20 de dono domini, vj s. viij d. Diuersis mynours operantibus in quadam sue juxta castrum de Welle de dono domini, lxvj s. viij d. Cuidam valetto magistri de Nyueland presentanti dominum cum j boue, iiij ouibus, et ij pauonibus ex parte dicti Marescalli apud sedem de Welle, vj s. viij d. Cuidam Gunner sagittario coram
25 domino ad t"ıū[d] super murum castri de Welle, per manus domini

---

[a] That is Livland, like Nicole for Lincoln. The master of Livland, Wennemar of Bruggenoie, had joined the army. Scriptores rerum Prussicarum, ii. p. 643. [P.]

[b] Christburg. Werner von Tettingen was commander at this time. [P.]

[c] In this and the two instances next following of the word reis' the adjective is masculine in the MS., viz: totum, indicating reisum. But according to Duncange and the examples there given the right form appears to be reisa, as above printed. It is generally called le Reys elsewhere in the MS., the word le, however, cannot here be taken as indicative of gender.

[d] What this contraction stands for is doubtful, trajectum is suggested as likely in meaning, but it requires the long r to be taken as j, whereas the letter j in this MS. is always the short i. Prof. Prutz suggests tractum (p. 98).

papiro contentas, vt in Ciiij marc. iij scot. ij s. iiij d. pr.; que faciunt Anglice, xxxij li. xij d.

Et in diuersis custubus et expensis dicti hospicii in officio speciarie factis per manus Curteys, prout patet per parcellas et per dictas in quodam rubio papiro contentas et super hunc compotum 5 examinatas, vt in CCxxij marc. xxij d. pr., que faciunt Anglice lxviij li. vj s. iiij d. st.; le noble ad xxvj scot., videlicet per totum tempus quo dominus stetit in partibus Prucie predictis.

Summa pagine de parcellis et abbreuiamentis, CCCiiij^{xx} ix li. vj s. v d. ob. qr. st. 10

DONA DATA CONTENTA IN ROTULO OSTENSO DOMINO PER CAMERARIUM.

fo. 39. / Hankyn Steresman de naui domini versus Pruciam de dono domini apud Dansk, xiij s. iiij d. Et diuersis ministrallis ibidem
August 11. die Jouis in crastino sancti Laurencii, nunciante camerario, vj s. 15 viij d. Et ij wafreres ibidem eodem die existentibus, nunciante camerario, xij d. Et cuidam homini portanti litteras de castello de Halyngburgh vsque regnum Anglie, xiij s. iiij d. Et diuersis sergeantes de Dansk, laborantibus super prouidenciam domini faciendam ibidem, xiij s. iiij d. Et diuersis botemen nauis domini de 20 dono domini quando venerunt cum corpore Christi de naui vsque Dansk, vj s. viij d. Et domino Hugoni Waterton ibidem de dono domini, x li. Et Johanni Norbery ibidem de dono domini, x li. Et domino Ricardo Kyngeston thesaurario ibidem de dono domini ibidem, lxvj s. viij d. Johanni Payn de dono domini ibidem, xl s. 25 Magistro Willelmo Cook de dono domini ibidem, xl s. Diuersis
August 10. ministrallis in festo Sancti Laurencii per manus Johannis Payn ex preceptis domini, j marc. pr. Cuidam ballino de Dansk eunti cum Johanne Payn ad monstrandum ei vina, bere, et mede et alia necessaria tangentia officium suum ibidem, j marc. pr. Diuersis 30

GIFTS WHILE IN PRUSSIA.   105

ministrallis apud Meluyng die dominica in vigilia Assumptionis   Angust 13.
Beate Marie, nunciante camerario, j marc. pr. Item Beuere
de Dansk eo quod laborabat circa prouidenciam domino apud
Dansk, xx s. st.   Johanni Whytwyk pro eadem causa, vj s.
5 viij d. Johanni Gray eo quod laborabat cum domino de Dansk
vsque Conyngburgh, xxvj s. viij d. Cuidam Gallico presentanti
dominum cum j cursero ex parte cuiusdam militis Francie,
nunciante camerario apud Conyngburgh, xiij s. iiij d. Roberto
Barbour de dono domini apud Dansk, xiij s. iiij d. Cuidam valetto
10 domini de Bourser, eo quod recepit vexillum primo super muro
ciuitatis de Welle, xl s.   Cuidam homini de Prucie eo quod
inuenit vnum noche domini ibidem, iij s. iiij d. Cuidam garcioni
domini Marescalli eo quod presentauit dominum cum vno cursero
ibidem, xiij s. iiij d. Diuersis ministrallis magistri de Nyueland[a]
15 facientibus ministraleiam ibidem, de dono domini, x s. Cuidam
valetto domini Camaundour de Kerseburgh[b] presentanti dominum
cum j cursero, vj s. viij d. Item ij valettis Prucianis de Reynete
existentibus cum domino per totam reisam[c] circa tentoria sua, ij
noble, ij flor. v s. iiij d. Cuidam cryour domini Marescalli ibidem
20 de dono domini, vj s. viij d. Diuersis mynours operantibus in
quadam sue juxta castrum de Welle de dono domini, lxvj s. viij d.
Cuidam valetto magistri de Nyueland presentanti dominum cum j
boue, iiij ouibus, et ij pauonibus ex parte dicti Marescalli apud
sedem de Welle, vj s. viij d. Cuidam Gunner sagittario coram
25 domino ad t"iū[d] super murum castri de Welle, per manus domini

---

[a] That is Livland, like Nicole for Lincoln. The master of Livland, Wennemar
of Bruggenoie, had joined the army. Scriptores rerum Prussicarum, ii. p. 643. [P.]

[b] Christburg. Werner von Tettingen was commander at this time. [P.]

[c] In this and the two instances next following of the word reis' the adjective is
masculine in the MS., viz: totum, indicating reisum. But according to Ducange
and the examples there given the right form appears to be reisa, as above printed.
It is generally called le Reys elsewhere in the MS., the word le, however, cannot
here be taken as indicative of gender.

[d] What this contraction stands for is doubtful, trajectum is suggested as likely
in meaning, but it requires the long r to be taken as j, whereas the letter j in this
MS. is always the short i.   Prof. Prutz suggests tractum (p. 98).

CAMD. SOC.   P

Willelmi de Wyloby, vj s. viij d. Diuersis engynours apud castrum de Welle de dono domini per manus Gybbethorpe, vj s. viij d. Cuidam venienti cum domino de Haff vsque Conyngburgh reducenti hackeneys domini, xl s. pr. Fratribus de Wylhoughe de dono domini ibidem, j marc. pr. Cuidam herald de Almannia 5 per manus Lancastri le heraud ibidem, in festo sancti Romani episcopi, xx s. st. Cuidam heremite de dono domini ibidem, xx s. st. Duobus militibus de Prucia existentibus cum domino per totam le reisam, pro regardo eis facto* ibidem in vigilia Omnium Sanctorum, nunciante camerario, xiij li. vj s. viij d. Thome de 10 Kempstone militi et vexillatori domini per totam reysam, pro regardo sibi facto, x li. Willelmo Wyloughby militi in festo Apostolorum Simonis et Jude pro regardo suo, ibidem, x li. Radulpho Staneley de dono domini ibidem, v marc. st. Item Mersyngton de dono domini, xx s. Item a Chalons de dono domini, 15 xx s. st. Et eidem pro j jak de dono domini, j marc. di. pr. Item a Hermann scutifero comitis Northumberland[a] de dono domini apud Conyngburgh, C s. Item a Hanz Duche ibidem scutifero domini, C s. Domino Roberto Elkyngton ibidem, C s. Willelmo Freman ibidem, xxvj s. viij d. Johanni Wyndesore ibidem, xiij s. 20 iiij d. Ricardo del Ewre ibidem, xx s. Johanni Peek in festo Omnium Sanctorum de dono domini. x s. st. Kikkeley de dono domini ibidem, vj s. viij d. Johanni Duffeld de dono domini ibidem, x s. Henrico de coquina de dono domini ibidem, x s. / Item Fyssher jun. de dono domini, vj s. viij d. Petro de coquina 25 de dono domini, vj s. viij d. Johanni Norway de dono domini, di. marc. pr. Item octo sumptermen de dono domini, iiij li. Roberto Waterton de dono domini ibidem, pro j equo perdito in passagio de la Memele, xl s. st. Willelmo Graceles de dono domini ibidem, j marc. pr. Cuidam scutifero de Dansk de dono domini 30 ibidem pro regardo suo pro le Reys, xl s. Ricardo Ryggeley de

* This must be an esquire of Henry Percy (father of Hot-spur) E. of Northumberland, d. 1407—8. The Earl was keeper of the castle of Merke, near Calais, from 1st Nov. 1389 to Feb. 1391.

dono domini ibidem in festo Omnium Sanctorum, xiij s. iiij d. November 1.
Item a Seland le heraud in festo apostolorum Simonis et Jude, October 28.
existenti cum domino in le Reys, xx s. Item a Dampier le heraud
eodem die existenti vt supra, xx s. Nicholao de camera de dono
5 domini in festo Omnium Sanctorum ibidem, xiij s. iiij d. Date a November 1.
Lancastre le heraud v die Nouembris eunti versus partes Anglie November 5.
cum litteris domini, nunciante camerario, xx li. Item dati iij
pursuantes de Francia existentibus cum domino, in festo Omnium
Sanctorum, nunciante camerario, viij nobles. Cuidam naute November 1.
10 Anglico portanti noua de partu Hounfredi filii domini mei, nunciante camerario, xiij s. iiij d. Duobus Prucianis presentantibus
dominum cum iiij haukes iij⁰ die Nouembris, nunciante camerario, November 3.
xiij s. iiij d. Item ij^bus Prucianis presentantibus dominum dominica
prima aduentus sui ibidem cum maulardis, nunciante camerario,
15 vj s. viij d. Diuersis ministrallis gallicis facientibus ministraleiam
suam in camera domini, x die Nouembris, nunciante camerario, xx s. November 10.
Johanni Cope pro sepultura Willelmi Abbegode, de [dono] domini
ibidem, vj s. viij d. Roberto Chalons pro regardo sibi facto ibidem,
pur le Reys, xxxiij s. iiij d. Thome Goter vna vice per totos
20 denarios per ipsum lucratos de domino ad tales, iiij li. Et eidem
Thome ab vice pro eodem lucro ad tales, xxvj li. xiij s. iiij d. Et
clericis ville de Conyngburgh in festo Sancti Nicholai cantantibus December 6.
coram domino sospitati, j marc. pr. Willelmo Rigmayden de dono
domini ibidem, xxij⁰ die Nouembris, nunciante camerario, lxvj s. November 22.
25 viij d. Thome Toty eodem die de dono domini ad soluendum pro
j coleria sibi data per dominum, xl s. Reginaldo Curteys eodem die
de dono domini, xl s. Item a Croyslett herald domini Ducis Gloucestre, pro j scuto armorum domini, nunciante camerario, xiij noble.
Johanni Payn pro regardo sibi facto pur la Reys, xl s. Magistro
30 Willelmo Cook pro regardo sibi facto pur le Reys, nunciante
camerario, xxvj s. viij d. Petro Hausemann de dono domini ibidem,
xv die Nouembris, xxvj s. viij d. Johanni Leuyngton de dono November 15.
domini pro regardo sibi facto pur le Reys, xx s. Johanni Edenham
de dono domini pur regardo sibi facto pur le Reys, nunciante

camerario, xxvj s. viij d. Roberto Sumpterman de dono domini ibidem, iij s. iiij d. Johanni Colle de dono domini, vj s. viij d. Item a Derby le heraud eunti versus regem Polonie cum litteris domini pro deliberacione ij militum suorum, xl s. Johanni Braylle-fford pro regardo sibi facto de dono domini, vj s. viij d. Johanni 5 dei Ewer pro regardo sibi facto de dono domini, iij s. iiij d. Cuidam valetto domini Marescalli presentanti dominum cum iiij roos, xviij die mensis Nouembris, vj s. viij d. Cuidam valetto socii Marescalli presentanti dominum cum iiij roos, xx die Nouembris, iij s. iiij d. st. Johanni Dalyngrugg militi pro vna cathena auri quam dominus 10 cepit ab eo, vj li. xiij s. iiij d. Johanni Beuer portanti certas pecunias de Dansk vsque Conyngburgh, vj s. viij d. Johanni Gylder eunti cum litteris domini de Tapio versus Angliam, nunciante camerario, xl s. Et eidem Johanni redeunti de Anglia vsque Conyngburgh pro skippagio, conductione equorum, et aliis expensis per 15 ipsum factis in Anglia, nunciante camerario, C s. Item dati a vn Piper Duche per manus Johannis Waterton ex precepto domini, ix s. Item eidem per manus Johannis Norbery de dono domini ibidem, xxx s. Clericis ville cantantibus coram domino quodam die dominico ibidem per manus Ricardi Dancastre, x s. pr. Item 20 dati a Derby le heraud apud Conyngburgh pro j scuto domini ex precepto domini ibidem, xxxiiij nobles. Item dati ij carectariis marescalli pro cariagio harnesii domini versus le Huntyng, xl s. pr. Item iiij prucianis facientibus focum in le huntyng, xx s. pr. Item dati officiariis domini marescalli per manus Simeonis, xl s. st. Roberto 25 Jonson pro regardo sibi pur le Reys de dono domini ibidem, vj s. viij d. Johanni Peck pro regardo sibi de dono domini ibidem, vj s. viij d. Willelmo Fyssher pro regardo sibi ibidem, iij s. iiij d. Johanni Syde pro regardo sibi ibidem de dono domini ibidem, nunciante seneschallo, xx s. st. Item iiij valettis marescalli portantibus faucons 30 *l* domino per ij vices, xxvj s. viij d. Roberto Pepur pro regardo sibi facto pur le Reys de dono domini, vj s. viij d. Item dati a Jenico eunti versus Angliam cum litteris domini nunciante camerario, xiij li. vj s. viij d. Cuidam Pruciano presentanti domi-

GIFTS WHILE IN PRUSSIA. 109

num cum iij^bus vrsulis xx die Decembris, nunciante camerario, December 20.
xij scot. Cuidam famulo Episcopi de Sameland presentanti dominum cum j tabula commensali de Prucia, vj s. viij d. Item dati
vni Heer pro capella Sancti Antonii, nunciante camerario,
5 lxvj s. viij d. Cuidam Pruciano presentanti dominum cum ij^bus
hyndes, x die Decembris, x scot. Cuidam famulo domini de December 10.
Lekirke presentanti dominum cum j equo in primo aduentu suo
apud Conyngburgh, xiij s. iiij d. Item dati ij fratribus die Natalis December 25.
Domini per manus Johannis Norbery ibidem ex precepto domini,
10 xxx s. pr. Item data famulo vnius presentantis dominum cum
vno oore^n in vigilia Natalis Domini, vj scot. Ricardo Chelmes- December 21.
wyke pro j pylche sibi data per dominum de beuere, viij noble.
Item iij^bus fithelers facientibus ministralciam suam coram domino
in festo Natalis Domini, xij s. viij d. Cuidam tumblere eodem die
15 facienti ministralciam suam coram domino, vj scot. Item dati
heraldis et ministrallis in die Natalis Domini, nunciante camerario,
x li. st. Item data ministrallis ville de Conyngburgh in festo Sancti
Johannis Evangeliste, ij marc. di. pr. Et duobus famulis mares- December 27.
calli de dono domini eodem die pro portacione vnius hert et vnius
20 hynde, j marc. pr. Item diuersis heraldis in die Circumcisionis January 1.
Domini ibidem, lxvj s. viij d. Item ministrallis domini pro eo quod
venerunt ad cameram domini mane faciendam ministralciam suam,
xl s. st. Ministrallis ville eodem die ibidem, xiij s. iiij d. Item
valettis camere domini eodem die de dono domini ibidem, xl s.
25 Item officiariis coquine eodem die de dono domini ibidem, xx s. st.
Item hospiti domus domini ex precepto domini eodem die, xx s.
st. Item officiariis buterie et paneterie eodem die, de dono domini
ibidem, xx s. st. Item ministrallis et wafters per manus Roberti
Waterton eodem die, vj s. viij d. Item dati nuncio socii Marescalli
30 pro eo quod portauit certa noua de marescallo iij° die Januarii,
vj s. viij d. Item eodem pro lusu domini ad tales ex precepto, viij
noble. Item data ministrallis de Conyngburgh in vigilia Epiphanie January 5.
Domini, ij flor. Item eodem die a j wawfroer, j flor. Item

* Ure-ox, wild bull, *urus* [Pauli].

diuersis harpours ibidem eodem die de dono domini, xvj s. pr.
Item diuersis heraldis de dono domini in festo Purificationis Beate
Marie ibidem, xiij li. vj s. viij d. Item eodem die dati ministrallis
de Conyngburg de dono domini, viij s. st. Willelmo Freman
cunti versus Angliam de dono domini ibidem, lxvj s. viij d.
Cuidam cissori occiso ibidem de dono domini ibidem, x marc.
prue. Cuidam Pruciano presentanti dominum cum piscibus, x°
die Febr., x s. pr. Item data Swethe le herald pro j scuto domini
faciendo ex precepto domini, xvij noble. Item dati aurifabro
facienti flores domini apud Conyngburg pro beueragio, vj s. viij d.
Item Johanni famulo Morley de dono domini ibidem, nunciante
camerario ibidem, vj s. viij d. Item data a Horne le herald de
dono domini ibidem pro j scuto faciendo, nunciante camerario
ibidem, xiiij noble. Item ij fratribus Carmelitis per manus
domini Hugonis Herle de dono domini, di. marc. pr. Willelmo Gracelesse de dono domini ibidem vj° die Febr. ex precepto domini, j marc. viij scot. Thome Waterton eodem die ex
precepto domini, iij s. iiij d. Item Cok de Byngeley de dono domini,
xij die Febr., xxvj s. viij d. Item a Derby le herald de dono
domini ibidem, x° die Febr., xl s. Item cuidam valetto custodienti le Hothous apud Dansk, de dono domini, vj s. viij d. Item
Nicholao Pruceman de dono domini apud Dansk, xviij die Febr.,
vj s. viij d. Item data ij^{bus} fythelers expectantibus cum domino
/per sex dies apud Dansk, iij marc. pr. Item dati a Lancastre le
heraud apud Dansk in festo Sancti Edmundi Archiepiscopi pro
pecuniis traditis domino per manus ipsius ad talos, nunciante
senescallo, xxx s. st. Cuidam fisiciano de Maryngburgh visitanti
dominum, nunciante senescallo, xl s. Roberto Chalons de dono
domini per manus senescalli ibidem, xxvj s. viij d. Item a le
Trumpetor per manus senescalli de dono domini ibidem, xxiij s.
iiij d. Item vxori hospitis domini apud Meluyng in vltimo exitu
suo ibidem, de dono domini ibidem, xiij s. iiij d. Item famulis
Norbery et thesaurario presentantibus dominum cum nouo dono*
in die Circumcisionis Domini, x s. Item quibusdam clericis

GIFTS WHILE IN PRUSSIA. 111

cantant*ibus* **coram** domino apud Dansk in hospicio Godesknawt, ex
precepto domini, vj s. viij d. Item cuidam Pruciano presentanti
dominum cum pykes de Burgensibus ville de Dansk, per manus
Johannis Payn, iij s. iiij d. Cuidam Pruciano portant*i* torticios
5 cor*am* domino de villa de Dansk vsque manerium domini, xij s. pr.
Item in die Pasche officiariis coquine per manus thes*aurarii* ex   March 26.
precepto domini, xx s. Item officiariis buterie per manus ejusdem
de dono domini ibidem, xx s. Item dati iij^{bus} sumptermen die lune
in septimana Paschali de dono domini per manus thes*aurarii*,   March 27.
10 x s. st. Item duobus fauconers portant*ibus* faucons de Magistro
de Prucia* per manus Norbery, xiij s. iiij d. Item octo ministrallis
ville de Dansk in die Pasche, nunci*ante* Camerario, vj s. viij d.   March 26.
Item iij^{bus} valett*is* de Prucia seruient*ibus* in coquina apud Conyngburg et apud Dansk, nunci*ante* senescallo, x s. st. Cuid*am* valetto
15 presentanti dominum cum venison de dono domini per manus
Croyslett, iij s. iiij d. Item dat*i* hospiti*sse* domini apud Dansk, in
recessu domini, vj li. xiij s. iiij d. Item, famulo ejusdem hospittisse
de dono domini, vj s. viij d. Item dat*i* vni pullener per manus
camerarii apud Dansk, vj s. viij d. Item diu*ersis* ministral*is* ville
20 de Dansk in festo Annunciacionis Beate Marie per manus senescalli,   March 25.
vj s. viij d. Item a Derby le heraud eunti de Dansk versus Regem
Polonie cum litteris domini, nunciante camerario, lxvj s. viij d. Item
data pro sepultura Willelmi Hauir facta apud Conyngburg per
manus domini Hugonis Herle, v marc. xvij scot. pr. Cuid*am* militi
25 de Scotia pro viij virgis panni blodei de Lira, de dono domini, le
virge iiij s. vj d., in festo Circumcisionis domini, nunci*ante*   January 1
camerario, xxxvj s. Item hospiti de Conyngburg existenti cum
domino in le Reys de dono domini apud Conyngburg, xl s. Item
predicto hospiti in recessu suo de Conyngburg, xl s. de dono
30 domini ibidem. Item Fratri Johanni de ordine predicatorum apud
Dansk per manus camerarii de dono domini ibidem, xx s. Item
eidem Fratri pro celebratione pro anima Bryan de Stapleton militis,

---

* Conrad van Wallenroth, previously Marshal, was elected Grand-Master of the
Teutonic Order on 12th March, 1391.

nunciante camerario, xxxiij s. iiij d. Item Galfrido Baker xj° die
Febr. de dono domini apud Conyngburg, vj s. viij d. Item fratribus
predicatoribus de Brekenok pro anima Guidonis Bryan militis,
nunciante camerario, xxxiij s. iiij d. Item Roberto Chalons pro
j coler de dono domini apud Conyngburg, xl s. Item Johanni 5
Malet, militi, de dono domini apud Conyngburg, v° die Januarii,
vj li. xiij s. iiij d. Ricardo Dancastre de dono domini, eo quod
perdidit diversa harnesia in le Reys, xl s. st. Item Cok de
Byngeley pro j equo de dono domini, xxxiij s. iiij d. Willelmo
Algood, piper, pro ij^{bus} equis, xlvj s. viij d. Willelmo de York, 10
piper, pro j equo, xxvj s. viij d. Magistro Johanni Nakerer pro
ij equis, xlvj s. viij d.; et eidem pro j cella, vj s. viij d.; et eidem
pro j pilche, vj s. viij d., in toto lx s. Johanni Brothir et sociis suis
pro ij equis emptis, liij s. iiij d. Et eisdem pipers et thrumpours pro
vj sackes de fostyon ex precepto domini, lx s. Et Johanni Waterton, 15
Roberto Chalons, Ricardo Ryggeley, Nicholao de Camera, Henrico
Maunsell, Henrico Morley, Johanni Leuyngton, Roberto Waterton, Kykeley, Waltero Hausman, Johanni Peek, Roberto Hethecote cuilibet illorum j pylche, precium vj s. viij d., in toto iiij li.
/Willelmo Freman pro j equo, xxvj s. viij d., et eidem pro j pilche, 20
vj s. viij d. Henrico de Camera pro j equo, xx s. et eidem pro j
pilche, vj s. viij d., in toto xxvj s. viij d. Roberto Litton pro j pilche,
vj s. viij d. Roberto Barbour pro j equo, xxvj s. viij d., et pro
j pilche, vj s. viij d., in toto, xxxiij s. iiij d. Ricardo Catour pro
j equo, xxvj s. viijd., et pro j pilche, vj s. viij d., in toto xxxiij s. 25
iiij d. Willelmo Harpedene pro j equo, xiij s. iiij d., et pro j
pilche, vj s. viij d., in toto xx s. Willelmo Habbegode pro j equo,
xxvj s. viij d. Johanni Cudeworth pro j equo, xxvj s. viij d.
Ricardo del Ewre pro j equo et pro j pilche, xxvj s. viij d. Roberto
Peper pro j equo et j pilche, xx s. Ricardo Sandehill pro j equo 30
et j pilche xxvj s. viij d. Roberto de Spayn, pro j equo et j pilche,
xx s. Roberto Knyghton pro j equo et j pilche, xvj s. viij d.
Johanni Fissher, baker pro j equo et j pilche, xx s. Willelmo
Wyndesore pro j equo et j pilche, xxvj s. viij d. Petro Hauseman

pro j pilche ibidem, vj s. viij d. Willelmo Graceles pro j pilche de dono domini ibidem, vj s. viij d.

Summa donorum vsque huc, CCCiiij**vj li. xij d. st.; et in moneta Pruciana xxxvj marc. di. x scot. vj d., qui sunt in moneta Anglica, 5 xj li. vij s. ij d. ob., le noble ad xxvj scot. *Probatur.*

Dona data non contenta in Rotulo predicto.

Nicholao Pruciano de dono domini ibidem, xl. s. Jacobo Fauconer de dono domini ibidem, xxvj s. viij d. Quatuor ministrallis domini in recessu eorum de domino, iiij li. Johanni Brailleford de dono 10 domini ibidem, xiij s. iiij d. Hans Weyn seruienti in coquina domini apud Dansk, xij scot. Johanni Morley, sumpter man, de dono domini, xij s. vj d. Willelmo Baker de dono domini ibidem, xx s. Balliuo manerii Episcopi pro custode de les Lettowes, de dono domini, xx s. Johanni Beuere pro expensis Willelmi Graceles de 15 dono domini, vj s. viij d. Hans Peyntour de dono domini per manus Johannis Elys militis, iij s. iiij d. Johanni Dounton pro j equo de dono domini, xiij s. iiij d. Johanni Clifton, militi, pro tabelers et meisne per ipsum emptis, de dono domini, xliij s. iiij d. vj scot. Cuidam valetto portanti harnesium domini ad hastilidiandum, iiij 20 nobles. Cuidam carectario portanti roos domino, xij scot, de dono domini ibidem. Bernardo Hauseman pro necessariis suis emendis, de dono domini, j marc. pr. Roberto Bolton de dono domini ibidem, xiiij scot. Dati prisonis apud Dansk per manus senescalli de dono domini, vj s. viij d. Cuidam naute naviganti dominum de le 25 Wyslec vsque Dansk, per manus Norbury, iij s. iiij d. Cuidam clerico ville de Conyngburg scribenti les prames et carectas ibidem, xiij s. iiij d. Item iij fithleres existentibus cum domino apud Dansk in quadragesima per manus senescalli ex precepto domini, xiij s. iiij d. Fratribus minoribus apud Brounesburgh de dono 30 domini ibidem, xij scot. Item fratribus predicatoribus de Dar-

114   THE EARL OF DERBY'S EXPEDITIONS

[At the side of the
Summa is the
following note,]

*Inquirendum cum
cancellaria pro istis
parcellis.*

*Summa pagine
denariorum non conten-
torum in Rotulo,
xxiij li. xv s. x d. st.
Et monete Pruciane
in mare. xvj scot.,
que faciunt xxij s.
vj d. ob. q^r.*

fo. 41 v°.

* [Corrected to
xv s. iiij d. in the
margin.]

sowe de dono domini ibidem, iij s. iiij d. Clericis cantant*ibus*
ad hostium domini apud Meluyng, de dono domini ibidem, xx s.
pr. Duobus Fratribus Carmelitis de dono domini apud Dansk,
viij s. st. Dati a le Trumpet de dono domini ibidem, xxiiij s.
viij d. Willelmo Baker de dono domini ibidem, xx s. st. Roberto 5
Barbour de dono domini ibidem, xiij s. iiij d. Item Hans
Hornpiper, xiij s. iiij d. Johanni Peek de dono domini
ibidem, xiiij s. st. Johanni Syde de dono domini ibidem, x s.
st. Galfrido Baker de dono domini ibidem, xxvj s. viij d. st.
/ Thome Watton de dono domini ibidem, vj s. viij d. Roberto 10
Jonson de buteria de dono domini ibidem, vj s. viij d. Henrico de
coquina de dono domini ibidem, xiij s. iiij d. Roberto Duffeld de
dono domini ibidem, x s. pr. Willelmo Fyssher de dono domini
ibidem, xiij s. iiij d. Petro Hausman de dono domini ibidem, xl s.
Laurencio de sentellaria de dono domini ibidem, xvj s. viij d. 15
Willelmo Kykeley de dono domini ibidem, xiij s. iiij d. Ricardo
Benteley de dono domini ibidem, xvj s. viij d. Thome Knapp de
dono domini ibidem, xvj s. viij d. Willelmo Wytlok de dono
domini ibidem, xxiij s. iiij d. Waltero Hausman de dono domini
ibidem, xxxiij s. Roberto Hughet de dono domini ibidem, x s. 20
Thome Swyllyngton de dono domini ibidem, xvj s. viij d. Johanni
Assheby de dono domini ibidem, xx s. iiij d.* Willelmo Higham
de dono domini ibidem, xvj s. viij d. Johanni Knyghton de dono
domini ibidem, xiij s. iiij d. Ricardo Walshman de dono domini
ibidem, xvj s. viij d. Johanni Norway de [dono] domini ibidem, 25
xxx s. Willelmo Graceles de dono domini ibidem, ij marc. pr. viij
scot. Cuidam valetto ciuis presentanti dominum cum j equo et j sella
ex parte dicti ciuis apud Hull, receptis denariis de magistro Willelmo
Cook de dono domini ibidem, vj s. viij d. Cuidam gyde ducenti
dominum viam de Barton vsque Bullyngbrok, de dono domini vj s. 30
viij d. Et per manus Roberti Waterton in primo aduentu domini
apud Dansk diuersis minstrallis de dono domini ibidem, ex precepto domini, vj s. viij d. st. Et per manus eiusdem cuidam famulo
Reynepot militis Francie, presentantis domino apud Conyngburg

GAMES OF DICE.

cum j courser, xiij s. iiij d. st. Et per manus thesaurarii dati Roberto Burton adiuuanti ipsum ad scribendum librum suum, xx s. st. Et data j pipere, socio Hans Hornpipere, per manus ciusdem, di. marc. pr.

5 Summa xviij li. xvj s. viij d. st. Ostendantur i-parcelle cames

Summa in moneta Pruciana iij marc. pr., qui faciunt xviij s. v d. ob. sterlingorum.

LUSUS AD TALOS.

In primis apud Conyngburg per manus Johannis Waterton,
10 xiij s. iiij d. Et liberate in festo Sancte Elizabete per manus proprias apud Dansk in nobilibus et florenis tempore quo stetit ibidem, xxv marc. st. Et liberati domino per manus Radulphi Staneley ibidem, lxvj s. viij d. Et liberate domino per manus seneseulli per ij vices ibidem, xiij marc. st. Et liberati Thome
15 Goter ex precepto domini, nunciante Camerario, xij nobles. Et liberati domino viij° die Januarii per manus proprias, xij nobles. Et liberate domino per manus proprias ad ludendum cum domino Johanne Rye per ij noctes, xlij marc. st. Et liberati domino per manus Simeonis xx d. st. Et liberata domino per manus ciusdem j
20 florena viz.,* ij s. viij d. Et liberati domino pro lusu suo ad tales in naui versus Pruciam, xxxiij s. iiij d. Et liberati domino in naui, nunciante camerario, xl s.ª

Novembris 19.

January 8.

* Ostendantur domino vel cam

Summa lxix li. iiij s. iiij d. st.

Summa istius Pagine   iiij^{xx}viij li. xix s. v d. ob.

25 / Summa totalis donorum in foliis precedentibus, Dxj li. vj s. qr. st.

fo. 42.

* Two items are here struck through, "quia scribitur in alio loco," as is explained in the margin.

ELEMOSINE ET OBLACIONES.

[fo. 42 verso is blank].

fo. 43. / In primis liberati domino Hugoni Herle pro elemosinis domini
August 9—17. distributis a ix die Augusti vsque xvij^m diem eiusdem mensis, per
compotum secum factum, xxj s. ob. st.   Et eidem pro oblacionibus
per idem tempus, v s. ij d. st.   Et liberati domino Willelmo Pomfreit
August 17--October pro oblacionibus domini, de xvij° die eiusdem mensis vsque vlti-
31. mum diem Octobris per xliiij dies, xliiij s. pr.   Item eidem pro
quodam Ducheman defuncto apud Conyngburg in oblacione domini,
vj s. viij d.   Item in elemosinis domini, videlicet oblacionibus distri-
November 1— butis fratribus et pauperibus, a primo die Nouembris vsque vlti-
December 31. mum diem Decembris, per manus dicti domini Willelmi et Rogeri
Messyngham, iij marc. xv scot.   Item in oblacione domini in festo
November 1. Omnium Sanctorum in ecclesia predicta, iij s. iiij d. st.   Et in
oblacione domini apud Sanctum Georgium in recessu suo, iiij s. pr.
January 1—31. Item in oblacionibus domini cotidianis a primo die Januarii vsque
vltimum diem eiusdem per xxxj dies, capiente per diem j s., in toto
xxxj s. pr.   Item in oblacionibus domini cotidianis factis a primo
February 1—28. die Februarii vsque vltimum diem eiusdem mensis, vtroque computato per xxviij dies, capiente per diem j s. pr., xxviij s. pr.
Item liberati domino per manus dicti domini Hugonis pro elemosinis, xj s. pr.   Et liberati domino per manus dicti domini
Hugonis pro oblacionibus suis ad Sanctam Annam, iij s. iiij d. st.
Et dati Rogero Hous et Johanni Gray ad Sanctam Annam de
elemosinis domini ibidem, vj s. viij d. st.   Item apud Dansk de
elemosinis domini datis per manus thesaurarii in die Cene,
Mar. 23. iiij marc. pr.   Et per manus Johannis Dyndon pro panno russeto
per ipsum empto apud Dansk ad distribuendum pauperibus in die
Cene, xij marc. vj scot. ij s. pr.   Et per manus eiusdem pro xxiiij
paribus sotularium per ipsum emptis ibidem pro eisdem pauperibus,
nunciante camerario, j marc. di. vj s. pr.   Et liberati domino
February 2. per manus thesaurarii in die Purificacionis Beate Marie apud
Conyngburg pro oblacionibus suis ibidem, v s. st.   Et liberati

ALMS AND OBLATIONS.   117

domino pro oblac*ionibus suis* apud Beuerley *per manus* Rygmayden, viij scot.   Et *per manus* eiusd*em* pro oblac*ionibus domini* apud Brytlyngton, vj s. viij d.   Et pro factur*a* pannor*um* dictor*um* paup*erum,* x s. st.   In oblac*ionibus* dom*i*ni cotidian*is* fact*is* apud
5 Dan*s*k, a primo die Mart*ii* vsq*ue* vlt*imum* diem eiusd*em* mensis   March 1-31.
p*er* xxxj dies, cap*iente* p*er* diem j s. pr., xxxj s.   In oblac*ionibus*
domini fact*is* in C*ena D*om*ini* ad ij missas vltra oblac*ionem* cotidia- Mar. 23.
n*am,* ij *s.* pr.   In oblac*ionibus* dom*i*ni fact*is* in die p*a*rasseuen orando March 24.
crucem, v s. pr.   Et in consimil*ibus* oblac*ionibus* dom*ini* fact*is*
10 orand*o* crucem in die Pasche,[a] v s. pr.   In oblac*ione* dom*i*ni fact*a* March 26.
in die Pasche vltra oblacionem cotidian*am,* j s. pr.   Et in obla-
c*ionibus* domini fact*is* apud Dansk tempore p*er*egrinacionis sue de
absolu*cione* sibi concess*a* a Papa no*s*tro Bonefacio, videl*icet* a pena
et a culpa, ad iiij*or* ecclesias ibid*em* p*er* vij dies continuos, viz. ad
15 qu*am*libet ecclesi*am* xvj d. pr., in to*to* xxxvij s. iiij d. pr.   Et in
elemosynis domini distributis pauperibus per diuersas vices tempore peregrinacionis sue, xvj s. pr.   Et in elemosynis domini dis
tributis per manus sui ipsius in die parasseue, l s. pr.   In
elemosynis datis hospicio Sancti Spiritus de Dansk ex precepto
20 domini, vj s. viij d.   In elemosynis domini datis apu*d* Dansk per
manus Johannis Norbury, xvj scot.   In oblacionibus domini apud
Brydlyngton, ad piliñ[b] nup*er* Priorem ibid*em,* rec*eptis* denariis de
Gloucestre, xx d. st.   In elemosynis domini distributis per viam
inter Brydlyngton p*er* manus Gloucestre, x d.   In oblac*ionibus*
25 domini fact*is* ad missas de requie apud Hulle cum oblacione
cot*idiana,* v d.   In oblac*ionibus* domini fact*is* ad magnum altare in

[a] The adoration of the Cross seems to be what is intended above, both on Good Friday and Easter Day.
[b] This contracted word is difficult to interpret, and I must leave it unsolved; *piissimum* suggested by Prof. Prutz is a quite inadmissible reading, owing to the shape of the *ll*. The Prior was probably John de Tweng, well known as John of Bridlington, who died in 1379, and was afterwards canonized, a commission having been issued in 1386 to inquire into the miracles performed at his tomb. See Hist. of **Priory Church of** Bridlington, by Rev. M. Prickett. Cambridge, 1835. Pp. 25, 61, 85.

ecclesia prioratus de Spaldyng, receptis denariis de Ricardo Dancastre, iij s. iiij d. st.

Summa pagine, iiij li. iiij d. st., et monete Pruciane, xxvj marc. xxij scot. x d. pr.; qui faciunt Anglice, viij li. v s. viij d. ob. qr.

[Seven pages blank here. 43 v°—46 v°].

VADIA MILITUM, SCUTIFERORUM ET VALETTORUM, TAM IN PARTIBUS PRUCIE QUAM IN ANGLIA, VT PATET PER NOMINA ET PARCELLAS EORUNDEM INFERIUS ET CONSEQUENTER DIUISIM ANNOTATA. 5

fo. 47.

May 9—25. / Decem valettis Willelmi Bagot militis pro vadiis suis extra curiam, existentibus apud Caleys a ix° die Maii vsque xxv^m diem eiusdem mensis, vtroque computato, per xvij dies, quolibet eorum capiente per diem xij d., in toto . . . . viij li. x s. 10

Et quinque valettis eiusdem pro regardo eisdem facto eo quod recesserunt versus partes Anglie, nunciante camerario xxxiij s. iiij d. 15

May 9—25. Willelmo Ferrour pro vadiis suis a ix° die Maii vsque xxv^m diem eiusdem mensis, vtroque computato per xvij dies, capienti per diem iiij d., in toto . . . . v s. viij d.

May 9—31. Rogero Smart pro vadiis suis a ix° die Maii vsque vltimum diem eiusdem mensis vtroque computato, per xxiij dies, capienti per diem vj d., in toto . . . . xj s. vj d. 20

Johanni Cudworth pro vadiis suis infra curiam vt supra, xj s. vj d.

May 9—31. Thome Toty pro vadiis suis infra curiam ad viij d., et vnius sagittarii extra curiam ad xij d. per diem xx d., a ix° die Maii vsque vltimum diem eiusdem mensis, per xxiij dies, in toto 25
xxxviij s. iiij d

May 9—31. Roberto Waterton pro vadiis suis infra curiam ad viij d., et vnius sagittarii extra curiam ad xij d. per diem, xx d., a ix° die Maii vsque vltimum diem eiusdem mensis, per xxiij dies, in toto
xxxviij s. iiij d. 30

Thome Gloucestre pro vadiis suis infra curiam ad viij d., et vnius sagittarii infra curiam ad vj d. per diem, inter se xiiij d., a ix° die Maii vsque vltimum diem eiusdem mensis, per xxiij dies, in toto . . . . . . xxvj s. x d. May 9—31.

5 Ricardo Dancastre pro vadiis suis infra curiam ad viij d., et vnius sagittarii extra curiam ad xij d. per diem, inter se in toto xx d., a ix° die Maii vsque vltimum diem eiusdem mensis, per xxiij dies, in toto . . . . xxxviij s. iiij d. May 9—31.

Johanni Payn pro vadiis suis infra curiam ad viij d. et vnius sagit-
10 tarii extra curiam ad xij d., per diem xx d., a ix° die Maii vsque vltimum diem eiusdem mensis, vtroque computato, per xxiij dies, in toto . . . . xxxviij s. iiij. d. May 9—31.

Summa pagii
xx li. xij s. ij
fo. 47 v°.

/Johanni Waterton pro vadiis suis infra curiam ad vj d., a ix° die Maii vsque vltimum diem eiusdem mensis, per xxiij dies vtroque
15 computato, in toto . . . . . xj s. vj d. May 9—31.

Ricardo Sandehill pro vadiis suis infra curiam ad iiij d. per diem, a ix° die Maii vsque vltimum diem eiusdem mensis, per xxiij dies, in toto . . . . . . vij s. viij d. May 9—31.

Nicholao de camera pro vadiis suis infra curiam ad vj d. per diem,
20 a viij° die Maii vsque vltimum diem eiusdem mensis per xxiiij dies . . . . xij s. May 8—31.

Ricardo Ryggeley pro vadiis suis infra curiam ad vj d. per diem, a ix° die Maii vsque vltimum diem eiusdem mensis per xxiij dies, in toto . . . . xj s. vj d. May 9—31.

25 Willelmo Freman pro vadiis suis vt supra, capienti per diem vt supra . . . . . . xj s. vj d.

Willelmo Wylloughby militi pro vadiis ij sagittariorum, quilibet capiens per diem extra curiam xij d., a ix° die Maii vsque vltimum diem eiusdem mensis, vtroque computato, in toto pro
30 xxiij dies . . . . xlvj s. May 9—31.

Magistro Willelmo Cook pro vadiis suis infra curiam a ix° die Maii vsque vltimum diem eiusdem mensis, capienti per diem viij d., per xxiij dies . . . . . . xv s. iiij d. May 9—31.

Rogero Langeford pro vadiis suis infra curiam ad viij d. et vnius

May 9—31.	sagittarii extra curiam ad xij d. per diem, xx d., a ix° die Maii vsque vltimum diem eiusdem mensis per xxiii dies, in toto xxxviij s. iiij d.
May 9—31.	Ricardo Wolfley pro vadiis suis ad iiij d. per diem, a ix° die Maii vsque vltimum diem eiusdem mensis, per xxiij dies, vtroque computato . . . . . vij s. viij d. 5
May 9—31.	Edmundo Stancysshe pro vadiis suis infra curiam ad viij d. per diem, a ix° die Maii vsque vltimum diem eiusdem mensis, in toto xv s. iiij d.
May 9—31. Summa pagine x li. xv s. ij d.	Johanni Assheley pro vadiis suis infra curiam ad viij d., et vnius sagittarii extra curiam ad xij d. per diem xx d., a ix° die Maii vsque vltimum diem eiusdem mensis per xxiij dies, vtroque computato, in toto . . . xxxviij s. iiij d. 10
fo. 48. May 9—31.	[Johanni Dounton pro vadiis suis infra curiam ad iiij d. per diem, a ix° die Maii vsque vltimum diem eiusdem mensis, per xxiij dies, in toto . . . . . vij s. viij d. 15
May 9—31.	Willelmo Sewarby pro vadiis suis infra curiam ad viij d., a ix° die Maii vsque vltimum diem eiusdem mensis per xxiij dies, in toto xv s. iiij d.
May 9—31.	Johanni Dalynggrugge pro vadiis suis infra curiam ad viij d., et vnius sagittarii extra curiam ad xij d. per diem, xx d., a ix° die Maii vsque vltimum diem eiusdem mensis per xxiij dies, in toto . . . . . xxxviij s. iiij d. 20
	Thome Asshedon pro vadiis suis et vnius sagittarii sui, vt supra, xxxviij s. iiij d. 25
	Radulfo Stanelcy pro vadiis suis et vnius sagittarii, vt supra, in toto . . . . xxxviij s. iiij d.
May 9—31.	Henrico Langdon pro vadiis suis infra curiam ad v d. per diem, a ix° die Maii vsque vltimum diem eiusdem mensis per xxiij dies, in toto . . . . ix s. vij d. 30
	Roberto Spayn pro vadiis suis infra curiam, capienti per diem, vt supra . . . . ix s. vij d.
May 9—31.	Johanni Countershawe pro vadiis suis infra curiam ad vj d. per diem, a ix° die Maii vsque vltimum diem eiusdem mensis, vtroque computato, in toto xj s. vj d. 35

WAGES OF KNIGHTS, ESQUIRES, AND VALETS. 121

Ingelfeld pro vadiis suis infra curiam ad viij d. per diem, et vnius
sagittarii extra curiam ad xij d. per diem, xx d., a ix° die Maii May 9—31.
vsque vltimum diem eiusdem mensis per xxiij dies, in toto
. . . . xxxviij s. iiij d.
5 Newport pro vadiis suis infra curiam, capienti per diem vt supra, et
vnius sagittarii capientis vt supra, in toto . xxxviij s. iiij d.
Christofori Langton pro vadiis suis infra curiam ad viij d. per diem, May 9—31.
a ix° die Maii vsque vltimum diem eiusdem mensis, vtroque
computato . . . . . . xv s. iiij d. Summa pagin xiij li. viij d.
10 / Ricardo Rygmayden pro vadiis suis infra curiam ad viij d. per fo. 48 v°.
diem, et vnius sagittarii extra curiam per diem ad xij d., in May 9—31.
toto xx d. per diem, a ix° die Maii vsque vltimum diem eiusdem
mensis vtroque computato, in toto . xxxviij s. iiij d.
Domino Thome Swynford pro vadiis suis infra curiam ad xij d., et
15 vnius sagittarii infra curiam ad vj d. per diem xviij d., a ix°
die Maii vsque vltimum diem eiusdem mensis, vtroque compu- May 9—31.
tato, in toto . . . . . xxxiiij s. vj d.
Domino Willelmo Pountfreyt pro vadiis suis infra curiam ad vj d.,
a ix° die Maii vsque vltimum diem eiusdem mensis, vtroque May 9—31.
20 computato, in toto . . . . xj s. vj d.
Willelmo Hauir pro vadiis suis infra curiam ad iiij d. per diem a
ix° die Maii vsque vltimum diem eiusdem mensis, vtroque May 9—31.
computato, in toto . . . . vij s. viij d.
Willelmo Wollaton pro vadiis suis infra curiam ad viij d., et vnius
25 sagittarii extra curiam ad xij d., in toto xx d., a ix° die Maii May 9—27.
vsque xxvij^m diem eiusdem mensis, vtroque computato, per
xix dies, in toto . . . . xxxj s. viij d.
Johanni Cope pro vadiis suis infra curiam ad viij d. per diem, a
ix° die Maii vsque vltimum diem eiusdem mensis, vtroque com- May 9—31.
30 putato, per xxiij dies . . . . xv s. iiij d.
Et eidem pro vadiis vnius sagittarii extra curiam, a dicto ix° die
Maii vsque vltimum diem eiusdem mensis, vtroque computato, May 9—31.
capienti per diem xij d., in toto . . . xxiij s.
Roberto Litton pro vadiis suis infra curiam ad vj d. per diem, a

CAMD. SOC. R

ix⁰ Maii vsque vltimum diem eiusdem mensis, vtroque die
computato, per xxiij dies . . . xj s. vj d.

Johanni ap Henry pro vadiis suis infra curiam ad viij d. per diem,
et vnius sagittarii extra curiam ad xij d. per diem, inter se per
diem xx d., a xij⁰ die Maii vsque vltimum diem eiusdem mensis, 5
vtroque computato, per xx dies, in toto . xxxiij s. iiij d.

Johanni Bodenhale sagittario pro vadiis suis extra curiam ad xij d.
per diem, a ix⁰ die Maii vsque vltimum diem eiusdem mensis,
vtroque die computato . . . . xxiij s.

Thome Haseldene pro vadiis suis infra curiam ad viij d. et j sagit- 10
tarii extra curiam ad xij d. per diem, inter se xx d., a ix⁰ die
Maii vsque vltimum diem eiusdem mensis, vtroque die computato, in toto . . . xxxviij s. iiij d.

/ Roberto Hethcot pro vadiis suis infra curiam ad iiij d., a ix⁰ die
Maii vsque vltimum diem eiusdem mensis per xxiij dies, vtroque 15
computato, in toto . . . . vij s. viij d.

Ricardo Messenger pro vadiis suis infra curiam ad vj d., a ix⁰ die
Maii vsque vltimum diem eiusdem mensis per xxiij dies,
xj s. vj d. Et eidem pro vadiis suis extra curiam misso de Caleys
vsque London cum litteris domini, eundo et redeundo per iiij 20
dies, capienti per diem xij d., iiij s., . . xv s. vj d.

Hugoni Herle pro vadiis suis infra curiam ad xij d., et vnius
sagittarii ad vj d., per diem xviij d., a ix⁰ die Maii vsque
vltimum diem eiusdem mensis, vtroque computato, per xxiij
dies, xxxiiij s. vj d., deductis inde ij s. eo quod recepit nobles. 25
xxxij s. vj d. Et eidem pro vadiis suis infra curiam ad xij d.
per diem, a primo die Junii vsque viij diem eiusdem mensis
per viij dies, vtroque computato, viij s. in toto . xl s. vj d.

Quinque valettis Willelmi Bagot militis pro vadiis suis extra curiam,
a xxvj die Maii vsque ij diem Junii, vtroque computato, per 30
viij dies, capiente quolibet eorum per diem xij d., in toto xl s.

Et eisdem pro regardo eis facto euntibus versus Angliam, nunciante
camerario . . . . . xxvj s. viij d.

Johanni Countershawe pro vadiis suis infra curiam ad vj d., a primo

WAGES OF KNIGHTS, ESQUIRES, AND VALETS. 123

die Jun*ii* vsq*ue* ij diem eiusdem mens*is*, per ij dies, vna cum   June 1—2.
regardo ei * facto apud **Caleys**, nunc*iante* camerar*io*, in toto • The MS. ha
         vj s. viij d.
Radul**pho** Rocheford *pro* **vad***iis* **suis infra curiam ad viij d.** *per*
5   *diem*, a ix° die Maii vsq*ue* vl*timum* diem eiusdem mens*is*,   May 9—31.
vtroq*ue* comp*utato*, *per* **compotum secum** factum apud Caleys
iij° die Jun*ii*, **in** to*to* . . . . xv s. iiij d.
Joh*anni* Levnthorpe *pro* **vad***iis* suis infra curiam **ad vj d.** *per diem*,
a ix° die Maii vsq*ue* vl*timum* diem eiusdem mens*is* per xx   May 9—31.
10   dies," x s. Et eidem pro vad*iis* suis **extra curiam**, misso de
Caleys vsq*ue* Hertford cum *litteris* **dom**ini per iij dies, ad xij d.
per diem, **in** to*to* . . . . . xiij s.   May 9—31.
Burghwell *pro* redditu vadiorum suorum a ix° Maii vsq*ue* vl*timum*   Summa pagin
diem eiusdem mens*is*, nunc*iante* camerar*io*, in toto vj s. viij d.   viij li. xij s.
15 /**Derby le heraud** *pro* **vad***iis* suis infra curiam **ad vij d. ob.** *per*   fo. 49 v°.
diem, a ix° die Maii vsq*ue* tercium diem Jun*ii*, vtroq*ue* com-   May 9—June
putato per xxv dies, **in toto** . . . xv s. vij d. ob.
Thome Stokes *pro* **vad***iis* **suis infra curiam ad x d.** *per diem*, et
vni*us* **sagittarii extra curiam ad xij d.** *per diem*, inter se xxij d.
20   a ix° die Maii vsq*ue* vl*timum* diem eiusdem mens*is*, vtroq*ue*   May 9—31.
comp*utato*, **in** to*to* . . . . xlij s. ij d.
Joh*anni* **Holcot** *pro* **vad***iis* **suis infra curiam ad vj d.** *per diem*,
a ix. die Maii vsq*ue* vl*timum* diem eiusdem mens*is*, vtroque   May 9—31.
comp*utato*, *per* xxiij dies, in to*to* . . xj s. vj d.
25 Joh*anni* Leg *pro* **vad***iis* **suis extra curiam** *per* **diem ad xij d.**, a ix°
die Maii vsq*ue* vl*timum* diem eiusdem mens*is*, vtroq*ue* com-   May 9—31.
putato, *per* xxiij dies . . . . . xxiij s.
Wyll*elmo* Hykelyng *pro* **vad***iis* suis **infra curiam ad x d.**, et vni*us*
valetti ad vj d., *per* diem inter se xvj d., a ix° die Maii vsq*ue*   May 9—31.
30   vl*timum* diem eiusdem mens*is*, **in** to*to* . . xxx s. viij d.
Thome Toty *pro* vad*iis* suis infra curiam **ad viij d.**, et vni*us* valetti
extra curiam ad xij d., *per* diem inter se ad xx d., a primo die

* So in the MS., but by the usual mode of reckoning both days, it should be
twenty-three days.

124   THE EARL OF DERBY'S EXPEDITIONS.

June 1—10.   Junii vsque x diem eiusdem mensis, vtroque computato per
              x dies, in toto . . . . . . xvj s. viij d.
              Ricardo Messenger pro vadiis suis per diem ad vj d., a primo die
June 1—8.   Junii vsque viij^m diem eiusdem mensis, vtroque computato, in
              toto . . . . iiij s. 5
May 9—June 13. Henrico Maunsell pro vadiis suis ad vj d. per diem, a ix° die Maii
              vsque xiij diem Junii, vtroque computato, in toto per xxxvj
              dies . . . . xviij s.
              Johanni Prendregest sagittario pro vadiis suis extra curiam ad viij d.
May 9—27.   per diem, a ix° die Maii vsque xxvij^m diem eiusdem mensis, 10
              vtroque computato, per xix dies, in toto . xij s. viij d.
              Hugoni Waterton pro vadiis suis infra curiam ad xij d. per diem,
              et ij sagittariis, quolibet eorum ad vj d. per diem, inter se ij s.
May 9—June 10. per diem, a ix° die Maii vsque x^m diem Junii, vtroque com-
Summa pagine putato, per xxxiij dies in toto . . . . lxvj s. 15
xij li. iij d. ob.
         fo. 50. / Cuidam valetto Nuport assignato pro corpore domini, pro vadiis suis
May 9—31.   extra curiam ad xij d. per diem, a ix° die Maii vsque vltimum
              diem eiusdem mensis, vtroque computato, per compotum secum
              factum apud Caleys, in toto . . . . xxiij s.
              Christofori Langton pro vadiis suis infra curiam ad viij d. per 20
June 1—3.   diem, a primo die Junii vsque iij^m diem eiusdem mensis, vtroque
              computato, in toto . . . . . . ij s.
              Domino Willelmo Elman pro vadiis iij sagittariorum extra curiam,
May 18—June 7. a xviij° die Maii vsque vij diem Junii, vtroque computato,
              capientium per xxj dies per diem inter se iij s., in toto 25
              lxiij s.
              Willelmo Porter pro vadiis suis infra curiam ad vj d. per diem, a
June 1—10.   primo die Junii vsque iij diem eiusdem mensis, xviij d. Et
              eidem pro vadiis suis a dicto iij die Junii vsque x^m diem
              eiusdem mensis per vij dies, capienti per diem iiij d., ij s. iiij d., 30
              in toto . . . . iij s. x d.
              Ricardo Dancastre pro vadiis suis apud Caleys, et vno sagittario
June 1—5.   capientibus per diem xx d. per v dies, viz. a primo die Junii
              vsque v^m diem eiusdem mensis, vtroque computato, viij s. iiij d.

WAGES OF KNIGHTS, ESQUIRES, AND VALETS. 125

    Et eidem pro vadiis suis infra curiam per xviij dies sequentes, capienti vij d. ob. per diem, xj s. iij d., in toto .   xix s. vij d.
    Johanni Cope pro vadiis suis per x dies, viz. a viij° die mensis Augusti vsque xvij diem eiusdem mensis ad vij d. ob. per diem, vj s. iij d. Et eidem per ix dies vsque vltimum diem eiusdem mensis, v s. vij d. ob. Et eidem apud Caleys per v dies iij s. iiij d., in toto   .   .   xv s. ij d. ob.   [August 8—17. August 23—31]
    Magistro Willelmo Cook pro vadiis suis per v dies apud Caleys in mense Junii, quolibet die ad viij d., iij s. iiij d. Et eidem pro v diebus versus Kylyngworth ad vij d. ob. per diem infra curiam, iij s. j d. ob., in toto   .   .   vj s. v d. ob.   [June (1—5. ?) Cf. first dates Dancaster abov of Stanley, fo. first item.]
    Johanni Waterton pro vadiis suis apud Caleys per v dies, ij s. vj d., Et eidem redeundo versus Angliam per v dies infra curiam, xx d., in toto   .   .   iiij s. ij d.
    Willelmo Porter pro vadiis suis vt supra per v dies, ij s. vj d. Et eidem per vj dies in Anglia ad iiij d. per diem, ij s., in toto   iiij s. vj d.
    Roberto Litton pro vadiis suis vt supra, per v dies ij s. vj d. Et eidem infra curiam per v dies versus Angliam, xx d., in toto   iiij s. ij d.   [Summa pagine vij li. v s. xj d. fo. 50 v°.]
    /Johanni Cudeworth pro vadiis suis apud Caleys per v dies, ij s. vj d. Et eidem per v dies extra curiam in Anglia, xx d. Et eidem pro xxx diebus apud Boston, capienti per diem viij d , xx s. in toto   .   .   xxiiij s. ij d.
    Henrico de Camera pro vadiis suis apud Caleys per v dies infra curiam, ij s. vj d. Et eidem per v dies in Anglia, xx d., in toto   .   .   iiij s. ij d.
    Cok Pulter pro vadiis suis infra curiam apud Caleys per v dies, capienti per diem iiij d., xx d. Et eidem per v dies extra curiam, xx d., in toto.   .   .   iij s. iiij d.
    Johanni Hethecote pro vadiis suis infra curiam apud Calcis pro v diebus ad iiij d. per diem, et pro v diebus infra curiam in Anglia, in toto   .   .   ij s. vj d.
    Ricardo del Ewery pro vadiis suis vt supra, in toto   ij s. vj d.

126   THE EARL OF DERBY'S EXPEDITIONS.

Willelmo Hauyr pro vadiis suis apud Caleis per v dies, capienti per diem infra curiam iiij d., xx d. Et eidem per v dies in Anglia infra curiam ad ij d. per diem, x d., in toto   ij s. vj d.
Ricardo Sendille pro vadiis suis, capienti vt supra, in toto ij s. vj d.

May 9—June 6.   Roberto Pepir pro vadiis suis a ix° die Maii vsque vj diem Junii, 5 vtroque computato, per xxviij dies, capienti per diem iiij d., ix s. iiij d. Et eidem per v dies infra curiam in Anglia, capienti ij d. vt supra, in toto   .   .   x s. ij d.
Roberto Spayn pro vadiis suis vt supra, in toto   ij s. vj d.

May 9—June 3.   Petro Bucton militi, senescallo, pro vadiis suis infra curiam per 10 xxvj dies, videlicet a ix° die mensis Maii vsque iiij diem mensis Junii, vtroque computato, capienti per diem xij d., et pro ij sagittariis, quolibet ad vj d. per diem, in toto   .   lij s.

loquendum cum domino et camerario pro istis vadiis.

Et eidem Petro pro vadiis suis extra curiam ex precepto domini Ducis Lancastrie, equitando super negocium domini Comitis 15 Derbye in Angliam ad diuersa loca [a] per xxiij dies, capienti per diem v s., in toto   .   .   .   .   v li. xv s.

Johanni Payn pro vadiis suis apud Caleys per v dies, capienti per diem viij d., iij s. iiij d. Et eidem in Anglia pro xiij diebus

Summa pagine xiij li. iij s. iij d. ob.

infra curiam, viij s. vij d. ob. Et eidem pro xxxj diebus extra 20 curiam, capienti per diem xij d., xxxj s., in toto
     xlij s. xj d. ob.

fo. 51.   / Radulpho Stancley pro vadiis suis infra curiam per v dies, a primo
June 1—5.   die Junii vsque v diem eiusdem mensis, vtroque computato, capienti per diem viij d., iij s. iiij d. Et eidem pro octo diebus 25 infra curiam in Anglia, capienti per diem vij d. ob., v. s., in toto   .   .   .   .   .   viij s. iiij d.
Johanni Dounton pro vadiis suis extra curiam, capienti per diem iiij d. de Caleys vsque London per x dies coligenda armatura

* From a repetition of this item on fo. 51, differently written out, but afterwards struck through, quia scribitur infra, we find that, between 3 and 17 June, Bucton went to "Boston, de Boston vsque Bullyngbrok, de Bullyngbrok vsque Lincoln, de Lincoln vsque Hull, de Hull vsque Bolyngbrok;" his other seven days extra curiam were from 29 June to 5 July.

WAGES OF KNIGHTS, ESQUIRES, AND VALETS. 127

domini, iij s. iiij d.   Et eidem de London versus Kelyngworth
per ij dies, viij d.   Et eidem de Leycestre vsque London, et de
London versus Boston per xvij dies, v s. viij d.* in toto
                ix s. viij d.

5 Johanni Walker et x sociis suis pro vadiis suis apud Caleys, a ix°
die Maii vsque xiiij diem eiusdem mensis, vtroque computato, May 9—14.
quolibet eorum capiente per diem ij d. per vij dies, in toto
                xij s. x d.

Et eidem Johanni et sociis suis pro vadiis suis, per diem ad iij d.
10 per viij dies sequentes per manus Assheby, a xv die eiusdem May 15—22.
mensis vsque xxij^m diem eiusdem mensis, vtroque computato,
nunciante camerario, in toto . . . xxij s.

Eisdem Johanni et sociis suis a xxiij die eiusdem mensis, vsque
vltimum diem eiusdem mensis, vtroque computato, capienti May 23—31.
15 per diem vt supra, in toto . . xxij s.

Waltero Hauseman capienti pro vadiis suis a xvj die Maii vsque
vltimum diem eiusdem mensis, vtroque computato, per xvj dies, May 16—31.
capienti per diem iij d., in toto . . iiij s.

Johanni Walker et sociis suis pro vadiis suis a primo die Junii
20 vsque ix diem eiusdem mensis, vtroque computato, quolibet June 1—9.
eorundem capiente pro ij diebus existentibus apud Caleys per
diem, iij d.   Et pro vij diebus euntibus versus Angliam, per
diem ij d., in toto . . . xviij s. iiij d.

Domino Willelmo Pomfreit pro vadiis suis infra curiam a primo
25 die Junii vsque xix^m diem Julii, vtroque die computato, per June 1—July 1
xlix dies, capienti per diem vj d. . . xxiiij s. vj d.

Summa pagine vj li. xx d.

* This item was at first written vj s iiij d., making the total x s. iiij d., but stands corrected as above.

VADIA MILITUM SCUTIFERORUM ET VALETTORUM A IX° DIE
MENSIS AUGUSTI VSQUE VLTIMUM DIEM MENSIS OCTO-
BRIS, VTROQUE COMPUTATO.

fo. 51 v°. / Domino Petro Bucton pro vadiis suis infra curiam a ix° die
August 9—October   mensis Augusti vsque vltimum diem Octobris, per iiij**iiij 5
31.   dies, vtroque computato, capienti per diem ij s., viij li. viij s.
Et eidem pro vno valetto pro lxvj diebus pur le Reys, capienti per diem vj d., xxxiij s., in toto . x li. xij d.
Domino Hugoni Waterton pro vadiis suis per tempus predictum
infra curiam, capienti per diem vt supra, et pro ij^{bus} valettis 10
sagittariis pur le Reys, capientibus vt supra, in toto
xj li. xiiij s.
Domino Thome Swynford pro vadiis suis vt supra, viij li. viij s.
Item eidem pro j valetto pur le Reys, xxxiij s. iiij d. in toto
x li. xij d. 15
Johanni Norbury pro vadiis suis vt supra. Et pro vadiis ij
sagittariorum, quolibet capiente vt supra, in toto xj li. xiiij s.
Domino Hugoni Herle pro vadiis suis infra curiam, capienti per
diem xij d. per tempus predictum, in toto . iiij li. iiij s.
Radulpho Staneley pro vadiis suis infra curiam per tempus predic- 20
tum, capienti per diem xij d., in toto . . iiij li. iiij s.
Ricardo Dancastre pro vadiis suis, capienti per diem vt supra, in
toto . . . . . . iiij li. iiij s.
Thome Toty pro vadiis suis, capienti per diem vt supra, in toto
iiij li. iiij s. 25
Rogero Langeford pro vadiis suis vt supra infra curiam, capienti
vt supra . . . . . iiij li. iiij s.
Willelmo Sewarby pro vadiis suis per idem tempus, in toto
iiij li. iiij s.
Johanni Assheley pro vadiis suis, capienti per diem vt supra, in 30
toto . . . . . . iiij li. iiij s.
Johanni Payne pro vadiis suis per idem tempus, in toto iiii li. iiij s. j

VALETS OF THE LORD'S CHAMBER.

Magi*s*tro Willelmo Cook pro vadiis suis per idem tempus, vt supra . . iiij li. iiij s. *Summa pagine iiij*xj l. vj s.

/ Thome Gloucestre pro vadiis suis infra curiam, a ix° die mensis Augusti vsque vltimum diem Octobris, vtroque computato, 5 capienti per diem xij d., in toto . . iiij li. iiij s. fo. 52. August 9—Oct 31.

Johanni Waterton per idem tempus pro vadiis suis infra curiam, in toto . . . . . iiij li. iiij s.

Lancastre le herald pro vadiis suis per idem tempus, capienti vt supra . . . . . . iiij li. iiij s.

10 Roberto Waterton pro vadiis suis infra curiam per idem tempus, ... iiij li. iiij s.

Domino Willelmo Pountfreyt pro vadiis suis infra curiam per idem tempus, capienti per diem, vij d. ob . . lij s. vj d.

VALETTI CAMERE DOMINI.

15 Johanni Dyndon pro vadiis suis infra curiam a ix° die mensis Augusti vsque vltimum diem mensis Octobris, per iiij^{xx}iiij dies, vtroque computato, capienti per diem vj d., in toto . . . . . . xlij s. August 9—Oct 31.

Ricardo Ryggeley pro vadiis suis infra curiam per idem tempus, 20 capienti vt supra . . . . . xlij s.

Nicholao de Camera pro vadiis suis infra curiam per idem tempus, capienti vt supra . . . . . xlij s.

Willelmo Freman pro vadiis suis infra curiam per idem tempus, capienti vt supra . . . . . xlij s.

25 Henrico Maunsell pro vadiis suis infra curiam per idem tempus, capienti vt supra . . . . . xlij s.

Henrico Morlee pro vadiis suis per idem tempus infra curiam, capienti vt supra . . . . . xlij s.

Roberto Litton pro vadiis suis per idem tempus infra curiam, 30 capienti vt supra . . . . . xlij s.

Johanni Cudeworth pro vadiis suis infra curiam per idem tempus, capienti vt supra . . . xlij s.

130   THE EARL OF DERBY'S EXPEDITIONS.

Ricardo Catour pro vadiis suis infra curiam per idem tempus, capienti vt supra . . . . . xlij s.
Willelmo Habbegood pro vadiis suis infra curiam per idem tempus, capienti vt supra . . . . . xlij s.
Henrico de Camera pro vadiis suis infra curiam per idem tempus, 5 capienti per diem v d., in toto . . . xxxv s.
Willelmo Pulter pro vadiis suis infra curiam per idem tempus, capienti per diem iiij d. . . . . xxviij s.
Johanni Wyndesore pro vadiis suis per idem tempus, capienti vt supra . . . . . . xxviij s. 10

Summa pagine xlvj li. vij s. vj d.

Johanni Hethecote pro vadiis suis per idem tempus, capienti vt supra, in toto . . . . . xxviij s.

fo. 52 v°.
August 9—October 31.

/ Ricardo del Ewerie pro vadiis suis infra curiam, capienti per diem iiij d., a ix° die Augusti vsque vltimum diem Octobris, vtroque computato, in toto . . . . xxviij s. 15
Roberto Barbour pro vadiis suis infra curiam per idem tempus vt supra, capienti per diem vt supra . . xxviij s.
Willelmo Hauyr pro vadiis suis per ix dies infra curiam, videlicet

August 9—17.

a ix° die Augusti vsque xvij^m diem eiusdem mensis, vtroque computato, capienti per diem iiij d., in toto . . iij s. 20
Johanni Dounton pro vadiis suis extra curiam misso de Dansk vsque Conyngburg cum armatura domini per vj dies, capienti per diem iiij d., ij s. Et eidem pro vadiis suis infra curiam, capienti per diem ij d., per iij dies vj d. Et eidem pro vadiis

August 18—October 31.

suis infra curiam, a xviij° die mensis Augusti vsque vltimum 25 diem Octobris, per lxxv dies in le Reys, vtroque computato, capienti per diem iiij d., xxv s., sic in toto . . xxvij s. vj d.

August 9—17.

Roberto Pepir pro vadiis suis infra curiam, a ix° die Augusti vsque xvij diem eiusdem mensis, capienti per diem ij d., xviij d. Et

August 18—October 31.

eidem pro vadiis suis infra curiam per lxxv dies in le Reys, 30 capienti per diem vt supra xxv s., in toto . . xxvj s. vj d.
Willelmo Wyndesore pro vadiis suis infra curiam per idem tempus, capienti vt supra . . . . xxvj s. vj d.
Roberto Spayne pro vadiis suis infra curiam per idem tempus, capienti vt supra . . . . xxvj s. vj d. 35

Johanni Fyssher baker pro vadiis suis infra curiam per tempus
predictum, capienti vt supra . . . xxvj s. vj d.
Roberto Cnyghton pro vadiis suis infra curiam per idem tempus,
capienti vt supra . . . xxvj s. vj d.
5 Johanni Gylder pro vadiis suis infra curiam per x dies, capienti
per diem ij d., in toto . . . . xx d.
Ricardo Sendehill pro vadiis suis infra curiam per iiij^{xx}iiij dies,
capienti per diem iij d. . . . . xxj s.
Johanni Cawode pro vadiis suis infra curiam per idem tempus, Summa pagine
10 capienti vt supra . . . . xxj s. xiij li. ij s. viij

VADIA MILITUM ET SCUTIFER*ORUM* PUR LE REYS.

/ Domino Thome Erpyngham pro vadiis suis extra curiam, a xviij° fo. 53.
die mensis Augusti vsque xxij diem mensis Octobris, vtroque August 18—Oc
computato, per lxvj dies, capienti per diem ij s., vj li. xij s. 22.
15 Et eidem pro j scutifero per idem tempus, capienti per diem
xij d., lxvj s., et sic in toto . . . ix li. xviij s.
Domino Thome Kempston pro vadiis suis per idem tempus, capienti per diem vt supra . . . vj li. xij s.
Domino Johanni Clifton pro vadiis suis per idem tempus, capienti
20 per diem vt supra . . . . vj li. xij s.
Domino Ricardo Goldesburgh pro vadiis suis per idem tempus,
capienti per diem vt supra . . . vj li. xij s.
Domino Johanni Loucyn pro vadiis suis per idem tempus, capienti
per diem vt supra . . . vj li. xij s.
25 Johanni Dalyngrugg pro vadiis suis extra curiam, capienti per
diem xij d. per idem tempus . . . lxvj s.
Radulpho Racheford pro vadiis suis per idem tempus, capienti per
diem vt supra, in toto . . . . lxvj s.
Johanni Cope pro vadiis suis per idem tempus, capienti per diem
30 vt supra, in toto . . . . lxvj s.
Johanni Gybbethorpe pro vadiis suis per idem tempus, capienti
per diem vt supra, in toto . . . . lxvj s.

Iue Jeke pro vadiis suis per idem tempus, capienti per diem vt supra, in toto . . . . . . lxvj s.
Roberto Burton pro vadiis suis per idem tempus, capienti per diem vt supra, in toto . . . . . lxvj s.
Thome Goter pro vadiis suis per idem tempus, capienti per diem vt supra . . . . . . lxvj s.
Edmundo Hastynges pro vadiis suis per idem tempus, capienti per diem vt supra . . . . . . lxvj s.

Vadia Ministrallorum.

August 13—17.

Johanni Brothir, trumpour, pro vadiis suis infra curiam a xiij° die mensis Augusti vsque xvij diem eiusdem mensis, vtroque computato, per v dies, capienti per diem iiij d.; eundo de Dansk vsque Conyngburg, xx d. Et eidem pro vadiis suis a xviij° die eiusdem mensis vsque xxij^m diem mensis Octobris, vtroque computato, per lxvj dies, capienti per diem vj d., xxxiij s. Et eidem Johanni pro vadiis suis infra curiam a xxiij die mensis Octobris vsque vltimum diem eiusdem mensis, per ix dies, vtroque computato, capienti per diem iiij d. ij s., et sic in toto . . . . . . xxxvij s. viij d.

August 18—October 22.

October 23—31.

Roberto Krakyll socio suo pro vadiis suis per idem tempus, capienti per diem vt supra in toto . . . xxxvij s. viij d.

August 9—17.

Willelmo Byngeley pro vadiis suis infra curiam a ix° die Augusti vsque xvij^m diem eiusdem per ix dies, vtroque computato, capienti per diem iiij d., iij s. Et eidem pro vadiis suis infra curiam a xviij die eiusdem mensis vsque xxij diem Octobris, vtroque computato, capienti per diem vj d., per lxvj dies, xxxiij s. Et eidem pro vadiis suis infra curiam, a xxiij die Octobris vsque vltimum diem eiusdem, vtroque computato per ix dies, capienti per diem iiij d., iij s., summa totalis xxxix s.

August 18—October 22.

October 23—31.

Summa pagine lxx li. vij s. iiij d.

Willelmo de York, pipere, pro vadiis suis per idem tempus, capienti per diem vt supra . . . xxxix s.

Numbers in right margin (top to bottom): 10, 15, 20, 25, 30

/ Will*elmo* Alg*od* pr*o* vad*iis suis* inf*ra* curi*am* p*er* idem temp*us*, fo. 53 vº.
cap*ienti* vt Willelmus Byngeley infr*a*, in to*to* .   xxxix s.
Mag*istro* Joh*anni* Nakerer pr*o* vad*iis suis* inf*ra* curi*am*, capi*enti*
vt sup*ra* p*er* idem t*em*p*us*, xxxix s.

5 [It has not been thought necessary to continue the *italics* signifying
extension of contracted words.]

VADIA MILITUM SCUTIFERORUM ET VALETTORUM A PRIMO DIE NOUEMBRIS VSQUE VLTIMUM DIEM DECEMBRIS, VTROQUE COMPUTATO.

10 Domino Petro Bucton pro vadiis suis infra curiam, a j die Nouembris   November 1—
    vsque vltimum diem Decembris, vtroque computato, vz. per   December 31.
    lxj dies, capienti per diem xij d., in toto . . lxj s.
    Domino Thome Erpingham pro vadiis suis infra curiam per idem
    tempus, capienti vt supra . . . . lxj s.
15 Domino Hugoni Waterton pro vadiis suis per idem tempus, capienti
    vt supra, in toto . . . . . lxj s.
    Domino Thome Swynford pro vadiis suis infra curiam per idem
    tempus, capienti vt supra . . . . lxj s.
    Domino Johanni Dalyngrugg pro vadiis suis infra curiam per idem
20   tempus, capienti vt supra . . . . lxj s.
    Domino Hugoni Herle, confessori, pro vadiis [suis] per idem tempus,
    capienti vt supra, in toto . . . . lxj s.
    Johanni Norbery pro vadiis suis per idem tempus, capienti vt supra,
    in toto . . . . . . lxj s.
25 Rudulpho Racheford pro vadiis suis infra curiam, a xxiij die mensis   October 23—
    Octobris vsque vltimum diem Decembris, vtroque computato,   December 31.
    per lxx dies, capienti per diem vij d. ob. . xliij s. ix d.
    Roberto Waterton pro vadiis suis infra curiam, a primo die Novem-   November 1—
    December 31.

134   THE EARL OF DERBY'S EXPEDITIONS.

  bris vsque vltimum Decembris, vtroque computato, per lxj dies,
capienti per diem vij d. ob., in toto   xxxviij s. j d. ob.
Thome Toty pro vadiis suis infra curiam per idem tempus, capienti
per diem vt supra . . . xxxviij s. j d. ob.
Thome Gloucestre pro vadiis suis infra curiam per idem tempus, 5
capienti per diem vt supra . . xxxviij s. j d. ob.
Johanni Waterton pro vadiis suis infra curiam per idem tempus,
capienti per diem vt supra . . xxxviij s. j d. ob.
Johanni Payn pro vadiis suis infra curiam per idem tempus, capienti
per diem vt supra . . . xxxviij s. j d. ob. 10
Magistro Willelmo Cook pro vadiis suis infra curiam per idem
tempus, capienti per diem vt supra . xxxviij s. j d. ob.
Rogero Langeford pro vadiis suis infra curiam per idem tempus,
capienti per diem vt supra . . xxxviij s. j d. ob.
Johanni Assheley pro vadiis suis infra curiam per idem tempus, 15
capienti per diem vt supra . . xxxviij s. j d. ob.
Johanni Cope pro vadiis suis infra curiam per idem tempus, capienti
per diem vt supra . . . xxxviij s. j d. ob.
Ricardo Chelmeswyk pro vadiis suis infra curiam, a xiiij die mensis

December 14—31.   Decembris vsque vltimum diem ejusdem mensis, viz. per xvij 20
dies, capienti per diem vt supra . x s. vij d. ob.

December 21—31.   Henrico Houghton pro vadiis suis infra curiam, a xxj die Decembris

Summa pagine   vsque vltimum diem eiusdem mensis, per x dies, capienti per
xlvli. viij s. ix d.   diem vij d. ob., vtroque computato, in toto . vj s. iij d.

fo. 54.   / Derby le heraud pro vadiis suis infra curiam, a xvj° die Nouembris 25

November 16—   vsque xxij^m diem Decembris, vtroque computato, per xxxvij
December 22.   dies, capienti per diem vij d. ob., in toto . xxiij s. j d. ob.

November 1—   Radulpho Staneley pro vadiis suis infra curiam, a primo die Nouem-
December 31.   bris vsque vltimum diem Decembris, vtroque computato, per
lxj dies, capienti per diem vij d. ob., in toto xxxviij s. j d. ob. 30
Willelmo Sewardby pro vadiis suis infra curiam per idem tempus,
capienti per diem vt supra . xxxviij s. j d. ob.
Ricardo Dancastre pro vadiis suis infra curiam per idem tempus,
capienti per diem vt supra . . xxxviij s. j d. ob.

KNIGHTS, ESQUIRES, AND VALETS. 135

Willelmo Rygmayden pro vadiis suis infra curiam, a vij° die
Nouembris vsque vltimum diem Decembris, vtroque com- November 7—
putato, per lv dies, capienti per diem vij d. ob., in toto   December 31.
            xxxiiij s. iiij d. ob.
5 Edmundo Bugge pro vadiis suis infra curiam, a iij die Decembris
vsque vltimum diem eiusdem mensis, vtroque computato per December 3—;
xxviij dies, capienti per diem vij d. ob. . xvij s. vj d.
Domino Willelmo Ponfreyt pro vadiis suis infra curiam, a primo
die Nouembris vsque vltimum [diem] Decembris, vtroque com-
10 putato, per lxj dies, capienti per diem vj d., in toto xxx s. vj d. November 1—
                  December 31.

VADIA VALETTORUM.

Johanni Dindon pro vadiis suis infra curiam, a primo die Nouem- November 1—
bris vsque vltimum diem Decembris, vtroque computato, per December 31.
lxj dies, capienti per diem iiij d., in toto . xx s. iiij d.
15 Ricardo Ryggeley pro vadiis suis infra curiam per idem tempus,
capienti per diem vt supra . . . xx s. iiij d.
Nicholao de Camera pro vadiis suis infra curiam per idem tempus,
capienti vt supra . . . . xx s. iiij d.
Henrico Maunsell pro vadiis suis infra curiam per idem tempus,
20 capienti vt supra . . . . xx s. iiij d.
Henrico Morlee pro vadiis suis infra curiam per idem tempus,
capienti vt supra . . . . xx s. iiij d.
Wilielmo Freman pro vadiis suis infra curiam per idem tempus,
capienti vt supra . . . . xx s. iiij d.
25 Johanni Cuddeworth pro vadiis suis infra curiam per idem tempus,
capienti vt supra . . . . xx s. iiij d.
Roberto Litton pro vadiis suis infra curiam per idem tempus,
capienti vt supra . . . . xx s. iiij d.
Henrico de Camera pro vadiis suis infra curiam per idem tempus,
30 capienti per diem iij d., per lxj dies, vtreque computato, in
toto . . . . xv s. iij d.   Summa pagine
                   xix li. xvij s. ij

fo. 54 v°. / Roberto Hethecote pro vadiis suis infra curiam, a primo die
November 1—   Nouembris vsque vltimum diem Decembris, vtroque compu-
December 31.   tato, per lxj dies, capienti per diem iij d., in toto   xv s. iij d.
Ricardo Catour pro vadiis suis infra curiam per idem tempus,
    capienti per diem iiij d., in toto   .   .   xx s. iiij d.
Ricardo del Ewerye pro vadiis suis infra curiam per idem tempus,
    capienti per diem iij d.   .   .   .   xv s. iij d.
Jacobo Fauconer pro vadiis suis infra curiam per idem tempus,
    capienti per diem vt supra   .   .   .   xv s. iij d.

VADIA DEL GROMES.

Willelmo Harpeden pro vadiis suis infra curiam, a primo die
November 1—   Nouembris vsque xxiiij^m diem Decembris, vtroque computato
December 24.   per liiij dies, capienti per diem ij d., ix s. Et eidem a xxv°
    die Decembris vsque vltimum diem eiusdem mensis, per vij
November 1—   dies, capienti per diem iij d., xxj d., in toto   .   x s. ix d.
December 31.   Roberto Pepir pro vadiis suis infra curiam a primo die Nouembris
    vsque vltimum diem Decembris, vtroque computato, per lxj
    dies, capienti per diem ij d., in toto   .   .   x s. ij d.
Johanni Dounton pro vadiis suis infra curiam per idem tempus,
    capienti per diem vt supra   .   .   .   x s. ij d.
Willelmo Wyndesore pro vadiis suis infra curiam per idem tempus,
    capienti per diem vt supra   .   .   .   x s. ij d.
Johanni Fyssher pro vadiis suis infra curiam per idem tempus,
    capienti per diem vt supra   .   .   .   x s. ij d.
Roberto Spayne pro vadiis suis infra curiam per idem tempus,
    capienti per idem vt supra   .   .   .   x s. ij d.
Roberto Knyghton pro vadiis suis infra curiam per idem tempus,
    capienti per diem vt supra   .   .   .   x s. ij d.
Johanni Gybler pro vadiis suis infra curiam ab vltimo[a] die No-

---

[a] "A secundo" must have been intended instead of "ab ultimo." "Decembris" was originally written and corrected to "diem ejusdem mensis," as above.

uembris vsque vltimum diem eiusdem mensis per xxix dies,
vtroque computato, capienti per diem ij d., in toto   iiij s. x d.
Johanni Cawode pro vadiis suis infra curiam a primo die Nouembris vsque vltimum diem Decembris per lxj dies, vtroque com- November 1—
putato, capienti per diem vt supra, in toto   . x s ij d. December 31.
Johanni Braylleford pro vadiis suis infra curiam per idem tempus,
capienti per diem vt supra .   .   .   x s. ij d.
Willelmo Kykeley pro vadiis suis infra curiam per idem tempus,
capienti per diem vt supra. .   .   .   x s. ij d

Vadia Ministrallorum.

Johanni Brothir, Trumpour, pro vadiis suis infra curiam, a primo November 1—
die Nouembris vsque vltimum diem Decembris, vtroque com- December 31.
putato, per lxj dies, capienti per diem iiij d., in toto xx s. iiij d.
Roberto Crakyll, Trumpour, pro vadiis suis per idem tempus, capienti per diem vt supra .   .   .   . xx s. iiij d.
Willelmo Byngley, pipere pro vadiis suis per idem tempus, capienti
per diem vt supra .   .   .   . xx s. iiij d.
Willelmo Algood, pipere pro vadiis suis per idem tempus, capienti
per diem vt supra .   .   .   . xx s. iiij d.
Magistro Johanni Nakerer pro vadiis suis per idem tempus, capienti
per diem vt supra .   .   .   . xx s. iiij d.
Willelmo de York, pipere pro vadiis suis per idem tempus, capienti Summa pagi
per diem vt supra .   .   .   . xx s. iiij d. xiiij li. xv s.

/Vadia Militum, Scutiferorum, et Valettorum a primo fo. 55.
die Januarii vsque vltimum diem Aprilis, vtroque
computato.

Domino Thome Erpyngham pro vadiis suis infra curiam, a primo
die Januarii vsque vltimum diem Aprilis, vtroque computato, January 1—
per vj^{xx} dies, capienti per diem xij d., in toto .   . vj li.

Domino Hugoni Waterton pro vadiis suis infra curiam per idem
tempus, capienti per diem vt supra . . . vj li.
Domino Petro Bukton pro vadiis suis infra curiam per idem tempus,
capienti per diem vt supra . . . . vj li.
Domino Thome Swynford pro vadiis suis per idem tempus, capienti
per diem vt supra . . . . . vj li
Domino Johanni Malet pro vadiis suis per idem tempus, capienti
per diem vt supra . . . . . vj li.
Domino Johanni Dalyngrugg pro vadiis suis per idem tempus,
capienti per diem vt supra . . . . vj li.
Domino Hugoni Herle pro vadiis suis per idem tempus, capienti
per diem vt supra . . . . . vj li.
Johanni Norbery pro vadiis suis per idem tempus, capienti per
diem vt supra . . . . . . vj li.
Henrico Houghton pro vadiis suis per idem tempus, capienti per
diem vij d. ob., in toto . . . . lxxvs.
Rogero Langeford pro vadiis suis infra curiam per idem tempus,
capienti per diem vt supra . . . . lxxv s.
Johanni Cope pro vadiis suis infra curiam per idem tempus, capienti
per diem vt supra . . . . . lxxv s.
Roberto Waterton pro vadiis suis infra curiam per idem tempus,
capienti per diem vt supra . . . . lxxv s.
Thome Toty pro vadiis suis infra curiam per idem tempus, capienti
per diem vt supra . . . . . lxxv s.
Johanni Gloucestre pro vadiis suis infra curiam per idem tempus,
capienti per diem vt supra . . . . lxxv s.
Radulpho Racheford pro vadiis suis infra curiam per idem tempus,
capienti per diem vt supra . . . . lxxv s.
Ricardo Chelmeswyk pro vadiis suis infra curiam per idem tempus,
capienti per diem vt supra . . . . lxxv s.
Radulpho Stancley pro vadiis suis infra curiam per idem tempus,
capienti per diem vt supra . . . . lxxv s.
Ricardo Dancastre pro vadiis suis infra curiam per idem tempus,
capienti per diem vt supra . . . lxxv s.

KNIGHTS, ESQUIRES, AND VALETS.

Johanni Waterton pro vadiis suis infra curiam per idem tempus, capienti per diem vt supra . . . . lxxv s.

Thome Haseldene pro vadiis suis infra curiam per idem tempus, capienti per diem vt supra . . . . lxxv s. *Summa pagine iiij^{xx}xiij li.*

5 /Derby le herald eunti versus Regem Polonie, pro vadiis suis extra curiam a xxiij° die Decembris vsque xxx^m diem Januarii, vtroque computato, capienti per diem xij d. per xxxix dies, in toto . . . . . . xxxix s. *fo. 55 v°. December 23— January 30*

Johanni Payn pro vadiis suis infra curiam, a primo die Januarii
10 vsque vltimum diem Aprilis, vtroque computato, per vj^{xx} dies, capienti per diem vij d. ob. in toto . . lxxv s. *January 1—A[*

Magistro Willelmo Cook pro vadiis suis infra curiam per idem tempus, capienti per diem vt supra . . lxxv s.

Ricardo Rygmaydene pro vadiis suis infra curiam per idem tempus,
15 capienti per diem vt supra . . . . lxxv s.

Edmundo Bugge pro vadiis suis infra curiam per idem tempus, capienti per diem vt supra . . . . lxxv s.

Reginaldo Curteys pro vadiis suis infra curiam per idem tempus, capienti per diem vt supra . . . . lxxv s.

20 Johanni Assheley pro vadiis suis infra curiam per idem tempus, capienti per diem vt supra . . . . lxxv s.

Domino Willelmo Pountfreit pro vadiis suis per idem tempus, capienti per diem vj d. in toto . . . . lx s.

VADIA VALETTORUM.

25 Johanni Dyndon pro vadiis suis infra curiam, a primo die Januarii vsque vltimum diem Aprilis, vtroque computato, per vj^{xx} dies, capienti per diem iiij d., in toto . . . xl. s. *January 1—A*

Ricardo Ryggeley pro vadiis suis infra curiam per idem tempus, capienti per diem vt supra . . . . xl. s.

30 Nicholao de Camera pro vadiis suis infra curiam per idem tempus, capienti per diem vt supra . . . . xl. s.

140 THE EARL OF DERBY'S EXPEDITIONS.

Henrico Maunsell pro vadiis suis infra curiam per idem tempus, capienti per diem vt supra . . . . xl. s.
Henrico Morley pro vadiis suis infra curiam per idem tempus, capienti per diem vt supra . . . . xl s.
Johanni Cuddeworth pro vadiis suis infra curiam per idem tempus, 5 capienti per diem vt supra . . . . xl s.
Ricardo Catour pro vadiis suis infra curiam per idem tempus, capienti per idem vt supra . . . . xl s.

January 1—Feb. 4. Willelmo Freman pro vadiis suis infra curiam, a primo die Januarii vsque iiij^{m} diem Februarii, vtroque computato, per xxxv dies, 10 capienti per diem iiij d., in toto . . xj s. viij d.

January 1—April 30. Roberto Litton pro vadiis suis a primo die Januarii vsque vltimum diem Aprilis, vtroque computato, per vj^{xx} dies, capienti per
Summa pagine xliiij li. viij d. diem iiij d., in toto . . . . . xl s.
fo. 56.
January 1—April 30. /Henrico de Camera pro vadiis suis infra curiam, a primo die 15 Januarii vsque vltimum diem Aprilis, vtroque computato, per vj^{xx} dies, capienti per diem iiij d. . . . xl s.
Ricardo del Ewerie pro vadiis suis infra curiam per idem tempus, capienti per diem iij d. . . . . xxx s.
Roberto Hethecote pro vadiis suis infra curiam per idem tempus, 20 capienti per diem vt supra . . . . xxx s.
Willelmo Pulter pro vadiis suis infra curiam per idem tempus, capienti per diem vt supra . . . . xxx s.

January 1—March 31. Johanni Leuyngton pro vadiis suis infra curiam, a primo die Januarii vsque vltimum diem Martii, vtroque computato, per 25 iiij^{xx}x dies, capienti per diem iij d., in toto . xxij s. vj d.

January 1—April 30. Jacobo Fauconer pro vadiis suis infra curiam, a primo die Januarii vsque vltimum diem Aprilis, vtroque computato, per vj^{xx} dies, capienti per diem iij d., in toto . . . xxx s.

Vadia del Gromes.

Johanni Gylder pro vadiis suis infra curiam, a primo die Januarii vsque vltimum diem Aprilis, vtroque computato, capienti per diem ij d. per vj^{xx} dies . . . . . xx s.   January 1—.

5 Johanni Cawode pro vadiis suis infra curiam per idem tempus, capienti per diem vt supra . . . . xx s.

Roberto Knyghton pro vadiis suis infra curiam per idem tempus, capienti per diem vt supra . . . . xx s.

Roberto Pepir pro vadiis suis infra curiam per idem tempus, 10 capienti per diem vt supra . . . . xx s.

Roberto Spayn pro vadiis suis infra curiam per idem tempus, capienti per diem vt supra . . . . xx s.

Willelmo Wyndesore pro vadiis suis infra curiam per idem tempus, capienti per diem vt supra . . . . xx s.

15 Johanni Fyssher, baker, pro vadiis suis infra curiam per idem tempus, capienti per diem vt supra . . . xx s.

Johanni Dounton pro vadiis suis infra curiam per idem tempus, capienti per diem vt supra . . . . xx s.

Johanni Braylefford pro vadiis suis infra curiam per idem tempus, 20 capienti per diem vt supra . . . . xx s.

Willelmo Kykeley pro vadiis suis infra curiam per idem tempus, capienti per diem vt supra . . . . xx s.   Summa pagit xix li. ij s. vj

Vadia Ministrallorum.

/ Johanni Brothir, Trumpour, pro vadiis suis infra curiam a primo   fo. 56 v°. 25 die Januarii vsque vltimum diem Aprilis, vtroque computato,   January 1—. per vj^{xx} dies, capienti per diem iiij d. . . . xl s.

Roberto Crakyll socio suo pro vadiis suis per idem tempus, capienti per diem vt supra . . . . . xl s.

Willelmo Byngeley, pipere, pro vadiis suis per idem tempus infra 30 curiam, capienti per diem vt supra . . xl s.

Willelmo Algode, pipere, pro vadiis suis per idem tempus infra
curiam, capienti per diem vt supra . . . xl s.
William de York pro vadiis suis infra curiam per idem tempus,
capienti per diem vt supra . . . . xl s.
Magistro Johanni Naker pro vadiis suis infra curiam per idem
tempus, capienti per diem vt supra . . . xls.

Summa totalis vadiorum, Dlxiiij li. viij s. viij d. ob. Probatur.

ALLOCACIO PRO PERDICIONE FLORENARUM.

Et in perdicione de xxv^{ml} floreyns, vnde singule iij floreins faciunt
le noble, et sic le floreyn ad ij s. ij d. ob. di.-q^r, vj pars q^r, et non
stetit in valorem vltra ij s. j d. q^r; et sic est perdicio cuiuslibet
floreyne j d. q^r di.-q^r vj pars q$^{r.n}$, et sic est perdicio cujuslibet noble
iiij d. q^r, et de qualibet marca viij d. ob.; et sic de singulis M^l marc.
xxxv li. viij s. iiij d., vnde summa Cxlvij li. xj s. iiij d. ob. Inde
deducti xiiij li. xv s. j d. q^r, de M^{l}M^{l}D flloreyns que steterunt ad
verum valorem iij pro le noble vt supra, et sic est summa perdicionis,
Cxxxij li. xvj s. iij d. q^r.

/ SUMMA OMNIUM EXPENSARUM ISTIUS LIBRI, M^l M^l M^l M^l
CCClix li. xvij s. j d. ob. q^r.

Et sic debet xxiij li. xj s. j d. ob. q^r. Et postea oneratur de
li. receptas de Johanne de Londeham milite in partibus Prucie, vt
pro tot denariis quos ipse recepit de domino de prestito in Anglia,
vt in vna tallia de recepta scaccarii regis facta domino de majori
summa de quodam assignamento sibi facto per ipsum Regem. Et
sic debet lxxiij li. xj s. j d. ob q^r. De quibus allocantur ipsi

---

* That is, the loss on every florin (with the exception stated below) was one
penny farthing, half a farthing, and a sixth part of a farthing, reckoning it at its
full value of one-third of a noble (6 8).

computanti xiij li. vj s. viij d., pro duobus equis trotters cum duabus sellis per ipsum emptis ad opus domini in partibus Prucie de servientibus predicti Johannis de Londeham, post mortem ejusdem defuncti in partibus de Lettowe. Et allocantur eidem computanti, xxix li. xij s. iiij d. pro vadiis suis tam infra Angliam quam apud Caleys et in partibus de Prucia, tam infra curiam quam extra, per totum tempus compoti quo stetit in officio suo, vt patet per parcellas et per dietas in quodam Rotulo de papiro contentas super hunc compotum examinato, remanente inter waranta et memoranda hujus compoti; hic allocati ex precepto domini oretenus existentis apud Petreburgh, xix die Januarii anno quintodecimo, et super hoc nunciante Hugone Waterton milite, camerario ipsius domini existenti ibidem eodem tempore. Et eidem, xiiij li. vj s. vt pro vadiis suis tam infra curiam quam extra, inter vltimum diem Aprilis anno quartodecimo et xviij diem Januarii proxime sequentem, anno xv°, extra tempus compoti, existenti in diuersa negocia domini officium suum tangentia, tam apud Boston quam London et alibi, et pro mora sua apud Petreburgh pro factura hujus compoti, vt patet per consimiles parcellas et dietas in predicto Rotulo contentas, &c , hic allocati forma et modo quo supra. Et allocantur eidem, vij li., pro duobus lodesmen de Boston, videlicet Johanni Gray et Rogero Attehous venientibus cum domino in nauibus suis de Dansk in partibus Prucie vsque in Angliam vsque ad portum de Kyngestone super Hulle, mense Aprilis anno xiiij°, non allocate superius inter alias parcellas, hic allocate forma et modo quo supra. ET SIC DEBET ix li. vj s. j d. ob. q^r. De quibus allocantur eidem xxij s. viij d. soluti Roberto Waterton pro baytyng et aliis custubus per ipsum appositis inter Cantuariam et Dauentre, mense Maii anno xiiij°, vt patet per parcellas examinatas super hunc compotum.

ET SIC DEBET viij li. ij s. v d. ob. q^r. Qui onerantur in proximo compoto eiusdem Ricardi in viagio versus partes Prucie et Sanctum Sepulcrum. Et sic hic eque.

January 19, 1

April 30, 139
January 18, 1

April, 1391.

May, 1391.

COMPOTUS RICARDI KYNGESTON clerici, Thesaurarii guerre domini Henrici Comitis Derbie pro viagio suo versus partes Prucie et Sanctum Sepulcrum, a xvj° die mense Julii anno regni regis Ricardi secundi xvj° vsque xvj^m diem eiusdem mensis anno xvij°, per vnum annum integrum.

[16 July, 1392—16 July, 1393].

TREASURER'S ACCOUNTS OF THE EARL OF DERBY'S EXPEDITIONS.

PART II.

SECOND JOURNEY TO PRUSSIA, AND THENCE TOWARDS PALESTINE,

16 JULY, 1392—16 JULY, 1393.

Receipt^a of Derby's treasurer, Richard Kyngston, for 3000 marks supplyed by Duke John, 19 July, 1392.

/ [Hec indentura] testatur quod dominus Ricardus Kyngeston Thesaurarius domini Henrici Lancastrie Comitis Derbye pro viagio
5 dicti domini versus partes Prusye recepit [de Willelmo] Louency clerico garderobe predicti domini Comitis super viagio eiusdem domini Comitis versus predictas partes Prusye per literam ipsius domini Comitis [predicti] tria milia marcarum, de quibus idem Willelmus Louency oneratur per dominum Robertum Whitby
10 generalem receptorem domini Johannis ducis Aquitanie et [Lancastrie per in]denturam de eadem summa factam. Data apud Lenn Episcopi xix^o die Julii Anno regni regis Ricardi Secundi post conquestum Anglie sextodecimo.^a

^a This and the following document are on long strips of parchment (torn and in bad condition) attached at one end to the edge of the front cover of the book.

*Writ ordering the audit of Richard Kingston's Accounts.
Leicester, 4 January, 1394—5.*

/ Henry de Lancastre Conte de Derby, de Herford et de Northampton, Sieur de Brekenok, a nos tres cher et bien amez sire Thomas
Hardwyk et Thomas de Wombewell auditours des accomptes de noz
ministres et officiers saluz. Purce que nostre trescher et bien ame clerc
Sire Richard de Kyngeston, Arcediaken de Herford ad este nostre
tresorer pur la guerre es diuerse parties outre le meer, del sezisme
jour de Juyllet l'ann du regne nostre tresredoute Seigneur le Roy
Richard second puis le conquest sezisme tanque a moisme le iour
l'ann du regne nostre dit seigneur le Roy dys et septisme, et ad
paie noz deniers pur les dispenses de nostre hostel es dictes parties
come ycelle office demande,——Nous vous chargeons que vous
preignez du dit sire Richard raisonnables accomptes de tous noz
deniers qil ad paie en le dit office et ly facez dehue allouance en son
accompte de tout quanque il ad raisonablement mys et paie en le
dit office, come l'ordre d'accompt demande et requiert; et outre ce
vous enuoions vne rolle ensealluz de nostre signet de diuerses paie-
mentz faitz par le dit sire Richard de nostre commandement en le
dit iournee, et vous mandons que de touz ycelles sommes contenuz
en le dit rolle facez au dit sire Richard dehue allouance en son
accompte. Et cestes noz lettres vous em serront guarrant. Donne
soubz nostre seal a Leycestre le quart jour de Januer, l'ann du Regne
nostre dit seigneur le Roy dys et octisme.

/ Compotus Ricardi Kyngeston clerici, Thesaurarii guerre excellentissimi domini, domini Henrici Lancastre, Comitis Derbie, pro
viagio suo versus partes Prucie et Sancti Sepulcri a xvj" die mensis[b]
Julii Anno regni regis Ricardi Secundi sexto decimo vsque xvj^m
diem ejusdem mensis, anno ejusdem Regis decimo septimo, per
vnum annum integrum, per commissionem domini datam apud
Petreburgh, xv^o die Julii Anno regni regis Ricardi Secundi xvj^o

[b] The MS. has *mense*.

II. MONIES RECEIVED.

et per aliam literam domini de warranto auditori directam pro isto
compoto capiendo, datam apud Leycestre quarto die Januarii anno   January 4, 1394
regni regis Ricardi Secundi xviij°. Que quidem commissio cum
litera Domini de warranto predicta huic compoto sunt* annexate.[a]   * Sic.

[RECEPTA DENARIORUM].

Idem recepisse de[b] viij li. iij. s. [5d.] ob. q[r] de arreragiis vltimi com-   Arreragia.
poti sui de primo viagio domini versus partes Prucie prout patet
in pede ibidem.[c] .   .   Summa viij li. iij s. [5d.] ob. q[r].

De Roberto de Whitteby generali receptore domini Johannis Ducis   Recepta denari
Aquitanie et Lancastrie per manus Willelmi Loueney clerici   de Roberto de V
garderobe ipsius domini comitis, mense Julii anno supradicto,   generali recepto
recipiente denarios apud Lynne de predicto Willelmo tem-   domini ducis A
pore predicto, vnde M¹M¹ marce de prestito facto per dominum   tanie et Lancas
Ducem ipsi domino comiti, prout notatur in compoto predict
Roberti de anno xvj° .   .   .   M¹M¹M¹ marc. st.

De Johanne Leunthorpe generali receptore ipsius domini comitis   Recepta denarii
recipiente denarios eisdem mense et anno supradictis prout   de Johanne Le
continetur in compoto Johannis Leuthorpe de eodem anno   thorpe generali
                                                                 ceptore domini.
                                                        C. li.

De marescallo Prucie apud Dansk anno supradicto, vnde idem   Recepta denarii
computans onerat se gratis receptis apud Conyngburgh, prout de marescallo P
idem computans fatetur super compotum   .   CCCC. li. st.

---

[a] This Commission of 15 July, 1392, to Kingston, as treasurer "for war" a second time, is missing (compare the similar document given to him for the first expedition, p. 1. and see p. 3). We have here instead his acknowledgment for a sum supplied by Derby's father towards the present journeys; cf. fo. 1 with the second item in these receipts.

[b] The full form of this contracted phrase is "Idem se onerat recepisse de," &c. See, for example, the accounts of Robt. de Whitteby, receiver-general to John of Gaunt, for 15 and 16 Richard II., Duchy of Lancaster Records, Class 28, Bundle 3, No. 2, fo. 1

[c] See before p. 143.

Forincera Recepta de Priore Sancti Johannis Jerosolimitani.	De priore Sancti Johannis Jerosolimitani[a] apud Venys et in galeia, prout continetur in compoto predicti Roberti de Whitteby generalis receptoris domini de anno xvij^(mo) . M^l. vij^c. ducati
Forincera Recepta apud Venys redeundo.	De denariis receptis apud Venys redeundo de Sancto Sepulcro per manus Lumbardorum de societate Albertinorum per viam excambii vt de M^l iij^c xxxiij li. vj s. viij d., prout continetur in compoto predicti Roberti de Whitteby de anno xvj^o viij^m viij^c iiij^xx viij duc.
fo. 4 v°. Adhuc Forincera Recepta. April 12, 1393.	/ De moneta recepta de Nicholao de Luca et sociis suis, xij^a die Aprilis apud Venys, vt in excambio pro v^c mare st., anno supradicto viz. anno xvj^o . . M^lM^l iiij^xx xv duc.
Adhuc Forincera Recepta.	De moneta recepta de Francisco Nearle, Lumbardo, et sociis suis, vt in precio v^c mare., fr. ad iij s. iiij d., prout notatur in compoto Roberti de Whitteby de a^o xvij^o . . M^lM^l fr.
Adhuc Forincera Recepta. November 6, 1392.	De denariis receptis vt pro expensis domini et familie sue apud Wene per iiij dies, recipientibus denariis de seneseallo et mareseallo ducis Ostrichie vj^to die Nouembris, etc., unde onerat se gratis . . . . Cxxiij flor.
Ad hnc Forincera Recepta.	De consimilibus denariis receptis vt pro expensis domini et familie sue per vnam noctem in Friola, cum mareseallo Patriarche ibidem, etc., vnde onerat se gratis . . vij flor.
Ad hnc Forincera Recepta de mercimonio excambii.	De denariis prouenientibus et receptis de incremento excambii diuersarum monetarum in diuersis locis per tempus compoti vj duc. di.
	De denariis provenientibus de proficuis excambii iij^ml clvj duc. di., pro pecia ij d., vltra xij^m vij^c xv duc. di. onerati de quadam summa de xv^ml viij^c lxxij ducatis allocata vt inferius xxvj li. vj s. j d.
Ad hnc Forincera Recepta de exitibus officii sui.	De denariis receptis pro j curru veteri vendito in Friola per thesaurarium et Wilbram . . . . iij flor.
Nov. 26, 1392.	De denariis receptis de exitibus xij bouum apud Portgrwer, xxvj Nouembris . . . . xxvj duc.

* The MS. has Jeresomital' both here and in margin.

II. MONIES RECEIVED.

De consimilibus denariis receptis de exitibus bonum venditorum provisorum pro hospicio domini, vnde idem computans onerat se gratis in quadam billa super compotum ostensa vltra xxvj duc. oneratos superius, &c. . . xlix s. iij d.

5 De diuersis victualibus remanentibus in quadam naue ducente partem familie domini de partibus Prucie vsque in Angliam, et postea venditis per Willelmum Pountfreit clericum ad hoc deputatum per dominum, per diuersas parcellas ostensas super compotum &c. . . . . xj li xv s. iij d.   Ad huc Forincec Recepta de victu venditis.

10 Summa totalis recepte, cum arreragiis, computata in sterlinges   [Totals of fore-;
                    $M^lM^lv^cxlviij$ li. xiij s. vij d. ob. q^r.

Item recepta vt in xij^{ml} vij^c xv duc. di, ad iij s. ij d.   ducats,
                        M^lM^lxiij li. v s. ix d.

Item recepta vt in M^lM^l fr., pecia ad iij s. iiij d.   francs,
15   CCCxxxiij li. vj s. viij d.

Item vt in cxxxiij flor. ad iij s. &c. . . xix li. xix s.   florins].

Summa totalis recepte* istius libri cum arreragiis
                            iiij^{ml}ix^{c}xv li. v s ob. q^r.   [Grand total £4,915 5 0$\frac{1}{4}$].

EXPENSE PRO PROUIDENCIIS INFRA ANGLIAM.

IN PARTIBUS ANGLIE.
20

/ Diuersis hominibus de Petreburgh pro iiij batellis ab ipsis con-   fo. 5.
ductis pro cariagio diuersorum victualorum et harnisiorum domini
de Burgh vsque Linne, per compotum cum eis factum apud Linne,
xvj° die Julii, xxxij s. Et per manus eorundem pro expensis   July 16.
25 diuersorum hominum custodientum dicta victualia et harnesia in
dictis batellis per iij dies inter Burgh et Linne, eodem die, xj s.
x d. CLERICO speciarie per manus thesaurarii pro iiij vergis panni

---

* The contraction in the MS. is Re^{te}, for recepte, receipt, in the singular, which was the form in old accounts. Cf. the phrases "receipt of Exchequer," "receipt of custom" (Luke, v. 27). Recepta before p. 3, and above p. 149, is nominative singular.

viridis pro j countingcloth per ipsum emptis apud Linne, verga ad ix d., iij s. SUPER officio scutellarie per manus Laurencii Trauers pro j sacco per ipsum empto pro vasis ligneis imponendis eodem die, vj d. Et pro emendacione ij coffres coquine eodem die, xxij d. CLERICO speciarie per manus Roberti Walpooll pro xlij vlnis tele 5 de Reynes, vlna ad ij s. vij d., ab ipso emptis ibidem eodem die, cviij s. vj d. SUPER officio salsarie per manus Moryce Baker pro farina ab ipso empta ibidem eodem die, iij s. Et per manus Laurencii Trauers pro j pare powder-baggs, iiij d. CLERICO speciarie per manus Rogeri Goldsmyth pro iiij*xij vlnis Westuall, 10 vlna ad vij d. ob., et pro j pare balaunces, ij s. x d., ab ipso emptis ibidem eodem die, in toto liiij s. j d. Et per manus Roberti Walpool pro xiij vlnis de Westuall ab ipso emptis ibidem xix° die Julii, vlna ad iiij d., iiij s. iiij d. CLERICO coquine per manus Simonis Feldwelle pro viij qr. salis grossi, qr. ad v s. iiij d.; et pro 15 viij qr. salis albi,[a] qr. ad ij s. iiij d., ab ipso emptis eodem die; in toto ij li. ix s. iiij d. CLERICO panetrie per manus Willelmi Tyrington pro ix qr. frumenti ab ipso emptis ibidem eodem die, qr. ad iiij s. iij d., xxxviij s. iij d. Et pro furnagio x qr. frumenti ibidem, et in furnagio pro naui, iiij s. Johanni Leunthorpe pro 20 emendacione j coffre pro thesauro ibidem eodem die, xij d. CLERICO panetrie per manus Johannis Fyscher pro cariagio panis, farine, et furnagii, de terra vsque nauem apud Linne eodem die, xij d. CLERICO marescalcie per manus Roberti Watertone pro iij capistris et malepanel ab ipso emptis ibidem, v s. Et per manus Roberti Pitte pro 25 j equo ab ipso conducto de Linne vsque Petreburgh et redeundo, per conuencionem factam, iij s. Roberto Wesnam de Linne pro worstede alb', et rub', ac pro bokeram, et factura de ij getens de armis Sancti Georgii, vj s. iij d. ob. SUPER OFFICIO scutellarie per manus Cudeworth pro ij bokets, vj d,, pro ij cordes pro dictis 30 bokets ij d., per ipsum emptis ibidem eodem die, in toto viij d. Et

[a] Salt, both coarse and white, here seems to be measured by the quarter, in the same way as wheat. See the following items. It should be noted, however, that the same contractions stand for *quart* and *quarter*.

II. NECESSARIES PROVIDED IN ENGLAND. 153

pro cariagio iiij^{mt} belet de terra vsque nauem, vj d. Et pro cariagio lx barellorum cum carne, pisce, et aliis diuersis victualibus vt supra, iiij d. CLERICO speciarie per manus Rogeri Goldsmyth pro xlviij vergis cancuas ad iiij d. ab ipso emptis ibidem, xvj s. Et pro v
5 duodenis pergameni, le xij ad ij s., emptis ibidem eodem die, x s. SUPER OFFICIO scutellarii per manus Alani Brasyer pro j peluc ab ipso empta ibidem eodem die pro camera domini, ij s. CLERICO coquine per manus Stephani Payee pro ijC vij crabbes et lobsteres ob ipso emptis apud Linne xx° die Jullii, vij s. ij d. CLERICO   July 20.
10 panterie per manus Morice Baker pro pane albo ab ipsum empto ibidem eodem die, v s. CLERICO coquine per manus Hamon Hamell pro j barello Wich[mar beer], viij s. iiij d. Et pro xxxvij barellis vacantibus pro aqua imponenda, barellus ad iiij d, in toto xij s. iiij d. SUPER officio scutellarie per manus Johannis Pye pro
15 xiiij q^ur carbonum, q^ur ad vij d., ab ipso emptis ibidem, viij s. ij d. SUPER officio salsarie per manus Morice Baker pro j bz. flowr ab ipso empto ibidem, ix d. CLERICO coquine per manus Johannis Siselden pro iiij^{xx} chelinges, lxviij s. Et pro j porco et j apro, xiiij s. CLERICO buterie super ceruisia per manus eiusdem pro ij pipes
20 ceruisie, xxx s. Et pro ij pipes vacantibus pro dicta ceruisia imponenda ab ipso emptis ibidem, ij s. iiij d. Et pro cariagio vj doliorum aque ad nauem ibidem, ij s. vj d. SUPER officio aule et camere per manus Braylefford pro cirpis per ipsum emptis ibidem pro naui, iiij d. JOHANNI Siselden pro ij peluibus, j lauacro, j skemour,
25 j ladell, ab ipso emptis ibidem, vj s. viij d. Et per manus eiusdem pro j pare balaunces nonarum empto ibidem, ij s. iiij d. Johanni   July 18.
Skette de Linne pro xviij vergis panni albi et blodei ab ipso   Summa pagine
emptis ibidem xviij° die Jullii, xxxiij s. CLERICO speciarie per   xxviij li. xviij
/ manus Roberti Hatfeld pro xx lb. piperis. lb. ad xiiij d., per   viij d. ob,
30 ipsum emptis apud London, xxiij s. iiij d. Et pro xx lb. gingiberis   fo. 5 v°.
ad xxij d., xxxvj s. viij d. Et pro iij lb. croci ad x s., xxx s. Et pro xx lb. canellis ad xiiij d., xxiij s. iiij d. Et pro xij panibus sugri coffetini, ponderantibus inter se xxxvj lb. di., et lb. ad xxiij d., lxix s. xj d. ob. Et pro vj lb. maces ad ij s., xviij s. Et

CAMD. SOC.   X

156

July 16.

Duobus carpintariis conductis ibidem per Cudworth per ij dies, ij s. CLERICO panterie per manus Johannis Fischer pro x hurdell, ij sparrez, ij bulters pro officio suo in naue per ipsum emptis ibidem per compotum secum factum, vj s. x d. Clerico panetrie per manus eiusdem pro xxviij qr. frumenti per ipsum emptis apud Linne xvj⁰ 5 die Julii, qr. ad iiij s. iij d.; cxix s. Et pro bulting et paring dicti frumenti ibidem, viij s. Et pro cariagio dicti frumenti ad diuersos locos, ix s. iiij d. SUPER officio scutellarie per manus Cudworth pro portagio, iiij M fagetes et x, et pro mundacione lxj barellorum et pro portagio ij C vessellarum lignearum, ij gemens pro barellis pro 10 vinegre, et ij bollecouerez per ipsum emptis ibidem eodem die, per compotum secum factum, in toto ix s. CLERICO buterie super ceruisia per manus Baron, pro iij doliis j pipe ceruisie per ipsum emptis ibidem, dolium ad xxx s., per compotum secum factum ibidem eodem die, cv s. Et pro j last de beer, xxx s., et pro ij 15 barellis ceruisie, barellus ad iij s. ix d., in toto, xxxvij s. vj d. CLERICO coquine per manus Baron pro vij duodenis lampredarum, duodena ad iiij s. vj d., per ipsum emptis ibidem, xxxj s. vj d. CLERICO buterie super ceruisia per manus eiusdem pro ciij qr. ciphorum ligneorum per ipsum emptis ibidem, xv s. SUPER 20 officio aule et camere per manus eiusdem pro j carecta liture empta ibidem, ij s. Johanni Baron pro iij doliis voidez pro seruisia imponenda, dolium ad ij s. ij d., et pro j pipa vacante pro seruisia imponenda, xx d., per ipsum emptis ibidem eodem die, in toto viij s. ij d. Et pro vj hurdel pro diuersis officiis, ij s. Et pro 25 x waynescotz, vj sparres, ij C di. clauorum emptis ibidem pro j cabana pro senescallo in naui, v s. vj d. Et pro vj operariis per ij dies, capientibus inter se per diem, iij s., vj s. Et pro iij pipes voidez pro seruisia imponenda, pipa ad xx d., v s. Diuersis hominibus de Linne pro xiiij doliis vacantibus, ij pipes, v hoggeshedes, ij laste 30 barellis vacantibus,—dolium ad ij s. ij d., pipa ad xx d., hoggeshedz ad xij d., j laste barellus ad v s., xxij hurdell xj s. iiij d., et pro portagio bordez sparrez vj d., ab ipsis emptis ibidem eodem die, per compotum cum eisdem factum, in toto, lx s. vj d. Et pro cariagio

II. NECESSARIES PROVIDED IN ENGLAND.

xx doliorum vsque nauem, iij s. iiij d. Et pro cariagio iiij doliorum
seruicie, viij d. Et pro runagio, iij s. iiij d. CLERICO speciarie
per manus Ricardi Wolfle pro factura diuersarum mapparum ibidem,
xx d. Et pro lx lb. candelarum cepi, lb ad j d. ob., emptis ibidem,
5 vij s. vj d. Cuidam carpintario operanti super cabanam senescalli
per j diem, vj d. CLERICO panterie per manus Johannis Milnere
pro xxiij qu. frumenti, ad v s. per ipsum emptis ibidem, cxv s. Et
pro multura liij qr. frumenti, vna cum cariagio, xvj s. viij d. Et
pro bulting ciusdem frumenti, ij s. x d. SUPER officio scutellarie
10 per manus diuersorum pro cariagio v barellarum[a] aque frisee vsque
nauem per diuersas vices, iiij s. ij d. CLERICO speciarie per
manus Johannis Siselden pro j streynour per ipsum empto apud
Lynne xx° die Julii, iiij d. ob. CLERICO buterie super seruisia July 20.
per manus ciusdem pro iiij barellis cervisie continente le barell
15 xxiiij galones, galo ad j d. ob., xij s.; et pro iiij barellis vacantibus
pro dicta seruicia imponenda, ij s. ab ipso emptis ibidem eodem die,
in toto xiiij s. DIUERSIS carpintariis facientibus aulam, cameram, et capellam in naue, per compotum cum eis factum apud
Linne xix° die Julii, xxxiij s. ix d. Et ij latoners per ij dies July 19.
20 ij s., et xij carpintariis per ij dies xij s. Pro spiking xij s. v d., Summa pagine
/ pro vj ston flax, iij s x d.; pro xxvj vlnis canevas pro j cabana xxxiiij li. xj d.
domini, xj s. iij d.; pro j virga tele Flandrie pro j fenestralla, vj d.; fo. 6 v°.
pro ij hokes et ij pair hinges, viij d.; pro xxxiiij deles, xxxiiij s.;
pro ij C weynescotes bordez et x., xlv s. viij d.; pro C sparrez emptis
25 pro diuersis cabanis coqui et aliorum diuersorum officiariorum factis
in naue domini, xviij s., per compotum cum eis factum ibidem eodem
die, in toto, vij li. iiij d. Et pro xxviij C clauis emptis ibidem pro
eodem opere eodem die ad diuersa previa, xiij s. x d. Et per manus
Baron pro ij C x bordez, centena ad xxij s., xlvj s. j d.; pro iiij^{xx}ij
30 sparrez, xxiij s.; pro xxxiiij deles xxxiiij s., pro vj regal. ij s.; pro
xiij oken sparrez, iiij s. x d.; pro xiij ferren bordez, xvij d.; pro
vj ferren deles, xx d.; pro vj ston flax, iiij s.; pro limine tegulis pro

* The MS. has batell'.

coquina, iij s. vij d., pro xxvij vlnis canevas xj s.; pro j vlna tele
Flandrie, vj d.; per ipsum emptis ibidem pro reparacione nauis, in
toto vj li. xij s. Et per manus eiusdem pro dole bordez sparrez et
aliis diuersis per ipsum emptis ibidem pro reparacione nauis in qua
equi steterunt, vz. pro rakkes, mangers, et aliis diuersis necessariis
factis in dicta naui, xviij s. iiij d. CLERICO coquine per manus
Johannis Baunche de Linne pro j kibderkyn di. de storgon, xvj s.
viij d., et pro canevas, iij s. ix d., ab ipso emptis[a] ibidem, in toto
xx s. v d. DIUERSIS carpintariis facientibus j cabanam Ottoni
Graunson, pro domino Willelmo Wyluby, pro camerario et
thesaurario et aliis diuersis militibus et scutiferis, per compotum
cum eis factum ibidem, xlij s. iiij d. SUPER officio pulletrie per
manus thesaurarii pro ij caponibus per ipsum emptis apud Hecham,
vj d. SUPER officio scutellarie per manus Cudworth pro tunges et
aliis necessariis per ipsum emptis apud Linne, xx° die Julii, vj s.
viij d. Johanni Fischer pro j trow per ipsum empto apud Linne
pro officio suo in naui, xij d. CLERICO marescalcie per manus
Roberti Kent pro xx qrt. auenarum ad ij s., ab ipso emptis apud
Linne xvj° die Julii, xl s. Et pro batillagio auenarum de terra
vsque nauem, vj d. Et pro xxj vlnis canevas pro saccis, vlna ad
iiij d., vij s. Et pro paethred [pro] dictis ligandis, iij d. Et pro
iiij"viij vergis wadmoll ad ij d. ob. pro saccis, xviij s. iiij d. Et pro
factura eorundem, xiiij d. Et pro feno empto ibidem eodem die,
xx s. Et diuersis operariis facientibus ropez de dicto feno pro diuersis
equis in naui, vij s. Et pro batillagio dicti feni de terra vsque
nauem cum j batella, viij d. Et pro iij lepez, vj d. Et pro iij
bollis, xv d. Et pro bokets, vj d. Et pro xx fadom cordez, iiij d.
Et pro batillagio equorum domini de terra vsque nauem, vj d. Et
pro cariagio piparum, barellorum, et aliorum vasorum vacantium de
terra vsque nauem per diuersas vices, xvj d. Et pro ligacione iij
bollarum, iij d. Et pro j pecco ligneo[b] pro mensura auenarum,

---

[a] Empt' is also found after "canevas" in this phrase, apparently a slip of the pen.
[b] This seems to mean a wooden peck measure.

II. NECESSARIES PROVIDED IN ENGLAND. 159

iiij d. Et pro cariagio aque frisce vsque nauem, ij s. Et pro feno   July 18.
empto apud Hecham xviij° die Julii, iij s. iiij d. Et pro cariagio
eiusdem feni de terra vsque nauem, vj d. Et pro cariagio aque frisce
ibidem vsque nauem, vj d. Et pro ij gemelettes ferreis, vj d. Et
5 pro vadiis Johannis Wilbram extra curiam, existentis apud Linne per
iiij dies pro dictis ibidem prouidendis, capientis per diem vj d., ij s.
Clerico speciarie per manus Wilbram pro ij magnis quarterniis
papiri pro officio thesaurarii per ipsum emptis ibidem, ij s. ij d. Et
pro j pennario cum corner empto ibidem, vij d. Et pro uno quar-
10 ternio papiri, vj d. Et pro batellagio diuersorum officiariorum de
Linne versus nauem per diuersas vices, x s. Et pro x batellis conductis de Linne vsque Hecham pro towing naues, xxvj s. viij d.
Super officio scutellarie per manus Cudworth pro cariagio aque de
Hecham vsque nauem, iij s. ij d. Clerico buterie super vino per
15 manus Baron, pro j pipa vini Vasconie empta apud Linne pro hospicio domini ibidem, liij s. iiij d. Clerico buterie super beer per
manus thesaurarii pro ij last de beer per ipsum emptis ibidem,   remanent j me
lxxviij s. Et pro cariagio eiusdem, vj s. viij d. Johanni Siselden   bras j pestell
de Linne pro j morter de bras, et pestell de ferro et xx vlnis strey-   July 21.
20 nour per ipsum emptis ibidem, xxj° die Julii, xxvj s. viij d.
Clerico panetrie per manus Ricardi Oret pro pane albo ab ipso
empto ibidem eodem die, vj s. Et per manus Fischer pro j qrt.
farine, iiij s. vj d. Et pro cariagio eiusdem, iiij d. Clerico
coquine per manus Godefridi Fyschere pro j qrt. salis ab ipso empto
25 ibidem eodem die, iiij s. vj d. Et pro crabbes et floundrez, xj d.
Et per manus Johannis Sparwe pro cariagio diuersorum harnesiorum
officii coquine de Hecham vsque nauem, xij d. Et per manus
Baron pro pastura boum per ipsum conductorum ibidem, xiiij s.
iiij d. Clerico coquine per manus Willelmi Worcestre pro dimidio   July 19.
30 carcoisii bouis per ipsum empto apud Linne xix° die Julii,   Summa pagine
vj s. vj d. Et pro iiij carcoisiis multonum, vij s. vj d. Et pro j vitulo,   xxxvij li. xxij
ij s. Et pro j kede, xv d. Et pro j porco, ij s. Clerico speciarie   fo. 7.
/ per manus Cudworth pro maas et clowis per ipsum emptis ibidem,
xij d. Super officio scutellarie per manus Laurencii Trauers pro

busca per ipsum empta ibidem, xxij d. Roberto Hattefeld contrarotulario pro vadiis suis extra curiam, misso de Burgh vsque London pro speciebus et aliis diuersiis per ipsum emptis ibidem pro viagio domini, eundo, morando, et redeundo per viij dies, capiente per diem, iij s. iiij d., xxvj s. viij d. Johanni Repon botman de Linne pro cariagio diuersorum harnesiorum de Burgh vsque Linne cum j battella, iiij s. CLERICO panetrie per manus diuersorum pro pane albo ab ipsis empto apud Hecham, x s. CLERICO buterie per manus Baron super vino pro xvij sextariis vini Vasconie per ipsum emptis apud Walsingham, ad iij s. iiij d., lvj s. viij d. Et per manus eiusdem pro xx sextariis ij picher vini vasconie, sextarium ad ij s. viij d., per ipsum emptis apud Linne, liiij s. viij d. CLERICO buterie super seruisie per manus diuersorum pro lviij galonibus seruicie, ad j d. ob., cum auenis ab ipsis emptis ibidem, vij s. iij d. Et pro xxvij ciphis ligneis, ij s. CLERICO speciarie per manus Baron, pro xlviij lb. cere per ipsum emptis ibidem, xxiiij s. CLERICO coquine per manus Harpeden pro ix baconis et j vitulo per ipsum emptis apud Hecham, xxiij° die Julii, xxvij s. viij d. CLERICO buterie super vino per manus * Johannis Payn, pro xix doliis et j pipa vini per ipsum emptis apud Linne, xvj° die Julii, cxxv li. xiij s. iiij d. CLERICO speciarie per manus Willelmi Rowham, pro ij lb. piperis, iij s. iiij d., et pro j lb. de canella, ij s. Et pro di. quarter macez, x d. Et pro j vncia clows, vj d. SUPER officio salsarie per manus eiusdem, pro iij galonibus vinegri per ipsum emptis ibidem, xxj d. Hamoni Hamell, pro xxxvij barellis vacantibus, ad iiij d. ab ipso emptis ibidem, xij s. iiij d. CLERICO coquine per manus eiusdem pro di. barelli de samone ab ipso empto ibidem eodem die, viij s. iiij d. SUPER officio scutellarie per manus Nicholai Narford, pro ij C vessellis ligneis ab ipso emptis ibidem, vj s. Et pro v trowes pro diuersis officiariis, xv d. Et pro ij sakkes, iij d. SUPER officio scutellarie per manus Johannis Essex pro couperagio, circulando, et emendacione diuersorum barellorum apud Linne, vij s. Et pro ij laste barellis voidz, ad iiij s., viij s. CLERICO coquine per manus Johannis Blaunche, pro j kilderkin

July 23.
July 16.

* lo[quendum] cum J. Payn butellario pro istis xix doliis j pipa vini : respondet Payne.

II. NECESSARIES PROVIDED IN ENGLAND.   161

de storgon ab ipso empto apud Linne, xvj s. viij d. Et per manus
Willelmi Inglewode, pro vj duodenis laumprez, duodena ad
iiij s. vj d., xxvj s. Et pro iij galonibus grece, ad x d., ij s. vj d.
Et pro j barello pro dicto imponendo, vj d. SUPER officio scutellarie
5 per manus eiusdem, pro vj cheynes, et ij axis pro naui, emptis
ibidem, vj s. CLERICO coquine per manus Johannis Gebon,
pro iiij salmonibus ab ipso emptis ibidem, xiij s. iiij d. SUPER
officio scutellarie per manus Cudworth pro iiij^{mt} belet, M^l ad
viij s., per ipsum emptis ibidem, xxxij s. Et soluti Henrico
10 Hull, pro xij barellis voidez, ad iiij d., iiij s. CLERICO buterie
super seruisia per manus Baron, pro j last de beer per ipsum empta
apud Linne de Gerard Fouk, xxxiij s. iiij d. st. Et per manus
eiusdem, pro xij barellis voidez ab ipso emptis ibidem per manus
Baron, iiij s. st. SUPER officio aule et camere per manus Kikkele
15 pro litura per ipsum empta apud Linne, v d. st. JOHANNI
Fyscher pro vadiis suis extra curiam existenti apud Linne pro
prouidenciis ibidem faciendis versus partes Prucie, per xiij dies,
capienti per diem vj d., per compotum secum factum, vj s. xj d. st.
JOHANNI Cudworth pro vadiis suis extra curiam, existenti apud
20 Linne pro prouidenciis ibidem faciendis versus partes Prucie, per
xxj dies^a vna cum rewardo sibi facto per idem tempus, xx s. st.
CLERICO buterie super ceruisia, empta per manus Roberti Hwet j
barello ibidem, iij s. iiij d. st. CLERICO coquine per manus Claws
/ de Norwey pro iij bouiculis ab ipso emptis ibidem, xviij s. viij d.
25 st. SUPER officio pulletrie per manus eiusdem pro v polettis, iiij d.
st. CLERICO coquine per manus Johannis Benet pro j oue per
ipsum empta, x d. st. CLERICO speciarie per manus Willelmi
Pomfret pro di. lb. gingibris et piperis, xv d. CLERICO buterie
super vino per manus Roberti Jonson pro tractagio ij doliorum et
30 iiij piparum de celario domini vsque le crane, vj s. viij. d. st. Et
per manus eiusdem pro tractagio j last et di. de beer, ii s. pr. Item
eidem pro j nouo cado per ipsum empto pro vino imponendo et
cariagio dicti cadi vsque le crane, v s. pr. Item soluti pro locione

Summa pagine
Cxlvij li. ix s. ii
fo. 7 v°.

* MS. has diem.

CAMD. SOC.   Y

j streynour domini ibidem per manus eiusdem, v s. pr. Item Johanni Whytlok pro locione mapparum tam apud le Mount quam apud Norwey, xiij d. st. Item Johanni Benet, lodesman, famulo hospicii domini, conducto de Dansk versus Angliam ex conuencione facta cum eodem per consilium domini,* iiij marcz. st. Item cuidam 5 steresman nauis, de dono per consilium Johannis Dyndon, iij s. iiij d. st. Item Willelmo Gibbeson de Linne pro cariagio harnisii domini de Hulle vsque Linne, ex conuencione facta cum eodem per consilium domini,† xxxiij s. iiij d. st. Item cuidam botman de Linne pro batillagio harnisii domini de Linne vsque Petreburgh, xx s. st. 10 CLERICO panetrie per manus Roberti Jonson pro pane albo per ipsum empto apud Hulle, ij s. viij d. CLERICO coquine per manus Johannis Fleschewer pro carne boum et ouium per tempus predictum, vij s. ij d. Et per manus Johannis Windsouere et Galfridi pro allecibus rubeis et piscibus recentibus per ipsos emptis per tempus 15 predictum, iij s. j d. Super officio palletrie per manus Galfridi pro iiij aucis per ipsum emptis, xvj d. Item per manus eiusdem pro butiro, iiij d. Et per manus eiusdem pro iij columbellis et j gallina, iiij d. Et per manus eiusdem pro iiij caponibus, v d. Et per manus eiusdem pro j pecco farine auenarum, iij d. CLERICO buterie super 20 ceruisia per manus Roberti Jonson et Johannis Jonson pro xix di. galonibus seruicie, galo ad ij d., ij s. iij d. Et in expensis domini Willelmi factis eundo de Hulle vsque Eboracum et ibidem morando et redeundo per v dies, vna cum conductione ij equorum, pro mutuacione^a C marcarum de Thesauro Anglie solutarum pro fraghtage nauis, 25 vj s. SUPER officio buterie super vino, pro windario [et] celeragio ij doliorum vini Vasconie, et ij piparum vini Vasconie et Rochell, xij d. Et solutus cuidam mulieri mundanti dicta dolia et pipes, j d. CLERICO coquine per manus Roberti Crane pro carne boum et ouium ab ipso empta, iij s. ij d. ob. SUPER officio scutellarie per manus 30 Johannis Jonson pro focali ibidem expendito per tempus predictum, ij s. iiij d. CLERICO speciarie per manus Johannis Whitlok et

* quia nisi xxxiij s. iiij d.

† qua xl s.

* The MS. has mitune'.

Johannis Jonson pro iij lb. candelarum cepi, iiij d. ob. CLERICO marescalcie per manus Roberti Hwet pro expensis iiij equorum domini, ij equorum Roberti Waterton, ij equorum custodis leopardi, et j hakenay Henrici conuersi, apud Hecham in feno, ix d. Item in litura, iij d. Item in auenis pro eisdem iiij bz. p^c,^a xx d. Item in rewardo pro eisdem vz. in pane equino, v d. Et per manus Johannis Aschby pro emendacione j malesadell, iij d. CLERICO speciarie per manus custodis leopardi pro candelis cereis emptis pro leopardo, iiij d. ob.

Summa pagine viij li. xiiij s. iiij d. ob.
Item de moneta Prucie xix s. pr., qui faciunt ij s. j d. st.

Summa istorum iij foliorum de prouidenciis in Anglia cccxxj li. viij s. ix d. st.
Item de moneta Prucie xix s. pr., qui faciunt ij s. j d. st.

IN PARTIBUS PRUCIE. DANSK.[b]

/ DIUERSIS hominibus pro tribus equis ab ipsis conductis pro equitacione domini et ij henksmen apud Dansk x° die mensis Augusti, xv s. pr. Et pro conductione iij carrectarum pro equitacione diuersorum famulorum domini ibidem eodem die, xxxvj scot. Et pro j curro * conducto pro Totty et Payne, v scot. Et pro cariagio diuersorum harnesiorum de naui vsque terram per manus Wilbram, Cudworth, et Thome Knapp, j marc, iiij scot. xiij d. Et pro cariagio et portagio diuersorum harnesiorum de terra vsque hospicium domini ibidem, ix scot. Et per manus Henrici de Camera pro emendacione vnius zone domini cum les flours ibidem eodem

fo. 8.
August 10

* [Sic.]

---

* This seems to mean four bushels one peck of oats.
[b] In the MS. for these first three folios Dansk alone stands as title. From 9 v° and onwards "In Partibus Prucie" is written at the head of every folio, evidently as a second thought as the items show it to be the more correct

die, ix scot. Clerico marescalcie per manus Johannis Wilbram pro j carecta feni per ipsum empta apud Dansk xx° die mensis Augusti, iiij scot. Et per manus eiusdam pro j serura empta ibidem eodem die, pro clausura hostii domus in qua dictum fenum includitur, iij s. pr. Clerico speciarie per manus Johannis Theplond, 5 pro iij C di. viij lb. amigdalarum ab ipso emptis ibidem xij° die Augusti, xxij marc. xx scot. pr. Clerico marescalcie per manus Johannis Wilbram pro feno per ipsum empto ibidem eodem die, vj scot. Et per manus eiusdem pro j quarter. j bz. auenarum emptis ibidem eodem die, xix s. vj d. pr. Super officio aule et camere 10 per manus Kykkele pro mattes per ipsum emptis ibidem eodem die, v s. pr. Hans Ducke pro expensis suis misso super negocium domini de Dansk ad magistrum de Prucia existentem apud Lype, vna cum conductione vnius carri* eundo, morando, et redeundo per v dies et. v noctes, per compotum secum factum apud Dansk, ij marc. xj scot 15 xvj d. pr. Diversis portatoribus portantibus diuersa harnesia et victualia de terra vsque le prame versus Kenesburgh, xliiij s. pr. Clerico buterie super seruicia per manus vnius lodesman pro j barello seruicie et pro j caseo empto apud Hecham, iiij s. xj d. ; et Johanni Chermon pro tonsura xij vergarum blanket ibidem, vij s. 20 pr. Cuidam carectario carecte misso de Dansk vsque nouam Abathiam cum j pipa vini, v scot. Clerico buterie super le beer, pro seruicia empta apud Dansk, xx d. st. Johanni leche pro camfor et staunche per ipsum emptis apud Dansk, vij nobles. Item pro conductione ij equorum pro Goter misso super negocium domini 25 de Dansk vsque Quenesburgh, xxxij scot. Item Gerard Fouk pro expensis diuersorum garcionum existentium cum equis in naui, iij noble. Henrico henksman pro j pare ocrearum per ipsum empto ibidem, xxx s. pr. Bernardo henksman pro emendacione ocrearum et sotularum emptarum ibidem, xij s. pr. Clerico marescalcie per 30 manus Uphill pro grece empt' ibidem pro equis domini, xij d. pr. Johanni Dounton pro emendacione j paris de bracez domini, viij scot. Et pro portagio harnesii garderobe domini versus les prames, ij scot. Super officio scutellarie per manus Laurencii

August 20.

August 12.

* MS carr'.

II. EXPENSES IN PRUSSIA.

Trauers pro busca per ipsum empta apud Dansk a xj° die Augusti   Aug. 11—23.
vsque xxiij diem eiusdem mensis, vtreque computato, per xiij dies
per manus diuersas, vna cum factura j dressynbord et diuersorum
necessariorum dicto officio contingentium per idem tempus, v marc.
5 iiij scot. ij s. pr. CLERICO coquine per manus Ducheman pro
j bacon empto apud Dansk, xij scot. Et pro diuersis carnibus recentibus emptis ibidem eodem die, v scot. SUPER officio pulletrie
per manus eiusdem pro xvj gallinis emptis ibidem, ix scot. xviij d.
pr. Et pro farina auenarum empta ibidem, viij d. pr. SUPER
10 officio salsarie per manus eiusdem di. galo vinegri, iij s. pr. CLERICO
coquine per manus eiusdem pro piscibus recentibus emptis ibidem,
viij s. pr. CLERICO panetrie per manus eiusdem pro chiriez emptis
ibidem, ij s. pr. SUPER officio aule et camere per manus eiusdem
pro litura empta ibidem, viij s. pr. SUPER officio salsarie per
15 manus Laurencii Trauers pro xvj galonibus di. venegri per ipsum
emptis apud Dansk, per compotum secum factum, j marc. vj s. pr.
CLERICO marescalcie per manus Wilbram pro feno per ipsum empto
ibidem, xxiiij die Augusti, v scot. CLERICO buterie super vino   Aug. 24.
per manus Henrici Wymmon' pro j dolio vini de Rochell per
20 ipsum empto ibidem eodem die, xvj marc. di. pr. Et per manus
Dedrick Fyk pro j fat vini de Rochell ab ipso empto ibidem   Summa pagine xij marc. ij sc[ot]. pr.
eodem die, viij marc. pr. Et per manus eiusdem pro j dolio
vini de Rochell, xv noble; SUPER / officio scutellarie per   fo. 8 v°.
manus Laurencii Trauers pro* herbis ibidem emptis eodem die,
25 xxvj s. vj d. pr. Et per manus Payne pro piris, pomis, chiriez,
et aliis diuersis fructubus per ipsum emptis ibidem eodem die,
iiij marz xxiij scot. ij d. pr. CLERICO buterie super beer, per
manus Payne pro xvj. barellis de beer per ipsum emptis ibidem
eodem die, v marc. vij scot. xv d. pr. CLERICO panetrie per manus
30 eiusdem pro pano albo per ipsum empto ibidem eodem die,
per compotum secum factum, vj marc. xvj scot. pr. CLERICO
buterie super vino, per manus eiusdem pro lvij stopes vini ad

* MS. has per.

diuersa precia per ipsum emptis ibidem, per compotum secum
ibidem eodem die, ij marez, xiiij scot, ij s. iiij d. pr. Clerico
coquine per manus Harpeden pro xxxj bacons per ipsum emptis

August 24. apud Dansk xxiiij die mensis Augusti versus Quenysburgh,
xiij marc. pr. Super officio salsarie, per manus Laurencii Trauers 5
pro j bus. di. flowr per ipsum empto apud Dansk eodem die, xx s.
viij d. pr. Super officio scutellerie per manus eiusdem pro ij
trowes ij boketes et aliis necessariis per ipsum emptis ibidem eodem
die, iiij scot. Clerico marescalcie per manus Johannis Smyth pro
ferrura omnium equorum domini apud Dansk, per compotum 10
secum factum ibidem, xx scot. iij s. pr. Clerico speciarie per
manus Johannis del Chaandrye pro xv lb. candelarum cepi per
ipsum emptis ibidem, vj scot. Clerico panetrie per manus Johannis Fyscher pro j. qrt. ij bz. flour per ipsum emptis ibidem
eodem die, ij marez di. pr. Et pro furnagio empto ibidem apud 15
Dansk, vj scot. Clerico marescalcie per manus Johannis Wilbram

August 25. pro ferris equinis per ipsum emptis ibidem, xxvᵒ die mensis
Augusti, ij s. pr. Super officio aule et camere, per manus Johannis
Selby pro hemmyng et emendacione diuersarum mapparum domini
ibidem, iiij scot. Cuidam Dovcheman pro conductione iij equorum 20
pro equitacione Roberti de Waterton et aliorum, vna cum j gyde,
euntium ad diuersos locos pro equis emendis pro domino, per
conuencionem factam, j marc. pr. Henrico Henksman pro j pare
sotularum per ipsum empto ibidem, ij s. pr. Henrico Henksman et Bernard Henksman pro factura de ij gounis ibidem, per 25
conuencionem factam, xviij scot. Clerico coquine per manus
Johannis Venere pro xxx bacons per ipsum emptis ibidem eodem
die, xv marez pr. Clerico speciarie per manus Ricardi Wolflee
pro locione mapparum domini ibidem eodem die, di. marc. pr.
Item Johanni de Watterton pro panno albo, rubeo, et nigro per 30
ipsum empto ibidem pro j sella domini araianda ibidem, xix scot.
Domino Wilelmo Wylughby pro j careeta per ipsum conducta apud
Dansk, die quo dominus iuit ad nauem cum processione cum
cropore Cristi, j nobll. Rectori ecclesie de Dansk pre sepultura

Hans et famuli sui, per conuencionem secum factam per dominum
Hugonem Herlee ibidem eodem die, vij noble v s. st. CLERICO [See after, p. 27:
panetrie per manus diuersas pro pane albo ab ipsis empto apud
Darsowe xxvj° die mensis Augusti, xvij s. pr. Et pro piris et August 26.
5 pomis, iij s. pr. CLERICO buterie super vino per manus eorundem
pro vino ibidem empto, ij marc. xxij scot. ij s. pr. Clerico buterie
super beer, pro beer empta ibidem ix scot., viij d. pr. CLERICO
speciarie per manus Johannis del Chaundrye pro iij lb. candelarum
cepi, iij s. pr. CLERICO marescalcie per manus Wilbram pro feno,
10 iiij s. viij d. pr. Et pro iij bz. auenarum, iiij scot. CLERICO panetrie per manus Fyscher pro ij schofull flour emptis apud Melwyn
xxviij die mensis Augusti, xxxij s. pr. CLERICO speciarie per August 28.
manus Willelmi Pomfret pro diuersis speciebus per ipsum emptis
ibidem, j marc. xj scot. vj d. Et pro xxxiiij lb. cere, j marc. di.
15 xvj d. pr. Et pro xiiij lb. candelarum cepi, xiiij s. pr. CLERICO
marescalcie per manus Wilbram pro ix l z. auenarum emptis ibidem,
ix scot. Et pro baytyng domini et famulorum apud Brounesburgh
vltimo die mensis Augusti, viz., in pane albo, vino, beer et aliis August 31.
diuersis victualibus emptis ibidem, j marc. iiij scot. xiiij d. pr.
20 CLERICO pantrie per manus Payn pro pane albo per ipsum empto
apud Helebell primo die mensis Septembris, xij s. pr. CLERICO September 1.
buterie super beer, pro beer empta ibidem eodem die, xj scot. Et
pro mede empto ibidem, xvj s. pr. SUPER officio scutellarie per
manus Laurencii Trauers pro herbis per ipsum emptis ibidem,
25 xij d. pr. CLERICO speciarie per manus Johannis del Chaundrye
pro ij lb. candelarum cepi, ij s. pr. Et pro conductione ij equorum
de ibidem usque Conyngsburgh et redeundo, xij scot. Et pro bayting
domini et famulorum suorum apud Brandeburgh eodem die, viz., in
vino, pane, bere at aliis victualibus, vj scot. xij d. pr. CLERICO
30 speciarie per manus Willelmi Pomfret pro diuersis confectionibus per ipsum emptis apud Dansk, vj marc. xj scot. Summa pagine
viij d. pr. Thome Goter pro expensis suis misso de Dansk iiij^{xx} j marc. di. scot.
/ vsque Conyngburgh super diuersa negocia domini ad magistrum
Prucie ibidem, j marc. pr. CLERICO marescalcie per manus fo. 9.

Graunsom Bastard pro expensis equorum existentium apud Dansk, j marc. pr. Et pro factura j selle domini apud Dansk eodem die, j marc. ij s. pr. CLERICO buterie super vino per manus Payne pro j fat vini per ipsum empto, v marc. pr. SUPER officio aule et camere per manus Selby pro locione mapparum apud Melwyn vltimo 5

August 31.
August 23.

die mensis Auguste, v scot. Et per manus eiusdem pro locione mapparum domini apud Dansk, xxiij die Augusti, xij scot. Johanni Marwicsire henksman domini pro j pare ocrearum, xxx s. pr. CLERICO speciarie per manus thesaurarii pro coopertorio tele Westvall pro dresseur per ipsum emptis apud Dansk, xij s. pr. 10 Johanni Frenschman pro j pare sotularum per ipsum empto ibidem eodem die, x s. pr. SUPER officio salsarie per manus Laurenci Trauers pro diuersis salsiamentis per ipsum emptis ibidem eodem die, xx s. pr. SUPER officio scutellarie per manus eiusdem pro carbonibus, xviij scot. Item pro batillagio domini, famulorum suorum et 15 harnesiorum suorum vltra aquam de Wissell apud Darsowe, ij marc. xij d. pr. CLERICO speciarie per manus Johannis Wilbram pro xxiiij vergis de Westuall per ipsum emptis apud Conyngburgh ij die

September 2.

mensis Septembris, xviij scot. iij s pr. Et pro j gallone melli empto ibidem, vj scot. iij s. pr. CLERICO marescalcie per manu 20 Johannis Wilbram pro feno per ipsum empto apud Conyngburgh eodem die, vj s. pr. Et pro litura empta ibidem, iiij s. pr. Et pro cariagio auenarum de Brauns vsque castellum ibidem, per conuencionem factam, j scot. Et pro j serura empta pro hostio auenarum ibidem, ii s. pr. CLERICO panetrie per manus Gylder pro pane 25 albo per ipsum empto ibidem eodem die, j marc. xvj scot. CLERICO buterie super vino, per manus eiusdem pro vino empto ibidem, vj marc. ij s. viij d. pr. Clerico buterie super beer pro iij barellis beer emptis ibidem, j marc. vj scot. Item pro iiij^{xx}x bykers emptis ibidem, vj scot. Et pro iiij^{xx} verrez emptis ibidem, xij scot. 30 JOHANNI Gylder pro reparacione panterie, buterie, celerie, vna cum mundacione domorum apud Conyngburgh, iij marc. x scot. xx d. pr. Johanni Blaeden pro factura j coquine de nouo, facte ibidem infra mansionem Episcopi, videlicet in clauis, bordez, deles,

II. EXPENSES IN PRUSSIA.

postes et aliis necessariis dicte coquine contingentibus ibidem, per compotum secum factum ibidem, vj marc. xiiij scot. xiiij d. pr. Thome Knappe pro emendacione et reparacione stabulorum ibidem in predicta mansione, j marc. v scot. ix d. pr. CLERICO coquine 5 per manus Willelmi Harpeden pro j carcoisia bouina, xiij carcoisiis multonum, iiij vitulis, v porcis, xviij porcellis, et pro sagmine, per ipsum emptis apud Conyngburgh iij die mensis Septembris, xj marc. iiij scot. Et per manus eiusdem pro xj carcoisiis multonum, iij marcz. vj scot. Et pro ij vitulis, xviij scot. Et per 10 manus eiusdem pro ij carcoisiis bouinis, ij marcz. xviij scot. Et pro j apro, ij marc. pr. SUPER officio scutellarie per manus Laurencii Trauers pro busca et carbonibus emptis ibidem, ij marcz. pr. Et pro ij barellis voidez pro discis ligneis imponendis, emptis ibidem, vj s. pr. SUPER officio salsarie per manus eiusdem pro 15 flowr et furnagio emptis ibidem, xx scot. Et pro j galone, iij qrt. venegr', vj scot. Et pro cenapi et vergus, vij s. pr. SUPER officio scutellarie per manus eiusdem pro ij C discis ligneis emptis ibidem, vj scot. xv d. pr. CLERICO coquine per manus Thome Peyntour pro pictura diuersorum ciborum ibidem eodem die in 20 coquina, x scot. Item vni homini operanti in coquina ibidem eodem die, iiij scot. Diuersis operariis facientibus vnam nouam coquinam infra castrum de Conyngburgh, per conuencionem cum eis factam ibidem, ij marc. pr. Et cuidam cementarii facienti j herth in dicta coquina, ij scot. ij s. pr. SUPER officio scutel-25 larie per manus Hans Douche pro conductione j magne patelle ad coquendam carnem ibidem eodem die, x s. pr. Et vni homini operanti in dicto officio ibidem eodem die, v s. pr. CLERICO coquine per manus Willelmi Cook, pro ij schuldrez brawn per ipsum emptis ibidem, xxv s. pr. Cuidam peyntour pro pictura 30 diuersorum armorum domini, militum, et scutiferorum ibidem eodem die, j marc. vj s. pr. SUPER officio salsarie per manus Blaedon pro flowr per ipsum empto ibidem, vj s. pr. SUPER officio scutellarie per manus Laurencii Trauers pro ij C discis ligneis per ipsum emptis ibidem, j marc. pr. CLERICO coquine per manus Har-

Margin notes:
Emptiones Ha solute per Thesaurium.
September 3.
Summa pagine lxiiij marc. di. scot.

fo. 9 vº.

peden pro sale albo per ipsum empto ibidem, xiiij scot. CLERICO / marescalcie per manus Wilbram pro feno et litura per ipsum emptis ibidem, xx s. pr. SUPER officio scutellarie per manus diuersorum operantium in coquina ibidem, xiiij scot. DIUERSIS operariis operantibus in diuersis officiis apud Conyngburgh eodem die, xviij s. pr. Et pro cariagio diuersorum harnesiorum officiariorum, aquarum et candelarum ibidem, vj s. pr. CLERICO speciarie per manus Johannis del Chaundrie pro xij lb. candelarum cepi emptis ibidem eodem die, xij s. pr. Et pro consuetura mapparum et locione ibidem eodem die, x s. pr. CLERICO marescalcie per manus Wilbram pro feno et litura per ipsum emptis apud Brendeburgh iiij die Septembris, iiij s. ij d. pr. Et pro iij bz. auenarum emptis ibidem eodem die, vij s. pr. CLERICO panetrie per manus Payne pro pane albo per ipsum empto ibidem, xiij s. ij d. pr. CLERICO buterie super beer, pro beer emptis ibidem, xij scot. viij d. pr. Et pro mede, vj scot. iij s. pr. SUPER officio pulletrie per manus Pepyr pro ouis et lacte emptis ibidem, xij s. iiij d. pr. CLERICO pantrie per manus Payne pro pane albo per ipsum empto apud Brounesburgh vᵗᵒ die mensis Sept., xxij s. pr. CLERICO buterie super vino, per manus eiusdem, pro vino empto ibidem, v marz. di. pr. CLERICO buterie super beer, pro beer empto, ibidem, x scot. Et pro mede, ij s. pr. Item pro expensis Cudworth, Harpeden, precuntium ibidem pro prouidenciis ibidem faciendis, iiij s. pr. SUPER officio salsarie per manus Laurencii Trauers pro vergus, cenape, et venegri emptis ibidem, ij scot. CLERICO maresca'cie per manus Wilbram pro feno empto ibidem, iiij s. viij d. pr. Et pro iij bz. di auenarum, ix s. ix d. pr. Et pro ferrura equorum ibidem. iiij s. v d. pr. CLERICO speciarie per manus Johannis del Chaundrie pro iij lb. candelarum cepi, iij s. pr. CLERICO pantrie per manus Payne pro pane albo per ipsum empto apud Melwyn vjº die Sept., xvij s. pr. CLERICO buterie super vino per manus eiusdem pro vino per ipsum empto ibidem eodem die, v marez., ij scot. xv d. pr. CLERICO buterie super beer pro beer per ipsum empto ibidem, xj scot. vj d. pr. CLERICO marescalcie

September 4.

September 5.

September 6.

II. EXPENSES IN PRUSSIA.

per manus Wilbram pro feno per ipsum empto ibidem eodem die, vij s. pr. Et pro iij bz. auenarum, ix s. pr. CLERICO coquine per manus Harpeden pro iij carcoisiis multonum emptis apud Melwyn vj die Sept., xviij scot. Et pro di. flyche bacon, xvj s. 5 pr. Et pro sale albo, iiij s. pr. Et pro j kede empt' ibidem, ix s. pr. CLERICO pantrie per manus Payne pro pane albo per ipsum empto apud Darsowe vij die mensis Sept., xj s. pr. CLERICO *September 7.* buterie super vino per manus eiusdem, pro vino per ipsum empto ibidem eodem die, xxvj s. pr. CLERICO buterie super beer pro 10 beer per ipsum empto ibidem, x scot. CLERICO coquine per manus Harpeden pro j storion empto ibidem, j marc. viij scot. Et pro j salmone recenti, vj scot. CLERICO buterie super beer, et pro mede, xvj s. pr. CLERICO pantrie per manus Payne pro fructubus emptis ibidem, iiij s. pr. SUPER officio scutellarie per manus 15 Laurencii Trauers pro herbis emptis ibidem, ix s. pr. CLERICO speciarie per manus Ricardi del Chaundrie pro cera empta ibidem, xiij s. pr. Et pro vj lb. candelarum cepi emptis ibidem, vj s. pr. SUPER officio scutellarie pro j ketell eneo empto ibidem, xx s. pr. CLERICO marescalcie per manus Wilbram pro feno 20 empto ibidem eodem die, iiij s. viij d. Et pro iij bz. auenarum, iiij scot. CLERICO coquine per manus Harpeden pro sale albo per ipsum empto, iij s. iiij d. SUPER officio scutellarie per manus Laurencii Trauers pro vj last. carbonum per ipso emptis apud Dansk xvj die Sept., ij. marez vj scot. SUPER officio scutellarie per manus *September 16.* 25 Thesaurarii pro bollez, trowes per ipsum emptis apud Conyngburgh, iij° die Sept., ix s. pr. JOHANNI Dounten pro emenda- *September 3.* cione j haberion domini ibidem eodem die, viij scot. CLERICO speciarie per manus Thesaurarii pro xj lb. de datilibus emptis ibidem, xj scot. Et pro diuersis confectionibus emptis ibidem, xliiij scot. 30 SUPER officio aule et camere per manus eiusdem pro cirpis emptis ibidem, vj s. pr. HENRICO henksman pro sotularibus per ipsum emptis apud Dansk, vj s. pr. CLERICO buterie super vino per manus Payn, pro vino per ipsum empto apud Conyngburgh, xiiij scot. CUIDAM Pruciano pro ij equis ab ipso conductis de Halybell

172   THE EARL OF DERBY'S EXPEDITIONS.

Summa pagine xxvij
marc. di. iiij scot.
xj d.

fo. 10.
September 16.

September 16.

September 17.

vsque Brownesburgh, vj scot. SUPER officio aule et camere, per manus Johannis Dauy pro cirpis per ipsum emptis ad diuersos locos per diuersas vices, vj scot. ij s. pr. CLERICO marescalcie per manus Thome Swylyngton et Thome Vphill pro expensis iiij equorum domini de Melwyn vsque Dansk, per compotum cum /eisdem factum apud Dansk, xvj die mensis Sept., vj scot. vj s. x d. pr. CLERICO panetrie per manus Payne pro pane per ipsum empto apud Dansk eodem die, ij marcz di. pr. CLERICO buterie super beer, pro beer empta ibidem eodem die, xl. scot. Clerico buterie super vino per manus Payne, pro vino empto ibidem, v marcz pr. Et pro pertagio j dolii et ij pipez vini ibidem, xij scot iiij s. pr. Et pro xx stope vini de Reynes, xxj scot. x d. Et pro bykeres emptis ibidem, xxvj s. pr. Et pro fructubus, x s. pr. Clerico buterie super vino per manus Payne, pro vino empto ibidem ; x marcz pr. Et pro vino Renis empto ibidem, vj marc. di. vj scot. Clerico buterie super beer, pro iiij barellis de beer emptis ibidem, xxx scot. Et pro ij barellis beer emptis ibidem, xxij scot. Et pro portagio dicte beer, xj s. pr. JOHANNI Dyndon pro xv vlnis de fustyan, vlna ad iiij s., per ipsum emptis ibidem eodem die, j marc. pr. Et pro viij vlnis tele Pruciane, vlna ad iij s. iiij d., xxvj s. viij d. pr. Et pro vj lb. cotonis, lb. ad vj s. iiij d. emptis ibidem, xxxviij s. Et pro filo empto, ij s. pr. THOME Gloucestre pro j carecta per ipsum conducta pro equitacione sui, Goter, et Johannis Wilbram de Holyed vsque Dansk, per conuencionem factam ibidem, xviij scot. Et pro expensis eorundem in eodem itinere per idem tempus, xij scot. Duobus carectariis pro ij carectis ab ipsis conductis de Conyngburgh vsque Sconee pro cariagio diuersorum harnesiorum et victualium domini, per conuencionem cum eis factam apud Dansk xvj die mensis Septembris, iiij marc. di. iiij scot. CLERICO marescalcie per manus Hans Ferour pro ferrura duorum equorum Yonger* Johan apud Dansk, xvij die mensis Septembris, x s. p. JOHANNI Dounton pro j pusayne, et emendacione

5

10

15

20

25

30

* i. e. Junker Johan.

II. EXPENSES IN PRUSSIA. 173

j paris gloucz de plate per ipsum empti apud Melwyn, per compotum
secum factum ibidem xij die Septembris, j marc. di. pr. Diuersis September 12.
carectariis pro iiij carectis ab ipsis conductis de Dansk vsque Melwyn
et redeundis, xij marc. viij scot. Et pro j carecta conducta de Dansk
5 vsque Conyngburgh et redeunda per convencionem factam, iiij
marcz di. pr. JOHANNI Gylder pro cariagio viij doliorum x pipes
flowr, beer, et aliorum diuersorum victualium de naui vsque hospicium
domini, et de hospicio vsque nauem apud Conyngburgh, per compotum secum factum apud Dansk xx° die Septembris, viij marc. Sepetmber 20.
10 viij scot. CLERICO marescalcie per manus Johannis Wilbram pro
cariagio feni et auenarum vsque hospicium domini apud Dansk xj°
die Augusti, ix scot. Et per manus Cawod pro cariagio diuersarum August 11.
sellarum et aliorum diuersorum harnesiorum, iij scot. CLERICO
speciarie per manus Cawod pro diuersis baggez pro diuersis speciebus
15 imponendis per ipsum emptis ibidem eodem die, x scot. ROBERTO
de Waterton pro cariagio diuersorum harnesiorum domini de naui
vsque terram, et de terra vsque hospicium domini, xviij scot. SUPER
officio aule et camere, per manus Wilelmi Kykkele pro j bagge et
xxiiij crochettes per ipsum emptis apud Dansk, xviij scot. iiij d. pr.
20 Duobus carpentariis facientibus diuersa necessaria in hospicio domini
ibidem, xiij s. pr. Johanni Dounton pro emendacione diuersorum
harnesiorum domini de armatura, xxviij scot. Et pro emendacione
j pipa et ij fattes ibidem, iiij scot. Et pro j doseyn blanket emptis
ibidem pro ij henksmen et aliis, iij nobles xij scot. Johanni Cud-
25 worth pro v barellis voidez per ipsum emptis apud Dansk, xj s. pr.
ET PER manus Johannis Gylder pro vadiis suis extra curiam existentis
apud Conyngburgh pro dictis* cariagio et custodia per xviij dies ad vj d.
per diem, ix s. ster. COK de camera pro cariagio et portagio diuersorum harnesiorum domini de la garderobe de terra vsque nauem et
30 de naui vsque terram apud Conyngburgh, vna cum expensis suis
ibidem per idem tempus, j marc. xxj scot. xij d. pr. SUPER officio
aule et camere per manus Kykkeley pro cirpis emptis ibidem, ix s.

* This seems to refer to the items in l. 6 above, and l. 31, p. 168.

174   THE EARL OF DERBY'S EXPEDITIONS.

<small>September 15.</small>

pr. Johanni Dounton pro emendacione j paris plates ibidem pro domino xv die mensis Septembris, j marc. di. pr. Henrico de camera pro emendacione diuersorum harnesiorum domini eodem die, xvij s. iiij d. pr. Super officio scutellarie per manus Laurencii Trauers pro carbonibus per ipsum emptis ibidem, j marc. di. pr. 5 Cok de camera pro portagio clothsakkes de le prame vsque hospicium domini ibidem, ij s. pr. Johanni Payne pro j pare bagges pro argento imponendo, vj s. pr. Clerico buterie per manus eiusdem pro vino Renis per ipsum empto ibidem eodem die, viij marcz xxj scot. Thome / Gloucestre pro vadiis suis extra curiam, per iiij dies ad xij d. 10 per diem, iiij s. st. Thome Gerard pro baytyng domini et partis famulorum ejus apud Pursk* primo die aduentus domini super terram, x s. pr. Super officio buterie super beer, pro bykerez et portagio vini et beer vsque hospicium domini, vna cum emptis fructubus ibidem, per compotum factum ibidem, j marc. viij scot. 15 iiij d. pr. Cuidam pramoni pro j prame ab ipso conducta de Dansk vsque Conyngburgh et redeunda, per conuencionem factam, xiij marc. pr. Super officio aule et camere per manus Johannis Syde pro locione pannorum lineorum domini apud Dansk, xiiij die mensis Septembris, x scot. Thome Knappe pro tabulis clauis per 20 ipsum emptis apud Conyngburgh pro reparacione stabulorum ibidem in domo, et pro ferrura equorum ibidem, viij scot. Et eidem pro vadiis suis extra curiam existenti ibidem circa facturam eorundem, per viij dies, capienti per diem iiij d, ij s. viij d. st. Clerico marescalcie per manus Wilbram pro feno per ipsum 25 empto apud Dansk pro equis in naui versus Angliam, xx die mensis Septembris, j marc. j scot. Et pro factura de ropes de dicto feno, viij scot. Et pro conductione vnius domus pro dicto feno imponendo, vj scot. Et pro xij barellis voidez pro aqua imponenda pro equis in naui, ix scot. Et pro ij payles ligneis, ij s. pr. 30 Et pro ij skeppes, ij s. pr. Et pro iiij bollis ligneis, iij scot. Et pro iiij deles pro clausura stabuli in naui, iiij scot. Et pro ij C clauorum emptis ibidem, iij scot. Et v carpentariis operantis in naui circa facturam stabuli, xvj scot. Et pro skippagio equorum domini

<small>Summa pagine iiij^{xx} viij marc. di. ix scot. fo. 10 v°.</small>

<small>* Sic.</small>

<small>September 14.</small>

<small>September 20</small>

ibidem, xvij s. pr. Et pro cariagio feni et auenarum et barellorum de terra vsque nauem, vj scot. Et pro cariagio auenarum de terra vsque nauem apud Conyngburgh, vj s. pr. Et pro expensis unius garcionis ibidem custodientis harnesium domini ibidem, vj scot.
5 Johanni Trepelond pro harnesio j carecte per ipsum conducte ibidem eodem die, x scot. CLERICO buterie super ceruisia per manus Nicholai Steynour de Dansk, pro iiij last de beer ab ipso emptis ibidem, lxxiij s. iiij d st. Johanni Dounton pro emendacione diuersorum harnesiorum domini apud Dansk, xviij die   September 18.
10 mensis Septembris, receptis denariis de Hugoni Herlee, xvij scot. Et pro batellagio senescalli, Hugonis Herlee et aliorum de naui vsque Dansk, vj s. pr. CUIDAM carmon pro j carceta ab ipso conducta de Dansk vsque Conyngburgh et redeunda, per conuencionem factam, j marc. di. pr. Thome Goter pro vadiis suis
15 extra curiam misso de Dansk vsque Conyngburgh, pro herburgagio per viam et ibidem, per x dies, eundo, morando et redeundo, per compotum secum factum, capienti per diem xij d. st, x s. st. JOHANNI Wyndesor pro vadiis suis extra curiam existenti apud Lynne pro prouidenciis ibidem faciendis, eundo, morando et redeundo
20 per xj dies, capienti per diem iiij d. st., iij s. viij d. st. Johanni Blacdon pro vadiis suis extra curiam existenti apud Conyngburgh pro officio suo ibidem ordinando, eundo, morando et redeundo, per viij dies, capienti per diem vj d., iiij s. st. Johanni Blacdon pro diuersis victualibus per ipsum emptis apud Conyngburgh
25 pur le prame versus Dansk, viz., in pane, beer, carne, piscibus per ipsum emptis ibidem pro diuersis hominibus existentibus in le prame, xxij scot. iiij s. viij d. pr. CLERICO marescalcie per manus Johanni Gybson pro feno ab ipso empto apud Dansk, xx die   September 20. Septembris, xx scot. Et Galfrido Newton pro feno ab ipso
30 empto ibidem eodem die, ij marcz. viij s. st. Et per manus eiusdem, pro lxxv bz. auenarum, bz. ad. iij s. pr., iij marc. xviij scot. Et per manus Thome Ferour pro emendacione et reparacione diuersarum sellarum domini ibidem, vna cum iij horscombes, j marc. vij s. pr. CLERICO panetrie per manus Roberti Jonson, pro

176   THE EARL OF DERBY'S EXPEDITIONS.

piris, pomis, nucibus, et aliis fructubus per ipsum emptis ibidem eodem die., xv scot. iij s. vj d. pr.   SUPER officio aule et camere per manus Johannis Selby pro locione mapparum ibidem eodem die, per compotum secum factum ibidem, xij scot.   CLERICO marescalcie per manus Thome Ostelcer pro expensis ij equorum 5 Johannis Bauen ibidem, per compotum secum factum eodem die, xj scot. xij d. pr.   Johanni Payne pro vno pari batell de steell per ipsum empto ibidem, xij scot.   CLERICO buterie super vino per manus Johannis Payne pro vino per ipsum empto ibidem eodem die, xlij marcz. pr.   Et per manus eiusdem super beer, 10 pro xxiij barellis de beer ad diuersa precia emptis ibidem eodem die, ix marcz xiiij scot.   Clerico buterie super beer per manus Gylder, pro j barello de beer, pro portagio et tractagio beer et vini, vna cum emendacione / vnius selle del cuphous ibidem eodem die, ij marc. xix scot. x d. pr.   CLERICO pinetrie per manus Payn pro pane albo per ipsum 15 empto ibidem eodem die per compotum secum factum, xj marcz, x s. pr.   Et per manus Fyscher pro ij qrt. iij bz. flowr per ipsum emptis ibidem eodem die, iiij marcz. xviij scot.   DOMINO Willelmo Pomfreit pro batillagio senescalli et aliorum de Dansk vsque le Movnt ad remeandam nauem domini, iiij s pr.   Et eidem pro ex- 20 pensis camerarii, senescalli, et famulorum domini de Melwyn vsque Dansk et ibidem per viij dies, per compotum secum factum, omnibus computatis, vt patet per parcellam, xxxvj marcz. di, v scot. x d. pr. CLERICO marescalcie per manus Johannis Wilbram pro cariagio auenarum de naui vsque Dansk per compotum cum ipso factum 25 ibidem, xxj° die Septembris, viij scot.   Clerico marescalcie per manus Thome Ferour pro ferrura equorum ibidem domini apud Dansk, per compotum secum factum xxj die mensis Septembris, eodem die, j marc. ix s. pr.   Bernardo et Henrico Tylman henksmen domini pro sotularibus per ipsos emptis ibidem eodem die, 30 ix s. pr.   SUPER officio scutellarie per manus Laurencii Trauers pro iij laste barellis vidz * pro aqua imponenda pro naui, j marc.

Summa pagine Cij marc. vj scot. ij s. pr fo. 11.

September 21

* Vidz, empty; perhaps an error for voidez.

di. pr. Et pro busca empta ibidem pro naui, j marc. xxij scot. Et pro carbonibus empto ibidem, iij marcz xxij scot. pr. CLERICO marescalcie per manus Godfrey Newton pro feno ab ipso empto ibidem, x scot. iiij s. pr. Et pro ij qrt. ij bz. auenarum emptis 5 ibidem eodem die, j marc. pr. DUOBUS hominibus pro j prame ab ipsis conducta de naui vsque Dansk cum equis et aliis harnesiis garderobe domini, per conuencionem cum ipsis factam iij marcz di. pr. Thome Ferour pro factura vnius pontis pro equis domini superambulandis ibidem eodem die, viij scot. SUPER officio salsarie per 10 manus Laurencii Trauers pro ij bz. iij peccis flowre per ipsum emptis ibidem eodem die, j marc. pr. SUPER officio marescalcie per manus Thome Ferour pro j countresengle per ipsum empto pro sella domini ibidem, v s. pr. JOHANNI Dyndon pro j cista per ipsum empta ibidem pro garderoba domini, xv scot. SUPER officio 15 salsarie per manus Laurencii Trauers pro cenape, venegre, vergus per ipsum emptis ibidem eodem die, j marc. xiiij scot. CLERICO marescalcie per manus Whitlok pro ferrura equorum domini ibidem, iiij s. pr. CLERICO speciarie per manus Johannis del chaundrye pro C lb. candelarum cepi per ipsum emptis ibidem eodem die, lb 20 ad xij d. pr., j marc. xvj scot. JOHANNI Peck pro j mantica pro capella[a] per ipsum empta ibidem, xij s. pr. SUPER officio scutellarie, per manus Johannis Tynker pro emendacione j olle ence ibidem, viij scot. CLERICO speciarie per manus Johannis del chaundrye pro iiij lb. cere per ipsum emptis ibidem, xij s pr. Johanni Yonge pro 25 j dowblet per ipsum empto ibidem pro semetipso, et aliis necessariis, j marc. pr. SUPER officio salsarie per manus Laurencii Trauers pro venegre per ipsum empt' ibidem, j marc. xvj scot. DIUERSIS hominibus pro diuersis harnesiis per ipsos emptis pro ij carectis domini, ij marc. xiij scot. viij d. pr. Johanni Dyndon pro diuersis 30 carpentariis per ipsum conductis, vna cum emptione pyche, tarre, hempe pro factura j cabane pro garderoba domini in naui, j marc.

---

[a] MS. capell', it might be either *capella* or *capellano*. In l. 6, p. 178, the same contracted word evidently means *capella*.

xviij scot. Johanni Dyndon pro iij gounis per ipsum emptis pro domino, camerario et senescallo ibidem, iij marc. iiij scot. di. SUPER officio scutellarie per manus Laurencii Trauers pro busca et carbonibus per ipsum emptis ibidem, ij marcz vj scot. Hugoni Herle pro batellagio apud Dansk, vj s. pr. CUIDAM peyntour pro ij tabulis ab ipso emptis pro capella domini ibidem, iiij marc. di. pr. CLERICO buterie super beer, pro iij barellis beer per ipsum emptis ibidem, xxx scot. Graunsom bastard pro j tabler per ipsum empt' ibidem pro domino, xij scot. JOHANNI Dounton pro batellagio harnesiorum domini de naui vsque terram, vna cum busca, carbonibus per ipsum emptis ibidem, ij marcz pr. Et per manus Thome Goter pro batellagio senescalli et aliorum de Dansk vsque nauem, xij scot. Willelmo Pomfreit pro batellagio sui et aliorum ibidem, xvj s. pr. Et per manus eiusdem pro beer per ipsum empta ibidem propter famulos domini ibidem, xviij s. Duobus carectariis pro ij saccis per ipsos emptis ibidem, vj s. pr. SUPER officio scutellarie per manus Trauers pro busca et carbonibus per ipsum emptis ibidem, ix scot. CLERICO buterie super le beer per manus Swan, pro ij C xl bykeres et pro j barello pro discis imponendis, xvij scot. Et per manus eiusdem pro spongyng j laste barello vna cum batellagio sui et aliorum diuersorum, xxij s. pr. JOHANNI Syde pro locione pannorum lineorum domini ibidem eodem die, iiij s. pr. CLERICO buterie super beer pro cariagio beer, bikeres, fructubus et locione pannorum del buterie per compotum secum factum, viij scot. ij s. pr. SUPER officio scutellarie, per manus Johannis / Beuer pro discis ligneis per ipsum emptis apud Melwyn, x scot. Eidem pro cariagio de ij tables de Conyngburgh vsque Dansk, vj scot. JOHANNI Dyndon pro batellagio et cariagio harnesiorum garderobe domini de naui vsque Dansk, xvj scot. Eidem pro emendacione diuersorum furrours domini ibidem, eo quod deteriorata fuerunt in naui, vj nobles. SUPER officio scutellarie per manus Newton pro carbonibus et busca, j marc. pr. JOHANNI Payne pro j barhide per ipsum empt' ibidem pro j carro,[a] ij marcz, pr.

Summa pagine iiij^{xx} xix marc. viij scot. vij. di. pr.
fo. 11 v^m.

5

10

15

20

25

30

* The MS. word is carr', in the second case (p. 179, l. 5) carr' eq.

Clerico marescalcie per manus Johannis Beuere pro expensis
j equo domini existentis apud Dansk, per xviij dies, per compotum
secum factum ibidem, xij scot. Clerico coquine per manus
Harpeden pro j homine conducto et operante in officio coquine, per
5 compotum factum, xij scot. Johanni Beuer pro j carrecta* equo per
ipsum empto ibidem. v scot, ij d. pr. Cuidam lotrici pro locione
del couertowres ibidem, v s. pr. Clerico pantrie per manus
Fyscher pro iij bz. flowr emptis ibidem per ipsum, xviij scot. Et
pro conductione vnius furni ibidem, eodem die, xvj s. pr. Johanni
10 Dauy pro cotone per ipsum empta ibidem eodem die, xj s. pr.
Clerico pantrie per manus Fyscher pro furnagio per ipsum empto
ibidem eodem die, x s. pr. Et pro furnagio empto ibidem pro
naui, xvj s. pr. Et pro pane albo empto ibidem, xxiij die Septembris, ij marc pr. Clerico butrie super vino per manus
15 Johannis Payne pro vino per ipsum empto ibidem eodem die,
xxj marc. pr. Et pro j barello de beer, x scot. Et pro portagio
vini et beer ibidem, x s. pr. Clerico speciarie per manus
Triplord pro j lb. croci empta ibidem eodem die, j marc. pr.
Clerico butrie super vino per manus eiusdem pro vino per ipsum
20 empto ibidem eodem die, iiij marc. pr. Super officio aule et
camere per manus Selby pro locione mapparum ibidem eodem die,
v s. pr. Super officio scutellarie per manus Johannis Kepe pro
busca et carbonibus ab ipso emptis ibidem, lj s. pr. Clerico
marescalcie per manus Thome Ferrowr ibidem eodem die, x s. pr.*
25 Clerico coquine per manus Johannis Beuere pro diuersis victualibus per ipsum emptis ibidem primo die aduentus domini super
terram, viij marc. pr. Johanni Beuere pro ij carectis per ipsum
conductis de Dansk vsque Conyngburgh et redeundis, vj marc. pr.
Super officio scutellarie per manus Laurencii Trauers pro emenda-
30 cione vnius cofre de scutellaria, per compotum factum, viij s. pr.
Et domino Ottoni Graunsom pro scriptura et sigillacione vnius
saueconducti Ducis de Stulpez, ij marez. xviij scot. Johanni
Dyndon pro j camera per eum conducta pro rebus domini
custodiendis apud Dansk post recessum domini ibidem, per xj dies,

180   THE EARL OF DERBY'S EXPEDITIONS.

et pro rebus ablatis ibidem eodem tempore, xxx scot. Item eidem
pro portagio et batillagio dicte garderobe versus nauem, xij scot.
Item pro vadiis dicti Johannis extra curiam per dictos xj dies, v s.
vj d. st. Item pro tabulis, pyche, clauis et lyno pro kalfact' in
predicta naue pro garderoba et armaria, ix scot. et. di. Item in 5
Anglia, pro vadiis suis pro iij diebus inter Hulle et Peterburgh,
xviij d. Item ij waynemen de Haylesbergh cuntibus cum domino
versus Sconce cum ij carectis, iiij marcz. pr. Duobus waynemen
de Dansk pro eodem viagio, iiij marcz. pr. Cuidam waynesman
de Dansk in eodem viagio, ij marcz pr. JOHANNI Dounton pro 10
mundacione harnesiorum domini apud Dansk post recessum domini,
viij s. st. Item in ij sellis emptis pro dictis carectis per manus
thesaurarii ibidem, xij s. st. Et per manus eiusdem vxori Godes-
September 10.   knayth x die mensis Septembris pro j pecia panni linei, v marc. pr.
Et per manus eiusdem pro^a trays, capistris et aliis diuersis 15
harnesiis, vna cum cepo pro dictis carectis, xxvj scot. Item pro
j curro conducto de Schynelben vsque Prake cum iiij equis per
senescallum et thesaurarium de Hanz Fycele, xvj noble. Item pro
xv vlnis de fustyan, pris le vlna iiij s. pr., j marc pr. Item par
viij vlnis drape lynge, pris le vlna iij s. iiij d., xxvj s. viij d. Item 20
pur vj lb. du* coton, pris le lb. vj s. iiij d., xxxviij s. pr. Item pur
* Sic.   ille, ij s. Item j lb. du* coton, pris vj s. iiij d. CLERICO panetrie
per manus Roberti Jonson pro pane albo per ipsum empto apud
Dansk post recessum domini, xiij s. pr. CLERICO coquine per manus
Johannis Wynaesouere pro xij bremes, xij s. pr., et C. allecum 25
recentium, ij scot.; pro j schok roches, ij scot.; et pro vj sertes, ij scot ,
per ipsum emptis ibidem, in toto x scot. ij s. pr. SUPER officio
scutellarie, per manus Henrici Brerley pro ij laste v barellis carbonum
Summa pagine Cij   per ipsum emptis ibidem, xxiiij scot. v d. pr. CLERICO speciarie
marc. pr.
fo. 12.   / per manus Whytlok pro vij lb. candelarum cepi per ipsum emptis 30
ibidem, vij s. pr. Et per manus eiusdem pro locione mapparum
domini, vj s. pr. CLERICO coquine per manus Johannis Wyn-

* The MS. has per.

II. EXPENSES IN PRUSSIA.

desore pro allecibus recentibus, playces, et aliis piscibus recentibus per ipsum emptis per j diem, x scot. xv d. Et per manus eiusdem pro diuersis piscibus recentibus per ipsum emptis, xxiiij s. pr. Et per manus ejusdem pro j carcoisio bouino, xx scot. Et per manus
5 eiusdem pro iiij carcoisiis multonum, xiiij scot. Et per manus eiusdem pro j carcoisio multonis, vj scot. CLERICO buterie super seruicia per manus Payn pro j laste de bona beer, v nobl. engl. xij scot. SUPER officio pulletrie per manus Geffr. pro j barello pisarum albarum per ipsum empto, x scot. Et per manus eiusdem
10 pro j schoful farine auenarum, v scot. Et per manus eiusdem pro j schofull cepi, iiij s. pr. CLERICO buterie super seruicia per manus Blaedon pro beer per ipsum empta apud le Mownt, ij scot. SUPER officio scutellarie per manus Henrici Brerlay pro j carecta focalis vocati aschelers per ipsum empta, iiij scot. Et pro batil-
15 lagio diuersorum victualium domini una cum batillagio mei,[a] ipsius, et aliorum officiariorum domini per diuersas vices, j marc. di. viij scor. vj d. CLERICO coquine per manus Johannis Wyndesouere pro di. carcoisii bouini et ij carcoisiis multonum, xviij scot. SUPER officio pulletrie per manus Geffr. pro iij duodenis pullettorum per
20 ipsum emptis, xiiij scot. ij s. Cuidam homini de la Mount pro j armilausa ab ipso furata in hospicio ubi familia[b] domini fuit hospicata, vj scot. CLERICO buterie super seruicia per manus Johannis Waterdene pro j laste di. de beer ab ipso emptis, iij marc. di. pr. SUPER officio scutellarie per manus Henrici Brerley pro diuersis
25 herbis emptis ibidem et pro stauro pro naui, iiij scot. ij s. CLERICO panterie per manus Johannis Swan apud Lecheco exeundo pro pane albo per ipsum empto ibidem, x s. vj d. pr. CLERICO buterie super seruicia per manus ejusdem pro j barello de beer, di. marc. pr. Clerico panterie per manus Swan apud Lecheco pro pane

---

[a] *i. e.* of the treasurer himself.
[b] The contracted word in the MS. is written famul' here and in a few other cases in Part II., which I render *familia* or *familie*, following the use of the word (spelt in the usual manner) in Part I., and required in this instance by the words "fuit hospicata" which are written in full.

albo, xij s. pr. Clerico buterie per manus eiusdem pro j barello di. de beer, xxij scot. CLERICO speciarie per manus Johannis Selby pro j lb. candelarum cepi, xij d. pr. Et pro batillagio equorum partis famulorum domini ad diuersa loca inter Melwyn et Dansk. j marc. xiiij scot. SUPER officio scutellarie per manus Henrici 5 Brerley, pro ij laste carbonum per ipsum emptis apud Dansk, redeundo de Melwyn cum parte familie domini, xvj scot. CLERICO speciarie per manus Willelmi Poumfret, pro di. lb. gingibri, v scot.; di. lb. piperis, ij scot.; di. qrt. croci, iiij scot. xv d.; iij lb. amigdalarum, vj s.; ij lb. dattilorum iiij s.,—in toto xv scot. xv. d. pr. 10 CLERICO coquine per manus Wyndesouere pro ij bobus, ij marc. xvij scot.; pro vj carcoisiis multonum, j marc. xx scot.; pro j porco et di., di. marc. j scot.; et per ij vitulis, xiiij scot.,— v. marez. di. iij scot. Et per manus eiusdem pro j storion recente, ij marc. pr. Et per manus eiusdem pro j salmone recente, ix scot. 15 Et per manus eiusdem pro aliis piscibus, viz., sardis, roches et codlynges, xx scot. Et per manus eiusdem pro xlij bremes, xiiij scot. Et pro j samone recente, ix scot. Et per manus eiusdem pro aliis diuersis piscibus recentibus per ipsum emptis viz. sardis, anguillis, roches et codlynges, xij scot. ij s. pr. Et per manus eiusdem pro 20 iij schok allecum, precium, v scot. Et pro iij anguillis grossis, ij scot. Et pro iiij schok rochez, v scot. Et pro xx sardez, vj scot. ij s. pr. Et di. samonis recentis, iiij scot. Et pro j trouhte, ij s. pr. Et pro j dolio salis, xij scot. xij d. pr. CLERICO speciarie per manus W. P.[a] pro j quartrono de clows, vj scot.; di. lb. piperis, ij 25 scot.; vj lb. sugre caffetin, lb. ad. ix scot., ij marez., vij scot.; di. lb. maces, vij scot.; vj lb. amigdalarum, v scot., iij marc. ij scot. Et per manus eiusdem pro j uncia et di. de sugre, iij s. pr. Et per manus Johannis Dalahow pro j lb. amigdalarum, ij scot. SUPER officio scutellarie per manus Henrici Breerley pro ij waynes 30 aschelers pro focali, vj scot. ij s. pr. CLERICO coquine per manus Wyndesouere pro xlij bremes, xiij scot. x d. pr. Et per manus

[a] i.e. William Pomfreit.

II. EXPENSES IN PRUSSIA. 183

eiusdem J. W. pro vj carcoisiis bouinis per ipsum emptis ad diuersa *Summa pagine.*
precia, v marcz. xiiij scot. Et per manus eiusdem pro xxx mul- *marc. di. ij scot*
tonibus ad diuersa precia, v marcz. iij scot. /CUIDAM currario *fo. 12 v°.*
ducenti currum cum vice domini de Dansk vsque Melbing, per
5 manus domini Hugonis Herle, xx s. pr. ITEM Johanni Peek pro
ij boket emptis apud Dansk pro elemosinis domini, v s. pr. ITEM
soluti Johanni Gray, pro cariagio ij tabularum pro capella domini
de Dansk vsque Boston, ix s. st.

10   CLERICO marescalcie per manus hospitis de Sconee pro feno ab *September 24*
ipso empto ibidem, xxiiij die Septembris, xvij s. pr. Et pro x bz.
auenarum ibidem, xij scot. CLERICO panterie per manus eiusdem
pro pane ab ipso empto ibidem, xij scot. CLERICO buterie super
beer, pro beer empta ibidem, xj scot. xij d. pr. CLERICO speciarie
15 per manus eiusdem pro iij lb. candelarum cepi, iij s. pr. CLERICIS
cantantibus coram domino ibidem, v s. pr. CLERICO speciarie per
manus Johannis del Chaundrye[b] pro ij lb. candelarum cepi ibidem,
ij s. pr. CLERICO marescalcie per manus hospitis apud Sconehow
pro x bz. auenarum ibidem eodem die, xij scot. Et pro feno empto
20 ibidem eodem die, viij s. pr. CLERICO panterie per manus eiusdem
pro pane albo per ipsum empto ibidem, iiij scot. CLERICO buterie
super beer, pro beer empta ibidem, xij scot. CLERICO speciarie
per manus Johannis del Chaundrye pro v [lb.] candelarum cepi
emptis ibidem, v s. pr. Et pro j gyde conducto per duos dies,
25 viij scot. SUPER officio pulletrie pro ij gallinis emptis, ij s. vj d.
pr. SUPER officio scutellarie pro busca diuersa empta ibidem, v s.
pr. CLERICO speciarie per manus Johannis Chaundrie pro * iij lb. *MS has per.*
candelarum cepi per ipsum emptis apud Conyngburgh, xxv die
mensis Septembris, iij s. pr. PRO expensis Cudworth et aliorum *September 25.*
30 precuntium per viam per iij dies, per compotum factum ibidem,
xij s. pr. Et pro locione mapparum ibidem, iiij s. pr. CLERICO

    * About a third of the page is left blank here, perhaps with the intention of
inserting some forgotten items.
    [b] This word generally appears as Chaundr' in the MS.

marescalcie per manus hospitis ibidem pro xj bz. di. auenarum
emptis ibidem, xiij scot. ij s. pr. Et pro feno empto ibidem, vj scot.
ij s. pr. CLERICO panterie per manus eiusdem pro pane albo empto
ibidem, xij scot. ij s. pr. CLERICO buterie super beer empta ibidem,
xvij scot. xij d. Et pro mede empto ibidem, iij s. pr. CLERICO
buterie super vino per manus eiusdem, pro vino empto ibidem,
xviij scot. iiij s. pr. CLERICO panterie per manus eiusdem pro
piris et pomis emptis ibidem, iij s. pr. HOSPITI ibidem pro j
lintheamine furato ibidem, j marc. pr. Et pro ferrura j equi
domini per viam, xvj d. pr. CLERICO marescalcie per manus
hospitis apud Hamestede pro feno empto ibidem, x s. pr. Et pro
x bz. di. auenarum emptis ibidem, xxvj die Septembris, xij scot.
CLERICO buterie super beer, pro beer empta ibidem, v s. pr.
CLERICO panterie per manus eiusdem pro pane albo empto,
viij scot. Et pro j barello beer empto ibidem, xiiij scot. Clerico
panterie per manus hospitis apud Polessine, xxvij° die Septembris,
xxiiij s. pr.

/Summa totalis monete de Prucia de Dansk vsque le Mark
vij^c xviij marc. x scot. xiij d. pr.

Qui faciunt in sterlinges   ccxxxix li. ix s. iiij d. st.

vnde memorandum quod xxiiij scot. faciunt j marc. pr.; et j marc.
pr. facit j noble st.; et ij s. vj d. faciunt j scot.; et lx s. pr. faciunt
j marc.

/ IN PARTIBUS DE LA* MARKE.ᵃ

IN LE* MARKE.

CLERICO buterie super beer empta apud Polyschene per manus
Payn, iiij marcz. iiij s. ff. CLERICO marescalcie per manus eiusdem

* The Mark here comprises that part of Brandenburg called the Neumark.

pro feno empto ibidem, xxviij d.; et pro x bz. auenarum, ij marc. di.
Et pro ij bz. di. auenarum, x s. ff.; et pro feno et litura, vj d. ff.
Super officio scutellarie per manus eiusdem pro busca et carbonibus, iiij s. ff. Super officio salserie per manus eiusdem pro venegre
5 empt' ibidem, viij d. ff. Clerico coquine per manus Harpedene
pro piscibus recentibus emptis ibidem, xij s. ff. Et pro bayting
domini et famulorum suorum apud Schenelbene eodem die, xij s. ff.
Et pro bayting ibidem eodem die, xiij s. ff. Clerico panterie
per manus hospitis apud Drawyngburgh, xxviij° die Septembris, September 28.
10 pro pane albo empto ibidem, j marc. ff. Clerico buterie super
beer, pro beer empta ibidem, ij marc. vj s. ff. Clerico speciarie
pro iij lb. candelarum cepi, iij s. ff. Clerico marescalcie per
manus eiusdem pro feno et litura emptis ibidem, j marc. ff. Et
pro x bz. di. auenarum emptis ibidem, ij marc. iii s. ff. Clerico
15 speciarie per manus Johannis de Chaundrye pro ij lb. candelarum cepi, ij s. ff. Item cuidam gyde de Drawyngburgh vsque
Arneswold, j marc. ff. Clerico speciarie per manus Johannis
de Chaundrye pro j lb. cere empta ibidem, iiij s. ff. Et pro ij lb.
candelarum cepi, ij s. viij d. ff. Cuidam gyde conducto per
20 iij dies, x s. st. Clerico speciarie per manus Johannis Chaundrye pro viij lb. candelarum cepi per ipsum [emptis] apud Arneswold,
viij s. ff. Item pro emendacione ij carectarum apud Arneswold,
per manus eorundem*, j marc. xvj d. ff. Super officio salsarie per ✱ Sic.
manus Laurencii Trauers pro cenape, vergus, venegre per ipsum
25 emptis ibidem, vj s. ff. Clerico marescalcie per manus Thome
Swylington pro emendacione j selle domini, ij s. viij d. ff. Et pro
ferrura j equi ibidem, xvj d. ff. Clerico buterie super beer, pro
beer empta ibidem vltimo die Septembris, v. marc. ff. Clerico September 30.
panterie per manus Payn pro pane albo per ipsum empto ibidem,
30 ij marc. x s. ff. Clerico buterie super vino per manus eiusdem,
pro vino per ipsum empto ibidem eodem die, v. marcz. vij s. vj d. ff.
Clerico marescalcie per manus Gylder pro emendacione j selle
del cuphous ibidem, xxij d. ff. Clerico marescalcie per manus
Thome Ferour pro ij quarteriis auenarum emptis, iiij marcz. ff.,

Et pro litura, iiij s. ff., et pro feno, ix s. iiij d. ff. CLERICO buterie super vino per manus eiusdem, pro vino empto ibidem, j marcz, iiij s. x d. ff. CLERICO panterie per manus Payne pro pane albo per ipsum empto apud Londesburgh j° die Octobris, j marc. viij s. ff. CLERICO buterie super beer, pro beer empta ibidem, ij marcz. x s. viij d. ff. CLERICO marescalcie per manus Willram 5 pro feno per ipsum empto ibidem eodem die, vj s. viij d. ff. Et pro x bz. di. auenarum emptis ibidem, j marc. xv s. vj d. ff. CLERICO speciarie per manus Johannis de Chaundrye pro v lb. candelarum cepi per ipsum emptis ibidem, v s. ff. Et pro litura empta ibidem, vj s. xj d. ff. Item pro ij gydes conductis per 10 ij dies, iiij s. st. Item vno alio gyde conducto per j diem, j marc. ff. CLERICO marescalcie per manus Goter pro expensis j equi domini ibidem, ij s. viij d. ff. Et pro feno et litura emptis apud Dresse ij° die Octobris, j marc. ff. CLERICO panterie per manus Payne pro pane albo per ipsum empto ibidem, j marc. v s. 15 iiij d. ff. Et pro xj bz. di. auenarum, ij marc. ff. CLERICO speciarie per manus Johannis del Chaundrye pro iij lb. candelarum cepi emptis ibidem, iij s. ff. Cuidam carmon pro tarr pro rotis carecte sue empto ibidem, ij marc. xj s. viij d. ff. CLERICO buterie super beer, pro beer per ipsum empta ibidem, ij marcz. ff. 20 CLERICO coquine per manus Goter pro sale albo ibidem empto, iiij s. ff. Et ibidem cuidam gyde conducto per j diem, vj s. f. Item cuidam capellano celebranti coram domino ibidem, xj s. f. CLERICO coquine per manus Mowbray herold, pro ij pikes per ipsum emptis ibidem, iij s. f. Cuidem guyde per ipsum conducto 25 ibidem, per j diem, xiij s. xiij d. f. Item eidem pro iij vergis panni albi pro sella domini per ipsum emptis ibidem, x s. Item eidem / pro ij gides per ipsum conductis per j diem, x s. viij d. f. CLERICO coquine per manus Yonge per ipsum empto ibidem eodem die, pro bacon pro j equo infirmo,* ij s. viij d. f. 30 CLERICO marescalcie per manus Thome Ferour pro ferrura equorum domini ibidem, eodem die, j marc. f. ij s. viij d.

Summa monete in le Mark vocate ff., lxij mare. iiij s. xj d. ff. Et sic, xvj s ff
Qui faciunt in sterlinges, cum xiiij s. st., vij lb. xxij d. st.
faciunt j mare.
et iij marez. ll
faciunt j noble
sterling.

FFRANKFORTH [on the Oder]. Ffrankforth.

CLERICO buterie super vino per manus Payn pro vino per ipsum
5 empto apud Frankforde, viij noble xiij gr. Clerico buterie super
beer, pro beer per ipsum empto ibidem, iiij die Octobris, xxvj gr. October 4.
CLERICO panetrie per manus eiusdem pro pane albo per ipsum
empto ibidem eodem die, xl gr. CLERICO buterie super beer,
pro portagio beer ibidem eodem die, v gr. CLERICO marescalcie
10 per manus Johannis Wilbram pro feno per ipsum empto ibidem
eodem die, xxj gr. Et pro ij qrt. vj bz. auenarum ibidem eodem
die, lxiij gr. Item pro locione diuersorum harnesiorum domini
ibidem, vij d. bem. SUPER officio scutellarie per manus Laurencii
Trauers pro busca et herbis per ipsum emptis ibidem eodem die,
15 xviij gr. Cuidam carrectario pro emendacione j carecte ibidem
eodem die, vj gr. CLERICO speciarie per manus Johannis del
Chaundrye, pro iij lb. candelarum cepi emptis eodem die, iij gr.
Item pro j gyde per j diem, viij gr. CLERICO panetrie per manus
Payn pro pane albo per ipsum empto apud Gobin, v⁰ die mensis October 5.
20 Octobris, xxvj gr. CLERICO buterie super vino per manus eiusdem
pro vino empto ibidem, xl gr. Clerico buterie super beer pro beer
empta ibidem, xxiiij gr. CLERICO marescalcie per manus Wilbram
pro feno et litura emptis ibidem, x gr. Et pro x bz. auenarum
emptis ibidem eodem die, xxxvij gr. Thome Goter pro j corrio* pro * The MS. has
25 factura j bag pro ciphis argenteis cariandis per viam, vij gr.
CLERICO buterie super vino per manus Payn, pro vino per ipsum
empto ibidem, xxvij gr. CLERICO speciarie per manus Goter, pro
ij lb. candelarum cepi emptis ibidem, ij gr. Item j gyde conducto
per j diem, viij gr. CLERICO panetrie per manus thesaurarii pro
30 nucibus et aliis fructubus per ipsum emptis ibidem eodem die, iiij gr.

188   THE EARL OF DERBY'S EXPEDITIONS.

October 6.

CLERICO marescalcie per manus Thome Ferour, pro ferruris equorum domini ibidem et aliis locis per diuersas vices, viij gr. CLERICO speciarie per manus Johannis del Chaundrye, pro ij lb. candelarum cepi per ipsum emptis apud Treboll vj° die Octobris, ij gr. CLERICO panetrie per manus Payn pro pane albo per ipsum empto ibidem die, xviij gr. CLERICO buterie super beer per manus ejusdem, pro beer empta ibidem, lxxij gr. CLERICO marescalcie per manus Wilbram pro feno et litura per ipsum emptis ibidem, xiiij gr. Et pro vj bz. auenarum emptis ibidem eodem die, xxv gr. Et per manus Payn pro iij bz. auenarum per ipsum [emptis] apud Ornesbold, xiij gr. di. CLERICO speciarie per manus Wilbram pro puluere piperis per ipsum empto apud Gorlech, vij° die Octobris, ij gr. 5

10

October 7.
xx grossi faciunt j florenum et vj d. faciunt j grossum.

Summa pagine, viij noble st. Item, vCxliij gr. iiij d. boem.

fo. 15.

IN PARTIBUS BOEMIE.   15

October 7.

Clerico panetrie per * manus Payn pro pane albo per ipsum empto ibidem, xviij gr. Item pro emendacione rote unius curri domini, iiij gr. Item pro ij gides conductis per j diem, xx gr. CLERICO buterie super vino per manus eiusdem pro vino empto ibidem, ix^{xx}viij gr. di. Clerico buterie super beer per ipsum empta ibidem, xlviij gr. Clerico buterie super vino per manus eiusdem, pro vino per ipsum empto ibidem, x gr. CLERICO marescalcie per manus Wilbram pro feno et litura per ipsum emptis ibidem, xj gr. Et pro vij bz. auenarum per ipsum emptis ibidem, xxxv gr. CLERICO speciarie per manus Wilbram pro peperi, gingibre per ipsum emptis apud Zitaw, vij° die Octobris, iiij gr. Clerico buterie super vino per manus Payn, pro vino per ipsum empto 20

25

---

* In the MS these three words are on the preceding leaf, the items running on from " Frankforth " to " in partibus Boemie," as the same money was in use throughout. This latter title continues to the end of fo. 16 ; see p. 194.

ibidem eodem die, iiij^xxj gr. CLERICO coquine per manus
Johannis Cudworth pro j boket pro diuersis victualibus inde custodiendis per viam, v gr. CLERICO speciarie per manus Goter pro
ij lb. candelarum cepi per ipsum emptis ibidem, iij gr. Item pro
5 ij gides conductis de Trebull vsque Gorlech, xxviij gr. CLERICO
coquine per manus senescalli pro iij leporaī* per ipsum emptis   *This must be
ibidem, v gr. CLERICO marescalcie per manus Clyderow pro ferruris error for lepori leporibus.
equorum ibidem, vj gr. CLERICO panetrie per manus Payn pro
pane albo per ipsum empto apud Zitaw, ix° die Octobris, xlv gr. October 9.
10 CLERICO buterie super vino, per manus eiusdem pro vino per
ipsum empto ibidem eodem die, vj^{xx} gr. Clerico buterie super
beer, per manus eiusdem pro iij barellis beer per ipsum emptis
ibidem, liiij gr. CLERICO marescalcie per manus Wilbram pro feno
et litura per ipsum emptis ibidem, xxviij gr. Et pro xiiij bz. di.
15 auenarum emptis ibidem eodem die, lxxij gr. iij d. bem. CLERICO
buterie super beer pro beer empta in hospicio domini ibidem, viij gr.
Clerico buterie super vino per manus Payn pro vino per ipsum
empto apud Nemance, x° die Octobris, cxij gr. CLERICO panterie October 10.
per manus eiusdem pro pane albo per ipsum empto ibidem, xviij gr.
20 iij d. bem. CLERICO buterie super beer per manus eiusdem, pro
beer per ipsum empta ibidem, xxxix gr. Et pro ij ollis luteis,
ij gr. CLERICO speciarie per manus Selby pro locione mapparum,
iij gr. Et pro iiij lb. candelarum cepi emptis ibidem, vij gr. Item
pro ij gides conductis per j diem, per manus Erpingham apud
25 Scheuelbene, j noble. CLERICO marescalcie per manus Wilbram
pro feno et litura per ipsum emptis ibidem, xiiij gr. Et pro
viij bz. auenarum emptis ibidem, bz. ad iiij gr., xxxij gr. Et pro j
gyde conducto ibidem, x gr. CLERICO buterie super vino per manus
Payn, pro vino per ipsum empto ibidem, viij gr. Item cuidam
30 carmon pro saguine per ipsum empto ibidem pro carecta sua, vj gr.
Clerico buterie super beer, pro beer per ipsum empta ibidem die
sequente, viij gr. CLERICO panetrie per manus Payn pro pane
albo per ipsum empto apud Whytwater, xi° die Octobris, xvij gr. October 11.
CLERICO buterie super beer per manus eiusdem, pro beer per

ipsum empto ibidem eodem die, xviij gr. Clerico buterie super vino per manus eiusdem, pro vino per ipsum empto ibidem die, lx gr. Et per manus eiusdem pro vino empto ibidem, eodem die, xvj gr. CLERICO marescalcie per manus Wilbram pro litura per ipsum empta ibidem, vj gr. Et pro feno empto ibidem, ix gr. iij d. 5 Et pro vj bz. auenarum emptis ibidem, xxiiij gr. CLERICO panetrie per manus Payn pro pane albo per ipsum empto apud Brounslowe, *October 12.* xij^o die Octobris, ix gr. CLERICO buterie super vino per manus eiusdem, pro vino per ipsum empto ibidem eodem die, clx gr. Clerico buterie super beer, pro beer per ipsum empto ibidem eodem die, 10 lxij gr. CLERICO marescalcie per manus Wilbram pro feno et *Sic.* litura per ipsum emptis ibidem, x gr. Et pro vj bz. p^c *auenarum emptis ibidem, xxv gr. CLERICO speciarie per manus Goter pro cera per ipsum empta ibidem, ix gr. CLERICO buterie super beer, pro beer per ipsum empta ibidem, xix gr. Item pro beer empta 15 ibidem, viij gr. CLERICO panetrie per manus Payn pro pane albo Summa pagine, m^l per ipsum empto ibidem, viij gr. Item pro ij vitris, ij gr. v^c xxvj grossi. CLERICO speciarie per manus eiusdem, pro ij lb. candelarum cepi Item, j noble sterling. fo. 15 v°. / emptis ibidem, ij gr. CLERICO marescalcie per manus Roberti Hethcote, pro expensis iiij equorum valettorum camere domini per 20 †The MS. has Math us. ij noctes et ij dies, xv gr. Matheo † Casson pro j curro* ab ipso con- *Sic. ducto cum iiij equis de Scheuelbene vsque Prake, xvj noble. Et eidem pro j curro conducto de Dansk vsque Scheuelbene cum iiij equis, v nobl. Item cuidam gyde conducto apud Gorlech, xix gr. SUPER officio salsarie per manus Trauers pro cenape, vergws, 25 vinegre, et crabbes emptis ibidem, vj gr. LANCASTER Herald pro diuersis armis domini pictis ad diuersos locos, xxij gr. CLERICO panetrie per manus diuersorum pro pane albo et fructubus *October 13—21.* ab ipso emptis apud Prake a xiij^o die Octobris vsque xxiiij diem eiusdem mensis, vtroque computato, vj^c xxxix gr. CLERICO 30 buterie super vino, per manus Payn pro vino empto ibidem per idem tempus, ij^mxxiiij gr. Clerico buterie super beer per manus eiusdem, pro beer per ipsum empta per idem

tempus, vij^c gr. CLERICO speciarie per manus diuersorum pro
peperi, gingibre, canella, sugre, amigdalis confectis, cera, candelis cepi, papiro, et pro locione mapparum ab ipsis emptis
ibidem, per idem tempus, vj^c lxxj gr. CLERICO coquine per manus
5 diuersorum pro carne bouum, multonum, et vitulorum, porcis et
salsis ab ipsis emptis ibidem pro thesaurario et parte familie domini
existentibus ibidem per iij dies, tempore quo dominus fuit apud
Bedeler cum Rege Bemie, iij^c gr. SUPER officio pulletrie per
manus diuersorum pro aucis, caponibus, pullis, pulcinis, columbellis,
10 malardez, et farina auenarum, emptis ibidem per idem tempus, pro
thesaurario et parte familie domini, lxxxij gr. di. SUPER officio
scutellarie per manus diuersorum pro busca et carbonibus ab ipsis
emptis ibidem, a xiij^o die Octobris vsque xxiiij diem ciusdem
mensis, vtroque computato, iij^c gr. ij d. ITEM pro diuersis carectis
15 conductis per diuersas vices, pro diuersis victualibus cariandis de
Prake vsque Bedeler, lxvj gr. SUPER officio salsarie per manus
diuersorum pro vergus, vinegre, senape, et aliis diuersis salsis
emptis ibidem per idem tempus, ij^c xxxiii gr. CLERICO marescalcie
per manus diuersorum pro feno et litura ab ipsis emptis ibidem,
20 per idem tempus, cij gr. Et pro xiiij quarteriis j bz. di. auenarum
ab ipsis emptis ibidem per idem tempus ad diuersa precia, ij^c liiij gr.
Et pro ferrura equorum ibidem per idem tempus, lxj gr. Et pro
emendacione diuersarum sellarum domini ibidem, lxxiiij gr. Et
pro expensis iiij equorum j carri conducti de Dansk vsque Prake
25 existentium ibidem per iij noctes, xlvj gr. Cuidam homini de Prake
pro j curru ab ipso conducto de Prake vsque Preda, xxvj gr.
CLERICO marescalcie per manus Wilbram pro feno et litura per
ipsum emptis ibidem, xviij gr. Et pro vj bz. di. auenarum, xxvj
gr. CLERICO panetrie per manus Payn pro pane albo empto
30 ibidem, x gr. CLERICO buterie super beer, pro beer empta ibidem,
xxxij gr. Clerico buterie super vino per manus eiusdem, pro vino
per ipsum empto ibidem, lxiij gr. iiij d. Et pro j barello vacante
pro vino imponendo, ij gr. CLERICO panetrie per manus Payn pro

192

pane albo empto ibidem, vij gr. CLERICO buterie super vino per manus eiusdem pro vino empto ibidem, xxvi gr. di. Clerico buterie super beer, pro beer empta ibidem, xxiij gr. CLERICO marescalcie per manus Wilbram pro feno et litura per ipsum emptis ibidem, xx gr. Et pro vij bz. auenarum, xxviij gr. CLERICO 5 speciarie per manus Johannis de Chaundrye pro iij lb. candelarum cepi, xij gr. SUPER officio scutellarie per manus Trauers pro carbonibus et busca emptis ibidem eodem die, xv gr. CLERICO panetrie per manus Payn pro pane albo per ipsum empto apud Chastelet, xxvj° die Octobris, viij gr. d. CLERICO buterie super beer, pro 10 beer empta ibidem eodem die, lviij gr. ITEM pro ij carectis conductis de Preda vsque Chastelet per conuencionem factam, xxvj gr. CLERICO marescalcie per manus Wilbram pro feno empto ibidem eodem die, vj gr. iiij d. b. Et pro litura, iiij gr. iiij d. Et pro viij bz. auenarum emptis ibidem, xxxij gr. Et pro expensis j 15 equi Wyncell per ij noctes, iiij gr. SUPER officio scutellarie per manus Trauers pro busca et carbonibus emptis ibidem eodem die, xv gr. Clerico marescalcie per manus Paule pro iij paribus trays emptis ibidem pro curru domini, iiij gr. CLERICO buterie super vino per manus Payn pro vino per ipsum empto 20 ibidem, xxiij gr. CLERICO panetrie per manus eiusdem pro pane albo per ipsum empto apud Deuchebrede xxvij die Octobris, xij gr. CLERICO buterie super vino per manus eiusdem, pro vino empto ibidem, vj gr. Clerico buterie super beer, / pro beer empta ibidem, xvj gr. CLERICO marescalcie per manus 25 Wilbram pro feno et litura, xviij gr. Et pro vij bz. di. auenarum, xxxvij gr. SUPER officio scutellarie pro busca et carbonibus emptis ibidem, xxiiij gr. Et pro vno lintheamine furato ibidem, viij. gr. Item pro j curru conducto ibidem eodem die, xviij gr. CLERICO panetrie per manus Payn pro pane albo per ipsum empto apud 30 Mederess', xxviij° die Octobris, xv gr. CLERICO buterie super vino per manus eiuslem pro vino empto ibidem, xvj gr. Clerico buterie super beer, pro beer per ipsum empta ibidem eodem die,

October 26.

October 27.
Summa pagine, xxi nobile st.
Item, vj^m cxxvj gr. ij d. boem.
fo. 16.

October 28.

xiiij gr. Item pro j gyde conducto per j diem, ij gr. CLERICO marescalcie per manus Thome Ferour pro butiro per ipsum empto ibidem pro j equo infirmo, iiij gr. Cuidam carrectario cum vno curru de Chastelet vsque Broune per ij dies cum iiij equis, lx gr.
5 Et pro feno et litura emptis ibidem, xiij gr. Et pro vij bz. auenarum emptis ibidem, xxviij gr. Et pro conductione j currus de ibidem vsque Broune per j diem, xxvi gr. CLERICO buterie super vino per manus Payn, pro vino empto ibidem, xvij gr. CLERICO coquine per manus eiusdem pro sale albo per ipsum empto ibidem,
10 vj gr. SUPER officio scutellarie per manus Trauers pro busca et carbonibus emptis ibidem, xxx gr. CLERICO marescalcie per manus Payn pro cariagio auenarum, feni, et litura ibidem, x gr. CLERICO speciarie per manus Johannis de Chaundrie pro vij ib. candelarum cepi emptis ibidem, vij gr. Et pro conductione ij equorum de
15 Gedding vsque Wiskirke per j diem, per conuencionem factam, vj gr. Et pro batillagio domini et partis familie sue ibidem, xxv gr. CLERICO marescalcie per manus Wilbram pro conductione ij equorum de Wiskirke vsque Drysing per j diem di, xviij gr. Et pro ferrura vna cum sagmine empto ibidem pro ij curribus, xvj gr.
20 Et pro feno empto apud Broune, iiij gr. Et pro litura empta ibidem, xxix° die Nouembris, xiiij gr. Item pro quodam gyde conducto per j diem, x gr. CLERICO panetrie per manus Payn pro pane albo per ipsum empto apud Drysing primo die Nouembris, viij gr. CLERICO buterie super vino per manus eiusdem, pro vino
25 per ipsum empto ibidem eodem die, ij schok gr. CLERICO marescalcie per manus Wilbram pro litura per ipsum empta apud Wiskyrke eodem die, xviij gr. Et pro feno per ipsum empto apud Drysing eodem die, vj gr. Et pro j quarterio vij bz. auenarum di.* emptis ibidem eodem die, xxxj gr. Et pro ferrura equorum ibidem
30 eodem die, xij gr. CLERICO buterie super vino per manus Payn, pro vino per ipsum empto ibidem eodem die, xlv gr. SUPER officio scutellarie per manus Trauers pro busca per ipsum empta ibidem eodem die, xx gr. CLERICO panetrie per manus Payn pro pane albo per ipsum empto apud Sconekirke iij° die Nouembris,

194   THE EARL OF DERBY'S EXPEDITIONS.

xxx gr. CLERICO buterie super vino per manus eiusdem, pro vino per ipsum empto ibidem, lj gr. Et per manus eiusdem pro j ostrich empto ibidem, xij gr. Item cuidam gyde conducto per j diem, viij gr. CLERICO marescalcie per manus Wilbram pro ij quarteriis di. bz. auenarum per ipsum emptis ibidem eodem die, xxxiij gr. Et pro feno et litura, xx gr. Et pro expensis j equi Winslowe per j noctem, iiij gr. Et pro litura, iij gr. Et pro ferrura equorum ibidem, xij gr. CLERICO buterie super vino per manus Gilder pro vino per ipsum empto ibidem, xv gr. SUPER officio scutellarie per manus Trauers pro busca empta ibidem, vij gr. Et pro viij ollis luteis emptis ibidem, viij gr. Item pro j curru conducto de Drysing vsque Wene per ij dies, per conuencionem factam ibidem, lvj gr. Et pro batillagio domini et harnesiorum suorum apud Wene vltra aquam de Donewe eodem die, iij flor.* CLERICO speciarie per manus Wilbram pro di. lb. canelle, et di. lb. gingibris per ipsum emptis ibidem eodem die, xx gr. CLERICO marescalcie per manus Thome Ferour pro ferrura equorum domini ibidem eodem die, xxxij gr. Clerico marescalcie per manus Roberti Litton pro expensis equi sui de Dansk vsque Prake per l dies, per compotum secum factum ibidem eodem die, lxiiij gr. CLERICO buterie super vino per manus eiusdem, pro vino per ipsum empto apud Chekirke per manus Gilder eodem die, xlvj gr. Roberto Duffeld pro j pare sotularum per ipsum empto ibidem, iiij gr. di. CLERICO marescalcie per manus Thome Ferour pro iiij capistris per ipsum emptis apud Wen iiij° die Nouembris, xij gr. Et pro iiij horscombes, v gr. CLERICO speciarie per manus Johannis de Chaundrie pro candelis per ipsum emptis ibidem eodem die, ix gr. Item pro j gyde conducto pro Harpeden per j diem de Whitwater vsque"

5
10
15
20
25

Summa totalis de Francford in partibus Boemie vsque huc ix^mccclxv grossi boemici,—qui faciunt in sterlynges lxxj l. viij s. ix d., cum iij florenis Hungaricis, precia ix s. x d. st.

30

* [Hungarian florins, see Summa.]

Incipit Wene.
November 4.
Summa pagine m^l clxvij grossi. iiij d. Bogm. Item iij floreni Hungarici.

* In the margin is the following explanation of the English value of the Bohemian money up to this page, "Vnde, xliiij gr. faciunt j noble vsque huc, tamen, et j gros. valet j d. ob. q^r. iiij^d pars q^r."

II. EXPENSES AT VIENNA. 195

/ HIC INCIPIT WENE IN OSTRICIA.ᵃ

Goby, vij gr. CLERICO buterie super vino per manus Payn, pro fo. 16 vº.
vino per ipsum empto ibidem eodem die, xviij gr. Item j gyde
conducto per j diem, viij gr. CLERICO panetrie per manus Payn
5 pro pane albo per ipsum empto ibidem, I gr. CLERICO buterie
super vino per manus eiusdem, pro vino per ipsum empto ibidem,
iij schok, xxxiv gr. Super officio aule et camere per manus Henrici
Maunsell, pro ij vitreis per ipsum emptis ibidem pro domino, vj gr.
Et pro xij crochets, iiij gr. Et pro j lb. cotonis empta ibidem pro
10 domino, ij gr. CLERICO speciarie per manus Wilbram pro xl lb.
cere per ipsum emptis ibidem, vjº die Nouembris, cxxix gr. Et pro November 6.
lumine per ipsum empto ibidem, viij gr. iij d. Item pro batillagio a
Henrico Maunsell vltra aquam iuxta mansionem Regis Hungarie,
ij gr. CLERICO marescalcie per manus Wilbram pro iiij saccis pro
15 auenis in eisdem capiendis pro diuersis equis domini, per ipsum
emptis ibidem eodem die, vij gr. Clerico buterie super beer, per
manus Payn pro xxx bikeres per ipsum emptis ibidem eodem die,
vij gr. Clerico marescalcie per manus j carrectarii pro emendacione
diuersorum necessariorum ibidem eodem die, xvj gr. CLERICO
20 panetrie per manus Gilder pro pane albo per ipsum empto apud
Wene, vijº die Nouembris, lxx gr. CLERICO buterie super vino
per manus eiusdem, pro viij barellis vini per ipsum emptis November 7.
ibidem, ciiijˣˣviij gr. Et pro locione pannorum panetrie et
buterie ibidem, viij gr. CLERICO panetrie per manus eiusdem,
25 pro j trenchurknyff per ipsum empto ibidem eodem die, xij gr.
CLERICO buterie super beer per manus eiusdem pro portagio
vini ibidem eodem die, iiij gr. ij d. Et pro ij doliis vacantibus pro
dicto vino imponendo per ipsum emptis ibidem, iiij gr. CLERICO
marescalcie per manus Wilbram pro feno per ipsum empto ibidem
30 eodem die, lv gr. Et pro litura, xl gr. Et pro iiijˣˣiij bz. auenarum per ipsum emptis ibidem eodem die, clxviij gr. Et per

ᵃ After this the running title of four folios is "In Ostricia" only.

manus Selby pro expensis equi sui ibidem eodem die, viij gr. ij d. SUPER officio aule et camere per manus eiusdem pro locione mapparum domini ibidem, xvj gr. Et pro emendacione vnius serure de j hampere pro peluibus argenteis imponendis, iiij gr. CLERICO speciarie per manus Johannis de chaundrie pro iiij lb. candelarum 5 cepi emptis ibidem, iiij gr. SUPER officio scutellarie per manus hospitis pro busca, carbonibus et ollis luteis ab ipso emptis ibidem die, x flor. Item pro ij capistris emptis ibidem eodem die, xiij gr. Super officio scutellarie per manus Laurencii Trauers pro herbis per ipsum emptis per viam ad diuersos locos, per compotum secum 10 factum ibidem eodem die, xxiiij gr. CLERICO marescalcie per manus Wilbram pro feno per ipsum empto apud Arskirke viij° die Nouembris, ix. gr. Et pro litura ibidem empta ibidem eodem die, xviij gr. Et pro xxij bz. auenarum emptis ibidem eodem die, xl gr. iij d. CLERICO panetrie per manus Gilder pro pane albo 15 per ipsum empto ibidem, v gr. CLERICO buterie super vino, per manus eiusdem pro vino per ipsum empto ibidem eodem die, xxj gr. Et pro busca empta ibidem eodem die, xij gr. CLERICO speciarie per manus Johannis de chaundrie, pro vij lb. candelarum cepi per ipsum emptis ibidem eodem die, vij gr. CLERICO 20 marescalcie per manus Aschby pro emendacione vnius freni et vnius selle apud Newekirke, ix° die Nouembris, ij gr. Et pro ferrura vnius equi ibidem eodem die, ij gr. SUPER officio scutellarie per manus Trauers pro carbonibus per ipsum emptis ibidem, xiiij gr. Et pro herbis, iij gr. iij d. CLERICO marescalcie per 25 manus Wilbram pro feno per ipsum empto ibidem, xj gr. Et pro litura, x gr. Et pro xvj bz. di. auenarum, xxxij gr. iij d. CLERICO panetrie per manus Gilder pro pane albo per ipsum empto ibidem, xix gr. ij d. CLERICO buterie super vino per manus eiusdem, pro vino per ipsum empto ibidem, liiij gr. ij d.[a] 30

/ Et pro busca empta ibidem, xij gr. Clerico buterie super vino

---

[a] Summa pagine, m^l cclx gr. ij d. Wene. At the bottom of the margin is this note : xxj grossi iiij d. faciunt j Florenum, et ij Floreni iiij grossi faciunt j noble.

II. EXPENSES IN AUSTRIA.

per manus Gilder, pro vino per ipsum empto ibidem ix° die *November 9.*
Novembris, xxx gr. CLERICO panterie per manus Gilder pro pane
albo per ipsum empto apud Mersolach x° die Nouembris, j flor. *November 10.*
CLERICO buterie super vino per manus eiusdem, pro vino per
ipsum empto ibidem eodem die, viij flor. iiij gr. ij d. CLERICO
marescalcie per manus Wilbram pro feno per ipsum empto ibidem
eodem die, ix gr. ij d. Et pro xviij bz. auenarum emptis ibidem
eodem die, ij flor. xj gr. SUPER officio scutellarie, per manus
Trauers pro busca empta ibidem eodem die, xij gr. SUPER officio
aule et camere, per manus Wilbram pro litura per ipsum empta
ibidem eodem die, vj gr. SUPER officio pulletrie pro butiro per
ipsum empto ibidem per manus Thome Ferour pro equis infirmis,
iiij gr. Clerico buterie super vino per manus Gilder, pro vino per
ipsum empto xj° die Nouembris, iij flor. CLERICO marescalcie per *November 11.*
manus Thesaurarii pro emendacione rotarum currus ibidem, x gr.
CLERICO panetrie per manus Gilder, pro pane albo per ipsum
empto apud Kimber eodem die, j flor. CLERICO buterie super vino,
per manus eiusdem pro vino per ipsum empto ibidem, iiij flor. xvj gr.
ij d. CLERICO marescalcie per manus Wilbram pro feno per ipsum
empto ibidem, x gr. iij d. Et pro litura empta ibidem, v gr. Et
pro xx bz. auenarum emptis ibidem, ij flor. vj gr. iiij d. SUPER
officio scutellarie per manus Trauers pro busca per ipsum empta
ibidem eodem die, viij gr. CLERICO speciar'e per manus Wilbram
pro ij lb. cere per ipsum emptis ibidem eodem die, xiiij gr. Et pro
cepo empto ibidem, iij gr. Et pro j galone vinegri empta ibidem
eodem die, iij gr. iij d. CLERICO marescalcie per manus Wilbram
pro xxix bz. auenarum per ipsum emptis apud Lowbon, xij° die *November 12.*
Nouembris, lxxij gr. iij d. Et pro feno empto ibidem, x gr. ij d.
Et pro litura empta, iiij gr. Et pro ferrura equi ibidem, iij gr.
CLERICO pantrie per manus Gilder pro pane albo per ipsum empto
ibidem, xviij gr. iij d. Et pro fructubus emptis ibidem, iiij gr.
CLERICO buterie super vino per manus eiusdem, pro vino per
ipsum empto ibidem, clxix gr. SUPER officio scutellarie per manus
Trauers pro busca empta, xiiij gr. Item pro conductione j currus per

j diem, vna cum emendacione ij curruum' per viam, lxiiij gr. iij d.
CLERICO marescalcie per manus Petri Fremon pro ferrura equorum
charecte ibidem eodem die, vij gr. Et pro expensis v equorum
scutiferorum conductorum per viam cum j curru, v gr. Et pro
expensis equi cuiusdam scutiferi per iiij noctes conducti per viam
pro domino, ij flor. v. gr. ij d. CLERICO buterie super vino per
manus Gilder, pro vino per ipsum empto ibidem, xiiij° die Nouembris, xliiij gr. ij d. CLERICO panetrie per manus Gilder, pro pane
albo per ipsum empto apud Knettesfeld, xiiij° die Nouembris, xliiij gr.
ij d. Clerico buterie per manus Gilder super vino, pro vino per
ipsum empto ibidem, vj flor. xiij. gr. ij d. CLERICO marescalcie
per manus Wilbram pro feno per ipsum empto ibidem, vij gr. Et
pro xxvij bz. auenarum, ij flor. x d. Et pro litura, vij gr. CLERICO
speciarie per manus einsdem, pro croco per ipsum empto ibidem,
vj gr. iiij d. SUPER officio scutcilarie, per manus eiusdem pro busca
per ipsum empta ibidem, vij gr. Et pro ollis luteis emptis ibidem,
vj gr. iiij d. CLERICO speciarie per manus eiusdem pro cepo empto
ibidem, iiij gr. CLERICO buterie super vino, per manus eiusdem
pro vino per ipsum empto ibidem eodem die post prandium,* vj gr. ij d.
Item pro expensis thesaurarii, Hethcote, Maunsell et aliorum cum
xiij equis de currubus extra curiam apud Sanctum Michaelem per
vnam noctem, viz. in pane, vino, carne, prebendis equorum, per compotum factum ibidem eodem die, vj flor. viij d. Johanni de Chaundrie et Roberto, pro sotularibus pro ipsis emptis ibidem eodem die,
vj gr. iiij d. CLERICO panterie per manus Johannis de Chaundrie
pro pane empto, vj gr. CLERICO buterie super vino per manus
eiusdem, pro vino per ipsum empto ibidem, xxiiij gr. CLERICO
marescalcie per manus Wilbram pro feno per ipsum empto ibidem,
j flor. CLERICO coquine per manus hospitis pro piscibus per ipsum
emptis ibidem, ix gr. CLERICO speciarie per manus eiusdem, pro
cepo empto ibidem, vj gr. Et pro expensis Henrici Maunsell pro*
prandio suo, vj gr. iiij d. Item pro ferrura equi ibidem, xiiij d.
Item pro conductione j currus per iiij dies per conuencionem factam
ibidem, vij flor. Item pro sagmine empto ibidem pro curru, vj gr

iiij d. Item pro reparacione ij curruum domini cum diuersis harnisiis,
correo, canabo, ligno, ferro, et diuersis necessariis pro ipsis emptis
ibidem eodem die, ix flor. CLERICO marescalcie per manus T.
Ferour pro ferrura diuersorum equorum domini apud ª / Jonden- fo. 17 vº.
5 bargh, xv die Nouembris, xvij gr. iij d. Et pro emendacione November 15.
diuersarum sellarum domini ibidem eodem die, vij gr. Et
pro viij ferris emptis ibidem, vj gr. CLERICO panterie per manus
Gilder pro pane albo per ipsum empto ibidem xvº die Nouembris,
vj flor. viij gr iij d. CLERICO buterie super vino per manus eiusdem,
10 pro vino per ipsum empto ibidem, xj flor. xxix gr. ij d. CLERICO
speciarie per manus eiusdem pro cepo per ipsum empto ibidem
eodem die, xj gr. ij d. Et pro cressets emptis ibidem, vij gr. SUPER
officio scutellarie pro busca empta ibidem, xviij gr. CLERICO
marescalcie per manus Wilbram pro feno per ipsum empto ibidem
15 eodem die, j flor. v gr. j d. Et pro lxv bz. auenarum, v flor. x gr.
vj d. Et pro expensis vnius equi Johannis Trumpet ibidem, viij gr.
ij d. Et pro litura, x gr. Et pro expensis ij equorum cuiusdam
scutiferi ducentis domino viam per iiij noctes, xxxj gr. CLERICO
marescalcie per manus Wilbram pro feno per ipsum empto apud
20 Fresak, xvjº die Nouembris, vij gr. ij d. Et pro viij bz. auenarum November 16.
emptis ibidem, xlviij gr. Et pro litura empta ibidem, xij gr.
CLERICO panetrie per manus Gilder pro pane albo per ipsum empto,
j flor. v. gr. iiij d. CLERICO buterie super vino per manus eiusdem,
pro vino per ipsum empto ibidem, vj flor. xvij gr. CLERICO
25 speciarie per manus eiusdem pro croco per ipsum empto ibidem, j gr.
Super officio scutellarie per manus eiusdem pro busco,* v gr. iiij d. * sic.
Clerico speciarie per manus eiusdem pro cepo empto, iiij gr. iiij d.
CLERICO buterie super vino per manus Gilder, pro vino per ipsum
empto ibidem, xvijº die Nouembris, xx gr. CLERICO speciarie per November 17.
30 manus eiusdem pro candelis cepi per ipsum emptis ibidem, xiiij d.
Et pro croco et pipere, vij gr. iij d. CLERICO marescalcie per manus

* Summa pagine, iiijˣˣix flor. iiij d. Wene. On the lower margin is written the
following : xxj grossi iiij denarii faciunt j florenum, et ij floreni iiij grossi faciunt
j noble.

Wilbram pro expensis ij equorum et j gyde et le Trumpet, per
j noctem, vij gr. j d   CLERICO panetrie per manus Gilder pro
pane albo per ipsum empto apud Felkirke xviij° die Nouembris,
xvij gr. iiij d.   Et pro fructubus, vij gr.   CLERICO buterie super
vino per manus eiusdem, pro vino per ipsum empto ibidem, vij flor. 5
xj gr. ij d.   SUPER officio scutellarie per manus hospitis pro busca
empta ibidem, v gr.   CLERICO marescalcie per manus eiusdem pro
feno per ipsum empto ibidem, xx gr.   Et pro viij bz. auenarum,
xlviij gr.   Et pro litura, iiij gr.   Et pro ferrura equorum ibidem,
vj gr.   CLERICO speciarie per manus Selby, pro cera et cepo 10
emptis ibidem, xiiij gr. iij d.   Et pro expensis j garcionis cuiusdam
guyde, pro prandio et cena per ij dies, vj gr.   CLERICO marescalcie
per manus Wilbram pro ij bz. auenarum emptis ibidem, vj gr. ij d.
CLERICO panetrie per manus Gilder pro pane albo per ipsum empto
apud Fillak xviij°die Nouembris, j flor. ij gr. ij d.   CLERICO 15
buterie super vino per manus eiusdem, pro vino per ipsum empto
ibidem eodem die, viij flor. iij gr. iiij d.   CLERICO speciarie per
manus hospitis ibidem pro cepo empto ibidem, iiij gr. iiij d.   Et
pro iij lb. cere di., xvj gr.   SUPER officio scutellarie per manus
eiusdem pro busca empta ibidem, xvj gr.   Et pro carbonibus emptis 20
ibidem, vj gr.   Clerico marescalcie per manus Wilbram pro feno
per ipsum empto ibidem, xx gr. iiij d.   Et pro xxviij bz. auenarum,
vj flor. v. gr. ij d.   Et pro iij singulis equinis, iij gr.   Et pro litura,
viij gr. ij d.   Et pro capistris equinis, iij gr. ij d.   Et pro ferrura
equi domini ibidem eodem die, vj gr.   Clerico buterie super vino 25
per manus Gilder, pro vino per ipsum empto ibidem eodem die,
ij flor. xvj gr. ij d.   Item pro j faucone empto ibidem, x gr.   Item
diuersis fabris facientibus ferrum ibidem, iiij gr. ij d.   Clerico pantrie
per manus Gilder pro pane albo per ipsum empto apud Malberget
xix° die Nouembris, xxxviij gr.   Clerico buterie super vino per 30
manus eiusdem, pro vino per ipsum empto ibidem eodem die,
lxxij gr. ij d.   SUPER officio scutellarie per manus hospitis ibidem
eodem die, x gr.   Clerico speciarie per manus eiusdem pro cepo
per ipsum empto ibidem, vij gr.   CLERICO marescalcie per manus

II. EXPENSES IN AUSTRIA.

Wilbram pro feno per ipsum empto ibidem eodem die, ix gr. j d.
Et pro xxxiij bz. auenarum, iiij^xx x gr. iiij d. Et pro litura, xij gr.
Et pro expensis j gyde, pro prandio et cena, iiij gr. v d. Et pro
iij bz. auenarum per ipsum emptis ibidem, xx° die Nouembris,
5 x gr. iiij d. Clerico marescalcie per manus Wilbram pro xiiij bz.
auenarum per ipsum emptis apud Peselthorpe, xx° die Nouembris,
lxiij gr. Et pro feno per ipsum empto ibidem eodem die, xx gr. iij d.
Clerico panetrie per manus Gilder pro pane albo per ipsum empto
ibidem eodem die, xv gr. Super officio scutellarie, per manus
10 hospitis pro busca ab ipso empta ibidem, xvj gr. iiij d. Clerico
speciarie per manus hospitis pro v lb. cere albe emptis [a] / ibidem
eodem die, xiij gr. ij d. CLERICO marescalcie per manus Thome
Ferour pro ferrura equorum ibidem eodem die, viij gr. Et pro
expensis vj equorum vallettorum camere domini ibidem eodem
15 die, j flor. CLERICO buterie super vino per manus Gilder, pro
vino per ipsum empto apud Malberget, vj flor. xvj gr. Clerico
panetrie per manus Gilder pro pane albo per ipsum empto
ibidem eodem die, xj gr. CLERICO buterie super vino per manus
eiusdem, pro vino per ipsum empto ibidem, vj flor. xiiij gr. ij d.
20 Item duobus carectariis conductis de Dansk vsque Venis, per conuencionem cum eis factam ibidem, viij noble. CLERICO pantrie
per manus Gilder pro pane albo per ipsum empto apud Cysele,
xxiiij° die Nouembris, vj flor. vj gr. CLERICO buterie super vino
per manus eiusdem, pro vino per ipsum empto ibidem eodem die,
25 xix flor. x gr. CLERICO marescalcie per manus hospitis ibidem,
pro expensis xxviij equorum ibidem eodem tempore per ij noctes,
xxj flor. CLERICO speciarie per manus Selby pro cera per ipsum
empta ibidem per ij noctes, xx gr. ITEM pro expensis domini
Petri Bucton senescalli hospicii domini, domini Petri Solatour
30 militis, Johannis Payn, Johannis Mowbray et aliorum, cum xiiij
equis euntibus de Wene vsque Venis pro galeia ordinanda et aliis

---

[a] Summa pagine, iiij^xx viij flor. v gros. j d. The note as to the values of the Austrian money at the end of fo. 17 (p. 199) is repeated here and on the two following pages.

diuersis victualibus ibidem emendis et prouidendis pro viagio domini versus Terram Sanctam; eundo et morando per x dies, per compotum cum eis factum apud Venis, xiij° die Nouembris, lv flor. xvj gr. iiij d. b. DIE sabbati xiiij° die Nouembris apud Newmark per manus Litton ad prandium pro vj personis, viz. in pane, j gr. iiij d.; ob.; item in vino pro eisdem, vij gr.; item in coquina, vij gr. Item in stabulo, viz. in feno pro vj equis ibidem, xij gr. iij d.; item in auenis pro eisdem, xij gr.; item in lumine, iiij d.; item in sagmine pro carrectis domini ibidem, vj d. DIE Dominica xv die eiusdem mensis ad prandium pro eisdem in mane, viz. in pane, v. d.; item in vino, v gr.; item in carne, iiij gr. Eodem die pro j gyde, iiij gr. Item eodem die apud Frisak pro bait' vj equorum et hominum, iij gr. Item pro j wheleband, j scho pro curru, et emendacione currus, v gr. Eodem die ad cenam apud Scintſete, viz. in pane, j gr. iiij d.; item in vino, xj gr.; in carne, vij gr. Item in focale et lumine, ij gr. iiij d. Item eodem die ibidem pro feno et litura pro viij equis, xij gr. v d. Item in auenis pro eisdem, xv gr. Item in ferrura ibidem, pro clauis et emendacione currus domini, vij gr. Item pro cambicione j currus domini cum ij paruis curribus,* causa vie stricte, v guldyn hungarici. Item in sagmine empto ibidem pro curru, ij gr. DIE Lune xvj° die eiusdem mensis ad prandium, viz. in pane, j gr. ij d; item in vino, vij gr.; item in carne, vij gr. Item in emendacione j rote domini, xj gr. iiij d. Eodem die pro cena apud Stamford, viz. in pane, j gr. iiij d.; item in beer, vj gr.; item in carne et piscibus, vj gr. In feno et litura pro vj equis ibidem, iiij gr. iiij d. In auenis pro eisdem, viij gr. Item pro j noua seturi empt' ibidem pro curru, iiij gr. iij d. DIE Martis xvij° die eiusdem mensis apud Felowe, pro prandio, xvj gr. iij d. In bayt' ibidem cum vij equis, v gr. Item in vno pare sotularum empto ibidem pro Nicholao Guyde, iij gr. Item in 30 sagmine pro curru domini ibidem, ij gr. In emendacione et ligamentis ferreis pro curru domini, vij gr. Item ibidem pro pictura clipeum armature domini, xxj gr. ij d. Item apud Horleston pro cena vij personarum eodem die, xv gr. Item in octo equis ibidem, viz. in feno et litura, iiij gr. iij d.; in auenis pro eisdem, xv gr.; in lumine, iiij gr.; in ferrura ibidem, vij gr. Die Mercurii xviij° eiusdem mensis ibidem, pro prandio corundem in mane,* ix gr. Eodem die ad cenam apud Pontafle pro eisdem, xiiij gr. Item in stabulo viz. in feno et litura pro viij equis, vij gr. iij d.; in auenis pro eisdem, xxxi gr. iij d.; in ferrura ibidem, iij gr.; in lumine ibidem, j gr.; in sagmine empto ibidem pro curru, ij gr. Die Jouis xix° die eiusdem mensis ad prandium ibidem mane, xj gr. Eodem die ad cenam apud Posidolfe, xiiij gr. Item in feno pro viij equis ibidem, vj gr. Item in auenis pro eisdem, xl gr. Die Veneris xx° die eiusdem mensis pro prandio mane ibidem, vj gr. ij d. In lumine, iiij d. Eodem die pro cena apud Spillingberk, xij gr. Item in feno, litura, et auenis ibidem pro viij equis, xxxiij gr. In sagmine pro curru domini, vj gr. Die Sabbati xxj° die eiusdem mensis, mane ad prandium, vij gr. Eodem die apud Gecur pro batillagio viij equorum, xvj gr. Eodem die ad cenam apud Conigliano, xx gr. Item in feno, litura et auenis ibidem pro viij equis, xlvj gr. Die Dominica xxij° die eiusdem pro prandio mane ibidem,* /xiiij gr. Eodem die ad cenam apud Trevise, xviij gr. Item in feno et litura et auenis pro viij equis ibidem, xlvj gr. iij d. Die Lune xxiij° die eiusdem mensis pro prandio viij personarum, xviij gr. Eodem die pro cena ix personarum ibidem, xx gr. In feno, litura et auenis ibidem, xlvj gr. In ferrura ibidem, vj gr. Die Martis xxiiij die eiusdem mensis pro prandio mane, xx gr. Eodem die ad noctem apud Pontegla pro batillagio equorum domini et currus domini, vj gr. Item pro ferrura ibidem, vj gr. Item in potu ibidem carrectariis, j gr. Eodem die ad noctem apud Mote pro cena v personarum, xx gr. In feno, litura et auenis pro vij equis ibidem, xvij gr. Die Mercurii xxv° die eiusdem mensis pro uno guyde ibidem, vj gr. Item pro prandio in mane, xxj gr. Item in ferrura equorum, iij gr. Item in emendacione duarum rotarum curruum et ligamentis ferreis, xliij gr. Item in sagmine empto

November 18.
* [The MS. នោ nau'.]

November 19.

November 20.

November 21.

November 22.
fo. 18 v°.

November 23.

November 24.

November 25.

* Summa pagine, viij noble st.; Item in moneta boemici, cxlv flor. ix gr. v d. ob. Wene. Item in alia moneta, v guldynes hungarici.

ibidem pro curru, v gr. Item in potu per viam eodem die, iij gr. Item in expensis v equorum senescalli a primo die Octobris vsque vij diem Nouembris, per xxxviij dies vtroque computato, capienti per diem xx d., in toto lxiij s. iiij d. st. Item in expensis iiij equorum thesaurarii a primo die Octobris vsque xxiiij diem Nouembris, vtroque computato per lv dies, capientis per diem xvj d., in toto lxxiij s. iiij d. st.*

Summa pagine, vj li. xvij s. ij d. sterlinges.
Item de moneta Boemica, xiiij flor. xvj gr. j d. bem.

Summa totalis de Wene in Ostricia vsque huc, m¹cccciiij^{xx}xij grossi.
Item iij^c xlvj floreni cum ix li. x s. vj d. in nobilibus st., et cum v guldyns precii v florenorum qui valent xv s. iiij d. ob. st. Et sic summa totalis computata in sterlinges, lxxiij li. xij s. ix d. ob. sterl.*

PORTGRWER, IN FRIOLA.

/ CLERICO coquine per manus Johannis Wilbram pro iij quarteriis bouis per ipsum emptis apud Portgruer, xxiiij die Nouembris, iiij duc. di. Et pro ij porcis, iiij duc. di. Et pro vj multonibus per ipsum emptis ibidem eodem die, iij duc. xxxj s. ven. SUPER officio pulleterie per manus eiusdem pro caponibus, gallinis, pullis, pulcinis per ipsum emptis ibidem eodem die, ij duc. xxxj s. ven. SUPER officio scutellarie per manus Laurencii Trauers pro busca et carbonibus per ipsum emptis ibidem eodem die, iiij duc.

* In the margin of the MS. opposite these two payments to the steward and the treasurer is the note "quia non receperunt vadia." The total given at the bottom of the leaf is not correct, being 6d. too much.

di. Clerico coquine per manus Jacobi le gyde, pro ij bacons, iiij duc. liij s. Super officio pulleterie pro ijC ouis emptis ibidem eodem die, j duc. Item pro sepo, vij s. Item pro j stara salis per ipsum empta ibidem eodem die, j duc. xj s. Clerico speciarie per manus Johannis Wilbram pro j lb. sugre caffetin empta ibidem eodem die, xx s. ven. Et per manus eiusdem pro candelis cepi per ipsum emptis ibidem eodem die, j duc. Et per manus Jacobi le guyde pro ij fesauntes per ipsum emptis ibidem eodem die, xxv s. Clerico coquine per manus eiusdem pro j quarterio bouis per ipsum empto ibidem xxv die Nouembris, j duc. xv s. Et pro iiij multonibus, j duc. x s. Et pro j porco, ij duc. vij s. Super officio pulleterie per manus eiusdem pro gallinis, pullis, pulcinis, per ipsum emptis ibidem eodem die, j duc. xij s. Et pro farina auenarum, v s. Clerico coquine per manus Wilbram pro sale albo per ipsum empto pro pantria, xxxj s. Super officio scutellarie per manus Thesaurarii pro busca per ipsum empta ibidem eodem die, j duc. l s. Et pro factura de rakkis et aliis necessariis in coquina per manus Johannis Cudworth, j duc. Et pro expensis ij equorum j gyde ibidem, j duc. Et pro factura de rakks et mangers in diuersis stabulis domini ibidem, ij duc. xvij s. Clerico coquine per manus Jacobi le guyde pro xij malardes et xij tele per ipsum emptis ibidem, j duc. v s. Super officio scutellarie per manus Johannis Cudworth pro vj ollis luteis, vj spets et meremiis pro rakks et pro aliis necessariis in coquina, j duc. vij s. Super officio salsarie per manus Laurencii Trauers pro vinegre, vergws, cenape et cepo et alleo, tempore quo dominus stetit ibidem, ij duc. lj s. Clerico buterie super vino, per manus Gilder pro j pipe de Maluesye per ipsum empta ibidem eodem die, xx s. Et pro tabulis, clauis, ligno emptis ibidem pro diuersis rakks et mangers faciendis in stabulis domini, iiij duc. xlviij s. Cuidam carpentario laboranti circa mangers et rakks per iiij dies, xlvj s. Clerico coquine per manus Willelmi Harpeden pro piscibus recentibus per ipsum emptis ibidem, xxvj die Nouembris, vij duc. lxj s. Et per manus eiusdem pro iiij gallinis et iij pulcinis per ipsum emptis

ibidem, xxxij s. Et per manus eiusdem pro oleo, xlviij s.
Et pro ijC ouorum, j duc.. Item pro lacte, xij s. CLERICO
coquine per manus Jacobi le guyde, pro crevys et floundres
per ipsum emptis ibidem, j duc. lxxiiij s. Et per manus eiusdem
pro ij malardz et iiij tele, xvj s. Et eidem pro j multone, xlij s. 5
Et pro j galone Maluesye per manus eiusdem, xx s. SUPER officio
scutellarie pro busca et carbonibus ibidem emptis per senescallum,
iij duc. di. Et per manus eiusdem pro ij bacon per ipsum emptis
ibidem, vij duc. xlvij s. Et per manus eiusdem pro ij fesauntes,
xxiij s. CLERICO coquine per manus Johannis Wilbram pro j 10
boue, iiij duc. di. Et eidem pro vj castronibus, iij duc. vij s. Et pro
iiij porcis, j duc. SUPER officio pulleterie per manus Wilbram,
iij duc. lv s. Et pro xij malardz, xlviij s. Et pro viij pertrices,
lxxv s. Et pro j roo, ij duc. Et pro iijC ouorum, iiij li. Et pro
lacte, xxv s. Et pro herbis emptis, xl s. Et pro sagmine, xj s. 15
Super officio scutellarie pro busca et carbonibus emptis ibidem
eodem die, iij duc. di. Clerico buterie super vino, iij ga'onibus de
Maluesye, lx s. SUPER officio scutellarie per manus Laurencii
Trauers, pro iiij ollis luteis, xij s. Et per manus eiusdem pro iiij
bollis et v barellis voidez, iij duc. Item pro j barga conducta de 20
Portgruer vsque Venis pro diuersis officiariis domini precuntibus
circa ordinacionem faciendam, v duc. Et pro expensis eorundem,
iiij duc. Et pro j alia magna barga conducta pro diuersis harnisiis
domini cariandis ibidem, ix duc. SUPER officio aule et camere pro
lectis conductis ibidem, j duc. di. Item diuersis hominibus laboran- 25
tibus in coquina tempore quo dominus stetit ibidem, j duc. xij s.
CLERICO speciarie pro cera operata, amigdalis, et aliis speciebus,
xj duc. Et pro caseo empto ibidem per manus senescalli, lv s.[a]
SUPER officio scutellarie per manus Laurencii Trauers pro
discis, platers, salsariis, ollis luteis, per ipsum emptis ibidem, j duc. 30
xv s.. Et pro iiij besoms ad mundandum coquinam, v s. Et iiij
hominibus laborantibus circa mundacionem domorum et stabulorum

---

[f] Summa pagine, cxxix ducati di. lxij s. venetiarum:—vnde iiij li. v s. faciunt j
ducatum, et computatur ibidem per ducatos simpliciter.

in hospicio domini ibidem, ij duc. CLERICO speciarie per manus Wilbram pro vij lb. candelarum cepi emptis ibidem, xxx s. CLERICO panetrie per manus Gilder pro pane albo per ipsum empto tempore quo dominus stetit ibidem, et per tres dies precedentes, 5 pro diuersis officiariis ibidem existentibus, xj duc. di. CLERICO buterie super vino per manus eiusdem, pro vino empto ibidem per idem tempus, xxvj duc. iij li. vij s. Et per manus eiusdem pro diuersis fructubus ibidem emptis, iij duc. di. Et per manus eiusdem pro locione le towaill de panetria ibidem, vij s. Et pro 10 lx vlnis panni linei emptis ibidem per* thesaurarium, le vlna ad vij s., xxj li. CLERICO marescalcie per manus Johannis Wilbram pro feno per ipsum empto apud Portgruer tempore quo dominus stetit ibidem, viij duc. di. Et per manus Mowbray pro feno per ipsum empto ibidem, ij duc. di. Et per manus eiusdem pro lxij 15 starris de spelta pro prebendis equorum domini per idem tempus, xxij duc. Et pro litura empta per manus eiusdem pro lectis et litura equorum ibidem, iiij duc. Et per manus Thome Ferour pro ferrura equorum domini ibidem, ij duc. xvij s. DIUERSIS hominibus de Portgruer pro iiij batellis conductis de ibidem vsque Venis cum 20 domino et familia sua, per conuencionem cum eis factam per senescallum et thesaurarium, xxj duc. Et ix hominibus frangentibus glaciem inter Portgruer et Venis, per conuencionem cum eis factam, ix duc. SUPER officio pulleterie per manus Jacobi Judei pro xxviij caponibus, xxxj gallinis per ipsum emptis ibidem pro 25 prouidenciis, viij duc. liiij s. Et per manus Couns Douche pro xx caponibus et xl gallinis, ix duc. Et pro mactacione xij bouum pro galeia, ij duc. lxx s. Et pro mundacione exitus duodecim bouum, xxiiij s. ven. Et pro vj barellis voidez pro carne saliendo, emptis ibidem, ij duc. lxx s. Item pro couparagio viij vasorum, xxj s. 30 Item pro iij barellis voidez pro carne omni imponendo, j duc. xxxvj s. Item ij hominibus operantibus ibidem in larderio, xiiij s. Item pro conductione j domus pro larderio per j septimanam. di. duc. Et pro viij staris salis, viij duc. Clerico speciarie per manus Cudworth, pro ij lb. candelarum cepi emptis ibidem, v s.

Clerico buterie super vino per manus eiusdem, pro vino per ipsum empto ibidem pro souse, xxxiij s. Item pro iij lectis conductis pro garcionibus domini stabuli apud Portgruer per j mensem, j duc. lxvij s. Super officio poletrie per manus Wilbram pro putura pullorum, l s. Et pro expensis iiij bouum de Portgruer vsque Venis, xx s. Et pro tabulis emptis ibidem pro factura mangers et rakks pro equis valettorum camere domini, viz. Gilder, Harpeden, et Schelford, xxxij s. Johanni Wilbram et Johanni Cudwerth pro expensis suis existentibus ibidem per iij dies pro diuersis carnibus ibidem saliendis, et diuersis victualibus ibidem emendis pro galcia, et pro j batella de ibidem conducta usque Venis per iij dies, in toto viij duc. CLERICO speciarie pro lv bras panni linei emptis apud Portgruer, v duc. xj s. Et per manus Johannis Payn pro iij butts de vino Mark per ipsum emptis erga aduentum domini Venis, xxiiij duc. di. Item pro ij butts vini de Treuyso, xij duc. xlvij s. Et pro xij butts vacantibus pro vino imponendo, xj duc. xv s. Item pro busca per ipsum empta ibidem et cariagio eiusdem, x duc. di. Et pro portagio vini, xlvj s. Item pro iij baskets pro panetria, xxxvj s. Item pro emendacione clauium, xxiiij s. Item pro mundacione domus, xx s. Item pro barka Venis et morundo inter Venis et Seint Jeorges, lx s. Item in trenchors, vij li. Item in trowes lxx s. Item in xij cadis pro eue, et pro ij grossis quynes et pro iiij paruis, et iij galonibus pro vino, et pro ij coruis pro pane, xij duc. xlj s. Item pro iij canellis pro trere[a] vinum, ij duc. di. Item pro carbonibus, vij duc. Item pro xvj gallinis, j duc. xvj s. Item pro prandio predictarum gallinarum, viij s. Item pro C scutellis ligneis, iij ladel, j morter cum j pestell, iij duc. di. Item pro prandio pro gallinis, vj s. Item pro vitreis[b] / et ollis, xlj s. Item pro vinegre, vij s. Item pro cenape, vj s. Item pro portagio, iiij s. Item pro ij C ouorum di., vj li. Item pro ij gallinis et pro portagio ad hospicium, vij s. Item pro carne,

5

10

15

20

25

30

[a] i.e. trahere.
[b] Summa pagine, celix duc. di. xxvij s. ven. At the bottom of the margin is this note : iiij li. v s. faciunt j ducatum, et computatur per ducatos et non vltra.

II. EXPENSES FROM PORTOGRUARO TO VENICE.

lxxviij s. Item pro puluere de canella, vj s. Item pro sepo, vij s. Item pro j barka de villa ad hospicium, iij s. Item pro portagio ad barkam, iij s. Item pro j paruo cade de Romoneye, vj li. di. Item pro piscibus, vj li. Item pro puluere piperis, xxxij s. Item pro
5 oleo ad prandium, xxviij s. Item ad bargemen, j duc. Item vni fabro de quo conduximus cacabum et alia necessaria, j flor. Item pro xxvj gallinis et vj pulcinis, iij duc. Item pro xvj gallinis, ij duc. xij s. Item pro xix gallinis, ij duc. vij s. vj d. Item pro vij gallinis, j duc. xij s. Item pro piscibus, vj duc. vj s. Item pro
10 botagio, xj s. Item pro ouis, j duc. xx s. Item pro ij doliis pro pane imponendo, lx s. Item pro ij staris salis, ij duc. lxix s. Item pro C vitreis, xxxvj s. Item pro vij vlnis de panno lingio ad tegendum cupbord, j duc. xx s. Item pro factura dictorum cupcloth et manutergiorum, viij s. Item pro portagio, ij s. Item pro j butt
15 vini ibidem empto per manus senescalli, viij duc. ij s. CLERICO pantrie per manus Gilder pro pane albo per ipsum empto apud Gauerley, xxviij die Nouembris, ij duc. CLERICO butrie super *November 28* vino per manus eiusdem, pro vino per ipsum empto ibidem, vj duc. xlij s. CLERICO coquine per manus Wilbram pro piscibus per
20 ipsum emptis ibidem, iiij duc. I s. Et pro piscibus per thesaurarium emptis ibidem, j duc. vij s. Et pro portagio corundem, iiij s. Et pro vj^{xx} ouorum ibidem emptis, xxv s. Et pro lacte, xj s. Et pro amigdalis, viij s. Et pro cenape, veriws, et cepo, xvj s. Et pro candelis cepi, xvij s. Et pro busca empta ibidem, iij duc.
25 vj s. Item duobus famulis servientibus in coquina, et pro aqua carianda, xij s. CLERICO panetrie per manus Gilder pro pane albo per ipsum empto apud Leo, xxix° die Nouembris, ij duc. CLERICO *November 29* buterie super vino per manus eiusdem, pro vino per ipsum empto ibidem, vij duc. xlvij s. CLERICO coquine per manus Wilbram pro
30 piscibus recentibus per ipsum emptis et per Wiluby, vij duc. iij li. Et pro busca, sepo, sale, vergws, farina, iij duc. vij s. Et pro lectis ibidem et apud Gauerley, ij duc. xij s. ITEM Willelmo Harpeden pro expensis suis apud Venis post recessum domini versus Iherusalem, et eundo de ibidem vsque Portgruer, j duc. xlij s. ven. Et

CAMD. SOC. 2 E

eidem pro expensis suis eundo de Portgruer versus Venis pro
moneta ibidem querenda, eundo morando et redeundo per vj dies,
ij duc. xliij s. Et eidem pro expensis suis, Thome Ferour, cok
Kikeley, Thome Swylington, Johannis Aschby, Roberti Hwet,
Johannis de Chaundrie, Johannis Maye et Henrici Hamond, custo- 5
dientium equos apud Portgruer per xix dies, xv duc. xxx s.
Et eidem^a pro expensis suis eunti de Portgruer vsque Venis,
eundo, morando et redeundo per v dies, xlij s. Et eidem pro
expensis suis eunti alia vice de Portgruer vsque Venis pro
moneta ibidem querenda, eundo morando et redeundo per vj dies, 10
ij duc. Et eidem pro expensis suis et Johannis Wilbram, euntibus
de Portgruer vsque Portlown pro auenis ibidem emendis, eundo
morando et redeundo, iiij li. Et eisdem pro expensis suis euntibus
de Portgruer vsque Venis erga aduentum domini de Iherusalem, per
ij dies et ij noctes, j duc. vij s. Et eidem pro iij lectis per ipsum 15
conductis apud Portgruer pro garcionibus stabuli per iij menses,
v duc. xxxj s. Et eidem pro candelis cepi per ipsum emptis ibidem
per idem tempus, j duc. x s. Et eidem pro expensis j hominis
conducti ad equitandum cum dicto Harpeden in patriam pro feno,
auenis et litura emendis, pro xxvij diebus, ij duc. Et eidem pro 20
expensis Johannis Maii et Henrici Hamond ibidem per j mensem,
ij duc. Et eidem pro feno per ipsum empto ibidem, a xxix^e die
Octobris vsque vltimum diem Martii, xlvj duc. Et eidem pro M^l
clauorum, xlvj ferris equinis per ipsum emptis ibidem per idem
tempus, iij duc. xlvj s. Et eidem pro vadiis Thome Ferour, Will- 25
elmi Harpeden, Willelmi Kikkeley, Thome Swylington, Johannis
Aschby, Roberti Hwet, Johannis de Chaundrie et Johannis Maye,
a xx° die Januarii vsque vltimum diem Martii, vtroque computato,
xlix duc. lxiiij s. Et eidem pro expensis ij hominum euntium de
Portgruer vsque Guydel, pro Johanne Wilbram ibidem querendo 30
existente ibidem infirmo, iij li. x s. Et pro factura j stabuli pro

^a In this and the two following items *eisdem* is written, but the singular *eidem*
appears to be meant on comparison with previous items, and noticing the sums paid.
Harpeden was evidently the officer responsible for these payments.

II. BETWEEN PORTOGRUARO AND VENICE. 211

equis valectorum camere domini, Harpeden et Schelford, j duc. Et eidem pro expensis suis cuntibus de Treuiso per aquam vsque Venis, xxiiij s. Et eidem pro iijCxxxiij staris auenarum per ipsum emptis ibidem ad diuersa precia per tempus vt supra, Cl duc.
5 xxxiij s. Et eidem pro factura rakks, mangers pro equis domini ibidem, ij duc. Et eidem pro expensis equi Thome Totty ibidem a xxix° die Octobris vsque vltimum die Marcii, xxvj duc. x s. Et Oct. 29—Marc eidem pro feno empto pro j equo Thome Swylington, ibidem per idem tempus, ij duc.ᵃ / Et eidem pro expensis equi Hugonis fo. 20 v
10 Waterton ibidem per idem tempus, xliij duc. xxviij s. Et in cera operata, diuersis speciebus, et confectis per manus Payn emptis erga aduentu domini Venis, xxvj duc. iij li. vij s. Et pro litura per ipsum empta ibidem pro lectis, v duc. Et pro batillagio et cariagio dicte liture de Sancta Lucya vsque Sanctum Georgium, j duc. viij s.
15 Et pro emendacione camini in camera domini apud Sanctum Georgium, ij duc. di. Et pro expensis domini vidz. pro pane, vino, carne, pullis, pulcinis et carbonibus ibidem emptis apud Leo, primo Dec. 1. die Decembris, vij duc. di. Item duobus hominibus conductis ad remeandum in batella domini de ibidem vsque Venis, ij duc. Item
20 dati hospiti pro perdicione scutellarum de pewter et j pilwe, per manus thesaurarii, xl s. Et pro pane empto per manus Gilder per Friola vsque h iij dies, vj duc. di.ᵇ non vltra.

Summa totalis de Portgrwer in Friola vsque huc. viijClxxix duc. di. xxxv s. vj d. ven.

25 VENYS

CLERICO coquine per manus Jacobi le guyde pro di. bouis pei ipsum empto Venis, die dominica prima die Decembris, iiij duc. Dec. 1. Et pro vj castronibus, iiij duc. Et pro j porco, iij duc. Et pro

---

ᵃ Summa pagine, vt extra. That is, the sum of this folio is included with the few lines over the leaf which conclude the expenses incurred in Friuli.
ᵇ Summa pagine cum alia parte, iiij‹liij**ix duc. di. xxxj s. vj d.

j bacon, liij s. Et pro ij porcellis, xxv s. Et pro j roo, j duc. viij s. Et pro vj paribus columbellarum, iij li. ij s. Et pro ij duodenis de parvis volatilibus, xxxvj s. Et pro portagio et batillagio dictorum victualium, xj s. SUPER officio scutellarie per manus Laurencii Trauers pro ijC scutellorum, discorum, salsariorum, litura per ipsum 5 emptis apud Venis eodem die, ij duc. liij s. Et pro iiij besoms pro mundacione coquine, iij s. SUPER officio salsaiie per manus eiusdem pro cenape, vergws, vinegre per ipsum emptis ibidem eodem die, ij duc. CLERICO speciarie per manus Johannis Wilbram pro vij lb. candelarum cepi per ipsum emptis ibidem eodem die, xxxv s. Et 10 per manus eiusdem pro cepo per ipsum empto ibidem, di. duc. CLERICO coquine per manus Jacobi le guyde pro di. bouis per ipsum empto ibidem, ij° die Decembris, ij duc. xxv s. Et pro viij multonibus, iiij duc. vij s. Et pro viij partricibus, iiij li. Et pro ij fesauntes, xl s. Et pro ij malardz, iij li. ij s. Et pro batillagio et 15 portagio dictorum victualium, viij s. Et per manus Johannis Gilder pro pomis et aliis fructubus per ipsum emptis ibidem eodem die, xxx s. SUPER officio scutellarie per manus Laurencii Trauers pro farina et herbis ibidem per ipsum emptis eodem die, xj s. SUPER officio pulleterie per manus Hans de Colon pro lacte, xvij s. Et 20 pro C ouorum, xxj s. Et per manus eiusdem pro x lb. candelarum cepi, l s. Et pro batillagio et portagio, iiij s. Et pro vij brochis, x s. CLERICO coquine per manus Jacobi le guyde pro iij quarteriis bouis per ipsum emptis ibidem ij° die Decembris, v duc. Et pro v castronibus, ij duc. l s·; et pro j bacono ij duc. xxxij s.; et pro 25 j roo, j duc ; et pro iiij porcis xxxiiij s. SUPER officio pulleterie pro iiij partricibus, xl s.; et pro ix paribus tele, lv s.; et pro j duodena de snytes, xxvj s.; et pro batillagio et portagio corundem victualium, ix s. SUPER officio salsarie per manus Laurencii Trauers pro cenape, vergws, vinegre, emptis ibidem eodem die, 30 j duc. v s. JOHANNI Selby pro locione mapparum, xj s. CLERICO coquine per manus Jaccbi le guyde pro pykes per ipsum emptis ibidem, iiij° die Decembris, j duc. xl s. Et pro xl plays grossis, ij duc. v s.; et pro anguillis grossis, xlv s.; et pro burl utts, lx s.; et

II. EXPENSES IN VENICE.

pro moletts, xxxviij s. Et pro schrympes, xliiij s.; et pro ostreis,
lxx s.; et pro xxx crabbes, xxxv s.; et pro C hornekek, lxviij s.
Et pro cokkes,ᵃ xxj s. Et pro batillagio et cariagio, vij s. Et pro
pisis, xvij s. Et pro oleo, lv s. Et pro floundres pro cena, j duc.
5 Et pro lacte, xvij s. Et pro butiro, xij s. Et per manus thesaurarii
pro busca per ipsum empta ibidem eodem die, iiij duc. Et pro
cariagio eiusdem, vj s. Et per manus Johannis Gilder pro fructubus per ipsum emptis ibidem eodem die, xv s. Et pro ij partricibus,
xxj s. Et pro iiij telis, xij s. CLERICO coquine per manus Jacobi
10 guyde pro j di. bouis per ipsum empto ibidem vº die Decembris, December 5.
iij duc. xxxj s. Et pro ij porcis, xxxij s.; et pro vij castronibus,
ij duc. lj s.; et pro j porco, ij duc. xliiij s.; et pro ij fesauntes, xlj s ;
et pro iiij partricibus, xlij s.; et pro iij paribus columbellarum,
xxxij s.; et pro x malardes, iij li. iiij s. SUPER officio salsarie pro
15 cenape, vergws, vinegre, xxviij s. CLERICO speciarie per manus
Hans de Colon pro vj lb. candelarum cepi, xxx s. Et pro farina et
herbis, ix s. CLERICO coquine per manus Jacobi guyde pro ostreis
per ipsum emptis, vjº die Decembris ibidem, lxx s. Item pro lx plays December 6.
grossis.ᵇ / ij duc. Et pro ffloundres et burbutts, j duc. xl s.; item   fo. 21.
20 pro schrimpes, xxxij s.; item pro crevys, xx s. ; item pro xxxiij
crabbez, xxiiij s. Et pro tenche, xxxviij s.; et pro molettes
xxiiij s.; et pro xiij pikerell, xxxij s.; et pro C. hornekek, lxviij s.;
et pro burbuttes, lx s.; et pro kokks, vij s. Et pro iij barces
grossis, xxiiij s. Item pro batillagio, viij s. Item in pisis, xv s.
25 Et in oleo, xl. s. Et in cepo, x s. Et in amigdalis, xxj s. Et per
manus Gilder pro fructubus, xj s. CLERICO speciarie pro iiij lb.,
candelarum cepi, xx s. Et pro emendacione j hostii de celario vna
cum emptione j cerure pro dicto hostio, xix s. CLERICO coquine
per manus Jacobi Guyde pro piscibus per ipsum emptis ibidem
30 vijº die Decembris, viz. pro ostriis, xlij s. Item pro creues, xl s. Item December 7.

ᵃ Evidently a sort of fish; see the same item a little further on, l. 23. It seems
to be the same as the cokkels, i.e. cockles, on p. 215, l. 3.
ᵇ Summa pagine de parte de Venys, lxxiij duc. di. xxxij s. Venetiani :—vnde, iiij
libri xij denarii faciunt j ducatum, et ij ducati et ix solidi faciunt j noble.

pro anguillis, lj s. Item pro burbutts, j duc. xl s. Item pro pikes et tench, j duc. xl s. Item pro fllowndres et plays, iij duc. Item pro crabbes grossis, xxij s. Item pro pisis, xvij s. Item pro oleo, lv s. Item pro lacte, xviij s. Item pro ovis, xv s. Item in amigdalis, xij s. Clerico coquine per manus Jacobi Guyde pro j boue 5 per ipsum empto viij° die Decembris ibidem, x duc. lx s. Et pro viij multonibus, iiij duc. xxj s. Et pro ij baconis, v. duc. di. Item pro j porco. ij duc. xxxvj s. Et pro iij porcellis, xlviij s. Et pro ij roos, ij duc. xxj s. SUPER officio pulleterie per manus eiusdem, pro xij gallinis, j duc. xxxviij s. Et pro xx pulcinis, j duc. Et pro 10 xxij columbellis, j duc. vij s. Et pro j duodena tele, xl s. Et pro portagio et batillagio victualium, vij s. SUPER officio salsarie pro cenape, vergws, et venegre per manus Laurencii Trauers, xlj s. SUPER officio scutellarie per manus eiusdem pro farina auenarum, xx s. Et pro oleribus et aliis herbis, x s. CLERICO speciarie per 15 manus eiusdem pro vj lb. candelarum cepi, xxxj s. CLERICO coquine per manus Jacobi Gyde, pro vj multonibus per ipsum emptis, ix° die Decembris ibidem, iij duc. xj s. Et pro xviij partricibus, ix li. Et pro iiij fesaunts, iiij li. Et pro vj paribus columbellarum, iij li. iij s. Et pro ij duodenis de parvis volatilibus, xxxvj s. 20 Item pro x paribus malardz, vj li. iiij s. Item pro ix paribus tele, lvj s. Et pro batellagio et portagio, vij s. SUPER officio [? scutellarie] per manus Laurencii Trauers pro carbonibus per ipsum emptis ibidem eodem die, v duc. Et pro cariagio, vj s. Et per manus eiusdem pro cepo per ipsum empto ibidem eodem die, x s. Johanni 25 Selby pro locione mapparum ibidem, xv s. Et per manus Laurencii Trauers pro j stara salis per ipsum empta ibidem eodem die, j duc, xxj s. CLERICO coquine per manus Jacobi Guyde pro j di. bouis per ipsum empto ibidem x° die Decembris, iiij duc. di. Et pro vj multonibus, iij duc. xvij s. Et pro di. porci, j duc. xlvj s. SUPER 30 officio pulleterie pro ix gallinis, j duc. viij s.; et pro xx pulcinis, j duc.; et pro xij columbellis, xlviij s.; et pro vj aucis, iij li. xij s. Et pro ij caponibus, xvj gallinis. xxiiij pulcinis, emptis ibidem per Jacobi Gyde, iiij duc. xvij s. CLERICO coquine per manus Jacobi

Gyde pro piscibus per ipsum emptis ibidem xj° die Decembris, viz. December
pro ostreis, lij s. Et pro gra-peys, j duc. di. Item pro batillagio,
iiij s. ; et pro portagio, iiij s. Et pro floundres et cokkels pro cena,
xlij s. ; et pro oleo, xliij s.; et pro lacte, xv s.; et pro ijC ouorum,
5 xl s. ; et pro butiro, x s.; et pro cepo, v s. ; et pro iiij lb. candelarum
cepi, xx s. CLERICO coquine per manus Jacobi Gyde pro di. carcoisii bouini per ipsum empto ibidem xij° die Decembris, v duc. December
Et pro vj castronibus, iiij duc. xvij s. ; et pro di. porci, j duc. li s. ;
et pro ij porcellis, xxxij s.; et pro j roo, j duc. vij s. SUPER
10 officio pulleterie per manus eiusdem, pro xij gallinis, vj li.; et
pro xvj pulcinis, lxiiij s.; et pro iiij ffesaunts, xli s. ; et pro xij
columbellis, iij li. iij s.; et pro C. ouorum, xx s. SUPER officio
salsarie pro cenape, vergws et vinegre per manus Laurencii,[a]
/ xvij s. Et per manus eiusdem pro herbis, v s. Et pro busca empta fo. 21 v
15 per Thesaurarium ibidem eodem die, vj duc. Et pro portagio, v s.
CLERICO coquine per manus Jacobi le Gyde, pro piscibus per
ipsum emptis ibidem, xiij° die Decembris, viz. pro burbuttes, xl s. ; December
item pro pikerell et tench, j duc. xx s ; item pro xiij trowtes,
j duc.; item pro xxvj cheuens, j duc. lx s.; item pro pikerell et
20 creuez, j duc. lxviij s.; item pro squames, xl s.; item pro kokkel, xxij s.
Item pro oleo, xlij s. Item pro pisis, xv s. Item pro sale, xxviij s.
CLERICO coquine per manus Jacobi Gyde, pro piscibus recentibus
per ipsum emptis ibidem xiiij° die Decembris, viz. pro burbutts, l s.; December
item pro xx anguillis, lxx s.; item xxxij cheuens, j duc. lxxvj s.;
25 item pro xxvj pimpernol, xvj s.; item pro xj pik, xl s.: item pro
j trowte, x s.; item pro xx tenche, j duc. xx s.; item pro creuez,
xxij s. Item pro sale, xxviij s. Item pro ouis, xx s. Item pro
lacte, xij s. CLERICO coquine per manus Jacobi Gyde pro j boue
per ipsum empto ibidem xv° die Decembris, x duc. lx s. Item pro December
30 j bacono, ij duc. lxiij s. Item pro vj multonibus, iiij duc. Item
pro xvj gallinis, viij li. Et pro xij pulcinis, xlviij s. Item pro

---

[a] Summa pagine, C ij duc. di. xxxviij s. Venitiani ; and on the margin beneath is the following note : vnde, iiij li. xij d. faciunt j duc., et ij duc. et ix s. faciunt j noble.

ij porcellis, xxxij s. Et pro portagio victualium, viij s. Et pro vj partricibus, iij li. Et pro oleribus, x s. Et pro sepo, vj s. Item pro viij lb. candelarum cepi, xl s. CLERICO coquine per [manus] Jacobi Gyde pro v castronibus per ipsum emptis ibidem xvj° die Decembris, ij duc. l s. Item pro j porco, ij duc. xxvij s. Et pro j roo, j duc. vij s. Item pro ix gallinis, j duc. xx s.; et pro x columbellis, lv s.; et pro j fesaunt, xx s.; et pro vj tele, xxj s.; et pro portagio eorundem, ij s. SUPER officio salsarie per manus Laurencii Trauers pro cenape, vergws, vinegre per ipsum emptis ibidem eodem die, j duc. Et per manus eiusdem pro herbis, vij s. Item pro busca per ipsum empta ibidem eodem die, iiij duc.; et pro portagio, vj s. Et per manus eiusdem pro sale, l s. CLERICO coquine per manus Jacobi Gyde pro di. carcoisio bouine empto ibidem xvij° die Decembris, iiij duc. liij s.; et pro iiij multonibus, ij duc. xj s. et pro j bacon, ij duc. iij li.; et pro ij porcellis, xxxiij s. SUPER officio pulletrie per manus eiusdem, pro j capone, xxx s. Item pro vj gallinis, j duc. xvj s. Item pro ix pulcinis, lij s. Item pro vj malardz, xlvi s. Item pro lacte, xix s. Item pro iiC ouorum, xl s. Et pro cepo, v s. Item pro herbis, iiij s. Et pro batillagio et portagio victualium, vij s. CLERICO speciarie per manus Hankyn de Colon, pro iiij lb. candelarum cepi per ipsum emptis, xx s. Et pro fructubus, xj s. CLERICO coquine per manus Jacobi Guyde pro piscibus per ipsum emptis xviij° die Decembris viz. pro ostreis, liij s. Item pro barbutts, xl s. Item pro pikerell et tench, j duc. xx s. Item pro xiij trowhtes, j duc. Item pro xxvj cheuens, j duc. lx s. Item pro pikerell et crevez, j duc. lxviij s. Item pro squamez, xl s. Item pro kokkel, xl s. Item pro pisis, xxviij s. Item pro alleo, xl s. Item pro cepo, xv s. Item pro j stara salis, j duc. xxxv s. Item pro lacte, xxj s. Item pro vj lb. candelarum cepi, xxx s. Item pro portagio et batillagio victualium, xj s. Item pro carbone per manus Laurencii Trauers, iiij duc. Item pro portagio et batillagio eorundem, viij s. Clerico coquine per manus Jacobi Guyde pro di. carcoisie bouine per ipsum empto ibidem xix° die Decembris, iiij duc. lxiij s. Item pro v multonibus, ij duc. lxxvj s. Item pro j bacono, ij duc. liij s. Item pro j roo, j duc. v s. Item pro ix gallinis, j duc. viij s. Item pro xx pulcinis, j duc. Item pro x malardz, iij li. iiij s. Item pro j fesaunt, xx s. SUPER officio scutellarie per manus Laurencii Trauers pro cenape, vergws, et vinegre per 5 ipsum emptis ibidem eodem die, j duc. Item per manus eiusdem pro farina auenarum, xxij s. Item per manus eiusdem pro herbis emptis ibidem eodem die, vij s. Et per manus Johannis Selby, pro locione mapparum, xxxij s. Item per manus eiusdem pro C lb. candelarum cepi, xxv s.* Item pro portagio et batillagio victualium,[b] 10 viij s. CLERICO coquine per manus Jacobi Guyde pro piscibus   fo. 22. per ipsum emptis ibidem xix° die Decembris, viz. pro burbuttes, December 19. l s.; item pro xx anguillis, lxx s.; item pro xxxij cheuens, j duc. lxxvj s.; item pro xxvj pimpernol, xvj s.; item pro xj pikes, xl s; item pro j trowhte, x s ; item pro xx tenches, j duc. xx s.; item 15 pro crevez, xxij s.; item pro schrimpes, xxviij s. Item pro butiro, xj s. Item pro pisis, xij s. Item pro lacte, xxiij s. Item pro ijC ouorum, xl s. Item pro cariagio victualium, vij s. Item pro iij lb. candelarum cepi, xv s. Item pro busca empta per manus thesaurarii, v duc. Item pro portagio, vij s. CLERICO coquine per manus 20 Jacobi Guyde pro piscibus per ipsum emptis ibidem xxj° die Decem- December 21. bris, viz. pro pikes et carpes, j duc. lxxvj s.; item pro iiij troztes, xvj s.; item pro crevez, xviij s.; item pro temele, j duc.; item pro anguillis, j duc.; item pro tenches, j duc.; item pro burbutts, xl s.; item pro cheuens, lx s.; item pro schrimpes, lxx s. Item pro 25 oleo, xxx s. Item pro portagio et batillagio, viij s. Item pro ostreis, xl s. Item pro pisis, xj s. Item pro alleo, xxij s. Item pro vj lb. candelarum cepi emptis ibidem eodem die, per manus Johannis Selby, xxx s. CLERICO coquine per manus Jacobi Guyde pro j carcoisio bouino per ipsum empto ibidem xxij° die Decembris, December 22. 30 x duc. Item pro ij bacons, v duc. xxij s. Item pro viij multonibus,

* Compared with the price of candles in other items, this figure seems to be a mistake. Five shillings a pound is the usual price paid.

[b] Summa pagine, eiij duc. xvj s. veniciani ;—rude, iiij li. xij d. fac. j duc., et ij duc. et. ix s. fac. j noble.

iiij duc. xxxiij s. Item pro j roo, j duc. xv s. Item pro iiij porcellis, xlj s. Super officio pulleterie per manus eiusdem pro xxj gallinis, ij duc. xlvj s. Item pro xvj pulcinis, lxiiij s. Item pro iiij fesauntes, iiij li. Item pro x paribus malardes, vj li. iiij s. Item pro ix paribus tele, lvj s. Item pro ij duodenis de parvis volatilibus, xxxvj s. Item pro xij partricibus, vj li. ij s. Item pro portagio et batillagio victualium, ix s. Et per manus Laurencii Trauers pro cenape, vergws, vinegre, et herbis, lvij s. CLERICO coquine per manus Jacobi Gyde pro vj. castronibus per ipsum emptis, xxiij° die Decembris, iij duc. xj s. Item pro iij gallinis emptis ibidem per manus eiusdem eodem die, j duc. xliiij s. Item pro xiiij pulcinis emptis ibidem, liiij s. Item pro x malardes emptis ibidem eodem die, iij li. iiij s. Item pro viij tele, xxviij s. Item pro v partricibus, liiij s. Item pro portagio et batillagio victualium, vij s. Item pro cenape, vergws, vinegre, herbis, et farina auenarum, xlij s. Item pro iiij lb. candelarum cepi, xx s. Item in busca et carbonibus emptis per manus Laurencii Trauers, vj duc. di. Et pro portagio eorundem, iiij s. Item pro pomis emptis per manus Johannis Gilder, vij s. Item pro locione mapparum per manus Johannis Selby, xxij s. Item pro C ouorum, xx s. CLERICO coquine per manus Jacobi Gyde pro j quarterio bouis empto ibidem, xxiiij° die Decembris, ij duc. di. Item pro v castronibus, ij duc. liij s. Item pro j bacon empto ibidem eodem die, ij duc. xlvij s. Item pro j roo, j duc. xj s. Item pro ij porcellis, xxxij s. Super officio pulletrie pro ix gallinis, j duc. vij s. Item pro x pulcinis, xlj s. Item pro iiij aucis, xlv s. Item pro vj malardes et viij tele, iij li. Item in herbis, v s. Item in ouis, x s.ᵃ / CLERICO panterie per manus Johannis Payn pro pane albo per ipsum empto de Jacobo Pimbeour per xxj dies, tempore quo dominus stetit [apud] Venys, per compotum secum factum, lj duc. Et eidem Jacobo per manus eiusdem in pane pro trenchors, v duc. di. CLERICO baterie super vino per manus eiusdem, pro xij butts vini de

December 23.

December 24.

fo. 22 v°.

5

10

15

20

25

30

ᵃ Summa pagine, iiij^xx duc. vij s. ;—iiij li. xij d. faciunt j duc. ; noble computato vt supra. This note is repeated on the next three folios.

Mark, iiij^{xx}xiij duc. Item pro x buts vini de **Trevise** (?) per manus eiusdem, lx duc. CLERICO speciarie per manus Wilbram pro diversis speciebus per ipsum emptis de Anton Potecario tempore quo dominus [stetit] ibidem, viz. croco, maces, gariofilis, sugre
5 candy, sugre caffetin, amigdalis et rys, xij duc. xxiij s. Item pro iij ollis luteis et iiij ladel, et sale emptis apud Venis per Johannem Cudworth, xxj s. Item pro factura de ij rakks ibidem, xiiij s. ven. Item pro factura j reredos pro eisdem ibidem, xij s. Item pro sale albo, pomis. lotrice, et cupcloth manitergis, et acucione cultellorum,
10 emptis ibidem, per manus Johannis Gilder, iij duc. xx s. Item pro glikes vna cum portagio ad bargam, iij duc. vj s. Item pro portagio et batillagio panis et vini, ij duc. di. Item pro factura cultelli domini, xxxj s. Item pro lembic' manitergiorum, iiij s. Item pro locione manitergiorum et pro ij cupcloth, botr' et liggs, x s.
15 Item pro batillagio, v s. Item pro j lb. anneys de comfyt, xxviij s. Item pro j lb. de colyandre, xxviij s. Item pro ij lb. de pistaqiis, lvj s. Item pro ij lb. de zitronade, lvj s. ITEM pro batillagio thesaurarii per diuersas vices de Sancto Georgio vsque Venis et redeundo, xxxj s. Item cuidam bargeman expectanti apud Sanctum
20 Georgium cum carbonibus per j septimanam. j duc. di. Item pro expensis Thome Toty et Thome Gloucestre per iij dies existentibus extra curiam super negocium domini, iij duc. xij s. Item pro expensis domini Roberti capellani, et diuersorum famulorum domini, de Portgruer usque Venis vna cum conductione j batelle, iiij duc.
25 di. Item pro expensis Willelmi Kikkeley de Venis vsque Portgruer, xx s. ET PER manus Johannis Gilder pro pane albo per ipsum empto ibidem per ij dies ante recessum domini de Venis, iiij duc. di. Et per manus senescalli, thesaurarii et Johannis Payn pro tabulis, ligno, sparres, clauis, et aliis diuersis circa cabanas in
30 galeia faciendas pro diuersis officiariis, xxj. duc. d. Et diuersis carpentariis facientibus dictas cabans in galeia et alia necessaria ibidem, vij duc. Item in batillagio thesaurarii de Sancto Georgio apud Sanctum Nicholaum, xij s. ven. Et per manus eiusdem pro iiij malardz, ibidem emptis, et iij galinis, lv s. Et per manus

eiusdem pro batillagio domini, militum et scutiferorum suorum de
Sancto Nicholao apud Sanctum Georgium, iiij duc. xx s. ven.
Item pro busca ibidem empta, ij duc.

Summa pagine,
cciiij**xiiij duc. di.
xviij s. vj d. ven.

Prouidencia apud Venys.

fo. 23.
November 20.

/ In primis pro xvj bobus emptis apud Ochen, xx° die Nouembris, per Mowbray heraud et Willelmum Harpeden, iii**xij duc.
Item pro expensis eorundem bouum per ij dies et j noctem, xlvij s.
ven. Et pro ij hominibus conductis ad idem cum eisdem ad diuersas ferias* et nundinas pro dictis bobus emendis, ij duc. Et pro
expensis eorundem Mowbray, Harpeden, et ij gydes cum vj equis
per iiij dies, per compotum cum eis factum, vj duc. di. Item pro
iiij vasis vacantibus conductis per Mowbray ad Portgruer pro carne
salienda, l s. ven. Item in expensis Mowbray, Cudworth, et Harpeden ad Portgruer pro dicta carne salienda, vj duc. Item pro
expensis senescalli domini, Petri Solatour et Mowbray apud Sanctum Danielum, vj duc. xv s. Super officio pulleterie per manus
Harpeden, pro C gallinis per ipsum emptis Venis, xxx° die Nouem-
bris, ix duc. xxxiij s. Et eidem pro ij^m ij^c di. ouorum, viij duc.
iij li. xiij s. Et pro putura pullorum, vna cum conductione j domus
pro officio pulleterie, j duc. v s. Et per manus Hankin de Colon
pro xxxviij caponibus, vj duc. Et pro C gallinis emptis ibidem,
viij duc. liiij s. Item pro diuersis piscibus salsis emptis per Jacobum
Gyde pro prouidenciis domini versus galeiam, iiij**vj duc. Item
pro retibus emptis de patrono per senescallum, xiiij duc. Item pro
piscibus recentibus emptis per manus eiusdem, xv duc. Item pro
vij doliis pro aqua imponenda in galeia, vj duc. di. Item pro iiij
barellis pisarum et fabarum emptis per manus Willelmi Harpeden,
xxvj duc. di. Item pro casco per ipsum empto ibidem pro galeia,
xxxiij duc. xxiij s. Item pro oleo, xxj duc. viij s. Item pro pisci-

November 30.

---

* The MS. has diuerso- feros.

bus recentibus, ouis, et oleo emptis ibidem, xvij duc. xvj s. Item in
prandio pro putura, viij duc. Item pro emendacione de le vessell
pro larderio, viij li. Item pro oleribus, xxj s. Item pro expensis
Wilbram de Portgruer vsque Venis, di. duc. Item pro piscibus
5 salsis, ouis, et oleo, emptis Venis per manus eiusdem, ij duc. Item
in carne bouum, multonum, porcorum, et bacono emptis Venis de
Jacomello carnifice pro galeia per Jacobum Gyde et Hankin de
Colon, et pro portagio et batillagio eorundem per diuersas vices,
per compotum cum eis factum, cxxxij duc. xlv s. ix bag.[a] Item
10 pro j morter empt' ibidem per manus Johannis Wilbram, iij duc.
di. Item pro vinegre, vj duc. Item pro cenape empto ibidem,
iij duc. di. Item pro lino empto ibidem per ij vices, x duc. Item
pro m^l lb. amigdalarum, precium lb. iiij s. j d., in toto, l duc. xiij s.
iiij d. ven. Item pro iiij C lb. rys, precium lb. xviij d., in toto,
15 vij duc. di. Item in racemis ijClxxv lb., precium lb. iiij s., in toto,
xiiij duc. iij li. Item in datilis ij^m, xiiij li. Item pro C lb. candelarum cere, le lb. vij s. iij d., in toto, viij duc. iij li. xvij s. Item
in sugre caffetin, xxij lb., prec. lb. xviij s., in toto, v duc. Item in
sugre candy, xxiiij lb., prec. lb xl s., in toto, xij duc. xij s. minus.
20 Item in gingibre pist' xij lb., prec. lb. xxiiij s., in toto, iij duc.
xxxvij s. Item in sitronade xij lb., prec. lb. xxviij s., in toto,
iij duc. xxxvij s. Hony, xl lb., prec. lb., xxviij d., in toto, iiij li.
xiij s. iiij d. ven. Item in pot[b] sugre, xx lb., prec. lb. xij s., in
toto, iij duc., iij s. minus. Item in gariofilis, xxx lb., prec. lb.
25 lxviij s., in toto, xxv duc. xv s. Item in maces, xxiiij lb., prec. lb.
lxij s., in toto, xviij duc. xxx s. ven. Item in diuersis confectionibus
ibidem emptis, xiiij duc. Item in xij staris salis, xiiij duc. Item
in alleo et repo ibidem emptis, vj duc. Item in vno cado de graspeys, xj duc. Item pro securis, serruris, haspis, gemewis et clauis
30 pro galeia, iiij duc. Item pro xij lucernis, ij duc. xxiij s. Item pro
caboch et oleribus, j duc. xlij s. ven. Item pro porris, xxiiij s. Item

---

[a] Bagantine, a very small Venetian copper coin ; see it again p. 281, l. 15.
[b] This word does not occur among the descriptions of sugar in Hudson Turner nor in Douët d'Arcq.

222   THE EARL OF DERBY'S EXPEDITIONS.

pro farina auenarum, j duc. xv s.   Item pro vergws, ij duc. xl s.
Item pro j cado pro vergws imponendo, xij s. ven. . Item
pro ij paribus balaunces, ij duc. xiij s.   Item pro j pixide et
tunder, fyryren et broches, j duc. xx s.   Item pro ij C lb. candelarum cepi, xj duc. xxix s.   CLERICO panterie per manus 5
Johannis Payn pro C staris frumenti per ipsum empto ibidem
de Jacomello pistore pro galeia, le stara ad xiiij li. / xiiij s. iiij d.
per compotum secum factum, in toto ij^{c}lxiiij duc.   Item eidem
pro factura et pistrinura,[a] de le stara pro biscwhit, xx s., in
toto xxiiij duc. di. xv s. iiij d.   Item pro vj staris de farina ab 10
ipso emptis ibidem per manus Laurencii Trauers, le stara ad xv li.,
xxij duc.   CLERICO buterie per manus Johannis Payn, pro xiiij
amphoris vini per ipsum emptis ibidem de Francisco Tylemer', le
amphora ad xlviij li., in toto clxv duc. iij li. xv s.   Et eidem per
manus eiusdem pro vj amphoris vini emptis ibidem, le amphora, 15
xlvj li. lxviij duc. xij s.   Item per manus Johannis Payn pro ij butts
de Algarbe, xxxv duc.   Item per manus eiusdem pro iij butts vini
de Mark, xxv duc.   Item pro xl saccis pro pane imponendo emptis
per Johannem Payn, ix duc.   Et pro portagio saccorum de le Ryoll
ad pistrinam, iiij s.   Item pro j butt' de Romoneye cum vasis, xiij duc. 20
Item pro iiij vasis pro vino imponendo, iiij duc.   Item pro xij cadis,
iij galeys, et iij buttes, vj duc.   Item xij hominibus auxiliantibus
implere vinum in vasis, vij li. iiij s.   Item pro portagio panis de
pistoria vsque ad bargam, xl s.   Item pro ij limbis portantibus panem
ad galeiam, xl s.   Item pro j cado de Romonye, vj li.   Item pro 25
portagio de vj cadis, vj s.   Item pro ij bargeis trahentibus vinum
vsque le galeye, iij duc.   Item pro lino pro vasis et pro vno homine
mundando dicta vasa, ij s. iiij d.   Item pro vj mattes ad cooperien-
dum le biscwhit in galeia, vj li. xij s.   Item pro j buta vini empta
apud Sanctum Nicholaum, viij duc. xx s.   Item vni carpintario pro 30
tabulis et clauis, iij duc.   Item pro j vase de Maluesye, iiij duc.

[a] The contracted word is pist*a. which might stand for pistura if there could be
such a word, but the verb pistrinare appears to require pistrinura. The word is not
found in Ducange.

II. PROVISION AT VENICE FOR SEA-VOYAGE.

Item pro amphora et vitreis, ij duc. Item in. pane pro galeia, viij duc. Item pro j buta vini, vij duc. iij li. xvj s. Item pro vitreis et pomis, j duc. Item pro portagio et batillagio victualium de Sancto Nicholao vsque Sanctum Georgium, et pro batillagio
5 unius bute vini, j duc. Item pro pane et vino emptis apud Sanctum Nicholaum, vij duc. Item in pane recente empto per manus Payn ibidem in recessu domini pro galeia, vij duc. Item pro j buta de Riboll pro galeia, xj duc. Item pro x buttes pro vino imponendo vacantibus, per ipsum emptis ibidem, ix duc. Item in expensis
10 Johannis Payn existentis circa dictum vinum trahendum, adimplendum et cariandum, ij duc. xx s. Item per manus eiusdem pro ligno, tabulis, clauis, emptis ibidem pro galeia, xij duc. Item pro stipendiis et labore iiij carpintariorum laborantium in galeia, vj duc. Item per manus eiusdem pro j barella de storgon per
15 ipsum empta ibidem, viij duc. xlvij s. Item per manus eiusdem pro lx lb. cere non operate, v duc. l s. Item per manus eiusdem pro pane recente empto ibidem in recessu domini, xij duc. Item per manus eiusdem pro conductione diuersorum vasorum pro coquina, v duc. Item per manus eiusdem, dati Janyn Pimbecour carnifici,
20 laboranti circa carnes emendas, ij duc. Cuidam bargeman laboranti cum dicto Johanne circa vinum querendum per iij dies, ij duc. Item, dati cuidam herdman pro custodia quorundam bouum [apud] Venis, di. duc. Item pro diuersis necessariis emptis per Johannem Cudworth in galeia tangentibus officium suum, vij duc. Item pro
25 putura pulleterie, vz. pro ordeo empto ibidem per Willelmum Harpeden, x duc. Item pro pomis, ficubus, chasteins et aliis diuersis fructubus emptis pro galeia per manus thesaurarii de Francisco, fruturer, xvj duc. xlv s. Item pro iiij barellis pro fructubus imponendis, ij duc. Et per manus Jacobi Gyde,
30 pro j barella butiri per ipsum empta ibidem, iiij duc. vij s. Item pro busca et carbonibus emptis per Laurencium Trauers pro galeia, xvj duc. Et per manus eiusdem pro xij barellis vacantibus pro aqua imponenda, viij duc. Item per manus Jacobi Gyde pro xx paribus malard, ad pinsendum pro galeia, xij li.

Summa pagine, ix^{c}xxxix duc. x viij d. ven.

xvij s. Item pro xx partricibus per ipsum emptis ibidem, x li. / Item pro ij roos per ipsum emptis ibidem, iij duc. Item pro pistrinura,ᵃ xlv s. Item pro iiij peciis panni linei emptis ibidem per thesaurario pro galeia, de iiijˣˣ vlnis, le vlna pro vj s., in toto vj duc. vj s. minus. Item pro smigmate empto per Johannem Selby pro galeia, j duc. Item pro vasis ligneis emptis per manus Johannis Payn pro galeia pro coquina, pro panetria, et pro aliis diuersis officiis, viz. tubbes, trowes, boketes et basketes, vj duc. lviij s. Item pro emendacione vasorum de larderia, iiij li. Item per manus eiusdem pro bollis, ciphis et ollis luteis per ipsum emptis ibidem pro galeia, ij duc. xl s. Et per manus eiusdem pro j towaill pro speciebus, j duc. Item per manus eiusdem pro iiij paribus flaskis de tyn per ipsum emptis pro vino imponendo, in galeia, vj duc. Item pro iiij cages emptis pro putura in galeia per Willelmum Harpeden, iiij duc. xxv s.

Summa Pagine, xxxj duc. iiij li.

Summa totalis de Venys vsque huc, MᵖMᵖCCClxxix duc. di. xxviij s. vj d. ven.

RODES EUNDO.ᵇ

Johanni Selby pro locione mapparum apud Lisca et apud Curfu, xxxvj s. ven. Item apud Curfu pro oleribus et herbis ibidem emptis, xlij s. Item apud Curfu per manus eiusdem pro j porco recente ibidem empto, xiiij li. xj s. Item ibidem pro piscibus recentibus, iij duc. xlj s. Item apud Modon pro locione mapparum per manus Johannes Selby, xxiiij s. Item pro ix castronis vini ibidem emptis per manus le scalk ᶜ et Jacobi Gyde, x duc. xviij s. Item in ouis emptis ibidem, ij duc. xl s. Item in iiij partricibus,

---

ᵃ See note above, p. 222.
ᵇ The heading Rodes continues for the three pages following.
ᶜ This is the Italian scalco, meaning head-cook or steward. The word is another form of the Mid-High-German schalc and A.S. secale, a servant or valet.

iij harez, j duc. di. Item pro citrons emptis ibidem, viij s. Item
pro xlviij anguillis grossis, iij duc. di. Item pro pane per ipsum
empto ibidem, ij duc. xl s. Item in herbis et oleribus, xxiiij s.
Item per manus le scalk pro spelt per ipsum empt' ibidem pro
5 putura, j duc. xvj s. Item pro lacte per ipsum empto ibidem,
xxiiij s. Item pro pomis d'orrange per ipsum emptis ibidem,
xvij s. Item apud Rodes pro M^l ouorum emptis per Jacobum Gyde,
cxliij aspers. Item in ij pixidibus de dragge, ij duc. xxj asp.
Item in pane recente ibidem empto per manus Johannis Payn,
10 iiij duc. d. Item in herb's, oleribus, et porro, j duc. xij asps. Item
in j boyste de sugre roseto pro domino, ij duc. Item in vj partricibus, ij duc. iij asps. Item in piscibus recentibus ibidem emptis per
manus le scalk, iiij duc. xj asps. Item in lx anguillis per ipsum
emptis ibidem, iij duc. xxj asps. Item pro x fernecal et pro viij
15 ollis, xvj asps. Item pro portagio de vj saccis de pane ad galeiam,
iiij asps. Item pro portagio de xx jaris aque ad galeiam, vj asps.
Item pro locione pannorum lineorum de boteria et paneteria vna
cum batillagio ad galeiam pro diuersis rebus officii panetrie, viij asps.
Item pro reparacione j tymon per le scriuen ibidem, vj duc. xxj asp.
20 Item pro j pare sotularum pro Henrico henksman, iiij gr. di. siccez
Item in piscibus apud Jaffe, vj gr. siccez. Item pro j asino ibidem
conducto pro victualibus cariandis apud Rames, vj gr. Item in ij
castronis emptis ibidem, iij duc. Item in gallinis et ouis emptis ibidem
per manus Antonii le Gyde, iij duc. Item pro vj kyd, xij gr. Item pro
25 ij castronis emptis ibidem per le scalk, iij duc. Item apud Rames^a
/ per manus Mowbray Herald pro vino, aqua sugurata, ouis et aliis fo. 24 v°.
victualibus per ipsum emptis ibidem, v duc. Item pro j equo
conducto per Herr* henksman de Rames vsque Iherusalem, vj gr. * This is Harry,
this henksman's n
was Henry, see al

* Summa pagine de parte de Rodes, lxxv duc. xiij s. vj d. ven. j gr. di. siccez.
In the margin are the values, as follow :—

         iiij li. xij d. fac. j duc.
         xxviij asps. fac. j duc.
         xviij gross. siccz fac. j duc.
         ij duc et ix s. faciunt j noble st.

Item apud Iherusalem pro vino empto, per manus thesaurarii, xiij gr. Item pro candelis cere emptis ibidem pro domino, vj gr. Item apud Rames redeundo pro j asino ibidem conducto pro Henrico henksman, iiij gr. Item pro candelis emptis ibidem per gardianum, xxiiij gr. Item apud Jaffe pro ij castrons et vj gallinis emptis per manus j Lumbard, iij duc. Item pro ligno empto ibidem, viij gr. Item soluti pro xj gallinis emptis ibidem, ij duc. xv gr. Item in vj gallinis per senescallum emptis ibidem, j duc. vij gr. Item pro vj gallinis et xj pulcinis emptis ibidem per manus thesaurarii, j duc. xj gr. Item in vino, pane et ouis emptis ibidem per Gilder, ij duc. xvj gr. Item in racemis emptis ibidem, xj gr. Item in viij C ouorum emptis ibidem, iiij^{xx} vj gr. Item pro pane empto ibidem per senescallum, viij duc. v gr. Item pro piscibus recentibus ibidem emptis per manus Antonii, ij duc. xvij gr. Item in nucibus et pomis ibidem emptis per manus eiusdem, vij gr. Et pro ouis per ipsum emptis ibidem, v gr. Item apud Famagost per manus le scalk pro pane albo per ipsum empto, xvij gr. Item in vino empto ibidem, per manus eiusdem, xxxviij gr. Item pro iij castronibus, iij duc. ix gr. Item per manus eiusdem pro gallinis et ouis ibidem emptis, v duc. xij gr. Item per manus Laurencii Trauers pro ligno et salsa ibidem expenditis et emptis pro galeia, viij duc. Item per manus Johannis Selby pro locione mapparum, j duc. Et per manus eiusdem pro oleribus et herbis emptis ibidem pro galeia, j duc. iiij gr. Et per manus le scriuen pro pinguedine pro reparacione galeie ibidem, xxiij duc. Item pro clauis emptis ibidem pro galeia, xj besaunts. Item in expensis domini prioris Sancti Johannis, domini Otes Graunsom et aliorum militum et scutiferorum euntium versus regem Cyprie de Famagost vsque Nikasye, vna cum conductione equorum, per compotum secum factum, xix duc. Item per manus Jacobi Gyde pa. iij castronibus emptis pro galeia, iij duc. Item pro xx gallinis per ipsum emptis, ij duc. iij besaunts. Item pro C anguillarum empta ibidem, iij duc. Item pro piscibus recentibus, ij duc. ij besaunts iiij gr. Item in ouis per ipsum emptis ibidem, ij duc.

iij besaunts j gr. Item in oleo et ficubus, iiij bes. Item apud
Rodes, redeundo, per manus Mowbray Herauld, pro viij tabulis per
ipsum empt:s ibidem pro scochons domini, militum et scutiferorum
suorum faciendis in Castello, iij duc. di. Item pro pictura dicta-
5 rum tabularum, ix duc. di. Item ad pendendum dictas tabulas in
Castello et pro cheynes, clauis, hokes, j duc. di. Item pro pane
empto ibidem per v dies per manus Johannis Payn, xij duc. xxiiij
aspers. Item per manus eiusdem pro vino ibidem empto, xxiij duc.
Item pro carnibus bouinis, motulinis, porcinis per Jacobum Guyde
10 emptis ibi lem, xv duc. xliiij aspers. Item per manus eiusdem pro
amigdalis et aliis diuersis speciebus ibidem emptis, vj duc. xxv asp.
Et per manus eiusdem pro xlv gallinis per ipsum emptis ibidem,
ij^{cli} asps. Item pro viij partricibus emptis ibidem, xxvj asp. Item
per manus eiusdem pro vj porcellis emptis ibidem, xxxvij asp. Item
15 pro parnis volatilibus emptis ibidem per manus eiusdem, xvij asps.[a]
/ Item in vC ouorum per ipsum emptis ibidem, lxx asps. Item pro fo. 25.
ij baskets per ipsum emptis ibi lem pro victualibus portandis, iiij
asps. Item pro j roo per ipsum empta ibidem, j duc. xiij asps.
Item pro lacte per ipsum empto ibidem, xiij asps iij gr. Et pro
20 oleo per ipsu n empto ibidem, x asps. Et per manus eiusdem pro
ij C anguillarum salsarum per ipsum emptis, iiij^{xx}xvj asps. Item
pro aliis piscibus salsis et recentibus per ipsum emptis ibidem tempore quo dominus stetit ibidem, ix duc. xv asps. Et per manus
Laurencii Trauers pro busca et carbonibus per ipsum emptis tempore
25 quo dominus stetit ibidem, vij duc. xj asps. Et pro portagio eiusdem, ij asps. Item per manus eiusdem pro cenape, vergws, vinegre,
herbis, farina et pisis ibidem expenditi, iiij duc. xxij asps. Item
per manus eiusdem pro sale empto ibidem tempore quo dominus
stetit ibidem, ij duc. xiij asps. Item pro discis, platers, salsaris
30 emptis ibi lem per manus eiusdem, j duc xvij asps. Et per manus
eiusdem pro conductione diuersorum vasorum pro coquina, tempore

---

[a] Summa pagine, ccj ducati di. vj grossi iij besantz, iiij aspers :—unde, xviij gr.
s'eez. faciunt j ducatum ; Item x besantz faciunt j ducatum ; Item xxviij aspers
faciunt j ducatum ; nobile computato vt supra.

quo dominus stetit ibidem, xxiij asp. Et per manus thesaurarii pro ligno et tabulis et j carpintario operante circa diuersa necessaria in hospicio domini, xvj asps. Et per manus eiusdem pro domibus in hospicio domini mundandis, et per manus Jacobi Gyde pro xij lb. candelarum cepi, tempore quo dominus stetit ibidem, xxiiij asps. Item pro xij lucernis emptis ibidem per manus Johannis Payn, iij duc. xv asps. Item per manus Jacobi Gyde pro portagio victualium tempore quo dominus (stetit) ibidem, xiij asps. xxv s. ven. Et per manus Johannis Gilder pro pomis, nucibus, et aliis fructibus per ipsum emptis ibidem, vij asps. ix s. ven. Et per manus eiusdem pro locione pannorum lineorum de panetria, et pro panno lineo empto pro ij portours ibidem, et pro emendacione cultellorum de panetrie, xvij asps. Et per manus eiusdem pro sale albo per ipsum empto ibidem, iiij asps. Et per manus eiusdem pro xij ollis luteis per ipsum emptis ibi lem, vij asps. Et pro iij vlnis streynour per ipsum emptis ibidem, iiij asps. Et per manus eiusdem pro j panyer per ipsum empto ibidem, ij asps. Item per manus eiusdem pro portagio xx jarrorum aque ad mare, ix asps. Et pro batillagio eiusdem ad galeiam, vj asps. Et pro batillagio domini et aliorum diuersorum de galeia usque terram in primo aduentu suorum ibidem, iiij duc. xxj asps. Et pro ouis emptis ibidem per seneseallum, j duc. iiij. asps. Item in diuersis speciebus emptis ibidem pro galeia, viz. croco, pipere, zinzubero, canella, et ficubus, vna cum iiij lb. confeccionum, per Johannem Payn ibidem emptis, viij duc. xiij asps. Et per manus eiusdem pro sugro et surrip et pro j pot de sitronade, iij duc. Et per manus Laurencii Trauers pro cenape empto ibidem pro galeia, iiij duc. xvj asps. Item pro aceto empto ibidem per manus eiusdem, vj duc. viij asps. Item pro busca empta ibidem pro galeia, per manus eiusdem, v duc. Item per manus eiusdem pro herbis, oleribus, porris et pisis emptis ibidem pro galeia, ij duc. Item pro C piscium salsorum empta vocatorum sardyns, per manus eiusdem ibidem, l asps. Item per manus eiusdem pro iij C anguillarum salsarum per ipsum emptis ibidem, cxxxj asps. Item pro ij saccis ibidem emptis per manus eiusdem pro piscibus imponendis,

II. EXPENSES IN RHODES AND CYPRUS.

iij asps. Item pro xx lb. candelorum cepi per ipsum emptis ibidem pro galeia, xliiij asps. Item pro ligno et tabulis per ipsum emptis ibidem pro j caban faciendo pro leopardo, j duc. Item pro iiij castronibus ibidem emptis per manus Jacobi Gyde pro dicto leopardo,
5 iiij duc. xiiij asps. Item pro diuersis speciebus per magistrum leopardi ibidem emptis pro dicto leopardo, iiij duc. vij asps. Item pro pane albo* / ibidem empto per manus Johannis Gilder pro galeia, vij duc. xvij asps. Item diuersis hominibus pro cariagio et portagio panis, vini et aliorum victualium de Castello ad galeiam, ij duc. xij asps. Item
10 pro oleo empto per manus Jacobi Gyde pro galeia, iiij duc. Item in piscibus salsis emptis ibidem pro galeia per manus eiusdem, xij duc. Item pro piscibus recentibus emptis ibidem per manus eiusdem pro galeia, iij duc. vij s. Item pro sepo per ipsum empto ibidem pro galeia, xl s. Item pro lviiij storgons salsis emptis
15 ibidem per manus le scalk, xxviij duc. di. Item pro iiijC piscium salsorum, vij duc. iiij s. Item pro vC anguillarum, ix duc. vj s. Item pro iij C sgomery,* vj duc. Et pro xj moges emptis ibidem, vij duc. iiij s. Item pro li. di. rolle de figges, iij duc. xix s. Item pro magna olla olei, vj duc. Item pro portagio eorundem ad
20 galeiam, ix s. Et per manus eiusdem pro confectionibus pro galeia, xxvj s. Item pro sugre, xxvj s. Item pro candelis cere, ij duc. v asps. Item apud Niksy in pane et herbis ibidem emptis per manus Jacobi Gyde, iij duc. Item in vino empto ibidem per manus Payn, vj duc. xliiij s. Item in oleo empto ibidem per manus
25 Jacobi Guyde, ij duc. Item in piscibus recentibus emptis ibidem per manus eiusdem, iij duc. Item pro piscibus salsis emptis per manus le scalk ibidem, ij duc. xliiij s. Item in oleo empto ibidem, per manus Jacobi Gyde, ij duc. Item pro iiij gallinis emptis ibidem pro falconibus, xxiij s. Item pro ij castronibus pro leopardo,
30 j duc. di. Item pro cariagio et batillagio victualium et aque recentis de villa vsque galeiam, xlv s. Item pro petrosilio et porris

[Sgomery, a p[robable] error for Skom (σκυμβρί), the fish mackerel.]

fo. 25 v°.

---

* Summa pagine, iiij**xv duc. xxxiiij s. ven., iij gros. siccz, xvij asps :—vnde xviij gros. siccz. faciunt j ducatum. Item, xxviij aspers faciunt j ducatum.

ibidem emptis per manus Jacobi Gyde, 1 s. Et per manus eiusdem pro alleo ibidem empto, j duc. Item pro cariagio et batillagio j but vini dati per Ducem ibidem, et alterius empti de castello ad galeiam, j duc. Et per manus le scalk pro busca per ipsum empta apud Baffa, iiij duc. xxiij s. Item pro x lb. candelarum cepi per ipsum emptis ibidem, lxiij s. Et per manus eiuslem pro batillagio de galeia vsque villam et redeundo, vij s. Item pro j lecto et j selaueyn emptis de Gilberto famulo patroni pro Henrico baptizato,[*] ij duc. xxvij s. Item pro camisia eidem et caligis et sotularibus, iiij duc. vij s. Item apud Langow pro cariagio et batillagio j but vini et panis datorum domino per magistrum ibidem, xxvij s. Item pro oleribus, petrosilio et porris ibidem emptis per manus Laurencii Trauers, j duc. xliij s. Item apud Modon reddite per manus Jacobi Guyde pro iij C anguillarum, v duc. xxxv s. Item pro xxij lb. olei, ij duc. xliij s. Item pro piscibus recentibus per ipsum emptis ibidem, iij duc. xxxvij s. Item pro porris, petrosilio, et cauleriis emptis ibidem per manus eiusdem, liiij s. Item pro sale empto ibidem, xxiij s. Item pro iiij castronis emptis pro leopardo, xij li. xxij s. Item pro vj gallinis ibidem emptis pro falconibus, xlv s. Item in croco empto ibidem, per thesaurarium, ij duc. Item pro vino empto ibidem per manus eiusdem, iiij duc. viij s. Item pro piscibus per ipsum emptis ibidem, ij duc. Item pro pane empto ibidem per manus Johannis Payne, vij duc. di. Item pro iij magnis battes vini de Romanye ibidem emptis per manus eiusdem, xxxiij duc. Item pro busca empta ibidem per manus Laurencii Trauers, vj duc. xliij s. Item per manus eiusdem pro cenape et aceto ibidem empto, ij duc. di. Item in sepo et farina per ipsum emptis ibidem, xxiij s. Item pro portagio victualium de villa ad galeiam, xj s. Item pro xiiij paruis barellis empeis pro vino imponendo ibidem, iiij duc. xxxvj s. Item per manus Johannis Payn pro tractura portagio et batillagio dicti vini de villa vsque galeiam, j duc. xlv s. Item pro melle ibidem empto per

[Marginal numbers: 5, 10, 15, 20, 25, 30]

* This Henry was evidently a Turkish convert, we find a little further on, in March, a toga was made for Henry the Turk.

manus eiusdem, I s. Item in Cornoua per manus le scalk pro pane, xij li. v s. Item pro porris et petrosilio et cauleriis per manus eiusdem,[a]

Per mare redeundo versus Venys.

5 / liiij s. Item pro piscibus emptis ibidem por manus eiusdem, lxij s. fo. 26. Item apud Ragusam pro v C anguillarum emptis ibidem, xiiij duc. di. Item pro nucibus, lij s. Item pro porris et petrosilio et cauleriis, lxvij s. Item ad portandum mandel et pisces, vj s. Item pro j gallina per ipsum empta ibidem pro falconibus, xiiij s. Item pro ij
10 castronibus emptis ibidem per manus eiusdem pro leopardo, ij duc. di. Item pro candelis cepi emptis ibidem, vj li. xxxiij s. Item pro amigdalis, xxv s. Item apud Curfu reddite pro pane ibidem empto per manus Johannis Payn, iiij duc. di. Item pro ij castronibus emptis pro leopardo, j duc. xxiij s. Item pro vj gallinis emptis pro fal-
15 conibus, liiij s. Item pro oleribus, herbis, et porris emptis ibidem per manus Laurencii Trauers, I s. Item pro nucibus et ficubus emptis itidem per manus Johannis Gilder, xxiij s. Item apud Jar pro busca empta ibidem per manus le scalk, ij duc. Item per manus eiusdem pro j castrone pro leopardo, xlvij s. Item per
20 manus eiusdem pro porris, petrosilio et pisis, xxxiij s. Item ibidem pro ostreis, viij li. iiij s. Item pro batillagio corundem, viij s. Item in vino ibidem, xvj duc. Item in estreis ibidem, iij duc. Item pro cenape, vergws, vinegro emptis ibidem per manus Laurencii Trauers, j duc. xl s. Item pro emendacione de le tymon per manus
25 le scriuen, iiij duc. Item pro filo empto pro eodem per manus eiusdem, ij duc. xv s. Item pro portagio et batillagio dictorum victualium ibidem, xv s. Item pro locione mapparum per manus Johannis Selby ibidem, j duc. Item pro xij lb. candelarum cere ibidem, j duc. lxvij s. Item apud Lissinner pro pane empto per

[a] Summa pagine, ccxviij duc. di. r s. vj d. ven., vj asps.:—vnde iiij li. xij d. faciunt j ducatum; xxviij asps. faciunt j ducatum; nob. comp. vt supra.

manus Johannis Payn, ij duc. lj s. Item pro vino empto ibidem per manus eiusdem, xj duc. d. Et pro portagio, tractura et batellagio dicti vini de villa vsque galeiam, xlvij s. Item pro piscibus salsis et anguillis recentibus et piscibus, v duc. lij s. Et pro portagio et batillagio victualium, v s. Item pro j gallina pro falconibus, xiij s. Item pro oleribus, herbis, et porris per manus Laurencii Trauers, xxij s. Item apud Pola per manus le scalk pro pane, piscibus et herbis per ipsum emptis ibidem, v duc. xlvij s. Item pro j castrone pro leopardo, xliij s. Item cuidam Greco in galeia pro j barella vini de Mark empta pro domino, iiij duc. xlvij s. Item eidem per manus Jacobi Gyde pro farina empta in galeia per diuersas vices, iij duc. di. Et eidem per manus eiusdem pro piscibus emptis ab eodem in galeia per diuersas vices, ij duc. xxix s. Item pro vino de Romonye empto per manus Johannis Payn in galeia de Gilberto famulo patroni, vj duc. Item eidem pro gallinis et ouis emptis apud Jaffam per manus senescalli, ij duc. di. Item pro vino empto de Johanne Cudworth per manus Johannis Payn, xxiiij duc. Item pro j barella de Romonye empta in galeia de Jacomello famulo patroni per senescallum, v duc. vij s. ven. Item soluti Johanni Payn pro vino de Romonye et de Mark per ipsum empto in galeiam de diuersis galeymen per diuersas vices, per compotum cum eis factum, xij duc. iij li. xvj s. Item pro diuersis piscibus salsis emptis in galeia per le scalk de diuersis galeymen per diuersas vices per compotum cum eis factum, xxvj duc. xxv s. Item pro diuersis piscibus emptis ibidem per senescallum per diuersas vices de le seryuen, per compotum cum eo factum, xj duc. l s. Item pro ij barellis vini de Romoneye emptis ibidem de Gilberto, famulo patroni per thesaurarium, iij duc. di. Item pro diuersis piscibus per ipsum emptis ibidem per diuersas vices, v duc. xviij s. Item pro fabis, oleo, et ficubus per ipsum emptis ibidem de vno Greco, ij duc. xj s. Item pro piscibus recentibus emptis ibidem per Dominum Willelmum Wiluby, iiij duc. xxj s.[a]

---

[a] Summa pagine. CCiiij duc. xxxvij s. vj d. ven.:—vnde iiij li. xij d. fac. j duc. j duc. et ix s. fac. j noble. This note of values is repeated on the next five pages.

II. EXPENSES IN VENICE AND TREVISO.

VENYS REDEUNDO.

/CLERICO panetrie per manus Johannis Payn pro pane albo per ipsum empto apud Venys redeundo de Sancto Sepulchro a xxj. die mensis Marcii vsque xxix^m diem eiusdem mensis, vtroque compu-
5 tato per ix dies, per compotum secum factum, xviij. duc. xxij s. CLERICO butrie super vino, pro vino per ipsum empto ibidem per idem tempus per compotum secum factum, lij duc. CLERICO coquine per manus Jacobi Gyde pro piscibus per ipsum emptis ibidem per idem tempus, per compotum secum factum, iiij^{xx}j duc.
10 xxxv s. CLERICO speciarie pro diuersis speciebus et confectionibus ibidem emptis per manus Johannis Payn per idem tempus, per compotum secum factum, xj. duc. iij. li. xv s. Item per manus eiusdem pro cera operata, viij. duc. xvij s. Super officio scutellarie per manus Laurencii Trauers pro sale, herbis, farina, busca et carboni-
15 bus per ipsum emptis ibidem per idem tempus, xviij. duc. vij s. Super officio salsarie per manus ciusdem pro cenape, vergws, vinegre, per ipsum emptis ibidem per idem tempus, iij duc. xxj s. CLERICO coquine per manus Jacobi Gyde pro carne et gallinis per ipsum emptis ibidem pro leopardo et iiij falconibus per idem tempus, vij. duc
20 xxxix s. CLERICO speciarie per manus Johannis Selby pro xxxij lb. candelarum cepi per ipsum emptis ibidem per idem tempus, ij duc. Item per manus eiusdem pro locione mapparum ibidem per idem tempus, iij li. Item pro factura de broyiours et correccione mapparum, xx s. Item pro correctione de coffris de
25 chaundry et ewery, xx s Item pro factura toge Henrici Turk.'* iij li. Item pro portagio panis, vini, et omnium dictorum victualium per idem tempus, per compotum cum officiariis factum, lvij s. Et per manus Johannis Wilbram pro scutellis ligneis, trowes, tubbes, basketes et aliis barellis et cadis per ipsum emptis ibidem
30 pro diuersis officiis, xj. duc. Et pro cariagio et batillagio corundem, vij s. Item pro vessellis de pewter emptis ibidem per thesaurium, iiij noble, l s. Item pro batillagio et portagio, v s. Item per

fo. 26 v°.
March 21-29,

* See note ab

234   THE EARL OF DERBY'S EXPEDITIONS.

manus ciusdem pro batillagio diuersorum harnisiorum domini, et portagio de galcia vsque terram, ij duc. Item per manus ciusdem pro

March 24. lv bras panni linei emptis Venys xxiiij° die Marcii, v li. xj s. Item cuidam carpintario pro tabulis emptis et factura diuersorum necessariorum in aula domini apud Sanctum Georgium, ij duc. CLE- 5 RICO panetrie per manus Johannis Payn, pro pane per ipsum

March 30—April 10. empto ibidem, a xxx° die mensis Marcii vsque x^m diem Aprilis, vtroque computato per xij dies, de Francisco pistore, xxvj. duc. CLERICO butrie super vino, per manus Johannis Payn pro vino de Rochelle empto de quodam Lumbardo vocato Bonefacio, xvj. duc. 10

March 22. xvij s. CLERICO speciarie per manus Jacobi Gyde xxij° die Marcii, pro vno streynour, x s. Et pro j quarterno papiri, viij s. Item pro xxxvj lb. amigdalarum, viij. li. xij. s. Et pro vj lb. cere, xlviij s. Et pro iij. vergis tele pro j gelicloth, xviij s. Et pro xij. lb. candelarum cepi, lx s. Super officio scutellarie per manus Laurencii 15

March 31. Trauers ibidem vltimo die Marcii, in sale empto, j duc. di. Item per manus eiusdem pro farina per ipsum empta apud Venesiam eodem die, xlj s. Et pro ligno per ipsum empto ibidem, v duc. Et pro ligno empto per manus senescalli, iij. duc. lx s. Et per manus eiusdem pro herbis, xlj s. Et per manus eiusdem pro aceto per 20 ipsum empto ibidem, ij duc. Item Mowbray herald. pro viij tabulis apud Sanctum Marcum cum armatura domini, militum, et scutiferorum suorum, et cum clauis ad pendendum dictas tabuias ibidem, xij. duc. xx s. Item pro pictura corundem armorum apud Sanctum Georgium, vj duc. di. Et pro dictis tabulis iij. duc. Item pro 25 manus Johannis Gilder pro locione dictorum towailles et cupcloth de panetria, tempore quo dominus stetit ibidem, xxj s. Item pro sale albo per ipsum empto ibidem pro panetrie, xxxij s. Item pro ij sincturis et ij stopell' pro botellis domini per manus eiusdem, xxiiij s. Item pro diuersis fructubus per ipsum emptis 30 ibidem per idem tempus, xxxvj s. Clerico butrie super vino,

March 30—April 10. pro vino per manus Payn ibidem empto, a xxx° die Marcii

Sic. vsque x^m diem Aprilis post prandium per xij dies, per compotum serum factum, lxxij duc. di. CLERICO coquine per manus

Johannis Wilbram pro piscibus et carne per ipsum emptis ibidem,[a]
/ per idem tempus, per compotum secum factum, clviij duc. xij s. fo. 27.
vj bag. CLERICO speciarie per manus Hans de Colon pro diuersis
speciebus per ipsum emptis ibidem per idem tempus, vna cum cera
5 operata et amigdalis, xxxvj duc. di. Et pro batillagio ipsius et
portagio diuersarum specierum et aliorum victualium per ipsum
emptorum per diuersas vices, per compotum secum factum, xxxiij s.
Et per manus eiusdem pro carne pro leopardo et gallinis pro
falconibus per ipsum emptis ibidem, per diuersas vices, iiij duc. di.
10 CLERICO speciarie per manus Johannis Selby pro candelis cepi
per ipsum emptis ibidem per idem tempus, j duc. xxx s. Et per
manus eiusdem pro locione mapparum per idem tempus, j duc.
xx s. SUPER officio scutellarie per manus Laurencie Trauers pro
carbonibus per ipsum emptis erga festum Paschale, vij duc. Item
15 per manus eiusdem pro busca per ipsum empta ibidem, v° die April 5.
Aprilis, v duc. Item pro portagio et batillagio dictorum carbonum et
busce, vij s. Item per manus thesaurarii pro busca per ipsum
empta ibidem, vij° die Aprilis, iiij duc. xliij s. Et pro batillagio et April 7
portagio eiusdem, iiij s. Super officio salsarie per manus Lau-
20 rencii Trauers pro cenape, vergws, et venegre, et sale per ipsum
empto ibidem per idem tempus, per compotum secum factum,
iiij duc. xxiij s. Et pro locione naperie et couertours coquine per
ipsum ibidem per diuersas vices, xxxvij s. Et per manus eiusdem
pro iiij besoms ad mundandum coquinam et larderiam, iij s. Et
25 per manus eiusdem pro mundacione domorum apud Sanctum
Georgium per ij famulos, viij s. Et per manus eiusdem Laurencii
pro j secure et ij schan pro dressing bord, xxxiij s. Et per manus
Johannis Payn pro conductione diuersorum vasorum pro coquina
tempore quo dominus stetit ibidem, v duc. Et per manus Johannis
30 Gilder pro ollis luteis per ipsum emptis ibidem, iij li. iij s. Et
per manus eiusdem pro glases et verres per ipsum emptis ibidem,
ij duc. Item pro portagio et batillagio corundem, v s. Item per

[a] Summa pagine, iiij noble st. Item de moneta, ij^{c}lxxvij duc. xxxix s. vj d. ven.

manus eiusdem pro mollicione cultellorum domini et cultellorum panetrie ibidem, viij s. Et per manus Laurencii Trauers pro mollicione dressyng knyues et aliorum cultellorum coquine, x s. Item per manus thesaurarii pro xl bras panni linei pro couertours et naperia diuersorum officiariorum, erga festum Paschale per ipsum emptis ibidem, le bras ad vj s., xij li. Et per manus eiusdem pro lxx bras per ipsum emptis ibidem pro naperia, le bras ad viij s , xxviij li. Et per manus Laurencii Trauers pro farina per ipsum empta ibidem ad pinsendum diuersas carnem et pisces tempore quo dominus stetit ibidem, iij duc. Et per manus eiusdem Francisco pasteler, pro furno suo ab ipso conducto vna cum busca ibidem expendita, j duc. di. Item pro manus thesaurarii iij seruientibus in coquina tempore quo dominus stetit ibidem, j duc. di. Item Jacobo Pimbeour, carnifici laboranti extra Venisiam pro carne querenda et emenda per diuersas vices, ij duc. Et eidem pro batillagio [apud] Venys, de villa vsque ad Sanctum Georgium per diuersas vices, xxxij s. Item per manus eiusdem Hans de Colon laborantis per diuersas vices circa diuersa victualia et alia necessaria querenda ibidem, ij duc. Item camerario Sancti Georgii pro clauibus perditis et emendacione serure ibidem per manus thesaurarii, j duc. di. Item per manus thesaurarii pro expensis senescalli, Toty, marescalli et aliorum diuersorum officiariorum domini euntibus ad Treuyse pro ordinacione domini ibidem facienda pro domino, vna cum conductione batelle de Venys vsque Portgruer pro equis domini et aliorum famulorum suorum ibidem querendis, et de ibidem vsque Treuyse, vna cum expensis eorundem redeuntium vsque Venys, per iiij dies per compotum cum eis factum, in toto, xl duc. Clerico marescallcie per manus Wilbram pro xxx staris auenarum per ipsum emptis Venys, iij⁰ die Aprilis, xvij duc. iij s. Et pro cariagio eorundem de ibidem vsque Trevyse, j duc. xij s. Et pro portagio eorundem, iiij s. Et pro tollagio pro eisdem apud Venys, xxvj s. Et pro expensis Wilbram et Harpeden existentium apud Treuisam pro eisdem, et pro aliis victualibus ibidem emendis per iij dies, per compotum cum

II. EXPENSES IN VENICE AND THE NEIGHBOURHOOD. 237

eisdem factum, j duc. Item pro ij equis pro eisdem conduc- Summa pagine
tis de Meistre vsque Treuyse et de ibidem vsque Meistre, CCCxiij duc. i ven.
/ xl s. CLERICO speciarie per manus eiusdem pro j quarterno fo. 27 v°.
papiri pro officio thesaurarii per ipsum empto apud Venis eodem
5 die, xvj s. Johanni Wilbram pro vj batellis per ipsum conductis
de Venis vsque Meistre pro domino et tota familia sua, ij duc.
xlviij s. Et per manus eiusdem pro j cista per ipsum empta ibidem
pro officio speciarie, lx s. Clerico speciarie per manus eiusdem pro
lxxxij lb. cere per ipsum emptis apud Venis pro Treuise eodem die,
10 vij duc. lxvj s. Item pro amigdalis, speciebus ibidem emptis pro
Treuise, xiij duc. xlvj s. ven. CLERICO panetrie per manus Gilder
pro pane albo per ipsum empto apud Meistre, xij° die Aprilis pro April 12.
cena domini, j duc. xix s. CLERICO buterie super vino per manus
eiusdem, pro vino per ipsum empto ibidem, iij duc. lx s. CLERICO
15 coquine per manus diuersorum pro carne bouina, mutulina, vitulina
per ipsos emptis ibidem, ij duc. l s. CLERICO marescalcie per manus
Wilbram pro feno per ipsum empto ibidem, j duc. Et pro auenis
emptis ibidem, ij duc. v s. Et pro busca et carbonibus ibidem, j duc.
x s. Johanni Wilbram pro j carecta per ipsum conducta de Meistre
20 vsque Trevyse cum diuersis harnisiis domini ibidem, j duc. Et pro
ij equis conductis in eodem itinere eodem die, xxx s. Cuidam
carectario de Treuise pro j carrecta ab ipso conducta pro cariagio
harnisiorum domini de aqua ibidem vsque fratres de Treuise, per
conuencionem secum factum ibidem, xiij° die Aprilis, xx s. CLERICO April 13.
25 speciarie per manus Wilbram pro j quarterno papiri per ipsum
empto apud Trevyse, xiiij° die Aprilis, viij s. Item pro expensis April 14.
in homine misso de Venis vsque Treuyse pro salua custodia harnisii domini, eundi per ij dies et j noctem, ij duc. Et pro expensis
leopardi per ij dies apud Treuyse, per compotum factum ibidem,
30 xxx s. Et pro j batella conducta de Venis vsque Treuyse pro
cariagio diuersorum harnisiorum domini per conuencionem cum ipso
factam apud Venis xj° die Aprilis, ij duc. xl s. Clerico speciarie per April 11.
manus Selby pro candelis cepi per ipsum emptis apud Trevise, xiiij° April 14.
die Aprilis, j duc. Clerico marescalcie per manus Thome Ferour pro

diuersis vnguentibus per ipsum emptis ibidem eodem die, j duc. CLERICO speciarie per manus Wilbram pro j lb. amigdalarum per ipsum empta ibidem eodem die, vj s. THOME Ferour pro j corio equino per ipsum empto apud Treuyse pro emendacione frenorum, capistrorum pro diuersis equis domini, j duc. lij s. Et per manus 5 eiusdem pro emendacione diuersorum sellarum, frenorum, capistrorum, ibidem eodem die, per compotum factum ibidem, ij duc. xxxviij s. CLERICO batrie super vino per manus Payn pro j carte

April 24. vini per ipsum empt' apud Treuyse, xxiij die Aprilis, xj duc. CLERICO speciarie per manus Jacobi Gyde pro x vergis streynours 10 per ipsum emptis ibidem eodem die, j duc. Clerico marescalcie per manus Wilbram pro j pole et x vergis de gerthwebbes per ipsum emptis ibidem eodem die, xxiiij s. Et per manus Wilbram pro horscombes, warrokes, et sagmine emptis ibidem pro equis

March 30—April 27. domini, xxij s. Et pro ferris emptis ibidem apud Treuyse a xxx° 15 die Marcii vsque xxvij diem Aprilis, vtroque computato, xxxiij duc. vj s. Et pro litura empta ibidem, iiij duc. Et pro lvij staris auenarum j quarter emptis ibidem per idem tempus, ad lx s. xlij duc. xxxiij s. Et pro ferrura equorum domini ibidem per idem tempus, ij duc. Item pro batillagio thesaurarii et aliorum officiari- 20 orum domini, de Sancto Georgio, cum diuersis coffris et aliis diuersis harnisiis domini, j duc. iiij s. Item pro vj batillis conductis de Venis vsque Meistre pro domino et parte familie sue per manus eiusdem, v duc. Clerico pantrie per manus Johannis Payn

April 11-25. pro pane albo per ipsum empto apud Treuise, a xj° die Aprilis 25 vsque xxviij diem eiusdem mensis, vtroque computato, per xviij dies, per Herman Clyne pistorem, per compotum secum factum, xlj duc. Et per manus eiusdem pro pane empto pro trenchors de eodem Herman, vj duc. xxviij s. Clerico batrie super vino, per manus eiusdem pro vj butts vini de Treuise, xxxvj duc. Et per 30 manus eiusdem pro j magn' but vini de Chastelfrank per ipsum empt' ibidem de Antonio Ferestell, xxxij duc. Et per manus eiusdem pro ij buttes vini de Mark pro domino, emptis Venys de Jacomello Ferar, xvij duc. Et per manus eiusdem pro j but de

Romonye empt' ibidem pro domino, v duc. Et per manus eiusdem Summa pagi
pro vj   CCiiij^xxvij d
                                                                xxxij s.

Treuyse* in partibus de Venys.

/ buttes emptis ibidem de Jacobo Furnour pro vino de Treuise fo. 28.
5 imponendo, iij duc. xliiij s. Item pro portagio et cariagio dicti
vini de villa ad fratres, iij duc. xvj s. Et per manus eiusdem pro
tabulis pro ostio camere, et pro tabulis pro le dressour et pro le
barra butrie et pro cupbord in aula, vna cum clauis et j carpintario
pro dictis facient', per conuencionem secum factam, vij duc. di.
10 Et per manus eiusdem pro diuersis seruris et clauibus de j fabro, per
ipsum emptis ibidem pro ostiis buterie, panetrie et camere domini,
j duc. Et per manus eiusdem pro glasez et verrez emptis ibidem,
ij duc. di. Et per manus Johannis Gilder pro sale albo per ipsum
empto pro panetria, iiij duc. Et pro mollicione cultellorum domini
15 ibidem, vj s. Et per manus eiusdem pro burnesching de tassis
domini, xviij s. Clerico speciarie per manus Jacobi Gyde pro
diuersis speciebus et confectionibus per ipsum emptis Ven. xx° die April 20.
Aprilis, ix duc. liij s. Et pro cera operata per ipsum empta ibidem,
iiij duc. Et pro portagio et cariagio eorundem de Venys vsque
20 Treuis, di. duc. Super officio scutellarie per manus Laurencii
Trauers pro busca et carbonibus per ipsum emptis ibidem tempore quo
dominus stetit ibidem, xvj duc. lvij s. Et pro portagio eorundem,
xxxiiij s. Super officio salsarie per manus eiusdem pro cenapio,
vergws, et vinegre per ipsum emptis, tempore quo dominus stetit
25 ibidem, vij duc. di. Et per manus eiusdem pro oleribus, herbis,
porris, pisis, et farina auenarum per ipsum emptis ibidem per idem
tempus, v duc. Et per manus eiusdem pro ij staris salis per ipsum
emptis ibidem, ij duc. 1s. Et per manus Johannis Gilder pro

---

* The u in this word looks like m in the MS. and in the marginal repetition the heading the word is Threu; but there can be no doubt that Treviso, frequently mentioned, where many purchases were made during April and May, is the place intended. Treviso is 16 miles from Venice.

litura pro lectis empta ibidem, iij duc. Et pro portagio et cariagio, xij s. Et per manus eiusdem pro locione de les towayll et cupcloth panetrie per idem tempus, xxxij s. Et per manus ciusdem pro ollis luteis per ipsum emptis ibidem, xxxiij s. CLERICO speciarie per manus Johannis Selby pro xx lb. candelarum cepi per ipsum 5 emptis ibidem, v li. Item pro vj lb. smigmatis per ipsum emptis ibidem, xxiij s. Item in batillagio thesaurarii de Treuise vsque Venis per iij vices redeundo, iij duc. xliiij s. Et in batillagio Roberti Hethecote euntis, per ij vices super negocium domini, j duc. Et pro batillagio aurifabri venientis de Venis vsque Treuise cum coleriis et aliis 10 harnisiis domini, vna cum conductione j equi ibidem, iij duc. Et per manus Thome Ferour pro butiro, corda, reyne per ipsum emptis ibidem, ij duc. di. Et pro j equo conducto pro Roberto Portour per iiij dies, j duc. Item pro ij currubus conductis de Treuise vsque Padowe pro cariagio harnisii domini, ix duc. ITEM pro j matte 15 empt' ibidem pro leopardo, xij s. ven. Item pro j equo conducto cuidam homini portanti lez faucones domini de Treuise vsque Vicens, j duc. Et eidem pro expensis suis et equi sui per idem tempus, j duc. Et pro sotularibus Henrici de Rodez,* ibidem, xviij s. ITEM pro expensis thesaurarii existentis apud Venis per 20 xiiij dies post recessum domini de ibidem, pro liberationibus domini emendis et aliis necessariis et victualibus ibidem emendis, vna cum expensis camerarii, Wilbram, Henrici de camera, et aliorum venientium ibidem per diuersas vices pro diuersis negociis domini ibidem, xxvij duc. Et pro batillagio eorundem de Meistre vsque Venys 25 redeuntium, v duc. di. Item cuidam fratri de Treuise custodienti cameras ibidem domini et famulorum suorum pro perdicione clauium et aliorum necessariorum fratrum ibidem, iij duc. Item pro conductione diuersorum vasorum pro coquina ibidem per manus Johannis Payn. ij duc. Item Thomas Ferrour pro panno laneo per 30 ipsum empto ibidem pro coopertura vnius selle domini, ij duc. Et pro factura eiusdem, xij s. CLERICO coquine per manus Johannis

* This Henry of Rhodes is probably the Turk who was baptized; see before.

II. PASSING THROUGH NORTH ITALY; PIEDMONT.

Wilbram pro diuersis carnibus, piscibus et aliis diuersis victualibus per ipsum emptis apud Treuise a xiij° die Aprilis vsque xxvij diem eiusdem mensis, vtroque computato, per compotum secum factum ibidem, Cxxxvj duc. xij d. SUPER officio poletrie per manus
5 Willelmi Harpedene pro caponibus, gallinis, pullis, pulcinis, lacte, butiro, columbellis, capriolis et aliis diuersis victualibus per ipsum emptis ibidem, per idem tempus, per compotum secum factum ibidem, xlij duc. lxviij s. ven.

April 13-27.

Summa pagine. CCCxiij duc. d xxvj s. vj d.

IN PARTIBUS PYMOND'.

10 / CLERICO panetrie per manus Johannis Payn pro pane albo per ipsum empto apud Norwall, xxix° die Aprilis, j duc. xix s. CLERICO butrie super vino, per manus eiusdem pro vino per ipsum empto ibidem eodem die, iiij duc. xlviij s. CLERICO marescalcie per manus Wilbram pro expensis equorum domini ibidem eodem die,
15 lxxviij s. Et pro expensis ij equorum, j gyde, ibidem per j noctem, xxx s. CLERICO marescalcie per manus Wilbram pro emendacione ij sellarum somerariorum camere domini apud Pauy, x° die Maii, vij gr. Et pro ij cordis per ipsum emptis ibidem pro ligacione j ciste fracte, vj gr. Et pro ferrura equorum domini apud Ladde,
20 vna cum emendacione sellarum ibidem, lx s. Item pro ferrura equorum domini apud Papyam, iij duc. Item pro clauis et ferris equinis ibidem emptis per Thomam Ferour, ij duc. xl s. Item pro panno laneo viridi ibidem empto per thesaurarium, pro diuersis sellis cooperiendis et pro diuersis harnisiis domini ibidem faciendis,
25 vij duc. di. Item apud Pauy pro factura j case pro iiij ciphis de ouo j ostrich ibidem eodem die, vj s. CLERICO marescalcie per manus Totty pro ij harnisiis et ij sellis domini per ipsum emptis apud Melane, xiij° die Maii, vna cum emendacione frenorum, capistrorum, per conuencionem ibidem factam, vj duc. CLERICO speci-
30 arie per manus Wilbram pro j quarta encausti per ipsum empta ibidem, xv die Maii, j gr. imperialis. Item eidem pro iij coffre de

fo. 28 v°.

April 29.

May 10.

May 13.

May 15.

nouo factis per ipsum emptis ibidem pro officio candelarie et aliis
rebus, per conuencionem factam ibidem, iiij duc. Et eidem pro
xl fadome corde per ipsum emptis ibidem eodem die pro eisdem
coffre ligandis, viij gr. Et per manus Thome Ferour pro ferrura
equorum domini ibidem, xxj gr. imperiall. Johanni Wilbram pro 5
j somersadell et j male per ipsum emptis ibidem, xv⁰ die Maii,
viij duc. CLERICO marescalcie per manus eiusdem pro emendacione j selle apud Vercelli, xviij⁰ die Maii, vj gr. Et pro iiij barhides per ipsum emptis apud Cheuaux eodem die, vij duc. Et pro
sagmine empto ibidem, vj gr. imperiall. CLERICO marescalcie per 10
manus Thome Ferour pro ij paribus fausteropes et aliis harnisiis pro
sellis domini per ipsum emptis apud Melan, vna cum ferrura
equorum ibidem, vij duc. CLERICO coquine per manus Harpeden
pro diuersis piscibus per ipsum emptis apud Toryn, xxj⁰ die Maii,
vj duc. xj gr. Et per manus thesaurarii pro j carcoisio bouino per 15
ipsum empto ibidem, vij duc. xxvj s. Et pro iiij carcoisiis multonum, iiij duc. xxiiij s. Et pro iiij kedes, j duc. xix s. CLERICO
panetrie per manus Payn pro pane albo per ipsum empto ibidem,
iij duc. CLERICO butrie super vino per manus eiusdem pro vino
per ipsum empto ibidem, viij duc. vj s. CLERICO panetrie per 20
manus eiusdem pro ceresis per ipsum emptis ibidem, xxij s. SUPER
officio scutellarie per manus hospitis ibidem pro busca et herbis,
v duc. xvij s. CLERICO marescalcie per manus Wilbram pro prebendis equorum ibidem, vj duc. xvj s. Et pro expensis Mowbray,
Wilbram, Harpenden precuntium per j diem et j noctem, j duc. 25
xviij s. Item Cowns Douche laboranti in eequina pro rebus faciendis ibidem eodem die, j duc. CLERICO pantrie per manus eiusdem
pro pane albo et vino emptis ibidem pro jantaculo domini, j duc.
vj s. Item iij carectis conductis de Toryn vsque Velayn, vij duc.
Item pro quodam curru conducto de ibidem vsque Cheuaux pro 30
cariagio harnisii domini eodem die, j duc. CLERICO butrie super
vino per manus Johannis Payn pro vino per ipsum empto apud
Auylan, x s. imperiall. Item per manus Zonge pro capistro et
emendacione j selle, j duc. Item pro pane albo empto apud Toryn

per manus Johannis Payn, xxj die Maii, ij duc. ij gr. Item pro May 21.
vino empto ibidem per manus eiusdem eodem die, viij duc. ix s.
Item pro fructubus emptis ibidem eodem die, xxj s. viij d. Item
pro busca et carbonibus emptis ibidem, v duc. Item pro lxiiij pre-
5 bendis equorum ibidem, vj duc. xvj s. Item pro expensis Mowbray, Wilbram, Harpeden, j duc. xx s. Item pro feno empto ibidem
per manus eiusdem, j duc. Et pro vino empto et pane supra montem, viij gr. Et pro ferrura equorum ibidem, viij gr. CLERICO
coquine per manus diuersorum pro iij carcoisiis multonum ab ipsis
10 emptis apud Velayn, xxij° die Maii, iiij duc. iiij s Et pro di. car- May 22.
coisii bouini, iij duc. xj s. CLERICO pantrie per manus Payn pro pane
albo per ipsum empto ibidem, iij duc. viij gr. CLERICO butrie super
vino* / per manus eiusdem pro vino empto, xiij duc. xij s. CLERICO fo. 29.
pantrie per manus eiusdem pro ceresis, pomis, emptis ibidem, vj gr. Ad huc in parti
15 SUPER officio pulletrie per manus eiuslem pro kedes, gallinis,   Pymond'.
pulcinis, emptis ibidem, vj duc. v gr. CLERICO coquine per manus
eiusdem pro sale empto ibidem, ij gr. xvj d. SUPER officio scutellarie
per manus eiusdem pro broche rakks emptis ibidem, xij gr. xvj d.
Item pro expensis Mowbray, Harpeden, preeuntium per j noctem,
20 vij gr. CLERICO marescalcie per manus Wilbram pro lxvij prebendis equorum emptis ibidem per j noctem, ix duc. viij gr. Et
pro feno empto ibidem, j duc. Item pro j pewter pot et aliis vasis
ibidem perditis in seruicio domini, j duc. CLERICO coquine per
manus Harpeden pro diuersis piscibus per ipsum emptis apud
25 villam de Sehusa, xxiij° die Maii, viij duc. Et pro xvij anguillis May 23.
emptis ibidem, xlv gr. SUPER officio pulleterie per manus hospitis * i.e. Six hundr.
ibidem pro vij C ouorum di., lvij gr. di.* CLERICO panetrie per manus and a half of eg
eiusdem pro pane albo per ipsum empto ibidem, iiij duc. v gr.
CLERICO butrie super vino per manus eiusdem pro vino empto
30 ibidem, xv duc. viij gr. SUPER officio scutellarie per manus eiusdem

* Summa pagine, Cxlvij duc. di. ij gr. ij d. ren.; vnde xiiij grossi faciunt j
ducatum. Item iiij li. xij d. faciunt j ducatum; noble computata vt supra.
Besides this latter note at the foot, a note of the value of the ducat in grossi stands
at the top of each of these four pages.

pro herbis ab ipso emptis ibidem, xij gr. SUPER officio salsarie per manus eiusdem pro cenape et vinegre emptis ibidem, viij gr. CLERICO coquine per manus eiusdem pro xvij anguillis emptis ibidem, xxiiij° die Maii, ij duc. ij gr. Et pro sale albo empto ibidem, iij gr. Item pro iiij^{or} verrez emptis ibidem, ix gr. Item pro expensis Gloucestre, 5 Mowbray, Harpeden, preeuntium pro prouidenciis ibidem faciendis erga aduentum domini illuc pro j nocte, xx gr. Item pro iiij lb. amigdalarum emptis apud Sebusa eodem die mensis Maii, iiij gr. Item pro di lb. sugre, vj gr. Item pro xlviij allecibus albis, xxvj gr. Item pro lacte eodem die, vij gr. Item pro pane albo empto ibidem 10 per manus eiusdem xxv° die Maii, iiij^{xx}xvj gr. Item pro vino empto ibidem per manus eiusdem, xxij duc. xx gr. Item pro viij carcoisiis multonum, xiiij duc. vij gr. di. Item pro bacon, ij duc. j gr. Item pro j carcoisio bouino, vij duc. j gr. Item pro vj caprellis, viij duc. vj gr. Item pro sagmine, vj gr. Item pro 15 C ouorum, vj gr. Item pro butiro, viij gr. Item pro farina auenarum, vj gr. Item pro verrez, ix gr. Item pro sale, xij gr. Item pro candelis cepi emptis ibidem eodem die, viij gr. Item pro oleo, di. gr. Item pro carbonibus, xviij gr. Item pro xl pulcinis, xxvj gr. Item pro herbis, ix gr. Item pro farina, viij gr. Item 20 pro C ouorum, vj gr. Item pro carbonibus, viij gr. Item pro prebendis equorum, ibidem per ij dies, xxj duc. Item pro seresis, vj gr. Item pro vino empto ibidem alias vices per manus eiusdem, xxij gr. di. Item pro pane albo ibidem per manus eiusdem, xj gr. Item pro vj multonibus, vij duc. vij gr. vj d. Item pro j carcoisio 25 bouino, vij duc. di. iiij s. Item pro iiij kides, xxx gr. Item pro pane albo empto apud Launcebrugge per manus Johannis Payn, xxvj° die Maii, xxvj gr. Item pro vino empto ibidem per manus eiusdem eodem die, C xj gr. Item pro iiij C multonibus, iiij^{xx}xvj gr. Item pro iiij vitulis, xxx gr. di. Item pro xj gallinis, xxxvj gr. 30 Item pro ij capriolis, vj gr. Item pro x pulcinis, vj gr. di. Item pro expensis Gloucestre, Mowbray, et Harpeden, vj gr. Item pro lxvij prebendis equorum, lxvij gr. Item in feno ibidem, j duc. vij gr. Item in pane albo empto apud Forneworht per manus

Johannis Payn, xxvij° die Maii, xxj gr. Item pro vino empto   May 27.
per manus eiusdem ibidem, lxvij gr. Item pro prebendis equorum
emptis ibidem, xxij gr. Item pro j vitulo, viij gr. Item pro xij
pulcinis, xj gr. Item pro j kede, viij gr. Item pro marescallo,
5 Mowbray, et Harpeden, vj gr. Item pro pane, vino, emptis ibidem,
xvj gr. di. Item pro feno empto ibidem eodem die, viij gr.
Item in pane albo empto apud Sanctum Michaelem per manus
eiusdem xxvij° die Maii, xxxv gr. Item in vino empto ibidem   May 27
eodem die, vij duc. x gr. Item pro xxxij prebendis equorum,
10 xlviij gr. Item pro expensis Gloucestre, Mowbray, et Harpeden,
precuntium, vj gr. Item pro iij vitulis di., xxvij gr. Item pro
di. bacon, x gr. Item pro j carcoisio multonis, xviij gr. Item
pro vj caponis et vij pulcinis, xxxj gr. Item pro ix anguillis
grossis, precium xxviij gr. Item pro ij lb. candelis cepi, vj gr.
15 Item pro busca et carbonibus emptis ibidem eodem die, vij duc.
viij gr. Item pro pane albo empto per manus Johannis *
/ Payn apud Chamboury, xxviij° die Maii, xxvij gr. Item in vino   fo. 29 v'
empto ibidem eodem die, lxvij gr. di. Item in lacte empto ibidem,   May 28.
vj gr. Item in feno empto ibidem, j duc. Item pro vjC. ouorum
20 emptis ibidem, xviij gr. Item pro caseo, vj gr. Item pro butiro,
vj gr. di. Item pro prebendis equorum ibidem, xxij gr. Item
pro pomis et ceresis ibidem emptis, vij gr. Item pro carne empta
apud Sanctum Michaelem pro jantaculo domini ibidem, j duc.
viij gr. Item pro vino albo empto apud Chambourell, xxiiij gr.
25 Item pro oleo pro leopardo, vij gr. Item pro ferrura diuersorum
equorum ibidem eodem die, ij duc. Item in feno empto ibidem,
j duc. viij gr. Item pro pane albo empto apud Egbell xxix° die   May 29
Maii, xxx gr. Item pro vino empto ibidem eodem die, lxviij gr.
Item in piscibus apud Chambour, xxviij° die Maii, vj duc. Item
30 pro ceresis emptis apud Egbell, xxix° die Maii, j gr. di. Item pro
iij lb. candelarum cepi emptis ibidem, vij gr. Item pro prebendis
equorum ibidem, lx gr. Item pro pane albo empto apud Jan per

---

* Summa pagine, CClxj duc. ij gr.

manus Johannis Payne primo die Junii, lxxviij gr. Item in vino empto ibidem eodem die, xix duc. xj gr. Item pro herbis, discis, ligno, carbonibus, busca, vinegre, cenape emptis ibidem, vij duc. Item pro herbis pro diuersis cameris emptis ibidem, xij gr. Item pro prebendis equorum ibidem per ij dies. ij duc. ix gr. Item pro iiij carcoisiis multonum, xlviij gr. Item pro vj vitulis di. lxxvij gr. Item pro x bordez, xxv gr. Item pro vij gallinis, xvj gr. Item pro iiij capriolis, xxxix gr. Item pro ouis et lacte, viij gr. d. Item pro di. quarterii bacon, vj gr. Item pro expensis marescalli, Mowbray, et Harpeden, p—ecuntium, xvj gr. Item pro batillagio domini et famulorum suorum vltra aquam eodem die, vij duc. Item in feno, j duc. gr. Item pro pane albo empto apud Rosselyon per manus eiusdem ij die Junii, iij duc. Item in vino empto per manus eiusdem, lxvj gr. di. Item pro prebendis equorum ibidem, lxj gr. Item pro locione mapparum ibidem. j gr. di. Item pro feno empto ibidem eo lem die, j duc. vj gr. Item pro prebendis equorum domini apud Sehusa, xxiij°, iiij°, v°, and vj° die Maii in mane, xxviij duc. di. Item in expensis Walteri Juteburgh euntis super negocium domini de Auelan ad Otes Graunson in Burgundia, ix duc. Item in expensis equorum gardiani et custodis leopardi apud Sehusa, xlv gr. Item pro ferrura equorum eorundem ibidem ad diuersos locos per viam, xix gr. Item pro lectis, busca, candelis ibidem, xv gr. Item pro diuersis speciebus et vnguentis ibidem emptis pro leopardo, ij duc. xj gr. Item pro camisiis, braccis, caligis, sotularibus custodis leopardi, ibidem emptis, j duc. ix gr. Item in cera operata et diuersis speciebus et confectis ibidem emptis, iij duc. xij gr. di. Item in ferrura equorum domini ibidem, iij duc. xvij gr. Item in sagmine empto ibidem pro equis domini per manus Thome Ferour, viij gr. Item in prebendis equorum domini apud Jan in festo Trinitatis, lxxij gr. Et in prebendis equorum gardiani et custodis leopardi ibidem, xx gr. Item apud Chauce pro carne bouina, motulina et vitulina, ij caponibus, vij gallinis, xvj pulcinis, herbis, farina et vergws, vij ffranks, xj

II. THROUGH PIEDMONT AND SAVOY.

blanes.[a] Item in expensis Roberti Porter cuntis cum les mulis de Auclan vsque Troys, vna cum ferrura equorum suorum et batillagio, iij franks, xvij bl. Item in batillagio domini et familie sue in una aqua inter Saboldiam et Burgundiam, iiij franks. Item in ferrura 5 equorum domini apud Chamboury vna cum sagmine empto pro ij equis infirmis et diuersis vnguentis per manus Thome Ferour, iiij duc. xj gr. Item pro j heuse pro sella domini de coreo, ij sur-sengulis, iij gerthis, j pole, vna cum emendacione diuersarum sellarum domini ibidem, et les somersadles per manus eiusdem, 10 iij duc. viij gr. Item pro diuersis expensis factis per Walterum Juteburgh de Chalons vsque Parys cum diuersis officiariis prece-dentem, xj franks xxj bl. Item in expensis equorum gardiani et custodis leopardi apud Auclan, Ryuols, Egbell, et Chambour, vna cum ferrura equorum, oleo, et aliis speciebus ibidem et per viam 15 per le libardmen emptis, vij duc. x gr. d. Et pro j pare ocrearum per ipsum empto apud Chambour, j duc. v gr.[b]

SOBOLDIA.

/ Item pro pano albo empto apud Sarombert iij die Junii, fo. 30 xxvj gr. Item pro vino empto per manus eiusdem ibidem eodem June 3. 20 die, vj duc. viij gr. Item pro prebendis equorum ibidem eodem die, xxxvj gr. Item pro bacon, vj gr. Item pro pisis, herbis, et [* xiiij grossi in pro portagio, viij gr. Item pro ix pulcinis, ix gr. Item pro   j ducatum. diuersis piscibus, vj gr. Item pro iiij vitulis emptis ibidem, vij duc. ix gr. Item pro feno empto ibidem, j duc. x s. imp. Item in pane 25 albo empto apud l'ompenet per manus Johannis Payn, iiij° die Junii, xxvj gr. Item pro vino empto ibidem per manus eiusdem, June 4.

---

[a] Here at Chance is the first use of French money; 24 blancs made a franc. The blanc was a small silver coin introduced under Philip of Valois about 1340, in the place of the gros tournois.

[b] Summa pagine, xxvij ffr. j bl. **Item** de ducates,[*] CCij duc. di. ij gr.   [* Sic.

clxij gr. Item in prebendis equorum ibidem, lx gr. Item pro
j carcoisio motulino, vj vitulinis, j quarterio bacon, vj kedes, xj
columbellis; et pro expensis Gloucestre, Mowbray, et Harpeden
ibidem eodem die, c'xvj gr. di. Item in vino empto ibidem pro
jantaculo domini, xx gr. d. Item pro feno empto ibidem eodem 5
die, ij duc. Item per manus ciusdem pro cheveyns et vmbres
emptis apud Fownteney eodem die, iiij duc. Item apud Breine
pro pane albo empto ibidem eodem die, ij duc. ix gr. d. Item pro
vino empto ibidem eodem die, vj duc. xvij gr. Item pro prebendis
equorum ibidem, vj duc. ix gr. Item in pomis et ceresis emptis 10
ibidem, j duc. Item pro verrez emptis ibidem. j duc. Item pro iiij
vitulis, xxxvij gr. Item pro vj carcoisiis motulinis, viij duc. Item
pro xij carpez, xxiiij s. Item pro bremes, xxj gr. Item pro
anguillis, viij gr. Item pro viij kedes, vj duc. di. Item pro viij
pulcinis, xviij gr. Item pro lacte, vij gr. Item pro iij C ouorum, 15
xvj bl. Item per manus ciusdem pro pane albo per ipsum empto
apud Bagea v° die Junii, xxvij gr. Item in vino empto ibidem
eodem die, vij duc. Item pro ij carcoisiis motulinis, iij vitulinis et
iij kedes emptis ibidem eodem die, vj duc. vj gr. Item in ceresis
emptis ibidem, vij gr. Item pro expensis Gloucestre, Mowbray, et 20
Harpeden, xvij gr. Item pro prebendis equorum, viij gr. Item in
vino empto ibidem eo lem die, per manus ciusdem, post dormitacionem domini ibidem, xj gr. Item pro vino empto apud Jan die
Sancte Trinitatis, per seneseallum, xvj gr. Item pro ferrura equorum vna cum clauis equinis emptis eodem die Junii, vz. v° apud 25
Yan, xj gr. Et pro sagmine empto ibidem pro equis infirmis,
vij gr. Item in feno empto ibidem, j duc. vj gr. Item in vino
empto apud Makon, vj° die Junii, ij^{c}iiij^{xx}xiiij bl. Item in pane
albo empto ibidem eodem die, lxxiij bl. di. Item in fructubus
ibidem eodem die, xxx bl. Item pro iiij carcoisiis motulinis, 30
lxxij bl. Item pro iij vitulis. lx bl. Item pro iij kedez, xxiiij bl.
Item pro xxvij pullis, xxvij bl. Item pro xl carpes, xviij pykes,
xx anguillis, perches, et roches emptis ibidem, xvj frank. xxij bl.
Item pro C ij ouorum, xj bl. Item pro pisis, xv bl. Item pro lacte,

II. PASSING THROUGH BURGUNDY. 249

vij bl. Item pro herbis, vj bl. Item pro sale albo empto ibidem,
xij bl. Item pro vinegre, vergws, emptis ibidem, xj bl. Item pro
x lb. cere facte emptis ibidem, ij frank, vj bl. Item pro viij lb.
candelarum cepi, xvj bl. Item pro carbonibus, xv bl. Item pro pre-
5 bendis equorum ibidem eodem die, ciiij^{xx} bl. Item in feno empto
ibidem, iij duc.^a

BURGUNDIA.

/ Item in pane albo empto apud Traues, vij° die Junii, xxvj gr.   fo. 30 v°.
Item in vino empto ibidem, clxx bl. Item in diuersis piscibus   June 7.
10 emptis ibidem pro prandio, viij frank. vij bl. Item in lucerna,   xxiiij blanca f.
vj bl. Item pro herbis, ij bl. Item pro pomis, viij bl. Item pro   j fr. xij grossi
ceresis, vj bl. Item pro sale, viij bl. Item pro pisis, viij bl. Item   j duc.
pro prebendis equorum ibidem, lxxiij bl. Item in feno empto
ibidem, j duc. viij gr. Clerico marescalcie per manus Thome
15 Ferour pro ferrura equorum domini apud Macon vij° die Junii,
xxxiiij bl. Item in pane albo empto apud Chalons per manus
Johannis Payn, viij° die Junii, iij frank. ij bl. Item in vino   June 8.
empto ibidem, per manus eiusdem xij frankes vj bl. Item pro
pomis et ceresis emptis ibidem, j frank. xvj bl. Item pro herbis
20 emptis ibidem eodem die, ix bl. Item pro diuersis piscibus emptis
ibidem, vij frank. vj bl. Item pro iij C ouorum, xv bl. Item pro
j quarter bacon, ij vitulis, ij carcoisiis motulinis di., iij frank. viij bl.
Item pro iij qrt. bouis, iiij vitulis, emptis ibidem, vj frank. xiiij bl.
Item pro iiij porcellis, xvij bl. Item pro farina auenarum, vj bl.
25 Item pro j qrt. bouis, ij vitulis, ij carcoisiis motulinis emptis
ibidem, iij frank. xvj bl. Item pro portagio, vij bl. Item pro
veriws, viij bl. Item pro confectionibus, xj bl. Item pro candelis
cepi, xv bl. Item pro prebendis equorum, ix duc. xij bl. Item

^a Summa pagine, lv franks iiij bl. di. Item in ducates,^a **Cxxiiij duc. di. ij gr. di.**   ^a Sic.

pro expensis equi gardiani. xv bl. Item pro feno, j duc. d. Item pro pane albo empto apud Beaume per manus eiusdem ix° die Junii, j frank. xx bl. viij d. Item pro pomis et ceresis, vij bl. Item pro vino empto ibidem eodem die per manus eiusdem, vj frank. j bl. vj d. Item pro vj vitulis, iij motulinis, vij frank. Item pro xxx pulcinis, 5 j frank. vj bl. Item pro herbis, vj bl. Item pro farina auenarum, j bl. Item pro ouis, j bl. Item pro ij caponibus, x bl. Item pro sale empto ibidem, viij bl. d. Item pro larde, vj bl. Item pro vj pulcinis pro jantaculo domini ibidem, vj bl. Item pro vj lb. candelarum cepi, ix bl. Item pro expensis Gloucester, Moubray, 10 Cudworth et Harpeden, preeuntium, xvij bl. Item pro prebendis equorum ibidem, xlvj bl. Item pro prebendis equorum ibidem, xxxix bl. Item pro cenape ibidem empto, vj bl. Item pro cera empta ibidem, viij bl. Item pro expensis equorum gardiani ibidem, ix bl. Item pro feno empto ibidem, ij duc. Item 15 pro pane albo empto apud Floreyn, x° die Junii, per manus eiusdem, lij bl. di. Item pro vino empto ibidem, clix bl. Item pro pomis emptis ibidem. vj bi. Item pro prebendis equorum ibidem, v frank. j bl. Item pro busca et carbone, vj bl. Item pro iiij carcoisiis motulinis, lxviij bl. Item pro ij vitulis, xxxv bl. Item 20 pro xxxiij pulcinis, xxxvj bl. Item pro j kede, xij bl. Item pro sale, vj bl. Item pro piscibus, viij bl. Item pro herbis, vij bl. Item pro iiij carcoisiis motulinis pro cena ibidem, xlviij bl. Item pro ij vitulis, xxxij bl. Item pro vino empto ibidem pro jantaculo domini, xxj bl. Item pro feno empto ibidem, iij duc. Item in 25 pane albo empto apud Chauce per manus Johannis Payn, xj° die Junii, iij frank. Item in vino empto ibidem, vij frank. vj bl. Item pro sale albo empto ibidem, xij bl. Item pro prebendis equorum ibidem, iiij frank. vij bl. Item pro expensis equi gardiani, ix bl. Item pro cera empta ibidem, xvij bl. Item in feno empto 30 ibidem, ij duc. j gr. Item in pane, vino, piscibus emptis apud Floreyn pro jantaculo domini, ij frank. ix bl. Item pro pane, vino, pulcinis, bacon pro jantaculo domini ibidem, iij frank. xij bl. Item in feno et prebendis equorum emptis ibidem, ij duc. Item in pane

II. EXPENSES PASSING THROUGH FRANCE.

albo empto apud Maynilambard, xij° die Junii, j frank. j bl. Item June 12.
pro vino empto ibidem, vj frank. Item pro expensis equorum [a]

IN PARTIBUS FRANCIE.

/ ibidem eodem die, xxxvij bl. Item pro busca et carbonibus emptis   fo. 31.
5 ibidem eodem die, xvj bl. Et pro expensis equi gardiani ibidem,   xxiiij blank.
vij bl. Item pro feno empto ibidem, iij duc. Item pro iiij vitulis   fac. j frank.
emptis apud Chauce, lxvij bl. Item pro iij carcoisiis motulinis,
lvij bl. Item pro xij pulcinis, xj bl. di. Item pro expensis preeuntium, viij bl. viij d. Item pro vij Conorum, xxxv bl. Item pro lacte,
10 viij bl. Item pro expensis equi Walteri Juteburgh, vj bl. di. Item
pro iij vitulis et j carcoisio motulino empto apud Mencyllambard,
lxxij bl. Item pro xxj pulcinis, xx bl. Item pro expensis preeuntium ibidem, vj bl. di. Item pro expensis equorum Walteri
Jutebergh, vij lb. Item pro pane albo empto apud Chastelon,
15 xxj bl. viij di. Item in vino empto ibidem, vj frank. vj bl. viij d.
Item pro pomis, pescodes, et ceresis ibidem, ix lb. Item pro expensis
equorum gardiani ibidem, vj bl. Item pro expensis eiusdem Gardiani
ibidem eodem die, x gr. Item pro expensis equorum domini ibidem,
iij frank. xvij bl. Item pro ij vitulis, iij carcoisiis motulinis, ij kedes,
20 iiij**viij bl. di. Item pro vij pulcinis, viij bl. Item pro di. multonis
a larde,* xij bl. di. Item pro expensis precuntis pro jantaculo domini,   • Sic.
vj bl. Item pro expensis equorum leopardi ibidem, ix bl. Item
pro ferrura equorum ibidem, vij bl. di. Item Henrico Sompterman
pro sotularibus emptis ibidem, vj bl. Item pro creues emptis ibidem,
25 viij bl. Item pro pane, vino, emptis pro jantaculo domini ibidem,
xvj bl. Item pro feno empto ibidem eodem die, j duc. Item pro
pane albo empto apud Berce, xiij° die Junii, j frank. Item pro   June 13.
vino empto ibidem per manus eiusdem, vij frank. viij bl. di. Item
pro expensis precuntium pro cena, xij bl. Item pro anguillis emptis
30 ibidem, pikes, creves, perches, et aliis piscibus, vj franks, vij bl. di.

* Summa pagine, Cxlij fr. di. viij bl. di. Item de ducates, xxiij duc. ij gr. ij d.

252   THE EARL OF DERBY'S EXPEDITIONS.

Item pro lacte, viij bl. Item pro fabis et pisis, xij bl. Item pro vj C ouorum, xviij bl. Item pro ceresis, vj bl. Item pro sale, viij bl. Item pro petrosilia empta, j bl. Item pro veriws, vij bl. Item pro caseo, vj bl. Item pro flawne, vj bl. viij d. Item pro farina, vj bl. Item pro herbis, j bl. Item pro prebendis equorum ibidem, iij frank. xvj bl. Item pro feno empto ibidem eodem die, ij duc. Item pro pane, vino, ceresis, emptis ibidem per manus eiusdem pro jantaculo domini, xix bl. Item pro iiij torches et perches emptis apud Troys per manus eiusdem xv° die Junii. viij frank. Item in pane albo empto ibidem per manus eiusdem, j frank. xix bl. ij d. Item in ceresis et pomis, viij bl. Item in vino empto ibidem, xviij frank. Item pro diuersis piscibus emptis ibidem, xj frank. xvj bl. Item pro diuersis carnibus, pullis, pulcinis ibidem emptis, viij frank. xvj d. Item pro j quarterno papiri empto ibidem, vj bl. di. Item pro herbis emptis ibidem, vij bl. Item pro cenape empto ibidem, vj bl. Item pro di. C. ouorum, vj bl. Item pro sale albo emptis ibidem, j fr. Item pro vij lb. candelarum cepi, ix bl. Item pro croco empto ibidem, vij bl. Item pro vinegre, veriws, emptis ibidem, vj bl. Item pro expensis equorum ibidem, iiij frank. Item pro expensis equorum gardiani et leopardi ibidem, xix bl. Item pro pisis emptis ibidem, viij bl. Item pro vino empto ibidem pro jantaculo domini eodem die, xviij bl. Item pro feno empto ibidem eodem die, iij duc. Item apud Graunt Pauelon pro batellagio domini ibidem eodem die, vj frank. xxj bl. Item in pane albo empto apud Marin per manus eiusdem xv° die Junii, xviij bl. Item pro ceresis emptis ibidem, vj bl. Item in vino empto ibidem, ix frank. xvj bl. Item pro busca, vij bl. Item pro carbone, xij bl. Item pro veriws, vinegre, vj bl. Item pro sale et larde emptis ibidem, viij bl. Item pro herbis, j bl. Item pro iij lb. candelarum cepi ibidem, vij bl. Item in stramine pro cameris domini, vj bl. Item pro prebendis equorum ibidem, vj frank. x bl. Item pro expensis [a]

June 15.

June 15.

---

[a] Summa pagine, Cxxxix fr. di. iij bl. di. Item de ducates, x ducat di. ij d. imperiall.

II. PASSING THROUGH FRANCE. 253

/equorum gardiani et leopardi ibidem, xij bl. Item pro expensis fo. 31v°.
precuntis ibidem pro jantaculo domini, ix bl. Item pro feno xxiiij pl. fac.
empto ibidem, iij du*. Item pro pane albo empto apud Nougent xij gr. j duc.
per manus eiusdem xxj° die Junii, xxiij bl. ij d. Item in vino June 21.
5 empto ibidem per manus eiusdem, vj frank. xvj bl. ij d. Item pro
ceresis emptis ibidem, vj bl. Item pro vinegre, verius, emptis
ibidem. vj bl. Item pro sale empto, vj b!. Item pro fabis et pescodes, viij lb. Item pro crenez, vj bl. Item pro viij carcoisiis
multonum et baconum emptis ibidem, vj frank xviij bl. Item pro ex-
10 pensis equorum ibidem eodem die, xxxv bl. Item pro vino empto
ibidem post dormitacionem, viij bl. Item pro pane, vino, pulcinis,
ceresis emptis apud Marine pro jantaculo domini, j frank, iiij bl.
Item, in pane albo empto ibidem per manus eiusdem eodem die,
xvj bl. iiij d. Item pro fructubus emptis ibidem, xij bl. Item
15 pro vino empto ibidem eodem die, iiij frank xvj bl. j d. Item pro
expensis equorum pre cuntium ibidem, ix. bl. Item pro iij vitulis
emptis ibidem, ij frank. Item pro larde, vij bl. Item pro xlj. pulcinis, xxviij columbellis emptis ibidem, iiij frank bl. di. Item pro
croco, zinsubre, emptis ibidem, viij bl. Item pro herbis emptis
20 ibidem, vj. bl. Item pro prebendis equorum ibidem, ij frank, xiiij
bl. Item pro vj lb. candelarum cepi, ix bl. Item pro fabis et pescodes emptis ibidem. viij bl. Item pro expensis xj equorum domini
existentium in duobus aliis hospiciis ibidem per j noctem, xxxvi
bl. Item pro vino, pane emptis pro jantaculo domini, xvj bl. Item
25 pro pane albo empto apud Grauntpuisse, xvj. bl. di. Item pro
ceresis emptis ibidem, vj. bl. Item pro vino empto ibidem eodem
die, iij frank. viij bl. viij d. Item pro ij vitulis, iij carcoisiis motulinis
emptis ibidem, vj frank. vij bl. Et pro expensis precuntis ibidem
pro cena, v bl. ij d. Item pro sale albo empto ibidem, vij bl. Item
30 pro expensis equorum ibidem eodem die, xxj bl. di. Item pro expensis
j equi Walteri Jutebergh, vj bl. Item pro expensis x equorum existentium per j noctem apud Bricounte-Robert xxvij° die Junii, June 27.
xxxvj bl. Item in feno empto ibidem, ij duc. Item pro pane albo
empto [apud] Bricounte-Robert [x]x viij° die Junii, j frank. Item June 28.

pro ceresis, vj bl. Item in vino empto ibidem, vj frank. xj bl. Item
pro pane, xij bl. Item pro vinegre et veriws, vij bl. Item pro
herbis et cenape, vij bl. Item pro candelis cepi, viij bl. d. Item
pro expensis equorum domini, iij frank. xj bl. Item in feno empto
ibidem, j duc. di. Item pro pane albo empto apud Pountechareton
eodem die, xxj bl. Item pro zeresis, vj bl. di. Item pro vino
empto ibidem eodem die, iii frank. vij bl. Item pro caseo empto
ibidem, vj bl. Item pro butiro, vj bl. di. Item pro larde, vij bl.
Item pro herbis, j bl. Item pro sale, vj bl. Item pro prebendis
equorum ibidem, j frank. vj bl. Item pro vinegre, j bl. Item pro
xij pulcinis emptis ibidem, xxviij bl. parnis. Item pro ij vitulis,
iij carcoisiis motulinis, j anguilla emptis apud Bricount-Robert
eodem die, iiij frank. viij bl. Item pro ij caponibus, xij bl. Item
pro xx pulcinis, xxxv bl. Item pro pisis, j bl. Item pro allecibus
et mackerell, viij bl. Item pro caseo empto ibidem eodem die, vj
bl. Item pro feno empto ibidem eodem die, ij duc. di. Item in
expensis Thome Dent, fratris Ade, Thome clerici sui, domini Hu
gonis Heerle, Henrici baptizati, vnius falconis domini, euntium
cum diuersis harnisiis domini per aquam de Melan vsque Caleys, et
de Caleys vsque Peterburgh, vna cum conductione batelle, equorum,
guydes, et tollage per la Ryne, per compotum cum eis factum, in
toto, lxij duc. ci. iiij s. st. Item in iij mulis conductis de Auelan
vsque Troys en Champayn pro harnisiis domini cariandis, vna cum
expensis iij hominum euntium cum dictis mulis in montibus, xxviij
duc. Item in ij carectis conductis de Troys vsque Parys, xiiij
frank. Item in duobus carectis conductis de Paris vsque Amyas,
xij. frank.[a]

IN PARTIBUS FRANCIE ET ANGLIE.

/ Item in pane albo empto apud Douer per manus Johannis Payn
vltimo die Junii, ij s. xj d. st. Item pro xvj galonibus ceruisie ad

[a] Summa pagine, iiij s. st. Item in franc, Cij fr. di. ij bl. Item in ducates,
iiij^{xx} xix duc. di. iij gr. j d.

II. EXPENSES ON RETURN TO ENGLAND. 255

j d. ob. emptis ibidem eodem die, ij s. Item pro busca empta ibidem eodem die, viij di. Item pro vinegre, j d. ob. Item pro herbis, j d. Item pro ij carcoisiis motulinis, iij s. iiij d. Item pro sale albo empto ibidem, xij d. Item pro iiij lb. candelarum cepi 5 emptis ibidem, vj. Item pro farina auenarum empta ibidem, j d. Item in feno empto ibidem eodem die, ij s. Item pro auenis emptis ibidem, ij s. Item in feno alia vice, ij s. ix d. Item pro auenis emptis ibidem, iiij s. Item pro expensis xj hominum per j diem ibidem, iij s. iiij d. Item pro ferura equorum ibidem, ij s. iiij d. 10 Item pro portagio domini de naui vsque terram, xx d. Item pro fabis emptis ibidem, ij d. Item pro diskippagio equorum ibidem, x s. vj d. Item pro diskippagio militum, scutiferorum et aliorum ibidem, ij s. Item in feno empto ibidem, xij d. Item pro j quarterio iij bz. auenarum emptis ibidem, iij s. viij d. Item pro 15 litura, ij d. Item pro emendacione ij sellarum ibidem, vj d. Item pro busca empta ibidem pro jantaculo, iiij d. Item pro lecto domini, xij d. Item pro vino empto ibidem eodem die, xviij s. Item in feno empto apud Caunterbury primo die Julii, ij s. viij d. ob. Item *July 1.* pro j quarteria auenarum empta ibidem, iij s. Item pro expensis de 20 somptermen ibidem per j noctem, ij s. vj d. Item pro portagio et batillagio harnisiorum apud Caleys, xx d. Item in pane albo empto apud Sityngbourne j^o die Julii, ij s. x d. ob. Item pro ceresis, viij d. Item pro vino empto ibidem, xxvij s. Item pro seruicia empta ibidem, iij s. j d. Item pro expensis preeuntis pro prandio, ij s. ij d. 25 Item pro iiij lb. candelarum cepi emptis ibidem, vj d. Item pro busca empta ibidem, xiiij d. Item pro croco empto ibidem, vj d. Item pro ouis, j d. Item pro siliquis, j d. ob. Item pro v carcoisiis motulinis emptis ibidem, viij s. x d. Item pro feno empto ibidem, xij d. Item pro vij bz. pure auene emptis ibidem, iij s. Item pro 30 litura, iiij d. Item pro feno, iiij d. Item pro j bz. auenarum, v d. Item pro feno empto ibidem, xx d. Item pro v bz. auenarum di., xxvij d. ob. Item pro litura, iiij d. Item pro expensis equorum j char ibidem, xj d. Item pro ferrura ibidem eodem die, vj d. Item pro expensis iij equorum de leopardo eodem die, xij d. Item pro con-

256   THE EARL OF DERBY'S EXPEDITIONS.

[Newington-juxta-Sittingbourne.] ductione ij equorum de Newynton * vsque Rowchestre, viij d. Item pro ij chares conductis de Douor vsque Caunterbury, iij s. iiij d. Item pro j char conducto de Caunterbury vsque Sityngbourne, xx d. Item pro j equo conducto de Douor vsque Sitingbourne pro victualibus de ibidem cariandis, xiiij d. Item pro portagio iij barellorum ferrez de Douor, vltimo die Junii, iiij d. Item pro vino empto apud

June 30.
July 1.
July 2.

Sytyngbourne, primo die Julii, pro jantaculo domini, xiiij d. Item pro pane albo empto apud Rowchestre ij° die Julii, iij s. vj d. Item pro ceresis ibidem, iiij d. Item pro vino empto ibidem, xv s. viij d. Item pro xviij galonibus cervisie, galo ad j d. ob., ij s. j d. Item pro cenape, venegre, veriws, emptis ibidem, vij d. Item pro sale, iiij d. Item pro farina auenarum, ij d. Item pro busca et carbonibus, viij d. Item pro feno empto ibidem, vj d. Item iij bz. auenarum di., xviij d. Item pro expensis precuntis ibidem, ij s. Item pro expensis vj equorum gardiani et leopardi ibidem, xj d. Item pro j equo conducto de Rowchestre vsque Derteford, iiij d. Item pro ij carectis conductis de Sitingbourne vsque Derteford, iiij s. iiij d. Item in feno empto

July 3.

apud Derteford, iij° die Julii, v d. Item pro ij bz. auenarum, x d. Item pro herbis, ij d. Item pro vinegre, verjws ibidem, ij d. Item pro busca empta ibidem, x d. Item pro feno empto ibidem, xxij d. Item pro j qrt. iij bz. di. auenarum, ad iij s. iiij d., iiij s. ix d. ob. Item pro litura, iiij d. Item pro pane albo empto ibidem eodem die, iiij s. vj d. Item pro xij sextariis j picheria di. vini Vasconie ad ij s. viij d., xxxiij s. Item pro xxiij

fo. 32 v°.
xxiiij bl. fac. j ffz.

galonibus seruicie ad j d. ob. emptis ibidem, ij s. x d. ob. Item[a] / pro sale albo, iij d. Item pro xv pulcinis, ij s. ob. Item pro j picheria vini Vasconie empta apud Rowchestre, viij d. Item pro lectis, xij d. Item pro iij carcoisiis motulinis et j qr. bouum emptis ibidem, viij s. ij d. Clerico marescalcie per manus Wilbram pro

June 30.

ij capistris per ipsum emptis apud Caleys, xxx° die Junii, xx d. Et pro ferrura equorum ibidem, ij s. Et pro diuersis medicamentis emptis ibidem per viam pro j cursore domini infirmo, xxiij d. Et

* Summa pagine, xj li. v s. ix d. ob. st.

II. EXPENSES ON RETURN TO ENGLAND.

pro feno empto apud London v° die Julii, iij s. iiij d. Et pro   July 5.
litura, ij s. j d. ob. Et pro ij qr. vj bz. di. auenarum, qr. ad iij s.
iiij d.,—x s. ij d. ob.[a] CLERICO speciarie per manus eiusdem pro
di. lb. countours empta ibidem pro officio thesaurarii, ix d. CLERICO
5 marescalcie per manus Thome Ferrour pro ferrura diuersorum
equorum a primo die Junii vsque xiij^m diem Julii ad diuersos locos   June 1—July 1
per compotum secum factum, iiij frank. iij bl. Et per manus
eiusdem pro emendacione diuersarum sellarum per idem tempus ad
diuersos locos, j frank. Et pro herbagio empto per idem tempus pro
10 vno equo infirmo, xvj bl. Et pro sagmine, butir, et sewet emptis per
idem tempus pro diuersis equis infirmis, v. bl. Et per manus
Wilbram pro feno per ipsum empto pro ij equis Toty, a xxj° die   May 21—June
Maii vsque xvj^m diem Junii, eo quod fuit magister equorum domini,
ij frank. Item pro cirpis emptis apud Caleys, xvj d. Item pro iiij
15 battellis cariandis harnisia domini et famulorum suorum de naui vsque
terram, xxix° die Junii, iiij s. Item pro lecto, vino, candelis et   June 29.
pro aliis expensis, per le libardman ibidem, j scut. Item pro expensis equi gardiani, lecto, candelis, et ferrura equina ibidem,
ij s. vij d. Item in diuersis expensis factis per Johannem Dindon
20 in Prucia et in Anglia, pro diuersis harnesiis camere et garderobe
domini custodiendis post recessum domini, vna cum vadiis vnius
mensis, capiente per diem iiij d.—in toto xxvij s. viij d. Item in
diuersis expensis factis per Johannem Dounton custodem armature
domini in Prucia et in Anglia post recessum domini circa mun-
25 dacionem et custodiam harnesii domini, viij s. vj d. Item pro per-
gamine, encausto, pennis et countours emptis pro compotis domini
faciendis, v s. Item apud Parys pro ferrura equorum domini vna
cum emendacione sellarum et aliorum hernesiorum domini per
manus Thome Ferrour, iij frank. xvj bl. Item pro locione map-
30 parum ibidem, per manus Johannis Selby, j scut. Item pro sagmine empto ibidem pro equis, viij bl. Item pro oleo ut speciebus

---

[a] Between these two items occurs the following, which is crossed through:—" Et
pro lecto pro Gardiano sociis suis et le lebardman per ij noctes, iiij d."

emptis pro leopardo ibidem, xx bl. Item pro iij paruis towailles de opere Paris emptis ibidem pro panetria per manus Johannis Payn, j scut. Item pro ferrura equi apud Amyas per manus Thome Ferour, xix bl. Item in pane et seruisia emptis per manus Johannis Gilder in vigilia Apostolorum Petri et Pauli apud Caleys, v scut. Item pro candelis cepi, farina, herbis, et aliis salsiamentis ibidem emptis per manus Laurencii Trauers, ij s. iij d. st. Item in locione diuersarum mapparum ibidem per manus Selby, viij d. st. Item in sale albo ibidem empto per manus Johannis Gilder, v d.

Summa pagine, iiij li. vj s. vj d. ob. st.
Item in moneta Francie, xxij fr. di. iij bl.

Summa totalis de Rodes et in partibus de Venys, et redeundo per partes Pymondi et Francie, computata in sterlinges; vna cum xij gr. sicez, precium ij s. j d. st., et cum xxviij s. ij d. ven., precium xiij d. q^r st., et cum iij besauntz, prec. xj d. q^r st., et cum xxvij aspers, prec. iij s. ob. q^r st.—xvij li. x s. ij d. q^r st.

Item de moneta de Venys, M'M'ix lv. duc.
Item de moneta Francie, iiij^{c}iiij^{xx}ix fr. xxij bl. di.

/ PARCELLE WILLELMI HARPEDEN DE EXPENSIS HOSPICII per dietas non contente inter alias parcellas expensarum istius compoti.

Et in diuersis parcellis pro diuersis victualibus emptis pro hospicio domini per Willelmum Harpeden in isto viagio a decimo die Augusti a° xvj° vsque xxiiij diem Nouembris proxime sequentem a° supradicto, computatis per dietas, prout particulariter continetur in quodam rotulo inde facto, super hunc compotum liberato per ipsum computantem et predictum Willelmum. Que quidem parcelle non continentur inter alias parcellas huius libri prout idem computans et predictus Willelmus affidauerunt super hunc compotum. Qui quidem rotulus super hunc compotum postea examinatus per auditores remanet cum isto compoto cum alio rotulo de donis domini. Videlicet de diuersis summis computatis in sterlinges, cxxxli. xv s. v d. ob. st. Item de moneta de Venys xxxiiij duc.

5 Summa pagine computata in sterlingis, cxxx li. xv s. v d. ob. st. Item de moneta de Venys, xxxiiij duc.

/ BELCHERE IN DIUERSIS LOCIS. fo. 33 vº.

In primis in hospicio domini existentis apud Dansk per xv dies ante exitum suum versus Coningesburgh, xxj nobl. Item eidem 10 hospiti domini existentis apud Dansk per xx dies post recessum domini de Coningesburgh, xxx nobl. Et famulo eiusdem hospitis per ij vices, j marc. di pr. Item in hospicio senescalli et thesaurarii et partis famulorum domini, vna cum equis domini existentium in eodem hospicio per idem tempus, eundo et redeundo, xiiij nobl. 15 Et famulo eiusdem hospitis per idem tempus, j marc. pr. Item pro hospicio domini Otes Graunsom ibidem per idem tempus per compotum secum factum, ix marcz. di. pr. Item apud Darsow eundo et redeundo, iij marc. pr. Et famulis ibidem per ij vices. xviij scot. Item apud Melving fratribus Augustiniensibus eo tempore quo 20 dominus erat hospitatus ibidem, eundo versus Coningesburgh, x marc. di. pr. Et ibidem redeundo in villa, iiij marc. di. pr. Item apud Holypitt excundo pro belchere ibidem, j marc. pr. viij scot. Item apud Bramburgh excundo, iij marcz pr. vj scot. Et ibidem redeundo, j marc pr. vij scot. Item apud Coningesburgh, x marc. 25 pr. di. Et apud Brounesburgh redeundo, ij marc. pr. di. Item apud Sconee pro belchere, xij scot. Item pro belchere apud Sconee xxvº die Septembris, j marc. pr. Item pro belchere ibidem, September 25. xij scot. Item apud Polysene, vj marc. ff. Item pro belchere apud Hamerstede, xxvjº die Septembris xij scot. Item pro belchere ibidem, September 26. 30 xvij scot. Item apud Scheuebene xxvijº die Septembris, xxij s. ff. September 27.

Item apud Drawinglurgh xxviij° die Septembris, vj marc. ff. Item pro belchere xxix° die Septembris apud Orneswald, j nobl. Item apud Londspere, x s. viij d. ff. Item alia die pro belchere ibidem, viij s. ff. Item apud Frankford pro belchere, xvj gr. Et pro belchere senescalli et thesaurarii ibidem, iij nobl. Item dati 5 famulis ibidem, xij gr. Item apud Prake cum familia domini, xxiij nobl. Item apud Gobin v° die mensis Octobris, xij gr. Item pro belchere ibidem vj° die Octobris, xlj gr. Item pro belchere apud Gorlech, lviij gr. di. Item pro belchere apud Tribull, xxxv gr. Item apud Zitaw ix° die mensis Octobris, xxv gr. Item apud 10 Nemance, xxvij gr. Item apud Whitwater, xxix gr. Item apud Berne xxij° die Octobris, vj flor. Item apud Bronslowe xxiij° die Octobris, xxxiiij gr. Item apud Preda, xxvj° die Octobris, xxij gr. Item apud Chastelet xxvj° die Octobris pro belchere, xxij gr. Item apud Denchebrod, xxvij° die Octobris, xvj gr. Item apud 15 Misserich, xxviij° die Octobris, xxvj gr. Item apud Broune, xxix° die Octobris, iij nobl. j flor. Et apud Drising, ij° die Nouembris, xxxij gr. Item apud Sconekirke iij° die Nouembris, xxvj gr. Item apud Wene, iiij° die Nouembris, vj nobl. ij flor. Item die Veneris apud Drossekirk, viij° die Nouembris, xvj gr. Item die 20 Sabbati ix° die Nouembris apud Neukirke, xxij gr. Item die Dominica x° die Nouembris apud Slomrestowe, xviij gr. Item die Lune xj° die Nouembris apud Kimburgh, xx gr. Item apud Louban, xij° die Nouembris, xvj gr. Item apud Knotilfell, xiij° die Nouembris, xviij gr. Item apud Rowdingburgh, xiiij° die 25 Nouembris per ij dies, xxxiiij gr. Item apud Husak, xvj° die mensis Nouembris, xxviij gr. Item apud Fellekirke, xvij° die eiusdem mensis, xxviij gr. Item apud Fillawk, xviij° die Nouembris, xij gr. vj d. Item apud Malberget, xix° die Nouembris, xx gr. Item apud Posilthorpe, xx° die Nouembris, viij gr. Item apud 30 ciuitatem hostr' xxj° die Nouembris, xviij gr. Item apud Sanctum Danielem, xxij° die Nouembris, xviij gr. Item apud Chichon' xxiij° die Nouembris, xvj gr. Item xxiiij die Nouembris apud Gisill, vj flor.

II. DRINK-MONEY IN VARIOUS PLACES. 261

Summa nobilium, ej nobl.
Item de florenis, 1 flor. vj gr. di.   Summa istius pagine computata in
Item xij marca xl s. viij d. ff.   sterlinges, lx li. xvj s. v d. ob. qa. st.ᵃ
Item lij marca di. scot. pr.

5 / Item pro belchere apud Nowall xxviij° die mensis Aprilis, j duc.   fo. 34.
vij gr. Item apud Turryn pro belchere xxj° die Maii, vj duc. Item   April 28, 1393.
pro belchere apud Auylan, xxij° die Maii, vj duc. vij gr. Item   May 21, 22.
apud Ryweles, xxij° die Maii pro belchere, iiij duc. vj gr. Item
pro belchere apud Schusa, per iij dies, ibidem commorantes xxiij°   May 23, 26.
10 die Maii, xvij duc. Item apud Launcebrugg', xxvj° die Maii,
ij duc. vj gr. Item apud Furneworthe, xxvij° die Maii, iij duc.   May 27, 28.
viij gr. Item apud Sanctum Michaelem xxviij° die mensis eiusdem,
iij duc. vij gr. Item apud Chambour xxix die eiusdem, ij duc. vij gr. May 29, 30.
Item apud Egebelle, xxx° die Maii, vj duc. vj gr. Item apud
15 Floren xxxj° die Maii, iij frank. vj bl. Item apud Jan primo die   May 31—June
Junii pro belchere, iiij duc. vj bl. Item apud Russebon ij° die   June 2, 3.
Junii, iij duc. viij gr. Item apud Syrombert iij° die Junii, xxxix gr.
Item apud Pompinet iiij° die Junii, iij duc. viij gr. di. Item apud June 4, 5.
Fownteney v° die Junii, iij duc. vij gr. Item apud Bagg' vj die
20 Junii, ij duc. vij gr. Item apud Macon vij° die Junii, viij duc.   June 6, 7.
viij gr. Item apud Trauays viij° die Junii, vj duc. viij bl. Item   June 8, 9.
apud Chalons ix° die Junii, xij duc. xij bl. Item apud Bewme pro
belchere x° die Junii, iij duc. vj bl. Item apud Chause, xj° die   June 10, 11.
Junii, vj frank. xij bl. Item apud Melnyle Lambar' xij° die Junii, June 12.
25 iij frank. vj bl Item apud Chastelon xiij° die Junii, iij frank. June 13, 14.
xiij bl. Item apud Beree xiiij° die Junii, iij frank. vj bl. Item
apud Troys xv° die Junii, vij frank. xj bl. Et in hospicio senes-   June 15, 16.
calli et thesaurarii, j frank iiij bl. Item apud Marine xvj° die
Junii, lxij bl. Item apud Nogent xvij° die Junii, ij frank. vj bl. June 17.

ᵃ A note at the bottom of the page, somewhat illegible, runs as follows :—Et sic
j noble [facit] ij flor., et ix s. faciunt j noble ; vsque huc flor. et gr. de boemia,
xx gr. pro j flor. ; et le mare de prucia computatur pro j noble.

Item apud Prouince, xviij° die Junii, iij flor. xx bl. Item apud Grauntpuisse xix° die Junii, ij frank, vj bl. Item apud Vicount Robert xx° die Junii, ij frank. xviij bl. Item apud Pountchareton xxj° die Junii, j frank. xviij bl. Item apud Parys xxij° die Junii, xxij scut.*

Summa pagine computata in sterlinges, iiij li. xiiij s. iij d. st.
Item in moneta Francie, xlij frank. iiij bl. di.
Item in moneta de Venys, iiij^{xx}xvij duc.

Summa totalis de Belchere computata in sterlinges, lxv li. x s. viij d. ob. q^a st.
Item in moneta Francie vt supra, xlij frank. iiij bl. di.
Item de moneta de Venys, iiij^{xx}xvij duc.

/ EMPTIO EQUORUM.

In primis pro j equo sorrel empto per manus domini apud Dansk de quodam mercatore vocato Lankow xxij° die Augusti, xl nobl. Item pro ij equis emptis per Robertum Waterton, xxiiij nobl. Item pro j equo empto per Willelmum Harpedene, viij nobl. Item pro ij equis emptis de Ricardo Hasildene pro carrecta, xj marc. di. pr. Item pro j equo empto de domino Thoma Erpingham pro carrecta, vj marc. pr. Item pro j equo empto de Thoma Eton pro carrecta, viij nobl. Item pro j equo empto de capellano domini Henrici Peercy pro carrecta, viij nobl. Item pro j equo empto de Johanne Aleyn pro carrecta, vj nobl. Item pro j equo empto de Matheo Casson carectario, v nobl. Item Thome Gloucestre pro j equo ab ipso empto apud Prake, iij nobl. Item Ricardo Dancastre pro j equo ab ipso empto ibidem, x nobl. Item Thome Gloucestre pro j equo ab ipso empto apud Wene, x flor.

* Scutum valet iij s. iiij d. ob. st., et facit xxvij bl.; le Frank valet xxiiij bl. Et ij ducati et ix s. faciunt j noble. (Lower margin).

Item pro j equo empto de Laurencio de scutellaria pro carrecta, vj duc. Item pro j equo empto de Henrico Maunsell pro le Trumpet, xxj duc. Item Laurencio Trauers pro j equo ab ipso empto apud Portgruer primo die Nouembris pro carectario, vj duc. Item Jacobo November 1.
5 Gyde pro j equo ab ipso empto ibidem eodem die, vj duc. Item pro j equo empto de Johanne Payn apud Portgruer pro somario domini, xxj duc. Item pro j equo empto apud Cheuaux de quodam marescallo domini Comitis Virtutum, xxj duc. Item pro j equo empto apud Papyam pro le male de quodam scutifero, xxiiij duc.

10 Summa computata in sterlinges, xliij li. iij s. iiij d. st. Et Cx duc.

Lusus Domini.

In primis liberata domino apud Hecham xx° die Julii per manus July 20.
Willelmi Burgoyne, j nobl. Item eidem per manus domini Willelmi
Pumfreet apud Hecham xxiiij° die Julii, ij nobl. Item eidem per July 24.
15 manus thesaurarii per ij vices, j nobl. Item eidem in naui per manus eiusdem, j nobl. Item eidem apud Dansk per manus thesaurarii xv die Augusti, vj nobl. Item alia vice apud Brounes- August 15.
burgh pro lusu domini per manus proprias, ij marc. pr. Item liberata domino per manus proprias apud Sconech xxij die Septem- September 22.
20 bris, j nobl. Item eidem apud Zitaw per manus proprias, ij nobl. Item liberatus eidem per manus Chelmeswyk, j flor. Item eidem apud Gorlech per manus thesaurarii, ij nobl. Item liberati domino per manus proprias et valecto camere ex precepto eiusdem, xxj flor. Item eidem pro lusu domini ad l'almam,[a] receptis denariis de
25 Wilbram apud Treuiso, ij duc. Item eidem pro luso suo ibidem per manus camerarii, j duc. Item liberati domino in galcia per manus domini Petri Sciolatour, iij duc. Item liberati domino in galcia,

---

[a] This is the *jeu de paume*.

264   THE EARL OF DERBY'S EXPEDITIONS.

February 23, 1392-3.   xxiij° die Februarii per manus Nowell, iiij duc. Item liberati
February 25.   domino per manus senescalli in galeia xxv° die eiusdem, ludenti
                       cum patrono, iiij duc.   Item liberati domino per manus thesaurarii
                       et Chelmeswyk, diuersis vicibus, vj duc.   Item liberati domino in
                       galeia pro luso suo ad tabulas per manus Dene, famuli Chelmeswyk, 5
                       ludenti cum vno Gascono, iij duc.

                       Summa computata in sterlinges, vj li. st.
                       Item in ducates, xlv duc.

fo. 35.   / VADIA.

                            Domino Ottoni Graunsom militi pro vadiis suis infra curiam, 10
August 12—Sep-   a xij° Augusti vsque ultimum diem Septembris, vtroque computato,
tember 30, 1392.   capienti per diem ex precepto domini et consilii, iij s. iiij d. per
                       l dies, viij li. vj s. viij d.   Et eidem pro vadiis suis infra curiam a
October 1, 1392—   primo die Octobris vsque vltimum diem Maii, vtroque computato,
May 31, 1393.   capienti per diem v s., ex precepto domini et consilii per ij°xliij 15
                       dies, lx li. v s.   Domino Willelmo Wiluby pro vadiis suis infra
July 21—September   curiam, a xxj° die Julii vsque vltimum diem Septembris, vtroque
30, 1392.   computato, capienti per diem xij d. per compotum secum factum
October 1, 1392—   per lxxij dies, lxxij s.   Et eidem pro vadiis suis a primo die
June 30, 1393.   Octobris vsque vltimum diem Junii, vtroque computato, per ij°lxxiij 20
                       dies, capienti per diem ij s. per compotum secum factum, in toto,
July 1-4, 1393.   xxvij li. vj s.   Et eidem pro vadiis suis infra curiam a primo die
                       Julii vsque iiij^m diem eiusdem mensis in Anglia, per iiij dies,
                       capienti per diem, xij d., per compotum secum factum, iiij s. st.
July 21—September   Domino Hugoni Waterton pro vadiis suis infra curiam, a xxj° die 25
30, 1392.   Julii vsque vltimum diem Septembris, utroque computato, capienti
                       per diem xij d. per compotum secum factum, lxxij s.   Et eidem pro
October 1, 1392—   vadiis suis infra curiam a primo die Octobris vsque vltimum diem
June 30, 1393.   Junii, vtroque computato, capienti per diem ij s., per compotum
                       secum factum, xxvij li. vj s.   Et eidem pro vadiis suis infra curiam 30

II. WAGES OF KNIGHTS.

a primo die Julii vsque xiij^m diem mensis eiusdem, vtroque computato, capienti per diem xij d. in Angliam, per compotum secum factum, xiij s. Domino Thome Erpingham pro vadiis suis infra curiam a xxiij° die Septembris vsque ultimum diem eiusdem vtroque die computato, capienti per diem xij d., per compotum secum factum, viij s. Item eidem pro vadiis suis infra curiam a primo die Octobris vsque vltimum diem Junii, vtroque computato, capienti per diem ij s. per compotum secum factum, xxvij li. vj s. Et eidem pro vadiis suis infra curiam a primo die Julii vsque iiij^m diem eiusdem, vtroque computato, capienti per diem xij d., in toto, iiij s. Domino Petro Bucton pro vadiis suis infra curiam a xxj° die mensis Julii vsque vltimum diem Septembris, vtroque computato, capienti per diem xij d. per compotum secum factum, lxxij s. Et eidem pro vadiis suis infra curiam a xxiiij° die Nouembris vsque vltimum diem Junii, vtroque computato, capienti per diem ij s., per ij^c xix dies, xx li. xviij s. Et eidem pro vadiis suis infra curiam a primo die Julii vsque vij^m diem mensis eiusdem, capienti per diem xij d., infra Angliam, vtroque computato, vij s. Domino H. Herle, pro vadiis suis infra curiam a xxj° die Julii vsque vltimum diem Septembris, vtroque computato, capienti per diem xij d., lxxij s. Domino Radulpho de Wene, militi, pro vadiis suis infra curiam a vj° die Aprilis vsque vltimum diem Junii per iiij^{xx} vj dies, capienti per diem ij s., vtroque computato, viij li. xij s. Et eidem pro vadiis suis infra curiam, a j° die Julii vsque xiij^m diem eiusdem, capienti per diem xij d., vtroque computato, xiij s. Radulpho Rocheford, militi pro vadiis suis infra curiam a vj° die Aprilis vsque vltimum diem Junii, vtroque computato, capienti per diem ij s., viij li. xij s. Item eidem pro vadiis suis infra curiam a primo die Julii vsque iiij^m diem eiusdem, capienti per diem xij d., infra Angliam, iiij s. Et eidem a xij° die Augusti vsque vltimum diem Septembris infra curiam, excundo cum domino scutifero, capienti per diem vij d. ob. xxxj s. iij d. Et eidem pro vadiis suis infra curiam a primo die Octobris vsque v^m diem Aprilis, vtroque computato, capienti per diem xij d.—in toto, ix li. vij s. Item domino Ricardo

Margin dates:
July 1-13.
September 23-30, 1392.
October 1, 1392—June 30, 1393.
July 1-4.
July 21—September 30, 1392.
November 24, 1392—June 30, 1393.
July 1-7.
July 21—September 30, 1392.
April 6—June 30, 1393.
July 1-13.
April 6—June 30.
July 1—4.
August 12 - September 30, 1392.
October 1, 1392—April 5, 1393.

July 21—September 30, 1392.	Kyngeston pro vadiis suis infra curiam a xxj° die Julii vsque ultimum diem Septembris, capienti per diem xij d. utroque computato,
November 24—June 30, 1393.	lxxij s. Et eidem pro vadiis suis infra curiam a xxiiij° die Nouembris vsque vltimum diem Junii, per ij^{c}xij dies, vtroque computato, capienti per diem ij s. xxj li. xviij s. Et eidem pro vadiis suis
July 1-13.	infra curiam a j° die Julii vsque xiij^m diem eiusdem, capienti per diem xij d., xiij s. Item Ricardo Chelmeswyk pro vadiis suis infra
July 21—September 30, 1392.	curiam, a xxj° die Julii vsque vltimum diem Septembris, vtroque computato, per lxxij dies, capienti per diem vij d. ob., in toto, xlv s.
October 1—April 6, 1393.	Et eidem pro vadiis suis a primo die Octobris vsque vj^m diem Aprilis, vtroque computato, per C iiij^{xx}viij dies, capienti per diem
June 1-30.	xij d., ix li. viij s. Et eidem pro vadiis suis a primo die Junii vsque vltimum diem eiusdem, vtroque computato, capienti per diem xij d., per xxx dies, xxx s. Et eidem pro vadiis suis infra curiam
July 1-13.	a j° die Julii vsque xiij diem eiusdem, vtroque computato, capienti per diem vij d. ob., viij s. j d. ob. Petro Melbourne pro vadiis suis a
July 21—September 30, 1392. fo. 35 v°.	xxj° die Julii vsque vltimum diem Septembris, vtroque computato,^{a} / capienti per diem, vij d. ob., in toto, xlv s. Et eidem pro vadiis
October 1—June 30, 1393.	suis infra curiam, a j° die Octobris vsque vltimum diem Junii vtroque computato, capienti per diem xij d., per ij^c lxxiij dies, xiij li. xij s. Et eidem pro vadiis suis infra curiam in Anglia,
July 1-13.	a primo die Julii vsque xiij^m diem mensis eiusdem, capienti per diem vij d. ob., in toto viij s. j d. ob. Radulpho Stanele pro vadiis suis infra curiam, capienti vt Petrus Melbourne per idem tempus, et per tot dies, in toto xvj li. vj s. j d. ob. Thome Toty pro vadiis suis infra curiam per idem tempus, capienti vt supra, xvj li. vj s. j d. ob. Johanni Payn pro vadiis suis per idem tempus, capienti vt supra, xvj li. vj s. j d. ob. Thome Gloucestre pro vadiis suis infra curiam per idem tempus, capienti vt supra, xvj li. vj s. j d. ob. Magistro Willelmo Cook pro vadiis suis vt supra per idem tempus, capienti vt supra, xvj li. vj s. j d. ob.
July 21—August 13, 1392.	Roberto Waterton pro vadiis suis infra curiam, a xxj° die Julii

* Summa pagine, CClvij li. x s. ob.

II. WAGES OF ESQUIRES AND VALETS.

vsque xiij^m diem Augusti, vtroque computato, capienti per diem
vij d. ob., in toto xv s. Et eidem pro vadiis suis infra curiam,
a primo die Junii vsque vltimum diem eiusdem, vtroque com-   June 1—30, 1393.
putato, capienti per diem xij d., xxx s. Et eidem pro vadiis suis
5 infra curiam a primo die Julii vsque xiij^m diem eiusdem, vtroque   July 1-13.
computato, capienti per diem vij d. ob., viij s. j d. ob. Johanni
Watertone pro vadiis suis infra curiam, a xxj° die Julii vsque   July 21, 1392—
xiij^m diem mensis Augusti, vtroque computato, per diem capienti   August 13.
vij d. ob., xv s. Mowbray le herald pro vadiis suis per vij dies
10 mensis Septembris, capienti per diem vij d. ob., iiij s. iiij d. ob.
Et eidem pro vadiis suis a primo die Octobris vsque vj^m diem   October 1, 1392—
Aprilis, vtroque computato, capienti per diem viij d. per Ciiij^{xx}viij   April 6, 1393.
dies, vj li. v s. iiij d. Et eidem pro vadiis suis a primo die Junii   June 1-30, 1393.
vsque vltimum diem eiusdem, capienti per diem vt supra, xx s.
15 Et eidem pro vadiis suis infra curiam, a primo die Julii vsque   July 1-13, 1393.
xiij^m diem eiusdem, capienti per diem vij d. ob., viij s. j d. ob.
Item Bastard Graunsom pro vadiis suis a vij° die Augusti vsque   August 7—Septem
vltimum diem Septembris, vtroque computato, per l dies, capienti   30, 1392.
per diem vij d. ob., xxxj s. iij d. Et eidem pro vadiis suis a primo   October 1—Februa
20 die Octobris vsque xix^m diem Februarii, per Cxlij dies, vtroque   19, 1392-3.
computato, capienti per diem xij d., vij li. ij s. Francisco de
Lumbardia pro vadiis suis infra curiam, a primo die Junii vsque   June 1-30.
vltimum diem eiusdem, vtroque computato, per xxx dies, capienti
per diem xij d., xxx s. Et eidem pro vadiis suis infra curiam in
25 Anglia, a primo die Julii vsque xiij^m diem eiusdem, vtroque   July 1-13.
computato, capienti per diem vij d. ob., viij s. j d. ob. Ricardo
Dancastre pro vadiis suis infra curiam, a primo die Junii vsque   June 1-30.
vltimum diem eiusdem, vtroque computato, capienti per diem
xij d., xxx s. Willelmo Gyse pro vadiis suis infra curiam, a xij°   August 12—
30 die Augusti vsque xv^m diem Septembris, vtroque computato,   September 15, 1392
capienti per diem vij d. ob., xxj s. x d. ob. Thome Goter pro   * Incipiunt vadia d
vadiis suis per ibidem tempus, capienti vt supra, xxj s. x d. ob.   Prusia redeundo
Item Willelmo Pomffrett pro vadiis suis infra curiam a xxj° die Julii   July 21—Aug. 31.
vsque vltimum diem Augusti, vtroque computato, capienti per diem

iiij d., xiiij s. Et eidem pro vadiis suis infra curiam, a primo die
Septembris vsque xxiiij^m diem ejusdem, vtroque computato, capienti
per diem vij d. ob., xv s. Willelmo Bigmayden pro vadiis suis, a
xxj° die Julii vsque xv^m diem Septembris, vtroque computato, per
lvij dies, capienti per diem vij d. ob., xxxv s. vij d. ob. Edmundo
Buyge pro vadiis suis per idem tempus, capienti per diem vt supra,
xxxv s. vij d. ob. Roberto Litton pro vadiis suis infra curiam, a
xxj° die Julii vsque vltimum diem Septembris, vtroque computato,
per lxxij dies, capienti per diem iiij d., xxiiij s. Johanni Wilbram
pro vadiis suis per idem tempus, capienti vt supra, xxiiij s. Henrico
de Camera pro vadiis suis per idem tempus vt supra, xxiiij s. Henrico
Maunsell pro vadiis suis per idem tempus, capienti vt supra, xxiiij s.
/ Johanni Cudworth pro vadiis suis per idem tempus infra curiam,
capienti vt supra, xxiiij s. Johanni Schelford pro vadiis suis,
capienti per idem tempus vt supra, xxiiij s. Johanni Gilder pro
vadiis suis infra curiam per lvj dies, capienti per diem iiij d.,
xviij s. viij d. Item eidem pro vadiis suis extra curiam per xvj dies,
capienti per diem vj d., misso de Dansk vsque Coningsburgh, viij s.
Willelmo Harpeden pro vadiis suis per idem tempus, capienti vt
Henricus Maunsell, xxiiij s. Johanni Dyndon pro vadiis suis, a
xxj° die Julii vsque xxij^m diem Septembris per lxiiij dies, capienti
per diem iiij d., in toto xxj s. iiij d. Henrico Morley pro vadiis
suis per idem tempus, capienti vt supra, xxj s. iiij d. Johanni Yonge
pro vadiis suis per idem tempus, capienti vt supra, xxj s. iiij d.
Johanni Pek pro vadiis suis per idem tempus, capienti vt supra, xxj s.
iiij d. Ricardo Wolfile pro vadiis suis per idem tempus, capienti ut
supra, xxj s. iiij d. Ricardo Weston pro vadiis suis per idem tempus,
capienti vt supra, xxj s. iiij d. Johanni Robinson, porter, pro
vadiis suis infra curiam, a xij° die Augusti vsque xv^m diem Septembris, vtroque computato, capienti per diem iiij d., xj s. viij d. Thome
Sohow pro vadiis suis per idem tempus, capienti vt supra xj s. viij d.
Rogero Clyderow pro vadiis suis per idem tempus, capienti vt
supra, xj s. viij d. Thome Gerad pro vadiis suis per idem tempus,
capienti vt supra, xj s. viij d. Ricardo Aunterous pro vadiis suis

II. ESQUIRES, VALETS, AND MINSTRELS.

per idem tempus, capienti vt supra, xj s. viij d. Nicholao Leche
pro vadiis suis per xlij dies, capienti per diem iiij d., xiiij s. Johanni Trompetour pro vadiis suis infra curiam, a xxj die Julii   July 21—Septen
vsque xv^m diem Septembris, per lxij dies, capienti per diem vt   15.
5 supra; xix s. Johanni Algood, piper, pro vadiis suis per idem
tempus, capienti vt supra, xix s. Johanni Smyth, piper, pro vadiis
suis per idem tempus capienti ut supra, xix s. Johanni Aleyn, piper,
pro vadiis suis per idem tempus, capienti vt supra, xix s. Thome
Aleyn, trumpet, pro vadiis suis per idem tempus, capienti vt supra,
10 xix s. Thome trumpet pro vadiis suis per idem tempus, capienti ut
supra, xix s. Johanni Dounton pro vadiis suis a xxj° die Julii vsque
xxij^m diem Septembris, vtroque computato per lxiiij dies, capienti   July 21—Septen
per diem ij d., in toto x s. viij d. Roberto Peper pro vadiis suis per   22.
idem tempus, capienti vt supra, x s. viij d. Roberto Knyghton pro
15 vadiis suis per idem tempus, capienti vt supra, x s. viij d. Item
Laurencio Trauers pro vadiis suis per idem tempus, capienti vt
supra, x s. viij d. Willelmo Kikkeley pro vadiis suis per idem
tempus, capienti vt supra, x s. viij d. Item Willelmo Syde pro
vadiis suis vt supra, x s. viij d. Johanni Flete pro vadiis suis,
20 a xij die Augusti vsque xv^m diem Septembris, vtroque computato,   August 12—
capienti vt supra, v s. x d. Johanni Selby pro vadiis suis per idem   September 15.
tempus, capienti vt supra, v s. x d. Johanni Windesoure pro vadiis
suis per idem tempus, capienti vt supra, v s. x d. Johanni Swanne
pro vadiis suis per idem tempus, capienti vt supra, v s. x d.^a Item
25 Johanni Wilbram pro vadiis suis a primo die Julii vsque xiij^m diem   July 1-13.
eiusdem mensis, vtroque computato, capienti per diem iiij d., in
toto iiij s. iiij d. Item Roberto Litton pro vadiis suis per idem
tempus, capienti per diem iiij d., in toto iiij s. iiij d. Johanni Cudworth pro vadiis suis per idem tempus, capienti vt supra. iiij s. iiij d.   Summa pagine.
30 Johanni Schelford per idem tempus, capienti vt supra, iiij s. iiij d.   xxv li. xvij s.
/ Roberto Heathcote pro vadiis suis per idem tempus, capienti vt   viij d, st.
                                                                                                     fo. 36 v°.

^a Five items in as many lines occur here which have been crossed out. The
wages of John Wilbram were first written at vj d. per diem, total vj s. vj d. afterwards corrected as above.

270   THE EARL OF DERBY'S EXPEDITIONS.

supra, iiij s. iiij d. Henrico de Camera pro vadiis suis per idem tempus, capienti vt supra, iiij s. iiij d. Johanni Gilder pro vadiis suis per idem tempus, capienti vt supra, iiij s. iiij d. Johanni Selby pro vadiis suis infra curiam, a xxiij° die Septembris vsque vltimum diem Nouembris, vtroque computato, capienti per diem ij d., per lxviij dies,—in toto xj s. iiij d. Et eidem pro vadiis suis a primo die Decembris vsque ultimum diem Junii, vtroque computato, per ij^cxij dies, capienti per diem ij d., in toto xxxv s. iiij d. Et eidem pro vadiis suis infra curiam a primo die Julii vsque xiij^m diem eiusdem, vtroque computato, capienti per diem vt supra, ij s. ij d. Thome Toty et Johanni Payn pro vadiis suis extra curiam, existentibus apud Linne per xiiij dies pro prouidentiis ibidem faciendis versus partes Prucie, capientibus per diem inter se ij s., in toto xxviij s. Willelmo Freman pro vadiis suis extra curiam, misso de Linne versus Episcopum Norwycensem et deinde redeundo per duos dies, per compotum secum factum, capienti per diem vj d., xij d. Johanni Baron pro vadiis suis extra curiam, existenti apud Linne per xxvij dies pro diuersis prouidenciis ibidem faciendis, capienti per diem vj d., xiij s. vj d. Johanni Zonge pro vadiis suis extra curiam, misso de Peterburgh vsque Lynne pro salua custodia diuersorum harnesiorum domini ibidem per viij dies, capienti per diem vj d., iiij s. Clerico coquine pro vadiis suis extra curiam, misso de Peterburgh vsque Lynne pro diuersis victualibus emendis ibidem, per vij dies, capienti per diem vj d., iij s. vj d. Willelmo Worcestre pro vadiis suis extra curiam, misso de Peterburgh vsque Linne pro prouidenciis ibidem faciendis per vij dies, capienti per diem vj d., in toto iij s. vj d. Roberto Hethcote pro vadiis suis infra curiam a xxj° die Julii vsque vltimum diem Septembris, vtroque computato, per lxxij dies, capienti per diem iiij d., xxiij s. Willelmo Harpeden pro vadiis suis a primo die Julii vsque xiij^m diem eiusdem, vtroque computato, capienti per diem iiij d., in toto iiij s. iiij d. Roberto Brakill, trumpour, pro vadiis suis per idem tempus,^a capienti per

---

^a There is an interlineation here, partly illegible. "quo . . . cum ministral'," but owing to corrections it is impossible to say what Brakill's wages were per diem.

II. WAGES OF VALETS AND MINSTRELS. 271

diem vt supra, xix s. Roberto Pepir pro vadiis suis extra curiam, misso de Peterburgh vsque Linne pro prouidenciis ibidem factis circa larder per vj dies, capienti per diem iiij d., in toto ij s. Roberto Duffeld pro vadiis suis extra curiam per vj dies, capienti per diem
5 ij d, in toto xij d. Johanni Cudworth pro vadiis suis, a primo die Octobris vsque vltimum diem Junii, vtroque computato, per ij^clxxiij dies, capienti per diem vj d., in toto vj li. xvj s. vj d. Roberto Litton pro vadiis suis infra curiam, a primo die Decembris vsque predictum vltimum diem Junii, per ccxij dies, capienti per
10 diem iiij d., in toto[b] lxx s. viij d. Johanni Gilder pro vadiis suis per idem tempus, capienti vt supra, lxx s. viij d. Johanni Shelford pro vadiis suis a primo die Octobris vsque vltimum diem eiusdem, per xxxj dies, capienti per diem iiij d, x s. iiij d. Johanni Blaedon pro vadiis suis infra curiam, a xxj^o die Julii
15 vsque vj^m diem Septembris, vtroque computato, per xlviij dies, capienti per diem iiij d., in toto xvj s. Et eidem pro vadiis suis extra curiam, misso de Dansk vsque Conyngysburgh pro diuersis prouidenciis ibidem factis pro domino, a vij^o die Septembris vsque xxij diem eiusdem mensis, per xvj dies, vtroque computato, capienti
20 per diem vj d., in toto viij s. Johanni Fyscher pistori pro vadiis suis infra curiam, a xxj^o die Julii vsque xxij^m diem Septembris per lxiiij dies, vtroque computato, capienti per diem iiij d., in toto xxj s. iiij d. Thome Trumpet pro vadiis suis a primo die Octobris vsque xxiiij^m diem Nouembris, per lv dies, vtroque computato, ca-
25 pienti per diem iiij d., xviij s. iiij d. Et eidem pro vadiis suis a vij^o die Aprilis vsque xiij^m diem Julii, per iiij^{vx}xviij dies, vtroque computato, capienti per diem iiij d., xxxij s. viij d. Ricardo Dancastre pro vadiis suis a primo die Julii vsque xiij^m diem eiusdem mensis, vtroque computato, capienti per diem vij d. ob., viij s. j d.
30 ob. Lancastre Regi armorum pro vadiis suis infra curiam, a xxj^o die Aprilis vsque vltimum diem Junii, per lxxj dies, capienti per diem xij d., lxxj s. Howell Tyder pro vadiis suis a xij^o die Augusti vsque

Margin notes:
October 1, 1392–June 30, 1393.
December 1, 139 June 30, 1393.
October 1-31, 13
July 21—Septem
September 7-22.
July 21—Septem 22.
October 1—November 24.
April 7—July 13.
July 1-13.
April 21—June 3
August 12—September 15, 13

---

[b] Several corrections have been made here, and lines crossed through, it being noted as to wages to Wilbraham struck out " quia in alia parte istius c. ad vj d.

272   THE EARL OF DERBY'S EXPEDITIONS.

xv^m diem Septembris, vtroque computato, capienti per diem iiij d.,
xj s. viij d.   Et Johanni Biterley pro vadiis suis vt supra, xj s. viij d.^a
/ Willelmo Harpeden pro vadiis suis,^b a primo die Octobris vsque
vltimum diem Decembris per iiij^{xx}xij dies, capienti per diem vj d.,
in toto xlvj s.   Item a primo die Januarii vsque xvij^m diem Februarii, vtroque computato, ipse fuit super expensis domini.   Et
eidem pro vadiis suis a xviij° die Februarii vsque vltimum diem
Junii, per Cxxxiij dies, capienti per diem vj d., in toto lxvj s. vj d.^c
Thome Ferour pro vadiis suis a xxv° die Nouembris vsque ultimum
diem Decembris, capienti per diem iiij d. per xxxvj dies, in toto
xij s.   Et eidem pro vadiis suis a xx° die Januarii vsque xiij^m diem
Aprilis, per iiij^{xx}iij dies, capienti per diem iiij d., in toto
xxvij s. viij d.; quia a primo die Januarii vsque xvij^m diem Februarii
ipse fuit super expensis domini.   Item Willelmo Kykkeley, Johanni Aschby, Thome Swillington, Roberto Hewet et Johanni de
Chaundre per cxix dies, quolibet capiente per diem iij d., in toto
vij li. viij s. ix d.   Johanni Maye, et Henrico Hound, pagettis,
valettis camere domini, et Willelmi Harpeden, pro vadiis suis per
idem tempus, vtroque eorum capiente per diem j d. ob., in toto
xxix s. ix d.   Willelmo Kikkeley, Johanni Aschby, Roberto Hwet,
Thome Swilington, pro vadiis suis infra curiam, a primo die Julii
vsque xiij^m diem eiusdem, quolibet capiente per diem ij d., in toto
viij s. viij d.   Laurencio Trauers pro vadiis suis a xxviij° die
Aprilis vsque xiij^m diem Junii per lxxvj dies, capienti per diem
ij d., in toto xij s. viij d.

Summa pagine, xvij li. xij s.
Summa totalis vadiorum, CCCClxvij li. xiij d. st.^d

^a Summa pagine, xxxij li. xij s. iij d. ob.   Hic deficiunt Hethcote a primo die
Octobris vsque vltimam diem Junii, capienti per diem iiij d.   Et Henrico Mounsel
a j° die Octobris vsque primum diem Maij, capienti per diem vt supra.   Et Schelford
pro xiij diebus in Angliam, capienti per diem vt supra.
^b Here also are a couple of lines crossed out, because the items are entered on
the previous page.
^c Here is another item crossed through because it is on the previous page.
^d The sums total of this and of the last page are corrected, the figures first
written being struck out.

II. OBLATIONS AND ALMS.

/ Oblaciones et Elemosine.   fo. 38.

In oblacionibus domini in naui apud Lynne, xxviij° die Julii, July 28, 1392.
receptis denariis de domina Katerina Bromwych, xx d. st. Et in
elemosinis domini datis cuidam ankerisse de Lynne eodem die,
5 receptis denariis de domino Johanne elemosinario domini, vj s. viij d.
st. Item in elemosinis domini distributis pauperibus apud Linne,
receptis denariis de Willelmo Pomfreet, xx d. st. In oblacionibus
domini in prima villa de Prusia, receptis denariis de Henrico de
camera, ix scot. Item in oblacionibus domini apud Dansk in festo   August 13.
10 sancti Ipoliti, j nobl. Item in oblacionibus ibidem in festo Assump-   August 15.
tione Beate Marie, j nobl. Item in elemosinis domini distributis
per manus domini Hugonis Heerle, per diuersas vices, xvj s. pr.
Et pro oblacionibus domini in xv primis diebus adventus sui apud
Dansk, xv s. pr. Item in oblacionibus domini euntis de Dansk
15 vsque Conyngesburgh, per manus Johannis Peck, xiiij s. pr. Item
in oblacionibus domini distributis pauperibus per viam per manus
eiusdem, xxiij s. pr. Item pro oblacionibus domini apud Dansk
post aduentum suum de Coningesburgh, per manus domini
H. Heerle, xij s. pr. Item in batillagio domini H. Herle euntis
20 super negocium domini apud nauem ibidem, xij s. pr. Item
in elemosinis domini datis diuersis sororibus apud Dansk, xvj°   August 16.
die Augusti, xij s. pr. Item in elemosinis domini datis fratribus
predicatoribus ibidem eodem die, v s. pr. Item in oblacionibus
domini et familie sue apud Dansk, die sepulture Hans et familie
25 sue * vna cum elemosinis distributis ibidem diuersis pauperibus   * [Sic. See bc
eodem die, iij noble. Item in elemosinis domini distributis diuersis   p. 167. l. 1.]
pauperibus apud Holipill primo die Septembris, xij scot. Item in   September 1.
elemosinis domini datis fratribus apud Darsowe xxv. die Augusti,   August 25.
j nobl. Item in elemosinis domini distributis ibidem diuersis pau-
30 peribus vltimo die mensis Augusti, iiij scot. Item in elemosinis   August 31.
domini datis fratribus apud Holipill primo die Septembris, j noble.   September 1.
Item in oblacionibus domini apud abathiam de Melwyn, xxix die   August 29.

CAMD. SOC.   2 N

Augusti, receptis denariis de Hasilden, j noble. Item in elemosinis domini distributis pauperibus apud Brondeburgh, v° die mensis Septembris, iiij s. pr. Et in elemosinis domini datis fratribus ibidem eodem die, j marc pr. Item in elemosinis domini datis fratribus apud Darsowe, vj° die Septembris, di marc. pr. Item in elemosinis domini datis diuersis pauperibus ibidem eodem die, xxxv s. pr. Item in oblacionibus domini in capella Sancti Georgii apud Melwin, primo die Septembris, di marc. pr. Item in elemosinis domini distributis diuersis pauperibus apud Dansk, xvj° die Septembris, v s. pr. Item in oblacionibus domini apud Dansk in festo Beate Marie, vj scot. Item in oblacionibus domini apud Coningsburgh, iij° die Septembris, vij s. pr. Et in elemosinis domini distributis ibidem eodem die, xiiij scot. Item in oblacionibus domini ibidem eodem die, in ecclesia parochiali ibidem, j noble. Et in elemosinis datis diuersis pauperibus ad diuersa loca per diuersas vices, receptis denariis de H. Herice, xvj s. pr. Et in elemosinis domini eodem die apud Dansk et Conyngsburgh, xxvij s. pr. Et pro oblacionibus domini apud Coningsburgh et elemosinis ibidem per manus Peek, ix s. viij d. pr. Item in elemosinis domini datis monialibus apud Dansk per manus Payn, xv s. pr. Item in elemosinis domini distributis pauperibus apud Sconee, xv° die Septembris vj s. pr. Item in elemosinis domini datis fratribus ibidem, iiij scot. Item apud Londes per xviij° die Septembris, ij s. viij d. ff. Item apud Zitaw fratribus Carmelitis xx° die Sept., x gr. Item cuidam mulieri paupercule apud Prake xxij° die Octobris, xx gr. Item ibidem eodem die diuersis pauperibus, vj gr. Item ibidem per manus domini distributis diuersis pauperibus, x gr. Item apud Berne xix° die Octobris, viij gr. Item in oblacionibus domini xx° die Octobris in castello de Prake, ij noble j flor'. Item in oblacionibus domini xxj° die Octobris in eodem castello, j flor. Item in elemosinis domini datis fratribus ibidem eodem die, ij gr. Item in elemosinis domini ibidem per manus domini H. Herlee, iiij gr. Item *

---

* Summa pagine, iiij li. xviij s. ix d. st. Item de moneta Prucie, vij marc. di.

II. OBLATIONS AND ALMS. 275

/ in oblacionibus domini ibidem in die anniuersarii filii Lowys Clifford   fo. 38 v°.
xxij° die Octobris, xv gr. Item ibidem distributi fratribus eiusdem   October 22.
ville, iij gr. Item ibidem eodem die, xij gr. Item ibidem xxiiij   October 24.
die Octobris, iij gr. Item in oblacionibus domini apud Charleston
5 ad reliquias infra castrum, xxij° die Octobris, iij noble. Item in   October 22.
elemosinis domini apud Broune, ij flor. d'arragon. Item in oblacionibus domini xxx° die Octobris, vij gr. Item apud Wene viij°   October 30.
die Nouembris, xvij gr. Item in elemosinis domini apud Proda   November 8.
per manus proprias, iiij gr. Item apud Drysing, ij gr. Item in
10 elemosinis domini apud Mersolach xj° die Nouembris, viij gr. Item   November 11.
apud Fillak in elemosinis domini distributis diuersis pauperibus per
viam per manus Yong, ix gr. Item in elemosinis domini distributis diuersis pauperibus per viam, et j dwarff ibidem per manus
Hasildene, j flor. Item apud Chastelet, ij gr. Item in elemosinis
15 domini datis diuersis pauperibus distributis per manus Graunsom
bastard, per diuersas vices, xvij gr. Item in elemosinis domini
apud Malburget distributis diuersis pauperibus, ij gr. ij d. Item in
oblacionibus domini apud Venis in ecclesia Sancti Marci ij° die   November 2.
Nouembris, ij nobl. Item in elemosinis domini apud Chychell per
20 manus Wyluby, j nobl. Item in elemosinis domini datis diuersis
pauperibus iiij° die Decembris, per manus domini Roberti Story   December 4.
apud Venis, j duc. Item in oblacionibus domini apud Sanctam
Lucyam per manus Chelmeswyk, v° die Decembris, j duc. Item in   December 5.
oblacionibus domini apud Sanctum Nicholaum, Sanctam Agnetam
25 et Sanctum Antonium per manus eiusdem, iij duc. Item eodem
die in oblacionibus domini apud Sanctam Elenam per manus
Erpingham, j duc. Item per manus eiusdem apud Rodes, j duc.
Item in oblacionibus domini per manus eiusdem ibidem, ix gr.
Item in elemosinis domini distributis per totam istam viam per
30 manus Melbourne, xxxiiij s. ven. Item in oblacionibus domini apud
Sanctum Marcum in primo aduentu suo ad ducem ibidem, j nobl.

---

x scot. di. pr., qui faciunt lij s. xj d. st.; xliiij gr. computantur pro j noble ;
j flor. computatur pro iij s. st.; xij d. ffs. computantur pro j d. ob. vj* pars qr. st. ;
moneta de Prusia computatur vt supra.

Item apud Sanctum Georgium ibidem, j nobl. Item ibidem, iij duc.
Item in oblacionibus domini alia vice cum duce Venis, receptis denariis de domino Petro Scinlatour, iij gr. Item in oblacionibus
domini apud Sanctum Christoferum et apud Innocentes per manus
thesaurarii, ij duc. Et in elemosinis domini distributis pauperibus 5
per manus eiusdem, xviij s. ven. Item in oblacionibus domini apud
Rodes per manus eiusdem, v duc. Item apud Landa x° die Maii in
oblacionibus domini in capella domini ibidem, j nobl. Item in
elemosinis domini ibidem, receptis denariis de Wilby,* j duc. Item
in oblacionibus apud Toryn xxj° die Maii, j duc. Item in elemo- 10
sinis domini distributis pauperibus per viam eodem die, vij s. ven.
Item apud Schusa xxiiij° die Maii in e'emosinis domini, ix gr.
Item in elemosinis domini ibidem datis cuidam fratri Minori, j duc.
Et in elemosinis domini datis cuidam capellano ibidem, vj gr. Item
in elemosinis domini datis pauperibus xxv° die Maii per viam 15
ibidem, iiij gr. di. Item in elemosinis domini distributis leprosis
super Montem eodem die, v. gr. Item in elemosinis domini datis
cuidam hermite super montem Chat, j duc. Item in elemosinis
domini apud Troys apud Sanctum Antonium, j duc. Item in elemosinis domini datis hospitali ibidem, j duc. Item in elemosinis 20
domini distributis pauperibus, xxvij° die Maii apud Sanctum
Michaelem, iiij gr. Item apud Egebelle xxx° die Maii, j duc. Item
in elemosinis domini datis apud Wycencam, j duc. Item apud
Bewme ix° die Junii in elemosinis domini, xj bl. Item in oblacionibus domini datis x° die Junii apud Chalons, ij bl. Item in 25
elemosinis domini distributis per viam inter Caunterbury et London,
vij s. st. Item in oblacionibus domini apud Canterbury, x s. st.
Item in oblacionibus domini distributis pauperibus ibidem, xx d.
Item in elemosinis domini distributis diuersis pauperibus apud
Osprenge, ij° die Julii vj d. st. Item in oblacionibus domini apud 30
Amyas in festo Sancti Johannis Baptiste, per manus Staneley,

* Willuby seems to be the name intended.

II. OBLATIONS AND ALMS.

iij nobl. Item in elemosinis domini datis ibidem furioso ex[b] / precepto domini eodem die, vj scut. Item traditi Staneley pro elemosinis domini [apud] London, iij s. iiij d. st. Item tradite fratribus de Treuys pro elemosinis domini, xv° die April, v duc. Item in oblacionibus domini apud Jarr' die Natalis domini per manus thesaurarii, iij gr. sic. Item in elemosinis domini datis cuidam hermite ibidem x gr. sic. Item in oblacionibus domini apud Modhom exeundi versus terram Sanctam per manus Stanele, ij duc. Item in elemosinis domini datis diuersis pauperibus ibidem, v gr. sic. Item in oblacionibus domini super Montem per manus Chelmeswyk, j duc. Item in oblacionibus domini ibidem per manus thesaurarii in ecclesia de Rodez et apud sanctas reliquias in capella, vj duc. Item in oblacionibus domini in die Ramorum Palmarum, j gr. sic. Item in elemosinis domini distributis iiij mulieribus pauperculis de Portingal, ij duc. Item in elemosinis domini distributis diuersis pauperibus apud Sanctum Laurencium, ij gr. sic. Item diuersis pauperibus ibidem, xiiij s. ven. Item in oblacionibus domini apud Sanctum Georginm die parasceue ex precepto domini, ij duc. v gr. sic. Item in oblacionibus domini ibidem eodem die, per manus Melbourne, iij duc. Item in oblacionibus domini in die Pasche, iiij s. ven. Item in oblacionibus domini ibidem in ecclesia Sancti Marci, v duc. Item eodem die Pasche, j duc. Item in elemosinis domini distributis diuersis pauperibus ibidem, vij s. ven. Item in oblacionibus domini apud Sanctum Antonium, receptis denariis de Wilby, j noble. Item in elemosinis domini ibidem, receptis denariis de Melbourne, j duc. Item in oblacionibus domini redeundo apud Sanctum Antonium xxj° die Maii, j duc. Item in oblacionibus domini apud Landa per manus Wilby, j noble. Item in oblacionibus domini apud Sanctum Augustinum apud Papvam, iij noble. Item in oblacionibus domini et elemosinis datis diuersis

---

[b] Summa pagine, computata in sterlinges vj li. xj s. vj d. ob. Item in moneta de Venys, xxv ducat.—Li. de Venys, computatur ad. ix d. q', iiij pars q'. st.; xliiij grossi faciunt j noble; j blanc facit j d. ob. st.; flor. d'arragon ad ij s.; flor. de Beemie ad iij s.

super viam venientibus vsque Chambry xxviij° die Maii, ix gr.
Item in oblacionibus domini vna cum elemosinis eiusdem apud
Rodez, ij duc. Item in oblacionibus domini vna cum elemosinis
apud Sanctum Sepulcrum, vj duc. Item in oblacionibus domini
apud Rodez redeundo factis fratribus ibidem pro domino de Clifford, 5
per manus proprias, ij duc. Item in oblacionibus domini ibidem,
j duc. Item in oblacionibus domini in festo Sancti Johannis Baptiste apud Amyas per manus Stanele, j nobl. Item in elemosinis
domini datis pauperibus per manus Wode apud Rodes, xj aspers.
Item in oblacionibus domini apud Modhom ad Sanctum Leonem 10
per manus Erpingham, j duc. Item in elemosinis domini distributis
pauperibus ibidem per manus Paunsefot, xvj s. ven. Item in oblacionibus domini ad quandam crucem in Cipria per manus Graunsom,
iij duc. Item in elemosinis domini datis vni pauperi presbitero
ibidem per manus eiusdem, j duc. Item in elemosinis domini datis 15
mulieri paupercule apud Venis per manus Stanele, viij° die Aprilis,
xxiiij s. ven. Item in elemosinis domini distributis pauperibus
per dominum in die Cene, v duc. Item in elemosinis domini distributis per manus Stanele apud Raguse diuersis pauperibus, xv s.
ven. Item in elemosinis domini distributis pauperibus ad Modon 20
in redeundo per manus Erpingham, xv s. ven. Item dati pauperibus per manus Henrici Langedon ex precepto domini apud
Pado, xvij s. ven Item fratribus Carmelitis apud Linne, xix° die
Julii, in recessu domini versus Pruciam, xiij s. iiij d. st.[a]

/ Skippagium. 25

In primis de Anglia versus Pruciam pro iij nauibus conductis
pro domino et familia sua ex conuencione cum eis facta per senes-

[a] Summa pagine computata in sterlinges, iiij li. ix s. viij d. Item de ducatis,
l duc.
Summa totalis oblacionum et elemosinarum in sterlinges, xviij li. xij s. x d. ob. st.
Item de moneta de Venys, lxxv duc.
xviij grossi computatur ad j duc.; scutum comp. ad iij s. iiij d. st.; asper comp. ad
j d. qr. di. st.; lira de veu. comp. ad ix d. qr. st.

callum et thesaurarium, lij li. vj s. viij d. Et pro galeia domini
de Venis vsque portam Jaffe et redeundo Venis ex conuencione
cum eis facta per priorem Sancti Johannis Jheroso[li]mitalis in
Anglia, et per senescallum, ij^{ml} vij^c iiij^{xx}v duc. Et pro vj passaiours
5 et j balinger conductis de Caleys vsque Douer per conuencionem
cum eis factam per senescallum et thesaurarium; vna cum pontagio,
portagio, batellagio a Caleys vsque naues, et a Douore vsque terram;
et portagio harnisiorum domini de nauibus vsque hospicium domini,
per compotum cum eis factum, in toto xxv li. di. st. De C marc.
10 solutum Ludkyn Drankmaistre, magistro nauis conducte de Prucia
vsque partes Anglie cum parte familie domini et diuersis harnesiis
domini, nihil hic, quia solutum per manus Johannis Leynthorpe,
generalis receptoris domini.

Summa pagine, lxxvij li. xvj s. viij d st.
15 Item de moneta de Venys, m^l m^l vij^e iiij^{xx}v duc.

/ GARDEROBA.

In primis Henrico de Camera pro x vergis tele per ipsum
emptis pro domino per manus proprias apud Prake xv^o die Octobris,
clx gr. Item ij henksmen pro sotularibus ibidem emptis pro eisdem
20 ex precepto domini, viij gr. Item domino Hugoni Herlee pro ij super-
altaribus per ipsum emptis ibidem, xviij gr. Item pro imposicione
dictarum petrarum in tabulis, et seruientibus episcopi laborantibus
circa consecracionem earundem per manus dicti domini Hugonis
ibidem, xv gr. Item eidem pro registro argenteo portiforii domini
25 empto ibidem per manus eiusdem, viij gr. Item ibidem pro j sinctura
argentea et deaurata eodem die empta ibidem per Mowbray le
heraud, iiij duc. Item pro x tabellis armorum per Moubray le
heraud ibidem, ij duc. Item carpintario facienti tabellam ibidem
per manus eiusdem, j duc. Item pro iiij papiris armorum domini

280   THE EARL OF DERBY'S EXPEDITIONS.

emptis ibidem pro dicto heraud, j duc. Item Henrico de camera
pro panno per ipsum empto ibidem pro ij henksmen eodem die,
ij nobl. Item pro factura ij gounarum pro dictis hensmen ibidem
eodem die, xiiij gr. Item pro emendacione j paris de vambras
domini ibidem, iij gr. Item pro j vlna de satyn empta ibidem pro   5
domino per manus eiusdem, xxv gr. Item Hanz Goldsmyth, pro
xiiij colers, quorum ix sunt deaurati, ab ipso emptis apud Prake,
October 23.   xxiij die Octobris, per compotum secum factum, xix nobl. iiij gr.
Item Lancastre Heraud, pro pictura diuersorum armorum in aula
October 25.   domini apud Prake, xxv° die Octobris, j noble. Item pro pictura 10
armorum domini apud Wene per manus eiusdem, j noble. Item
pro pictura armorum domini apud Broune per manus eiusdem,
j nobl. Et per manus Moubray Heraud pro xij scochons papiris
armorum domini per eundem factis ibidem, iiij duc. Item per
manus eiusdem Henrici apud Prake pro j pilche fact' ibidem pro 15
October 17.   domino xvij° die Octobris, xxx gr. Item pro j pare de botes
furratis cum blanket pro domino, xxiiij gr. Item pro locione
pannorum domini ibidem, vj gr. Item Henrico de Camera per
manus eiusdem pro j pare caligarum apud Wene per ipsum empto
November 3.   vna cum j pare sotularum iij° die Nouembris pro domino, v flor. 20
Item pro locione diuersorum harnisiorum domini per viam, xiiij
Wener [?gr]. Item pro iij pannis ceresis de Damasco emptis per
December 15.   dominum xv° die Decembris apud Venis, liiij duc. Item pro j
December 18.   lorica empta pro domino ibidem xviij° die eiusdem mensis, per
manus proprias, xx duc. Item pro iij panni lanei de Frise 25
emptis pro domino per manus Henrici de Camera apud Venis, le
bras pro iij li., xxvij li. ven. Item pro linura^a eiusdem de blanket,
xiij bras, le bras pro xxiiij s., xv li. xij s. ven. Item pro j pare
caligarum et panno pro j capicio pro domino per manus eiusdem,
ij duc. xviij s. Item pro j furra pro jupa domini denigrata, vij duc. 30
Item dati cissori pro j coyfe et factura diuersorum harnisiorum
domini pro galea, iiij duc. xlviij s. Item dati armature pro

---

^a Linura here seems to be lining, it cannot mean linen garments.

j pare de vambraces, et emendatione aliorum diuersorum harnisiorum domini ibidem, iiij duc. Item sutori domini pro iiij paribus sotularum emptis pro domino ibidem, ij duc. Item lotrici pro locione diuersorum harnisiorum domini per diuersas vices ibidem exeundo, xxx s. ven. Item pro emendacione j zone domini ibidem, vj s. ven. Item pro batillagio Henrici de Camera euntis pro istis expediendis et faciendis, xx s. ven. Item per manus Roberti Hethecote, pro j chausour empt' Venys, xij° die Decembris pro domino, xl s. ven. Item per manus eiusdem pro factura de chesmeyne ibidem, xx s. Item per manus Henrici de Camera pro j coopertorio j scabelli domini ibidem, j duc. Item pro j lb. coton empta ibidem pro domino per manus eiusdem, ix s. Item per manus eiusdem pro mundacione de tapeto camere domini ibidem, vij li. Item pro xxx bras de Lyre ad faciendum j tapetum in modo lecti pro domino, le bras xx bag.ª, in toto vjᶜ bag. Item pro ij orynalibus per ipsum emptis ibidem, per manus eiusdem, ij s. Item pro portagio et batillagio diuersorum harnisiorum domini de villa vsque Sanctum Georgium, vj s. Item pro j laumpe ad pendendum in cabano domini in galeia, iij s. Item ij lb. cotoni emptis ibidem pro domino per manus Roberti Hethcote, xvij s. Et per manus eiusdem pro xiiij vlnis de canevas, le vlna ad vj s.; et pro cerucis eiusdem canevas, et pro iiij lb. cotoni et j matte pro galeia et pro viij orynalibus, pro corda, pro j tablerio, pro xiiij crochetis, emptis pro galeia per compotum secum factum, in toto vij duc. xxv s. Item per manus eiusdem pro j materas, j fetherbed cum j bolster, emptis pro domino in galeia, viij duc. xl s. Item pro ij peciis de baldekin viridi de x bras emptis pro ᵇ / liberata domini danda scutiferis suis per manus camerarii et thesaurarii xvj° die Maii, le bras, ij duc. xx duc. Item pro j pecia de v bras minus j quarte-

December 12.

fo. 41.
May 16.

ᵃ Bagatino, a small copper **coin of Venice.**
ᵇ Summa computata in sterlingᵢ, xij li. xix s. vj d. st. Item de moneta de Venys, Cxxj duc. Item de flor., v. flor
Viij li. xj s. ven. faciunt j noble st. Et xliiij grossi faciunt j noble st. In ista pagina sunt iijᶜxvij gr. Boem. et Wener.

rio, ix duc. Item pro iij peciis de xxx bras, le bras ij
duc. di.; in toto lxxv duc. Item pro j pecia de baldekin de
xxvij bras, le bras ij duc di., in toto lxvij duc. Item per manus
eorundem pro j panno de veluello viridi, de xxix bras, per ipsos
empto ibidem pro liberata domini et militum suorum ibidem, le
bras ij duc. di., in toto lxxij duc. di. Item pro j pece de veluello
viridi pro eisdem, de xvij bras, le bras iij duc., in toto lj duc. Item
pro j pece veluello viridi de xx bras, le bras ij duc. di., l. duc. Item
pro j pece veluello viridi de viij bras, le bras ij duc. di., xx duc. Item
pro j pece veluello viridi de xvj bras, le bras ij duc. di , xl duc.
Item pro j pece velnello de xiiij bras, le bras ij duc. di., xxxv duc.
Item pro xiiij bras de veluello viridi, le bras ij duc., in toto xxviij
duc. Item pro viij bras veluello albo pro manticis domini et militum,
le bras ij duc. di., xx duc Item per manus camerarii et thesaurarii
pro j pece de baldekin rouge pro liberata domini et militum suorum,
de vj bras, le bras ij duc. di., xv duc. Item pro ij peciis de baldekin
rouge, de x bras, xxj duc. Item pro j pecia de baldekin rouge de
grana empta pro domino, de vij bras, xxij duc. Item pro ij peciis
de baldekin rouge, de xiiij bras, j qrt., xxix duc. Item pro iij
peciis de baldekin rouge de xviij bras, xxxvij duc. Item pro iij
peciis de baldekin rouge, de xxviij bras, le bras pro ij duc. jqr., lxiij
duc. Item pro j pece de baldekin albo pro manticis domini, militum
et scutiferorum suorum, de vj bras, le bras ij duc. et j qr., in toto
xiij duc. di. Et pro j pecia de baldekin nigro pro eisdem de vj bras,
xiij duc. di. Item per manus eorundem pro iij peciis de satin rouge
emptis pro liberata scutiferorum, xxxv duc. Item pro iij peciis de
satin emptis ibidem pro eisdem, xxxiij duc. Item pro ix satellins
emptis ibidem pro eisdem, le pece xj duc., cj duc. Item pro iij
satellins de grana, xlvj duc. Item pro ij satellins emptis ibidem
pro eisdem, xxiij duc. Item pro lvj bras panni lanei viridis emptis
pro valettis camere domini et aliis, per manus thesaurarii et Payn,
le bras xxiij s., in toto xv duc. lx s. Item pro lxj bras panni lanei
viridis emptis pro gromes, sumptermen et pages domini, le bras xxiij s.,
in toto xvj duc. xlvij s. ven. Item per manus Henrici de Camera

pro xx bras panni de Lyre emptis pro domino xxij die Martii, le
bras j duc. di., in toto xxx duc. Et pro iiij bras panni albi pro
linura eiusdem, iiij duc. Item per manus eiusdem pro ij paribus
sotularum emptis pro domino, vij gr. sicc. Item pro locione pannorum domini ibidem, ij gr. sicc. Item per manus eiusdem pro j brest-
5 plate domini purgando ibidem, iij li. vij s. Item per manus eiusdem
pro factura j jupe apud Rodez, j duc. Item armature ibidem pro
emendacione diuersorum harnisiorum domini ibidem exeundo versus
Sanctum Sepulcrum, xxxviij aspers. Item pellipario ibidem per
manus eiusdem, xviij aspers. Item ibidem pro portagio diuersorum
10 harnisiorum domini de Rodes vsque galeiam, j duc. Item per
manus Mowbray le herald pro viij scochons armorum domini factis
ibidem per eundem, viij duc. Et per manus Hethcote pro ij canes
de cancuas per ipsum emptis ibidem pro domino, xiij aspers. Et per
manus eiusdem pro ij orynallibus per ipsum emptis ibidem, recepti,*
15 ij aspers. Et per manus eiusdem pro cariagio diuersorum harnisiorum domini de castro vsque galeiam ibidem, iij gr. sicc. Et per
manus eiusdem pro ij lb. cotoni per ipsum emptis ibidem pro domino,
vj aspers. Item Jacobo Francisco aurifabro pro j colera deaurata
facto ex precepto domini pro senescallo, et j alia colera deaurata pro
20 camerario ex precepto eiusdem, et seinctours pro eisdem, et pro xij
colers, vj deauratis et vj argenteis, vna cum factura eorundem et
expensis, ac batillagio dicti aurifabris de Venis vsque Trevisam,
per compotum secum factum, cxxxvij duc. di. Item pro j
panno Accaby empto apud Venys, xxvj° die Martii, nunciante
25 / camerario, xxvj duc. Item traditi Payn pro j arblast pro domino,
iij duc. Item pro diuersis necessariis emptis pro domino per
Henricum de Camera apud Venys eodem die, per compotum secum
factum, vj duc. iij pichon. Item pro xij bras panni viridis emptis
per Wilbraham et capellanum † Erpingham, per manus thesaurarii

* Summa pagine computata in sterlinges, xvij s. viij d. ob. st. Item de moneta de
Venys, MClxij duc.—xviij gr. siccez faciunt j duc.; viij li. xj s. ven. faciunt j
noble; xxviij aspers faciunt j ducatum, et j duc. valet iij s. ij d. st. In ista pagina
sunt lxxviij aspers xij gr sicc.

284   THE EARL OF DERBY'S EXPEDITIONS.

eodem die, nunciante camerario, xij duc. Item pro tonsura eiusdem panni, xxiiij s. ven. Item pro j bras de panno albo pro manticis ij henksmen, j duc. x s. minus. Item pro ij bras et j quarterio panni nigri pro caligis eorundem, vij li. ven. Item pro vj bras panni albi et blodei pro caligis domini ibidem, per manus Henrici de Camera, viij duc. Item pro sotularibus emptis Henrico Henksman et Yonge ibidem, per manus thesaurarii, j duc. Item pro j chapelet empto pro domino ibidem per manus Henrici de Camera, iij duc. xl s. ven. Item pro factura juparum et caligarum de les Henskamen ibidem, vj li. x s. ven. Item pro les corps sincture domini et j colera facta per senescallum, iij duc. di. Item pro sotularibus emptis ibidem Henrico de Rodez, xviij s. ven. Item pro vj bras panni viridis pro caligis domini, per manus Henrici de Camera, viij duc. Item pro ij furrours emptis pro domino de Meneuia per Henricum de Camera apud Venis xx° die mensis Martii, xl. duc. Item pro vij bras de veluello rubeo pro domino emptis per dictum Henricum ibidem eodem die, xviij duc. xl s. Item pro vij bras de veluello nigro emptis ibidem eodem die pro domino, per manus eiusdem, xxiij duc. Item pro j panno deaurato empto pro domino ibidem, per manus camerarii primo die Aprilis, lj duc. Item pro j bursa empta per manus thesaurarii eodem die pro vxore patroni, viij s. ven. Item pro furrura empta ibidem pro domino per manus Henrici de Camera eodem die, xvj duc. Item pro j rubeo pilio empto ibidem per camerarium eodem die, iiij duc. Item cuidam cissori pro xxvj jupis ad distribuendum pauperibus in die Cene, emptis per thesaurarium, xxvj duc. Item pro xxvj paribus sotularium eisdem pauperibus eodem die distributis, v duc. xxvj s. Item pro panno lineo empto pro pauperibus, pro towaill et naperons pro domino, militibus et aliis sibi seruientibus in die Cene, ix duc. Item pro ij furrours emptis pro domino, ij die mensis Aprilis, per manus Henrici de Camera, xxxvij duc. Item pro xx bras scarleti Anglici emptis per Henricum de Camera pro domino apud Venis, vj° die Aprilis, lxvij duc. Item pro ij

March 20.

April 1.

April 6.

April 2.

April 6.

5

10

15

20

25

30

furrours emptis pro domino, iiij° die Aprilis, per manus eiusdem April 4.
Henrici, xxxvj duc. Item pro j furrour empta pro domino eodem
die, per manus eiusdem, xvj duc. Item pro ij furrours emptis per
thesaurarium v° die Aprilis, xxxvj duc. Item pro ij clothsakk April 5.
emptis pro domino ix° die mensis Aprilis per thesaurarium, xix duc. April 9.
Item pro tonsura panni scarleti albi et nigri per manus Henrici de
Camera, iij duc. Item pro furrura iiij juparum domini per manus
eiusdem, ij duc. di. Item pro ij jupis pro ij henksmen domini per
ipsum emptis ibidem vj° die Aprilis, viij duc. Item pro viij bras April 6.
panni viridis emptis per camerarium pro thesaurario apud Venis iij° April 3.
die Aprilis, xij duc. Item pro j pare cultellorum empto pro domino
ibidem, vij° die Aprilis, per thesaurarium, ij duc. xxx s. ven. Item April 7.
pro j panno de chamelot empto pro quodam scutifero Ducis Ostricie
veniente cum domino de Wene vsque Venis, per thesaurarium,
x duc. Item pro j pilio nigro empto pro domino per manus eiusdem, iij duc. Item j pictori pro iiij papiris armorum domini,
viij duc. Item pro expensis Hethcote per ij vices de Treuise vsque
Venis, ex precepto domini, v li. ven. Item apud Venis pro corda
ad pendendum j kage, ex precepto domini, I s. ven. Item pro
factura j houpelond longe et j jupe pro domino, per Henricum de
Camera iiij° die Aprilis, v duc. Item dati operantibus ad potan- April 4.
dum per manus eiusdem, xij s. ven. Item pro reban aureo pro
domino ibidem per manus eiusdem, iij duc. Item pro portagio de
le popingay de Meistre a Treuyse ex precepto domini, xx s. ven.
Item pro expensis dicti Roberti Hethcote apud Venys, cum j equo
pro j nocte, j duc. Item pro portagio tabularum vltra la veill a
Treuise ad cameram domini, iiij s. ven. Item Hethcote pro
batillagio harnisiorum domini per ij vices, ibidem allocatus, j duc.
Item eidem pro batillagio harnisiorum domini de Trevise vsque
Venis vna cum expensis v hominum per j nocte, ij duc. xxviij s.
ven. Item pro diuersis caligis factis pro domino, per manus
Henrici de Camera, ex liberatione Regis Hungarie, broideratis cum
liberata dicti regis, xj duc. liiij s. ven. Item pro sendello pro

baners, ij bras, ij duc. di. Item dati factori le baner domini
per manus thesaurarii.ᵃ / iij duc. Item pro sendello empto
pro j jupa domini furrenda, per manus eiusdem, v duc.
lv s. ven. Item pro iij pannis, ij aureis et j de veluet, emptis
per dominum ibidem, ijᶜxlv duc. Item pro tonsura Cxviij
bras panni viridis ibidem, v li. x s. ven. Item cuidam cissori
nominato Graunsom pro factura panni domini per compotum
secum factum ibidem xiij° die Aprilis, xxxj duc. iij li. ven. Item
Henrico de Camera pro iiij paribus sotularium pro domino per ipsum
emptis apud ᵇ . . xvij° die Aprilis, xlviij s. ven. Item eidem pro
emendacione iij gladiorum ibidem eodem die, xxxvj s. ven. Item
per manus eiusdem pro ij vnciis cerici per ipsum emptis ibidem
eodem die, xxv s. ven. Item per manus eiusdem pro factura iiij pannorum lincorum pro domino, xxxij s. ven. Item per manus eiusdem
bas pann' pro locione pannorum lineorum* domini ibidem eodem die, xliiij s.
ven. Item per manus eiusdem pro batillagio per diuersas vices pro
officio suo apud Venis, xxx s. ven. Item Jacobo Francisco aurifabro
pro vj colers argenteis deauratis qui ponderant xvj vncias j octauus
minus. Et pro factura dictarum colerarum, le vncia ij duc. di.
Item pro vj colers argenteis ponderantibus xvj vncias ij qrt. di.
Et pro factura dictarum colerarum, le vncia j duc. di. Et pro
j coler de auro facta pro domino et j cathena de auro ad imponendam
in dicta coleria ; amount in toto cum ponderatione et factura per
compotum secum factum, iiijˣˣxix duc. Item Mowbray le herald
pro pictura et factura diuersorum armorum domini, militum et senti-
ferorum suorum, vna cum tabulis et stipendiis carpintariorum
easdem faciendorum, per compotum secum factum ibidem, lxiij duc.
Et per manus Hethcote pro j cage pro le popingay per ipsum
empto, xx° die Aprilis apud Ven., vj li. Et per manus eiusdem
pro xxx crochets per ipsum emptis ibidem pro camera domini

ᵃ Summa pagine computata in sterlinges, xxviij s. iij d. qᵃ st. Item de moneta
de Venys, vᶜxlviij duc. di.:—viij li xj s. ven. faciunt j noble, et j pichon valet j d.
ob qᵃ st.
ᵇ The scribe forgot to insert the name of the place.

II. WARDROBE EXPENSES.

eodem die, xl s. Et per manus eiusdem pro corda per ipsum
empta ibidem ad pendendum dict' cage, l s. ven. Et per manus
eiusdem pro j laumpe ad pendendum apud Trevisam in camera
domini, iiij s. ven. Item pro j pece de satin rouge empta per Mow-
5 bray apud Mediolanum per manus thesaurarii, xij duc. Item Thome
Trumpet pro frenge per ipsum empt' ibidem eodem die, viz. primo *May 1.*
die Maii, pro le baner de Trumpet, j duc. Item pro tapheta empta
pro domino per manus Henrici de Camera apud Mediolanum,
iiij duc. Item per manus eiusdem pro linga j ouche domini
10 ibidem facta xv° die Maii, ij duc. Item pro j magna ceroteca pro *May 15.*
le faweon ibidem empta eodem die, xvj s. imperiall. Item pro
j cipho et j ewer argenteis et deauratis emptis ibidem xxj° die *May 21*
Maii, per manus camerarii et thesaurarii, lxj duc. Item cuidam
aurifabro pro factura j gladii et iij ouches domini eodem die, vij duc.
15 Item apud Cheuaux pro ij coleris nouis argenteis ponderantibus
vj vncias cum di., vna cum emendacione j ouche et j zone domini,
ix duc. Item cuidam cissori per manus Henrici de Camera pro
factura iij gounarum domini, vij duc. Item Lancastre Herald, pro
j furro ab ipso empto pro domino eodem die, xxx duc. Item ij
20 sumptermen et ij garcionibus coquine pro sotularibus et caligis sibi
emendis ibidem, iij duc. Item apud Parys pro j capella rubea
empta ibidem pro domino per thesaurarium, x scut. Item pro
calcaribus emptis pro domino per Henricum de Camera ibidem,
xiiij franc. Item pro ij peciis de baldekin rubeo de xj bras, xxiij
25 duc. Item pro j annulo cum vno baleys empto per camerarium
pro domino ibidem, xv scut. Item pro sotularibus emptis Henrico
Sarasin ad Wycens, xviij s. ven. Item pro factura jupe Johannis
de Chaundrie ibidem, j duc. Item pro sotularibus emptis pro les
henksmen ibidem et aliis necessariis illic oportunis, ij duc. Item
30 pro sotularibus emptis apud Parys pro domino per manus Henrici
de Camera, j duc. Item apud Amyas pro j scochon miss' in hospicio domini ibidem, j scut. xxiij s. ven. Item cuidam Lumbard
pro frenges pro domino emptis ibidem, xxvij bras di., xiiij duc.
vij s. ven. Item pro j scochon fact' Venis, per Mowbray le herald

ex precepto domini, xxx duc. Item pro diuersis frenges
de auro et de diuersis cericis emptis ibidem pro domino xj°
die Aprilis, per manus Henrici de Camera, iiij duc. Et per
manus Henrici Langedon pro expensis suis circa negocium
domini Venis faciendum. In primis j pelipario* / furranti 5
j jupam domini, xj° die Aprilis, xx s. ven. Item j lotrici apud
Treuisam, xviij s. ven. Item j sutori ibidem pro factura j paris
chaussembles domini, xxiiij s. ven. Item apud Siron pro botening
j lorice, xiij pichons. Item j lotrici ibidem, iiij pich. Item apud
Pauys pro j pair chaussemble domini, ij pich. Item j lotrici ibidem, 10
vij pich. Item pro iiij braces de panno lineo ibidem, xij pich. Item
apud Cheuaux pro furrura j goune longe domini, di. duc. Item
j lotrici ibidem, viij pich. Item apud Melan pro bordez pro panno
de velewet et auro inuoluendo, iij pich. Item eidem pro batillagio
et pro expensis ij equorum existentium apud Meistre eo tempore 15
quo stetit Venys circa negocium domini expediendum et vestimentos
eiusdem faciendos ibidem, iij duc. Et per manus thesaurarii et
Henrici de camera pro j pecia veluelli blodei de x bras per ipsos
empta apud Melan pro domino, xxvij duc.

Item pro iij salers argenteis, j eorum deaurato, emptis de Willelmo 20
aurifabro domini Londoni de nouo factis ibidem de iij salers veteribus, pro factura et ponderatione sic factis ibidem ex conuencione
in grosso, v li. xiij s. iiij d. st.

Summa pagine computata in sterlinges, vj li. ij s. viij d. qr. st.
Item in moneta de Venys, xxxj duc. 25

Summa totalis Garderobe computata in sterlinges, xxvij li. ij s.
ij d. st.
Item de moneta de Venis, m'm¹v°xx ducati.

---

* Summa pagine comput. in sterlinges, Cxiiij s. st. Item de moneta de Venys,
vj°lvij duc. di. (this sum is written in the margin, the space here being blank).
Item de moneta Francie, xiiij fr. In ista pagina sunt xxvj scut., xiiij franks, xvj s.
imperiales ; xxxij s. pro le ducat ; scutum vel corona computatur ad iij s. iiij d.

Item de moneta Francie, xiiij franci.
Item de florenis Boemie, v floreni.

/ DONA DATA PER DOMINUM IN ISTO VIAGIO PER TOTUM
TEMPUS COMPOTI.

5 Et in diuersis donis datis per dominum in toto isto viagio per tempus compoti in diuersis locis et de diuersis monetis vt patet per parcellas in quodam rotulo contentas et vnatas, et super hunc compotum per ipsum dominum liberatas, et sub signetto suo sigillatas. Qui quidam rotulus remanet cum isto compoto, etc., videlicet.:

10 In nobilibus sterlinges, v^{c}iiij^{xx} iij li. ix s. st.
Item de moneta Prucie, xxxvij marc. di. xij d. pruc., qui faciunt in sterlinges, xij li. x s. j d. st.
Item in grossis Boemie, iiij^{xx}vj grossi, vnde xliiij faciunt j noble st., qui faciunt in sterlinges, xiij s. ob. st.

15 Item de florenis de Boemie, ccxxix floreni, vnde ij flor. et iiij gr. Boemie faciunt j noble, in toto in sterlinges, xxxiiij li. xviij s. x d. ob. q^a st.
Item de florenis d'Arragonie, lxxij floreni d'Arragon, pecia ad ij s., vij li. iiij s. st.

20 Item de moneta de Venys, xxiiij s. ven., quod valet in sterlinges, xj d. st.
Item de scutis, liiij scuta, vnde ij faciunt j noble, qui valent in sterlinges, ix li. st.
Item de aspers, viij aspers, et xxviij aspers faciunt j ducatum.
25 In sterlinges, xij d. ob. st.
Item des grossi sicvcz, ix grossi, et xviij faciunt j ducatum. In sterlinges, xix d. st.
Item des pichons, vj pichons, qui valent x d. ob. st.
Item des blanks, lxiij bl., vnde xxiiij faciunt j frank ad iij s. qui
30 valent in sterlinges vij s. x d. ob. st.
Item de moneta imperiali, xij s. imperiales, precium xv d. st., vnde xxxij s. faciunt j ducatum.

Summa istius pagine computata in sterlinges, vj^{c}xlviij li. viij s. vj d. ob. q^a st.

Item in moneta de Venys, m^{l}m^{l}m^{l}ix^{c}iiij^{xx}xij duc.

Item de moneta Francie, clxxiiij fr. di.

/ Summa omnium expensarum istius libri computata in sterlinges . . . . . . m^{l}m^l ccxv li. iiij s. vij d. ob.

Item vt in xv^{ml}viij^{c}lxxij ducatis lxiiij s. ven., pecia ad iij s. ij d. st. . . . . m^l m^d v^c xiij li. iij s. viij d.

Item vt in vij^{c}xx francis di. iij blancis, le franc ad iij s. iiij d., computatis in sterlinges . . . . . . cxx li. ij s.

Item vt in v florenis Boemie computatis in sterlinges . xv. s.

Et sic est summa omnium expensarum, computata in sterlinges, vltra c marcarum solutum pro skippagio de Prucia vsque Angliam solutum per manus Johannis Leventhorpe

iiij^{ml}viij^{c}xlixli. v^l s. iijd. ob.

Et debet lxv li. xix s ix d. q^a. De quibus allocantur eidem lxiiij li. xvij s. vj d., de diuersis peticionibus allocacionum factis per ipsum dominum de gratia sua speciali ; que quidem peticiones in diuersis parcellis per ipsum computantem ostense fuerunt ipsi domino apud London mense Februarii anno xviij^o. Et postea liberate auditoribus eiusdem domini apud London eodem mense a^o predicto, de allocacione inde facienda, nunciante et testante Hugone Waterton milite, camerario domini ; que quidem petitiones in quodam Rotulo contente, sub sigillo ipsius camerarii sigillato huic compoto sunt annexate. Et sic debet adhuc, xxij s. iij d. q^a.

/[ALLOCATIONES.] ª   fo. 44.

Ricardus Kyngeston, Thesaurarius guerre pro viagio excellentissimi principis Domini Henrici Lancastrie, Comitis Derbie, versus partes Prucie et Terre Sancte, petit allocationes vt infra.

5   In primis petit allocationem de M'lij'iiij'ˣˢ gr. sibi disallocatis vt in M'lij'iiij'ˣˢ fr., oneratis ad iij s. iiij d., vt patet in compoto ipsius computantis, quos idem computans soluit le franc ad iij s.

                                                     xxj li. vj s. viij d.

Idem petit pro diuersis parcellis de dono domini per ipsum datis
10 de rewardo, vt patet in summis subsequenter, Thome Gloucestre de dono domini . . . . liij s. iiij d.

    Francisco de Courte, xxviij s.
    Johanni Cornewayle, lxvj s. viij d.
    Thome Trumpet in viij duc., xxvj s.   ·   xij li. viij d.
15 Johanni Wilbram, lxvj s. viij d.

Idem petit allocationem de diuersis parcellis et expensis Domini Willelmi Pomfreit non scriptis in libro compoti per ipsum factis in Anglia cum ceteris equis summariis domini, de London vsque Hegham et rede-
20 undo ad Hertford, vna cum xx s. de prestito domino apud Hertford, nunciante camerario; et iij s. iiij d. prestitis Willelmo Kyghley, nunciante eodem camerario, pro diuersis expensis j cursarii domini de Hertford vsque Petreburgh, lx s. ij d. st.
25 Idem petit allocationem pro vadiis suis extra curiam   July 8-15, 1392. ab viij° die Julii vsque xvᵐ diem eiusdem, vtroque computato, per vij dies veniens de Hereford vsque Lynne pro officio suo Thesaurarii incipiendo, capiens per diem iij s. iiij d., xxiij s. iiij d.

ª The sheet (fo. 44) containing these items of allowance is stitched by one end on to the blank leaf at the end of the book (fo. 45); at the top are the remains of a seal, made on a small piece of parchment which is stitched on all round. This was the seal of Sir Hugh Waterton, Derby's Chamberlain, see before p. 290, l. 24.

Idem petit allocacionem pro vadiis suis extra curiam a xiiij° die mensis Octobris vsque primum diem Nouembris, vtroque computato, per xviij dies, veniens de Hereford vsque London per litteram domini causa certificationis faciende domino Duci Lancastre de diuersis debitis per diuersos Lumbardos prestitis in partibus transmarinis, capiens per diem vt supra, lx s. } xviij li. ij d.

Idem petit pro vadiis suis extra curiam a xij° die Januarii vsque xiiij^m diem Martii, vtroque computato, per lxij dies, veniens de Hereford vsque London per litteram domini et ibidem existens pro compoto suo faciendo, capiens per diem vt supra, x li. vj s. viij d.

Idem petit pro vadiis suis eunt' de Hereford vsque Leycestre pro compoto suo reddendo, per iij dies extra curiam, capiens per diem vt supra, x s.

Idem petit allocationem pro vadiis suis existens ibidem infra curiam pro eodem compoto suo reddendo per xxiij dies, a xxiij° die Decembris vsque xiiij^m diem Januarii, vtroque computato, tempore Natalis domini, capiens per diem xij d., xxiij s. } lv. s.

Idem petit allocationem pro vadiis suis infra curiam a xv° die Januarii vsque xvj^m diem Febuarii, vtroque computato, per xxxij dies, capiens per diem xij d., xxxij s.

Idem petit allocationem pro tot denariis solutis diuersis clericis pro compoto suo scribendo et ordinando, lxvj s. viij d.

Idem petit allocationem vt de dono domini pro expensis equorum suorum apud Portgruer tempore quo dominus stetit vltra partes transmarinas, xxvj duc., que faciunt iiij li. ij s. iiij d.

Item petit allocationem pro expensis ij cursariorum domini ductorum de Preda in Boemia vsque Angliam per Willelmum Drausfeld, scutiferum domini, nunciante camerario, lx s.

Idem petit allocationem pro expensis Thome Dent in Almandia querendi le Popingay domini, vj s.

Summa istius Rotuli, lxiiij li. xvij s. vj d.

NOTES.

Pp. 1, 2, 143, &c. *Richard de Kyngeston*, archdeacon of Hereford from 1379 to 1404 (when he resigned). For the special occasions of his two years of travels abroad, and primarily for the wars, 1390 and 1392, Derby appointed the archdeacon his treasurer. Little is known about him, but from the tone and freedom of his letters written at Hereford to Henry when king, as to the Welsh troubles in 1403, extant in a Cotton MS., it would appear that he was on intimate terms with Henry and of some local value (Ellis, Original Letters, 2nd. Ser., I., p. 17; Hingeston's Letters of Henry IV., Rolls ser., i., p. 155). It was in 1402 that Henry IV. made him Dean of St. George's Chapel, Windsor, giving him custody and prebend thereof. He died in 1418 (Pat. 3 Hen. IV. p. 2, m. ii.: Rot. Par. iv., 346 *b*.).

Pp. 2, 4, 80, &c. *Hugh de Waterton*, knight, held the manor of Ygglee in Essex from Derby by the farm of 20 marks annually; which sum in 1392 he paid to the Earl while abroad with him (Levnthorp's accounts, 15 to 18 R. II., D. of L. records, cl. 28, bdle. 3, No. 5, fo. 4). We find him acting as Derby's receiver of monies in 1377-8 and 1381-2, and as his chamberlain in 1386 (D. of L. rec. cl. 28, bdle 3, Nos. 1, 3; and ib. bdle. 1. No. 1), in which last office he continues through 1390-1. and probably 1392-3, the years of our accounts. He had charge of Henry's children Philippa and John at Berkhampstead in 1402 (Mrs. Everett Green's Princesses of England, iii., 343). A letter about 1403 (July) as to the troubles in Wales desires his influence with the king to go to the rescue (Ellis, Orig. Letters, 2nd ser., I. 20). and there is one from Hugh de Waterton himself to his master on the same subject (Hingeston's Letters of Henry IV., Rolls Ser., i., p. 149). In 5 and 7 Henry IV. he was one of the king's council (Rot. Par. iii., 530*a*, 572*b*). He married Ellen daughter of Thomas Mowbray, and died in 1409.

Sir Hugh belonged to one of the oldest families of commoners in England, taking their name from Waterton, a small place in the Isle of Axholme, Lincolnshire. Hugh's cousin William, who married the heiress of Thomas Methley of Methley near Pontefract, had two sons Robert and John Waterton, who were both also in the intimate employ of Derby, and afterwards of his son Henry V. All three were eminent men, in positions of trust. For further details see History of the Isle of Axholme, by Rev. J. B. Stonehouse, 1839, 447-455; also Nicolas, Scrope and Gros. Cont. II. p. 190. These belonged to the Axholme branch; another branch about Richard's reign settled at Walton Hall, near Wakefield, in Yorkshire, whence sprang in these latter days the fine naturalist and good man Charles Waterton, author of Wanderings in South America (died 1865).

Hugh Waterton had two daughters. Blanche, who in 1393 was wife to Robert Chalons, esquire, who served in the Reysa and received annuities and new year and other gifts with the rest of Derby's retainers in 1390-1 (pp. 107, 112; D. of L. cl. 28, bdle. 3, No. 5 fo. 7). Stonehouse speaks of him as Sir Robert Challons, and of his wife Blanche, in 1420; and Elizabeth, who married John ap Harry of Paston in Herefordshire (Stonehouse, p. 448). John ap Henry appears in Derby's accounts (p. 122) as receiving 20 days wages for himself and his archer for service in May, 1390.

Pp. 4, 13, 123. *John Leventhorpe*, esquire, was Derby's receiver general of monies arising from lands and estates, indeed to judge by his accounts still remaining he exercised the part of the Earl's general treasurer at home, giving account of important expenditure as well as of incoming receipts. (D. of L., cl. 28, bdle. 3, Nos. 4, 5, for greater part of four years 14-18 Ric. II.) He certainly was at Calais with Derby in May, 1390; but does not seem to have gone further abroad. The wages allowed him in 1391, for two years' official work were £6 13s. 4d. (ib. No. 4). Simon Bache, however, was treasurer of Derby's household. On Henry's death in 1413, and on the death in 1422 of Henry V., Leventhorpe acted as executor to both kings (Rot. Par. iv., 5a, 172b); and in a petition of Anne, countess of Stafford, in 1422, regarding her share of the Bohun property (Henry's share of which formed part of the Duchy possessions), John Leventhorpe as one of the Council of the Duchy is stated to have charge of the charters and muniments (ib. p. 176b).

A century later one Nicholas Leventhorpe was in the service of the Duchy, being receiver of Pontefract and keeper of artillery in that castle. (Rot. Par. vi., 341).

Pp. 5, 7, 31. *William Loveney* was keeper of the great wardrobe to Derby, otherwise "clerk of his wardrobe"; a full and most interesting book of his accounts for the year from 15 May, 14 and 15 R. II. (1391-2) still exists, and another for 17 R. II. (D. of L., cl. 28, bdle. 1., nos. 2, 3). He does not seem to have accompanied Derby on his travels; in Kyngeston's accounts he only appears responsible for the "Garderoba in Anglia" (p. 34, 35). Officers under him were John Dyndon "cissor robarum domini," a valet of the wardrobe, and John Dounton, keeper of the armour, who received regular wages for service abroad and who must have taken his place for the expenditure abroad pertaining to his office. Loveney continued in the same office when Henry became king, who granted him for life the manor of Worton, co. Surrey (Rot. Par. iv., 67a, 243a). In 1401 with Erpingham, Hugh

Waterton, and others he was warden of Thomas of Lancaster, the king's son ; and in 1406 Henry made William Loveney, esquire, temporary treasurer to his daughter Philippa, Queen of Denmark, Sweden and Norway, during her voyage thither, and for her escort there and back (Rymer, viii., 227, 446).

Perhaps of the same family was John Loveney, who succeeded Richard Kyngeston as archdeacon of Hereford in 1405, and was appointed archdeacon of Salop in 1417. (Le Neve's Fasti, i., 480, 483.)

Pp. 8, 20, 124. *William Elmham*, knight, was on service with the Duke of Lancaster in Artois in 1373, and otherwise in the wars in France ; also in Flanders with the Bishop of Norwich, where in 1383 he and others were convicted of having been bribed by the French (see Kervyn's Froissart, vol. 21, p. 137. and references in Index to Rolls of Parliament). Nevertheless he was, later, employed in several missions of trust, among them being the journey in 1390 from Calais to Paris to get letters of safe conduct for Derby from the French king, accompanied by Derby's esquire (John Stokes, Thomas is an error, and both entries refer to the same journey). This journey is not dated, but was probably made early in the financial year, and as Elmham and Stokes did not themselves go to Prussia (shown by the absence of wages on this account) it seems likely that the three archers, whose wages *extra curiam* from 18 May to 7 June Elmham received from Derby's treasurer, were for his service from Calais to Paris, and that we here find the date of that journey indicated occupying part or the whole of the three weeks.

In September 1390 Elmham was one of the knights appointed to treat with the French commissioners "de attemptatis reformandis," and in October was sent to Aquitaine on the king's business. In 1391 he was again employed on affairs concerning the treaty with France (Gascon Rolls, 14 R. II., m. 4, 3, 1). He was probably from the same place in Norfolk as Thomas Elmham, the Benedictine who wrote the Life of Henry V.

John Stokes, "scutifer domini," who accompanied Elmham on his mission in 1390, seems to be the same as the " mayster Johan Stokes, LL.D.," who was one of Henry IV.'s ambassadors to the king of Hungary in 1411 (MS. Cott. Vesp. F. 1, fo. 2), and is mentioned in a letter to Henry V. of 1419-20. There is a letter written by him to Henry V. from Heidelberg after the treaty of 1420 (Ellis, Original Letters, 2nd ser. i., p. 80 ; 3rd ser. i., p. 66) ; and the pages of Rymer (vol. ix.) show that he was employed in numerous embassies from Henry V.

P. 9, 29, &c. *Robert Chalons*, esquire, see note to Sir Hugh Waterton, p. 294.

Pp. 10, 108, &c. *John Waterton* esquire, **brother** to Robert, (*see note*, p. 293) was during the period of these accounts a constant attendant on Henry, receiving regular wages. his employment being apparently connected with the marshalcy, so that he naturally in after years succeeded his brother as Master of the Horse to Henry V. He was present at Agincourt, and later on became comptroller of the royal household for Henry V. and for his son. Died in 1430. (Stonehouse 452.) A letter from Henry V. when Prince, about 1402, with news of his successes to the keepers of the marches of Wales was sent by "notre tres-chier escuier John de Waterton," who could confirm it. (Ellis, Original Letters, 2nd series, 1827, vol. i. pp. 11-13.)

Pp. 11, 15, &c. *Robert de Waterton*, esquire, was Master of the Horse to Derby, and appears in this and various capacities throughout these accounts. He received a regular annuity from Derby (see Leventhorpe's Accounts, 15-18 Ric. II., D. of L. records, cl. 28, bdle. 3, no. 5). In 1406, while acting as king's messenger, he was taken prisoner, and only set free on his brother John becoming hostage for him (Rot. Par. iii., 605a). This is the same John Waterton, esquire, who is so frequently named in the present accounts, and who was evidently also attached to the household. Robert was employed in Flanders in 1401 (Fr. Roll, 2 Hen. IV. m. 4); he appears as chief steward of the Duchy of Lancaster north of Trent in 11 Henry IV, and was one of that king's executors (Rot. Par. iii., 610a; iv., 5a, 75b, &c.). Through the reign of Henry V. he had important employ, as ambassador and keeper of noble prisoners, &c., among others he kept the Duke of Orleans at Pontefract in 1417; he was Constable of Pontefract Castle, and was active till his death in 1424, 3 Hen. VI. In Sir H. Ellis's collection of Original Letters, 1st. ser., vol. i., p. 6, is one from Robert Waterton to Henry V. in 1420, just before the marriage to Katharine of France; reprinted in Stonehouse, History of the Isle of Axholme, where will be found a fuller account of this distinguished man, pp. 449-452.

P. 11, l. 11. *Comes de Saint Pol.* In 1390 the owner of this title was Waleran de Luxembourg, Comte de Ligny and de St. Pol in the Pas de Calais. He was prisoner in England (at first in the Tower of London) from February, 1375, till July, 1379 (Rymer, vii., pp. 58, 224), part of his ransom going to redeem Thomas Felton, taken prisoner by the French (ib. 265; the petition on Rot. Par. iii., p. 256a, should be dated 1378-9, not 1388-9). While in England he fell in love with and married Matilda, the young widow of Hugh Courtenay (son of the Earl of Devon, died 1374), daughter of Sir Thomas Holland and Joan of Kent, sister to Sir John Holland, and half-sister to King Richard II., "the most beautiful lady in England." The story is told by Froissart, Kervyn's edition, ix., p. 131-2. It was an incident at this lady's house (at Luchen in the county of St. Pol), followed by a duel for the honour of French knighthood, that was said to have given rise to the holding of the famous justs of St. Inglebert, in March-April, 1390 (Froissart, Johnes' ed. iv., 99 *et seq.*; Kervyn's ed. xiv., 44-55, 105-151) Derby and his friends were present there little more than a month before the date of our text. Through King Richard, and through John de Beaufort's wife, who was a Holland (niece to Matilda), Derby was doubly connected with that family and thus with St. Pol. In 1391 the

Countess was dead, as we find that Derby gave oblations at Westminster for the obit of the Countess St. Pol (D. of L. cl. 28, bdle. i., no. 2, fo. 5).* Waleran was one of the French Ambassadors sent to England concerning the recent truce, in July, 1390, and again in June of the following year (French Roll, 13 R. II., m. 23; 14 R. II., m. 13; see further Kervyn's Froissart, vol. 23, p. 78). He married a second time, and died in 1415.

P. 14, l. 28. *Seneseallus Francie.* Since the middle of the 12th century there had been no Steward of France, and the office as such did not exist in the time of Charles VI. (Anselme, Hist. Genealogique, vi., p. 37) though there were stewards of certain provinces (see Ducange). The officer intended here, however, was probably the *maitre d'hôtel* of the French king, who from his duties would be called steward by the English. Walsingham (Hist. Anglicana, ii., 206), speaking of the continuation of the truce arranged by Lancaster in 1391 and ratified 5 May, 1392, by Richard II., says the "Seneschallo Francie" came over to England to take the king's oath. Turning to Rymer (vii., 717, 720) the actual documents say that the oath was taken in presence of " Tanpyn de Chantemarle, chivaler, meistre del Hostiell " of the French king. Derby addressed him about two years before this incident, but the exact date is not given in the text.

P. 14, l. 30. *De la Haren usque ad pippem stantem in le Ras.* The haven at Calais, called at this time Paradis,† known later as " grand " and " petit " Paradis (E. Le Jeune, Hist. de Calais, 1880, p. 103), was partly enclosed by a long strip of bank parallel to the town, at the open end of which rose the castle of Rys-bank. Outside of this harbour was the open sea. On early maps two long parallel jetties project, one from the Rys-bank, the other from the town, protecting the mouth of the harbour. I have not found le Ras marked on any map of Calais, it cannot mean a race (Fr. raz) of water, as no ship would be placed to stand in a spot of rapid, contrary currents. It seems to mean the straits of Calais (pas de Calais), the ship (pippem=puppem, a ship) standing outside the harbour to be laden. The converse took place at Dover, where Derby and his men were conveyed in boats from the ship in the Roads to the Haven (p. 15, l. 21). It may be remarked, however, that in both cases " haven " indicates rather the dry land than water, perhaps used in a general sense it means the wharf. Taken thus, we may look for " le Ras " inside the harbour.

Pp. 15, 108, &c. *Derby le Herald* (whose name was John and probably Mowbray) accompanied Henry on his journey in 1390, and, as he received wages *infra curiam,* he must have remained abroad with him during the winter. When

---

* *Cf.* Chronique du Religieux de St. Denys, i. 739. (Doc. inéd. sur l'hist de France.)

† Rot. Par. iii., p. 371, col. a.

at Calais in May or June he was sent to France to seek a safe conduct for Henry, who intended to go to Barbary (see Introduction). for which he received a gift from his master, and, later on, another from the Duke of Lancaster (D. of L., cl. 28, bdle. 3, no. 2). From Königsberg he went with letters from Henry to Jagello, King of Poland, seeking the deliverance of two knights, taken prisoner, says Prof. Prutz, at the siege of Wilna; this journey was made between 23 December and 30 January, 1390-1, for which he received wages *extra curiam* (p. 108, 130). From Dantzic he went a second time about the end of March following (p. 111).

By Leynthorpe's accounts for 17 Rich. II. (1393), we find that "John Derby herawde" was paid on 26 Oct. for going to the King of Hungary, which perhaps refers to his heralding the visit of Henry to the King in the previous November on his way to Venice (cf. 195, l. 13; 233, l. 31); but more likely indicates a later mission.

On Henry's second journey, in 1392-3, we find his herald always called Mowbray, a John Mowbray is twice named (pp. 14, 201), so that he was probably the same as "Derby le Herald" of 1390. So important an official might well have a house at Calais, and his presence with Bucton and others at Venice making ready the galley before their lord's arrival, would impart authority to the party. His services were in constant requisition; for the greater part of the year he received 8d. a day, but 7½d. during the few weeks he was *infra curiam* (p. 267).

Pp. 17, 122. *Hugh Herle*, Derby's confessor (p. 133) and chaplain since at least 1376 (Beltz, p. 237), also in 1377 (account of Duke of Lancaster's receiver, D. of L., cl. 28, bdle. 3, No. 1, see extract in Furnivall's Trial Fore-words, Chaucer Society, 1871, p. 147), was Archdeacon of Durham in 1388 (Le Neve's Fasti, iii., 303); he accompanied the Earl on both journeys to Prussia, frequently acting as his almoner (17, 37, 116) receiving the same wages as a knight. Two others of the name, probably of the same family, were contemporary, Alexander de Herle was Archdeacon of Cleveland in 1387 (Le Neve), and a John de Herle *clerk*, going abroad in Feb., 1389, had as attorneys Hugh and Alexander de Herle, both *clerks*, no doubt the two archdeacons (French Roll, 13 R. II., m. 8). There was a John Herle *knight* in 1402 (Rymer, viii., 255). A Robert de Herle was Captain of Calais several years in the reign of Edward III. (Chron. of Calais, xxxiii.).

P. 19, &c. *John Norbury*, esquire (occasionally called *Northbury*), was one of Derby's retainers, receiving an annuity (D. of L., cl. 28, bdle. 3, Nos. 4 and 5). He must have been high in service and trust, as he received the same wages as a knight, accompanying Derby on his first journey, in 1390, but not on the second. He, together with Rempston and Erpingham, was with Henry when he landed in England in 1399, and was recommended by the Commons for his services (Rot Par. iii., 553). Henry as king granted to him and his wife Elizabeth the Manor and advowson of Cheshunt (Herts), which should pass to their sons Henry and John,—

Henry being the king's godson (Ib. iv., 460). He was one of Henry's standing Council in 1403-4 (Ib. iii., 530a, 669b). In 1 Henry VI. (1422) he appears in a charter as that king's treasurer (Ib. v., 432b).

P. 20. l. 2. *La Whithall usque le Clut.* I have been unable to find what places this paragraph refers to, whether in Boston or London. The well known Whitchall in London was in the fourteenth century called York Place, being the palace of the Archbishops of York, and therefore could not be here intended. "Whithall" seems to be the name of a house either belonging to Derby or used by him.

Pp. 28, 138, &c. *Ralph Staveley*, or *de Staveley*, esquire. Staveley is a Manor in Derbyshire; and Radulph de Staveley, armiger, I found, plainly written, as receiving money in one of Leynthorpe's accounts (D. of L., cl. 28, bdle. 3, No. 5), but unfortunately after the text was printed off. Owing to the similarity of u and n, and the invariable use of u for v in Stanele in these accounts, I mistook the word for the more familiar Stanley, and it is so printed throughout.

There was a Sir Ralph Stanley in 1414, who was the fourth son of Sir John Stanley then deceased. On the other hand the Staveleys were an old Yorkshire family which still exists (Burke, Landed Gentry).

Pp. 23, 24, 37, 38. *Chopchire.*
This place is not to be found on the Ordnance Survey, or on other maps of Lincolnshire, old or modern, as far as I can find. Nor do I find mention of it in any record or local historian. It seems to be a local name, for the point outside the port of Boston whence ships in the 14th century could set sail; it was also, as the third mention shows, a place on *terra firma*—not merely a beacon or sand-bank on the shoaly coast—to which carts could be taken with further baggage to be put on board. The spot that answers to this description is Skirbeck, an ancient town or village on the bend of the river Witham going out from Boston. This place derived its name from an old brook, the Scire-bec, long since dry land; but the name Skyrbeck being already fixed by the 14th century does not offer any help to the identification of Chopchire. The port of Boston was at this period in a flourishing condition, and the river channel must have been kept clear up to a high point to allow of the passage of the numerous foreign and other vessels entering.

Mr. W. H. Wheeler, C.E. of Boston kindly informs me that in the time of Henry IV. the navigation extended as far as Dog-dyke, several miles higher than Boston; but in the course of wide enquiries for his "History of the Fens of South Lincolnshire" he has not met with the name of Chopchire. On the outside coast, it has perhaps been washed away.

Pp. 31, 51, 106, 119. *William Willoughby* or *de Willoughby*, knight (Willoughby, a manor in Lincolnshire). Le Sire de Willoughby appears frequently on the Parliaments of Richard II's reign as a trier of petitions, and took part in several important incidents in the careers both of Richard and Henry, assenting to the imprisonment of the first, made a councillor by the last. He sent two archers to Calais in May, paid for by Henry, but did not go himself; he accompanied Henry afterwards to Prussia, receiving a good round reward for his work there (p. 106), but does not appear to have remained abroad through the winter, at least not attached to Henry's household. He formed, however, part of Henry's paid retinue throughout his travels in 1392-3.

P. 34, l. 25. *Domino de Scynpe de France.* Jean, sire de Sempy or Saint Py, belonged to a family of Picardy (Sampy is a village in the Pas de Calais), was captain of Artois in 1370, and took a prominent part in much honourable service for his king and country during the next twenty years. He and the Comte de St. Pol were eminent French leaders at the Battle of Rosebecque (against the Flemings) in Nov., 1382. He was chamberlain to the Duke of Burgundy, and he was one of the three French knights who threw open the jousts of St. Inglebert to foreigners in March and April, 1390; "companion in arms of Maréchal Boucicaut, and one of the most valiant knights of his time" (Delaville le Roulx, France en Orient, i., 235). He died before 1398, leaving no children, his brother Robert becoming his heir. (Partie inédite des chroniques de St. Denis, ed. par le baron J. Pichon, 1864, pp. x., xi; P. Roger, Noblesse et Chevalerie du Comté de Flandre, d'Artois et de Picardie, 1843, p. 154-157).

Eustache Deschamps the poet, friend and contemporary of Chaucer, wrote a "balade" on the death of "Le bon prodomme et chevalier Sampy," who must have been the Sire Jean. (Œuvres de E. Deschamps, Soc. des anciens textes Français, tom. I., p. 88). The precise date of his death is not yet ascertained.

Pp. 25, 126, &c. *Peter Bucton* (also in other documents Peter de Bukton), knight, and steward of Derby's household (*seneseallus*). He had Robert Burton for his esquire (p. 53, and p. 303). The poet Chaucer, who evidently was on familiar terms, addressed to him "the counseil of Chaucer touching mariage, which was sent to Bukton," a cynical poem written, Prof. Skeat thinks, towards the close of his life (Minor Poems, 204, 390, 392).

Sir H. Nicolas says that Bucton was a native of the north of England, living from 1350 to 1412, and that he served against both the Scots and the French, and notices several civil offices undertaken by him (Scrope and Grosvenor Controversy, ii., 466).

On 4 May, 1390, he took out letters of attorney for going abroad (French Rolls, 15 R. II., m. 12), though we find that he was again in England riding on his lord's affairs in June and July (p. 126, note). He was abroad with Derby throughout his second journey (p. 265). He was escheator of the county of York in 1397. Later, Henry as king granted him the office of chirographer of the Common Bench, which he was holding in 1402 (Rot. Par., iii., 496 a); and he was Mayor of Bordeaux in 1411 and 1412.

P. 35. *Domus Orwell extra Bysshopsgate.* It would be interesting to know what house this was, visited by Derby, whether it belonged to the Lancasters. His father's palace of the Savoy was burnt by the mob in 1381 : was this another house to which the family had resort? I find no mention of it in Stow, Riley, or Loftie. Dr. R. R. Sharpe of the Guildhall kindly informs me that among the City records there is a conveyance to Lancaster in 1377 of a house near Thames Street, formerly belonging to Alice Perers, but he does not find Orwell House. Mrs. Everett Green, 'Lives of Princesses', iii., 310, says that Derby had a large town residence in Bishopsgate Street, with a garden, but I have been unable to trace her authority for the statement.

P. 36 *note*. *Lord Thomas Percy* was younger brother to Henry Percy, first Earl of Northumberland. He was made Earl of Worcester in 1397, and was beheaded soon after the battle of Shrewsbury in 1403.

Pp. 38, 100, &c. *Thomas Swinford*, knight, was the son of Sir Hugh de Swinford, of Lincolnshire, and Catherine (de Roet) his wife, and grandson of another Thomas. His father died abroad on 13 Nov., 1371, at the age of 31, when Thomas was but four years old. (Inq. Post Mortem 35 Ed. III., pt. 2, no. 62; 46 Ed. III., no. 55). Catherine Swinford had performed various services to Blanche late duchess of Lancaster, Derby's mother (d. 1369) for which the wardship of her son's lands was granted her by the duke. (Beltz, Knights of the Garter, 134 *note*.) She afterwards resided at Beaufort, a Castle in Anjou belonging to the Lancasters, where she bore four children to the Duke, who married her in 1396 and had them legitimated in 1397, by the name of de Beaufort. John the eldest, who would be about 15 in 1390, when he joined the Barbary crusade starting under the Duke of Bourbon on 1 July, appears to be referred to in the text among the expenses of the return to England (p. 100, l. 3) ; as the unsuccessful crusaders returned to Europe at the end of September, Beaufort may have joined his half-brothers Derby and Swinford in Germany after the Reysa, or later in England. He was in Lithuania in 1394 (Wigand v. Marburg, Script. rer. Pruss. II., p. 653).

The connection of Thomas Swinford (who was nearly the same age as Derby), with the Lancasters seems to have been close. There is a charge (p. 31) in Kyngston's account for the expenses of bringing two of Derby's horses from Kettlethorpe, one of Swinford's Lincolnshire manors, to Bolingbroke. Duke John (who in his will, 1397, calls him "mon très chere bacheliere"), gave him an annuity of £20 ; in the accounts of Whittelby, his receiver general, for 15 Rich. II., Thomas Swinford's name stands next to that of John Beaufort (D. of L., cl. 28, bdle. 3, no. 2). This was the year following that of Derby's Prussian expedition. Swinford was with Derby at Calais in May, 1390, afterwards accompanying him on the Reysa and remaining with him throughout the year ; he received the same pay as Bucton and Hugh Waterton, besides finding an archer *infra curiam* at Calais, and a valet on the Reysa. He did not go with Derby on his second journey. According to Sir J. Ramsay (Lancaster and York, i. p. 22) he was Henry's instrument in procuring the death of Richard II. in Pontefract Castle, where he was at the time. He was sent conjointly with others on several important missions of treaty in France and Flanders in the years 1405-1410 (Rymer, viii., 391, 444, 452, 480. &c.). Some doubt having been cast on his legitimacy, he obtained in 1411 letters patent clearing his name, for the purpose of inheriting property in Hainault left him by his mother Catherine the late Duchess, who died 10 May, 1403. The seal of arms which he, his father, and ancestors had borne was annexed to this curious document (Pat. 13 Hen. IV., pt. i. m. 35). He died in 1432-3. (*See* Sir Harris Nicolas in Excerpta Historica, p. 152; Archæologia, xxxvi., p. 267 ; Archæol. Jnl., xxi., p. 254.)

Pp. 39, 105. *Dominus de Burser.* The lord here intended seems to be Sir John, second Lord Bourchier, K.G., a man of high military reputation and service in Parliament and Council, from the siege of Calais in 1346 till near the close of his life in 1400. He himself did not join Derby's company (he was about 60 years of age), but one of his men (the (the valet was probably an archer) was at the siege of Vilna, and was the first to receive Derby's flag to be planted on the wall (p. 105). Walsingham relates that " qui fuerunt de familia sua primi murum ascenderunt, et vexillum ejus super muros . . . . posuerunt " (Hist. Angl. ii., 198), words which, clearly pointing to an Englishman for the time in Derby's service, put it out of the question that a French lord Boursier might be referred to in the text. Bourchier was made vicegerent of Flanders and governor of Gant in 1384 ; if he had a house at Dantzig, according to the text, p. 39, his travels extended further than is commonly known.

Pp. 49, 131. *Sir Thomas Erpingham,* knight, a distinguished man, belonged to a Norfolk family, was born in 1357, and died in 1428 (Liber de Antiquis Legibus, Camd. Soc. ed. T. Stapleton, Pref. pp. clxxvii, clxxix, *notes*). He went to Spain with the Duke of Lancaster in 1386 (see letters of attorney in Rymer, vii., 508) ; accompanied Derby * on both his journeys to Prussia in 1390 and 1392, and was with him on his landing in England to take the Crown (Rot. Par. iii., 553a). We find Erpingham Constable of Dover Castle in 1102 (Collins, Peerage of England, v., p. 493), Sub-chamberlain in 1400, and Steward of the king's household in 1404 (Rot. Par. iii., 456, 669b). In 1421 we find him " a myghty and a gret supportour " of Walter Aslak, one of the enemies of William Paston the justice (Paston Letters, ed. Jas. Gairdner, vol. i., Introd., xxiv, 13-15). See further, Nicolas, Scrope and Grosvenor Controversy, ii., 194.

---

* Lancaster gave Erpingham 360 florens of Arragon (by warrant dated Pontefract, 10 August, 1392), towards his second journey to Prussia (D. of L., cl. 28, baic. 3, no. 2); he was there *infra curiam* in September (p. 265).

P. 50, 139. *William Pountfreit or Pomfreit* was Derby's clerk of the kitchen, called *clericus* (pp. 103, 151) and probably in orders; he is generally styled *dominus*, no doubt as a complimentary title, being at the head of an important department, just as the cook was "Magister William cook." No mention is found of him in general history, and the comparatively low rate of his wages (6d. a day) shows that his rank was not high. He is named in Leventhorpe's account for 16th Rich. II. as having paid for the freightage of a ship with Derby's wardrobe, &c. from Dantzic to Hull (D. of L., class 28, bdle. 3, No. 5, fo. 5 v°, see before p. liii.). He accompanied his master on both journeys.

Pp. 51, 123, &c. *Ralph Rochford*, who is mentioned as one of the sick on the Reysa, apparently received the pay of an esquire in 1390-1 and in the autumn of 1392, but in April, 1393, he is styled knight, and appears to have received knight's pay thenceforward.

When in 1386 armour and horses were needed for arming against the French, Ralph Rochford, knight, was one of those appointed to make proclamation to keep down the prices in the parts of Holland and Lincolnshire (Rymer, vii., 546).

A Ralph de Rochford, knight, was sworn among others in Lincolnshire to support the Lords Appellants in 11 Rich. II. (1387); there were also two Johns de Rochford (one knight, one burgess) sworn on the same occasion (Rot. Par. iii., 401*a*). An annuity for attending on the king's person was given by Henry VI. in 1433 to Ralph Rocheford, knight, when he must have been over sixty, if he were the same. (*Ib.* iv., 437).

P. 53. *Robert Burton* acted as esquire to Sir Peter Bucton the Steward; Kyngston states too that he helped him to write his book, *i.e.*, the book of accounts (p. 115); while to add to his manifold capacities he performed the offices of deputy-clerk of the kitchen and of the poultry from October 19 to November 30, 1390 (p. 103 l. 27, and *cf.* pp. 62, 65).

P. 53, l. 18. *Capellam sancte Katerine.* This place, apparently visited by Derby and his two chief officers, is identified by Prof. Prutz with Arnau, the church of which was dedicated to St. Katherine and was a place of pilgrimage.

Pp 53, 88, 142, 143. *John de Loudeham*, erroneously printed Londeham in the text, of Walton in Derbyshire, was the son of Sir John Loudham the elder, of Nottingham, &c. (who died in 1388). He went to Prussia and was on the Reysa with Derby, but died early in the expedition, "defunctus in partibus de Lettowe," his body being conveyed to Königsberg. From an inquisition *post mortem* which was taken in the third week of Feb. 1390-1 (first week in Lent, 14 Rich. II., No. 36), we find that he died on Sunday, 28 August, 1390, aged 25, leaving his sisters Isabella and Margaret his heirs. This agrees with the date in our text (p. 51, l. 14) of the Sunday when "the battle with the Pagans," was fought, in which he must have been slain, *i.e.* the battle on the banks of the Memel in which the combined

forces of the Marshall and Derby gained the day over Skirgal (see also John of
Posilge. Script. Rer. Pruss. iii., 165).

The chronicler Wigand von Marburg states that "quidam miles Johannes de
Lutam" was killed on approaching Wilna; he evidently intends Loudham, misplacing the date by a few days.

Loudham seems to have mortgaged his services to Derby for a loan of £30, part
of which was taken out after his death in the value of his two horses—"trotters"—
and saddles. No wages are entered as paid to him.

There was also another Sir John Loudham, of Suffolk, who was retained by the
Duke of Lancaster for life, and went to Spain with him in 1386 (when he was 34
years old), but when he died is not found. (Nicolas, Scrope and Grosvenor Controversy, ii., p. 175.)

P. 86. *Mende*, 162, 176, 181, *le Mount*. Prof. Prutz believes these both indicate
Münde, a place at the mouth of the Vistula, to-day Weichselmünde. The first
is the nearest phonetic shape of the word, and was used by the scribe of the first
accounts. Derby went thither by water from Dantzic; and on the second journey
some of his people were housed there (181).

P. 98, l. 21. *Abbot of Thornton*. Thornton-upon-Humber was an old Augustinian
House, lying between Boston and Bolingbroke, a convenient place to hire an extra
cart; the abbot in 1390 was Thomas de Gretham.

Pp. 101, 108, &c. *John Dalyngryg* or *Dalyngrugge* appears by the rate of his
wages to have been an esquire when he first joined Derby's retinue in 1390,
receiving 8d. a day *infra curiam*, and 12d. a day *extra curiam* on the Reysa, i.e. up
till the end of October. The knights on the Reysa received 2s. a day, but only 1s.
from 1 Nov. till April 30; Dalyngrugge however seems to have been promoted
after the siege of Wilna, as he is called *dominus* and receives wages equal to the
knights during these last five months. Sir John Dalyngrugge was knight for
Sussex in several Parliaments of Henry IV. and Henry V., and on Commissions of
Sewers between Hastings and Bexley (Collins, Peerage, ed. 1779, viii., 99, 100, 101).
In 1406 he was one of a Committee on the Safety of the Seas. (Rot. Par. iii., 569.)

According to Nicolas Sir John was son of Sir Edward Dalyngrigge, and made his
will in 1417 (Scrope and Grosv. Cont. ii., 371).

P. 106, l. 11, 131, l. 17. *Thomas de Rempston* (erroneously printed Kempston in
the text) was one of the knights having seen much military service who joined
Derby for the period of the Reysa of 1390, in which he held the honourable office of
Derby's standard-bearer. He did not go on the second journey of 1392. When
Henry landed at Ravenspur in 1399, Rempston was one of the "vaillantz
chivalers" who accompanied him (Rot. Par. iii., 553a); in 1400 he was Steward
of the king's household; in July, 1401 he was made Admiral of the West and a

keeper of the truce with France, in the following year Admiral of the South and West. He was drowned at London Bridge while attempting to row against a dangerous tide, on 31 Oct., 1406. (French Roll, 2 Hen. IV., m. 5; Rot. Par. iii., 512a, iv., 320a; Nicolas. Scrope and Grosv. Controversy, ii., 190).

P. 107. *Duke of Gloucester.* Thomas of Woodstock, sixth son of Edward III., married Eleanor eldest daughter and co-heir of Humfrey de Bohun, in whose right he was constable of England. He was created Duke of Gloucester in the 9th year of Richard II. He was thus uncle and brother in-law to Derby, whose wife was Mary, Bohun's other daughter and co-heir.

P. 108. *Jenico*, or Janico Dartache elsewhere, seems to have been a trusted esquire messenger, receiving higher pay for taking letters from Derby to England in 1390 than any other except Lancaster herald; perhaps they contained the news of the first successes at Wilna. In Dec. 1392, the Duke of Lancaster sent him to his son at Venice in order to cash the money transmitted to Derby through Alberti and Dyne of Florence; for in Whitteby's accounts we find "Janico Dartache" esquire named as a person who might receive money at Venice as Derby's attorney (see before, p. lv. *note*), and in the same account a payment is made by warrant dated London, 4 Dec., 1392, to "Janico Dartache, sentifero, cunti versus partes de Venys domino comiti Derbye." (D. of L., cl. 28, bdle 3, No. 2.)

P. 109, l. 2 *Episcopus de Samland.* The bishop of Samland, a northern province of Prussia, having his seat at Königsberg, from 1387 to 1395 was Henry II. Kuwal. About the gift which he sent to Derby in Königsberg, "j tabula commensali de Prucia" there may be some difference of opinion. Professor Prutz says that it cannot mean a specially Prussian table to eat at (Esstisch), but thinks that it indicates a table on the flat of which there was a map of Prussia inlaid in wood. (Rechunngen, p. 101, note 4). The learned professor does not give any reason for this conjecture, which appears to ignore entirely the word *commensali*. *Tabula* in the fourteenth century, besides a wooden board or broad plank, sometimes signified a cloth (Ducange), and it may be that the bishop sent a fair linen cloth, made in Prussia, to cover the festive board of the foreign prince. Cloths were used at the tables of rich men, the washing of the "mappas aule" (*e.g.* p. 85, l. 30) several times mentioned shows that Derby carried this habit with him; and we have "panni linei de Prucia" bought, p. 89, l. 15; so that such a gift was possible.

There does not, however, seem any difficulty in believing that a dining table from Prussia, such as a great man with his guests would use (probably a broad board with trestles) should have been bestowed. Derby took a "tabula comensalis" with a pair of trestles on the reysa (p. 49/18); and when he went to Dantzic one of the items of expenditure was for eight great boards (tabulis) "pro tabulis comensalibus in aula et in camera," where the same phrase is used (p. 75,15).

P. 111, l. 32. *Bryan de Stapleton*, knight, was the eldest son of the famous Sir Bryan de Stapleton, who was the first Bryan of his ancient house, bearing his mother's name. The father was of a Yorkshire family and took part in distinguished service for upwards of forty years, from the siege of Calais 1346, onwards. He died 25 July, 1394, and in September of that year Derby paid for masses for his soul (D. of L., cl. 28, bdle. 3, No. 5). But his eldest son died before him, (Inquis. Post Mortem, 18 R. II., No. 36), and Derby paid the Dominicans of Dantzic to celebrate mass for his soul about the new year, 1390-1 (Nicolas has, it seems erroneously, dated his death in 15 R. II., Scr. and Gr. Cont., ii., p. 289). Little is known about this son save that he took out letters of attorney to go to Spain in 1386.

P. 112, l. 3. *Guido Bryan, miles*, of Walwayn in Pembrokeshire, but sprung from an old Devonshire family, was long one of Edward III.'s valets. He was at the taking of Calais in 1346 (Add. MS. 6298, fo. 314), was made Knight of the Garter by Edward III, and was one of the lords appointed by Parliament in 1381 to enquire into the governance of the king's household (Rot. Par. iii., 101a; Rymer vii., 250). His name frequently appears in Rymer as occupying important positions of trust, the latest being in 1385. He died on 17 August, 1390, at the age of about 90 years (The Black Prince, ed. H. O. Coxe, Roxburghe Club, p. 319 ; Nicolas, Scrope and Grosv. Cont., ii., 215-6). His eldest son, also Guy Bryan, died in 1386, aged about 32. His second wife was a member of the Grandison or Gransuson family in England. The best account of this famous knight is given by Nicolas, 215-255.

P. 114, l. 34. *Reynepot, a knight of France*. This was Regnier or Rénier Pot, maître d'hotel to Jean sans Peur, Comte de Nevers, son of Philippe le Hardi, Duke of Burgundy, and chamberlain to the duke. He accompanied the Comte de Nevers on the crusade in aid of Hungary in 1396, and was among the prisoners taken at the disastrous battle of Nicopolis (Delaville le Roulx, France en Orient, 1886, i., p. 286, ii., pp. 83, 91, 94 ; Kervyn's Froissart, xxii., p. 383). His name is among those who received a *houpelande*, the French king's livery, on 1 May, 1400 (Douet D'Arcq, Pièces inédites, i, 164).

P. 116, ll. 22, 23. *Ad Sanctam Annam*. The chapel of the Order in the castle at Marienburg was dedicated to St. Anne ; Derby was at this place on 13 Feb. (p. 71).

Ib. l. 14. *Apud sanctum Georgium*. This appears to be a church in Königsberg, at which oblations were given on Derby's leaving that city, Feb. 9 (cf. pp. 167, 67).

P. 118, l. 9 ; 122, l. 29 *Sir William Bagot* himself is not recorded as receiving wages, nor is he entered among the knights on the Reysa ; he did not therefore accompany Derby in person ; but he sent 10 valets to Calais in May 1390, probably intended for the Barbary crusade (see Introduction). We find various mentions of William Bagot, who with Bussy and Green was on Richard's Council for many years, on the Rolls of Parliament (see also MS. Cleop. F. iii., fo. 8b): in 1393 he was concerned in a fray in Warwickshire, where he had a house at Coventry; in 1397 under the king's orders he was concerned in the murder of Thomas, Duke of Gloucester, at Calais (Ramsay, Lancaster and York, i., xlv., 7, 8): in 1399 he was one of the four king's councillors who managed the affairs of the kingdom under the Duke of York during Richard's absence in Ireland, and on the landing of Henry was the only one of these who escaped with his life. Having been apprehended in Ireland and examined in October 1399 he was left in the Tower, and the next year the Commons petitioned that his lands and possessions should be restored to him. In 1402 he was appealed against by John Bemyngton of Whitnash near Coventry. He and his wife Margaret were dead before 1421 (Rot. Par. iii., 326b, 458, 484; iv., 152).

Pp. 122, 139. *Thomas Hasleden*, esquire, of Steple Morden, co. Cambridge, appears as steward of Soham manor in the same county, Duchy property, in Levnthorpe's accounts, 16 Rich. II. He was the son of Christopher Hasleden and was born 1322. He was comptroller of John Duke of Lancaster's household, and his retainer for life (Nicolas, Scrope and Grosv. Cont. ii., 173).

P. 123. *Thomas Stokes* appears to have been an esquire, paid at an unusually high rate *infra curiam*, who also provided an archer during the three weeks' stay at Calais, May 9 to 31. The mention of his name on p. 20 must be an error for John Stokes, who was away with Sir Wm. Elmham at Paris, their expenses being paid independently (pp. 8, 20). That there were two Stokes', and that it was John, not Thomas, who accompanied Elmham is shown by the fact that no wages are entered for Elmham or for John Stokes except the large payment £13 3s. 0d. for the expenses of both. Elmham provided three archers *extra curiam* 18 May to June 7 (p. 124); if they were part of his following, and if this was the date of his journey to Paris, the existence of the two Stokes is certain. The point is of little importance except as connected with the date and motives of the Paris journey. See note to *Elmham*, p. 295.

P. 131. *John Loreyn* was one of the five lords who received knight's pay for the Reysa, but I have not been able to identify him. He seems to have been the heir of John de Lovein, and a minor at his father's death, as his lands were granted to Lord Burghershe about 1346 to hold till he should come of age (Beltz, p. 45). There was a Nicholas de Loveyn, who was lord of Bristow, co. Surrey, in the 44 Edward III. (Collins, Peerage, ed. 1812, viii., 250) whose daughter Margaret died in 10 Henry IV.; whether John belonged to this family I cannot say.

P. 131. Sir *John Gybbethorpe* was one of the deponents in the Scrope and Grosvenor cause in 1386, but Sir H. Nicolas was unable to find his name in pedigrees of the Gibthorpe family in Lincolnshire or to identify him. He is here among Derby's military company in 1390-1, with the pay of an esquire, and seems to have served under John of Gaunt in Spain (Nicolas, ii., 225.)

P. 131. *Richard Goldsburgh*, knight, was one of those sworn to support the lords appellant in Lincolnshire in 1387 (Rot. Par. iii., 401*a*); and he is mentioned in an inquisition in 1403 at Newcastle-on-Tyne. (Collins, Peerage of England, ed. 1812, i. 459.) In 1410 he was in a commission of array for the West Riding of Yorkshire against the Scots (Rymer, viii., 640.) He seems to have joined Derby in 1390 only for the Reysa.

P. 138. *John Malet*, knight, appears in the list of annuities paid by Derby (through Leventhorpe) for several years; after 18 Rich. II., however, the annuity ceases, because, as a side-note informs us, he is dead—"cesset ista annuetas quia mortuus est predictus Johannes" (D. of L. cl. 28, bdle. 3, Nos. 4 and 5). He accompanied Derby on his first journey and was with him in Königsberg at the New Year, when he received a large gift, (p. 112), but does not appear to have gone on the Reysa.

P. 150. *Prior Sancti Johannis*. The grand-prior of the English langue of the Order of St. John of Jerusalem at this time was John de Redington (1381-1399); and it seems probable that he, rather than the grand-prior of Venice (of the Italian langue) upon whom Derby could have no claim, supplied this contribution towards the expenses of the second journey. The account of Robert de Whitteby for 17 R. II., which would probably settle this question, unfortunately does not appear in the calendar of existing records of the Duchy. Redington and Bucton the steward made the agreement for the galley which took Derby from Venice to Jaffa and back again (p. 279; see Lutroit lviii), and the Prior seems to have accompanied him, and to have been sent with Granson on a mission to the King of Cyprus at Nicosia (p. 226). It will be remembered that the seat of the order at this time was in Rhodes, the ambitious and able Heredia being Grand Master (1376-1396).

John of Redington had already in 1386 been charged as special ambassador by Richard II. with the treating of affairs in Cyprus and Rhodes, and thus would be by his knowledge of those countries and their diplomatic relations a valuable guide for Derby. (French Roll, 9 R. II. m. 26, 5 Feb., printed by Mas Latrie, Hist. de l'Ile de Chypre, tom. II. pt. i. p. 401).

P. 150, l. 20. Aquileia, the ancient Roman city to the south of Friuli, was governed by a Patriarch from the sixth century, who in the tenth century had also obtained jurisdiction over Friuli. The Patriarchs later transferring their residence to Udine, they naturally became also known as Patriarchs of Friuli. From 1387 to 1394 John Sobieslaw, a son of the late and brother of the reigning Margrave of

Moravia, was Patriarch, having been translated from the bishopric of Olmütz. He was killed at Udine in 1391. (F. Ughelli, Italia Sacra, v., 116, 117.)

Pp. 158, 179, &c. Odo or Otto, familiarly Otes, third of the name, Sire de Granson (Granson, a castle and town near the lake of Neufchâtel), had rich possessions in Savoy and Vaud. He married in 1365, was at the siege of Rochelle, 1372, and at the defence of Cherbourg in 1379, and appears to have been several times in England, where he had numerous relations, and where a whole branch of his family was settled * (Louis de Charrière, Dynastes de Grandson, Tableau iv. a, cited by Ar. Piaget in Romania, xix., p. 238; see also Beltz, p. 176). He succeeded to his father's estates in 1389. In 1391 Amé VII., Count of Savoy, was poisoned, Granson became, as it appears unjustly, implicated; and, after an inquest, all his estates and property were, in 1393, confiscated. Meanwhile Granson had gone to England, perhaps early in 1392,† for we find that he accompanied Derby on his second voyage to Prussia in July of that year, a cabin in the ship being built for the accommodation of himself, Lord Willonghby, and others. Payments were made for short sojourns made by him at Königsberg and Dirschan (259). Passing through Stolpe, Pomerania, in September, he paid for Derby's safe conduct from the Duke there, and was with him also in Cyprus about the middle of February (226).

He received wages as *infra curiam*, by the grant of Derby and the Council of the Duchy of Lancaster, at higher rates than any other knight of Derby's company, viz. 3s. 4d. and 5s a day (the usual rate being 12d. a day), from the 12 August, 1392, till 31 May, 1393 (p. 264); about this latter date he probably went to Burgundy, at which court, Piaget says, he passed two years (Rom xix., p. 243), for Walter Jateburgh was sent by Derby from Avigliano, where he was on the 22 May on his way homewards through Italy, "to Otes Granson in Burgundia" (p. 246). On 1s Nov., 1393, after Derby had returned to England, Richard II. granted him a pension of £126 13s. 4d. In 1396 he returned to Vaud, but being again accused he was killed in a duel, 7 August, 1397 (Piaget, 247).

Some time before his father's death he received annuities from John of Gaunt; in 1377-8 he had £33 6s. 8d. (see Furnivall's Trial Fore-words, Chaucer Society, 1871, pp. 123, 148); in 1391-2 he had 100 marks or £66 13s. 4d. as annuity from the same nobleman (D. of L. records, cl. 28, bdle. 3, no. 2). Granson appears to have been not only a soldier and a courtier, but a poet; Chaucer calls him the flower of the poets of France—" flour of hem that make in France "—and translated

---

* Sir Guy Bryan married a Granson or Grandson. A century before this time one Otto Granson was warden of the Channel Islands under Edward I.

† In Loveney's accounts for the year ending 13 May, 1392 (14 and 15 Ric. II.), there was given to a servant of Otes Granson presenting Derby with a courser, 13s. 4d. (D. of L., cl. 28, bdle. 1, no. 2, fo. 19). This was before the second journey to Prussia.

310   THE EARL OF DERBY'S EXPEDITIONS.

a ballad from his French, calling it the *Compleynt of Venus* (Skeat's edition of Chaucer's Minor Poems, 1888, p. 206, 392, 395). He is also often referred to by Christine de Pisan and other French writers (Piaget, 237, 412).

There was also a "bastard Graunsom" in Derby's company, who was paid at the same rate as the esquires (see Index).

P. 167, l. 1, p. 273, l. 25. *Sepultura Hans et famuli sui.* John of Posilge, the historian of the Teutonic order, narrates that Lancaster (meaning Henry) came into Prussia in 1392 intending to join the knights on an expedition; and that, in Dantzic, his people killed a certain Hannus von Tergawisch, of the Witkop family, from the country (Script. Rerum Pruss., iii., p. 182), after which Henry withdrew from Prussian "nugereyset." Prof. Prutz identifies this man with the Hans of our text, and points out that Henry made due reparation; through his chaplain Herle arranging with the rector of the chief church, Marienkirche, of Dantzic for the burial of Hans and his servant (who must have been killed with him) at considerable expense, besides giving oblations and distributing alms to the poor at the funeral. The incident does not appear to have affected Henry's action, as he continued his journey to Königsberg.

P. 191, l. 8. *Cum Rege Bemie.* The King of Bohemia was Wenceslas, son of the Emperor Charles IV. of Luxemburg, to whom he succeeded in both dignities in 1378. Owing to his disorderly reign he was deposed from the empire in 1400; in Bohemia he tolerated the Hussites; died in 1419. Sigismund, King of Hungary (1386-1437), was his younger brother. Their sister Anne was the first wife of Richard II. of England (married 1382) and now queen; consequently Derby was a family connection. Bedeler, where Derby paid him a visit of three days, was a country seat or castle, the modern Bettlern, in Czechish Schebrak or Zebrak, a small town S.W. of Prague, on the way to Pilsen.

P. 195. *Regis Hungarie.* Sigismund, of Brandenburg, became king of Hungary in 1386 at the age of eighteen, marrying Mary, the young heiress to that kingdom; he became Emperor of Germany in 1411, and died 1437.

P. 210, l. 30. *Guydel.* May this be Cividale, north-east of Portogruaro? It is rather far east, and is out of Derby's route; but, as supplies were evidently sought in many places, it is possible that John Wilbram may have been specially sent there, and falling ill had to be fetched away. Cividale, or Civitas Austriæ, was the ancient capital of Friuli, under the Lombards.

P. 226, l. 28. *Regem Cyprie.* James I. de Lusignan, constable of Cyprus, second son of King Hugh IV., was king of Cyprus from 1382 to 1398, and titular King of Jerusalem. Part of the island was at this time under the dominion of the Genoese, who took it in 1373. The royal palace was at Nicosia, whence from Famagusta, the sea-port, was a tolerably long journey.

P. 230, l. , *per Ducem ibidem*. This personage who gave Derby a present of a butt of wine, was probably the Doge of Genoa; "ibidem" must refer to a seaport, as the wine was brought "de castello ad galeiam," and we know Derby was at Famagusta on his return voyage. Famagusta was at this time in the hands of the Genoese; contesting nobles occupied alternately the doge-ship for several years at this period, and whether the actual possessor or the one in retreat met with Derby at Famagusta he might well wish to be in the good graces of such a prince. The chief officers of the cities Nicosia and Famagusta were *ricomtes*, viscounts, (Mas Latrie, Hist. de l'île de Chypre, ii., pt. 2, p. 811, 814), but there hardly seems to be question of them here, neither of them could be called a "Duke."

P. 254, l. 2¹, *per la Ryne*. This word should be *ryne=rive*, i.e. river, the journey from Melun to Calais being made "by water," along the Seine to the sea, and toll paid along the river. It does not seem possible that Milan and the Rhine should be in question here; that the payment was made in ducats, does not disprove this view, as the ducat was used in several other payments in France and Burgundy. See Introd. p lxx.

P. 262. *Henry Lord Percy* was created Earl of Northumberland in 1377, and an esquire of his was with Derby at Königsberg in 1390 (p. 106). The item here does not show whether the chaplain (1392) were attached to Northumberland or to his son Harry Hotspur, and the horse may have been bought in England; there is nothing to indicate. From a letter of the King of Cyprus to Richard II., 15 July, 1393 (Raine's Northern Registers, p. 425), it seems that Henry Percy had recently been in Cyprus (no date given). Derby was there probably in February; the travellers possibly may have met, but it does not appear that Hotspur visited Cyprus in company with Derby, as surmised by Bishop Stubbs (Lectures on Mediæval and Modern History, 1887, p. 228).

P. 263, l. 8. *Dominus Comes Virtutum*. The powerful prince Gian Galeazzo Visconti, Seigneur of Milan (1378 to 1402), held the fief of Vertus, a county of Champagne in France, as the dower of his wife Isabella, daughter of King John of France (married 1360). He was known by this title till he was created Duke of Milan in 1396 by the Emperor Wenceslas.

P. 271. *Lancastre regi armorum*, i.e. king-at-arms; in other places he is called simply Lancaster herald (*see* Index). The herald of the famous Sir John Chandos, Chandos le herald, was called king-at-arms on one occasion in 1380 (*see* The Black Prince, ed. H. O. Coxe, Roxburghe Club, p. iii.) He was with Derby on the Reysa, receiving his wages (129), and on 5 November was sent with letters to England (107).

P. 273. *Lady Katerina Bromwych*. The only fact that I have gleaned about this lady, who appears to have paid some money to the treasurer on Derby's account at Lynn when sailing for Prussia in 1392, is that she held for life the manor of Michelhampton, a charge on which was granted to Joan (the second) queen of Henry IV., and which afterwards was to pass to the new Convent of Sion. (Rot. Par. iv., 213b.)

P. 276, l. 2. *Cum duce Venis.* Antonio Vernieri was Doge of Venice from 1382 till his death on 23 Nov., 1400, a period of renown for the republic, which acquired the marches of Treviso in 1388, and in 1390 restrained the power of the Duke of Milan. He received Derby in state, and the two princes appear to have paid their oblations at St. George's together.

P. 276, l. 19. *Apud Troys apud St. Antonium.* There was a monastery of St. Antony at Troyes, founded in the 13th or 14th century, a dependant of the diocese of Vienne. (Dictionnaire topographique du Département de l'Aube, par. MM. Théo. Boutiot et E. Socard, p. 140.)

P. 278. *Dominus de Clifford*; p. 275, l. 1. *In die anniversarii filii Lewys Clifford.* Roger 5th Lord Clifford had two sons; Thomas, a gallant knight and opponent of Boucicaut in the French wars, who died 4 Oct. 1391, 15 Ric. II. (Inq. P. M. 15 R. II., pt. 1, no. 17), at the early age of 28, seems to be the Lord Clifford for whom Derby gave oblations at Rhodes (in Feb. 1392-3). The younger son, William, died in 1418,——Sir Louis Clifford was probably brother to Robert and Roger the fourth and fifth Lords Clifford, (Whitaker's History of Craven p. 314; Nicolas, Scrope and G. Cont., ii. 469), but there is some doubt as to his exact relationship. He fought in the wars in France and Spain between 1352 and 1373, when he was with the Duke of Lancaster's army which marched to Bordeaux. From 1385 he filled civil offices of trust, being executor to Richard II's mother, and at various times to four other nobles. He was honoured by being elected knight of the garter in 1398. He had a son Lewis who was living in June 1390, being named in a grant of manors of that date, but nothing more is known of him. Possibly the "filius" of the text, whose death on 22 October 1391 Derby commemorates, on his anniversary, *i.e.* a year later, was this Lewis. He is also said to have had another son, William, but no proof of his existence is known. (See Sir Harris Nicolas, Scrope and Grosvenor Controversy ii., p. 427). For some years he was one of the principal supporters of the Wicliffites (Walsingham, Hist. Angl. i. 356, ii. 159, 216, 253), but in the last years of his life he informed against them and recanted. Dugdale prints his will, which refers to this (Baronage, i., 341): he died in 1404. It is a curious thing that Derby, afterwards so conservative and pious a churchman, should be giving oblations for the son of a man who already, in 1392, had been many years connected with the Lollards; but at this time his father, John of Gaunt, who strongly supported Wiclif, was still alive.

P. 275. *Dominus Robert Story.* Evidently one of Derby's English friends at Venice, perhaps of his company (though this is the sole mention of his name), as he handed

Derby money for alms to the poor on 4 Dec. This gentleman ("Robert Steri") was at the justs of St. Inglebert on 24 March 1390. (Pichon, Partie inéd. des Chron. St. Denis, p. 71.)

P. 284, l. 15. *Dominus de Menevia.* The bishop of St. David's (who also held manorial rights over that town) at this period (1389-1397) was John Gilbert, a Dominican friar and formerly bishop of Hereford. He held high positions of trust under Richard II., one being that of Treasurer of England (History of St. David's, by W. B. Jones and E. A. Freeman, 1856, p. 304). The costly furs bought for him at Venice were doubtless intended as a present.

POSTSCRIPT.

P. 113, l. 16. *John Elys*, knight, through whom Derby made a gift to a German painter in 1390-1, may possibly have been one of Lord Percy's men; we find him accompanying ("in comitiva") Henry Percy when going from Acquitaine to Gascony in 1393-4 (Gascon Roll, 17 Rich. II., m. 14). If so he would be the third man connected with the Percies mentioned in these accounts (*see note*, p. 311).

P. 168, l. 8. *John Marwicsire*, henksman. This name should be added to those of Derby's other henchmen, the Tylmans and Yonge, noticed on page xcvi.

Tradesmen dealt with, probably in London. In Loveney's Wardrobe Accounts, (1 Feb., 20 to 21 R. II., D. of L., cl. 28, balle. 1, No. 5), upon the last page he enters a list of Derby's creditors that year, among whom are found the following persons from whom purchases were made in 1390, and entered in this volume :—John Clee, draper (35); Henry Pomfreit, sadler (34); Mergarete Stranston, silkwyf (Thomas was perhaps her husband, p. 19); Thomas Grafton, malemaker (5, 6, 19), John Martyn, cordewaner (12).

INDEX I.—PERSONS.

Names which are taken from occupation, and therefore only descriptive, are placed under the name of the occupation with a small initial. A few cases of such names were already true surnames, as William Ferrour, and it is impossible to be certain in all cases, but the rule holds good in general.

All pages up to 140 are in Part I.; those after it in Part II., as indicated by an asterisk. The number of a line, in a page, is put in black type.

Abbegod. *See* Habbegod
Adam, Hansk, 54 ; frater, 254
Albertini at Venice, firm of the Lombards of, 150, liv.
Aleyn, John, piper, 262, 269
———, Thomas, trumpet, 269
Algood, John, piper, 269
———, William, piper, 112, 133, 137, 142
Almannia, herald from, 106
almoner to Derby, lord John, 273, xcii.
Alstrey, William, 32
Anchoress of Lynn, 273 **3**
Antony, ———, 226
Ap Henry, John, 122, 294
apothecary. *See* potecario
Aquitain, 3
Assheby, Aschby, John, valet, 52, 114, 127, * 163, 196, 210 ; wages, 272
Asshedon, Thomas, esquire, 120
Assheley, John, esquire, 94, 120, 128, 134, 139
Attehall, John, 18
Atteloft, Roger, 24
Attehous, Roger, pilot of Boston, 143
Angustus en Kenburghe, 11
Aunterous, Richard, valet, 268

Austria. *See* Hostrych, Duke of, Leopold III. (IV.), 150, an esquire of, coming with Derby, 285 **13**, lxxxiii.

Bache, Thomas, 24
———, Simon, treasurer of Derby' household, xci., 4, 294
Bagot, William, knight, 118, 122, 306
baker, Adam, 75
———, Francisco, 234, 236
———, Geoffrey, 112, 114
———, Hans, 42
———, Herman, 41, 42
———, John, of Boston, 23
———, Moryce, 152, 153
———, Thomas, at Leicester, 32
———, Walter, 12
———, William and John *See* Fyssher
bakster, Alan, 21
Bamburgh, Hans, 67
Barbour, Robert, valet, 105, 112 114 130
Barge, Richard, 36
Baron, John, 155, 156, 160, 161, 270
Bast, ———, 41
Bate, John, 36
Bauen, John, 176

Baydot the Prussian, 60
Beaufort (John), 100, xv., xxxv.
Bell, John, 27
Benet, John, pilot, 164
Benhow, Claus, master carpenter, 78
Benteley, Richard, 114
Bener or Bevere, John, merchant of Dantzic, 40, 41, 42, 87, 88, 96, 97, 105, 108, 113, 178, 179, xiii.
Bewford. *See* Beaufort
Biterley, John, 272
Blacdon, Blackdon, Blackden, John, valet of the kitchen, 6, * 168, 175, 181, 271
bladesmyth, John, 20
Blannehe, John, of Lynn, 158 **7**, 160
bocher, bucher, Henry, 8, 9
———, ———, Hankyn, 12, 49; Hans, 83, 96
———, ———, John, 18
Bode, John, 36
Bodenhale, John, archer, 122
Bohemia, Wenceslas IV., king of, 191, 310
Bohun, Mary de, 1, *note*, 27 **28**, lxxxi., lxxxii.
Bolton, Robert, 113
Boneface the Lombard, 234
Boniface IX., pope, 117
Bosse, ———, 36
botellerie or botery, Robert del, 49, 98. *See* Jonson and Payne
boteman, John, 7, 20, 24; Hans, 86
Bourchier (Burser, Bourser), lord de, 39, 105, 302
Brailleford, John, valet, 60, 63, 67, 69, 75, 85, 98, 108, 113; wages, 137, 141, * 153
Brakill, Robert, trumpeter, 270, **33**. *Should be* Crakyll
Brandyk, James Van, 67
Brank, John, Prussian, 52
brasyer, Stephen, 102
———, Hans, 102
———, Alan, 153
Breker, Peter, 64
Brerley, Birlay, Henry, 180, 181, 182
Bridlington, John of, 117 **22**
Broke, Affons, 58
Brome, Hankyn, 37
Bromwych, lady Katerina, 273, 311
Broshir, John, trumpeter, 112, 132, 137, 141
Broun, John, 18
———, Richard, 26

Brounham, Margerie, 13
Bryan, Guido, 112, 306
bucher=butcher. *See* bocher
Bucton, Peter, knight, steward of Derby's household, 35, 201, 300, xcii. ; his wages, 126, 128, 133, 138, * 265
Bugge, Edmund, esquire, 5, wages, 135, 139, 268 **6**
Burghwell, ———, 123
Burgoyne, William, 263
Burrek, Henry, 78
Burser. *See* Bourchier
Burton (Robert), clerk of the kitchen, 62, 65, 103, 115
Burtou, Robert, esquire to the steward, 53, 303 ; wages, 132
Busee, Robert, 18
Busshen, Henry, 17
Bussyn, John, 6, 14
Byngeley, William, piper, 132, 137, 141

cadeller = sadler, Saunder, 7
cage-maker, William, 25
camera, Henry de, valet, 46, 50, 89, 90, 92, 112 ; wages, 125, 129, 130, 135, 139, 140 ; * 165, 174, 240, 273, 279, 280, 284, 282, 283, 284, 285, 286, 287, 288 ; wages, 268, 270. *See* Morley
———, Nicholas de, valet, 31, 107, 112; wages, 119, 155
carpenter, Valerian, 26, 27
———, John, 26
———, Claus, 57, 82
———, Hans, 75, 83, 86
carter, Hankyn or Hans, 65, 67
carver (carrier), Hayne, 74
Casseleyn, James, carpenter, 79
Casson, Matthew, 190, 262
Catour, Adam, 17
Catour, Richard, valet, 37, 46, 47, 48, 49, 50, 53, 57, 58, 60, 63, 65, 66, 68, 70, 80, 83, 85, 86, 87, 88, 91, 92, 93, 95, 96, 97, 112 ; his burial, 89 ; wages, 130, 136, 140
Cawod, Cawode, John, valet, 23, 57, 58, 60, 61, 64, 65, 66, 67, 68, 69, 70, 71, 80, 84, 87 ; wages, 131, 137, 140
Chalons, Robert, armiger, 9, 29, 30, 31, 106, 107, 110, 112, 291
chaplain, Robert, the lord, 219 **23**. *See* Herle
Chancer's friends, lxxxii.
chaundeler, John, 11, 14
———, John of Calais, 14
———, Nicholas, 32

INDEX I.   317

chaundeler, Richard, 22
chaundrye, John de], valet, **166, 167, 170,**
  177, 183, 185, 187, 188, **191, 193, 194,**
  196, 198, 210; wages **and dress, 272,**
  287
———, Richard del, **171**
———, Robert, 198. See Whitlok
Chelmswyke, Richard, esquire, 109, **134,**
  138, 263, 275, 277; his servant Dene,
  264; wages, 266
Chermon, John, 164
Chewworth, William, 52
Clarence, George, Duke of, his household, lxxxix.
Clasenwright, Margerie, 32
Claus de Norwey, 161
Cle, John, of London, **35, 313**
clerk, Thomas a, 254
Clerke, John, 20, 24, 26
Clifford, lord de, oblations for, **278, 312**
———, Louis, knight, oblations for his
  son, 275, 312
Clifton, John, knight, 113, 131
Clyderow, Roger, valet, 268
Clyne (=Klein) Herman, baker, **238**
clokmaker, John, **19**
Codeworth. See Cudworth
Cok. See cook
Colendorf, Heyn, **55**
Colle, John, 108
Colon, Hans or Hankyn de, **212, 213,**
  216, 220, 221, **235, 236**
Colton, John de, **20**
colyer, Bartholomew, **59**
———, Hans, 59
cook de Byngeley, 110, 112; de camera,
  174
cook, Herman, **21**
———, John, 22, 23, 24, 25, 27, **30**
———, William, 169. See Kikkeley and
  Palter
———, Master William, 12, 29, **31,** 39, 51,
  53, 60, 96, 102, 104, 107, 114; wages,
  119, 125, 129, 134, 139, * 266
Cope, John, esquire, 107; wages, **121,**
  125, 131, **134, 138**
coquina, Lawrence of, 89; Henry of,
  89. See kitchen
Cornewayle, John, 291
Countershaw, John, valet, **120, 122**
Couper, Richard, 22, 23
———, Hans, 41
———, John, **23**
Courte, Francisco de, 291
Crakyll. See Krakyll and **Brakyll**

Cremere, Clans, 74
Cremer, James, 42, **63**
Cremeton, Hugh, 43, 50
———, Hans, 62
Cremeton van Torne, James, 68
Crochemere, Hans, 64, 66
Crokeler, Hans, 61
Croyslett, herald of Duke of Gloucester,
  107, 111
Crull, John, 16
Cruse, Hans, baker, 83
Cudworth, Cudeworth, **John,** valet, 18,
  20, 22, 23, **24,** 52, 112, * **152,** 155, 156,
  158, 159, **161,** 163, 170, 173, 183, 189,
  205, 207, 208, 219, 220, 223, 232,
  250, 271; wages, 118, 125, 129, 135,
  140, * 268, 269, 271
Curteys or Curteyn, Reginald, esquire,
  67, 102, 107, 139
Curteys, ———, 96, 104
Cyprus, King of, 226, **310**

Dalahow, John, 182
Dalyngrugg, John, esquire and knight,
  101, 108, 304; wages, 120, 131, **133.**
  138
Dampier le heraud, 107, xliv., lxxxii.
Dancastre, Richard, esquire, 13, 37, 38,
  79, 108, **112**; wages, 119, 124, 128,
  134, 138, 262, 267, 271
Dartache. See Jenico
Daventre, Henry, 32
Daveson, Richard, 11
David, John, 74, 91, 93, 99
Davy, John, 99, 172, 179
Dent, Thomas, 254, 292
Derby, Countess of, 1, note, 27 **28**
Derby, Earl of. See Lancaster
Derby, herald, 15, 108 **3, 21,** 110, 111;
  wages, 123, 134, 139, 297, xcii. See
  Mowbray herald
Deschamps the poet, lxxxii.
Douche, Conns, 207, 242
Dounce, Peter, 36
Dounton, John, garcio armurer (D. of
  L., cl. 28 belle 3, no. 5), 9, 35, 45, 46,
  91, 92, 93, 94, **113** * 155, 164, 171,
  172, 173, 174, **175, 178,** 180, 257;
  wages, 120, 126, **130, 136,** 141, * 262,
  xcii.
Drankmaistre, Ladkyn, 279
Drausfeld, William, 292
Drayton, John, 5
Duche piper, a, 108

2 T

Ducheman, 165, 166
———, Richard, servant of Lord T. Erpingham, 49, 60
———, Hans, 106; one died at Königsberg, 115
Ducke=Duche, Hans, 164, 169
Dutfield, John, 49, 53, 89, 90, 106
———, Robert, 114, * 194, 271
Dyndon, John, clerk of the wardrobe, 49, 74, 88, 89, 90, 91, 92, 93, 94, 116, * 172, 177, 178, 179, 257; wages, 129, 135, 139, * 268, xcii.
Dyscher, Nykell, 85

Ecton, John, knight, 37
Edenham, John, door-porter in the lord's hall, Königsberg, 58, 107
Edeyne, Hankyn, pastry-cook, 64, 67
Edwynes, Peter, 62; matrona, 63
Elchyn, Hans, 62
Elkyngton, Lord Robert, 106
Elnham, or Elnam, William, knight, 8, 20, 295; wages, 124
Elner, John, 10
Elys, John, knight, 113, 313
Eton, Thomas, 232
Erpingham, Thomas, knight, 302; wages, 131, 133, 137, * 189, 262, 265, 275, 278; his servant Richard Ducheman (i.e. the German), 49, 60; his chaplain, 283 29
Essex, John, 160
Emlith, the washerwoman, 58, 61
Everet, Claus, 60
Ewer, John def. 108
ewery, Richard de la, valet, 61, 63, 65, 87, 106, 112; wages, 125, 130, 136, 140

Fader, John, 14
Farrewyk, Gys, 42
Furys, ———, matron, 92. See Ferwey
fauconer, Hans, 64; Jacob, valet, 60, 66, 68, 88, 91, 92, 93, 113; wages, 136, 140
Feldwelle, Simon, 152
Ferar, Jacomello, 238
Ferestell, Antonio, 238
Ferronr, William, valet, 118
ferronr, or feronr [shoe-smith]
Hans, Hankyn, 12, 40, 61, 64, 65, 172
John, 33
Walter, 61

ferronr, Thomas, 155, 175, 177, 179, 185, 186, 188, 193, 194, 197, 199, 201, 207, 210, 237, 238, 240, 241, 242, 246, 247, 249, 257, 258; wages, 271
Ferwey, ———, matron, 68
Fethir, Gyse, 59
Fisher, John, 68. See Fyssher
Flet, Margaret de, 24
Flete, John, valet, 269
Flokton, John, 10
Fodringay, John, 17
Fosdyke, Thomas, 20
Fouk, Gerard, 161, 164
Fournour, Jacob, 239
Franch, William, 24
Francisco de Lumbardia, ? an esquire, 267
Francisco, fruiterer, 223
———, baker and pastry-cook, 234, 236
———, Jacob, goldsmith, 283, 286
Fremon, Peter, 198
Freman, William, valet, 106, 110, 112; wages, 119, 129, 135, 140, 270
Frenschman, John, 168
Freston, John of, 21
Friuli, John, of Moravia, Patriarch of, 150, 308
Frost, Nichel, 62
Friars, Augustinians at Elbing, 259 19
———, Carmelites, 110; at Dantzic, 114; at Lynn, 278; at Zittau, 274
———, minorites at Braunsberg, 113; at Susa, 276
———, preachers at Dirschan, 113; at Brecknock, 112; at Dantzic, 273
——— in Prussia, 109; at Treviso, 237, 240; of Wylhonghe, 106
———, John, of the Order of Preachers, 111
———, John of Sutton, 12
Fycele, Hans, 189
Fyk, Dedrick, 165
Fyscher, Godfrey, 159
fyssher, Hankyn, 40, 44
———, John, 58
———, Maryon, 12
———, Thomas, 20
Fyssher, junior, 106
Fyssher, Fyscher, John, the lord's baker, 68, 75, 80, 81, 82, 112, * 152, 156, 158, 161, 166, 167, 179; wages, 131, 136, 141, * 271
Fyssher, William, baker, 89, 108, 113, 114

INDEX I.   319

Galiard de Gaston, 24
Gamelyn, cofferer, 5, 6
Gardebrand, ——, 43
garderoba, Henry of, 88, 89, 90, 93
Gasteyn, John, 23
Gebon, John, 161
Geffr. ? = Geoffrey, ——, 181 *bis*
Geffrayson, Thomas, of Sutton, 20
Gelow, John, 6
Genoa, duke of, 230 **3**, 311
Gerard, Thomas, valet, 174, 268
Geykyn, Hans, 60
Gilbert, servant of the ship's captain, 230, 232 **15**
Gilder. *See* Gylder
Gloucester, Thomas, duke of, xv., lxxxii.
Gloucestre, Croyslett herald of duke, 100
——, Thomas, esquire, marshal, 16, 117, * 172, 174, 219, 244, 245, **4**, 246, **10**, 248, 250, 262, 266, 291; wages, 119, 129, 134, * 266
——, John (query error **for Thomas**), esquire, 138
Glouekyn, ——, 41
Golon, Robert, 24
Godesknawt, Godesknayth = Gottesknecht (Claus), 73, 111, * 180, xxxiii.
Godfrey, John, 24
Goldsburgh, Richard, lord, his wages, 131, 308
Goldsmyth, Roger, 152, 153
——, Hans, 280
goldsmyth, William, in **London**, 288
Gosseleyn, Hans, 97, 98
Goter, Thomas, esquire, 90, 107, 115, * 164, 167, 172, 175, 178, 186, 187, 189, 190; wages, 132, * 175, 267
Gracelesse, Graceles, William, valet, **106**, 110, 113, 114
Grafton, Grofton, Thomas, 5, 6, **19**, **313**
Graunson, Graunsom, Otto, Otes, knight, 158, 179, 226, 246, 259, 309, lxv., lxix., lxx.; wages, 261
Graunsom, a tailor, 286
——, bastard, esquire, **168**, **178**, **275**, 278; wages, 267
Gravenyng, Bartholomew, 9
Greeks, 232 **9**, **31**
Grenok, William, 11
Grey, Gray, John, **pilot of Boston, 22**, 105, 116, 143, * 183
Gromet, John, 12
Gromette, Heyn, 83

Gumme, Thomas, 15
guyde, gyde, Antony le, 225
——, Jacob le, *or* Jacob, 205, 206, 211, 212, 214, 215, 216, 217, 218, 220, 221, 223, 224, 225, 226, 227, 228, 229, 230, 232, 233, 234, 238, 239, 263
——, Nicholas, 202
Guylmyne, ——, 92
Gybbethorpe, John, esquire, 131, 307
Gybson, John, 175
Gylder, Gilder, John, valet of the chamber, 131, 208; 7, 10, 11, 18, 28, 33, 72, 74, 78, 79, 80, 81, 82, **85**, 87, 95, 98, 99, 100, 106, * 168, 173, 185, 194, 195, 196, 197, 198, 199, 200, 201, 205, 207, 208, 209, 211, 212, 213, 218, 219, 226, 228, 229, 231, 234, 235, 237, 239; wages, 131, 136, 141; * 268, 270, 271
Gyse, William, esquire, 267
Gyseley, ——, 32, 33

Habbegod, William, valet, 59, 112; his burial, 107; wages, 130
Halden, William, 24
Hale, James van, 66
Hamell, Hamon, 153, 160
Hamond, Henry, valet page, 210, 272 **17** (*Hound is error*)
Hankey, ——, butcher, 11
Hankyn, skipper of Dantzic, 37
Hans von Tergawisch and his servant, burial of, 166-7, 273, 310
Hardwyk, Thomas, Derby's auditor of accounts, 2, * 148, xci.
Harghtych, Hankyn, 42
Harpeden, William, valet of the chamber, 8, 9, 13, 14, 17, 23, 26, 31, 39, 40, 45, 47, 58, 60, 61, 62, 64, 65, 69, 73, 82, 83, 84, 87, 88, 93, 96, 97, 103, 112, * 166, 168, 170, 171, 179, 185, 194, 205, 208, 209, 210, 220, 223, 224, 236, 241, 242, 243, 244, 245, 246, 248, 250, 258, 262; wages, 136, 268, 270, 272
Harwood, Thomas, 26
Hasildene, 274, 275
Hasildene, Richard, 262
Haseldene, Thomas, esquire, **122**, **139**, 307
Hastynges, Edmund, esquire, 132
Hatfeld, Robert, controller of Derby's household, 153, 160, xcii.
Hansemann, Bernard, 91, 92, 93, 94, 113

320 INDEX I.

Hansemann, Peter, 107, 112, 114
Hansman, Walter, ? valet, 112, 114, 127
Hansemere, Peter, master of a ship, 56
Haner or Hauyr, William, valet, "clericus domini," 5, 8, 13, 36 *note*, 38, xcii.; burial of, 111 ; wages, 121, 126, 130
Haydon, ——, 96
——, Hans, 74
——, Robert, pilot, 87
henksman, Henry and Bernard. *See* Tylman *and* Marwiesire
Henry (or Herry), John ap, esquire, 36, 294; wages, 122
Henry,—baptised.—Turk,—of Rhodes,—Sarasin, 230, 233, 240, 254, 284 **12**, 287, lxvi.
herald, 107; from Almannia, 106; Dampier, 107; Croyslerf, 108; Horne, 110 **12**; Mowbray, 220, 225; Seland, 107 ; Swethe, 110 **8** ; gifts to, 109, 110. *See* Derby, Lancaster
Herdwyk. *See* Hardwyk
Herle, Hugh, clerk, Derby's chaplain and confessor, 17, 37, 92, 110, 116, * 167, 175, 178, 183, 254, 273, 274, 279, 298, xcii.; wages, 122, 128, 133, 138, * 265
Herman, skipper of Dantzic, 37
Hertyk, Henry, 98
Hethecote, James, 42
——, John, valet, 125, 130
Hethcote, Robert, valet, 12, 81, 87, 112, * 190, 198, 210, 281, 283, 285, 286 ; wages, 122, 136, 140, * 269, 270, 272 *note*
Heyne, ——, chandler, 68
Heyngere, Claus, 83
Heyngle, Hans, 84
Heynrych, Hanke, 56
Higham, William, 114
Hoges, William, 37
Hogull (Hogle), Heyne, beaker-maker 62, 86
Hoke, Hankyn, a Prussian **carter,** 68
Holeote, John, valet, **123**
Holste, Hanke, 55
Hoppemere, Bartholomew, 59
hosteler, Philip, 15, 16; Martyn, **17**; John, 18, 28
hostiler, de Lincoln, 31
——, Gilbert, 6 ; William, 6
Hostrych (= Austria), Kyrsten van, 83
Horne le Herald, 110
hornpiper, Hans, 114, 115
Houghton, Henry, esquire, **131, 138**

Hoult, Hanke, 55
Hous, Roger, 116
Howe, Robert, 98
Howman, Claus, 63
Hughet, Hogher, Hwet, Robert, valet, 93, 114, * 161, 163, 210 ; wages, 272
Hull, Henry, 161
Humphrey (duke of Gloucester), fourth son of Henry of Derby, his birth, 107, lxxxii.
Hungary, Sigismund, king of, 195 ; gaiters of his livery, 285 **31**, 310
Hykelyng, William, esquire, 16, 123

Inglefeld, ——, esquire, 124
Inglewode, William, 161

Jacob the Jew, 207 **23**
Jacomello, baker, 222
——, butcher at Venice, 221
Jacson, John, 27
Jeke, Ine, esquire, 132
Jekyll, Knuge, master of ship, 56
Jenico, Janico Dartache, 108, lv., *note*
Jerusalem, Prior of St. John of, at Venice, 150 ; in Cyprus, 226 ; in England, 279, 308, lviii., lxi.
Jonson, John, 163
Jonson, Robert, of the butery, 10, 49, 98, 108, 114, * 161, 175, 180
——, Peter, 37
——, Thomas, 20
——, Walter, 26
Junker, Johan, 172
Jnteburgh, Walter, 246, 247, 251, 253

kagemaker. *See* cage-maker
Kemp, John, 21
Kempston, *should be* Kempston, *which see*
Kent, John, of Calais, 14, 25
——, Robert, 158
——, Thomas, 37
Kepe, John, 179
Kesseleyn, Claus, 65
——, Hans, 85
Kikkeley, Kikkele, Kykeley, William, valet, 75, 99, 106, 112, 114, 161, 164, 173, 219 ; a "grome," 137, 141 ; wages, 137, 141, 210 **26**, 269, 272 ; cook, 210 **4**
kitchen, Henry, page of, 89, 98, 106, 114

INDEX I. 321

kitchen, **Peter of,** 106. *See* Lawrence
Knape or Knapp, Thomas, 52, 53, 99, 114, 163, 169, 172
Knyghton, Cnyghton, John, **83, 114**
———, Robert, grome or valet, **59,** 112, * 269; wages, **131, 136, 141**
Kogeler, Heyn, 55
Korme van Ederyke, Claus, **87**
Krakyll or Crakyll, Robert, **trumpeter,** 132, 137, 141. *See* Brakill
Krozier, Claus, 56
Kuer, Hermann, 56
Kyghley, William, 291
Kyleys, Saundre, 36
Kyngeston, Richard de, archdeacon of Hereford, Derby's treasurer for war and journies, 1, 2, 3, 5, 57, 104, * 147, 148, 205 **16**, 215, **15**, 291; his wages, 143 **5**, * 266, 292, 293, xcii., xcv.

Laghmere, Henry, 72
Lake, Martinus de, 41, 55
Lancaster, Henry of, earl of Derby, 2, 3, * 147, 148, 291; as dominus, *passim*; his position, lxxx.
Lancaster, duchess of, Constance of Castile, duke John's second wife, 8
Lancaster, John, duke of Aquitaine and, 3, 19, 31, 40, * 147, 149, 292, lxxxii-lxxxvii.
Lancastre le heraud, 18, 40, 106, 107, 110, 129, * 190, 280, 287; king of arms, 271 **30,** 311
Lange, Henrych, 56
Langdon, Henry, valet, 120, * 278, 288
Langeford, Roger, esquire, 119, 128, 134, 138
Langton, Christofer, esquire, 121, 124
laundour=washerwoman, Edith, 58 61, 81
Laurence of the kitchen, 89. *See* scullery and Travers
leche, John, 164
——— Nicholas, 269
Leg, John, esquire, 123
Lekirke=lord of, 109
Lettowe, **boys from,** 52 **26,** 65, 67, 68, 91, 92, 113, xxxi; **women and children from,** 89, 92; tradesmen, 52 **9, 26,** 53 **5**
Lettowe, Henry, 90, 91
Leveret, Thomas, 19
Levyngton, John, valet, 54, 60, 63, 80, 107, 112; wages, 140

Lewnthorpe, Levnthorpe, John, Derby's general receiver, 4, 13, * 149, 152, 279, 290, 294, xcii.; wages, 123
Lisle William de, lxiv. *note*
Lithuanians. *See* Lettowe
Litton, Robert, valet, 112, * **194, 202**; wages, **125,** 129, 135, 140, * **268, 269,** 271
Livland (Nyueland). Master of, Wenne- mar of Bruggenoie, 105
Loft, Roger, 23
Loge, Henke, pilot, 56
Loge, Henry, 85
Logere, Heyne, 74 (? this the same as the two last)
Lombard merchants, 287, 292; at Jaffa, 226 **6**; Boneface, 234. *See* Francisco
London', John, 7, 9
Longheyn, ———, 56
Lorell, Hans, 60
Loreyn, Peter, carpenter, 63
Loudeham (*erroneously printed* Londeham), John de, knight, 53, 88, 142; his death, 143, 303
Loneyn, John, lord, his wages, 131, 307
Loveney, or Lovenay, William, 5, 7, 34, 35 * 147, 149, 294, xcii., xcv.
Luca, Nicholas of, and Co., money changers, 150, lv.
Lynne, John, 14

Makenhagen, Claus, xxxiv, *note*
Malet, John, knight, 112, 138
Malkon, Henry, 89
Manere, Henry van, 61
Mannyngs, William, 10
Markesworth, Haukyn, 54
Marshall, John, 37
——— Nicholas, 102
Martyn, John, 12, 313
Marwiesire, John, henksman, 168, 313
Massyngham, Matilda, 22
Maunsell, Henry, valet, 37, 52, 98, 112, * **195,** 198, 263; wages, 124, 129, **135,** 140, * 268, 272 *note*
Maye, John, valet page, 210, 272
Melbourne, Peter, esquire, **275, 277**; wages, 266
Merenb., Hankyn, **79**
Mersyngton, ———, 106
messenger, or mensenger, Richard, 9, 10, 13, 16; wages, 122 124
Messyngham, Roger, 116
Milan, duke of, Comes Virtutum, 263, 311

milnere, mylner, John, 157
———, Thomas, 32
Moket, Hans, furrier, 92
Moore, Peter, 65
Moreyn, Edwyne, 86
Morley, Henry, valet, 37, 63, 112, 113; wages, 135, 140, 268; his servant John, 110
———, John, 44, 45, 46
Mot de Curterykes, 14
Moubray, Gelinna, 24
Mowbray, John, 14, 201
Mowbray, Moubray, le herald, 186, 220, 225, 227, 234, 279, 280, 283, 286, 287; wages, 267
Mowbray (seems to be the herald), 242, 243, 244, 246, 248, 250
Mustarder, Malkyn, 23
Mynter, Hans, 62

nakerer (musician), John, 112, 133, 137, 142
Narford, Nicholas, 160
Newport, ———, esquire, 121
Newton, Geoffrey, 175
Neerle, Francis, & Co., Lombard, 150
Norbery, or Norbury, John, esquire, 19, 30, 31, 50, 53, 86, 91, 104, 108, 109, 110, 113, 117, 298; wages, 128, 133, 138
Norkyn, Thomas, 12
Northoner, Yngram, 14
Northumberland, earl of, 311, Hermann esquire of, 106; chaplain, 262
Norton, William, 6, 19
Norway, John, 106, 114
Norwich, Bishop of (Henry Spencer, 1370-1406), 270/**15**, xlvii.
Nowell, 264
Nuport, ———, valet of the body, 124

Oret, Richard, 159
osteler, ostelcer, Thomas, 30, * **176**
———, Nicholas, 31
Ostremark, Mattes van, carpenter, 78
Onteredy, ———, of Calais, 12

pages, Gilbert, 24; John, 37; Maye and Hammd (*Hamnd* in *error*), 272, **17**
pasteler, Francisco, 236; Hans (*see* Edeyne), 67

Paule, ———, 192
Pannsefot, ———, 278
Payce, Stephen, 153
Payne, John, esquire, clerk of the buttery or butler, 6, 7, 11, 12, 16, 19, 20, 21, 27, 29, 30, 31, 38, 39, 41, 42, 43, 44, 45, 46, 50, 52, 54, 58, 61, 64, 67, 68, 69, 70, 71, 78, 81, 83, 85, 86, 95, 97, 102, 104, 107, 110, * 155, 160, 163, 165, 170, 171, 172, 174, 178, 179, 181, 184, 185, 186, 187, 188, 189, 190, 191, 192, 193, 195, 201, 208, 211, 218, 219, 222, 223, 224, 225, 227, 228, 229, 230, 231, 232, 233, 234, 235, 238, 240, 241, 242, 243, 244, 245, 246, 247, 249, 250, 254, 258, 263, 274, 283 ; wages, 119, 126, 128, 134, 139, * 266, 270, xcii.
Peck, John, 177, 183 (*error for Peek*)
Peek, Peke, Pek, John, valet, 31, 86, 106, 108, 112, 114, 273, 274; wages, 268
Peegolt, Pege, pilot, 56
Pepour, Pepur, Pepir, Pepyr, Poper, Robert, valet of the chamber, or "grome," 79, 108, 112, * 170 ; wages, 126, 130, 136, 141, 269, 271
Percy, Henry, lord, earl of Northumberland, his chaplain, 262 ; his esquire, 106, 311 ; Elys with, 313
———, Thomas, lord, his shippage from Dover to Calais, 36 *note*, 301.
Peter, Philip, 59
pewtrer, James, 65 ; Hans of Konigsberg, 101
peyntour, Hans, 113 ; John, 23 ; Thomas, 169
Pinlerour, Jacob, Janyn, 218, 223, 236
Poland, king of, Jagello, 108, 111/**22**, 139
Pomfreit, Ponfreyt, Ponmfret, Pumfreet, Pountfreyt, William, lord, clerk of the kitchen, 50, 52 **26**, 53 **16**; clerk, 103, 151 ; 116, * 151, 161, 167, 178, 182, 263, 273, 291, 303, xcii.; wages, 121, 127, 129, 135, 139, * 267
Pontfreit, Henry, 34, 313
Poppyn, James, 40, 42, 56
Porteier, William, 9
porter, portour, Haukyn, 70, 73, 78
———, John, 25
———, Robert, 247
———, William, 124, 125
potecario, Anton, 219
Prake (= Prague), Nicholas of, 54
———, Claus of, 69

Prendregest, John, archer, 124
Pruceman, Nichol, 51, 110
Prucianus, Bartholomew, 59
————, Claus, 56
————, Clekyn, 63
————, Hans, 49
————, Nicholas, 113
————, Peter, 62
Prussia, master of, 40/**7**. *See* Teutonic Order
Pruciani, 106 **8**, 107, 108 **'24**, 34, 109, 110, 111, 171/**34**
Puffyn, William, 13
Pulter, William, cok = cook, his wages, 125, 130, 140
Pusk (Putzig), John of, 40
pursuantes = pursuivants, of France, 107 **8**
Pye, John, 153
pybaker, Thomas, 12

Ragnit, commander of, 94/**3**
Rakebrond, ————, 7
Ravene, John, nephew of the marshal of Prussia, 90
Rede, John, 30
Redington, John, *see* Jerusalem
Rempston, Thomas of, 106, 304, lxxxi.; wages, 131
Renier Pot (Reynepot), French knight, 114, 306
Repon, John, of Lynn, 160
Retfurre, Thomas, 36
Reyneth, James van, 67
Rigmayden, Richard, esquire, 121, 139
————, William, esquire, 107, 117 ; wages, 135, 268
Robert, lord, the chaplain, 219 **23**
Robinson, John, porter, 268
Rochford, Racheford, Ralph, esquire, ill on the reysa, 51 ; wages, 123, 131 133 138, * a knight, 265, 303
Rocheforthe, Hans, 65
Rodebrond, Claus, carpenter, 79
Rotherford, Hans, 81
Rothir, Hans, 62
Roper, John, 24
Rowham, William, 160
Rubne, Huet, 80
Russe, Robert, 5
Ryggeley, Richard, valet, 106, 112 wages, 119, 129, 135, 139
Ryle, John, 25
Rye, lord John, 115

sadeler, John, 33
————, Richard, 7, 34
————, Peter, 13
Sadeler. *See* cadeller
Saintpyr (*i.e.* St. Pierre), Robert, 30
Salsale, James, 81
Samland, bishop of, 109, 305
Samland or Semeland Claus, 63, 68
————, Henry, 50
————, Hanke, 55
————, Jacobus, 41
Sandhill, Sendille, or Sendhille, Richar valet, 10, 15, 17, 18, 112 ; wages, 119 126, 131
Sandwich, John of, 37
Sandyk, Claus, 68
Satemere, Hans, 59
Scheffer, Hanke, 55
Schele, James, 55
Schelford, John, valet of the chamber 208 ; wages, 268, 269, 271, 272 *note*
Schone, Clank, 54
Schoneman, Claus, a carter, 52
Schulkes, Peter, 54
Schulshe, Hans, 55
Sconfeld, Hankyn 41
Scorell, John, 68, 89, 90
scullery, Laurence of the, 59, 60, 62, 63, 67, 70, 78, 80, 84, 85, 98, 114, 263. *See* Travers
————, Robert, of, 59
Seinlatonr. *See* Solatonr
Seland = Zealand, le herand, 107, lxxxii.
Selby, John, valet, 166, 168, 176, 178, 182, 189, 196, 201, 212, 214, 217, 218, 224, 226, 231, 233, 235, 237, 240, 257, 258 ; wages, 269, 270
Semond, Thomas, 21
Sempy (Seympe), lord, of France, 34, 300, xxxviii.
"Senescallus Francie," xxxix., 297
Sewarby, William, esquire, 120, 128, 134
Sholk, Matan, 62
Shone, Hans, 87
Simeon, 108, 115
Siselden, John, 153, 159
Skette, John of Lynn, 153
skypher = skipper, Hans, 81. *See* Herman skipper of Dantzic, Hankyn, 37
Smart, Roger, valet, 118
Smyth, John, piper, 25, 166 ; wages 269
————, Robert, of Gofforth, 10
smyth, John, 6, 31

Smith, Richard, 18, 22
―――, William, 24
Sohow, Thomas, valet, 268
Solatour, Seinlatour, Peter, knight, 201, 220, 263, 276, lviii.
Sompterman. *See* Sumpterman
Sotynges, Gyles, 14
Sparr, William, 36
Sparwe, John, 159
Spayne, Richard, 13, 15, 29, 30
Spayne, or Spaigne, Robert, valet or grome, 9, 12, 49, 58, 59, 60, 62, 64, 66, 67, 70, 72, 73, 74, 78, 81, 84, 186, 12; wages, 120, 126, 130, 136, 141
Sprank, Nicholas, 41
spicer, or spycer, Claus, 61, 62
――― Hankyn, 11
Squyrell, John, English merchant, 49, 61, 68, xiii.
Staneley. *See* Staveley
Stanerle, John, 12
Stancysshe, Edmund, esquire, 129
Stapleton, Bryan de, miles, 111, 306
Staveley (*erroneously printed* Staneley *throughout*), Ralph, esquire, 28, 31, 37, 39, 109, 115, * 276, 277, 278, 299; wages, 120, 126, 134, 138, * 266
St. David's, bishop of, 284, 313
Stedeman, Hans or Hankyn, 14, 35
Stenefeld, Hans, 59
Stereff, Hankyn, 59
steresman, Hankyn, 104
steynour, Ralph, of Westminster, 18
―――, Nicholas, of Dantzic, 175
Stokes, John, 8, 20 **9**, 295
―――, esquire, 123, 307
―――, Thomas (MS. error for John, 20), esquire, 123, 307
Stolpe (Stulpe), Bogislav von Stolpe, duke of, 170, xxxiv, *note,* lvi.
Story, Robert, lxxi, 275, 312
St. Pierre. *See* Saintpyr
St. Poul, St. Pol or Paul, earl of, 11 **'11**, 296
Stranston, Thomas, 19, 313
Stromburgh, Andrew, 50, 51
Sumptermann, Henry, 251
――――――, Richard, 93
――――――, Robert, 108
Swan, John, valet, 178, 184, 269
―――, Symon, 5
―――, Thomas, 20
Swethe le herahl, 110
Swinburne, Thomas de, lxiv., *note*

Swylyngton, Thomas, valet, of the marshalcy, 40, 69, 70, 71, 86, 87, 114, * 172, 185, 210, 211; wages, 272
Swynford, Thomas, knight, 38, 100, 301, xxxix.; wages, 121, 128, 133, 138
Syde, John, valet, 30 bis, 31, 108, 114, 174, 178
―――, William, 269

Talleworth, 17
Tanfeld, Alan, 12
taveruer, John, 6
―――― Martin, 11
――――, Nicholas, 16
――――, Thomas, 16, 18
――――, William, 15
Temman, John, 24
Teutonic order of Prussia, officers of—
  Grand masters (Zölner von Rotenstein) 40 **7**, 93 **31** (Conrad von Wallenroth), 111, 164 **13**, 167/ **33**
  Grand-commander and vice-gerent (Conrad von Wallewroth) 94 **1**
  Marshal (Engelhardt Rabe), 50, 53, 54, 55, 90-**31**, 105, 108, 109, * 149, xxix; his nephew (nepos) John Raveue, 90
  Master or commander of Ragnit, (Johann von Rumpenheim), 53/ **10**, 91 **3**
  Master of Livland (Wennemar von Bruggenoie), 105
  Commander of Christburg (Werner von Tettingen), 105
Theplond, John, 164. *See* Trepeland
Thorne, Edward, pilot, 87
Tollenere, Hans, pastrycook, 74
Toren (= Thorn) Poul de, 96
Torne (= Thorn), Henry van, 64, 66, 67, 74, 85
Toty, Totty, Thomas, esquire, 38, 86, 107, * 163, 211, 219, 236, 241, 257; wages, 118, 123, 128, 134, 138, * 266, 270
Travers, Laurence, (? same as L. of the scullery) valet, 152, 155 159, 164, 165, 167, 168, 169, 170, 171, 174, 177, 178, 179, 185, 187, 190, 191, 192, 193, 194, 196, 204, 205, 206, 212, 214, 216, 217, 218, 222, 223, 226, 227, 228, 230, 231, 232, 233, 234, 235, 236, 239, 258, 263; wages, 269, 272

INDEX I. 325

Trepeland, Triplond, John, 40, 42, * 175, 179, xiii.
trumpet, le, trompetour, 36, 37, * 200
———, John, 199, 269.3
———, Thomas, 269 **10**, 271 **23**, 287, 291
Turk baptised, *see* Henry
turnor, Thomas, 14
———, William, 17
———, Walter, 27
Tutbery, Thomas, treasurer to John D. of Lancaster, 3
Tweyfrend, or Tweyfrere, Peter, of Dantzic, 72, 81
Tweyford, Peter, 88
Tyder, Howell, 271
Tylemer, Francisco, 222
tyler, John, 23
Tylman, Bernard and Henry, the lord's henkmen, 164, 166, 171, 176, 225, **20, 28**, 284, xcvi.
tynker, John, 177
Tyrington, William, 152

Undreland, Christofer, 60
Uphill, Thomas, 164, 172

Vandaleyt, Bartelet, 59
Venere, John, 166
Venice, doge of, 276, 312
Vienna, lord Ralph of, knight, 265
Virintnm, Comes, 263 **8**, 311, lxxxiii.

Wace, John, of Lynn, 55
Wakfeld, Thomas, 32
Walker, John, 9, 35, 127
Wallowe, Henry, 92
Walpole, Richard, 65
———, Robert, 152
Walshman, Richard, 114
Walsoken, Bartholomew, 21, 24, 26
Warderer, Worsten, 55
Warwick, Thomas of, 13
Waterdene, John, 181
Waterman, John, **7**
Waterton, Hugh de, knight, chamberlain of Derby's household, 2, 4, 80, 104, 143, * 211, 290, 291; wages, 124, 128, 133, 138, * 264 ; 293, xcii.

Waterton, John, esquire, 10, 108, 112 115, *166; wages, 119, 125, 129, 134 139, * 267 ; 295
Waterton, Robert de, knight, master of the horse, 11, 15, 38, 43, 60, 90, 91, 91, 108, 109, 112, 114, 143, * 152, 163, 166, 173; wages, 118, 129, 133, 138, * 266 ; 296, xcii.
Waterton, Thomas, 110
Watton, Thomas, 114
Wegle, Heyne, 87
Wendell, or Wendehull, matron, 65, 67
Wendehull, ———, chandler, 65
Wene, Radulphus de, knight, 265
Weyn, Hans, 113
Wesnam, Robert, of Lynn, 152
Weston, Richard, valet, 268
Whitby, Whitteby, or Whytby, Robert, general receiver to John, duke of Lancaster, 3, * 147, 149, 150
Whitlok, Whytelok, Wytlok, or Wytelok, John, chandler, 60, 63, 65, 66, 67, 68, 71, 73, 74, 78, 80, 81, 85, * 162, 177, 180. *See* chaundrye
Whityk, or Whytyk, John, English merchant, 42, 72, 75, 79, 97, 105, xiii.
Wikerell, Adam, 21
Wilbram or Wilbraham, John, valet, 150, 163, 164, 165, 166, 167, 168, 170, 171, 172, 173, 174, 186, 187, 188, 189, 190, 191, 192, 193, 194, 195, 196, 197, 198, 199, 200, 204, 205, 206, 207, 208, 209, 210, 212, 219, 221, 233, 235, 236, 237, 238, 240, 241, 242, 243, 256, 257, 263, 283, 291 ; ill at Guydel, 210; wages, 268, 269
Wilby, *for* Willughby, **276, 277**
Winslowe, 194 **6**
Wode, ———, 278, **9**
Wolfley, Wolfle, Richard, valet, 120, 156, 166 ; wages, 268
Wollaton, William, esquire, 5, 121
Womlewell, Thomas, auditor of accounts, 148, xci.
Worcester or Wyrcestre, William, 20, 23, * 155, 159, 270.*
Wrake, William, 22
Wrangill, Thomas, 22
Wyghtman, Hans, 89
Wylhoughe, Friars of, 106
Wyllonghby or Wylnby, William de, miles, 31, 51, 106, 119, * 158, 166, 209, 232, 299 ; wages, 264, 275

Wynmnon, Henry, 165
Wynerll. ——, 192, **16**
Wynch, John, 22
Wyndesore, Wyndesonere, John, valet, 98, 106, 170,* 175, 180
————, William, grome, 112, 130, 136, 141, 181, 182, 269
wyndrawer, Hans, 62
Wytlok, William, 114

Ympyngham, William, 32

Yorge or Zonge, John (? valet, or henchman of, 1391-2, see p. xcvi. note), 177, 186, 242, 275, 281; wages, 268, 270
Yongfrowe, Hans, 81, 82
York, William of, piper, 112, 152, 137, 142

Zealand. See Seland
Zymmerman, Nikell, 55
Zonge. See Yonge

INDEX II.—PLACES.

The places are indexed under the modern names, the various old spellings are within brackets following. A few of the old names it has been found impossible to identify.

The Itineraries are on pp. xxxv., lxxii. of the Introduction.

Aiguebelle (Egbell), 245, 261, **276**
Almannia, 106, Almandia, 292
Amiens (Amyas), 254, 276, 278, 287
Arnau, chapel of St. Katherine at, 53 **18**, 303
Arnoldstein (Horleston). 202
Arnswald (Arneswold, Ornesbold, Orneswald), 185, 188, 260
Arragon, florens of, 3, 33, 103, 289, xcviii.
Arskirke. *See* Traiskirchen.
Austria (Hostrych, Ostricia). 83,* 195. 204
Avigliano (Velayn, Auylan, Avelan), 242, 243, 246, 247, 254, 261

Bafas (Baffa) in Cyprus, 230
Bage-le-châtel (Bagea). near Macon, 248, 261
Bar-sur-Seine (Berce), 251, 261
Barbary, intended journey thither, xxxvii.-xlii.; bows for, sold, 4; bargeman going there, 28; cloth for squires and valets going, 35 20, xl.
Barnet, 34
Barton [on Humber] 98, 99, 114
Beaune (Beaune), 250, 261, 276
Berkhampstead, 28
Berne, in Bohemia (? Bernau), 260, 274, lxxiii.
Bettlern, Zebrak or Schebrak (Bedeler), 191
Beverley, 98, 117
Bishop-gate, Orwell house without, 55, 301

Bohemia. 188, 191, 194, 289, 290, ci.
Bolingbroke (Bollyngbrok, Bullyngbrok), 20, 21, 24, 31, 98, 99, 114, 126 *note*.
Boston (St. Botulphs), **4**, 19, 20, 22, 23, 24, 25, 27, 29, 30, 32, **33**, 37, **38**, 98, 99, **125**, 126 *note*, 127, **143**,* 183; the haven, 23 / **28**. *See* Chopchyre
Boulogne (Boloigne), 16
Bourne (Bronn, Bruu), *Linc*., 31 **6.7**
Bramburgh *See* Brandenburgh.
Brandenburg (Brambergh, Brandeburgh. Brondeburgh), 44, 69, 71,* 167, 170, 259. 274
Braunsberg (Brounesbergh, Bronesberg. Brownesburgh). 44, 69, 71, 93, 103, 113, * 167, 168, 170, 172, 259, 263
Breeknock (Brekenok), 1; Dominican friars at, 112
Breme (not identified), 248
Bridlington, 98, 117 **3.22**
Brie - Comte - Robert (Bricomte-Robert Vicomit R.), 253, 254, 262
Brod, near Prague (Preda, Proda), 191. 192, 260, 275, 292
Bronn *See* Bourne
Brounslowe. *See* Jungbunzlau.
Brück (Weste), on the Putzig Wiek, south of Putzig, 38
Bruu. *See* Bourne
Brünn (Broune), 193, 260, 275, 280
Buntingford, 28
Burgh, or Peterborough, 151, 155, 160
Burgundy, 246, 247, 249; "water boundary between, and Savoy, 247, lxix.

Caistor (Castre), 98, 99
Calais, 7, 8, 9, 10, 11, 12, 13, 14, 15, 16, 17, 18, 20, 28, 34, 35, 36, 37, 38, 118, 122, 123, 124, 125, 126, 127, 143, * 254, 255, 256, 257, 258, 279, xxvi.; indenture dated at, 1; Derby's house at, 7 **6**; The Lanterngate, 8; The Haven, 10, 12, 14, 15; le Ras, 14, 297; St Nicholas' light, 37. *See* Whitsand *and* Gravelines
Canterbury, 6, 7, 15, 28, 143, 255, 256, 276
Castelfranco (Chastelfrank), near Treviso, 238
Cavallino ? (Gauerley), on coast n. of the Lido, Venice, 209
Caxton, 28
Chalon-sur-Saone, 247, 249, 261, 276
Chambery (Chaumbery, Chambry), 245, 247, 276, lxxvii. *See* La Chambre
Champagne, 254
Chanceaux (Chauce, *error for* Chance) Côte d'Or, France, 246, 250, 254, 261
Charenton (Pount-Charcton), 254, 262
Charleston. *See* Karlstein
Chastelet, 192, 193. *See* Czaslau
Chat, Mount du, in Savoy, 276
Chatillon sur Seine (Chastelon), 254, 261
Chekirke (not identified), 194
Chichen (not identified), 260, lxxv.
Chivasso (Chevraux), 242, 263, 287, 288
Chyrhell (not identified), 275
Chopchyre, Chopcherye, Chopehire, Chopchyre, near Boston, 23, 24, 37, 38 299
Christburg (Kerseburgh), 105
Cividale (civitas hostr.' Gnydel ?), 260 **31**, 240 **30**, 310, lxxv.
Clot, le (not identified), 26
Coluwa on the upper Wilia r. (Colu.), 52
Conigliano, 263
Conyngsburg. *See* Königsberg
Copenhagen (Hanen), 97
Corfu (Curfu), 224, 234
Cormena = Coroni in Morea, 231
Cos, island of Greece. *See* Lango
Cremitten (Cremeton), 45, 50
Crowland, 29
Cyprus, lxv., across in, 278; cloth of, 35. *See* Bafas, Famagusta, Nikosia
Cysele ? Savile, 201
Czaslau (Chastelet), 192, 193, 260, 275

Dantzic (Dansk), 37, 38, 39, 40, 41, 42, 43, 44, 45, 49, 55, 56, 57, 60, 68, 72, 73, 74, 75, 76, 80, 81, 83, 84, 86, 87, 88, 89, 90, 94, 95, 97, 102, 103, 104, 105, 106, 108, 110, 111, 113, 114, 115, 116, 117, 130, 132, 143, * 149, 162, 163, 164, 165, 146, 167, 168, 171, 172, 173, 174, 175, 176, 177, 178, 179, 180, 182, 183, 184, 190, 191, 194, 201, 262, 263, 268, 274; *muncrius* or Bergh Episcopi, 72, **13**, 75 **5**, **23**, 78, 79, **15**, 80, 81, 83, 85, 86, 113, 88; Hofhaus at, 110; Burgesses of, 111; New Abbey, 164; house of Gottesknecht (Gotieskuawt), 73, 111; hostess at, 96; the haven, 97; Dominican friar, 111/**30**; Carmelites, 114; belchere given there, 259; oblations and alms there, 273, 274, xxxiii.
Danube river (Doncwe), 194
Darsowe. *See* Dirschau
Dartford (Derteford), Kent, 6, 8, 16, 30, 256
Daventry, 143
Deutschbrod (Denchebrede—brod), 192, 260
Dirschau (Darsowe), 71, 72, 113, **30** * 167, 168, 171, 259, 273, 274
Dover, 7, 9, 10, 11, 13, 15, 16, 31, 36, 37, 254, 256, 279; le Rood and haven, at, 15; Derby's lodging at, 15 **17**
Dramburg (Drawyngburgh), 185, 260
Driesen (Drysing), 193, 194, 260, 275
Drossekirke. *See* Traiskirchen
Drossen (Dresse), 186
Dunstable, 18, 33, 34, 99.

Egbell. *See* Aignebelle
Elbing (Melwyn,—wyn,—wyng,—vyng,—bing), 44, 70, 71, 103, 105, 110, 114, * 167, 168, 170, 171, 172, 173, 176, 178, 182, 183; Augustinian friars, 259; abbey 273; chapel of St. George, 274
England, 80, 83, 87, 97, 98, 100, 108, 110, 118, 122, 142, * 151, 162, 174, 180, 278, 279. Wages paid for services in 125, 126, 127, 143, * 264, 265, 266, 267, 272 *note*

Famagosta 226; castle in ? 230 **3**
Feldkirch (Felkirke, Fellekirke), 200, 260
Felowe. *See* Villach
Fennystratford. *Bucks*, 18
Flanders, cloth of, 157, 158

Floreyn, between Beaume and Chanceaux (not identified), 250, 261
Fontrouverte (Furneworth, Fornewht), in Savoy, 214, 261, lxxviii.
Fossdyke, 35 '**29**
Fownteney, Ain (not identified), 248, 261
France, senescallus, 14, 297; kingdom of, 15, 251, 258; king of, 8, 20, 34; pursuivants of, 107; a knight of 105; money of, 290
Frankfort-on-Oder (Frankforde,—forth), 187, 191, 260
Frieston (Freston) near Boston, 21, 24
Friesack (Fresak, Frisak, Husak), 199, 232, 260
Friuli (Friola), 150, 204, 211, 308, lix., lx , cii.

Ganerley. *See* Cavallino
Gecur (? identified), 203, lxxv.
Georgenburg (Jorgynburgh) castle, 31
Gernade, 95
Göding (Gedding), 193
Gofforth, 10
Görlitz (Gorlech), 188, 189, 190, 260, 263
Gravelines (Grauonyng), near Calais, 9, 11
Graunt Pauclon, near Troyes, now Pavillon, 252
Graund-Puits (Graunt Puisse), Seine-et-Marne, near Naugis, 253, 262
Guben (Gobin), 187, 195 **2**, 260
Guydel (? identified), 210

Haff, le Hoff, the Curische Haff on the coast of East Prussia, 53, 54, 106
Halybell. *See* Heiligenbeil
Hammerstein (Hamerstede), 184, 259
Hauen. *See* Copenhagen
Hencham (Hecham), 158, 159, 160, 163, 164, 263, xlviii
Heiligenbeil, Helebell, Halybell, Holypill), 167, 171, 259, 273
Heilsberg (Haylesbergh), 180
Helsingborg ? (Halyngburgh), castle of, 101
Hereford, 291, 292
Hertford, 13, 28, 29, 123, 291
Higham-Ferrers (Hegham), *Northants*, 291
Holbeach, 22
Holyed (not identified), 172

Holy Land, 291. *See* Jerusalem and St. Sepulchre
Horleston. *See* Arnoldstein
Horncastle (Horncastell), 99
Hull, Kingston-on-, 19, 35, 98, 99, 114, 117, 126 *note*, 143, * 162, 189
Humber, 28, 36, 99
Hungary, 34, 195
Huntingdon, 29, 30

Insterburg, 53, 54

Jaffa (Jaffe), 225, 226, 232
Jan. *See* Yenne
Jar. *See* Zara
Jerusalem, 210, 225, 226. *See* St. Sepulchre, and Index I.
Jorgynburgh. *See* Georgenburg
Judenburg (Jondenburgh, Rowdingburgh), 199, 260
Jungbunzlau (Brounslowe), 190, 260

Karlstein (Charleston), Prague, 275
Kenilworth (Kylyngworth, Kelyngworth), 17, 31, 33, 125, 127
Kennington, 28
Kerman in Persia, 28 *note*
Kerschurgh. *See* Christburg
Kettlethorpe, *Linc.*, 31
Kindberg (Kimber), 197, 260
Klagenfurt (Stamford), 292
Knittelfeld (Knettesfeld, Knotilfell), 198, 260
Königsberg (Conyngburgh), 40, 42, 43, 45, 46, 49, 53, 54, 55, 56, 57, 60, 66, 67, 68, 88, 89, 90, 91, 92, 93, 94, 101, 102, 103, 105, 106, 107, 108, 109, 110, 111, 112, 113, 114, 115, 116, 130, 132 * 149, 167, 168, 169, 170, 171, 172, 173, 174, 175, 178, 179, 183, 259, 271, 273, 274 ; Kenesburgh, Quenesburgh, Quenysburgh, 164, 166, also mean Königsberg; the Bishop's house, near the cathedral, 168, **34**; castle at, 169 **22**; St. George's church, 116 ,**14**; St. Antony's chapel, 109 , **4**
Kowno, alt (old), or Kawen, xxx, xxxvi., cix.

La Chambre in Savoy (Chambour, Chamboury, Chambourell), 245, 261, 278, lxxviii.
Landsberg (Loudesburgh, Londespere), 186, 260, 271

Lango or Cos (Langow), an isle near Rhodes, 230
Lanslebourg (Launcebrugge), 244, 261
Leba (Lebe), 38, 77, 273 8, wine of, 95
Lecheco (not identified, ? le chequer) 181
Leicester, 31 32, 98, 127 * 148, 149 292
Leipe (Lype), near Lippniken, north of the lake of Culm, 104
Lekniko (not identified), 109
Lio, Lido (Leo) island near Venice, 209, 211, lxxvi.
Leoben (Lowbon, Lonban), 197, 260
Lesina (Lissiner), 231
Lincoln, 27, 30, 31, 35, 126 *note*
Lira (Lyra) near Evreux in Normandy, cloth of, 89, 90, 91, 111, 281
Lissa (Lisca), island near Dalmatia. 224
Lissiner. *See* Lesina
Lithuania (Lettow, Lettowe), 52, 53, 55, 65, 89, 92, 143,
Livland (Nyneland), 105
Lodi (Ladde, Lauda, *Lauda an error*), 244, 276, 277
London, 5, 6, 7, 9, 13, 16, 17, 18, 19, 20, 28, 29, 31, 33, 34, 35, 36 *note*, 98, 122, 126, 127 * 153, 160, 257. Orwell house extra Bishopsgate, 35; treasurer there, about accounts, 143, 290, 291, 292; messenger to, 122
Louth, 100
Lullyngham, 11
Lombardy (Lumbary), 17
Lyna episcopi, 117
Lynn (Linne, Lean), 149, 151, 152, 153, 155, 156, 157, 158, 159, 160, 161, 162, 175, 270, 271, 273, 278, 294

Macon (Makon), 248, 249, 261
Malborghet (Malberget, Malburget), 200, 204, 260, 275
Malvasier (Maluesye), 205, 206, 222
Marienburg (Marvnghurgh, Marnehurgh), 40, 71, 72, 95; physician of, 110; chapel of St. Anne at the castle there, 116 22, 336
Markerle. *See* Neumark
Marigny (Marine), Aube, 252, 253, 264
Melton Mowbray, 30, 31, 98
Melnyn. *See* Elbing
Melun in France (Melan), 251
Memel, river, 48, 54, 53, 105
Meneyllambard, Maynilarbard (? Mont-

bart, Côte d'or), near Chatillon s. Seine, 254, 261
Mestre (Meistre), 237, 238, 240, 285
Mesernsch, Gross (Mederess, Misserich), 192
Milan (Melane, Mediolanus), 241, 242, 254, 287, 288, ciii., civ.
Molhom? same as Modon, 277, 278
Modon, town on S.W. Cape of Greece, 224, 230, 278, lxviii
Montbart. *See* Meneyllambard.
Motta (Mote), on the Livenza, between Portogruaro and Ponte di Piave, 203
Mount (Mownd) le, near Dantzic, 162, 176, 181. *See* Weichselmünde and Münde
Münde (Mende), mouth of the Vistula, 86, 394
Mürzzuschlag (Mersolach and ? Slomrestowe), 197, 260, 260, 275

Neumarkt (Newmark), north of Friesack, 202
Neumark (le Marke), 184, 187, xcix.
Neunkirchen (Newekirke), 195, 260
Newark, 31
Newington, 16
Newington-juxta-Sittingbourne, 256
Niemes (Nemance) in Bohemia, 189, 260
Nikosia in Cyprus (Nikasye, Niksy), 226, 229
Norkitten (Nenerketon), 50
Noale (Norwall, Nowall), near Mestre, 241, 261
Nogent-sur-Seine (Nongent), 3, 261
Norway (Norwey), 161, 162
Nyneland. *See* Livland.

Ochen, near Portogruaro (not identified), 220
Osey, wine of, 12, 95
Ospringe, 6, 16, 276
Ostremark, 78

Palma (Padowe), 240, 278
Palestine, 262. *See* St. Sepulchre
Paris (Paryse, Parys), 8, 93, 247, 254, 257, 287
Pavia (Pany, Papya, Panys), 241, 263, 277, 288
Pavillon (Graunt Parelonn), Aube, 252
Penseldorf, *in Italica* Venzone (Peselthorpe, Posidolfe, Posithorpe), 201, 203, 260, lxxiv.
Peterborough, 2, 29, 30, 143, * 118, 152,

INDEX II. 331

162, 180, 254, 270, 271, 291, lxxxiv.
  See Burgh
Piemont (Pymond), 241, 258
Pola, in Istria, 232
Poland, 108, **3**, 111, 139
Po'eschken (Polessine, Polyrchene) near
  Pelzin, 184, 259
Pontafel, 203
Pont d'Ain, ? (Pompinet', 247, 261
Ponte di Piave ? (Pontegla), 203
Portlown. *See* Prodolone
Portogruaro (Portgrwer), 150, 204, 206,
  207, 208, 209, 210, 211, 219, 220, 221,
  236, 263, 292
Posidolfe, Posilthorpe, Peselthorpe. *See*
  Pensseldorf
Pountcharcton. *See* Charenton
Prague (Prake) 54, 69, * 180, 190, 191,
  194, 260, 262, 279, 280, castle 274
Preda, Proda. *See* Brol
Prodolone or Pordenone ? (Portlown),
  north of Portogruaro, 210
Provins (Province), 262
Prussia, (Pruscia, Prusye), 1, 2, 3, 4, 5,
  27, 35, 36, 38, 40, 87, 88, 89, 93, 95,
  98, 102, 104, 105, 109, 111, 115, 118,
  142, 143, * 145, 147, 148, 149, 151,
  161, 163, 164, 184, 257, 278, 279
Pulcrich (not identified) ? in Lincolnshire, 30 **1. 21**
Putzig (Pusk, Putsk), 38, 39, 40, *
  174

Quenesburgh. *See* Königsberg

Ragnit (Reynet.—neth,—nete) 53, 67,
  94, 105
Ragusa, 231, 278
Ramleh (Rames) in Judea, 225, 226
Rheims (Reymes), 152, 172
Rhodes, (Rodes), 224, 225, 258, 275,
  276 ; castle there 227, 229, 277, 278,
  283 ; money, ciii.
Rivoli ? (Ryuois, Ryweles), near Turin,
  247, 261
Rixhöft (le Ross benid, Rooshed), 38
Roston (Rooston), ? Derbyshire 30, **4,
  26, 31**
Rochester 6, 98, 256
Rossillon (Rosselyon, Russebou), Aube
  246, 261

Sacile ? (Cysele, Gisill), 201, 260
Samland, 109, 305
Sandwich, 37

Saône r. ? 247 **4**
Savoy (Saboldin, Soboldia), 247
Schievelbein (Scheuelbene, Schenebene,
  Schvnelben), 180, 185, 189, 190, 259
Schönberg (Schonebergh), 44, 45
Schonen (Scon), chief seat of herring
  fishery and trade, 47
Schöneck (Seonec, Sconchow), 172, 180,
  183, 259, 263, 274
Schönkirchen (Sconckirke), 193, 260
Scotland, knight of, 111
Siron, error for Viron, *i.e.* Verona, 288
Sittingbourne (Sytyngburne), 98, 255, 256
Sleaford, 30
Slomrestowe ? = Mürzzuschlag, 260 (*cf.*
  197)
Southam, Warwickshire, 18, 33
Spalding, 29, 118
Spilimbergo (Spillingberk), 203
St. Alban's (Seint Albon), 18, 33
St. Antony, chapel of, in Königsberg,
  109
St. Daniele, near Spilimbergo, 220, 260
St. Michael, south-west of Leoben, 198
St. Michel (Michael), Savoy, 245, 261,
  276
St. Rambert (Sarombert, Syrombert),
  Ain, 217, 261
St. Sepulchre at Jerusalem, 143 * 145,
  148, 150, 233, 278
St. Vito (Seintfete), 202
Stamford. *See* Klagenfurt
Stolpe (Stulpez), 179
Stralsund (le Sonde), 97, xxvii.
Stratford, 33
Susa (Sebusa), 243, 244, 246, 261, 276
Sutton, 12, 20

Tapiau (Tapiou,—io,—cowe,—iewe), 50,
  53, 54, 108
Thorn (Torne, Toren), 64, 66, 67, 68,
  74, 85, 96
Thornton, abbey of, 98, 304
Tournus (Tranes, *error for* Tranes,
  Turnays) near Macon, 249, 261
Towcester, 18, 33
Traiskirchen (Arskirke, Drossekirke),
  south of Vienna, 196, 260
Trappöhnen, xxix., cvii.
Treviso (Trevise, Trevyse) 203, 208
  211, 219, 236, 237, 238, 239, 240, 241,
  263, 277, 283, 285, 287, 288 ; friars at,
  246 **26**
Tritel, or Gross Triebel (Trebull, Tre-

bod) near the Silesian frontier of Brandenburg, 188, 189, 260
Troyes (Troys) in Champagne, Aube, 247, 252, 254, 261; St. Anthony in, 276, 342
Turin (Toryn), 242, 264, 276; St. Anthony at, 277

Velayn. *See* Avigliano
Venice, 150, 201, 202, 205, 207, 208, 209, 210, 211, 212, 218, 219, 220, 221, 223, 224, 231, 233, 234, 236, 237, 238, 239, 240, 258, 259, 278, 279, 280, 281, 283, 284, 285, 286, 287, 288, 289; the Rialto (le Ryoll) 222; duke of, 276, 277; St. Mark's 234, 275 *bis*, 277; St. Lucia, in or near Venice, 211, 275; St. Nicolo, on the Lido? (St. Nicholas), 219, 220, 222, 223, 275; St. George, island near Venice, 208, 211, 219, 220, 223, 234, 235, 236, 238, 276, 277; churches? in Venice, St. Agnes, St. Antony, St. Ellen, 275; St. Christofer, Innocents, 276; St. Lawrence, 277, lviii.-lxiii., lxvii., cii.
Venzone. *See* Peusseldorf
Vercelli, 242
Verona (Virona, *erroneously printed* Siron), 288 **8**
Vicenza (Vycens, Wycenca), 240, 276, 287
Vienna (Wene), 150, 194, 195, 201, 204, 260, 262, 275, 281, 285
Villach (Fillak, Felowe, Fillawk), 200, 202, 260, 275
Vistula, river (Wysle, Wissell), 41, 88, 97, 113, * 168

Walsingham, 160

Warwick, 28
Watton (Whatton), 98
Wash, the, 28, 35
Weichselmünde? (Mende, le Mount), 86, 162, 176, 181 [Prutz]. *See also* Münde
Weisskirchen (Wiskirke) in Moravia, 193
Weisswasser (Whytwater), 189, 194, 260
Weste. *See* Brück
Westminster, 18
Westphalia (Westvall), cloth of, 35 * 152, 168
Westvall. *See* Westphalia
Whithall (not identified)), 20, 239
Whytwater. *See* Weisswasser
Wilderness, *i.e.* forest between Insterburg and Ragnit, 49, 50, 53, xxix.
Wileny, formerly Willum or Welun (Wyllenghe), 106
Wilna (le Welle, Wylle), 51, 53, 54, 105; castle of, 105, 106, xxx.
Wismar (Wyshmer, Wyschemere), 57, 84, 95, 153
Wissant (Whitsand), 7, 8, 12, xxvi.
Woodstock, 36 *note*
Writtle, 28
Wyshmer. *See* Wismar
Wyslee. *See* Vistula

Yenne (Jan, Yan), Savoy, 245, 246, 248, 261
York (Eboracum), 162

Zara (Jar) in Dalmatia, 234 / **18**, 277
Zebrak, Czech for Bettlern in Bohemia
Zittau (Zitaw), 188, 189, 260, 263, 274

INDEX III.—GLOSSARIAL.

I must express my gratitude to MR. HENRY BRADLEY for his kind assistance with many glosses.

[Books referred to in short: "Inventories and Accounts of Finchale Priory," Surtees Soc., 1837; Theo. Hirsch, "Danzigs Handels-und Gewerbs-geschichte," Leipzig, 1817; W. Heyd, "Histoire du Commerce du Levant au Moyen-âge" (tr. from Germ.), Leipzig, 1886; "Collection of Household Ordinances," including Liber Niger of Edward IV, Ordinances of the Duke of Clarence, &c., Society of Antiquaries, 1790; "The Babees Boke," including The Boke of Curtasye, &c., ed. F. J. Furnivall, Early Eng. T. Soc., 1868; Alex. Henderson's "History of Ancient and Modern Wines," 1824. F. Kluge's "Etymological Dictionary of German," 1891; H. Bradley's edition of Stratmann's "Middle English Dictionary," 1891; "Promptorium Parvulorum," ed. A. Way (Camden Soc.); "The New English Dictionary;" and the dictionaries of Halliwell, Jamieson, Ducange, Godefroi, and Cotgrave.]

Abbreviamentum rolls, 102, 103, enrollments of the items of daily expense, or *dictæ*
Acetum, vinegar, 234
Acucio, sharpening, 219
Accounts.—
In the keeping of accounts three words meet us: *dicta* (102 **23**, 103 **6**, 258 **20**) was the daily petty expenditure and consumption of stores by each officer of the household, his day-book; *parcella*, which is distinct, seems to be the bill for any general or particular purchase, expenditure in gross, &c. ("billa de papiro," p. 6 **6**), but whether made out by the purchaser or the vendor I do not find; I suspect the purchaser. The *abbrevement* rolls seem to have been made out from the *dictæ* alone; the expenses of a day, shortly given under the head of each

Accounts—*continued*.
office, being grouped, day thus following day on the roll. Such a roll is Add. MS. 23,938, the expenses of Margaret of Anjou on coming to England in 1444-5. In the Northumberland Household Book (A.D. 1512) the "clerk of brevements" is to be daily at the "brevynge," and it is required that all the officers have "breved," *i.e.* taken in their accounts to be entered and checked (pp. 59, 60). "The clerke of ye cochyn shalle alle pyng breve," Boke of Curtasye (A.D. 1460) in Babees Boke, p. 317. See also Liber Niger, Edw. IV., p. 71. In our accounts Reginald Curteys and Burton performed this clerkship (102 **24**, 103 **27**) while in Prussia; and when Kyngston made up his full accounts these abbrevements and parcellæ or

334 INDEX III.

Accounts—*continued.*
  bills were part of his vouchers (102 **25**, 103 **6, 30**, 104 **5. 9**, 143, 258, 294.
  An agreement was sometimes made beforehand for the price of services (*see* Conventio), and payment was frequently made "per compotum factum," which appears to show that a written statement or account had been given (13, 35)
Alblastes stryngcs, 74, strings for a cross-bow; an alblast made, 93
Ale 7, 10, 12, 29, &c.
Allecium, allec, herring. 12, 14, &c.
Alleum, garlic, 69 **30**, 216 **27**, 218 **26**, 221
Almonds. *See* Spices
Allocacio, allowance, 143, 290, 291
Alms to the poor, 17, 27, 31; baskets and baskets for, 74; at Finchale, Yorkshire, in 1397 was a "skepe pro elemosyna," "to hold the broken meat intended for the poor." (Inventories of Finchale Priory, Surtees Soc., pp. cxviii, ccccxlvii). *See* before, p. xciii, *note*.
Alms in money, 116, 117, 273-278; in clothes. *See* Poor.
Altar in a ship, 26; table or board for, 49 **19**
Alumglas, alum, 64. New Eng Dict.
Amphoras of wine, 222
Amygdali, almonds, 21
Amydon, starch, 100 **9**
Ankers, 40
Ankerissa, a hermitess, 273
Anneys. *See* Spices
Anulus a gramauland, 28, probably a turquoise ring
Aper, a wild boar, 62 **29**, 153
Appenticium, a pent-roof, 63
Aqua ardens, a spirit? eau de vie, 60
Aqua zugurata, 225
Arblast, 283 **25**, a cross-bow. *See* Alblast
Armaria, place to put armour in, 180
Armatura, armour, 11 **27**, 43 **27**, 45, 175. On pp. 280 **32**, 283 **6**, the armouter is meant
Armilausa, a military under-vest, 181 **21**
Armour—
  gloves of plate, 173 **1**
  pusayne or gorget, 172 **32**
  hotell? = botelli = boots or hose of steel, 176 **7**

Armour—*continued.*
  basenett, 49, 91
  mailes, plates, 46 **16**
  lorica, or coat of mail, 74 **5**, 280 **24**, 288 **9**; harness of maill, 155
  toprnet and basinet. 91
  brake. bras, braas, 92 **19, 26**, a guard for the arm rest. 92
  haberion, habergeon, or breast-plate, 171, 283
  vambras, pair of, 280 **4**, 281 **1**, Fr. *avant bras*, the part which guards the arm from elbow to wrist
Armourerius, armorer, 45
Arms in heraldry, painted on wooden shields or scutcheons for hanging in houses, — clipens, tabella or tabula, 93 **19, 20**, 202 **33**, 227, 234 **21**, 279 **28**, 283, 286; scutum armorum, 107 **28**, 108 **21**. 110 **8**, p. lxxxiii.; painted by the herald, 190, 280, 286; painted on paper scutcheons, 279 **29**, 280 **13**, 285 **16**, 287 **31**
Arrows, sheaves of, 154
Aschelers for fuel, 181 **14**, 182 **31**, seem to be either (*a*) hewn timber cut into lengths or, (*b*) the odd remnants of a carpenter's shop: *cf.* senses in New Eng. Dict.
Asses hired at Jaffa, 225; at Rama, 226
Auca, a goose, 9 **20**, 11, 162
Avenae, oats: farina avenarum, oatmeal; *pura avena*, 255 **29**
Aula, tapestry, 18 **27**, 34 **11**, 154, a kind of stained hanging for the hall, being sold by the "steynour"; green cord for the aula, 19 **3**; hooks for hanging it, 25 **10**, 75 **21**
Aula domini at Boston, 25
Aula et camera, the lord's hall and bed-chamber, office of, 6, 13, 16; various articles for, viz. a lock, 58; linen 61, mappae, 166 (*see* Textiles); reeds, 63, 67, 85, 171; cupboard, 64; dinner-tables, 63 **22-25**, 75; beds, 206 **25**; carpet, 281 **13**; matts, 164; brass basin, 153 **6**; on board ship, 87 **25**, 153 **23**; litter for, 156 **21**, 161. *See* Ships, s. of the lord's hall
Aune, an ell, cloth measure
Anne, (? **2**, a cask, 3½ aunes = 1 pipe, German wine measure; mod. ahm of awne. *See* Measures
Axes, 18 **28**, 52, 58, 161 **5**, 224, 235

INDEX III. 335

Backgammon. *See* Games.
Bacon flitches, 21, 42, 155. *See* Brawn.
Bacons, 42, 52, 96, 160, 166, 204, 212, 214, 245, 247, &c.
Baggez, bags for spices, 173 **14**; for money, 174 **7**; leather, for silver cups, 187
Bailiff of Dantzig, 104
Bakers, 45, 222
Balance with weights for weighing spices, 65; pare balaunces, 152, 153 **26**, 222
Baldekin. *See* Textiles
Bale, a bundle, 154
Baleys, 287 **25**, a balais ruby, from Arab *balakh*, short for Balakhchan, a province on the upper Oxus and Jaxarte where rubies are found. Heyd, vol. ii. p. 654
Balinger, 279, a sea-going vessel; O. Fr. *baleinier*, a whale-ship.
Balista, 94, ancient ordnance for casting stones.
Ballid, 5 **23**, bald, horse marked with white
Bar of a buttery, 239 **8**
Barber lets blood, 10 **19**; of the King at Kennington, 28
Barga, a barge, 206 **20. 24**
Bargeman, 209, 219 **19**
Barhide, or bare-hide, *i.e.* without the hair, ? undressed leather, 5, 154, 242 **8**. Thomas Grafton who sold them was a male-maker (maker of trunks or leather-bags), 313; *query* was the barhide simply used as a tarpaulin. In 1611 Florio speaks of " a great hide to cover cartes, in court we call them beare-hides" (New Eng. Dict.), this appears to be the case on 178 **33**; on p. 154 they may be to cover the loads of the five sumpter-horses, *cf.* "sella pro cariacione cum barhyde," apparently as saddle-cloth. " Finchale Accts.," pp. clviii. ccccxix.
Bark, a boat, 81 **7**; at Venice, 208, 209
Barley for poultry, 47, 83
Barrels of whale 19, vinegar 22, beer 44, sturgeon 42, salt meat 42; for biscuit 41, flour 23, fat or lard 22, herring 77; empty for water, meat, &c., 22, 23, 48, 156, 233, &c.; locks, hasps, and hinges for these 25
Barrel-ferrers. *See* Ferrers

Barrel-heads, 41 **32**
Basenettum, bacinet, a light helmet, 49 **22**, 91
Basins, 153 **6. 24**
Basket, 86 **21**. *See* Skep *and* Lepe
Batella, a boat, 41 **27**, 54, 151 **26**, 208, 257
Batell. de steell, pair of, 176 **7**? an error for botell, thus a pair of steel boots or leg coverings; *botellus* = *bota*, *verea*, hose or boots (Ducange)
Batillagium, boatage, 7, 13, 15, 21, 36, 79, 178, 181 **15**, 194
Battle of Alt-Kawen, 51 **13**
Batella, a boat, 41 **27**, 54, 151 **26**, 208, 257
Bayte, baytyng, bait, feed of man or horse when on the road, 11 **26**, 16 **5**, 23, 18, 28, 98, 167
Beans for potage, 25, 31 **33**, 32
Beaver, tails to eat, 47 **24**; fur, 91 **9**: cap, 49 **30**; pilch, 91 **21**; jupe, 93 **27**
Beds of straw, 72 **31**
Bed, hung in the ship for Derby, 26 **18**, 76 **23**; cord for, 81 **8**; hooks for, 92; at Portogruaro, 206 **25**, 210; for a henksman, 230; of carpet, 281 **14**; in the galley, 281 **25**
Beer, bere, 39, 42, 47, 165, &c.; Wismar beer, 57, 81 **14**, 95, 153; English, 85: Dantzic, 95, bona, *i.e.* good beer, 181 **7**
Belechere, a present or fee given to the host, hostess, or servants of a hospice or lodging, *bela cara* or *pourboire*, 41 **20**, 44 **18** & **29**, 46 **11**, 50, 53, 69, 70, 71,259-262. Fr. *belle chier*, good cheer, pleasant countenance; degenerated into *belly cheer*. *See* New Eng. Dict.
Beler, a billet of wood, 153 **1**, 161
Bendes, bands or hoops, 86 **20**
Bere, beer
Besage, 42, Fr. *besace* or *bessache*, a double wallet or pair of saddle bags
Besoms, 206, 212, 235
Beste, beast, 91
Beting (beating) of stock fish, 155
Beuer, beaver
Beueragium, 110 **10**, drink money on striking a bargain
Billets (of wood), 7 **32**, 9 **32**, 12
Blanket, 8 **23**, 89, 90

Blaundrel, a kind of apple, 10 **10**;
blaundell, 11 **15**. Lib. Nig. Edw. IV.,
p. 82
Bholens, 34, 90. O. Fr. *bloi*, a kind of
blue or slate colour, blue-grey. *See*
Textiles
Boar, 62 **29**, 66 **2**
Boatage. *See* Batillaginm
Bokeram, 152, buckram
Bokete, bucket, 61, 73, 74, 86; for
victuals on the way, 189; for alms,
183 **6**, xciii, *note*
Bolls, bowls, 64, 73, 86, 224; bolle
coveres, 156 **11**
Bolting. *See* Bulting
Boot, bot, a boat, 19, 26; repair of,
26; Botesmen, 104
Body, 32 **19**
Botels de tyn, 49 **26**, tin bottles; de
Anglia, 72; stopell for, 72 **18**, 234;
fer croees, 74 **32**; pottle bottles, 154
Botening, 288 **8**, used with a coat of
mail, ? buttoning
Bow given by Derby to his father, 31
Bows and arrows bought, 34, 154;
broad, 34 **16**, **18**
Bowges, pair of, 16 **18**, protection for
the legs, ? of stuffed leather, like
modern cricketers' leggings, bowge
signifying bulged or raised work. "A
iether coofer maker or a bouge maker,"
Palsgrave.
Boyste, Fr. a box, 225 **11**
Brace, there seem to be three senses:
braas, brake, 92 **19**, **26**, 164 **32**, that
part of armour which covers the arms
(or is it the *bracer* used to guard the
arm in archery, Fairholt?); bracei,
breeches or drawers (in note on cloth
of Reynes, *see* Textiles; brasse, braas,
46 **26**, 94, part of a horse's harness.
See Bras
Bras, braces, a brasse, cloth measure of six
feet, Ital. *braccio*, 208, 234, 287 **11**
Brass pots and cauldrons, 102, 177
Brauderere, an embroiderer, 90
Brawn, shoulders of, i.e. of pig, 169 **29**
Bread, white, 12, 29, 15, 17, 78, 159, 165,
&c.; fresh, 223 **6**, 225 **9**
horse-bread. *See* Horse
pastry, 12 **17**
byspuyte, 17, 222. *See* Byspuyte
loaves for trenchers, 218 **30**. *See*
Trenchers
cost of baking, 222

Breakfast or lunch (officers *prandentes*)
on the ship preparing to sail, 77, **5**
Breen, 10, bran
Brevement, from abbreviare, to note down
in writing. *See* Accounts
Bridge for horses ? to walk on board
ship, 177, **8**
Broches, spits, 18 **30**, 162 **12**, 212 **22**;
broche rakks, spit racks, 243 **18**
Broylours, gridirons, 233
Bullokes, bullocks, 51, 52
Bulting or sifting of flour, 21 **8**, 156;
strainers for, 25 **11**; bulters, 156, bul-
tyng-cloths, 21 **11**, 80; boltyng house,
25, 80; bultynge-tonne, a large tub
into which the flour was sifted, 75
Burrew, 13 **27**, *borche*, the baer of a
lance, a projecting circular ring that
protected the hand, "Promp. Parv." p.
56. Here perhaps another form of
barghum, a dialectal word of many
forms, meaning a collar of a working
horse. New Eng. Dict.
Bursa, a purse or small bag, 284 **21**
Busca, firewood, 6, 12, 28, 33, 38, 177,
185
Busta, box, 5 **15**, boyste, 225 **11**
Butcher, 223 **19**
Butter, 8 **14**, 9 **21**, 11, 15, 25, 31, 97, 100
162, 213, 244; cask of, for the Reysa,
18 **21**; by the stone, 25; by the cista,
64 **10**; by the dolium, 97 **21**
Buttery, office for wine and beer, 15;
gate of, 57
Buttery sumpter-horse, 10 **13**; buttery
chest, 64 **10**; bar of buttery, 239 **8**
Bykeres, beakers, cups, 49, 57, 58, 61, 70,
80, 168, 174, 195
Byspuyte, panis vocatus b., biscuit, 11
29, 17, 32. This was put in barrels
for the Reysa. Baked for the galley,
222

Cabans, cabins, in the Venetian galley.
See Galley; to be made in the ship's
hull at Boston, 20 **7**, made with
canvas, 21 **8**, 157, and waynscot, 26 **5**,
76, 157; in the vessel between Dover
and Calais, 36, in the vessel at Dantzig, 76; materials for, in the vessel at
Lynn, being cabins for hall and
chamber, chapel, kitchen, &c., 157;
for horses, 158; for different knights
and officers, 158; for the wardrobe in
vessel returning to England, Sept.,

Cabans—*continued*.
1392, 177, **32**; lamp to hang in, 281, **18**
Cabul, a cable, thick rope. 48
Cacabus, a cauldron, 209 **6**
Cade, a cask or barrel, 233 ; of wine or herrings. 161 ; for water, 208 **22**
Caffetin, applied to loaf sugar. *See* Sugar.
Cages for hens, 25, 97,; hung up, 26 **3**; 48 **7**, **16**; for falcons, 91, 93; for the popingay, 286 **28**, 287 **2**
Caligæ, hose, gaiters, 89, 280, &c.
Calix, chalice ? for the Sacrament, 92 **29**
Calx, lime either of chalk or other metal, here used in the buttery, 64, **14**. New Eng. Dict.
Cambicio, exchange, 202
Caminus, a fireplace. 211 **15**
Canabum, canvas, 34
Candles. *See* Tallow and Wax
Candelabrum, 64
Canella, cinamon, 11 **20**, 79
Canellus, a small cane or tube for drawing wine. 208 **24**
Cannevas, canvas, 6 **26**, 10, 20, 21, 24 **14**, 35, &c
Capicinm. *See* Clothing
Caprella, a she-goat. 244 **15**
Careoisium, 32, a carcase, beef or mutton, whole
Carecta, a cart, 43, 173, 254, &c.; repaired while travelling, 185 **22**, 187 ; tar for the wheels, 186 **18**; fat or grease for, 189 **30**, 202
Carectarius, a carter, 43, 49, 51, 68, 98, 172, 173, 201 ; drink for, 203 **28**
Carmon, a carman, 175 **12**, 186 **18**
Carpenter's work, in a larder, 22 **25**; in a kitchen, &c., at Königsberg, 63, 64 ; tables made at Dantzic, 75, and stools, 75 **19**; in a house, 173 **20**, 228 ; in a stable, 205 **30**; at Venice, 234 ; at Treviso, 239 ; for wardrobe in a ship, 177. *See* Cabins *and* Ships
Carriage in Prussia, regulated by the marshal's officers, cost of, by land, 54 ; by water, 55-57
Caruca, a carriage, hung and covered, according to Ducange. But the 7 *carucæ nouæ* bought for the Reysa, 41 **8**, **13**, were probably forage waggons. *See* p. xxviii. *note*

Casks, empty, 57 **26**, 160, 161 ; fattes, wynfattes, 74 ; watertonnes, 74. *See* Barrel, Cade, Dolium
Castor, castrones, wethers, sheep, 206 **11**
Casula mesal, 34 **17**, a case for packing the broad-arrows in, but the meaning of the word is not clear; *casula missalis* was a mass-chasuble
Cauldrons, 18, 22, 102
Caundres, sanders. *See* Spices.
Celarium, cellar, 42 **33**, 63 **28**, 168, 213; seler, 72 **22**
Celarius, cellarius, saddler, 43 **33**, 94
Celeragium, cellarage, 162
Cella=sella, a saddle, 7, 31
Cementarius, a cementer, a mason, 169 **23**. *See* "York Plays," p. xxi. *note*.
Cenape, 16, sinape, 49, mustard
Cene, die, Holy Thursday, 116, 117
Centena, a sale hundred, as of eggs, &c., 84 **6**, 155, 157 **29**
Cepum, tallow, 6 **17**, 15 **20**, 27 **25**, &c.
Cera *for* sera, a bolt or lock, 64 **10**, 72, 75, 79
Cerica, ceresa, *for* serica, silk, 280 **22**, 288 **2**
Ceroteca, glove for the falcon, 287 **10**
Ceruca, a cord or rope for a sail, 281 **21**
Cerrura *for* serrura, a lock, 24, 93
Chalkyng furs, 93 **3**
Chapelet, a jewelled circlet, a wreath, 284 **8**. *See* Clothing
Chapel on board ship, 157; painted boards for, 178. *See* Altar
Char, chares, a sort of carriage, 255 **32**, 256
Chare de coyns, quince conserve (*chair, flesh*), 19 **5**
Chargeor, a charger or large dish, 100
Chasteins, chestnuts, 223 **26**
Chaundler Whytlok, his cloth sack to pack his things in, 78 **16**
Chaundry, office for lights, tallow, and wax, coffers for, 233 **25**
Chausour, 284 **8**, chaussure, breeches or trousers
Chausseralde, a pair of, bought at Paris, 287, sort of high boots. *See* Clothing
Chawfour, chafing pan to warm the hands, 87 **5**
Cheese, 25 **18**, 39, 48, 206 **28**, 245, 252, &c.
Chelynges, keeling or cod-fish, 153 **18**
Cherries, 29 **17**, ceresis, zeresis, 254, 256. *See* Fruit.

338 INDEX III.

Chesell, 35, chisel, instrument for cutting, possibly scissors
Chess, 49 **19**, 281 **9**
Chevens, cheveyns, chub or pollard. *See* Fish
Chernes, chains, 22, 76. 161, 227; of silver gilt, 104; of gold, 108 **10**
Ciphus, a cup, 6 **4**, 17 **25**, 224 **10**
Cirpus, sirpus (*for* scirpus), a rush or reed, 63, 67, 153, 257
Cista, a chest, 177. *See* Kist
Clare-bagges, probably bags for clarifying jelly or other cookery, 65 **26**
Cleansing, the larder, 24, 235; Derby's lodging at Boston, 25; the pantry at Dantzie, 72; barrels 156 **9**, 162 **28**
Clerks assisting the treasurer, 102 **24**, 103 **27**, 292 **25**
Clipeus, a shield in heraldry, 93, 292
Clock, carried in a basket from London to Bolingbroke, 19, 20
Cloos boketes, seem to be closed buckets, as they were provided with hasps, 86 **20**
Cloth of various kinds, linen and woollen, *pannus*. *See* Textile Fabrics
Clothing, various, bought by the Wardrobe office, 88-91, 279-288, money for, given at New Year, 112. *See* Furs, Textile, *and* Wardrobe
  rayed coats (*stragula*) 89
  petticoat (*jupa*), 91 **26**, 280, 283, 285; black, furred, for Derby, 91; of beaver, 93 **27**
  pilche, peltice, skin-coat or gown, 91, 93, 112, 280 **15**
  Jakkes, jacks or jackets, 106 **14**, generally used for defence. "Prompt. Parv."
  doublet, a lined or wadded garment, 92 **11**, 177 **25**
  sackes of fustyon for the six minstrels, a sort of upper garment or surtout, 112 **15**
  sclaveyn, pilgrim's gown, 230 **8**
  gowns for the henchmen, &c., 280 **3**. *See* Gowns
  hompeloud, 285 **20**. *See* Hompelond
  armilausa, 181 **21**, a military undervest
  mantica, a short mantle, 282, 284 **3**
  capicinm, 91 **17**, **32**, 280 **29**, a capuchon or hood
  capella, 287 **21**, a short cape or mantle

Clothing—*continued*.
  shirts, hose, and shoes, 89 **19**, 91, 92, 230 **9**
  chaussour or breeches, 281 **8**
  chaussemble, 287
  legging or boot (*ocrea*), 32 **19**, 164, 168 **8**
  pair pynsons, furred, 91 **14**, high unsoled shoes or rather leggings. "Prompt Parv."
  shoes (*sotulares*), 89, 90, 91, 164, 239, 279, 280, 286, 287
  boots furred with blanket, 280 **17**. The cordewaner made "boteux, sotulares, pynsons, chaussembles de baleyne, chaussembles bottes, galoches, ocreas." D. of L., cl. 28, bdle. 1, No. 5.
  hose or gaiters (*caligæ*), 280 **19**, 284, of green cloth, 284 **13**, 285 **31**, 287. In 1397-8 Henry had both scarlet and white *caligæ*: 4 pair took 3 yards of scarlet, 2 pairs took 1¼ yards white cloth, D. of L., cl. 28, bdle. 1, No. 5
  zone or belt, 91, 163 **25**, 281, 287; sinctura, 279, 283, a girdle. *See* Sinctura
  fourteen collars, 280 **7**; twelve collars, 286. *See* Silver
  coyfe or cap, 280 **31**
  chapelet, 284 **8**, a jewelled circlet or a wreath of flowers, here probably the former. It is depicted in MS. Roy. 20 B. 6 fo. 2, contemporary with our accounts
  hats, red and black, 284 **24**, 285 **15**. *See* Beaver
  gloves (*siroteces*) 92 **34**. *See* Ceroteca, webbe de kerches, a piece of material for kerchiefs, 91 **31**
Cloth-sak, 19, 78 **16**, 154, 174, 285, a sack or bag of worsted cloth, bought at the male-maker (trunk-m.) to pack clothes in. "Pro robis domini trussandis in clothsakkes, x ulnæ Westnall griseti;" "clothsakkes et mantice" (portmanteaus or leather wallets). D. of L., cl. 28, bdle 1, No. 5.
Coal, 185, 211, 219, in sacks, 9 **30**, 14 **3**; sold by the bushel, 15 **30**; by the father, 59, 62, 66, 84; by the cart, 59/ **3**, **8**; by the quarter, 153; by the last, 72, 76, 171, 180; by the tonel, 78

INDEX III.   339

Cobarde, 102 **10**, a rack or iron bar connected with the spit. It probably was the same as the cob-iron, though not yet proved so (New Eng. Dict.). Some of the college kitchens at Oxford still show the mediæval kitchen machinery. Two upright iron racks stand on either side of the fire-place; these were jacks; the branches of these supported long iron bars—the cobards—from which hung the spits, great or small, over the fire.
Coclear, a spoon for the table, 100
Cofre, a box or trunk for treasure, 41, 152; pairs of, 5 **8**, 19 **1**; for a shield, 91; for kitchen use 152, and scullery, 179
Coleria, a collar, 107 **26**, 112, 240, 280, **7**, 283
Commissariat on the Reysa, found by Andrew Strowsburg and other Prussians, 50, 51, 52
Compotus, an account, 13, 35
Comyne, cummin, 64
Conductio, hire, 13 **2**, 31 **28**, 98 **11**
Congrus, a conger eel, 16 **27**, 18
Conke, 64 **33**, 68 **10**, a vessel used in the bake-house
Contours, counters for reckoning accounts, 5 **15**, 257 **4**, **26**
Consuetura, sewing together, 170 **9**
Convencio, agreement as to payment, 43, 75, 172 **28**
Cooper's work, 155, 160; at Boston, 22; at Dantzig for the Reysa, 49
Cooperare, to cover, 40
Coperos, copperas, 64 **6**
Coquina, kitchen
Cords, 86, 158; for drawing water, 13; for packing, 35
Corf, 72 **17**; of figs and raisins, 79
Corkes, pair of, cork slippers or soles, 91 **19**
Corn bought and prepared for voyages, 21, 25, 80, 156, 157; bulting and paring of, 156 **6**. See Bolting.
Corner, 159 **9**, ink-horn.
Corphe, 58 **23**, corf or basket, here used for bread. See Jamieson
Cornis, 208 **23** ? baskets
Cotom, coton, cotton, 75, 87, 90, 92, 172, 179, 180, 281. "2 lb de filo cotonis," A.D. 1299, Wardrobe Accts of Edw. I., p. 144; "vj lb. de coton pro stuffura vestimentorum domini," and was used

Cotom—*continued*.
by the tailor for stuffing or padding doublets, slops, &c.; "2 lb coton for a slop of velvet at Bolyngbrok," D. of L., cl. 28, bdle. 3, No. 3, fo. 3; *ib*. bdle. 1, No. 2, fo. 10
Couertowres, covertures, or table-cloths, of washing material, 179 **7**; for the kitchen and offices, 235
Council of the Duchy of Lancaster, 162 **9**; their expenses waiting five days at Leicester, 32
Counting-board, green friese for, 10, **5**; green counting-cloth for, 152
Couper, a cooper, 43
Comperage, 207 **29**
Coyfe, a cap or head-covering, 280 **31**
Craieres, craiers, 99 **20**, **23**, slow trading ships of old times. Smyth's "Sailor's WordBook." Sea-going ships without yards to their masts, used in the N. of Europe
Crane, for hoisting, 161
Crem, creme, creem, cream, 29, 40, 82
Cressets, 199, 12
Crevys, cray-fish, 206
Crisma, 92 30, chrisma, the holy oil for anointing at baptism
Crochetes, hooks, 25, 75, 173, 195, 281
Crocus, saffron, 17, **31**, 28, 29; bottles for, 74
Crospeys, graspeys, *for* craspiscis, 19, 215 **2**, 221 **28**, a grampus or whale; on p. 19 a barrel of whale-oil may be intended, or of pieces of flesh
Cryour, cryer of the Prussian Marshall, 105 **19**
Cultellus coquine, kitchen knife 74, 236
Cuparius, a cooper, 73
Cupbord, a sideboard in the hall, 239 **8**; cupcloth to cover it, 209 **13**, 219, 231
Cuphons, 6 **8**, 7 **11**, 176 **14**, 185 **33**, seems to be a trunk in which the gold and silver plate was carried, on a special sumpter horse with a saddle.
Currants. *See* Spices.
Curin, court of the lord, the place where he is actually residing, bearing the same relation to him as the king's court to the king, lxxxix., xc., 118, 264
Currarius, a coachman, 183 **3**
Currus, a carriage, 150 **29**, 163, 183 **4**, 190, 192, 194 **11**, 240; with four horses, 180 **17**, 191 **24**, 193 **4**;

Currus—*continued.*
wheels mended, 188, 197; lard for, 193, 198, 202, 203; repair of, 199 **2**, 202; shoe for, 202 **13**; exchange of in Bohemia for two little ones, 202 **19**
Cuva, a tun or big vessel, 74 **30**

Dattili, dates, 8 **28**. *See* Spices
Deer, presents of, roes, 108; hinds, 109 **6**; hart, 109 **19**
Deles, deals, deal boards. *See* Wood. This appears to be the earliest use of the word yet noted. New Eng. Dict.
Denigrata, cleaned (applied to garments and furs), 280 **30**
Dice, play at. *See* Games.
Dieta. *See* Accounts
Dishes of wood, 9 **24**
Dishes and platters, 53 **14**
Diskippagium. *See* Skyppagium
Docer, dorser, tapestry hung round the hall at the back of the sitters, 25 **10**
Dolium, a tun, cask for wine, 19, 54; used for flour on board ship, 22
Donum, this is not merely a present, but money bestowed in return for casual service and many miscellaneous purposes, 104, 113
Drage, 19 **13**; 225 **8**, a digestive sweetmeat, Fr. *dragée*.
Drawing-yerne, 90 **12**, an iron employed in some part of tailor's work, perhaps a flat-iron
Dresser, planks to make, 22, 239; cover for, 52; dressynhord, 165, 235
Dressyng-knif for the scullery and kitchen, 20 **28**, 236
Drink given to workmen, 26, 203 **28**
Drinking vessels. *See* Byketes, Verres, *and* Wooden Cups
Dwarf, 275 **13**

Earthen pots, 10 **12**, 60
Eels, sold by the stick, containing twenty-five (Statutes, Record ed., vol. i 205), 20 **13**, 29. *See* Fish.
Eggs bought by the centena or hundred, 9, 15 **3**, 25 **17**, 53, 61, 82, 100, 208, &c.; salt for preserving, 25 **20**
Ememlacio, mending, repair, 175, &c.
Encaustum, ink, 5 **15**, 155, 241, **30** 257 **26**
Engrave, r., 34 **27**

Equitatio, riding, whether on horseback or in a vehicle, 166 **21**, 172
Esiamentum, the right of enjoying another person's house or goods, 14, **6**, **26**
Ewer, gilt, 6 **3**
Ewery, xciii., 318
Exitus, exitibus, sales by auction, 150 **31**, 151 **1**
Exitus multonum, 20 **17**, seems to be the offal of the sheep returned to the salesman; exitus 12 bouum, 207 **27**, offal of the oxen
Expenditns, paid for, 39 **12**, 44 **13**, 45, **27**, 46

Factura, *verbal noun*, the making, 73 **20**
Fagots, fagets, 29 **32**, 30, 155, 156
Falcons, 254 **18**, a falconer and house for, at Königsberg, 68 **20**; ? used in hunting near Königsberg, 108 **30**; cages for, 93; presents of, 108 **30**, 111 **10**; bought, 200 **27**; horse for man carrying in Italy, 240; glove for, 287 **10**. *See* Hawks, Tiercels.
Famulus, servant, 99, 110 **32**, 111, 114, 167, 239, 260
Farcost, farecost, a trading vessel, generally on the northern coasts, 97, 98
Fatte, German *fass*, Eng. *vat*, a cask, 58, 61, 68, 74; the word here used for purchases in Germany only; but this form is found in England. "empty pipes, hogges-hedeles, fattes." "Clarence Ordinances," p. 95
Fau-teropes, 242 **11**, apparently a kind of stirrups; *unexplained*
Fenestralla, a window, 157
Fernical, 225 **14**, seems to be some household vessel or implement; *unexplained*
Ferrers, 47 **5**, 256 **5**, a term applied to barrels in which wine or water were carried on horseback; New Eng. Dict. (O. Fr. *ferriere*, a travelling bottle; Bradley's Stratmann)
Ferrour, a smith, 94, 201, 237
Ferrum, a horse-shoe, 31, 199 **7**; ferri equini, 240 **24**. *See* Horsegear
Ferrura, shoeing of horses, 31, 33
Fesauntes, pheasants, 205
Fetherbed, 281 **25**

Figs, roll of, 228 **18**; roll here is a weight. rotola=nearly 2 lbs., still used in Malta, and found at Rhodes in 1392; "quatuor rotulos ceræ in tortices." Regist. Magist. S. Joh. Jer. at Valetta. (Arabic *ratl*, Italianised *rotola*)

Fish (a greater variety of poultry and fish were eaten during the weeks passed at Venice than anywhere else, and they formed large part of the food there. See pp. 211-218). (*Cf.* list of fish in "La Manière de Langage," ed. Paul Meyer, p. 393

salt and fresh, 8 **12**, 29, 44, 53, 86, 100, 164, 205, 220

whale or grampus. See Crospeys

herring (*allec*), 12, 29, 62, 65, 73, 182, 254; fresh, 180 **25**, 181; white, 62, 77, 96, 244 **9**; red, 77, 97; of Schonen, 47 **23**; salt (*allecibus poudris*), 29

cod (*morruda*), 12, 14, 18, 29

codelynges, 73 **14**, 87, 97, 182; salt, 47

chelynge, keeling or cod-fish, 153

conger eel (*congrus*), 16, 18

anguilla grossa, 29, 155, 212

eels, 29, 73, 82, 97, 182, 217, 248; salted, 42 **4, 10**, 73 **26**

stoks, stok-fisshe, stock fish, 22, 29, 30, 31, 42, 97, 100; beating of, 80 **23**, 155 **10**; winter-fish and half-waxen or half-grown, 21. The cod dried in the sun or air was called stok-fish. It became so hard that for cooking it required previous beating ("verberacione" 22) with a mallet and long soaking in liquid; apparently a distinction was made between the fish caught young and those fully grown about winter

flat-fyssh, 47; perhaps flack-fish is intended, a Dantzic name for stockfish. Hirsch, p. 247

great plat-fysshe, 96, 97

sturion, sturgeon, barrels of, 42, 47, 96, 158; fresh, 97, 182

perpoise, 58, 62, 70, 71, 72, 87, 97

pike or luce, 29, 30, 50, 51, 87, 155, 186, 212, 215

pykerelles, 73 **18**, 213, 215

salmon, 31 **32**, 42, 47, 160; salt, 96, 161, 171; fresh, 182

wych, 42 **4**; *unexplained*

Fish—*continued*
whelks, 29, 31

bremes, 73 **19**, 180 **25**, 182, 248

lampreys, 75, 156 **17**, 161

roches, roach, 53, 73, 180, 182, 248

tenches, tench, 73, 155, 213, 215

ray, 100 **8**

crabs and lobsters, 153, 159, 190, 213, 214

thornbacks, 155

plaice (plays), 155, 181, 212, 213

flounders, 159 **25**, 206, 213, 215

troulite, trowtes, troztes, trout, 182 **23**, 215, 217

crevys, cray-fish, 206 **3**, 213, 215, 251, 253

burbutts (or eel-trout), fresh water fish, 212, 213 **19, 23**, 214, 215, 217. "Borbotha be fisshes very slepery, somewhat lyke an ele." Lawr. Andrewe, quoted in "Babees Boke," p. 231

moletts, mullets, 213

schrympes, 213, 217

ostreæ, oysters, 213, 216 **23**, 231

cokkes, kokks, cokkels, cockles, 213, 215, 216

hornekek, 213, garfish or greenback

barce, 213, barse or bass, a name for the perch

chevens, 213, 217, 248, chevin, the poilard, says Cotgrave; the chub. New Eng. Dict.

squames, 215 **20**, 216. ? some sort of shell-fish with rough almost scaly exterior: *cf.* Lat. *squamosus*

sertes, sardes, 180 **26**, 182, sardines (Ducange), pilchards (Cotgrave)

sardyns, salted, 228 **31**

pimpernol, 215 **25**, a spitch-cock or dart, little fish extremely agile. (Cotgrave, Godefroi)

skombri (*sgomery*), mackarel 229

vmbre, 248 **6**, the omber or grayling, of which a delicious kind is found in the rivers of Auvergne and Savoy (Cotgrave)

carpez, carp, 217, 248

perches, 248 **33**, 251

mackerell, 254 **15**

tencle, 217 **22**, *unexplained*

Fishing nets, 22 **24**

Fithelers, fiddlers, 109 **13**, 110 **23**

Flags (*vexilla*), 43, 90, v.magna, 93; Derby's for the Reysa, 43 **32**; first

Flags—*continued.*
 taken on to walls of Wilna, 105 **11** ;
 standards, 90 **24** ; pennons of lances,
 34, 74 ; banners, 93 **12**. *See* Getens
Flasks of tin for wine in the galley,
 224. **12**. *See* Botels of Tin
Flawne, 252 **4**, pancake. Bradley's
 "Stratmann" ; "Promptorium." In
 "Babee's Boke," p. 287, flaunes are
 explained to be cheesecakes
Flax, six stone of, 157. *See* Linum
Flores domini, 101, 110, ornaments of
 silver gilt ; perhaps representing the
 Lancaster rose, or they may have been
 posies (mottoes), wound into a floral
 shape, or a combination of posy and
 flower. These ornaments seem to have
 been sown on parts of the dress. "pro
 emendacione unius zone domini cum
 les flours ibidem," p. 163 **25** ; in
 1391-2, we find Hen. Goldbeter paid
 "pro 320 fol. de *soucine rous de mey*"
 of silver gilt "pro j slop domini," and
 in 1397-8 Herman Goldsmith provides
 a "coler fact. cum esses et floribus de
 soueigne rous de moy pendentibus et
 annaill." (*i.e.* enamelled). D. of L., cl.
 28, bdle. 1, No. 2, fo. 15ᵛ ; *ib.* No. 5
Flour, 12, 13, 21, 22, 25, 153 ; farina
 frumenti, 47, 64, 97, &c.
Flycke, flykke, a flitch, 21, 23, 42
Focalis, fuel, 30. *See* Fuel
Fodder for horses, 10. *See* Prebends,
 Horses
Foraging near Venice, 220, 223
Fraghtage, freight-money, 162 **25**
Friese *See* Textiles
Fringe, for lance-pennons, 35, 74 ; for
 banners, 93, 287 **6** ; for sleeves, &c.,
 90, 287 **33** ; of gold and silk, 288 **1**
Fruits, 11 **2**, **6**, 40, 71, 171, 197, 212, 213,
 223, 228, 253
 apples and pears, 49 **1**, 69, 70, 87, 165,
  167, 176, 212, 226, 243, 248, 252
 cherries, 29 **17**, 165, 243, 248, 252,
  254
 nuts, 52, 69, 70, 87, 176, 187, 226, 228,
  234
 chestnuts, 223 **26**
 citrons, 225
 oranges, 225 **6**
 figs, 223 **26**, 227, 228, 231
Fuel (*focalis*), *i.e.* coals and wood,
 bought at Königsberg, 59 ; at Dantzig,
 78, 85 ; a stack of, 66 **9**, 67, 72 ;

Fuel—*continued.*
 waggon of, 76 ; called a-helers, 181 **14**.
 See Billet, Coal, Busca
Fogacio, the driving of cattle, 22, 24, 49
Furiosus, a madman, alms given to, 277
Furnaginm, 64 **31**, 152 **19**, 179, money
 paid for the baking of bread; on p. 23
 it appears to be for furnacing wheat
Furnus, a baker's oven or furnace, 75,
 179 **9**, 236
Furs damaged on the ship, 178
Furs and fur trimming, 90, 280, 284,
 285, 287, 288 ; chalkyng fur, 93 **3**
 beaver, 91 **9**, **21**. *See* Beaver
 minever, 92 **7**, **29**, 93 **5**
 martinet, 91 **12**, **16**
 grys, 92 **28**, 93 **1** ; the *vair* of the
  French. In Loveney's Wardrobe
  Accounts of 1397-8, "ermyns" head
  the list of furs, next comes "menever
  pur." used for trimming the "goun
  of Garters of the King's livery," and
  for velvet or baldekin gowns ;
  "grys" follows, used for gowns of
  black or red cloth ; the "martryns"
  come fifth, used for gowns of satin,
  scarlet, &c. D. of L., cl. 28, bdle. 1,
  No. 5
Fustyan. *See* Textile
Fyryren, fire-iron, 222

Galley, Venetian, for the voyage to
 Palestine, 201 **31** ; expense of navigating, 279 **1** ; meat provided for,
 207 **26**, and salted, 208, 220 ; fish
 salted for, 220 ; general provision for
 in meat, spices, flour, wine, fruit,
 poultry, and utensils, 221-224 ; cabins
 made in, materials and carpenters for,
 219 **29**, 223 ; windows or lights for
 the cabins, 221 **30**, 228 **6** ; cabin
 made in for the leopard, 228 **3** ; mats
 for coverings, 222 **29**, 281 **22** ; rudder repaired, 225 ; fat for repair of,
 226 **25** ; canvas and cords (*verueis*)
 for sails, 281 **21** ; bedding bought for,
 281 **25**. *See* Patronus
Galo, a gallon, 15
Galoner, a gallon pot of leather, 18, 154
Games on shipboard and journey, dice
 (*tales*), 28 **2**, 31, 35, 109, 110, 115 ;
 chess, 49 **19**, 281 **9** ; backgammon,
 113 **17**, 178 **8**, 264 **5** ; *jeu de paume*,
 263 **24** ; gains at dice by an esquire
 from Derby, paid, 107 **19**

INDEX III.   343

Garcio, a **groom**, 8 **4**, **23**, 9, 164 **27**, 208 **3**
Garderobe, office of. *See* Wardrobe
Gariselet, 13 **12**, a sort of spice. *See* Spices
Getens, 152 **28**, penons, small flags for the ship. "Item a gyton for the ship," MS. of 1437 ; the word appears to come from *Guydhome*, *guydon*, *gyton*; the two first forms are in a MS. of 1520. "Retrospective Review," 2nd Ser., vol. i. pp. 111, 114, 115
Gelicloth, for straining jellies, 234 **14**
Gemelettes, 159, ? gimlets
Gemewes, 25 **34**, 26, 221 **29**, hinges (*gemel*, a twin or pair); gemeus, 156 **10**, *misprinted* gemeus
Gifts or rewards for service on the Reysa (irrespective of wages), 105, 106, 107, 108; at new year, 109; to household officers, 114, at Easter, 111; to prisoners, 113; in money on the journeys, 289
Ginger. *See* Spices
Glas, verrez de, 58 **22**; glasez, 235 **31**, 239
Gloves, 46 **19**, 173 **1**
Glikes, 219 **11**, *unexplained*
Gobete, 19 **9**, Fr. *gober*, to swallow, a nice morsel; gobete real, a royal bit, evidently a sweet; *gobeter*, to eat delicious morsels, Godefroi
Gold-smith's ware, 6 **1-4**, 34. *See also* Silver Ware
Goldsmith of Calais, 34; of Venice, 240 **10**; of London, 288. *See* Index I.
Gouna, a gown
Gowns, for Derby, 35, 178, 287, 288 **12**; for various men, 35 **7**, 166, 178, 280
Grana, rouge de, scarlet (*cf.* mod. *in grain*), 282 **18**, **29**
Graspeys. *See* Crospeys
Gratour, a grater, 24, 58
Grece, grees, grease, 46, 64, 98, 161
Grome, a groom or valet, not necessarily serving horses, 136, 141
Gross, purchases in, 70 **14**
Gunner, archer, 105
Gyde, a guide, 114 **29**, 166 **21**, 183, 185, 186, 194, 205, 206, 220
Gymlottes, gemelettes, ? gimlets, 86, 159

Hakenay, hackney horse, **31**, **105**, **163**
Half-waxen, half-grown, 21
Hamper with lock, 196 **4**

Hammers for stock-fish, 80 **23**
Hares, 189 **6**
Harness, a general term for baggage; gear. "Prompt. Parv." gives four senses: (*a*) raiment, (*b*) weapons and armour, (*c*) household utensils, (*d*) horse harness; three of which are found in these accounts, *e.g.* (*a*) on 173 **29**, (*b*) 35 **12**, 173 **22**, (*c*) 170 **6**; (*d*) does not, I believe, occur
Hasps, 26, 29. *See* Iron
Hastilidiandum *for* hastiludiandum, justing, going to the just-, 113
Hausak, 20 **27**; ? *error for* hauersack, or bag for oatmeal
Hawks or falcons, hens bought to feed, 60 **25**, 61 **25**, 66 **5**, 68, 77, 88, 229, 230, 231, 232, 235; tields for carrying, 88; present of four, to Derby at Königsberg, 107 **12**
    Dame J. Berners says of mewed hawks, when she waxith nygh ferme geve hir hennys." "Boke of St. Albans," Stock's facsimile, sign. c cij
Hay, 158, 159, 164; bought by the waggon (*carnea*), 60; by the fothir, 62 **31**; by the stack, 72 **29**; hire of house for, 174 **28**
Hedynge casks, heads put in by the cooper, 22
Hemmyng of towels or napkins, 166. *See* Lembic?
Henksmen, 163 **17**, 164 **29**, 171 **31**, 173, 176, 225, 226, 230; clothing for, 279, 280, 285, 287
Herbs, for "sauce," 258 **6**; these were bought for the office of the scullery, but what kind of green they were does not appear, 12 **9**, 13, **33**, 15 **30**, 29 **10**, 63, 67, 78, 167, 196, 225, 249, 258
    In "Liber Cure Cocorum" (ed. Rich. Morris), p. 48, the recipe for " capons in erbis " shows that the " erbis " were what we still call " sweet herbs " in the kitchen, parsley, sage, savory, &c. *See also* how to dry them, *ib.* p. 34
Herburgagium, lodging at inns, &c., 175
Hermits, gifts and alms to, 106 **7**, 277 **7**
Hermittess, 273
Herthe, hearth made of tiles in the ship, 23; in the kitchen, **169**
Hokes, hooks, 48, 227
Honey, 9 **23**, 21, 31; by the gallon, 52, 65, 168 **19**, 221 **22**, &c.

344   INDEX III.

Hoggeshed, hoggeshed, a hogshead, 23, 156
Hooping casks, 22 **30**, 23 **19**
Horse-bread, only in England, 6 **20**, 23, 7 **2**, 9, 11 **28**, 16, 28, 99 **1**, 163
Horscombes, 46, 175, 194, 238
Horses bought, 46, 262; grey, white, sorel, bald, bay, 5; black, 7
  palfreys, 6, 9, 34
  trotters, 143
  hakeney, 34, 105 **4**, 163
  sumpter-horses (*somers*), 6, 7, 9, 11, 46, 47, 263; for the treasury, 7 **20**;
  maler, for carrying males (*i.e.* budgets or portmanteaus), 30 **4**, **5**, **25**, 31, 263 **9**
  cursors, coursers, 46 **24**, 53 **14**, 105, 7, **17**, 256, 292; Derby's white coarser, 64 **6**
  for a carriage, 198 **21**. *See* Currus
  for carts, 262, 263
  sick, medicine for, 11 **29**, 256; eight substances for curing, 64 **5**; bacon for, 186 **30**; butter, 193 **2**, 197 **11**, 257; suet (sewet), 257; lard, tallow, and other unguents, 46 **27**, 71, 164, 238 **1**, **14**, 247, 248 **26**, 257
  their food; oats, 11, 28, 48, 63, &c.; hay, 60, &c. (*see* Hay); hay in the ship, 174; spelt, 207; prebends, 207 (*see* Prebend)
  expenses of, 168, 169, 170, 172, 201, 253, 292, &c.
  ropes of hay for, 158, 174
  bridge for, (?) to walk on to the prame, 177
  beds and litter for, 207. *See* Litter
  keepers of at Portogenaro, 210
Horse-gear—
  saddles (*cella, sella*), 34, 46, &c.; stuffing of, 94 **8**; covered with cloth 240 **31**, 241 **23**
  sumpter-saddles, somer-sodell, 7, 13, 154, 241, 242; maler-saddle, 30, 44 **1**
  carriage-saddle, 7
  new panels, 46 **24**, 94 **6**, a kind of saddle; mule-panel, for a maler, 152 **24**
  leather sengles, 34 **19**, 200 **23**, straps or girths
  surcingle, surcingle, 7 **12**, 13, 46, 94 **31**, 247, a long upper girth which went over the saddle; counter-sengle, 177 **12**

Horse-gear—*continued*.
  stirrups and stirrup leathers, 46, 94. *See* Fausteropes
  halters (*capistra*), 41 **12**, 46 **26**, 94, 152 **24**, 180, 194; girths, 46, 48, 94, 256
  brace (brase, braas), 46 **26**, 94
  warroke, 238 **14**, a girth or strap; "j somer sadill cum j freno et j warrok." "Finchale Inventories," clvii. *See* Warroke
  reins, 13 **28**, 46 **24**, 94, 240 **12**
  traces (trays), 180, 192 **19**
  bridle (*frenum*), 34, 44, 94, 196 **21**, 238
  burrews, 13 **27**, ? horse-collars. *See* Burrews
  poles and girths, 7, 238, 247; girth weldes, 238
  spurs, 94 **4**
  mounce, a maund or basket, 61 **5**, **6**
  repair of various articles, 238
  shoesmith and shoeing, 10, 12, 31, 33, 34, 45, 48, 61, 69, 166, 172, 188, 193, 201, 207, 241, 256, 257; wages of shoesmith, 61 **7**
  leather sack to carry horseshoes for the Reysa, 13
Hospes, hospitis, host of lodgings, 59, 61, 65, 68, 184; on the Reysa, 114; his wife, 110 **31**, 259; servant of the, 259 **11**, **15**
Hospicata, hospitata, 184 **21**, 259 **20**, entertained
Hospicium, a house for which rent was paid, a hired house; probably also part of a house, as rooms at an inn. At Calais Chaundeler and Mowbray had hospicii, 11 **6**, **26**; Derby had one at Boston, 204 **4**; at Dantzic, 41, 88, 259; at Königsberg, 58 **13**, 67; money paid for this last, 68 **22**; at Königsberg H., 173 **7**; and Dantzig, 173 **11**
Hospicii expense, house expenses, 258
Hospitissa, hostess of lodging or inn, 41, 77, 111
Hostelers, innkeepers, 43 **10**
Hostia, door or gate to kitchen, larder, &c., 69 **5**, 72, 76 **22**, 85 **1**, 259; to layhouse, 164 **4**; to oats, 168; to cellar, 213
Hostilia, outhouse, part of a house, 85 **1**
Houpeland, 285 **20**, a loose upper garment or tunic (Fairholt) fashionable

Houpelond—*continued.*
   in reign of Richard II., introduced from France, probably from Spain originally. Planché's "Encycl. of Costume"
Hous, a covering, cup-hous, 6 **8**, 7 **11**; hous pro le bauer et j autre pro le penon, 46 **17**; for the lord's shield, 93 **16**; of leather for a saddle, 247,**7**
Housia, housing for a horse, 34
Hungarian leather, 31 **19**
Hunting in Prassin, horses shod for, 61 **26**; other items for, 108 **23**; ? falcons employed in, 108 **30**
Hurdells, 156

Ice between Portogruaro and Venice, expense of breaking, 207 **22**
Indulgences. *See* Religion
Ink. *See* Encaustum
Iron, ferri operati, wrought iron, 24 **25**, 26, 41, 209 **28**
   nails, 26, 69
   carpenter's tools, 26
   ferramentis, iron things for a door, 69 hokes, hynges or henges, and haspes, 76, 79, 221
   chains, 76

Jak, Jakke, a jack or jacket, short coat, 92 **10**, 106 **14**
Jakkes, pair of ? part of a spit, roasting machine, 102. *See* Cobard
Jars for water, 225 **16**, 228
Jantaculum, breakfast, 242, 248, 250, 253
Jobbes, pair of, some kind of vessel, measuring four gallons, 151
Jupa, petticoat worn by men, 91, 93. *See* Clothing

Kalefact', 180 **4**, caulking; Fr. *calfater*, to caulk
Karde. *See* Textile Fabrics
Kede, a kid, 171 **5**, 242
Kempe of herrings, 77 **22**, apparently a sale term for a large bulk of herrings. "Prompt. Parv."
Kercheo, kerchief, 94 **31**
Kerman land, 28 *note*
Kid meat, 40 **11**, 45 **16**. *See* Meat
Kist, cista, a chest, 23, **30**, 64 **10**, 177

Kitchen, in Dantzic hired from a woman, 41 **17**; fitted up and repaired, 79, 86 at Königsberg enlarged, 63; a door put, 69, **5**; new ones, 168, 169 **21** at Portogruaro fitted up, 205; besoms for cleaning, 206
   a furnace put in, 58
   vessels and pots in pewter, brass, and ? iron, 101, 102; broylours, ? gridirons, 233; ladles and skimmers, 21, 151, 219; parura and grater, 58; clarehagges, 65; trows, *i.e.* troughs and other implements, 24; knives, 74, 236
   fuel for, 59. *See* Coal, Fuel
   nappery and cloths for, 10 **3**
   valets of, 113 **10**, 287 **20**; servants, 209 **25**
Klikete, the part of a lock which hooks or catches, a lock with four kliketes, 57 **21**; O. Fr. *clike, clique* (Godefroi); *cleik,* to hook (Jamieson)
Knives sharpened, *acucio,* 219; *mollicio,* 236
Kranage, charge for hoisting casks by a crane on to the boat, 19

Laces, 90, **14**, whether a catch-pin, *fibu'a*, or a reticulated light web, *laqueum*, does not appear
Ladel, a ladle, 24, 219 **6**
Lard, 251 **21**, 252 **28**, 253 **17**
Larder, at Boston, 22, 24 **28**; at Königsberg, 60; at Venice, 207 **32**
Laton, a mixed metal, 154 **25**
Latoner, a worker in laton, 157
Latrina, 60
Lances, pensils for, 34
Lanterns for the ship, 87, 155
Laundress of nappery for the lord's hall and chamber, 13 **24**, 54 **13**, 57, 58, 61, 65, 70, 85, 217; for the buttery, 81, 178, 195, 225; for the pantry, 207, 225, 228
Laundry of linen, &c., 31 **14**, 43, 46, 74, 76, 162, 166, 168, 174, 179, 183, 194, **3**, 195, 233, 235, 257, 258, 280, 281, 284, 286, 288
Laumpe for cabin, &c., 281 **18**, 287 **3**
Lavacrum, a bath or laver, 153 **24**
Leather for making gloves, 92 **33**; for the lord's doublet, 90; for a bag, 187/ **24**; *corium equinum*, for mending bridles, &c., 238 **3**; measure-pots of, 18
Leche, a doctor, 164 **23**

346 INDEX III.

Leggharneys, ? armour for the legs, 46
Lembic, 219 **13**, ? for limbacione, the hemming (of towels)
Leopard lxv., his guardian and keeper, 163, 246 **29**, **30**, 247, 250, 251, 252, 257 ; clothes for keeper, 246 **25**, 247 ; "libard-men," 247, 257 ; his food and expenses, 229, 230, 231, 232, 233, 235, 237, 246, 258; expenses of horses, 163, 251, 253, 255, 256; a mat, 240 **15**, oil, 245 **25**
Lepe, a basket, 86 **29**, 158
Lepers near Susa, 276
Letters sent to England, 108 **12**, **33**, 122 **20** ; to Poland, 108 **3**, 111 **22** ; to Hertford, 125, **11** ; Derby to Kingston, 292
Leveyn, leaven, perhaps to make horsebread, with the bran named, 1016
Lewyn, 80 **15**, ? cloth of Louvain (Loveyne, Loeven), seems to have been used in making torches ; *cf.* " 12 ulnae de lewyn pro mappis." "Finchale Accts.," p. lii.
Liberationes, liveries or garments, money for certain, 240 **21**
Ligacio barcllorum, &c., hooping of barrels, 23, 158
Light on the journey, daily cost of, 222 **8**, **15**, 203 **8**
Limbus, *for* lembus, a small boat, 222 **24** ; " proij limbis portantibus necessaria nostra de galea usque ad Kairam." "Voyage d'un Maire de Bordeaux au 14th siècle." Archives de l'Orient Latin, tom. II. pt ii. p. 387
Linen cloth, 46, 61, 65; for the Reysa, 49 **33**, 50; for various offices, 61 **19**, 65. *See* Textile
Linga, tongue or pin of a brooch, 287 **9**
Linnoñ, 154 **20**, may mean wood of aloes, O. Fr. *ligné aloes*, *lingaloes*, *linon allouez*, and many other forms. Godefroi
Lintheamen, a sheet, 77 ; stolen, 184, 192
Linum, 41 **6**, 64 **5**, 76 **16**, 186 **4**, 221 **12** ; flax, ? tow for caulking. *See* Kalfast'
Litura, litter, for both men and horses, 7 **2**, 15 **11**, 20 **2**, 53 **23**, 70, 186, 187, &c.
Livery, and horses at new year, 1391; money given for, 112; given to squires in May, 1396, 284 **24**; of the lord

Livery—*continued.*
and his knights, 282 **5**; of the King of Hungary copied for Derby, 285 **33**. The word livery, *liberata*, is applied even to Derby's own dress, 282 **5**, and to that of the King of Hungary, 285/ **33**
Locio, washing of linen, 31, **14**. *See* Laundry
Locks, 25, 58, 64, 221
Lodesman, pilots, 37, 56, 87, 97, 143, 162
Loke, a lock, 25
Loss. *See* Theft
Lotrix, a laundress, 43 **18**
Lourica, Lorica, a coat of mail, 74
Luce, a pike (fish), 50, 51
Lucerna, a light or window like a skylight, evidently here meant for the cabin, 221 **30**, 228 **6**
Lucerna, 249 **10**, a plant ; Ducange says it is mullein
Lusus, play, at dice or tables, 28 **2**, 31, 35; money spent over, 115, 263
Lym, lime, 77
Lynsede, linseed, 64

Mailes, link or rings of which coats of mail are made, 46 **16** (Cotgrave)
Male, a wallet or travelling bag, 68 **8**, 242 ; male-panel, saddle for a horse carrying males, 152 **24**
Manche, a sleeve, 99
Mandel, Ital. *mandelora*, almonds, 231 **8**
Mannts, 64 **5**, **6**, baskets ; Fr. *manne*, An oblong wicker basket, used by masons, gardeners, and laundresses. The Picard form is *mande*, whence our *maund*. (Littré, Godefroi)
Mantica, a short mantle, 282, 284 **3**
Mantica, 177 **20**, a travelling bag or portmanteau. *See* Clothsack
Matrona, 67, 68
Materas, mattrass for the galley, 281 **25**
Mappae, napkins or cloths, 54, 61, 157, 166 ; comensales, table cloths, 46 ; mappa Paris, 154 ; opera Paris, 258 **2** (*see* Textile); hemming or sewing of, 166, 170 **9** (*see* Lembic)
Marescalcia, marshalcy, office concerning horses, 15, 46, 63, 71, 72, 166
Mats, 41 **22**, 74 **13**, 87, 222, 240, 281
Maungour, manger, 64

INDEX III. 347

Meade, 38 **25**; methe. 39 **21**; 57, 58, 64, 67, 69; meed, 43 **8**; mele, 47, 170

Meals, prandium, lunch or first meal, 44 **22**, 77 **5**, 198, 200; expenses of, for six persons, 202 **10**
cena, supper, 45, 75, 98, 200 **12**; expenses of, 202 **14**
jantaculum, breakfast, 242 **28**, 248

Measures—
Wine: two quarts = one pottle, 6 **14**
five pottles = one sextar, 15, 160, 256
picheria, pitcher, 21 **5**, 160, 256; the sextar and picheria were used with **Gascon wine**
barrel, 7, 10, &c.
olla, 21 **6**, a jar or pot
stoup, stopa, 9 **23**, 14, 39, 47, 164; stoup of honey, 9 **23**
dolium, tun, 42 **29**, contents variable
pipe and tonel, 24, 156
hogshead, 23, 156
last, of Rhine wine, 58 **27**
fatte, 58, 61, 68; Germ. *fass*, a large vessel or cask. Kluge

Beer and mead; gallon, 6, 10, 160
barrel, of 24 gallons, 157 **15**
last, of 12 barrels, 47 **10**, 58, 64, 67, 69, 71, 159
dolium, 58 **8**

Dry; peck and bushel, 6, 20 **24**, 29 **5**; peck of flour, 73 **31**
quarter, of oats, 7 **25**, 8, 191; of wheat, 20
cade of herring, 97 **12**. A cade contained 600; "Prompt Parv." Cades of red herring and sprats, Clarence Ord., p. 102. In Italy the cade or barrel was used for water and wine, 208 **22**, 209, 222
stone of butter and cheese, 25; of wax, 68, 75; of flax, 157
kynerkyn of salmon, 96; of eels, 97
kilderkyn of sturgeon, 158
stick of eels, 25 eels, 20 **14**, 29
tymbre, timber of fur skins, number from 10 to 40, 92 **28**. *See* Tymbre
roll of figs (or rotola) at Rhodes, 228 **18**. *See* Figs.
quire of paper, 159 **7**, **10**; ream of paper, 154

Measures—*continued.*
Long; yard (*virga*), 8, 90, &c.
ell (*ulna*), 35 **16**, 61
fadom, fathom of cord, 158, 242 **3**
Used in Prussia; fattes of wine; lasts of beer; stoups of wine, beer, or mead. The old Dantzic *stof* held 1¼ Prussian quarts. Hirsch, p. 262, *note.*
aune = forty gallons, 42, 47; 3½ aunes = one pipe. *Cf.* the *ohm* (containing 110 *stof,* which appears to be the English stopa or stoup) of Dantzic in 14th cent., and the modern *ahm* or *awm.* Hirsch, p. 261
schok, of beakers, 70 **19**, 72, 80; scok or schok of deals, 75, 76; shok of straw, 80. Mid. High Germ. *schoc,* three score; a lot of things, always 60. Three schok of wine, 195 **7**, must mean three schok of the measure, stoups or beakers
fothir, of coal, 59, 62; of litter, 60 **14**; of hay, 62 **31**; of straw, 63 **9**, 72
shephul, scheful, Germ. *scheffel,* a bushel, 48, 77, 81, 167, 181

Used in Italy; stara, of salt, 205, 214; of spelt, 207; of oats, 211; of flour, 222
Of wine.—cade, 209, 222; butt, galey, amphora, vasa, 222, 230; castron, 224 **25**
Long measure,—bras, of linen, &c., 208, 234, 236, 280, Ital. *braccio,* brasse, of six feet. A measure for stuffs. Daru's "Hist. de Venise," iii. 105
cane, *for* canna, a measure of canevas, 283 **12**

Measures, vessels to contain. *See* Poteller, Galloner, Peck

Meat, in carcase, of oxen, calves, sheep, lambs, 8, 9, **99**, 155, 169, 191, 204, 214, 248, 249, 253, 255, 256; at Calais, 10, **12**, 13, 61, 65; at Dantzic, 39, 45, 83; at Lynn, 159; on the Reysa, 50-52
salt in barrels, 42; fresh and salt, 53, 86, 95, 96, 194; salted down for a voyage, 220
pigs, porci, 51, 62, 65, 153, 159, 212, 214. *See* Bacon

Meat—*continued*.
 porcelli, 212, 214, 216; boar, 62,
  153
 kids, 40 **11**, 51, 52, 159, 241
 hares, 159 **6**, 225
 wethers, 206 **11**, 211 **28**, 213
 roes, 162, 113, 206, 212, 216, 217
Meats painted in the kitchen, 162 **19**
Medicaments—
 camphor and stanch, 164 **23**
 smigma, 224 **5**, 240
 for a horse, 236 **31**
Meisne, mainy or meiney, company of household servants or followers, 113, **18**
Meremium, timber, material for building ships or houses, 26, 41, 75
Methe. *See* Meade
Milk, 8 **14**, 11, 15 **3**, 30, 45, 100, 206, 209, 212, 227, 248; cow taken on Reysa for, 51
Mill near Pntzig, 33
Millaria, miles, 20
Miners at the siege of Wilna, 105
Minstrelcy, a term not confined to music, but signifying also entertainment by tumblers, 109 **15**
Minstrels. *See* Musicians
Mirrors of Paris, 93
Moges, 229 **17**, heifers. Godefroi
Mollicio, 236, sharpening, *mollire* for *molere*, Ducange. *See* Acucio
Money. All the pages of different kinds are gathered together under their countries in the Introduction, xcviii.-cv.
Morrods, a cod-fish (Fr. *morue*), 14, 18
Mortars, in the scullery, 23, 221; of brass, 159
Motulinum, carcoisium, mutton, sheep's carcase, 255
Mules, 247 **1**, 254 **22**
Multo, mutton, " multones a larde," 251 **21**
Multure, the miller's due for the grinding of wheat, 21 **10**
Musicians, generally called minstrels—
 pipers and minstrels at Dantzic, 39 **9**, 104 **14**, 105, 108, 111, 114, 115;
 clerks there singing, 111
 French musicians at Königsberg, 107 **15**
 clerks of Königsberg singing, 107 **22**, 108 **19**, 114; at Schonec, 123 **15**

Musicians—*continued*.
 Derby's minstrels, 109 **21**, 113
 minstrels of Königsberg, 109 **17**, **23**, 110
 fitheleys or fiddlers, 109 **13**, 113;
  harpers, 110
 Christmas gifts to, 109 **16**
 trumpet or trumpour, 114, 132;
  hornpiper, 114, 115; pipers, 132
 nakerer, 133. *See* Nakerer
 their wages, 132, 137
Mustard, 12 **12**, 22; by the gallon, 23, 155; by the stoup, 49 **3**, 50 **33**
Mustard-seed, 22, 155
Mutnacio, 162 **24**, borrowing. *See* " Finchale Inventories," cxii., cxlviii., where loans are made on securities

Nails, 26, 35, 41, 63, 75, 157, 174, 219, 222; clavis equini, 248
Nakerer, 133, 137, 142, a player on the nacaire or naquaire, a kind of cymbal, an Arab instrument, *naqqârich*, brought to Europe by Crusaders. F. J. Fétis, " Histoire Générale de la Musique," v. 219
Naperons for the kitchen, 10
Nauiagium, navigation, conveying by ship, 98
Nauta, sailor, 8 **6**, 43, 54, 98, 113 **24**
Node, 99 **28**, a bow or knot. Fr. *nœud*
Noche or nouche, a brooch, ornamented pin, 105 **12**
Notary paid for writing account of the prames and carts for the Reysa, 54
Nova, 107 **10**; news, 109 **30**
Nundina, a market-place, 220
Nuns and sisters at Dantzic, 273 **21**, 274 **20**
Nutmeg. *See* Spices
Nuts. *See* Fruit

Oats bought, 11 **31**, 28, 63
Oatmeal (*farina avenarum*), 25 **16**, 28, 39, 63, 98, 191, 218, 239, 249
Oblations abroad and in England paid by Derby in 1390-91, 116, 117; paid in 1392-93, 273-278
Ocrea, a legging or boot, 32 **19**, 164, 168 **8**. *See* Clothing
Offices built and repaired at Königsberg house, II. 168 **31**, **33**, 170 **5**

INDEX III. 349

Oil, 65 **12**, 80, 97, 206 ; at dinner, 209 **5** ; much used during stay in Italy, 213, 214, &c. Probably olive oil: "Oyle olif for Lent, 10 gallons at 124." Clarence Ord., p. 102
Olla, a measure for wine, 21 **6** ; of clay, 39 **11**, 189 **21**, 194, 206, 228 **14**
Olus, cole-wort, 63. *See* Vegetables
Ordeum *for* hordeum, barley, 223
Orynales. *See* Vrinales
Ostia *for* hostia, a door or gate, 239 **7**, **11**
Ostrich bought in Bohemia, 191 **2** ; ostrich eggs, cups from, 211 **26**
Ouche, a brooch, 287 **9**, **14**. *See* Noche

Pagettus, diminutive of *pagius*, a page or servant, 272 **17**
Painters of shields, 45 **28**, 169 **29** ; of meats, 169 **19**
Pakkyng, packing, 35
Pakthred, 24, 41, 158
Panels, a kind of saddle, 46 **24**, 91 **6**
Panetria, pantry, office for bread, 15, 20, 33, &c.
Pannus, a full piece of cloth, 35 **14**, **19**
Panyer, basket, 228 **14**
Paper ryal or real, 8 **16**, 13 **11**, 19, 191 ; ream of, 154 ; quires of, 5 **17**, 159, 234, 237, 252
Par cofres, pair of coffers, 5 **8** ; par trossyngcofres, packing boxes, 19 **1**
Par rakkes, pair of racks, 18
Par sengles corei cum plustula, pair of leather straps with a buckle, 34
Par bowges, 16. *See* Bowges
Par styrop, stirrups, 46
Par botels de tyn, 49 ; flaskis de tyn, 224
Par jobbes, 154
Par potel botels, 154, bottles to hold a pottle
Par trestellorum, 63 **24**
Par de balance, 65 **28**. *See* Balance
Par botelles de Anglia, 72 **15**
Par jakkes, 102
Parasceue, die, Good **Friday**, 117
Parcella. *See* Accounts
Parchment, 5 **14**, 8, 19, 153, 257
Partridges. *See* Poultry
Paruta, 58 **30**, some kind of kitchen implement
Pasteller, a pastry-cook, 236
Pastelleria, pastelli, pastry, pasties, 64 **29**, 67 **18**, 70, 74 **25**

Pasture, closing of, 24 **31**
Patella, 169 **25**, a sort of lamp (Ducange), or a big dish, perhaps a baking-dish, as the new kitchen and hearth would not be fully fitted
Patronus, captain of the Venetian galley, 220 **24** ; his servants, 230 **8**, 232 **15**, **19** ; his wife, 281 **22**
Paueys, pavesium, a large shield, 23, 90 **22**
Payles, pails, buckets, 171 **30**
Pea-cocks presented to Derby, 105 **23**
Peas and peas-cods. *See* Vegetables.
Peck measure, a wooden, 158
Pelliparo, pelterer, skinner or furrier, 90 **16**, 91, 283, 288
Penner, a sheath to hold pens hanging at girdle, 159 ; cum corner, with inkhorn
Penons, 8 **26**
Pens, 5 **17**, 257
Pensel, diminutive of penon, a small flag ; pensels of taffata for lances, 34 ; white and red fringe for them, 55, 74
Penydes, 19 **12**, Fr. *penide* (Cotgrave); pennets or barley-sugar. *See* Sugar.
Perches, stands or spikes for torches, 252 **8**
Pesteles, pestles, 22, 74, 159
Petrosilium, parsley, 229 **31**
Pewter, 101, 211, dishes and saucers, 154, vessels, 233
Pheasants. *See* Poultry.
Physician of Marienburgh, 110 **27**. *See* Leche.
Picheria, a pitcher (of wine), 21 **5**
Pichon, civ. *See* Money
Pictatio, painting, picking out in colours, 93 **18**
Pictor, a painter, 43, 79, 93, 285
Pilche, 91 **21**, a warm fur gown or pellice; sometimes of woollen; for kitchen valets, 93; a white one, 93/**26**; of beaver, 91 **21**, 109 **12**; for members of the household, 112
Pilius (pileus), a hat or cap, 281 **24**, 285 **15**
Pilots. *See* Lodesmen.
Pilwe, a pillow, 214 **20**
Pinguedo, lard or fat, 66 **6**, 86, 226
Pinsendum, braying or pounding, 223 **34**; or kneading, 236 **9**
Pipers. *See* Musicians.
Pippis, ? *for* puppis, a ship, 14 **30**
Pistor, a baker, 234

CAMD. SOC. 2 z

Pistrina, a bakehouse; pistrinrra baking, 222
Pixe, pitch, 41. *See* Pyche
Pixis, a box, 12 **28**, 41 **14**; for tinder, 222; the vessel containing the consecrated wafer, 77 **2**
Plastre, plaster used in repairs, 79
Plates, thin leaves of metal for plate armour, 46 **16**, 174 **1**; glove of plate, 173 **1**
Platers, wooden platters or plates, 154
Plostula, a buckle, 34 **19**
Pyche, pitch, 76, 180
Pynsons. *See* Clothing
Point, a tagged lace for dress, 35 **9**, 45
Poletria, poultry, 241
Poma d'orange, oranges, 225 **6**
Ponderatio, 280 **23**, weighing
Pontage or pountage, a toll paid for passing under or over bridges, 7 **17**, 85 **10**, 57
Poor, Easter gifts to, of petticoats, shoes, and linen, 116, 117, 284. The number of poor persons to whom these were given correspond to the years of Derby's age on his previous birthday, viz. 24 in 1390-91, and 26 in 1392-93. 32 tunics and hoods were given at Tutbury in 139s
Popinjay, a parrot, 285 **24**, 286 **28**, 292 **34**
Porters, 19 **5**, 164 **16**, 228 **12**; porter or janitor, *infra curiam*, 268 **28**. The porter's duties are well told in the "Boke of Curtasye," Babees Boke, p. 310. *See also* Fieta, lib. ii. cap. 24
Portagium, carriage on the back, 21, 23, 57, 70, 98, 230, 232, 283
Portiforium, a breviary, 279 **24**
Potage, 25 **22**
Potecarius, an apothecary, 219 **3**
Potted ducks for sea voyage, 223 **34**
Potell, a wine measure holding two quarts
Poteller, a pottle measure of leather, 18; a pot poteler, 154 **22**
Poudre, 33 **31**, of gynger, 31
Poudrez, anguillæ, salted eels, 73
Powder-baggs, ? for salt or flour, in the scullery, 152 **9**
Poultry, prandium for, 208 **26**. *See* Pntura.
capons, fowls, chicken (*capones, gallinæ, polæ, pulcini*), 8, 9, 11, 13, 25, 30, 32, 51, 53, 100, 162, 191, 204.

Poultry—*continued*.
205, 209, 214, 218, 250. The Finchale Accounts have "galli, gallinæ, pulli," p. cxxcix.
pullets, 181 **19**
geese (*auces*), 9 **20**, 11, 13, 30, 51, 162, 191, 214, 218
pigeons (*columbellæ*), 45 **16**, 53, 162, 191, 212, 214
mallards, wild ducks, 53, 82, 83, 84, 107, 191, 205, 206, 212, 214, 218
partridges, 82, 83, 84, 206, 212, 218, 224, 227
little birds, 82, 212, 214, 218, 227 **15**
pheasants, 205 **8**, 206, 212, 214, 218
peacocks, 165
teal, 205 **21**, 206 **5**, 212, 214, 218
snytes, snipes, 212 **28**
cages and baskets for living, 25, 48 **7**, 84
Pounce, 19 **17**
Poyntell, a style for writing on wax tablets, 5 **16**
Pramo, the owner of a prame, 174 **16**
Prames (*pranhm*, Low Germ., derived from Slavic, Kluge), open, flat-bottomed Prussian boats for transport, 38, **42**, 46, 164, **174**; repair and covering of, 40; anchors, sails, ropes, lines, and timber procured for, and other expenses in making ready, 40, 41; mats to cover the provisions in, 41; cables to drag them overland, 48 **13**; sheep-hatches and poultry-cages in, 48 **15**, **16**; cost of navigating and hire of, 55, 56; tables in, 56 **15**; pilots for, 56; help with, given by a serjeant of the city of Dantzic, 57; entered down by a clerk of Königsberg, 113. 41, Victualing a prame, 175 **24**; hired to carry wardrobe to Dantzic, 177
Prebenda, horse rations per day, 9 **14**, 188 **22**, 207, 243, 245 **9**, 250
Presents to Derby, in Prussia, 105, 107, 108, 109, 110, 111, 114; at Hull, 111
Presepe ovinum, 48, sheep-hatch on the prames
Prestitus, money advanced or lent, 140f **13**, 206 **20**, **22**, 292 **6**
Prisoners at Dantzic, 113
Providencia, provisions, things provided (not necessarily food), 5, 28, 34, 38, 47, 60, 104, 170, 220
Pulletria, office for poultry, eggs, milk, and butter, cheese, &c., 15, 17, 25, 45, 82, 83, 84, 241; house hired for, 220

INDEX III.   351

Putnra, food, usually here the food of poultry, 25 **31**, 64 **2 0**, 208 **4**, 220 ; of sheep, 96
Pu-ayne, a gorget. 172 **32**
Pylche. *See* Pilche
Pynenade, 19 **6**, conserve of the seeds or "nuts" of the pignon pine (? Pinus pinea, or p. pineaster, both Italian trees) or pinnote-tre. *See* London's "Encyclopædia of Plants," 1841, p. 806 ; Bradley's "Stratmann," p. 476 ; Pegge's "Forme of Cury," xxv.

Quarteria, a measure, the quarter, 8, 10, &c.
Quaternus, quire, 5 **17**, 159
Quynes, coyns, quinces, 19 **5**

Rakkes, pair of racks for hanging cauldrons, 18 **31** ; in a kitchen, 205 ; in stables, 205.
Real, royal, an attribute meaning the very best ; papir ryal, gobete, and drage real, 8, 19
Reeds or rushes (*cirpa*) for the floor, 16 **30**, 63 **14**, 67, &c.
Regal. *See* Wood
Regardum, reward, extra or special payment, 5 **12**, 122 **32**, 161
Registrum, 279 **24**, ? *for* regestum, a treasure-box or case for a book, &c. "Registra pro suo libro," D. of L., cl. 28, bdle. 1, No. 5.
Relics at Karlstein, Prague, 275 **5** ; in the chapel at Rhodes, 277 **12**
Religion, accessories of. *See* Altar.
chalice and chrism, 92 **30**
Corpus Christi brought from the ship to Dantzic, 104 **21** ; taken from Dantzic to the ship, 166
adoration of the Cross, 117
indulgences at four Dantzic churches at Easter, 117
"tables" for Derby's chapel taken from Dantzic to Boston, 183 **7**
celebration by chaplain at Drossen, 186 **23**
reredos, 219 **8**.
two stone super-altars and their consecration at Prague, 279 **21**
breviary with a silver case, 279 **24**
Reyne, reins, 240 **12**
Reys, reysa (Old H. Germ.: modern *reise*, a journey), 38, 40, 47 ; a march, military expedition ; provisions made

Reys—*continued.*
for in Dantzig, 45-50 ; beginning of, 50 **7** ; provisions bought during, 50-53
Reysyngs, raisins, 79
Rice. *See* Spices
Rings, turquoise, 28 ; Balais ruby, 287 **25**
Rollage, charge for rolling casks of wine to the boat, 19
Roos, roes, 108 **7**, **9**, 113 **20**. *See* Meat.
Ropes, 40, 48 **13** : to tie cattle to pasture, 48 **19** ; of hay for horses, 158, 174
Roseyne, rosin, 64 **6**
Rostern, a gridiron, 24 **7**
Ruban, ribbon, mottly 8 ; golden, 285
Rumage, 19 **25**, 23 **1**, 157 **2**, appears to mean the same as rollage
Rye. *See* Siligo.

Saculus, money-bag or purse, 6 **29**
Sacks and sack-cloth, 21 **9**, 54, 152, 154: sewing of, 25 **7**, 86 ; leather sacks, 43 **30** ; for spices 154, oats 195, bread 222, fish 228 **34**. Cloth sacks for clothes on a journey. *See* Cloth Sacks.
Saddles and saddlery 13 **27**, 46, 152 **24**, 154, 173, 175 ; repair of, 185, 191, 196, 199, 257 **8** ; cloth for arraying saddles, 166 **31**, 186 **27**
Safe conduct, 20 **10**, 179 **31**
Saginum, lard, hog's fat, 11, 189 **30**, 193, 202, 203
Sagitta, ? a stave in cooperage, 155
Sagittarius, an archer, 105 ; this was a gunner-archer. *See* Wages.
Saguen, fat, 21 **16**, "porco magno de saguine," a large fatted hog
Saler, a salt-cellar
Salseria, sausery, office for mustard, vinegar, verjuice, salt, &c., and salted vegetables (salsiamentis 258 **6**), 15, 22, 152, 177, 190
Salsarius, a saucer, *i.e.* a platter of pewter or wood for salted food and sauces, 154, 244
Salt, 12, 15, 29, 48, 72, 182, 211, 221: coarse salt (*sal grossus*) 152 ; white, 152, 186, 193
Saucers, 100 **28**, 101 **25**
Scabbard, 35 **12**, 94 **12**
Scabellum, a seat or stool, 48, 75, 281 **11**
Scaccarium, a chess-board, 49 **20**
Scalk, Ital. *scalco*, head-cook and steward on the galley, 224 **26**, 225, 226, 229, 232

Schan, 225 **27**; skain, a dressing knife for meat (Halliwell)
Schane, 20 **27**, 76 **32**, a kind of knife. "Schave, or schavynge knyfe," Prompterium; or it may be a misreading of schane, *i.e.* skain, a dressing knife, (Halliwell)
Schavyng-casks, in cooperage, 22
Schaveyn, a pilgrim's gown, 230 **8**
Scok = schok, a lot containing sixty articles, 75
Seomer, summer, 24
Scot, a Prussian coin, or money of account. *See* p. xcix.
Scope, a scoop, 86
Scriuen, 225 **19**, 226 **25**, 231, 232, ship's officer who wrote down expenses. *Scrivano*, a clerk or writer, adopted in our early ships from Portuguese or Spanish (Smyth's "Sailor's Wordbook"), but here it is in an Italian vessel
Scutcheons, *See* Arms.
Scutellæ, dishes, 211 **20**, 233 **28**
Scutellaria, scullery, *i.e.* office for bowls, troughs, plates, dishes, and fuel, 15, 59, 61, 72, 85, 154, 160, 171, 233; cups of wood, 17 **25**, 59; vinegar and mustard, 59, 155; brass basin, 153; brass kettle, 171 **18**; necessities provided for, 165, 166. *See* Dresser.
Scutifer, an esquire, 106, 128, 131, &c.
Scythes and sickles for the Keysa, 48
Seler, for cellar, 72
Sengle, a leather-strap, 34 **19**. *See* Horsegear
Sepum, *for* sebum, 209
Sepe *for* cepe, onions, 39 **26**, 40 **12**, 51, 69
Sercisia *for* cervisia, ale
Sewet, suet, 277 **10**
Sextarium, a sextar, wine measure, containing five pottles, 15, 16. It appears to be a French measure in use with the French wines.
Seyles, sails, 10
Sgomery *for* skombri, mackerel, 229
Shearing of cloth, linen, blanket, &c., 89, 90, 104, 284 **1**, 285 **6**, 286 **5**
Sheppel, shephul, Mid. H. Ger. *scheffel*, *schofull*, bushel, a German corn measure, 48, 60
Shield, scutum, Derby's, 94, 95
Shield in heraldry. *See* Arms
Ships. *See* Galley, **Frames**, Lodesman, Steresman

Ships—*continued*.
landing-bridge to bring horses from, 15 **15**
at Boston, master and servants of, 20
hearth of tiles made in, 23; towed from Boston haven, 23
cabins and other necessities made in, at Boston, 26 **8**, 27; at Dantzig, 76; at Lynn, 156
carpenters in, their materials and tools, 20, 26, 76; masters, men, and wages, 27, 76, 78, 156, 157, 174
pitch, timber, and other materials for, 76, 157; caulking, 180 **4**. *See* Linum
oven in the kitchen on Derby's ship, 77 **3**; office of pantry, 156
tools, vessels, and other articles provided for, 86, 87; lanterns, 87, 155
stable fitted up in, for the horses, 158 **4**, 174 **32**
windows (*fenestralla*) in, 157; lucarnes, lucerns, 221 **30**, 228 **6**. *See* Lucerna
rudder (tymon) mended, 225 **19**, 231 **24**
various vessels, farcost, farecost, ? a coasting boat, 97 **26**, 98 **5**, **6**; craiers, slow trading vessels, 99 **20**, **23** (Smyth's "Sailor's Word-book"); passaiours, 279 (appear to be boats of passage across the Straits of Dover); balinger, 279, a sea-going vessel
Ship of the lord's hall, 87 **25**, 97 **24**, 98. The vessel which carried the prince represented his dwelling and court for the time, and was called his hall and chamber (*aula et camera*) like that on land. So at Lynn the carpenters made a hall, chamber, and chapel in the ship for the second voyage to Prussia, 157 **17**. In this, as in household rules, Derby followed the royal custom at sea. *See* H. Nicholas' "Hist. of Navy," II., 101, 191, "Black Book of Admiralty," Rolls Ser., I., before II, and lxxxvii., lxxxviii.
Sick men in Prussia, 51 **12**
Siceez. *See* Money, ciii.
Siege of Wilna, miners and engineers at, 105, 106
Signet of gold, engraved with plume and collar, 34 **26**
Siligo, rye, 80 **9**, 97 **32**
Siliqua, rye, 225 **27**

Silk, in knots or bows, 90 **28** ; by the ounce, red, white, and ruby, 94
Silver and gold ware, weight and price, 100, 286 **18**, 287 **16**
   treacle box, 12 **27, 29**, 13
   six scales, 100
   thirteen spoons, 100 **23**
   charger, dishes and saucer, 100
   two [? 12] spice-plates ornamented with 12 shields of arms, gilt, 100, 101 **3**
   salt-cellars, silver gilt, 101, 288 **21**
   covercle or lid for a pot, 101
   cups, 187 **25**, 287 **12**; basins, 196 **4**; ewer, 287 **12**
   chains for Derby and Dalyngridge, silver-gilt, 101
   belts, 279, 283
   collars, some silver, some gilt, 280 **7**, 283 **21**, 286, 287 **15**
   gold collar and chain, 286
   flores domini. *See* Flores
Sinetura, 234 **31**, 279 **25**; belt, ? for bottles (like John Gilpin's), 234 **29**
Singulus, a girdle, ? of the coat of mail, 74 **5**; singulus equinus, a horse girth, 200
Siroteeæ, ceroteca, gloves or gauntlets, 46 **19**, 92 **34**, 287 **10**
Sirpus. *See* Cirpus
Sizan, civ. *See* Money.
Skales, scales of silver, 100
Skaldyng of pigs, 65, 68
Skep, a basket, 174 **31**
Skins, goat and sheep, 35 **10**; black, 35
Skypper, skipper or captain of a ship, 37
Skyppagium, money paid for sailing or navigation, 37, 108 **15**, 174, 278; diskippaginum, disembarking, 255 **11, 12**
Slypyng, 46 **14**; whetting, sharpening; a sword-slyper, one who whets swords (Jamieson).
Smigma, 224 **5**, 240 **6**. soap. " Finchale Accts.," p. cccexlvii.
Soap, 63 **13**, 85 **19**, 154 **3**
Somarius, somer, sumpter-horse, 5, 6
Sorel horse, 5
Sotulares, shoes, 89, 90, 91, 93, 164, 171, 194, 251
Sparrez, 156 **3, 26**
Speciaria, spicery, 11, 14, 21, 33
Speciebus, spices, 42, 67
   bags to put them in, 67
   bought in London, 160 **2**

Spelta, a kind of barley or inferior wheat, 207 **15**, 225
Spet, ? a spit, 205 **23**
Spices and dried fruits—
   almonds, 8 **27**, 62, 70, 153, 182, 213; bale of, 154; confected, 191 **2**, 219, 231
   ginger, 11, 19, 21, 29, 31, 32, 153, 182; ginger en confit, a confect, 19 **7**; green ginger in pots, 154; ginger pist, ? paste, 221;
   ginger madrean, ? Fr. *madré*, mapled or spotted, 19 **12** "Un livre de madrian," Douët d'Arcq, " Comptes de l'Argenterie," p. 246
   pepper, 11, 21, 29, 32, 182
   cinamon (*canella*) 11, 21, 79, 153, 191, 228; in powder, 209
   clowes, cloves, 11 **21**, 22, 154 **3**, 159, 182, 219, 221; clowes en confyt, a confect of cloves, 19 **8**
   dattiles, dates, 8 **28**, 11 **21**, 70, 73, 86, 171, 182, 221
   racemi de corene, currants, 11 **22**, 154, 221 **15**, 226
   crocus, saffron, 17, 21, 29, 32, 100, 153, 179, 182, 253; in bottles, 74, **32**
   carawey, 19 **7**, 154
   rice, 21, 154, 219, 221; floure de rys or ground rice, 22
   anneys en confyt, anys confecto, confect of anniseed, 19 **11**, 68, 219 **15**; anise, 154
   notemug, 19, nutmeg, 154
   mace, macez, 22, 153, 159, 221
   quibibbes, cubebs, 22, 154
   sanudres, sanders, 22, sandal-wood, used in tinting jellies, sweetmeats, &c.
   comyn, cummin, 22
   alkenade, alkenet, or wild bugloss, used for colouring in cookery, 151 **8**
   gariselet, 19 **12**. Is this an error of the scribe, either for Italian *girasole*, turnsole, or for *gariofile*?
   figs, 70, 73, 79, 228 **18**
   raisins, 79 **34**
   galingale, 154, a warm spice-powder made from the root of several plants Eastern and English, formerly much used as drug and condiment. " Prompt Parv.," 185; " Babees Boke," 216

Spices and dried fruits—*continued*.
  licorice, 154
  colyandre, coriander, 219
  zitromade, conserve of citrons, 219, 221, 228
  pynes, 154. *See* Pynenale
  pistaplis, pistachios, 219
  turnsole, 154, a drug used for colouring in cookery, and for dyeing. Pegge's "Form of Cury," p. 58, note x. The plant must have been one noted for turning to the sun. Landon and Littré say the heliotrope, "Babees Boke" has *Achillea tomentosa*, none suggest the sunflower itself, helianthus, a species of which comes from Asia. *Cf.* Ital. *girasole*.
Spiking, 157 **20**
Spits, large and small, 102
Spongyng a barrel, ? cleaning it, 178 **20**
Sprygelle, 72 **18**, an article used in the buttery, ? a tap
Spurs (in Paris), 287 **23**
Spyce-plates, 100 **25**, **29**, special plates for sweets, confections, dried fruit, &c. (*cf.* spices), answering to modern dessert-plates.
Spyks, spikes, a sort of nail, 26
Stables cleansed, 11 **33** ; repaired, 169, 174; mangers in, 61, 205, 208; at Portogruaro, racks in, 205 ; fittings for, 208 **2**, **6**, 211
Stak, stack, 66, **9**, 72, 77
Staples of iron, 26
Stara, an Italian dry and liquid measure, a sester or sextar. 205 **3**
Stationery provided by the clerk of the spicery, 19, *e.g.* paper, red wax, parchment, pounce
Staunche, 164 **23**, material to stay bleeding
Staurum, store for providing, 181 **25**
Stepyng yn, steeping in, a vat for, 74 **10**
Stereman, man at the wheel, 104 **13**, 162
Stewe of the bishop's house at Dantzie, 74 **19**, probably a fish pool
Stock-fish, hammers for, 80 **23**
Stocks, a pair of, bought, 102
Stopa, a stoup, liquid measure, as for honey, 9 **23** ; wine, 11 **21**, 39 ; and ale
Stopells for bottles, stoppers. 72 **18**, 234 **29**
Store, 61 **6**

Stowage, work of packing, 22, 155, **32**
Stragulum, a rayed or striped outer garment, 89, **11** ; sheared, *i.e.* the long nap taken off, 89 **16**
Straw, 54 **3**, 72, 74; for the lord's chamber, 252, **30**
Streynours, a cloth used for straining out, in cookery, 22, 67, 157, 228, 238 ; used in bolting flour, 25
Stryeage, *i.e.* strikage, 22.
Stuffura, stuffing, 46 **24**
Succades or conserves with sugar—
  drage real, a fine sweetmeat. 19 **13** ; box of dragge. 225 **8**
  pasta real. 19 **10** ; royal paste, a dried paste of sugar and spices, *see* recipe in Halliwell
  divers confections, 62, 68, 167 **30**, 171 **29**, 221, 228 **23**, 229, 233, 249
  gobete real, 19 **9**, a royal tit-bit
Sugar, 68, 70, 191, 229 ; in loaf, 77, 86
  loaf of caffetin, 11 **6**, **19**, 21, 153, 182, 205 **5**, 219 **5**, 221
  siprei, Cyprus sugar, 11 **19**, 21
  flat sugar, red and white, 19 **9**
  pot sngar, 221 **23**
  sugre roseto, 225 **11**
  sugar candy, 19 **10**, 219, 222
  penydes, 19 **12**, pennets or barley sugar ; "livre de pénites," Douët d'Arcq, p. 216 ; " in penettes emptis," Account Roll of Holy Trinity, Dublin, p. 3 (Soc. Ant. Ireland). Originally the Arab word *fanid*, Heyd, II. 683
  sugared water, 225 **26**
  surrip, syrup, 22 **25** Heyd gives the different kinds of sugar known in the fourteenth century ("Commerce du Levant," 1886, II. 691), among these were several sorts of loaf sugar, one being the *caffetino*, rounded at the top, white sugar of the second quality. A French ordinance of 1333 speaks of "bon suere caffetin en suere blanc" ; the French King John consumed many pounds of it, bought at Lincoln, during his sojourn in England in 1359-60. Douët d'Arcq, "Comptes de l'Argenterie," 1851, pp. 215, 231, 101. Another sugar was *poudre*, less firm; on transport of the moulds its particles fell apart ; it seems to answer to

Sugar—*continued*.
  our moist sugar. But as early as
  1265 the Countess of Leicester had
  what seems to have been white
  sugar pounded (Hudson Turner,
  "Manners and Household Expenses," Roxb. Club, pp. li. 71).
  The sugar grown in Cyprus, near
  Bafa and Limasol, was the finest
  in the Mediterranean. *Sugar candy*
  was in large morsels well crystallized (*candi* from the Sanscrit
  khanda, a bit or morsel, by way of
  Persia and Arabia). *Sugre roseto*
  was sugar perfumed with roses or
  rosewater. *Miel sucré* was the un-
  crystallized juice that ran through
  the cask, like our treacle. *Sucre
  plat* was one of the cheaper sorts
  of loaf, flattened at the top; its
  price here is 1s. per lb., while the
  caffetino is 4s.
Suiti, followers, 16 **33**
Sumpter-men, 100, 106 **27**, 108, 113,
  255
Sursengles, surcengula. *See* Horsegear
Sus, sow, a machine under cover of which
  the miners worked in the siege of
  Wilna, 105 **21**
Sutor, a shoe-maker, 281, 288
Sygle, sickle, 48

Tabelers et meisne, backgammon board
  and men, 113 **17**, 178 **8**, 264,5;
  meisne=meiny or mainy. O. Fr., household followers
Tabler, tablerinm, 178 **8**, 281 **23**, ? a
  towel or a knife. Ducange
Tables, 178 **27**
Tabula, comensalis cum uno pare tresteles, dining table with trestles, 49,
  63, 75; de Prussia, 109 **3**, 305
  pro altari, 49 **19**; for a dresser in the
  kitchen, 69 **6**; for the pantry, with
  two rests, 72; for a battery bar,
  239 **8**, 239; for coats of arms, *see*
  Arms
Taffata. *See* Textile.
Tailors employed, 35; one killed, 110 **6**
Tales, dice, 35 **26**. *See* Games.
Tallow candles, 6, 12, 14, 28, 32, 39, 60,
  63, 65, 71, 72, 75, 100, 167, 183, 187,
  214; tallow-melting, 86 **32**
Tapetum, a carpet or hanging tapestry,
  25, 281 **13**, **14**

Tar, 26, 41; for cart-wheels, 186
Tassa, 239 **15**, a leather purse or
  pouch. Riley's "Memorials of London," p. 360
Taverner, 39
Tela, 234, 279 **17**, a term for a stuff or
  web, usually applied to linens and the
  like.
Tele, a teal, sort of duck, 206 **5**
Tents and cords for the Reysa, 50;
  Prussian valets serving them, 105
Textile fabrics, panni, telæ, &c.—
  baldekyn, green, 281 **24**; white,
  282 **22**; black, 282 **24**; red,
  282 **15**, 287 **24**; red de grana, *i.e.*
  scarlet, 282 **17**. A rich stuff of
  silk, the weft often *broché* with
  gold, generally ornamented with
  figures; the name derived from
  Bagdad, where it was first made; it
  was afterwards made at Damascus
  and Cyprus. Heyd, II. p. 697.
  Loveney has "baldekyns auri de
  Cipre." D. of L., cl. 28, b. 1, No. 5
  gold cloth of Cyprus, 35 **5**. A costly
  silk interwoven with gold thread
  silk cloth of Damascus, 280; this was
  often in two colours. D. of L., cl.
  28, bdle. 1, No. 5
  gilt cloth (deauratus), 281 **19**; cloth
  of gold, 286 **4**
  taffata, tapheta, 31, 287; blue-grey,
  90. A Persian silk, Pers. *taftah*.
  Heyd, II. p. 700.
  satin, 280 **5**; black, 89; red, 282 **25**,
  287 **4**
  satellins, 282 **27**; a kind of dressed
  silk. Ducange
  silk, 89 **31**, 94, 286 **12**; bows of red
  and white, 90 **28**
  scendel, sendal, blue-grey, 94 **21**,
  285 **33**, 286 **2**. A kind of thin
  silk. Heyd, II. 701
  velvello, velvet, 286 **4**; green, 282;
  white, 282 **13**; red, 284 **16**; black,
  284 **18**; blue-grey, bought at Milan,
  288 **19**; velewet and gold, 288 **14**
  ribbon, golden, 285 **22**
  Attaby (*misprinted* Accaby), 283 **24**;
  a heavy silk mixed with gold:
  "pro j gonua longa domini furrata,
  ij peciæ Attaly auri," D. of L.,
  cl. 28, bdle. 1, No. 5. Attabya
  was the name of a quarter of Bagdad, *Attabi* the Arab name for a

Textile Fabrics—*continued*.
heavy rayed satin, whence came the word *tapis* (tappetum), applied to all heavy stuffs of silk or wool used as carpets, curtains, or other furniture. The makers of Asia Minor were specially famous for their *tapis*, Heyd, II. 706. Derby had some of both. *See* Tapetum.
cloth (no kind named), blue (*bloduus*), 89, 91, 153, 284; green, 283 **28**; black, 88, white, 153, 284, presented to great men, 93, 94; white for lining, 283 **3**; red, 88; scarlet, 89; English scarlet, 281 **32**; russet, 116
worsted, white and red, 152
Westnall, 152; used for packing, 35; for covering a dresser, 16: **10**. A worsted cloth, the name seems derived from Westphalia. "Westnall de worsted," white or red and black, used for lining of saddles, bed covers, &c., is found in Loveney's Wardrobe Accts., 1397-8, D. of L., cl. 28, blle. 1, No. 5. Hirsch, pp. 256, 257, says it was used for linings, sacks, &c.
Wadmoll, a coarse woollen cloth, 158
blanket, 173 **23**; for lining petticoats, 89, 280; shorn, 164 **20**
cloth of Frise, woollen friese, 280 **25**; blue, 8 **25**; green, 10
fustian, 30 **10**, 112 **15**, 172, 180
kersey, 89
kanle, a material, probably worsted, of which flags were made, 90 **24**, **26**
woollen cloth, for servants, 89 **18**; for liveries of valets, grooms, pages, &c., 282 **33**; for falcons' cages, 91; for covering saddles, 240 **30**; green, 241 **23**
bokeram, buckram, 152
linen cloth, 46, 89, 90, 91, 207, 234, 286; by the piece for towels, 61, 154; drape lynge, 180; lingio, 200 **12**
linen of Prussia, 89, 172 **20**; white of Dantzic, 89
mappa Paris, 151; opera Paris, 258 **2**. "Naperie" and "napkyns of Parice" occur in the Clarence Ordinances, 103, 104
cloth (*tela*) of Reynes, *i.e.* Rennes in

Textile Fabrics—*continued*.
Brittany, 152, ? fine linen. In the Wardrobe Accts., 1397-8, the things made of tela de Reynes are shirts and drawers ("iiij camisiis et vj braccis"), kerchiefs, sheets and pillow cases, and lining of a satin doublet. D. of L., cl. 28, blle. 1, No. 5
cloth (*tela*) of Flanders, 10, 11, 23, 24, 157, 158, ? a strong linen. Used to make a shirt under coat of mail, linings of sleeves, doublets, &c. D. of L., cl. 28, blle. 1, No. 5
lewyn, 80 **15**, ? cloth of Louvain. *See* Lewyn
canvas, 6, 10, 94, 153, 154, 157, 281, 283
streynour, cloth for sifting or straining, 159 **19**. *See* Bultyng, Streynour
the shearing of cloth, including linen, 30 **7**, 164 **20**, 285 **6**. *See* Shearing
cloth of Lyra, 89, 90, 281, 283; black, 91 blood-red, 111. Lire or Liere is a town of Brabant between Mechlin and Antwerp
Theft or loss made good by Derby, 181 **21**, 184, 192, 211 **20**, 236 **19**, 240 **27**, 243 **22**
Thourkeys, par de, 35 **11**; a pair of pincers, O. Fr. *truquaise* (Roquefort); *turkes*, Gawain Douglas, cited in "Finchale Inventories," Glossary, under *turked*
Thread, 86 **26**, 90 **9**, 172 **22**, 180 **22**
Tieldes, 88 **13**, for carrying the hawks. I can find no instance of this word in books of hawking or elsewhere, perhaps it was some kind of cover to put over the birds on the "cadge" or frame on which they were carried. In a list of tackle, &c., for a large barge are "ketels, teeldes, and skaltrowes," but this seems to be a pot or tub. Riley's "Memorials of London Life," p. 369
Toga, 233 **25**, for the baptized Turk
Tonella, tonel, small tun, 24, 79; used for flour, 25 **1**
Tonsura, shearing of linen and other cloth. *See* Shearing, Stragulum
Torches, 74 **17**, 75, 282; wick for, 66; hooks to hang, 68; iron ladles for making, 80

Torteys, tortices, 74, 75, 111. The tortay, *tortícius*, seems to have been a large wax candle: "torches and tortayes," brought by a "yeoman, cunnyng in waxemakinge," Lib. Niger. Edw. IV., and *see* Ducange, *tortisius*. The waxchandlers made them, Riley's "Mem. of London," p. 359. *Cf.* "Boke of Curtasye," ll. 825-827, in "Babees Boke," p. 327
Towels, 61 **13**, 154
Towaill, 207 **9**, 234, 258
Towandum, towing, 37
Tiles, 58 **2**
Tin, par botels de tyn, 49; flasks, 224
Travel, daily expenses of, during two months, Sept. 24 to Dec. 1, 1392, 183-211
Treacle, 12 **28**, 13 **10**, an antidote for poison, a medicine
Tractagium, tractura, drawing or dragging, 161, 176, 232
Trenchers, 208 **21**; bread for, 218 **30**, 238 **28**. Trenchers were cut from loaves specially made; and there were rules for cutting and properly laying them on the table, "Babees Boke," 200, 322, 323, 369. It seems to have been black bread; the minor canons of St. Paul's, in 1378, each had weekly "tres panes nigros vocentos trenchar-bred." W. Sparrow Simpson's "Registrum Statutorum St. Pauli," pp. 325, xxxv.: "No blacke breade but for trenchours or houndes," Lib. Niger. Edw. IV., p. 69
Trencher, v. to cut, 35
Trencherknyff, 195 **25**, a knife to cut trenchers from the loaves made for table-trenchers, 195 **25**.
Trestles, 86. *See* Tabula.
Trow, trough, 24, 25, 57, 61, 73, 208, 224; for the baker, J. Fisher, 158 **16**
Trussura, the act of packing or tying up; (Fr. *trossa* or *troussa*, a bundle), 34 **17**, 35 **15**
Tubbes, 224 **8**, 233
Tumbler, "making minstrelcy," 109 **15**
Tunges, tongs, 158 **14**
Tunder, tinder and box, 222 **4**
Turquoise ring, ? 28
Tymbre, timber, a packet of fur skins tied together as brought for sale, 92, 93; the number varied from 10 to 40 (Statutes, Record ed., I. p. 205)

Tymon, rudder of a ship, 225, 231

Ulna, an ell, 35
Unguents for sick horses. *See* Horses
Ure-ox, oore, 109

Vagina, a scabbard, 46 **15**
Valets, wages of, xcvii. *See* Wages gifts and rewards to, 105
Vambrace, armour for front of the arm, 280 **4**
Vasa, vessels in Italy (for salting meat), 220; for wine, 222. *See* Wooden Cups
Vat (fatte), empty for steeping, 74 **10**
Vegetables, sometimes called sauces, 78 **27**, 231. (*Cf.* modern "gardensauce")
leeks (*perra*), 48 **24**, 78, 221, 225, 229, 230, 239
onyons, 73. *See* Sepum, 97
various herbs, 49, 67, 214, 239. *See* Herbs
cole-wort (*oleribus*), 63, 67, 70, 78, 214, 221, 224, 225, 228, 230, 239; probably often salted, like sauerkraut. (*Cf.* 70 **27**
caboches, cabbages, 67, 78, 221
garlick, 69 **30**. *See* Alleum
peas, 25, 45, 48, 70, 73, 97, 181, 213, 228, 231, 239, 249
parsley, 229, 230, 231, 252
cauleria, 230 **17**, 231. Ital. *cavola*, a cauliflower, Ducange
peas-cods, 29 **1**, 251 **16**, 253
beans (*faba*), 252 **1**, 253, 255
Veill, la, at Treviso, 285 **26**. Placeword, unexplained
Venison, 111 **15**
Vergens, verges, vericus, verjnice (an acid liquid made from crushed crabapples, unripe grapes, or sorrel), 12, 14, 23, 155, 190
Verrez de glas, glass drinking vessels, 58; verres, 74 **18**, 168 **30**, 235, 239, 244. Hirsch mentions several kinds of drinking glasses at Dantzig, 257
Vesselamenta, all sorts of vessels, 34
Vexillatorus, standard-bearer, 16
Vexillum, flag, 40; leather bag for, 43
Village near Rixhöft, 38, 39
Vinegar, 12, 48 **22**, 59, 60, 74 **27**, 190, &c.

Vitrum, vitreum, a glass cup or drinking vessel, 190 **17**, 195 **8**, 208 **28**, 209, **12**, 222, 223
Virga, a yard (measure), 8, 21
Vmbre. *See* Fish
Voidz, empty, 169
Vrinales, ? urinals on, 75 **1**, and 92 **3**. According to Ducange the word also means *orarium*, a light cloth or kerchief, and it also appears to mean the border of a robe, which sometimes was lined or stuffed with cotton: the word occurring among the items of the Wardrobe, 91 **34**, 92 **3**, 281 **15**, 283 **14**, probably refers to one of these

Wadmoll, a coarse woollen cloth 158 **22**
Wafreres, 104 **16**, 109, makers of wafer-cakes; *waufre, gaufre*, O. Fr., a thin cake. "Gilberto j wafrer ministranti wafres ad mensam domini regis et regine et eciam ad mensam domini [*i.e.* Henry] tempore Parliamenti," A.D., 1396-7. D. of L., cl. 28, bdle. 3, No. 6.
Wages, 118-142, 264-272; of divers men—
  carpenters, 26, 27, 78, 79, 82, 169
  carters, 54, 68 **24**
  prame sailors, 55
  the shoe-smith, 64 **7** (his stipendium)
  pastry-cook, 64 **32**
  a painter of arms, 79
  of a painter of meats, 169 **19**
  knights, squires, and valets, 118, 133, 137, 264-268; special on the Reysa, 128-132
  archers, 118, 119, 120, 121, 122, 123, 124, 128
  minstrels, 132, 137, 141, 269, 271
  valets and grooms, 240 **25**,
  the herald, 267, 271 **30**
  the porter, 266 **28**
Wardrobe, office of, expenses in England, 31; in Prussia, 45 **7**, 46, 49 **21**, 88-95, 155. Woollen and linen cloth after it was bought often had to be sheared; the expense both of this and of making many of the garments of retainers, henchmen, &c., as well as of the lord, also of making flags, banners, and pennons, &c., belonged to the Wardrobe.

Wardrobe carried back to England, 177, 180, 257 **20**
Warrokes, 238 **14**, girths or straps. Warrok occurs as verb, to bind or restrain, "York Plays," p. 291, l. 525
Water, fresh, in casks and barrels, 22, 24, 83, 86, 153, 157, 159, 229; carriage of, 74; water tonnes, 74
Wax, 32, 52, 65, 75, 190; cera operata, 14, 22, 61, 160, 167, 206, 233, 235; non operata, 88, 223 **16**; red wax, 19 **14**, 154; candles, 221 **17**, 229
Waynemen, waynesmen, waggoners, carters, 180
Wayne, waggon, 182 **30**
Weapons. *See* Armour—
  bows and arrows, 31, 34, 154
  broad bows and broad arrows, 34 **16**, **18**
  axes, 48 **28**. *See* Axes
  alblast or crossbow, 74, 93
  balista, 94
  lances, 34 **29**, 74
  scabbard, 35 **12**, 94 **12**
  swords, 35 **3**, 46 **14**, 94 **11**, 286 **11**, 287 **14**
Weighing, of meat and fish at Dantzig, 87 **16**; of pewter and brass, 102
Weights—
  Goldsmiths', *i.e.* Prussian money, 100, 101
  Troy, 100 **28**
  for pewter and brass, the stone and pound Prussian, 101, 102
  uncia = ounce of sugar, 182
  lb. = pound *passim*
Wheat bought for the pantry, 20; carriage of it, 24 **34**, 25 **6**, **8**
Wheels mended, 188, 197, 202, 203 **32**
Wheel-band, 202
Windarium, the hoisting or moving by a windlass, 162 **26**
Wine, 68, 165, 172, &c.; bought by gallon at Barton-on-Humber, 99 **33**; tube or cane for drawing, 208 **24**; expenses over filling vessels for ship, and carriage of them, 222, 223
Wines, red, 27 **27**; white, 69 **2**, 75, 87, 95; sweet (dulcis), 77
  landewyn, 47 **8**, 81, country wine of Prussia, chiefly grown near Thorn at this period. Hirsch, p. 262
  of Leba, in Pomerania, 77
  Renyss, Rynen, Rhenish, 24, 42, 43, 47, 58, 80, 172, 174. In London in

Wines—*continued*.
14th cent. (1381) Rhenish was double the price of Gascon wine, and forty years later it was not only ordered that it should be put in separate cellars from wines of Gascony, Rochelle, and Spain, but taverners were forbidden to sell them together. Riley's "Mem. of London Life," pp. 181, 342; "Liber Albus," vol. iii. 269, 270
of Garnade, Gernade, 64 **15**. 66 **22**. 78, 81 **31**. 84. 95. Granada (*cf.* Chaucer's "In Gernade atte siege badde he be," Prologue, l. 56); wine from that province, perhaps wine of Malaga. Henderson, p. 395
Lepe, 95, a strong white wine of Spain; Lepe, a small town on sea-coast, between Ayamont and Palos, long celebrated for raisins, figs, and wine. Henderson, p. 396. Chaucer warns against "the white wine of Lepe" sold in London, the "famosile" of which brings the drinker "in Spayne, right at the toun of Lepe." "Pardoner's Tale"
Malvesye, malmsey, 205, 206, 222. A sweet wine of Greece, chiefly grown in Crete. Henderson, p. 287; "Informacyon for Pylgrymes," sign. C iij. v°
Romoneye, 209 **3**. 222, 230, 232, 239. A sweet wine made in Greece [*alias* Romania, Heyd, II., p. 696] Henderson, p. 288; grown at Axtin in Corfu and at Modon in Morea. Wey's "Itineraries" (Roxb. Club), pp. 94, 124; "Informycyon for Pylgrymes" (Roxb. Club), sign. C iij
Rochelle, 10, 11, 14, 16, 165, 234. Light red wines grown in Poitou, shipped at Rochelle; had been drunk in England since the time of K. John. Henderson, pp. 278-279
Vasconiæ, Gascony, 6, 7, 10, 15, 16, 17, 20, 21, 29, 159, 160, 256; at various prices, 18 **4**; red, 78 **14**. The consumption of wines from this province was very large in England during the 13th and 14th centuries in proportion to that of other wines; they appear to have been clarets and

Wines—*continued*.
other light kinds, for common use. Henderson, pp. 279-283
Osey, 42, 95, a sweet wine of Alsace. Hirsch mentions this wine in the Dantzic trade, but does not know it, p. 262. Langland has "white wyn of Oseye," P. Plowman, C. Pass. I., l. 228 (Clar. Press ed.); the forms Osoye (Rot. Par. III. 121) and Osay (Morte Arthur. Linc. MS., fo. 55) show the English form of Aussoy (Rom. of l'artenay, E. E. T. Soc.) and Aussay (Roquefort's Dict.), which, as pointed out by Prof. Skeat, mean Alsace. The editor of "La Bataille des Vins," a poem of 13th cent., shows that Aussai is Alsace, the wines of Aussai and of the Mousele (Moselle) are grouped together, and the wines of Rochelle address them as pleasing the Germans—
"Vous Aussai et vous la Mousele, Se vous paissiez cele gent herre." (Œuvres de Henri d'Andeli, ed. A. Héron, Paris, 1881, pp. 23, 27, 95). In the "Manière de Langage" (close of 14th cent.), Osey is one in the list of "vins doucetes" or sweet wines (ed. M. P. Meyer, Paris, 1873, p. 392), and the Clarence Household Ordinances have it in a similar list (p. 101). *See*, too, Henderson, p. 289.
bought in Italy:—of Mark, 208 **14**. 219 **1**, 222, 232, 238, 239
of Treviso, 208 **15**, 219, 238
of Algarbe, 222 **17** (Algarvé in Portugal)
of Riboll, 223 **8**
of Castelfranco (Chastelfrank), 238 **31**
at Avigliano, 212 **33**
Wood—
meremium, timber, 26 **25**, 41, 75, 79, 205; forty great trees, 76
tabula, 180 **4**, 219. *See* Tabula
planks, plaunches, 22, 43
ferren or fir deles, 157; fir boards, 157 **31**
deles, deals, 26, 40, 63, 75, 76, 79, 157
bord, border, boards, 26, 156, 157
waynscots, 26, 76, 156; postes, 160 **1**
spars, 156, 157, 219; oaken spars, 157
regal, 157 **30**. "v regaldes" were

Wood—*continued.*
  in the naval storehouse in 1338.
  Harris Nicolas, "History of the Navy," vol. ii., p. 476
Wooden cups, 17 **25**, 59 **17**, 62 **17**, 66, 152, 156 ; dishes, 23 **11**, 67, 72, 169 ; sold by a turner, 27,**1** ; vessels for the galley, 224
Worsted. *See* Textile

Writing [list] of prames and carts at Königsberg, 113,**26**, Kingston's book of account, 115
Writing materials, 5,**14-17**, 153,**5**, 159, 257
Wyke, wick. 67,**28**, 88

Zinsubero, zinziber, ginger, 42, 228,**23**, 253

Printed by Nichols & Sons, 25, Parliament Street, S.W.

REPORT OF THE COUNCIL
OF
THE CAMDEN SOCIETY.

READ AT THE GENERAL MEETING
ON THE 2ND MAY, 1893.

The Council of the Camden Society elected on May 2, 1892, regret the loss by death of one of their number, Mr. James Doyle, a careful and judicious Antiquary, whose presence at their Meetings was always much esteemed.

They have further to regret the loss by death of the following Members of the Society :—

    John Birkbeck, Esq.,
    Rev. W. E. Buckley,
    Rev. Herbert Hill,
    R. C. Nichols, Esq.

They also have to report the following accessions to the Society :—

    W. K. Marriott, Esq.,
    John Bruce Nichols, Esq.,
    G. W. Prothero, Esq.,
    Tom C. Smith, Esq.,
    Mrs. Verney;

and the following Libraries and Institutions :—

    Kimberley Public Library, South Africa,
    Detroit Public Library, Michigan, U.S.A.,
    Balliol College, Oxford,

REPORT OF THE COUNCIL, 1893.

EDINBURGH PUBLIC LIBRARY,
BAILLIE'S INSTITUTION, Glasgow,
HAMMERSMITH FREE PUBLIC LIBRARY,
WESTMINSTER PUBLIC LIBRARIES,
OLDHAM FREE PUBLIC LIBRARY,
THE PUBLIC RECORD OFFICE,
SOUTHPORT FREE LIBRARY,
WORCESTER PUBLIC LIBRARY,
MIDDLESBROUGH PUBLIC LIBRARY,
JUNIOR CONSTITUTIONAL CLUB.

The book for the year 1892-93 is as announced in last year's Report—
THE ACCOUNTS OF HENRY EARL OF DERBY. Edited by Miss TOULMIN SMITH.

The Council had hoped that this book would have been in the hands of Members before the Annual Meeting. It has, however, been a work of much labour, necessitating a good deal of correspondence with Germany, where the East and West Prussian Historical Society have undertaken to publish, simultaneously with the issue of the whole work by this Society, an edition of so much of it as concerns Prussia. Nevertheless there is every reason to expect that it will now be issued without much further delay.

For the year 1893-94 it is impossible to promise absolutely more than one volume, which will be a volume of Miscellany, containing, among other matters, Wentworth and (additional) Hamilton Papers, and a collection of Woodcuts illustrating rare ballad broadsides in the time of the Stuarts. It is a matter of much regret to the Council that the present resources of the Society do not enable them to present Members with a greater number of issues in return for their Subscriptions. An appeal to Libraries and Institutions has resulted in a small addition to the number of Subscribers; but the Council would urge all Members of this Society who have influence with such Institutions to press on their Committees the importance of giving their support to the Society.

SAMUEL RAWSON GARDINER, *Director*.
JAMES GAIRDNER, *Secretary*.

BALANCE SHEET 1892-93.

We, the Auditors appointed to audit the Accounts of the Camden Society, repor[t] [t]o the Society, that the Treasurer has exhibited to us an Account of the Receipts an[d] Expenditure from the 1st of April, 1892, to the 31st of March, 1893, and that w[e h]ave examined the said accounts, with the vouchers relating thereto, and find the sam[e t]o be correct and satisfactory.

And we further report that the following is an Abstract of the Receipts an[d] Expenditure during the period we have mentioned:—

Receipts.	£	s.	d.	Expenditure.	£	s.	d.
[Re]ceived on account of Members whose Subscriptions were in arrear at last Audit	30	0	0	By Balance	0	19	
[T]he like on account of Subscriptions due on the 1st of May, 1892	132	1	0	Paid for printing 500 Copies:—Abingdon Abbey Accounts	102	5	
[T]he like on account of Subscriptions due on the 1st of May, 1893	13	1	0	Paid for Miscellaneous Printing	8	12	
[O]ne year's dividend on £299 9 9 2¾ per Cent. Consols, standing in the names of the Trustees of the Society, deducting Income Tax	8	0	8	Paid for delivery and transmission of Books, with paper for wrappers, warehousing expenses, &c. (including Insurance)	18	0	
[Sa]le of £50 Consols	48	17	6	Paid for Binding	40	19	
[T]o Sale of Publications of past years	69	17	7	Paid for Transcripts	11	4	
				Postages, &c.	3	5	
				Clerical Assistance	7	19	
				Bankers' Charges, Sale of Consols, &c.	0	15	
				Indexing	2	2	
					£202	3	
				Balance	99	13	
	£301	17	9		£301	17	

John W. Hales. } Auditors.
Guy Pym.

April 20th, 1893.

REPORT OF THE COUNCIL

OF

THE CAMDEN SOCIETY.

READ AT THE GENERAL MEETING

ON THE 2ND MAY, 1894.

The Council of the Camden Society elected on May 2, 1893, regret the loss by death of the following members:—

    ROBERT HUMPHREY COOKE, ESQ, F.R.C.S.,
    SIR HARRY VERNEY, BART.,
    THE EARL OF WARWICK.

They also have to report the following accessions to the Society:—

    THE DUKE OF DEVONSHIRE, K.G.,
    H. J. BUSHBY, ESQ.,
    SIR REGINALD PALGRAVE, K.C.B.,
    THE LORD WELBY, G.C.B.

The Council much regret that "The Accounts of the Earl of Derby," the volume for the year 1892-3, has not yet been published. The delay, for which the Editor offers sincere apologies, has been entirely due to the unexpected amount of labour involved in its production, and it is hoped that the work, which has been so serious a task upon her energies, will be of special value in consequence. The difficulties in making out the itineraries, in consequence of the conflicting dates given in the MS., have been considerable, and the work of identifying the place-names has been no less troublesome. Care had to be taken in drawing up indices of persons and places especially, as but slight clues were sometimes offered. The introduction left by Dr. Pauli at his lamented death was imperfect and inadequate, whilst several of the positions adopted by Professor Prutz seemed to require re-investigation. It is now expected that the Volume will be out of the Editor's hands by the end of May.

The book for the year 1893-4 is

THE CAMDEN MISCELLANY, Vol. IX.

which will shortly be in the hands of Members of the Society.

The second volume of the Clarke Papers, edited by Mr. C. H. Firth, is in an advanced stage of preparation, and will, possibly with another volume in addition, form the issue for 1894-5.

SAMUEL RAWSON GARDINER, *Director*.

JAMES GAIRDNER, *Secretary*.

P.S.—Owing to the delay in the issue of the publications, the Report of the Auditors, commonly appended to the Report of the Council, cannot at present be circulated.

www.ingramcontent.com/pod-product-compliance
Lightning Source LLC
Chambersburg PA
CBHW051233300426
44114CB00011B/724